25 Years of the
NEPL

Steve Graham

Grosvenor House
Publishing Limited

This book is published by
Grosvenor House Publishing Ltd
Link House
140 The Broadway, Tolworth, Surrey, KT6 7HT.
www.grosvenorhousepublishing.co.uk

A CIP record for this book
is available from the British Library

ISBN 978-1-83615-093-0

This book is dedicated to my wife Carol, and
to my six grandchildren, Thomas Graham, Ava and
Arthur Graham and Edward and Elliott Lynn and Harriet Lynn.

Contents

Foreword

I am delighted to be asked to write a foreword to 25 Years of the North East Premier League by Steve Graham and I warmly commend it to you.

Coinciding with the new millennium in 2000 the existing league structure across the whole of the Northeast, Northumberland and Durham would dramatically change. The idea to create "Premier Leagues" across the whole of the country was put forward in a 1997 ECB report "Raising the Standard".

To accommodate such a huge change within the whole Northeast, a sub committee was formed consisting of members from both Northumberland and Durham Cricket Boards and League Officials from existing leagues. After much discussion and debate a North East Premier League was formed and began playing in the 2000 season.

Over the ensuing years the League itself has grown from one division to two and a pyramid structure created amongst other leagues in both Northumberland and Durham which allows for promotion and relegation. To run the League over this time has taken a great deal of time, work and commitment by all who have served on the Management Committee and equally by all members and club officials who have worked to support the League.

Having caused some ripples in its early days the League can be looked upon as a huge success, with some of its clubs reaching, and winning, the ECB National Club competitions on multiple occasions. Over 25 seasons, league champions have come from 6 different clubs, but the standout club has been South Northumberland Cricket Club, who have won it on 15 occasions.

It was widely felt that the standards of cricket did not help produce English Cricket to a high standard for what was needed to be an international force. Scrapping county second XI's and encouraging the formation of Premier Leagues were seen as a realistic option with opportunities given to the best recreational cricketers and aspiring junior players. It certainly can be said that it has "raised the standard" of club cricket in the North East with a good number of players being outstanding for many years.

The focus and vision of the clubs and leagues, as well as the ambitious young players, was challenged with "comfort zones" reshaped as the need to produce better players and tougher standards was recognised. Every level of cricket in 2024 now benefits to varying degrees on the back of those developments. We now have a system in structure unrecognisable to that of 25 years ago. There have inevitably been casualties along the way, but the future of young cricketers and their development background is undoubtedly healthier.

This is a very well researched book by an author steeped in cricket. It tells the story of opportunity, triumph and some of the challenges of establishing what can now be claimed to be, one of the best Premier Leagues in the country.

Bob Jackson, M.B.E

Introduction

Just before 4pm on Tuesday 5th August 1997 the Chairman, Lord Ian Maclaurin, of The England and Wales Cricket Board (ECB) published a new 33-page management blueprint for the future playing structure of cricket.

Poor results in the test arena in late 1996/early 1997 against New Zealand and Zimbabwe had led to a frantic desire to improve English cricket from the grass roots up.

Against two of the weaker test cricket playing nations England had played five test matches and won two, and played eight one day matches and won only two of those as well.

With the novel idea of doing exactly what the title said, the goal of "Raising the Standard" set out to improve the top tier of club cricket through the introduction of a Premier League System and to bridge the gap between recreational cricket and the first-class game.

Major changes to the professional game were also to be implemented, including the County Championship to be split and the amount of one day cricket cut.

At club level a national network of Premier Leagues was to be established, at the time of the report there were 38 ECB Counties, the original intention was to form no more than 15 Premier Leagues, it was accepted that counties like Yorkshire would have only one Premier League, others such as Durham and Northumberland would combine to form a joint Premier League.

Premier League teams were required to show a strong commitment to junior cricket and the assessment criteria of them required strong junior sections with a provision for cricket coaching and matches for the next generation of cricketers.

This was reflected in the likely criteria for a Premier League listed in a letter sent out by The Northumberland County Cricket Board Chairman, Bobby Smithson, to its members.

1. Standard of performance

This came with an acknowledgement that Durham was the stronger of the two counties and would therefore have more players of the required standard, it was suggested that a 12 team Premier League would have a 9;3 or 8;4 split between Durham and Northumberland.

2. Standard of facilities

Those forming the League wanted it to be the best possible, so this would include the ground, pavilion facilities, covers etc.

It's worth looking back to this time, I gave up playing in the mid-nineties, my club Seaton Burn played in The Tyneside Senior League, they, along with probably nine or ten other teams in the League at that time had no covers, this was the case for many North East Clubs at the time.

3. Practice and coaching facilities

This included outdoor net facilities. Again, going back to the early eighties when I started playing, I'm not sure how much formal coaching was done, for a long time Seaton Burn had no qualified coaches, only experienced players who would do what they could. Bill Graham qualified around 1990.

Practice at Seaton Burn was eight to ten indoor sessions from mid-February onwards and, weather permitting, a couple of grass sessions before the season began. Tuesday night was practice night, but also the night most cup games were arranged for and so it was not always regular, I'm sure this would have been replicated at clubs across the North East.

4. Youth Program Under 11 to Under 17 Years old

When I grew up in the late seventies, most clubs wouldn't have any provision for kids under 13 initially, invariably those who did play any formal cricket did so because their fathers played cricket.

Things had improved by the nineties, The Northumberland Cricket Association ran an under 13 and under 15 competition which ran from at least 1991, although it was mainly Northumberland County League clubs whose juniors participated.

5. Development Structure -For 6- to 11-year-olds to get involved with cricket at a much younger age.

Most state schools wouldn't play organized cricket until a child reached 13.

As cricket has developed, the "Chance to Shine" program, linking schools to clubs began in 2006.

In 2017 the "All Stars" program has opened up more opportunities for children aged between 5 years old and 8 years old, of both sexes, which previous generations didn't have.

The "Dynamos" program started two years later and provides a more focused schedule for 8- to 11-year-olds.

My own grandson, Thomas, who has just turned nine, has just completed his fourth year in The All Stars and is moving up to Dynamo's this upcoming 2024 season.

6. Financial Structure

Given that each Premier League team could employ an overseas player and the restriction on paying other players was now to be allowed, this was always going to be part of any restructuring. The ECB were to offer a grant of £1000 but clearly that wouldn't go very far, even back in 1997!

Promotion, relegation and a feeder system were also part of the plan.

The North East Premier League/First Division was an ECB Designated Premier League from its inception.

In March 1999 the 12 proposed founder members were announced, from the Durham Senior League, Chester le Street, Gateshead Fell, Sunderland and Durham Cricket Academy

The Durham Cricket Academy had opened in 1996 and joined the Durham Senior League in 1997, becoming Champions in 1998.

From the North Yorkshire and South Durham League, Norton and Stockton.

Four Northumberland County League Clubs had already made it known that they would form part of the newly formed Premier League, Benwell Hill, Newcastle (Formerly County Club /Jesmond), South Northumberland and Tynemouth.

These four clubs were selected from several criteria, but the new emphasis on junior cricket played a key part in the selection of these teams.

Benwell Hill Junior sides had performed well at National Level competitions.

South North had the indoor nets to support their claim, and while they weren't yet the cricket centre, they would become, their nets were still better than almost every other club.

Tynemouth had enjoyed a golden period with producing young talent, Barry Stewart, Gordon and Paul Muchall, Nicky Peng and Richard Coughtrie all coming through their juniors to play county cricket.

Newcastle were an obvious choice as they were the County Ground of the time at Jesmond, having staged the Callers Matches and numerous other high-profile games.

Ashington and Tynedale were both strong sides around this time and would both have been sound choices but neither wanted to apply.

The eight remaining County League Clubs were to amalgamate with the Tyneside Senior League.

Matches in the NEPL were to be 120 Overs, the side batting first restricted to 65 overs maximum.

Overseas players were to be allowed, with only one per team, they could also hire one Durham contract player at £75 per game, with no bar on paying others.

Not everyone was in favour of the new league, The NYSD refused to guarantee re-admission to any relegated clubs, although not an immediate issue as there would be no promotion/relegation for the first two years of the new format, the possibility of no re-admission was enough to give Bishop Auckland and Darlington pause for thought and they withdrew their application to join the Premier League, Norton were unsure what to do and were subsequently replaced by reserve side Blaydon, from The Tyneside Senior League, before Norton were then admitted following some negotiation!

It was said at the time that The NYSD believed they wanted to be a Premier League in their own right.

At club level many long serving players and officials thought that the new system would end village rivalries which had gone back decades, cricket acquaintances who you saw two or three times a year would fall away, sacrificed on the altar of ambition of a system which would benefit the few.

Some feared that any youngster who showed promise would be "simply hoovered up" by the powerful and wealthy Premier League clubs. Others were simply traditionalists who didn't like change!

The Durham Senior League North Section was founded in 1890, Sunderland being among the founder members.

Burnmoor were first recorded as members of the Durham Senior League in 1891, winning their first Durham Senior League Title in 1900, the League ended at the close of the 2012 season.

The North Yorkshire & South Durham League started as far back as 1893 and continues to thrive today, Saltburn Cricket Club taking the title in 2023.

It was said that almost all Tyneside Senior League Clubs were against the NEPL, certainly at my own club, Seaton Burn, that was the feeling amongst the lads I spoke to. The Tyneside Senior League had started in 1906 and still operates today as part of The Northumberland and Tyneside Cricket League.

The closing date for applications to the Premier League was Saturday 15th May 1999, ironically The Back Street Boys were on top of the British music charts on that day, with the aptly named tune "I Want it That Way!"

Perhaps more interestingly, the song on top of the American music charts on that day was a singer called Ricky Martin with "Living La Vie Da Loca", roughly translated "Living the crazy life", you pay your money you take your choice!

It's worth a look at the final league tables from which the founding clubs of the NEPL came.

TABLE 1   Durham Senior League Final Table 1999.

	Played	Won	Drawn	Tie	Lost	Points
Burnmoor	26	13	13	0	0	90
Chester le Street	26	9	13	0	4	73
Felling	26	8	13	0	5	64
Philadelphia	26	6	16	0	4	58
Durham CA	26	8	13	1	4	57
Eppleton	26	8	11	0	7	56
Gateshead Fell	26	6	14	0	6	47
Horden	26	5	11	1	9	47
Sunderland	26	4	17	0	5	47
Seaham Harbour	26	5	13	0	8	46
Whitburn	26	5	12	0	9	44
Durham City	26	4	14	0	8	41
Boldon	26	4	15	0	7	40
South Shields	26	2	13	0	11	24

TABLE 2   North Yorkshire & South Durham League 1999.

	Played	Won	Lost	Drawn	Points
Bishop Auckland	26	10	1	15	392
Darlington	26	11	7	8	316
Stockton	26	10	7	9	314
Northallerton	26	6	5	15	300
Guisborough	26	8	8	10	298
Hartlepool	26	10	6	10	295
Normanby Hall	26	6	4	16	294
Marske	26	5	6	15	282
Norton	26	6	8	12	280
Saltburn	26	7	11	8	278
Richmondshire	26	7	11	11	276
Blackhall	26	5	6	15	276
Middlesbrough	26	3	5	18	245
Darlington R. A	26	1	13	12	200

TABLE 3   Northumberland County League Final Table 1999.

	Played	Won	Drawn	Lost	Tie	Points
Benwell Hill	22	17	3	2	0	341
Ashington	22	17	3	2	0	339
Tynedale	22	16	0	6	0	329
Tynemouth	22	12	1	8	1	312
Jesmond	22	11	2	8	0	276
South Northumberland	22	10	2	9	1	262
Blyth	22	8	4	10	0	212
Backworth	22	6	1	15	0	205
Alnwick	22	7	2	13	0	202
Morpeth	22	5	2	15	0	199
Percy Main	22	5	2	15	0	190
Benwell & Walbottle	22	5	2	15	0	175

TABLE 4   Tyneside Senior League Final Table 1999.

	Played	Won	Drawn	Lost	Tie	Points
Annfield Plain	24	19	4	1	0	388
Blaydon	24	17	2	5	0	375
Lintz	24	16	2	6	0	353
Consett	24	15	1	8	0	326
Lanchester	24	13	2	9	0	296
Shotley Bridge	24	13	3	8	0	290
Sacriston	24	11	1	12	0	272
Ryton	24	10	2	11	1	250
Swalwell	24	8	3	13	0	218
Burnopfield	24	6	2	16	0	192
Seaton Burn	24	6	3	15	0	183
Whickham	24	5	3	16	0	164
Greenside	24	0	4	19	1	69

Under League Chairman Alan Mckenna, The NEPL Division 1 opened officially on Saturday 29th April 2000.

In the League handbook of the year each of the Club Chairman took the opportunity to reflect on their own Club history and what had gone before, whilst not going into it too deeply, it is worth having a look at the very early roots of the original eleven clubs and just how far in history those clubs go back.

Benwell Hill Chairman Stewart Allen started his message reflecting that his club had been formed in 1883, with young men, mainly juniors, and a 17-year-old captain, playing exclusively friendlies on various sites of Benwell Hill Hall (now St Cuthbert's School). A place in The Tyneside Senior League was taken up in 1905 and a League title in 1906.

As the club continued to evolve, including the hiring of a professional, George Milne, a move to land on Thorntree Farm on Denton Bank in the early 1920's was procured, such was the way of things they dismantled their pavilion and took it with them!

Benwell Hill joined the newly formed Northumberland League in 1934, continuing there until 1977 when the Northumberland County League was formed. A brick pavilion was built along the way, in 1952 and in the late 1960's a club professional was engaged once again, Doug Ferguson and Mike Younger being the first incumbents.

Blaydon Chairman Ken Foster also started his message right back at the very beginning, Blaydon CC being formed in 1861, playing at Ryton Willows from 1876. The club folded in 1897, many of the players joining Blaydon St Cuthbert's, driven by schoolmaster Tom Ryding, they became Blaydon CC in 1908.

Ryding had formed The Derwent Valley League in 1907, despite this Ryding applied to join The Tyneside Senior League in 1908! Drainage problems on the ground near the River Tyne prompted a move to Denefield in 1913. After spending ten years in The North Durham Senior League Blaydon joined the West Tyne League.

In the mid 1930's repeated unsuccessful attempts to join The Tyneside Senior League led to Blaydon withdrawing from The West Tyne League, missing the chance to apply for an enlarged North West Durham League and then finding themselves without a league when the latest application failed! A season of friendlies then led to The Northern Combination League.

Denefield became a wilderness during The Second World War but in 1950 they were elected to The North Durham League.

Professional Jack Oliver helped raise the profile of the club and election to The Tyneside Senior League was finally granted in 1972 and this was followed by a new pavilion in 1974.

Although Blaydon lost their league lead in the final Tyneside Senior League match of 1999 to Annfield Plain, they had won the title three of the previous four years and finished in the top four seventeen times and never outside the top eight in their 27 years in the league.

Left-handed opener Ian Somerville was set to start his NEPL career with 18,384 league and cup runs for Blaydon and would go onto become very well known to those who bowled in the newly formed league, as he made 2485 runs in the NEPL with 9 half centuries and 2 centuries!

Chester le Street Chairman J.H Ward could trace his club's roots back even further, the first recorded match involving Chester le Street was against Durham City was in 1834! The first cricket field in Chester le Street was in 1866, at Mordue's Field, Crown Farm, Ropery Lane, the Town's bypass now runs through the middle of it! A spell at Red Rose Terrace followed before they moved to their current location in 1886! In 1892 Chester le Street won the County Challenge Cup, beating Bishop Auckland in the final and thereby gaining a place in The Durham Senior League, Northern Division. In 1893 this League consisted of Chester le Street, Philadelphia, North Durham, South Shields, Sunderland and Whitburn.

In 1904 a new two storey pavilion was built, and the Ropery Lane Ground was purchased in 1948 for the sum of £1000. In 1966 another new pavilion was built, being further extended in 1972.

They won The Durham Senior League six times, the last in 1983, and were runners up seven times, the last being in 1999.

For obvious reasons Durham Cricket Academy Coach Geoff Cook had little local league history to call on with his preseason thoughts, though he did have enough to raise The Academy winning The Durham Senior League in 1998 and finishing fourth in 1999. Instead, he re-iterated the aims of The Academy, stressing that those aims do not change. That is, it (the NEPL) is a development ground for young players to show their suitability to move through to the next stage.

Cook went on to praise many of his current crop of young cricketers, most, if not all will be familiar to those interested in the NEPL, Chris Hewison, Ian Hunter, Gary Pratt, Ian Pattison, Graeme Bridge, Gordon Muchall, Mark Davies and Nicky Peng, amongst others.

Gateshead Fell Chairman, Doug Hudson, was another keen to emphasize the history of his club. Although records of the clubs' early days were destroyed in a fire in 1960 there was enough from various sources to paint a picture. The "Gateshead Observer" of 1867 had an extract which mentioned Gateshead Fell Cricket Club". In 1878 it is known that matches were played in a field adjoining St John's Church in the Parish of Gateshead Fell. In 1880 the club moved to its current ground.

In the early days the club would play only friendly matches until prior to the 1914 war they joined and then resigned from the North West Durham League and the now defunct North Durham Senior League.

In 1920 they became Gateshead Fell Cricket and Lawn Tennis Club, the cricket club also joining The Tyneside Senior League that year. It reverted to a cricket club only when the tennis section was disbanded after The Second World War. In 1958 a new pavilion was built, only to be burned down two years later in 1960.

This was also the year Gateshead Fell resigned from The Tyneside Senior League and were accepted into The Durham Senior League.

Newcastle Cricket Club Chairman Bill Peacock opened his message with a brief history of the club with confirmation of a name change at the end of it. The Northumberland County Cricket Club, also known for many years as County Club, was formed in December 1895 and started playing in the 1896 season at The Heaton Ground in Newcastle. In 1897 the club moved to its current ground in Jesmond, then known as The Constabulary Ground. Initially playing friendly cricket, they joined The Tyneside Senior League in 1909. They remained there until a breakaway league; The Northumberland League was formed in 1934.

The formation of The Northumberland County League was in 1978, and this became County Club's league home until 1999. With the commencement of the NEPL the club will now be known as Newcastle Cricket Club.

Following the historical theme of his fellow Chairmen, Norton Cricket Club Chairman, Ken Symington, laid out his club's long history. Founded in 1847 with the intention of "firstly, to afford to the young men of the village during their leisure hours the rational enjoyment of an innocent pastime; and secondly to bring together on one common and friendly footing, the different classes of society". Originally playing on the picturesque Norton Green until 1878 when it acquired seven acres of land on Station Road.

Over the years Norton have played cricket, they have been NYSD Champions eleven times, the last time in 1998.

South Northumberland Chairman Clive Goatman was another who could trace his club's history to the mid 1860's. South North were formed in 1864 as Bulman Village CC and it's first field was across the High Street in Gosforth. In the winter of 1864/65, they moved to their present ground.

In 1866 they became Gosforth Cricket Club before settling on South Northumberland Cricket Club in 1882. In July of that year the Roseworth Terrace ground hosted Northumberland against The Australians, a month later the tourists claimed The Ashes at The Oval.

They were a founder member of the Tyneside Senior League in 1906, winning the first four titles and joined the newly formed Northumberland League in 1934, between 1947 and 1967 they won the League seven times.

Goatman identifies the 70's and 80's as a transition period for the club, despite producing some good cricketers. It did find success in winning The Northumberland County League in 1988 and 1997, and various cups along the way, including the Just Sport Trophy in 1999.

A major refitting of the club's facilities in 1998, the indoor school, all-weather nets and the clubhouse, all benefiting but with a view towards the club's juniors, as well as taking on a coaching role formerly assumed by schools in the city.

Stockton Chairman Peter Davies could arguably go further back in history than almost anyone tracing his club history, so he did! The first mention of an established cricket club in Stockton was in 1816, although in 1814 a game against Yarm attracted 2000 spectators! In 1847 an All-England team played the first of several games against a Stockton and District team.

In 1891 the club joined "The New Durham League", this year was also the year the club found out their ground was to be turned into a park for the town, Ropner Park is still in use today.

They played their first game on The Grangefield Ground on 4th June 1892 against Constable Burton, a village from North Yorkshire. In 1896 the club joined The North Yorkshire and South Durham League. The ground was enlarged in 1921, and a purpose-built tearoom added in 1923 with a groundman's house added in 1953 and a new score box in 1955.

More recent times have seen dressing rooms extended, an electronic scoreboard and an indoor net facility also built. On the field the club has had success across many levels, including winning the NYSD three times.

Sunderland Cricket Club Chairman Peter Fenwick looked back to his clubs' ancestors for his message to the newly formed NEPL, his ancestors right back in 1801! It was that year in "The Newcastle Chronicle" that a match took place on 25th July 1801 between 11 gentlemen of Monkwearmouth "and an equal number from Sunderland."

By 1808 Sunderland CC were playing matches on The Old Town Moor, moving to Hendon in 1850, then Holmeside until 1876, then to Chester Road until 1887, when they moved to their current home at Ashbrooke. In 1890 the Durham League was being split into North and South, Sunderland playing in the North. One of the purposes behind the split was to provide a more competitive environment so the best players would come to the fore-does this sound familiar?

Sunderland met Norton in a Championship play off in both 1891 and 1892, losing both, before defeating Stockton in the 1895 play off. In 1903 The North Section broke away to form The Durham Senior League, Sunderland winning the first three titles.

By the time they resigned in 1999 from The Durham Senior League the club had 18 league titles to its credit. Over the years the ground has hosted all Test playing countries except Zimbabwe.

Tynemouth Chairman Alan Haley emphasized the fact that Tynemouth were formed in 1847 and was one of the oldest Northern clubs. The club moved to its present ground in 1885, in no small part due to the patronage of The Duke of Northumberland, who also opened the new pavilion at the ground in 1902. The club was at its strongest between the two world wars, winning The Northumberland League for the first three years of its existence from 1934.

The club has a long and proud history of introducing talented juniors to senior cricket, as far back as 1871 they had a 13-year-old, Shallett Crawford, playing in the second team, he would later captain Northumberland. The latest promising teenager is Nicky Peng, who played for the first team at 14 in 1997.

What struck me as I read the Chairman's messages from the first NEPL handbook, was that each and every one of them, whether intentionally, accidently or sub consciously, they had started with the very beginnings of their club, the long and rich history of their club, but they also raised the fact that each club, and this would also apply to many, many local league cricket clubs, had at some point moved leagues, often when doing so because a new league had started up, often to increase competition.

I don't think those Chairmen throughout history, or those in more recent times, took the decision to leave their established leagues lightly, but all did so and hence we have the NEPL.

At the very early stages of researching this book, I spoke to Phil Haves and Phil Nicholson at Benwell Hill CC. Phil Nicholson vividly recalled a conversation he and a couple of other players had been having two or three years before The NEPL was formed, the content of the conversation being that they felt the Northumberland County League was starting to feel a bit "stale", the top six was becoming very predictable, with Ashington and Tynedale the two standout sides, and it was starting to feel "like a league within a league".

Nicholson, who was 27 when the NEPL started, said that from a player's perspective it felt that the NEPL was going to test them further and be much harder cricket, he, and he said other players he spoke to, were excited at the prospect of playing in the new league.

And that is the crux of this book, the players, particularly the local players, those with Monday to Friday jobs, or doing shift work and trying to compete with the very best cricketers the North East had to offer.

There have been some incredible cricketers produced by Durham CCC, many who played in this league as teenagers, whether for The Durham Academy or at an NEPL side to gain experience, Ben Stokes, Mark Wood, Liam Plunkett, Graham Onions, Phil Mustard, Keaton Jennings, Mark Stoneman, to name just a few, but their exploits and deeds are recorded elsewhere, this book will touch on their achievements in this league and in the wider world, but it's purpose is to record the deeds of the out and out club cricketer, perhaps the guy who didn't get the break or that one big score that it took to make his dreams come true.

What I will try and do is to look at a little of the background of as many players as possible, to look at how they ended up in The NEPL, many were such stand out youngsters it would be impossible to list all the achievements of every player, so instead I will try and give one or two examples of each stepping stone or representative game they played, debut's, highest score, that type of thing.

I would also raise the subject of money and players being paid. I will just say this, in the past there was much speculation about players being paid on the quiet, the rules of the NEPL allow paid players, and that's all I need to know, if you're good enough to be paid to play cricket then good luck to you, that's between you and your club.

I would also point out that when I refer to The NEPL I am referring to the topflight of the league only, this book will only be covering the topflight, I realise that the league was known as Division 1 until 2013 when it became a Premier League with a Division 1 and later a Division 2 below it, but NEPL means the top flight for the purpose of this book.

For clarity, if I say someone made their NEPL debut on a given date, I mean his topflight debut in The Premier Division, not Division 1 or later, in Division 2. To spell it out, NEPL means the top division, not Division 1 or 2.

I would also point out that the figures I can find, and therefore use, are as accurate as I can find, in turn it has been pointed out to me that in the early days of the league, the figures weren't always accurate or complete.

I would humbly ask that you, the reader, for the sake of clarity, and my sanity, understand the two points I have made above.

And so, we had the opening fixtures of The Foster's North East Premier League on Saturday 29th April 2000. Matches were to start at 11.30am and be 120 overs duration with the side batting first allowed to bat for a maximum of 65 overs. Bonus points were to be awarded, 1 batting point for each of the following scores reached in the first 60 overs of the innings, 140, 170, 200, 230, 260. 1 bowling point for every two wickets taken, 2, 4, 6, 8, 10, if a side is dismissed 5 bowling points are awarded irrespective of number of wickets taken. Naturally there were more rules than that, but I think that's enough for anyone.

Here are the opening fixtures for the opening weekend of the NEPL.

Benwell Hill v Durham CA
Chester le Street v Gateshead Fell
Norton v Newcastle
South North v Stockton
Tynemouth v Blaydon
Sunderland had a free weekend.

At this point, as it's sure to come up, I must point out, I'm no relation to John Graham, I did play many years with his father Bill, and a couple of seasons with John at Seaton Burn but no, we are not related!

CHAPTER ONE

Sunderland 2000

Sunderland were the first NEPL Champions.

The very first weekend of NEPL fixtures took place on Saturday 29th April 2000, because of the odd number of teams in the league, Sunderland opened with a free weekend.

So, on Saturday 6th May 2000, Sunderland CC set about writing their NEPL history with a home fixture against Tynemouth. The first innings was limited to 65 overs and the match to 120 overs in total. They were led by Adam Applegarth who was to form a formidable opening bowling partnership with West Indian Professional Cameron Cuffy. Sunderland batted first, they scored 193 for 8 wickets declared, from an unknown number of overs. Wicketkeeper Ben Young had the distinction of scoring the first half century by a Sunderland player in the NEPL, 50 not out. Chris Beever, a leg break bowler, who would go on to play four games for Northumberland, was the best of the bowlers, with 3 for 43. The match was drawn. Greg Applegarth, who was around the team a lot at this time, both as the captain, Adam Applegarth's son and regular scorer, has cast his mind back to 2000 to remember this title winning side.

The Sunderland team who played that day was as follows.

Simon Old opened the batting with Simon Brown in the first ever Sunderland NEPL match. He faced the first ball and went on to make 30 in the innings. Old was a right-handed batsman, Greg Applegarth recalls that Old had joined the club from South Shields where he had been "a very good player, a very brave player, very gritty, although he was quick between the wickets, his team mates always thought he was going to get "timed out" before the game even started as he would take an age to get to the crease. Old always fielded in the mids, often diving to stop the ball, occasionally ending up "with his trousers round his ankles!"

He would play in all 17 NEPL matches Sunderland played this season, scoring 394 runs at an average of 26.40 with 1 half century and 1 century, 101 scored on 5th August 2000 against South North. He took eight catches this season.

Old took over the captaincy for the 2001 season, he continued to play for Sunderland in The NEPL until the end of the 2006 season when he retired. He represented Sunderland in 126 matches, having 119 innings with 8 not outs, he is credited with 3208 NEPL runs with a high score of 139 and an average of 28.90. He scored seventeen half centuries and five centuries. The highest score was on 28th August 2006 at home to Gateshead Fell, he also took 35 NEPL catches.

Simon M. Brown was the other opener in that first game, a right-handed batsman, he is not to be confused with Simon J.E Brown, who also played at Sunderland. He had a younger brother, Chris, who played for the club as a right-arm leg spinner.

Greg Applegarth states that Brown was "solid, dependable, exactly what you wanted in an opener, he had opened the batting with Philo Wallace in the last five or six years of The Durham Senior League. He was a tough batsman, another one who was brave, he used to nurdle the ball around, accumulate runs, he was a unique individual with his own style in the dressing room. "

He had two spells at Sunderland in the NEPL. The first was from 2000 to 2005, the second from 2013 to 2014. He opened the 2000 season against Tynemouth with a score of 12 and one catch and went on to play 10 matches in the NEPL, batting 7 times with 1 not out. He scored 47 runs with a high score of 14 and an average of 7.83. The high score of 14 could have been a pivotal one, more of that later.

At the end of his first spell at the club, in 2005, Simon Brown had played in 58 matches and batted 46 times, with 7 not outs, 596 runs at an average of 15.28 and a high score of 57, his only half century during this spell, coming on 23rd July 2005 away at Stockton.

He simply stopped playing for a while, returning to Sunderland for the 2013 and 2014 seasons.

He would play 21 matches in that period, batting 20 times with 4 not outs, scoring 387 runs with 2 half centuries at an average of 24.18. His highest score was 89 not out at home against Durham Academy on 15th June 2013, it came from 168 balls and contained 3 boundaries, he opened the innings this day and carried his bat as Sunderland batted 59.2 overs for the draw.

When all was done, his NEPL career with Sunderland covered 79 matches, 66 innings, 11 not out, 983 runs at an average of 17.87, with three half centuries. He took 30 career catches and had 2 stumpings.

Lee Rushworth batted at number three for the season opener at home to Tynemouth, scoring 13. He was a right-handed batsman; he is the older brother of ex Durham bowler and legend Chris Rushworth and cousin to Phil Mustard and his father Joe was well known on the Durham cricket scene, playing at Hylton.

Greg Applegarth recalls that Lee Rushworth was a "big hitting, swashbuckling batsman, he hit it everywhere, but playing cricket shots, he hit it straight if it was at the stumps, through or over the covers if it was on or outside off stump, he was incredibly talented but not necessarily driven about his cricket, that little bit of drive missing was probably the only thing which possibly stopped him going a bit further in cricket, he was a cool lad, vey laid back in the dressing room too. He just kind of drifted away from cricket in the end."

During the 2000 NEPL season Lee Rushworth played 17 matches for Sunderland, batting 16 times with 2 not outs, he scored 489 runs at an average of 34.92. He scored 3 half centuries and 1 century, the century, 117, was scored on 17th June 2000 at home to Gateshead Fell.

He bowled 23 balls in the NEPL in 2000, with 0 maidens, he conceded 80 runs and took 4 wickets at an average of 20.00. His best bowling figures were 2 for 31, taken on 13th May 2000 at home to Norton.

His first NEPL wicket was taken in the season opener on 6th May at home to Tynemouth when he dismissed Tynemouth opener Tony Lion, caught by Simon Old for 27. He took 5 NEPL catches in the 2000 season.

The first record of Rushworth came on 23rd July 1996, representing Durham Under 15's against Scotland Under 15's at Ampleforth. Scotland batted first, scoring 85 all out, D. Craig had 4 for 9, Rushworth taking 3 for 11 although he didn't get to bat as his side won easily for the loss of three wickets.

He played in the same fixture almost a year later, on 18th July 1997, this time at Bishop Auckland. Rushworth opened the batting with Ian Pattison and made 5, 83 not out from M. Smith saw Durham score 220 for 8 from their 50 overs. When Scotland batted, they were bowled out for 104, taking 2 for 12 as he opened the bowling with Paul Chivers, Chivers had 3 for 12 and Ian Pattison 2 for 15.

Rushworth was then selected to play for The English Cricket Association North Under 15's against their counterparts from the West Under 15's, in The Bunbury Festival, making his debut on 21st July 1997 at St Helens. Rushworth batted at three, scoring 33 not out, as Gary Pratt, 80 not out and John Sadler, 61, got North to a respectable 205 for 1 from 59 overs declared. The West side put together a solid batting performance and won by 6 wickets, Rushworth not getting a bowl.

He made 45 in the second Bunbury game two days later against The South side, future England wicket keeper Matt Prior among the opposition and scored 9 in both innings in the final match against The President's Headmasters Conference Schools side, again containing Matt Prior.

On 13th July 1998 Rushworth started a two-day match for Durham Under 16's against Scotland at Edinburgh. Only limited information is available, Rushworth scored 57 and 27 in a drawn match.

On 31st August 1999 Rushworth started a 4-day match for Nottinghamshire Seconds against Yorkshire Seconds at Trent Bridge, batting five in both innings, he scored 11 and 1.

After the NEPL had started Lee Rushworth would go on to play for both Durham Seconds and The Durham Cricket Board, his last NEPL game for Sunderland was on 9th July 2005 at Tynemouth, when he made 16.

His career stats in the NEPL with Sunderland were as follows, he played 89 matches, batting 85 times, with 8 not outs, he scored 2426 runs at an average of 31.50, with a high score of 133 not out, made on 14th June 2003 at Jesmond against Newcastle. He scored 15 half centuries and 3 centuries and took 28 catches. He would go on to play for Eppleton in The NEPL Division One.

Andrew Pratt batted at number four in the 2000 season opener, scoring 17. He was a left-handed batsman; he is the brother of Gary Pratt of Durham and Ashes run out of Ricky Ponting fame!

He was a Durham contracted player this season, he used to keep wicket for Durham but not for Sunderland, Greg Applegarth recalls that the feeling around the team was that they weren't always sure of his availability and so went with Ben Young as their regular keeper.

As a batsman Applegarth states that Pratt "had huge ability, he was a cool customer when batting, he was a very good player off the back foot, pulling and cutting, he hit the ball very hard, if it was pitched up, he would throw his hands at it.... hard! In the field he always had something to say, he played the game very hard, tough. He brought an element of the professional to the team."

Andrew Pratt first came to note on 30th May 1990 playing for Durham Schools Under 15's against Welsh Schools Under 15's. The Welsh batted first, scoring 187 for 4 declared from 59 overs. When Durham batted, Quentin Hughes, 27, and Robin Weston,67, put on 48 for the first wicket, Pratt, batting at four, scored 12 as Durham won by 5 wickets.

The next appearance of note for Pratt came on 31st May 1991 for Durham, against Durham University at The Racecourse Ground. Pratt didn't get a bat as Durham made 194 for 2 from their 55 overs, John Glendenen making 61 and Gary Brown, 61 not out. Pratt did keep wicket when the students batted, taking three catches, as they made 195 for 6 to take the win.

Representative games started piling up for Pratt, Durham Seconds and Under 19's initially, then on 14th May 1993 he made his debut for The Marylebone Cricket Club at Tunbridge Wells against The Club Cricket Conference. The weather seems to have ruined the game 25 overs into The M.C.C. bowling effort, Pratt hadn't got to bat when his side did. He represented the M.C.C from 1993 until 2006.

Andrew Pratt would go on to play 62 first class matches for Durham, this included 105 innings and 14 not outs, scoring 1974 runs at an average of 21.69, with a high score of 93, with 10 half centuries. He took 150 catches and had 12 stumpings.

He would also play 82 List A matches for Durham, batting 63 times with 15 not outs and scoring 988 runs at an average of 20.58, with a high score of 86. He took a further 89 catches and had 24 stumpings at this level.

Andrew Pratt's NEPL career with Sunderland started on 6th May 2000 and he played his last NEPL game for them on 4th September 2004, at home to The Durham Academy. During the 2000 NEPL season he played 9 matches for Sunderland, batting 8 times, with 0 not outs, he scored 195 runs at an average of 24.37. He scored 2 half centuries, with a highest score of 88, made on 13th May 2000 at home to Norton. He did not bowl in the NEPL in 2000, but he did take 5 catches that season.

He played 23 NEPL games for Sunderland, batting 21 times, with 1 not out, he scored 568 runs at an average of 28.40 and a high score of 96, the 96 was one of 5 half centuries he scored for Sunderland and came on 9th August 2003 at Philadelphia. He took 19 catches and had 2 stumpings.

He did return to The NEPL on 30th April 2005 for Newcastle at home to Stockton, he made 7. He played a total of 15 NEPL matches for Newcastle, batting 15 times, scoring 233 runs at an average of 15.53, and a high score of 65.

Adam Applegarth batted at five in the season opener, scoring 12, he was also skipper and opening bowler, taking 2 for 47 in the game. He was a right-handed batsman and right arm medium/fast bowler, he was also Chairman and captain and would be 37 by the time the season ended.

He played for Sunderland in The Durham Senior League and subsequently when they entered the NEPL. As a captain he had realized that the strength of their team, plus the points system of the time, a team got the maximum points if you bowled the other side out cheaply and then knocked the runs off, and that was his strategy as captain during the initial NEPL season.

He used to bat at three during The Senior League days, but son Greg recalls that he "realized that this was probably unrealistic, giving the bowling he was going to have to do plus the higher standard of cricket in the new league."

As a bowler Greg says his dad had been "sharp earlier in his career, he was now medium/fast rather than fast but he looked to hit the seam, bowling accurately and being miserly with the runs, he and Cuffy were a good fit, they were the top two wicket takers in the NEPL in that 2000 season."

A notable clash and sign of things to come took place on 27th April 1997 when Applegarth played an Abbot Ale Cup match for Sunderland against then Northumberland County side, Benwell Hill. Benwell Hill batted first, Lee Crozier, yes, that Lee Crozier, the spinner, made 66, David Weatherhead added 67 as Hill scored 217 for 4 from their 40 overs. Sunderland scored 113 all out in reply, Applegarth batting three, scoring 14, Crozier was the pick of the bowlers with 4 for 36.

On 16th May 1998 Applegarth represented Sunderland in a National Club Championship fixture at Backworth Welfare. Sunderland batted first, Applegarth again batting at three, made 167 for 7 from their 45 overs. Applegarth scored 18. Backworth, with Tim Brown scoring 78 and Darren Leason 61 not out, were comfortable winners by 7 wickets, Applegarth 0-28.

When the NEPL got under way on 29th April 2000, Sunderland had a free weekend. Therefore, they opened their very first NEPL campaign a week later on 6th May 2000, at home to Tynemouth. Sunderland batted first, 193 for 8 declared, Ben Young had the distinction of notching their first half century in the NEPL, exactly 50 not out as Sunderland declared. Adam Applegarth, skipper, batted at five, making 12.

In response Tynemouth scored 171 for 5, Applegarth opening the bowling with Cameron Cuffy, taking 2 for 47, his first NEPL wicket being Barry Stewart, whom he bowled. The match was drawn.

Applegarth played 17 matches in the NEPL in 2000, batting 11 times with 1 not out, he scored 70 runs at an average of 7.00. His highest score of the 2000 season in the NEPL was 21 not out.

He bowled 731 balls in the NEPL in 2000, with 41 maidens, he conceded 650 runs and took 39 wickets at an average of 16.66. His best bowling figures of the season were 6 for 39, taken on 9th September 2000 at Blaydon. He took 5 catches in the NEPL that season.

Adam Applegarth was named as the first ever NEPL Player of the Season in 2000.

Applegarth played his last NEPL game for nearly 10 years on 30th August 2004 at Norton. Sunderland batted first, Applegarth listed to bat at 10, did not bat as Sunderland declared on 208 for 8 from 60 overs. When Norton batted, they were dismissed for 128. Applegarth opening the bowling from one end and taking the wicket of Durham's Marc Symington for 19, to finish with 1 for 34.

His next appearance was on 2nd May 2015, a Division One fixture for Sunderland at home to Boldon. His son Greg was also playing for Sunderland in the game, taking 2-19 in the Boldon innings and scoring 11. Adam Applegarth didn't bowl and scored 12 with the bat as Boldon won by 9 runs.

When the curtain was drawn on his NEPL career he had played 74 NEPL matches with 42 innings, 17 not out's, scoring 715 runs at an average of 8.60 and a high score of 21 not out.

He was predominantly a bowler, and he bowled 4500 balls in the NEPL, with 168 maidens, conceding 2786 runs and taking 123 wickets at an average of 22.65, his best bowling figures were 6 for 27 and took place on 1st September 2001 at home to Tynemouth. He also took six wickets on three occasions and five wickets on three more occasions and 14 NEPL catches.

Ben Young batted at six in the season opener of 2000, top scoring with 50 not out, he was a right-handed batsman and wicket keeper and a remarkable man. Greg Applegarth recalls that Young was "In his mid-20's at this time, he had been struck by a childhood illness as a toddler, leaving him a deaf mute. He used sign language or wrote things down to communicate with his teammates, running between the wickets was obviously a challenge sometimes, but he rose to it. Remember, we could have had a Durham wicketkeeper behind the sticks, the team went with Young, that shows you the respect we had for him. As a batsman he was steady, he was very good off the front foot, hitting big, booming cover drives, he was brave, he seemed to get hit a lot, but it never deterred him, he was a competent batsman at this level and worth his place as a batsman or wicketkeeper."

Ben Young was one of several Sunderland youngsters who first featured on 16th May 1999 in a National Club Championship game for Sunderland at Backworth, he opened the batting that day, making 3.

He marked his NEPL debut in Sunderland's league opener on 6th May with the first half century by any Sunderland player in the NEPL, scoring exactly 50.

Young played 17 matches in the NEPL in 2000, batting 14 times with 3 not outs, he scored 217 runs at an average of 19.72. He scored 2 half centuries with a highest score of 53, made on 29th July 2000 at home to Chester le Street. He took 24 catches and had 2 stumpings in the NEPL in 2000.

He would go on to play NEPL cricket for Philadelphia and Gateshead Fell, as well as play at Eppleton.

Ben Young also represented his country, playing for England at The Deaf Cricket World Cup in India in 2005. He played against Sri Lanka on 17th November at Lucknow, he opened the batting, scoring 9 as England made 203 for 9 from their 50 overs. Sri Lanka were dismissed for 107 in 32.3 overs.

After scoring just a single in the next match, a 1 wicket loss to Australia, the next game was on 20th November again at Lucknow, against Nepal. Young once again opened the innings, scoring 107 from just 94 balls in 154 minutes, he struck 8 boundaries. England scored 362 for 6 from their 50 overs. Nepal were dismissed for 72, a very comfortable England win.

Young continued to give a good account of himself, making 43 opening in a loss to India, 20, batting at number seven in a loss to South Africa, 85 opening again against New Zealand in a win and 11 opening in a loss to Pakistan.

A second match against Australia, the semifinal of The Deaf World Cup, on 26th November, again at Lucknow, saw him make 50, opening the batting in a winning effort as England chased down 153 for a 4-wicket win. His 50 had come from 95 balls, in 118 minutes and contained 6 boundaries.

England Deaf Cricket Team played their Indian counterparts in The Deaf World Cup Cricket Final at Lucknow on 27th November 2005. India batted first and scored 218 for 9 from their 50 overs. When England batted, Young opened the innings and scored 17. His side never really got going, slipping to 139 all out in 46.1 overs as India won by 79 runs.

By the end of the competition Ben Young had played 9 times for his country, batting 9 times, scoring 343 runs at an average of 38.11, with a high score of 107, with 2 further half centuries to his credit.

He also represented the England Cricket Association for the Deaf three times, the first on 21st June 2010, he played at Lord's against The M.C.C. He scored 16 batting at five in a losing effort.

Young's last NEPL game for Sunderland came on 28th May 2001 at home to South North. He scored 37 in a Sunderland win.

He played 21 NEPL matches for Sunderland, batting 18 times, with 3 not outs, scoring 325 runs at an average of 21.66, he had a high score of 53, one of two half centuries he scored. His high score had come at home against title winning Chester le Street on 29th July 2001. As a wicketkeeper he took 28 catches and 2 stumpings for Sunderland in the NEPL.

He was the top wicketkeeper in the NEPL in 2000 with 24 catches and 2 stumpings.

His NEPL career, across Sunderland, Philadelphia and Gateshead Fell saw him play a total of 110 matches, batting 105 times, with 8 not out's, he scored 1500 runs at an average of 15.46, with 8 half centuries and a high score of 86, for Gateshead Fell away at South North on 25th August 2003.

As a wicketkeeper Young took 50 catches and had 4 stumpings in the NEPL, he played his last NEPL game on 25th April 2009 for Gateshead Fell at South Shields.

Cameron Cuffy batted at seven on the season opener of 6th May 2000 scoring 14. He was a tall, right arm fast bowler from St Vincent, he was listed at either 6 foot 7 or 6 foot 8 depending on your source! Greg Applegarth had him as 6 foot 8 so I will go with that. He also says that Cuffy wasn't the original pro that they had lined up, that was a certain Waqar Younis from Pakistan! Younis had agreed to come and play as he had fallen out with the then Pakistan captain, Wasim Akram and that meant he was available. Younis was recalled to the side, eventually taking over from Akram as captain and back in the national side and not available for Sunderland. So, they got Cameron Cuffy instead.

Greg Applegarth remembers that he was "quick, around the mid 80's, he hit the bat hard and because of his height he got a bit of extra bounce, often hitting the splice of the bat, he was very accurate on both his line and length, bowling inswing to the right hander, his bouncer used to follow right handed batsmen, as well as being a very, very good bowler he was an outstanding club pro, always bowling off his full run up, giving his all on every wicket, whether helpful or otherwise 100 % effort."

Applegarth remembers a story about Cuffy and a game at Tynemouth. Cuffy had forgot his white shirt, all he had was shirt from his days in The Caribbean, from playing in The Buster Cup, it was white with a multi-coloured chest, a mainly red multi-coloured chest, Applegarth says that he could only "presume that the Tynemouth batsmen didn't want to upset him, as no-one complained!" When Tynemouth batted, he had 1 for 50, his first NEPL wicket being P. Haynes.

During the 2000 season Cuffy took at least four wickets on eight occasions, his best bowling figures being 8 for 46 on 22nd July 2000 at Norton. Lee Rushworth had 89 not out in the same game as Sunderland picked up a comfortable eight wicket win.

In addition to Sunderland Cuffy would also play for the Windward Islands, Surrey and the West Indies.

He played 15 Test Matches and 41 One Day Internationals for the West Indies, and he also spent the 1994 season at Surrey CCC. His test debut was on November 18th, 1994, at Wankhede v India. It wasn't a memorable debut as he failed to take a wicket in the first innings and got a first ball duck in his first innings, caught and bowled by Anil Kumble. In the second innings he took his first test wicket, dismissing Kumble, caught by Carl Hooper. He did bat in the second innings, nought not out but didn't face a ball as a strong India side won by 96 runs.

His best bowling figures in test cricket were 4-82 in February 2002 v Pakistan in Sharjah, UAE.

His last Test Match started on 30th October 2002 at Eden Gardens, again v India. He took 2 wickets in each Innings in a high scoring match which featured five centuries across both teams.

Cuffy made his One Day International debut was on 17th October 1994 v India at Faridabad and his last took place on 3rd December 2002 in Dhaka against Bangladesh. His best bowling figures were 4 -24 against Zimbabwe on 23rd January 2001 in Sydney.

When his international career ended, and despite its inauspicious start, Cuffy had played 15 Test Matches, taking 43 wickets at an average of 33.83 each, including dismissing Sachin Tendulkar three times, and 41 One Day Internationals, taking 41 wickets at an average of 35.02.

Cuffy also had in his pocket, a rather unusual man of the match award. On 23rd June 2001 West Indies were playing a One Day International against Zimbabwe in Harare. West Indies batted first, 266 for 5, Cuffy didn't bat. Zimbabwe made 239 for 9 with Cuffy bowling his ten overs at a cost of twenty runs. The man of the match adjudicators decided Cuffy's bowling was the key factor in the game, so without scoring a run or taking a wicket, he was man of the match! Overall decent numbers and a good international career.

His NEPL career was limited to just this one season, playing 17 matches with 10 innings and 4 not outs, he scored 71 runs at an average of 11.83 and a high score of 19.

It was as a bowler that Cuffy made his impression, bowling 777 balls, 23 maidens, taking 54 wickets at an average of 13.66, he also took 3 catches.

He was recalled by the West Indies for the 2001 season and replaced by Franklyn Rose, a very capable cricketer who Greg Applegarth recalls "never quite made the impact in the league that Cuffy had."

He later moved on to be professional at Nelson Cricket Club in what was then The Lancashire League.

Richard Barnes, known to all as "Richie" batted at eight in the season opener, scoring 16, he was a right-handed batsman and right arm leg spin bowler.

Greg Applegarth recalls that he was "a lower order batsman, as a bowler he never realized his potential, he had played a lot in the Durham Senior League for the club as a leggy, he also had dyed blond hair at this time, comparisons with Shane Warne were inevitable. His cricket suffered when he ruptured his Achilles playing squash in 2001 with my dad."

Barnes played 12 matches in the NEPL in 2000, batting 9 times with 2 not outs, he scored 67 runs at an average of 9.57. His highest score was 29 not out.

He bowled 18 balls in the 2000 NEPL season, with 0 maidens, he conceded 24 runs and took 0 wickets., he did take 3 catches in that NEPL season.

Barnes played 30 matches for Sunderland in the NEPL, batting 24 times, with 8 not outs, he scored 241 runs at an average of 15.06 and a high score of 29 not out, made on 13th May 2000 at home to Norton.

He bowled 162 balls, with 5 maidens, conceding 105 runs and taking 5 wickets at an average of 21.00. His best bowling figures were 3 for 31 on 27th August 2001 at home to Gateshead Fell. He also took 7 NEPL catches for Sunderland.

After featuring regularly in the first team in 2000 and 2001, he played four more games in the NEPL for Sunderland in 2006, his last appearance was on 26th August 2006 at Blaydon when he scored 14.

Stuart Pattison batted at nine in the 2000 season opener, failing to score. He also got a bowl, 0 for 16. He was a right-handed middle order batsman, right arm medium pace bowler and is the brother of Durham bowler Ian Pattison. Greg Applegarth described him as "an attacking batsman who liked to play his shots, as a bowler he could swing it both ways and was the first change bowler after the prolific opening pair. He was a very good player, he left for Seaham Harbour around 2004, I think he's still there!"

He played 16 matches in the NEPL in the 2000 season, batting 14 times with 7 not outs, he scored 226 runs at an average of 32.28. He scored 1 half century, 65 not out, made on 1st July 2000 at home to Blaydon.

He also bowled 347 balls in the NEPL in 2000, with 13 maidens, conceding 435 runs and taking 21 wickets at an average of 20.71. His best bowling figures were 3 for 1, taken on 24th June 2000 at Newcastle. He also took 7 catches in the NEPL in the 2000 season.

Stuart Pattison was first featured in the history books on 16th May 1999 in a National Club Championship game for Sunderland at Backworth. He clearly had some pedigree before this as he would have been in his teens at this time, Sunderland batted first, and Pattison top scored with 58 in a score of 167 for 7 from 45 overs. Tim Brown, 78 and Darren Leason 61 not out saw Backworth home by seven wickets. The Sunderland side that day had several names who would play in the club's NEPL debut in 2000, Simon Brown, Ben Young, Adam Applegarth, Paul Goodwin and Michael Nunn.

Pattison would go on to play 80 NEPL matches for Sunderland, batting 71 times, with 14 not out's, he scored 1238 runs at an average of 21.71 and a high score of 91, made on 25th August 2001 at Stockton, he also had 4 for 24 that day for good measure! He scored 5 half centuries in The NEPL for Sunderland.

As a bowler Pattison bowled 3332 balls, with 121 maidens, conceding 1985 runs and taking 90 wickets at an average of 22.05. His best bowling was 5 for 24 at home against Norton on 31st August 2002. He took 15 catches for the club in the NEPL. His last appearance for Sunderland was on 4th September 2004 at home to Durham Academy.

Paul Goodwin batted at number ten in the season opener, scoring 8 not out, he also bowled, marking his NEPL debut with the wicket of Wayne Falla, as he took 1 for 27. He was a student at this time, a left-handed batsman, Greg Applegarth recalls "a proper tail end spinner, arm guard and all type, as a bowler he was right arm off spinner. As a bowler he absolutely hated giving runs away, to the point that we felt that he preferred miserly, tight bowling figures to wickets against his name, he mixed his bowling up well, bowling a lot flatter the more he went through his career, he could read batsmen and conditions quickly and work out quickly how to close a batsman's scoring down, he bowled with a very straight arm."

During the 2000 season Goodwin played 12 matches in the NEPL, batting 2 times with 1 not out, he scored 8 runs at an average of 8.00. His highest score was 8 not out.

He bowled 123 balls in the NEPL in 2000, with 0 maidens, he conceded 201 runs and took 9 wickets at an average of 22.33. His best bowling figures were 3 for 38, taken on 1st July 2000 at home to Blaydon. He took 6 catches in the NEPL that season."

Paul Goodwin first came to note of the record keepers as an Under 15, playing for Durham against their Scotland counterparts on 17th July 1997 at Brandon in a one-day match. Durham batted first, Goodwin at number three contributing 24, as they made 183 for 8 from their 50 overs. Dan Shurben top scored with 45 and Steven Lee Merrington had 32. When Scotland batted an opening stand of 125, saw them go on to win comfortably by eight wickets, Goodwin bowling eleven overs, 0 for 50.

He did play a further Under 15 match, against the same opposition, a couple of weeks later, on 30th July 1997, this time at Ampleforth. Scotland batted first, scoring 137 for 8 from 50 overs, Goodwin bowling four overs and taking 1 for 11. When Durham batted Goodwin opened and scored 51, with 9 boundaries, as his side won by 9 wickets with 18 overs to spare. Ian Pattison was the other opener that day and he had 72 not out.

His first recorded appearance for Sunderland came at Backworth on 16th May 1999 in The National Club Championship. Sunderland batted first, 58 from Stuart Pattison helping to 167 for 7 from their 45 overs, Goodwin, batting at seven, made 27 not out. When Backworth batted the Northumberland pair of Tim Brown, 78, and Darren Leason 61 not out, saw them home by seven wickets, Goodwin 0 for 32.

His next recorded appearance was that NEPL fixture on 6th May 2000 and his NEPL career was to last until 4th June 2005, when he played his last NEPL game, at home to South North, he was L.B.W to Lee Crozier.

In total Paul Goodwin played 35 NEPL matches, all for Sunderland, batting 18 times, with 6 not outs, scoring 194 runs at an average of 16.16 and a high score of 52 not out, made at home to Tynemouth on 30th April 2005 and this was his only half century.

He bowled 687 deliveries in the NEPL, with 13 maidens, conceding 561 runs and taking 25 wickets at an average of 22.44 and a best bowling of 4-40. That best bowling was at Norton on 30th August 2004. He took 11 NEPL catches.

Michael Nunn was a left-handed batsman and right arm off spinner, only a very occasional bowler. Nunn was the only Sunderland batsman who didn't get to bat in their first ever NEPL fixture, he was listed at number eleven, he didn't get to bowl that day either and that was symptomatic of this season for him.

Nunn played four NEPL games that season, he had just two innings, scoring 17 runs for an average of 8.50. His top score was 17, against Chester Le Street on 20th May 2000. His two dismissals were a run out and an L.B.W and he didn't bowl for the first team that season nor take a catch.

Greg Applegarth remembers Nunn as "a steady batsman, very stable, with a good defence, if you needed someone to stand up to the new ball or bat out an innings for a draw, Nunn would do a job for you, he was a very good second team cricketer, when he played in the first team, he gave everything, a wholehearted, dedicated cricketer."

He went on to play for Sunderland up to the end of the 2014 NEPL season, his last game coming on 13th September 2014 at Tynemouth.

There is one wrinkle in his statistics, he played for Sunderland on 4th July 2009, he next appeared in The NEPL for Tynemouth on 11th July 2009 against Chester Le Street, before re-appearing in Sunderland colours again on 1st August 2009 against South Shields.

He made 147 NEPL appearances for Sunderland, comprising of 113 innings, 34 not out's, scoring 1148 runs at an average of 14.53, with a high score of 74 not out, with 2 half centuries. His high score came on 5th September 2009 at home to Norton, he opened the batting that day, adding 180 in an unbroken second wicket stand with Stuart Walker, 98 not out, in a nine-wicket win.

He bowled 32 balls taking 0 for 42, he failed to score in his one appearance for Tynemouth.

His next NEPL appearance came for Washington at Hetton Lyons on 1st May 2021, he scored 17 and his last NEPL appearance was again for Washington on 11th September 2021 at home to Benwell Hill, opening the batting and scoring 13.

He appeared 17 times for Washington in the 2021 season, batting 17 times, he was dismissed in all 17 innings, scoring 242 runs at an average of 14.23, with a high score of 74 and 1 half century. The high score of 74 was on 28th August 2021 opening the batting at Burnopfield and was top score in the innings. He also played for Seaham Harbour.

To sum up his NEPL career, batting only, he played 165 matches, had 131 innings, scoring 1390 runs with an average of 14.32 and a high score of 74. He had 3 half centuries and took 40 NEPL catches.

Darren Blenkiron was a left-handed batsman and right arm medium pace bowler; he was signed by Sunderland for the final third of the 2000 season, he already had three years as a first-class cricketer when Sunderland signed him. He played 19 first class matches for Durham, with 33 innings, 3 not outs and 774 runs at an average of 25.80. His highest first-class score was 145 and this was one of three first class hundreds he scored, he also had 2 half centuries. The highest score of 145 was against Glamorgan over 29th -June to 3rd July 1995 at Swansea. He had scored 53 in the first innings and his century was one of four in a high scoring match.

Blenkiron also had 6 first class wickets to his credit, bowling 323 balls, with 10 maidens and conceding 187 runs, giving him an average of 31.16. His best bowling was 4 for 43.

He also played 24 List A matches for Durham, scoring 396 runs, with a high score of 56 and an average of 23.29. He also took 1 wicket and had 4 one day catches.

As a young man he played 1 Test Match for England Under 19's and 3 One Day matches and he also represented Durham at Minor Counties level.

Blenkiron made his NEPL debut for Sunderland on 29th July 2000 at home to Chester le Street. Sunderland batted first, Ben Young top scoring with 53, Blenkiron batted at four and was run out for 18 as Sunderland declared on 225 for 9. When Chester batted Ashley Thorpe had 91, there were 46 extras and Tony Birbeck had 31, despite 6 for 65 from Cameron Cuffy and two wickets for Adam Applegarth, Chester 211 for 9, hung on for the draw.

Blenkiron made 60 in his next game at South North on 5th August 2000. South North batted first, 86 from captain John Graham helping them to 259 for 7 declared, Paul Goodwin 3 for 38 the pick of the bowlers. Simon Old had 101, his first century for the club, and Blenkiron 60 as Sunderland 234 for 8, got a draw.

Blenkiron next contributed with the ball on 2nd September 2000 at home to Newcastle, Newcastle batted first, only two players scored double figures as they were bowled out for just 65. All four Sunderland bowlers used picked up at least one wicket, Cameron Cuffy 1 for 14, Adam Applegarth 4 for 17, Stuart Pattison 2 for 25 and Blenkiron had 5-0-6-3. When Sunderland batted 26 not out from Simon Old and 35 not out from Blenkiron saw Sunderland home by eight wickets.

When the season ended, Blenkiron had played 7 matches for Sunderland, batting 6 times with 2 not outs, he had scored 176 runs at an average of 44.00 and 1 half century, the 60 mentioned earlier.

He had also bowled 42 balls, with 1 maiden, conceded 7 runs and took 3 wickets at an average of 2.33.

He returned to Sunderland for the 2001 season, playing 18 matches in this season, with 16 innings and 3 not out, he would score 406 runs at an average of 31.23 and a high score of 118 not out. He would add one fifty and one hundred to his Sunderland career. That high score was at Tynemouth on 23rd June 2001, a game Sunderland won comfortably by 99 runs as they bowled Tynemouth out for 159, Franklyn Rose 4 for 69 and Ian Pattison 4 for 17.

When his Sunderland NEPL career was done, he had played 25 matches for them, batted 22 times, with 5 not outs, and scored 582 runs at an average of 34.23, with 2 fifties and 1 hundred. He also had 3 wickets for 12 runs from just 48 balls and 6 catches to his credit. He went on to play for Bishop Auckland and Bilton.

There were several other young lads who contributed throughout the 2000 season, Craig Burdon, Jimmy Butler, Chris Brown and Chris Robson.

Craig Burdon was a slow left arm bowler, he made his NEPL debut on 13th May 2000 at home to Norton, he took 2 for 53 when Norton batted first, Marc Symington had 45 and Graeme Bridge 40, as they made 205 for 5 declared. When Sunderland batted Burdon scored 12, despite 88 from Andrew Pratt the game just ended up in a draw, Sunderland 202 for 8. Marc Symington had 4 for 58 for Norton.

Burdon had already represented England several times at Under 15 level, the first time on 7th August 1996 against Canada, at Teddington, as part of the Lombard Challenge Cup, although he didn't get a bat as England made 344 for 5 from 55 overs. Michael Carberry and Graeme Bridge were in the same side and James Adams, who would go on to a long first-class career with Hampshire, scored 141 not out. When Canada batted, Burdon came on as first change, bowling 11 overs and taking 1 for 21, Canada scored 173 for 5, as England won comfortably.

England reached the semifinal of the competition, losing out to Pakistan, Burdon played in every game, with a best bowling of 3 for 19.

Burdon was selected by The ECB Schools East for a 2 day, 100 over fixture against ECB Schools West at Aldershot starting on 13th July 1999. When The West batted, he bowled 34.5 overs, taking 4 for 98, as they made 281 all out in 98.5 overs. He opened the batting, scoring 4 as his side were all out for 249, to lose by 32 runs.

Burdon played a two-day match for Durham Under 19's against Derbyshire Under 19's at Ilkeston, starting on 26th July 1999. Tom Lungley, who would go on to a first-class career with Derbyshire, scored 138 not out as their Under 19's made 388 for 7 declared, from 111 overs, Burdon had just 4 overs for 22. He did open the batting, scoring 42 in an opening stand of 94 with P. Gough, who top scored with 89 as Durham scored 337 for 9 from 93 overs and the match was drawn.

Returning to Burdon in the 2000 NEPL season, he played 16 matches, batting 16 times, with 2 not out's, he scored 180 runs at an average of 12.85 and a high score of 27.

He bowled 98 balls, with 1 maiden, conceding 181 runs and taking 10 wickets at an average of 18.10. His best bowling figures were 4 for 10 away at Tynemouth on 15th July. Cameron Cuffy had 4 for 45 in the game as Tynemouth were dismissed for 127. 84 not out from Lee Rushworth saw Sunderland win by 7 wickets.

Burdon would have a patchy career in The NEPL with Sunderland, after the end of the 2000 season he didn't re-appear in the first team until June 2003, playing four NEPL games that season, after a handful of other appearances, he did play regularly in the side in 2013 and 2016 and 2017. His last NEPL appearance came on 5th August 2017 at Burnmoor, he scored 4 opening the batting.

He played 47 times in The NEPL for Sunderland, batting on 43 occasions, he had 4 not out's, he scored 414 runs at an average of 10.61 and a high score of 34.

He bowled 104 balls, with 1 maiden, conceding 190 runs and taking 10 wickets at an average of 19.00. His best bowling was the 4 for 10 mentioned earlier and he took 8 NEPL catches.

Jimmy Butler was another relative youngster, "probably a student" around the time of the 2000 season. He was a right-handed batsman and right arm medium fast bowler. Greg Applegarth remembers him as a "very skilful bowler, he could swing it both ways, he rarely batted but he did achieve better things after 2000 before moving on to Percy Main around 2005."

He made his NEPL debut on 10th June 2000 at Stockton, he bowled five overs and took his first NEPL wicket, Hilton Wordsworth, caught by Lee Rushworth, 1 for 18 although he didn't bat.

He played 4 matches in the title winning side, batting just once, for 4 and he bowled 30 balls, 1 maiden, conceding 32 runs and taking 1 wicket. His 1 for 18 on debut was his best of the season and he took 2 NEPL catches that season.

His last appearance in The NEPL came on 3rd September 2005 at Gateshead Fell, he opened the bowling taking 1 for 58, Kyle Coetzer had 118 not out for Fell. He was L.B.W for nought when Sunderland batted in a 146-run loss.

His NEPL career, all with Sunderland took in 38 matches, although batting 15 times he was not a batsman. He bowled 1597 balls, 49 maidens, conceding 969 runs and took 37 wickets at an average of 26.18 with a best bowling of 6 for 60 on 14th May 2005 at home to Stockton and he took 13 catches.

Chris Robson also played for the first team in 2000, making his NEPL debut on 1st July 2000 at home to Blaydon. He played 9 matches in the NEPL in 2000, batting 5 times with 3 not outs, he scored 38 runs at an average of 19.00. His highest score was 27, made on 29th July 2000 at home to Chester le Street. He didn't bowl in 2000 but took 3 catches. His last NEPL match was on 2nd August 2008 at home to Benwell Hill.

He played 46 NEPL matches for Sunderland, batting 33 times with 7 not outs, he scored 254 runs at an average of 9.76, his highest score was 63, his only half century coming on 23rd July 2005 at Stockton. He didn't bowl but did take 13 catches.

Greg Applegarth recalls that Sunderland had, under his dad's strategy of bowling first, been bowling sides out relatively cheaply and picking up plenty of bonus points along the way, they had been going well, with only four games to go, on 19th August, they were playing The Durham Academy at The Riverside, on a wicket that was "damp" at one end. The Academy were pushing Sunderland all the way at this time, but it was a low scoring match.

Sunderland batted first and were 59 for 6 when Simon Brown came to the crease to join Darren Blenkiron. They were the only two players to make double figures, Blenkiron with 44 had the top score in the match, he and Brown took the score to 98 when they were separated, Brown dismissed for 14. There were 17 extras as they were dismissed for 104.

When the Academy batted, they lost an early wicket, Hiran Marambe bowled for a duck by Cameron Cuffy, five for one. Phil Walker 14, and Gordon Muchall 9, took the score to 30 before the Academy lost their next wicket, they lost another two at the same score and quickly fell to 39 for 5.

Phil Mustard was the top scoring batsman with 18, Chris Mann and Mark Davies had 11 each, 25 extras was the real top scorer! A ninth wicket stand of 20 took the score from 80 for 8 to 100 for 8, Stuart Pattison had mark Davies caught by Lee Rushworth, 100 for 9, then Pattison bowled the eleventh batsman, Jonathan Kean for a duck, Sunderland had won by four runs. Cuffy had 3 for 37, Adam Applegarth 4 for 27 and Stuart Pattison 3 for 25, his wickets being the last three to fall.

Sunderland subsequently saw the season out with an abandoned game at Gateshead Fell and then 2 big victories, both following their plan of bowl first, Newcastle 65 all out, Adam Applegarth 4 for 17 and Darren Blenkiron 3 for 6, then Blaydon 77 all out, Cuffy 4 for 35, Applegarth 6 for 39.

The Academy had two games abandoned and they then drew with South North, Sunderland were champions by 38 points.

Adam Applegarth was named as the first ever NEPL Player of the Year, son Greg remembers that the talk at the time was that the recipient of this award would be given some form of Durham contract, while that may have come true for the next winner, Ashley Thorpe, Greg Applegarth laughs that "it kind of fell on its backside a bit when my 37-year-old dad won it, not sure they had much use for a middle-aged seamer!"

Greg Applegarth has himself had a good NEPL career, making his debut on 2nd August 2003 for Sunderland at home to Stockton.

His statistics up to 9th September 2023 are that he has played 147 NEPL matches, all for Sunderland, batting 129 times, with 10 not out's, scoring 2174 runs at an average of 18.26, this includes 6 half centuries and 1 century, 123, scored on 4th May 2013 at Tynemouth.

He has also bowled 751 balls, 21 maidens, conceding 480 runs and taking 13 wickets at an average of 36.92, his best bowling is 3 for 85. He has also taken 33 NEPL catches.

As his name cropped up earlier in the 2000 season, I will take the opportunity to have a look at Phil Mustard in the NEPL. He made his NEPL debut on 13th May 2000 for The Durham Academy at Stockton.

Gary Pratt made 149 not out to start the season so Mustard didn't get to bat, Dawnely Joseph scored 134 not out in the Stockton reply, 483 runs were scored for the loss of just 4 wickets as The NEPL got off to a tough start for bowlers!

Mustard played his last game for The Academy in The NEPL on 7th September 2002 at The Riverside against Newcastle.

He made his NEPL debut for Benwell Hill on 26th April 2003 at home to Stockton, scoring 70 and played his last NEPL game for Hill on 30th August 2004 at home to Newcastle.

On 8th August 2008 Phil Mustard played his one and only NEPL game for Newcastle at Gateshead Fell, he scored 53 and took 3 for 54 bowling.

He next appeared in The NEPL for South North at home to Stockton on 27th June 2015. He took 0 for 3 and made 52. He would play just 2 more games for South North that season and in total.

On 28th April 2018 Mustard made his NEPL debut for his fifth NEPL team, Felling at The Riverside against The Durham Academy, his last NEPL game came for them was on 8th September 2018 at South North. South North batted first and Mustard took his last NEPL wicket when he bowled Adam Cragg for 13, Cragg got his revenge when Mustard batted, running him out for 26.

Across his five teams Phil Mustard played 88 games in the NEPL, batting 80 times, with 5 not out's, he scored 2333 runs at an average of 31.10. He scored 16 half centuries and 2 centuries. His highest score was 145 for Felling at Benwell Hill on 7th July 2018. Incredibly that wasn't the highest score of the day, Gerrit Snyman, Hill's South African pro had 173, James Schofield was another centurion that day as he scored 117 not out for Hill.

Mustard also bowled 402 balls in the NEPL, with 2 maidens, conceding 369 runs and taking 9 wickets at an average of 41.00. His best bowling figures were 3 for 36 on 26th June 2004 at Stockton for Benwell Hill. He also took 65 NEPL catches and had 5 stumpings. I asked John Graham about Phil Mustard's bowling; he describes it as "very average leg spin."

Fortunately, Mustard had his wicketkeeping and batting to fall back on, he played 10 One Day Internationals for England, batting 10 times, with 0 not outs, he scored 233 runs at an average of 23.30. He made 1 half century, his highest score of 83, made on 20th February 2008 at Napier against New Zealand. He also took 9 catches and had 2 stumpings for England.

He also played 2 Twenty20 games for England, batting 2 times, with 0 not outs, he scored 60 runs at an average of 30.00. His highest score was 40 on 7th February 2008 at Christchurch against New Zealand.

Mustard had a first-class career with Durham, Lancashire and Gloucestershire, playing 210 first class matches and scoring 8700 runs at an average of 30.41. He scored 52 half centuries and 7 centuries.

He took 1 wicket in first class cricket, but also had 670 catches and 19 stumpings.

He also played 205 List A matches, scoring a further 5484 runs at an average of 30.63, with 34 half centuries and 7 centuries. He had a further 214 catches and 48 stumpings at this level.

Phil Mustard also played 192 Twenty20 matches, scoring 4228 runs at an average of 24.43, scoring 22 half centuries. He also took 95 catches and had 38 stumpings in Twenty20 cricket.

Phil Mustard is now a respected NEPL umpire, his son Haydon is following in his father's footsteps at Benwell Hill.

Haydon Mustard is a right-handed batsman and wicketkeeper. He made his debut for England Young Lions on 22nd August 2023 at Loughborough against Australia Under 19's. Up to the end of February 2024 he has now played 3 matches for this side, with a highest score of 66.

He made his debut for England Under 19's in India on 22nd November 2023, up to the end of February 2024 Haydon Mustard had 4 now played matches for England Under 19'S, his highest score is 41.

On 29th March 2024 it was announced that Haydon has signed a 2-year rookie contract with Durham.

He came through the Northumberland pathway to represent Durham at Under 16 level.

He made his first-class debut and T20 debut in February 2024 in Harare with Durham, scoring 46 not out. He also made his professional debut in a T20 match for Durham on 3rd March 2024 in Zimbabwe against Mountaineers.

Haydon Mustard made his NEPL debut on 11th September 2021 for Benwell Hill at Washington. To the end of the 2023 season, he has now played 34 NEPL matches and has 3 half centuries and the highest score of 60 to his name. He has also taken 31 catches and had 2 stumpings.

One for the future, as no doubt is his younger brother, Rory!

If you are going to discuss Sunderland around this time you must mention Chris Rushworth and his association with the club. Although he played a lot for the Durham Academy and in first-class cricket, he made his debut on 19th May 2001 for Sunderland at home to Chester le Street.

Rushworth played 4 times in the NEPL for Sunderland that season, batting 2 times with 2 not outs, he scored 16 runs at an average of 8.00 with his highest score of 7 not out.

He bowled 120 balls for them, with 7 maidens, conceding 42 runs and taking 3 wickets at an average of 14.00. His best bowling figures were 2 for 20 on 28th May 2004 at home to South North.

His first NEPL wicket came in this game, South North captain, John Graham, bowled for 32.

Chris Rushworth made his NEPL debut for Durham Academy on 27th April 2002 at South North, his last appearance in the NEPL for them was on 3rd September 2005 at The Racecourse Ground against Blaydon, taking 4 for 57.

He played 62 times in the NEPL for The Academy, batting 30 times with 14 not outs, he scored 257 runs at an average of 16.06. He scored 1 half century, his highest score, 50, on 28th May 2005 at The Racecourse against Philadelphia.

He bowled 3112 balls for them, with 77 maidens, conceding 1924 runs and taking 72 wickets at an average of 26.72. His best bowling figures were 5 for 27 on 24th April 2004 at Newcastle. He took 13 catches.

He returned to Sunderland and next played for them in the NEPL on 29th April 2006 at home to Stockton and his last NEPL appearance for them was on 17th August 2013 at home to Hetton Lyons.

He had played 82 matches for Sunderland in the NEPL, batting 60 times, with 10 not outs, he scored 1087 runs at an average of 21.74 and scored 8 half centuries. His highest score was now 79, scored on 26th May 2012 at South Shields.

He bowled 5342 balls in the NEPL for Sunderland, with 193 maidens, conceding 2970 runs and taking 156 wickets at an average of 19.03. His best bowling figures were 7 for 39 on 24th April 2010 at home to Hetton Lyons and he took 32 catches in the NEPL for the club.

Chris Rushworth would play twice more in the NEPL, the first was for Chester le Street, on was on 19th May 2018 at Sacriston. His last NEPL appearance came on 12th June 2021 for Sacriston at home to Chester le Street, he took 4 for 41, his last NEPL wicket was Amaan Ulhaq, bowled for 4.

In his NEPL career, Chris Rushworth played 150 matches, batting 95 times with 26 not outs, he scored 1377 runs at an average of 19.95. He scored 9 half centuries with his highest score being the 79 mentioned earlier.

He bowled 8724 balls, with 283 maidens, conceding 4999 runs and taking 236 wickets at an average of 21.18. His best bowling figures were the 7 for 39 mentioned earlier. He took 45 NEPL career catches.

He played first- class cricket for Durham, The M.C.C and Warwickshire, playing 168 matches in total, he batted 222 times with 74 not outs, he scored 1765 runs at an average of 11.92 with 1 half century, his highest score of 57.

He bowled 29931 balls in first class cricket, with 1157 maidens, he conceded 14711 runs and took 656 wickets at an average of 22.42. His best bowling figures were 9 for 52 for Durham against Northants in September 2014. He took 37 catches in first class cricket.

He played 87 List A matches, batting 38 times with 19 not outs, he scored 215 runs at an average of 11.31. His highest score was 38 not out.

He bowled 3959 balls in List A cricket, with 47 maidens, he conceded 3416 runs and took 140 wickets at an average of 24.40. His best bowling figures were 5 for 31 taken in June 2013 against Nottinghamshire and he took 19 career catches in List A cricket.

Rushworth also made 85 appearances in Twenty20 cricket, batting 15 times with 9 not outs, he scored 20 runs at an average of 3.33 with a highest score of 5.

He bowled 1623 balls in Twenty20 cricket, with 3 maidens, he conceded 2121 runs and took 78 wickets at an average of 27.19. His best bowling figures were 3 for 14 and he took 18 catches in this format.

The other Sunderland player from this period we should have a closer look at is Simon Brown, to avoid confusion with Simon M. Brown who was covered earlier as part of the 2000 title winning side, I am now referring to S. J. E Brown, the left arm medium pace bowler.

To further avoid confusion, I will deal with his professional career first.

Brown played one test match for England in a game starting on 25th July 1996 against Pakistan at Lord's, he took 1 for 78 in the first innings. His first test wicket was opener Aamer Sohail, leg before for a single. He scored a single when he batted and then took 1 for 60 in Pakistan's second innings, the match was drawn. Brown was never given another chance at international level.

He did, however, have an excellent first-class career for Durham, he played 159 first-class matches, batting 221 times, with 221 not outs, he scored 1796 runs at an average of 12.05. He scored 2 half centuries, with the highest score of 69.

He bowled 28735 balls, with 935 maidens, conceding 15800 runs and taking 550 wickets at an average of 28.72. His best bowling figures were 7 for 51. He took 42 catches.

He also played List A cricket for Northamptonshire and Durham, playing 113 matches in total, his batting was in its early stages, and he had a high score of 18.

He bowled 5352 balls, with 66 maidens, conceding 4062 runs and taking 132 wickets at an average of 30.77. His best bowling figures were 6 for 30. He took 23 catches.

He made his NEPL debut for Sunderland on 26th April 2003 at home to Norton and he took his first NEPL wicket on 10th May 2003 Gateshead Fell, opener Philip Taylor caught by Michael Roseberry for a single.

His last NEPL game was on 8th September 2007 at home to The Durham Academy, he took 3 wickets that day, Scott Borthwick for 3, Ben Stokes for a duck and his last NEPL wicket, Paul Muchall, bowled for a duck, he finished with 3 for 17.

In total S.J.E Brown played 90 matches in the NEPL, all for Sunderland, he batted 42 times, with 17 not outs, he scored 243 runs at an average of 9.72. His highest score was 43, scored on 14th June 2003 at Jesmond against Newcastle.

He bowled 5303 balls, with 233 maidens, conceding 2478 runs and taking 162 wickets at an average of 15.29. His best bowling figures were 6 for 28 taken on 31st May 2003 at Blaydon. He took 28 NEPL catches.

To return to the NEPL and for completeness, this season's Banks Salver was won by South North.

TABLE 5   NEPL Final Table 2000.

	Played	Won	Drawn	Lost	Bonus Points	Points
Sunderland	20	8	11	1	86	261
Durham CA	20	6	11	3	78	223
Blaydon	20	6	10	4	69	209
South North	20	5	12	5	74	209
Norton	20	3	14	3	93	208
Chester le St	20	3	15	2	82	202
Benwell Hill	20	3	15	2	75	195
Gateshead Fell	20	4	12	4	63	183
Stockton	20	3	11	6	76	176
Tynemouth	20	1	14	5	66	151
Newcastle	20	0	11	9	51	106

TABLE 6   NEPL Batting Averages 2000.

Qualification 250 Runs.

40 Batsmen Qualified this season.

Player	Club	Inns	Not Out	H. S	Runs	Average
(1) G.J Muchall	Durham CA	11	4	153 no	545	77.86
(2) A.M. Thorpe	Chester le St	15	4	179 no	843	76.64
(3) D. Joseph	Stockton	17	3	159 no	1023	73.07
(4) M.J North	Gateshead Fell	14	3	163 no	770	70.00
(5) J.A Graham	South North	14	2	108	703	58.58
(6) Q.J Hughes	Chester le St	6	1	101	277	55.40
(7) C.J Hewison	South North	13	4	106	470	52.22
(8) S. Ball	Norton	17	2	114 no	693	46.20
(9) J.B Windows	Benwell Hill	13	2	74	485	44.09
(10) G.J Pratt	Durham CA	7	1	149	260	43.33
(11) P.J Nicholson	Benwell Hill	11	1	100 no	428	42.90
(12) M.J Symington	Norton	12	1	74	465	42.27
(18) L.J Rushworth	Sunderland	16	2	117	489	34.93
(28) S.J Old	Sunderland	16	2	101	344	24.57

TABLE 7   NEPL Bowling Averages 2000.

Qualification 15 Wickets.

30 Bowlers Qualified this season.

Player	Club	Overs	Mdns	Runs	Wkts	Ave	Best
(1) C. Cuffy	Sunderland	290.5	64	767	54	14.20	8-48
(2) S. Humble	Blaydon	115.5	60	515	33	15.61	5-19
(3) M.J Symington	Norton	141.9	31	408	25	16.32	4-36
(4) A.M Thorpe	Chester Le St	216.4	58	524	32	16.38	4-35
(5) A.J Applegarth	Sunderland	234.0	63	650	39	16.67	6-39
(6) N. Campbell	South North	218.3	69	564	33	17.09	5-27
(7) J. Walker	Blaydon	131.5	31	376	21	17.90	3-16
(8) G. Bridge	Norton	199.2	54	520	28	18.57	5-45
(9) J. Kean	Durham Academy	106.0	29	323	17	19.00	5-41
(10) B. Stewart	Tynemouth	122.5	22	306	16	19.13	4-21
(11) J.B Windows	Benwell Hill	130.5	33	412	21	19.62	4-52
(12) S. Pattison	Sunderland	152.2	33	435	21	20.71	3-1

Sunderland NEPL Champions.

Back Row L to R-Peter Fenwick, Chairman, Mike Smith, Secretary, Ben Young, Stu Pattison,
Joe Rushworth, Cameron Cuffy, Paul Goodwin, Luke Bowmaker, Scorer, Tommy Bowmaker, Life President.

Front Row L to R-Craig Burdon, Darren Blenkiron, Lee Rushworth, Adam Applegarth, Captain,
Chris Robson, Simon Old, Ron Young, Coach.

Adam Applegarth, Secretary Mike Smith,
Simon Old, Vice-Captain with The NEPL Trophy.

15

CHAPTER TWO

Chester le Street 2001

After finishing 6th in the inaugural NEPL season and winning The Just Sport Trophy, Chester le Street had plenty of cause for optimism as they approached the second NEPL season. In 2000 Aussie Pro Ashley Thorpe had scored three NEPL hundreds and both Quentin Hughes and Dan Shurben, had also scored a century. The same three batsman had also featured in the League batting averages; Thorpe being second placed to Gordon Muchall of The Durham Academy and finishing fourth in the bowling averages with 32 wickets. Hughes only played six NEPL games that season, and his greater availability was another cause for optimism on its own! Steven Lee Merrington was also placed in the bowling averages with 15 wickets. They had also added Mark Davies to the side he had already played for Durham Seconds and would go on to play first class cricket for both Durham and Kent.

Allan Worthy and Dan Shurben recall their memories of the 2001 season. In respect of the formation of the league itself, Worthy recalls that teams "weren't necessarily selected for their cricketing strength, Eppleton and Horden for example were both very strong sides in The Durham Senior League and were not to be in The NEPL, it was to be more about facilities first and build your side later. The Northumberland teams pretty much went with the local lads they had, Sunderland had some good local lads in their side to start with and added a superstar in Cameron Cuffy."

Worthy recalls that Tony Birbeck "had a clear plan for Chester le Street, in terms of both his recruitment of the team initially when they entered The NEPL, and as captain, in terms of tactics on the field. He was absolutely the mastermind and heartbeat of Chester le Street cricket at this time, in fact 25 years later he still is, he still has his passion for cricket, recently scoring a century for England Over 60's.

Going into the original NEPL season of 2000 Birbeck knew the local cricket scene very well, The Durham Senior League in particular. Birbeck took a different approach, he knew a lot of the Chester players prior to 2000 were probably not going to be good enough for the new league and so he recruited what he knew, and a lot of the existing players left."

Ashley Thorpe had played for two years at Eppleton with Birbeck, he had a good pedigree too, having played for Western Australia Under 19's and was signed as their overseas player. Worthy, who was to be vice-captain, was well known to Birbeck and Worthy describes himself as a "bit of a punt" as he was still recovering from a bad ACL football injury in his right knee in 2000 and had missed 1999.

Birbeck also recruited a handful of talented but raw youngsters in their late teens for the inaugural season, by 2001 Dan Shurben, Gary Hunter, Paul Chivers, Chris Dodsley and Steven Lee Merrington, would all shine in their second season with that years' experience behind them.

Quentin Hughes was a little older, in 2000, in his mid-twenties, having recently finished playing for Cambridge University when he joined Chester le Street, but he was an established and proven all-rounder with Durham City in The Durham Senior League." That season he joined he only played six NEPL matches, long enough to score 277 runs at an average of 55.40, with a hundred against Stockton on 9th September!

Wicket keeper David Wilson was the only Chester player from The Senior League days to transition to The NEPL.

Worthy recalls "Birbeck was an attacking captain, always wanting to bat first and take the game to the opposition, he liked runs on the board. He always liked a spinner in his side. His game plan for the bowlers was relatively simple, two young, raw, completely different styles of fast bowlers in Chivers and Dodsley, go hell for leather at the openers, with four slips, and try and get the opposition two or three down. During the title winning

2001 season when Mark Davies was available, he only played six NEPL games for Chester, Davies would replace Chivers and open the bowling with Dodsley. Then bring on the slower bowlers in spinners Quentin Hughes and Steven Lee Merrington.

This would be followed up by Ashley Thorpe and me, Thorpe was quicker than I (Worthy) was, and he was medium/fast. We both bowled off eight paces, with the fielders in a ring and challenged the batsman to score, we often "choked the life out of sides" as they found it hard to score."

Speaking to long standing South North captain, John Graham, about this Chester side, he well recalls that ring of fielders and the tactics and skill of Thorpe and Worthy in bowling to their field.

Worthy goes on "If needed the two openers were brought back to remove the tail."

Chester le Street opened their title winning season on 28th April 2001 at home to Tynemouth, Dan Shurben and Allan Worthy opened the innings, Shurben falling for 17, Worthy would go on to make 124 not out. Ashley Thorpe, batting at three, scored 53, and Quentin Hughes batting at four, made 50 not out, as they posted an impressive 265 for 2, declaring after just 53 overs.

Tynemouth were dismissed for 95, all five bowlers used make useful contributions, Davies 9.1-3-19-1, Dodsley 8-4-11-2, Thorpe 9-0-34-3, Chivers 9-2-19-1 and Merrington 4-0-5-3. Chester le Street had started the season with a statement win.

The Chester le Street side that day was-

Dan Shurben a left-handed batsman, he opened against Tynemouth that day, scoring 17. He recalls from a very early age, little more than a toddler, going to cricket with his father, Graeme Shurben. Dan says he "practically grew up at the cricket field."

He says his grandfather, Jim Shurben, was a key figure initially in his cricket upbringing. A former professional footballer with Sunderland in the 1950's as well as a good club cricketer, playing for Burnmoor and Chester le Street. Dan remembers his grandad throwing the ball at him for hours and him trying to belt it over the fence! He says that as he grew older his dad would take him to home games and his grandad to away games.

Dad Graeme had been a wicketkeeper and captain for around ten years at Burnmoor, he was captain when they won The Durham Senior League in 1990, Richie Richardson was amongst his charges, and he was also the leading wicketkeeper for catches ten years in a row. His father moved to Eppleton where he was captain also, batting in the lower middle order, Dan Shurben made his debut for Eppleton Second's aged 12 and Eppleton first team aged 13! He has fond memories of playing first team cricket for "around 18 months" with his father.

The first recorded innings I could find for Shurben was for a one-day match on 17th July 1997 for Durham Under 15's against Scotland Under 15's. Shurben batted at six and top scored with 45, fellow Chester le Street players, Steven Lee Merrington, who batted at four and scored 32 and Graeme Race, who was eleven and didn't get a bat, were also in the side as Durham scored 183 for 8 from their 50 overs. Scotland lost just three wickets as they won comfortably.

Shurben joined Chester aged 16 from Eppleton for their first NEPL season and opened the batting throughout the 2001 season. He made his NEPL debut for Chester on 6th May 2000 opening the batting away at Newcastle.

Shurben played 18 matches in the NEPL in 2001, batting 17 times with 1 not out, he scored 420 runs at an average of 26.25. He scored 4 half centuries with a highest score of 69, made on 30th June 2001 at home to Gateshead Fell. He didn't bowl in the NEPL in 2001 but did take 8 catches.

As well as being an integral part of the title winning side of the 2001 season, Shurben played seven seasons in total for them. He played his last NEPL game for Chester on 28th August 2006 at Stockton, opening the batting he top scored in the innings with 17.

His NEPL career with Chester saw him play 133 matches, batting 128 times, he was not out 6 times, scoring 3983 runs at an average of 32.64. He scored 19 half centuries and 8 centuries. His highest score was 138 on 29th May 2004 at Benwell Hill. The innings came from 135 balls and contained 20 fours and 2 sixes. He bowled 6 deliveries for them, 0 for 2 and took 50 NEPL catches.

Shurben made his debut for Northumberland on 13th June 2004 in a 3-day match at Suffolk, Chris Rushworth was a fellow debutant. The hosts batted first, 325 all out, John Windows had 6 for 57.

Shurben had made 8 opening the Northumberland first innings when he was bowled by Devon Malcolm, yes, that Devon Malcolm, the ex-England fast bowler! Allan Worthy top scored with 50 as Northumberland scored 199 all out, Malcolm had 4 for 50. Suffolk declared for 299 in their second innings. Shurben 75 and Adam Heather, 47, put on 117 for the first wicket, Allan Worthy made 85, Bradley Parker 55, John Windows 40 and Phil Nicholson 43 not out as Northumberland replied with 373 for 5 from 101.4 overs to get a draw. Malcolm had 1 for 89 in the innings.

Shurben would play for Northumberland for the next 20 years or so, playing his last match on 11th June 2023 at Bodicote against Oxfordshire. He opened the batting, making 42 as Northumberland won by 9 runs on Duckworth/ Lewis. He played 57 matches for Northumberland, batting 79 times, he was not out once, scoring 2679 runs at an average of 34.34. He scored 16 half centuries and 4 centuries. His highest score for Northumberland was 153 in a 3-day match which started on 17th July 2005 at Fenner's against Cambridgeshire. He bowled 11 career deliveries for the county, with 1 maiden and conceded 1 run for no wicket and took 22 catches.

Shurben made his NEPL debut for South Shields on 28th April 2007 at Blaydon, marking his debut with 73 not out opening the batting in a 5-wicket win. Mark Stoneman had opened the batting for Blaydon when they had batted. Dan Shurben played his last NEPL game for South Shields on 29th August 2009, scoring 5.

He had played 56 NEPL matches for them, batting 55 times with 10 not outs, he scored 1682 runs at an average of 37.37, with 10 half centuries and 1 century. The century came on 24th May 2008 at home to Chester le Street, he scored 132 opening the innings.

He bowled 210 balls in The NEPL for Shields, with 3 maidens, conceding 173 runs and taking 3 wickets at an average of 57.66 and a best of 2 for 33. He took 37 NEPL career catches for them.

At the end of the 2009 season Shurben was named in The NEPL Team of the Decade.

Shurben made his NEPL debut for Sunderland on 24th April 2010 at home to Hetton Lyons, opening the batting he made 82. His last appearance of this spell for Sunderland was due to be at Whitburn on 10th May 2014, the match was abandoned after the toss but before a ball was bowled.

Shurben had played 77 matches for them, batting 74 times with 6 not out's, he scored 2129 runs at an average of 31.30. He made 12 half centuries and 2 centuries. His highest score, 144 not out, came on 12th May 2012 at Tynemouth. He didn't bowl for Sunderland in The NEPL but did take 42 catches for them.

He moved across to Washington for the remainder of 2014, making his debut on 24th May in a rain affected game at Vigo Lane, Washington against Brandon in the NEPL First Division. He was out for 14 before the rain came after just 12.2 overs and the game was abandoned. For the record, Ashley Thorpe and Melvyn Betts were also in the Washington side that day.

He batted 15 times in the season for Washington, with 0 not outs, he scored 316 runs at an average of 21.07 and a best of 68. Washington were runners up in the league to a strong South Shields in 2014, Shields being promoted to The NEPL for the 2015 season.

Shurben made his NEPL debut for Whitburn on 18th April 2015 at home to Blaydon, opening the batting he made 19, his last appearance for Whitburn was at Eppleton on 9th September 2017, he made 38 opening the batting.

Shurben played 60 matches in The NEPL for Whitburn, batting 59 times with 6 not outs, he scored 1691 runs at an average of 31.90. He made 7 half centuries and 3 centuries. His highest score, 180 not out, came on 30th May 2012 at home to Gateshead Fell. The innings took 175 balls and contained 25 fours and 5 sixes. He didn't bowl for Whitburn in The NEPL but did take 35 catches for them.

Shurben returned to play for Sunderland in The NEPL Division 1 for the 2018 season, playing his first game of this spell on 21st April at home to Gateshead Fell, he made 136 as he opened the batting. The innings came off 151 balls and contained 8 fours and 10 sixes. Sunderland were promoted back to The NEPL at the end of 2021.

Shurben played 21 NEPL matches for Sunderland in 2022, batting 20 times with 2 not outs, he scored 584 runs at an average of 32.44, with 3 half centuries and 1 century. The century, 105 not out, had come on 2nd July 2022 at home to Chester Le Street. It contained 16 fours and a six and took 153 balls. He didn't bowl in 2022 but took 16 catches. Sunderland were relegated back to Division 1 at the end of 2022. His last appearance to date was in The NEPL Division 1, was for Sunderland on 9th September 2023 at Philadelphia, he made 4. Although, he did go on to play in the NEPL throughout the 2024 season and updates on him will appear there as part of the weekly roundup.

To the end of 2023, Dan Shurben had played 347 NEPL matches in his career, batting 336 times with 30 not outs, he scored 10069 runs at an average of 32.90, with 51 half centuries and 15 centuries. His highest score was the 180 not out for Whitburn mentioned earlier.

He bowled 216 balls in his NEPL career, with 3 maidens, conceding 175 runs and taking 3 wickets, at an average of 58.33.

His first NEPL wicket had been Uzair Mahomed who was playing for The Durham Academy against South Shields on 26th May 2007. He was caught by Oliver Stedman. Shurben took 180 catches in the NEPL.

In addition to the years in The Premier Division, Shurben played 2018 to 2021 plus 2023 in Division 1.

John Graham, South North captain of many years, recalls that Shurben was "a brilliant player of seam and fast bowling, in a league of good players of this type of bowling, Shurben was a "standout," he was a good player off both front and back foot, very strong through the covers and a good player of spin."

Graham did say that if Shurben had a weakness South North thought it was against the very, very best spinners, they would open the bowling against him with Lee Crozier, partly in this belief and partly because they knew how good he was against the faster stuff.

Allan Worthy opened the innings with Shurben at the start of the 2001 season, he started the season quietly, 124 not out! He started his cricket career as a junior at South Hetton in The Durham Coast League. He was a right-handed batsman and right arm medium/fast bowler.

His first recorded innings of note was on 8th September 1991 for Durham Under 19's against Northumberland Under 19's side at Benwell Hill. Northumberland, with Graeme Hallam in their side, scored 184 for 4 from their 40 overs. Worthy opened the batting with Paul Dumighan, they scored 158 for the first wicket when Dumighan was out for 68. Worthy ended up 75 not out, with 12 fours, as Durham won by 9 wickets.

Another notable innings followed on 22nd June 1992 for Durham Club and Ground against Cumberland Second team. Worthy made 84 out of 222 all out. Cumberland 142 for 8 in response, match drawn.

On 23rd June 1994 Worthy played for Derbyshire Second's against Durham Second's at Bunker Hill, Philadelphia in a Bain Clarkson Trophy match of 55 overs each. Durham batted first, 209 all out. Worthy 5 overs for 16. Dominic Cork was batting at three for Derbyshire, Worthy batting five, top scored with 38 as his side fell just short, 198 for 9.

On 2nd August 1994 Worthy was selected for a League Cricket Conference Under 25 side to play against a touring India Under 19 team at Wellington College, Berkshire. India batted first and Anil Muzumdar had 101 not out and V.V.S Laxman 54 not out as they scored 266 for 2 from their 55 overs. Worthy bowled just four overs and when his side batted, he was stumped for a duck as the Indians proved too strong, dismissing their hosts for 127 to take a comfortable win.

In 1995 Worthy was selected to play for English Universities North against Irish Universities at Finchampstead Park, Berkshire in a one-day match. He opened the batting making 24 as his team posted 228 for 8 from their 55 overs. He also opened the bowling, taking 3 for 29 from nine overs as the Irish were bowled out for 187.

As he made his way into senior club cricket, he played for South Hetton in The Durham Coast League. He contributed with bat and ball as they won the league in 1993, 1994 and 1995. He was top of the most runs scored one year and top wicket taker the next!

Worthy joined South Moor CC in The Tyneside Senior League in 1996. He says he had a choice of clubs he could have signed for but chose South Moor as he knew they had a poor side, he felt that he knew he would have the opportunity to participate with bat and ball and that the only way was up for them!

On 4th July 1996 he was selected to play for The Durham Cricket Association against Durham Second's at The Riverside, Chester le Street. Michael Gough, Robin Weston, Chris Hewison, Ian Jones, Ian Hunter and Neil Killeen were amongst the opposition. Worthy's teammates included Paul Veitch, Ian Somerville, Quentin Hughes and Wayne Ritzema. Worthy dismissed Weston and Michael Foster as he took 2 for 30 from 7 overs but rain stopped and then finished play before The Association side could mount any meaningful response.

Worthy joined Sacriston in The Tyneside Senior League as professional for the 1997 and 1998 seasons. On 7th September 1997 Worthy represented The Tyneside Senior League in a President's Trophy match against Derbyshire County Cricket League. Worthy, batting three, scored 14 as his side posted 223 for 5, Dave Jackson top scored with 72 not out. Despite Worthy taking 2 for 31 from six overs, Derbyshire won by 5 wickets.

On 17th May 1998 Worthy made his debut in Minor Counties Trophy matches for Durham Cricket Board at Lincolnshire. Batting at four, Worthy scored 42 as his side scored 240 all out. When the hosts batted, they scored the required runs for the loss of four wickets.

Three days before the 1999 season Worthy tore his ACL in his right knee, this would prevent him from bowling throughout the 2000 season.

Worthy should have made his NEPL debut on 29th April 2000 for Chester le Street at home to Gateshead Fell but the match was abandoned without a ball being bowled.

So, on 6th May 2000, Worthy made his NEPL debut away at Newcastle, opening the batting with Dan Shurben. He made 32 before being bowled by Graeme Angus as Chester le Street were all out for 158. Newcastle could only muster 103 in response, Paul Chivers took 4 for 9 and Chris Dodsley, 3 for 16.

Shurben recalls the Allan Worthy of 2001, he remembers that he was "one of the best cricketers in the Northeast at this time, he was an aggressive, often explosive batsman who set out to completely dominate the bowler. He was powerful, especially on the front foot, he liked to hit it through the covers and offside. He trusted his own technique and trusted his own method, "he was phenomenal in his second season, 2001, especially when you think he missed 1999. He was supportive, very supportive of his team mates and was known to get in a batsman's ear to support his bowlers."

Shurben, in later years would also play against Worthy, he says that as an opposition player, "he would be fair, if an opponent did well, Worthy would praise them and tell them so."

Worthy played 18 matches in the NEPL in 2001, batting 17 times with 2 not outs, he scored 740 runs at an average of 49.33. He scored 5 half centuries and 2 centuries, his highest score was 124 not out, scored in the season opener on 28th April 2001 at home to Tynemouth. His other century, 104 not out, was scored on 2nd June 2001 at Blaydon.

He also bowled 724 balls with 35 maidens, conceding 322 runs and taking 22 wickets at an average of 14.63. His best bowling figures were 8 for 12 taken 18th August 2001 at home to Blaydon. He took 4 catches in the NEPL in 2001.

Allan Worthy was named as NEPL Player of the Year for his efforts, and deservedly so.

Ashley Thorpe batted at three in the 2001 season opener, making 53 with the bat, he also took 3 for 34 with the ball. He was a left-handed batsman who also bowled right arm off breaks or medium pace. He was from Scarborough in Western Australia and had played for Australia Under 19's. He had also previously played for Whitburn and after Chester le Street would also go on to play for Sunderland and Washington.

He played 18 matches in the NEPL in the 2001 season, batting 17 times with 3 not outs, he scored 1003 runs at an average of 71.64. He scored 4 half centuries and 5 centuries with a highest score of 132 not out.

His first century of the season, the 132 not out, was scored on 23rd June 2001 at Stockton, the second century, 109, was scored on 21st July 2001 at Norton, the third, 128, was scored on 25th August 2001 at South North, the fourth, 106, was scored on 1st September 2001 at home to Stockton and the fifth, 115, was scored on 8th September 2001 at Gateshead Fell. He actually scored three centuries in his last four innings of the 2001 season.

Thorpe also bowled 1318 balls in the NEPL in 2001, with 70 maidens, he conceded 524 runs and took 33 wickets at an average of 15.87. His best bowling figures were 7 for 14, taken on 28th July 2001 at home to Sunderland. He took 2 NEPL catches in the 2001 season.

He played nine first class matches for Durham, making his debut on 7th May 2002 against Sri Lanka at The Riverside, Durham. Paul Collingwood, batting four, scored 190 in Durham's first, and only innings of the game, Thorpe batted at six and made 26. Phil Mustard weighed in with 75 down the order at eight, as Durham made 469 all out in 93.2 overs.

Sri Lanka were bowled out for 167 in their first innings, Marc Symington with 4 for 27 the pick of the bowlers, and then made 282 for 4 following on as the match was drawn. Thorpe had two overs for fourteen in the first innings and six overs for eighteen in the second innings.

Thorpe made his County Championship debut on 16th August 2002 at The Riverside in a Division Two match against Glamorgan. Almost the entire Durham side would have NEPL connections at some time, Michael Gough, Gary Pratt, Nicky Peng, Danny Law, Ian Pattison, Andrew Pratt, Nick Philips, Mark Davies and Neil Killeen all would play in the League. Only Steve Harmison didn't play in the NEPL and his connections to current NEPL side Ashington are well known! Robert Croft, Mathew Maynard and Michael Kasprowicz were among others in the Glamorgan side.

A low scoring game scheduled for four days was completed in two! Durham batted first and made 124 all out, Thorpe batted at three and scored four before Kasprowicz had him caught. Mark Davies had 5 for 61 and Steve Harmison 3 for 75 as Glamorgan registered 233 all out in reply. Thorpe wasn't required to bowl. Durham fared even worse in the second innings, despite a decent start from Michael Gough and Gary Pratt and a 77-run opening partnership, they slumped to 114 all out. Thorpe making five before Kasprowicz bowled him. Glamorgan duly scored the runs needed and at 9 for 0, won by ten wickets.

Thorpe would go on to play nine times for Durham, having sixteen innings, with two half centuries and a highest score of 95 and an average of 20.06. The 95 came against Essex at The Riverside in September 2002. It lasted 162 minutes and 150 balls, containing 16 fours.

Thorpe also played 11 List A (One Day Matches) for Durham, making two half centuries, with a best of 76 against Northamptonshire on 7th September 2003. He had a best of 2 for 49 with the ball, against Leicestershire on 11th August 2002.

Thorpe also played 5 T20 matches for Durham in June 2003, with a high score of 35 not out and best bowling of 3 for 20.

He made his Chester le Street debut when the club did, on 6th May 2000 at Newcastle. When his first Chester le Street NEPL stint was over, he had played 52 matches, batting 48 times, with 12 not out's, scoring 2416 runs at an average of 67.11 and a high score of 179 not out, made on 1st July 2000 at home to Stockton, he took 4 for 35 in the game too, but Stockton still fought hard and got a draw.

With the ball he bowled 3330 deliveries, with 144 maidens, conceding 1693 runs and taking 96 wickets at an average of 17.63. His best bowling figures in this time were 7 for 14 on 28th July 2001 at home to Sunderland. He also took 6 catches. His last game in this spell with Chester took place on 16th August 2003 at South North.

He would go on to play first class cricket for Durham, playing 9 times, with 16 innings, he was out in each innings, scoring 321 runs at an average of 20.06 and a high score of 95. He had two half centuries.

He bowled 48 deliveries for Durham in first class cricket, no maidens conceding 32 runs and not taking a wicket.

He also played 11 List A matches for Durham, batting 11 times, 0 not outs, scoring 243 runs at an average of 22.09 and a high score of 76.

With the ball he bowled 132 balls in List A games, 0 maidens, conceding 149 runs and taking 2 wickets at an average of 74.50.

Thorpe also played T20 cricket 5 times for Durham, batting 5 times, with 2 not out's, scoring 79 runs at an average of 26.33 and a high score of 35 not out.

He would go on to play for Whitburn, Chester le Street, Sunderland and Washington and played regularly for Chester le Street in the 2023 and 2024 season.

Quentin Hughes is a left-handed batsman and right arm off break bowler, he batted at four in the 2001 season opener, scoring 50 not out. Like Allan Worthy and Dan Shurben, he is probably worth at least a chapter on his own!

Hughes played 18 matches in the NEPL in the 2001 season, he batted 16 times with 11 not outs, he scored 463 runs at an average of 92.60. He scored 4 half centuries, with a highest score of 82 not out made on 30th June 2001 at home to Gateshead Fell.

He also bowled 168 balls in the NEPL in 2001, with 7 maidens, conceding 100 runs and taking 4 wickets at an average of 25.00. His best bowling figures were 3 for 30, taken on 8th September 2001 at Gateshead Fell. He took 3 catches in the NEPL that season.

His first recorded game of note came on 30th May 1990 for the Durham Schools Cricket Association against The Welsh equivalent at Swalwell in a one day, one innings match. Melvyn Betts, who originated from Sacriston, and would go on to play for Durham, Warwickshire and Middlesex, was also in the Durham side that day, along with

Andrew Pratt. Pratt would also play first class cricket for Durham. The Welsh Schools batted first and scored 187 for 4 and declared after 59 overs, 2 catches for Hughes and 11-4-28-0, Betts had 7-2-18-0. Hughes opened the batting with Robin Weston, Weston another who played for Durham, then moving on to Derbyshire and Middlesex, he also played for England Under 19's. Hughes scored 27 in an opening stand of 48, Weston would go on to top score with 67, as Durham won by 5 wickets with nearly five overs to spare.

Just one year later, 5th June 1991, Hughes was good enough to play for Durham City against Benwell Hill in a National Club Championship fixture at Denton Bank. It was a 20-over game with Benwell batting first and scoring 115 for 5, Hughes had 0 for 21. Despite a strong Durham City side, containing both Gary and Andrew Pratt and Peter Birtwisle, Hughes batted at six, making 3 before being run out as Durham won by 5 wickets.

Just over a month later, 19th August 1991, Hughes was selected for Durham in a Minor Counties fixture with Norfolk at The Racecourse, Durham. John Glendenen, Geoff Cook and Simon Brown were also in the Durham side. Hughes didn't get a bat as Durham scored 226 for 5 declared from 49.1 overs, Gary Brown, who later played for Middlesex and Durham, top score of 81. Hughes was the most successful of the Durham bowlers, 3 for 61, two of them caught and bowled, as Norfolk declared their first innings on 191 for 6 after 50 overs. When Durham batted again an opening stand of 155 between John Glendenen, 80, and the left-handed Stewart Hutton, 112 not out, set up a good score and a good game of cricket. Hutton went on to play first class cricket for Durham, scoring 3341 runs at an average of 29.56, a high score of 172 not out, including four hundreds and thirteen half centuries.

Hughes would go on to represent Durham in a few different ways over the years, Under 19's, Second XI, Durham Young Cricketers and Durham Cricket Association. He would also go on to represent and captain Cambridge University on many occasions, quite frankly Hughes played so much representative cricket it's difficult to know where to start!

Hughes played 23 matches for Durham Second XI, from his debut on 27th April 1992 until the last on 23rd August 2000. He had 40 innings, with 3 not outs, and scored 1209 runs at an average of 32.67 and a best of 223. He scored 3 half centuries and 3 centuries. The 223 came on 7th-9th September 1999 against Worcestershire Seconds at The County Ground, Worcester. Worcestershire batted first and were all out for 146 from 62 overs, Ian Hunter, Marc Symington and Chris Hewison among the Durham bowlers. When Durham batted opener Chris Hewison had 70, Chris Mann had 50, and Hughes had his 223 as Durham scored 483 all out. Worcestershire batted again, 150 all out this time, as Durham won by an innings and 187 runs. Slow left arm bowler, Steven Chapman, who would later play a few games for Durham firsts, had 6 for 22.

As a bowler for Durham Seconds, Hughes bowled 697 balls, 42 maidens, he conceded 301 runs and took 13 wickets at an average of 23.15, his best bowling was 7 for 68, taken in his debut match for the side, against Leicestershire at Grace Road on 27th-29th April 1992. Durham batted first, Hughes did not get a bat, as opener Stewart Hutton made 168 not out, as they scored 300 for 3 declared. Leicestershire, with future England Internationals Paul Nixon 45, and Darren Maddy 48, in their side, were bowled out for 275. Hughes 0 for 43 from seventeen overs. Durham's second innings 238 all out, 50 from opener Jimmy Daley the best of them, Hughes had 13. Set 264 to win, the Leicester openers put on 40 for the first wicket before a run out. Andrew Roseberry came in at three but was dismissed for 10. Hughes then took his first wicket at this level, opener Martyn Gidley, caught by Steven McEwan and he went on to have figures of 14.1-1- 68-7 as Durham won by 44 runs. He also took 19 catches for Durham Second XI at this level.

Hughes played his first match for Cambridge University on 15th April 1997 against Derbyshire; it should be noted that University matches are classed as First-Class appearances. Across his university career Hughes played 28 matches, with 42 innings and 8 not outs, he scored 1086 runs, with a high score of 119, and an average of 31.94. This included 5 fifties and 2 hundreds. That high score came in his last appearance for Cambridge University in The Varsity match at Lord's against Oxford University on 11th-13th July 2000. It came off 213 balls and contained 13 fours and took 287 minutes. Together with James Pyemont, who scored 124, Hughes added 177 for the third wicket. Rain ruined the game with Oxford 71 for the loss of no wickets and Hughes had one over for seven before the deluge.

As a university bowler, Hughes bowled 479 balls, 11 maidens, conceded 323 runs and took 5 wickets, with a best of 2 for 73 and he also took 7 catches.

When Hughes joined Chester for the 2000 season, he didn't play his first game until July, as he had been playing for Cambridge University. He arrived having scored the last century, 119 to be precise, in a Varsity Match to be held at Lord's.

That first NEPL game for Hughes came on 15th July 2000 at home to Newcastle. Ashley Thorpe, with 124 not out set the tone, Hughes, batting four, made 49 as Chester scored 240 for 4 declared from 60 overs. Despite 52 from opener Wayne Ritzema, Chester proved too strong, each of the bowlers used taking wickets, Ross McLaren 2 for 32, Paul Chivers 3 for 34, Ashley Thorpe 3 for 31 and Steven Lee Merrington 2 for 33 as Chester won by 101 runs.

It's worth noting that throughout the 2001 season several NEPL players were playing for The Durham Cricket Board as they got as far as the semifinals of The ECB 38 County Cup, Allan Worthy and Hughes both representing Chester.

The rest of the Chester team, who did not bat on that opening day of the 2001 season was as follows-

Anthony (Tony) Birbeck was captain and a right-handed bat and a right arm medium pace bowler, he was the brother of another well-known local Durham cricketer, Shaun Birbeck and was listed to bat at four.

He played 17 matches in the NEPL in the 2001 season, batting 10 times with 4 not outs, he scored 173 runs at an average of 28.83. He scored 1 half century, 60, made on 27th August 2001 at home to Newcastle. He bowled 12 balls in 2001, conceding 3 runs and not taking a wicket, he did take 4 catches in the NEPL that season.

Worthy remembers "a genius of a captain who knew the game and the local leagues inside out. As a batsman he was a good player, an elegant, touch, player, he was strongly built who liked to stand on the back foot and was a lovely cutter and good puller, he loved the ball short outside off stump, he would accumulate runs rather than bludgeon them, placing the cricket ball rather than smacking it."

Tony Birbeck played seven times for Durham in The Minor Counties Championship, debuting on 8th July 1989 in a two-day match against Northumberland at Eastwood Gardens, Gateshead. Northumberland batted first, opener Jon Benn top scoring with 62, Graeme Morris 43 and my old friend, Kevin Corby, who I played with at Seaton Burn, had 21 in a total of 208 for 8 declared from 55 overs. Durham legend Steve Greensword had 5 for 42. Durham made 214 for 4 from 54 overs before declaring, Ashok Patel top scored with 93 not out, Paul Burn 61 and Steve Greensword 35 not out with the bulk of the runs, Birbeck, batting at five, made 5. Northumberland successfully played for a draw in their second innings, 170 for 8, John Tindale, who would later go on to play in the NEPL, had two wickets.

Birbeck's seven Minor Counties matches for Durham brought him eleven innings, one of which he was not out, 176 runs, at an average of 17.00. His highest score was 51, opening the batting on 30th July 1989 away at Lincolnshire in a drawn game.

Birbeck made his NEPL debut on 6th May 2000 at Newcastle, top scoring with 44 in a low scoring win, a more detailed look at Tony Birbeck can be found later in the book.

Gary Hunter was a left-handed batsman and right arm off break bowler, he was listed to bat at six and is the son of Tyneside Senior League and Consett CC legend Gordon Hunter.

Gordon Hunter had started playing junior cricket for Consett in the 1960'S, making his senior debut in 1965. He was a stylish left-handed batsman and a right arm slow bowler; he would regularly feature in both the league averages and league representative sides. After five years as a pro at Langley Park, he returned to Consett and became captain.

His last game was in 2004, he is credited with 14,276 runs at 29.83, with five T.S.L hundreds and a best of 108 not out. His T.S.L bowling record is incomplete, but he has at least 394 wickets and a best of 8 for 34.

He played 8 matches for Chester le Street in the NEPL in 2001, he batted 4 times with 1 not out, he scored 69 runs at an average of 23.00. His highest score was 29, made on 26th May 2001 at home to Benwell Hill. He didn't bowl in the NEPL in 2001, but he did take 4 NEPL catches that season.

Gary started out at Consett, in his father's footsteps and on 23rd July he was selected for Durham Under 15's in a fixture at Ampleforth against Scotland. Future NEPL players Ian Pattison and Lee Rushworth were selected in the same side. Scotland were bowled out for just 85, Rushworth taking an impressive 3 for 11 as he swept away the tail. When Durham replied, Hunter, batting four, made 17 not out and Ian Pattison had 21, as they won by 7 wickets.

Hunter also represented Durham at Under 19 level, featuring in a two-day match at Derbyshire which started on 26th July 1999. Ian Pattison was also in this side, along with Phil Mustard. Derbyshire scored 388 for 7 declared from 111 overs after winning the toss. Tom Lungley, who would go on to play first class cricket for Derbyshire and Lancashire, with 138 not out. When Durham batted, three batsmen scored half centuries, Hunter making 4, but they fell a little short on 337 for 9, but this was still good enough for a draw. Hunter batted at four when Chester made their NEPL debut on 6th May 2000 at Newcastle and scored 9.

He was a young lad with a lot of promise, but, because of the strength of Chester's top four, his opportunities were limited and so, after being part of the title winning side of 2001, he moved to Tynedale for the 2002 season.

Mark Davies was a right-hand bat and right arm medium pace bowler; he would go on to play first class cricket at Durham and Kent as well as England Under 19's and was listed to bat at seven on debut, in the 2001 season opener. He opened the bowling, taking 1 for 19 from 9.1 overs, bowling Chris Beever to take the last wicket and seal the win.

He made his NEPL debut on 13th May 2000 for Durham Academy at Stockton but didn't get a bat, nor did many others, Gary Pratt run out for 149 and Ian Pattison 53 dominating an Academy score of 241 for 3 declared from 59 overs. He did bowl in the Stockton response, 0 for 23, the star of the show though was Stockton's West Indian Pro, Dawnley Joseph, who scored 134 not out as his side won by 9 wickets! For the record, Rob Lake also had 71 in an opening stand of 172.

Davies last NEPL game for Chester came on 30th June 2001 at home to Gateshead Fell, he didn't bat but took 1 for 18 in a drawn game. His contribution to Chester winning The NEPL title in 2001 was also his NEPL career with them, he played 6 matches for them, batting just once, scoring 3 not out.

He bowled 415 balls, with 27 maidens, conceding 140 runs and taking 8 wickets at an average of 17.50, his best bowling was 5 for 45, against Durham Academy on 5th May 2001.

He played one game for Tynemouth in the 2003 season, taking 1 for 29 and failing to score on 10th May at South North.

He made his first-class debut for Durham in 2003, on 13th June against Nottinghamshire.

Davies again re-appeared in The NEPL in the 2004 season, playing 5 times for Norton, he also played once for Norton in 2005.

Dan Shurben recalls that "Davies was always going to be pro, he could be a match winner with the ball, he was very accurate, moving the ball in off the pitch with a good bowling action, he was just a young lad at this time, but he was a great lad in the dressing room, and we had some good nights out in Durham!"

Five NEPL appearances for Stockton in 2007 was followed by three games for Durham Academy in 2009.

Mark Davies had a stop start NEPL career at best, this is undoubtedly because he was playing first class cricket at the time, there is no doubt that Durham have used the NEPL to help players get back to fitness or form over the years and I suspect the nature of Davies NEPL career is an example of that.

Davies had a good first-class career at Durham, being awarded his cap in 2005 and went on to play for Kent. In total he played 109 first class matches, batting 138 times, with 49 not outs, scoring 1118 runs at an average of 12.56 and a high score of 62 for Durham against Somerset in May 2005.

He also bowled 16386 deliveries, with 802 maidens, conceding 7064 runs and taking 315 wickets, at an average of 22.42, his best bowling was 8 for 24.

Davies was called in to an England Test squad in 2009, but he wasn't required, injury undoubtedly prevented an England career, his last first-class appearance came on 31st July 2013 for Kent at Sussex, a shoulder injury eventually finishing his first-class career.

Steven Lee Merrington was a slow left arm orthodox bowler, a left-handed off spinner in more common terms! He was listed to bat at eight and he bowled four overs and took 3 for 5, removing most of the lower order.

He played 18 matches in the NEPL in 2001, batting 8 times with 3 not outs, he scored 124 runs at an average of 24.80. He scored 1 half century, 51 not out, made on 30th June 2001 at home to Gateshead Fell.

He bowled 768 balls in the NEPL in the 2001 season, with 31 maidens, conceding 392 runs and taking 13 wickets at an average of 30.15. His best bowling figures were 3 for 5, taken in the season opener on 28th April at home to Tynemouth. He also took 2 catches that season.

Dan Shurben, who was the same age, played a lot of cricket with Merrington, as teenagers, they would also go and watch Durham CCC together as well, said of Merrington "he would bowl it flat, flat and accurate is the best way to describe his style. In his own age groups growing up, Merrington was more of an all-rounder than a bowler only. He was, a nice lad, a good lad from Hetton. He left for Sunderland for the 2002 season, also going on to play for Hylton, where he still plays."

He first featured on 17th July 1997 for Durham Under 15's against Scotland Under 15's in a 50-over match at Brandon. Merrington batted at four and scored 32, Dan Shurben, 45, and Phil Mustard 4 not out, were also in the side, as Durham made 183 for 8. An opening partnership of 125 for Scotland saw them to a seven-wicket win, Merrington not getting a bowl.

Merrington was part of the successful Chester le Street side that won the 2000 JustSport Trophy on 10th September, taking 1-31, as Chester beat Benwell Hill by 5 wickets.

He would also play for Durham Under 19's, featuring in two matches against Scotland in July 2001. He took 1 for 30 and scored 6 in the first game and scored 3 and had 2 for 38 in the second.

David Wilson was a right-hand bat and wicketkeeper who was listed to bat at nine, he took two catches and a stumping, so he played a part. He had played a decent level of cricket prior to The NEPL but was happy to concentrate on his wicketkeeping and bat down the order, Allan Worthy describes him as "a fantastic wicketkeeper."

Wilson played 17 matches in the NEPL in 2001, he batted 6 times with 1 not out, he scored 100 runs at an average of 20.00. He scored 1 half century, 60, made on 26th May 2010 at home to Benwell Hill. As a wicketkeeper he excelled, taking 14 catches and making 3 stumpings in the 2001 season.

He first came to attention on 16th June 1986 for Worcestershire Under 25's against Somerset Under 25's in a 40 over match at Kidderminster, although he didn't bat as Worcestershire won by 3 wickets.

A three-day version of the same game started at Taunton just two days later, Wilson took one catch behind the stumps as Somerset were dismissed for 96 in the first innings. When Worcestershire batted, they scored 203 all out, Wilson, batting at eleven, scored 13. Somerset were shot out in their second innings for just 85, Wilson taking two more catches as his side won by an innings and 22 runs.

He played a third uneventful match for Worcestershire against Warwickshire at the end of the month.

On 24th May 1989 Wilson played a one-day game for Durham Seconds at Appleby against Cumberland Seconds. Batting first, Cumberland made 245 all out in 60.2 overs, wicketkeeper Wilson taking two catches. When Durham batted, they struggled to 93 for 7 from 43 overs, Wilson scoring 9, as the match was drawn.

Wilson was selected to play for The National Fire Service on 3rd July 1989 in a 55 over match at Aldershot against The Army Under 25 side. Opening the batting, he scored 16 in 175 all out from their overs as the Army lost three wickets, two of them to catches by Wilson, as they won by seven wickets.

Wilson also played for The British Fire Service, playing a fixture on 22nd August 1989 at Horsham against Sussex Seconds, he made 33, opening the batting, this was joint top score for the firemen as they were 172 all out. A couple of unbeaten seventies saw Sussex home by eight wickets.

Wilson further represented The National Fire Service on 7th July 1993 in another fixture against The Army, again at Aldershot, taking 3 catches as The Army posted 150 all out from 50 overs. Wilson opened the batting, making 80 not out from 78 balls with ten boundaries, as his side won by eight wickets.

Wilson made another notable appearance on 5th September 1999 in a 45-over match at Corsham when he represented The Durham Senior League against The County of Alliance of Cricket Clubs. The hosts batted first, Quentin Hughes with 4 for 51 the best of the Durham bowlers, Wilson taking one catch behind the stumps as they scored 250 for 9 from their allotted overs although Durham had an off day with the bat, 91 all out, Hughes making 5 and Wilson 2.

Like many of this team, Wilson's NEPL debut came with the club, away at Newcastle on 6th May 2000. He failed to score but took two catches in the Newcastle innings.

Dan Shurben also recalls that Wilson was "one hell of a keeper, I remember a game at Chester on 18th August, in the Championship winning season, against Blaydon."

Blaydon batted first and despite losing Ian Somerville for seven, were making good progress, Paul Underwood, who had opened made 52 and West Indian pro Nehemiah Perry at three, had 59. The game changed when Allan Worthy came on to bowl, although I have no fall of wicket details, Worthy bowled 8.4-4-12-8, bowling both Underwood and Perry along the way. Shurben remembers an hour of remarkable cricket and that David Wilson stood up to the stumps throughout Worthy's spell, Worthy, despite his knee injury, was still a very capable medium/fast bowler. Of Worthy's eight victims, Wilson accounted for five of them, four catches and a stumping. Shurben had 52 and Ashley Thorpe 43 as Chester won the game by 3 wickets.

Paul Chivers was a right-handed bat and right-arm fast bowler, he was listed to bat at ten, he took 1 for 19 from nine overs to start the 2001 season.

He played 18 matches in the NEPL in 2001, he batted 3 times, scoring 18 runs with a highest score of 9 not out, he also bowled 854 balls, with 31 maidens, he conceded 529 runs and took 28 wickets at an average of 18.89. His best bowling figures were 6 for 36, taken on 1st September 2001 at home to Stockton and he took 4 catches in the NEPL that season.

Chivers first came to notice as a youngster, being selected for a Bunbury Under 15 game between English Schools Association North v West at The Oval, St Helens on 21st July 1997, others in The North side were Gary Pratt, Lee Rushworth and Nicky Peng. North batted first and made 205 for 1 declared, Gary Pratt 80 not out, John Sadler 61, and Lee Rushworth 33 not out, from 59 overs. The runs were chased down for the loss of four wickets. Chivers 1 for 43.

He played another game in the same competition just two days later, at Aigburgh, Liverpool, against The South. Pratt, 68, and Rushworth 45, opened the batting and with support from the middle order at six, from R. McFarlane, 53 not out, they scored 241 for 6 declared from 74 overs. Chivers, made 2 not out.

Future England Test wicketkeeper batsman Matt Prior opened the innings for The South. Chivers had him caught behind for 15 and finished with the excellent figures of 5-3-8-1. The South eventually made 101 for 9 from 46 overs as they hung on for the draw.

On 8th June 1999 Chivers played for the Durham Cricket Board against their Northumberland counterparts at Ropery Lane, Chester le Street. Rain reduced the game to 22 overs a side, Durham scoring 117 for 5 from their overs, although Chivers didn't bat. Northumberland won by six wickets with two balls to spare, Andy Hayhurst top scoring with 46 not out, he would go on to play for Lancashire, Somerset and Derbyshire. Chivers had two overs for eleven runs.

Two days later, 10th June 1999, Chivers represented The Durham Cricket Board, at Hullen Edge Ground, Elland, against Yorkshire. The hosts made 181 for 8 wickets from their 50 overs, Chivers 2 for 36, future teammate Mark Davies 2 for 21. Durham, fell just short in their reply, 166 all out, Chivers making 6 not out.

Chivers was another who made his NEPL debut on 6th May 2000 at Newcastle.

On 30th May 2000 Chivers started a Durham Second XI four-day fixture at Northampton. The hosts batted first, 310 all out in 100 overs. Chivers had 4 for 73, one of whom was stumped by Phil Mustard. The NEPL was well represented that day as all of the bowlers used in the first innings would, at some point in their career, feature in the league. They were Marc Symington, Mark Davies, Ian Pattison, Chivers and Graeme Bridge. When Durham batted, they were all out for 194, Marc Symington top scored with 42, Chivers failed to score. Northamptonshire batted again, 223 all out, Chivers 11-4-30-0. Chivers made 28 in Durham's second innings as the game ended in a draw.

Chivers played a second game for Durham seconds a week later, away at Glamorgan. In a low scoring game, only one batsman made fifty for either side, Durham's Ian Pattison 55, although Syed Ali made 100 not out in Durham's second innings as Durham won by 250 runs. Chivers scored 11 and 11 not out and had bowling figures of 5-1-18-0 and 4-1-13-0.

Chivers would later go on to represent The Durham Cricket Board before later playing for Esh Winning.

Worthy recalls that Chivers had come to Chester from Durham City and was around 18 during the 2001 season. "Physically he was five foot six or seven and solidly built, that he used to bowl off around ten paces and always had a smile on his face when bowling, he would get the ball, practically jog to his mark, turn round then sprint to the wicket. Because of his height he was a skiddy bowler, he would only bowl two lengths, full and straight, often resulting in flying stumps, or bouncers, again because of his height, his bouncers tended to be always around the batsman's throat, making hooking and pulling a dangerous shot. He was a real handful if he got it right, because of the two lengths, if he got the full ball wrong, and given Birbeck's attacking fields, he could leak a few runs. A "lovely kid" is how Allan Worthy remembers Paul Chivers.

Chris Dodsley was a right-hand bat and right arm fast bowler, listed at number eleven, he opened the bowling, taking 2 for 11 from eight overs.

He played 18 matches in the NEPL in 2001, batting 2 times with 0 not outs, he scored 1 run, he also bowled 882 balls with 34 maidens, conceding 482 runs and taking 22 wickets at an average of 21.90. His best bowling figures were 5 for 36, taken on 2nd June 2001 at Blaydon and he took 3 catches in the NEPL in 2001.

Near the end of this season, on 13th September 2001 Dodsley made his first, and last appearance, for The Durham Cricket Board in a List A two-day fixture against Buckinghamshire at Beaconsfield in The Cheltenham and Gloucester Trophy. Buckinghamshire batting first were 187 all out in 47.3 overs. Dodsley opened the bowling, 0 for 18 with Marcus North, the best of the bowlers, 4 for 26. Durham never really got going, four L.B.W decisions disrupting the innings, 166 all out from 46.1 overs, extras, 35, was the top scorer. Dodsley was 1 not out.

Dodsley did represent The Durham Cricket Board on two occasions in Minor Counties Trophy Matches, both against Northumberland. The first was on 24th June 2001 at Preston Avenue, North Shields in a 50 over match. Durham batted first, 297 for 7 from their 50 overs. Half centuries for Gary Pratt, 65, Allan Worthy, 52 and "extras", 53! John Graham had 2 for 38 for Northumberland. When Northumberland batted, they were bowled out for 207, Wayne Ritzema 53, top scored, Dodsley 0 for 33.

On 19th May 2002 the above fixture was reversed, played this time at Philadelphia and with Northumberland batting first. Ex Yorkshire player Bradley Parker top scored with 70 and with solid support from Wayne Ritzema,41, John Windows, 26 and David Rutherford 26 not out, posted 237 for 6 from their 50 overs. Dodsley took the first wicket of the game, bowling Steven Chapman for three and finished with 1 for 24 from nine overs. Liam Plunkett, with 2 for 31 the most successful Durham bowler. Despite being a strong team, full of NEPL connections Durham were bowled out for 181. Ashley Thorpe top scoring with 32. John Graham, with his right arm medium pace, did most of the damage, 4 for 40.

Worthy remembers Dodsley joining Chester le Street from Felling "He was very tall, all arms and legs, with a long stride and a long run up. He was open chested when he bowled, looking inside his front arm as he bowled. Worthy particularly remembers, a proper Felling accent, and describes him as a massive Newcastle United fan, Toon daft."

He also recalls that he was another "really nice lad", again young and raw, only lacking a bit of venom and sometimes a bit of self-confidence, both probably down to his age, Worthy said he was "brisk" on his day, his inswinger regularly uprooting stumps and causing batsmen all sorts of problems.

Together with Chivers, Dodsley formed a dynamic opening bowling pair, different in style, but often doing a great job for the team of grabbing a couple of early wickets.

Dodsley played a Second XI Championship game for Leicestershire in 1998, starting on 10th August against Sussex, future Chester team mate Ross McLaren was in the same side. Sussex made 456 for 9 declared from 100 overs. Dodsley 0 for 67 and McLaren 1 for 45. McLaren made 6, Dodsley didn't bat as Leicestershire declared on 311 for 9. When Sussex batted again, Dodsley took 1 for 21 from five overs and McLaren 1 for 36 from six overs, as Sussex declared on 205. McLaren scored 27 in the second innings, Dodsley again didn't bat, as his side, 300 for 8, hung on for a draw.

Dodsley, through Ashley Thorpe, went to play cricket in Perth, Australia, he subsequently met and married an Australian girl, and emigrated around 2003/2004. He is still there, Worthy last seeing him, "a couple of years ago," he recalls a lovely lad of nice character who hadn't changed a bit", he had brought his family over "to buy the new Toon kit!"

There were several other club members who made valuable contributions to the team that year.

Graeme Race was in his late teens at this time, a right-handed batsman and right arm fast/medium bowler. He played for Durham at Under 15 and Under 17 level, his first recorded Under 15 game coming on 17th July 1997 at Brandon in 50 over game against Scotland. Future team mates Steven Lee Merrington and Dan Shurben were also in the Durham side that day. Race did not bat, as Durham scored 183 for 8 from their 50 overs, Merrington batting at four, had 32, Shurben, batting at six, had the top score of 45. When Scotland batted, Race came on as first change, 5-2-7-0 as Scotland got the runs for the loss of three wickets.

He played for Durham Under 17's in a two-day match on 10th and 11th July 1998 at Edinburgh again, against Scotland. Majid Haq scored 112 of the in the Scots first innings 185 all out, Kyle Coetzer, who would go on to a long and distinguished cricket career with both Scotland and in the NEPL, was also in the Scot's side. Race opened the bowling and had seven overs for nineteen. Dan Shurben opened for Durham, making 21, but it was Phil Mustard at three, who took the eye, 78 not out, Durham scoring 150 for 5 declared. Other Durham lads of note, Craig Symington was another one for the future, as part of Burnmoor's title winning side of 2019, and Phil Bell, who I came across at Benwell Hill.

Bell had a fascinating sports career, playing cricket for a number NEPL clubs, Gateshead Fell, South Shields, South North, Whitburn and Benwell Hill and also turning out for Marsden and Eastcote and playing for Northumberland. In addition to his cricketing prowess, he also played football for Blyth Spartans, York City, Whitley Bay and Ashington. In the short time I have photographed The NEPL I've seen Bell play a couple of very destructive innings at Denton Bank.

Returning to Graeme Race and Durham Under 17's, Scotland were bowled out for 115 in their second innings, Race had 1 for 27. As all their top order made double figure contributions, Durham won by five wickets.

Race made his NEPL debut on 19th May 2001 for Chester away at Sunderland, the hosts batted first, Darren Blenkiron 94 not out, 220 for 9 declared from 65 overs. Dodsley 2 for 36, Chivers 2 for 57, Thorpe 3 for 45, Worthy 1 for 14, Race had 0 for 18. When Chester batted, despite 51 from opener Quentin Hughes, they never really got going, settling for 169 for 7 declared from 55 overs as the match was drawn. West Indies pro Franklyn Rose had 3 for 42.

Race had to wait until 2nd June 2001 for his next match, away at Blaydon, where he took his first NEPL wicket, Blaydon legend Ian Somerville bowled for 19.

He played 12 matches in the title winning season of 2001, batting 5 times, with 2 not outs, he scored 65 runs at an average of 21.66 and a high score of 29 on 27th August at home to Newcastle.

He bowled 168 deliveries that year, with 7 maidens, conceding 98 runs and taking 2 wickets at an average of 49.00and a best of 1 for 8.

He played his last NEPL match for Chester on 25th August 2003 at Benwell Hill, he didn't get to bat or bowl in a low scoring 9 wicket win for Chester, Allan Worthy had 4 for 14 and 58 not out.

In total he played 42 matches for Chester, batting 20 times, with 6 not out's, he scored 224 runs at an average of 16.00, with a high score of 32. The high score was on 10th May 2003 at home to Blaydon.

He bowled 776 balls, with 25 maidens, conceding 496 runs and taking 12 wickets at an average of 41.33 and a best of 3 for 22. The best bowling came on 27th April 2002 at home to Blaydon. He took 8 catches in The NEPL for the club.

Race would move to Benwell Hill for the 2004 season and play there until he joined Washington in 2016.

He made his NEPL debut for Benwell Hill on 24th April 2004 at Blaydon, making 1 not out as Hill were 132 all out, Phil Mustard had top scored with 43. Graham Onions took 5 for 27 for Blaydon. When Fell batted Race opened the bowling, taking 2 for 34, his first Hill wicket in The NEPL was Paul Underwood, caught by Phil Mustard for 1 but 53 from Ian Somerville saw Blaydon home by 4 wickets.

Race played his last NEPL game for Benwell Hill on 5th September 2015 at Jesmond against Newcastle. It wasn't a memorable game for him, Hill 75 all out as Callum Harding took 8 for 17 from just 13.5 overs. Matthew Muchall took 4 for 33 but he couldn't stop Newcastle winning by 4 wickets, Race didn't get to bowl.

During his Benwell Hill career he played 220 matches in The NEPL for them, batting 149 times, with 20 not outs, he scored 1856 runs at an average of 14.38, with 6 half centuries. His highest score was 78 on 1st September 2007 at home to Chester Le Street.

He bowled 8203 balls for them, with 209 maidens, conceding 5139 runs and taking 176 wickets at an average of 29.19. His best bowling figures were 5 for 34 on 2nd June 2012 at home to Gateshead Fell. He took 53 NEPL catches for Benwell Hill.

During his NEPL career, to the end of 2015, Graeme Race played 262 NEPL matches, batting 169 times, with 26 not outs, he scored 2080 runs at an average of 14.54, with 6 half centuries. His highest score was the 78 on 1st September 2007 at Chester le Street.

He bowled 8979 balls, with 234 maidens, conceding 5635 runs and taking 188 wickets at an average of 29.97. His best bowling figures were 5 for 34 on 2nd June 2012 against Gateshead Fell. He took 61 NEPL catches.

Ross McLaren played half a dozen times in the title winning side of 2001, he was in his early twenties at this time, he was a right-handed batsman and right arm medium fast bowler. His father David McLaren was well known in local cricket circles. I have had the pleasure of his company numerous times on the boundary since I started photographing NEPL games in the last couple of years, he describes himself as "a wicketkeeper and slogger." I'm sure he was more than that, he played across five decades in The Durham Senior League, for Durham County, Durham City and Bishop Auckland, that is testimony to his undoubted quality, he did sign for a first-class county, but went to Sydney, playing grade cricket for three seasons.

On his return from Australia he played for Sunderland, he won the league on six different occasions with five different teams over the course of his career. He fondly recalls some of those he played with and against, describing Peter Birtwisle as the best amateur batsman he came across, Stan Stoker the best amateur bowler, Steve Greensword the best English pro, David Chardon, the best overseas pro, Tom Angus the quickest bowler and Frank Greenshields the best sledger. He is of the opinion that the Durham Senior League between the 70's and 80's was the strongest league in the North.

Ross McLaren first came to light playing for Durham School against Dame Allan's School on 11th May 1994 at The Playground, Durham. Durham scored 204 for 7 from their 40 overs. John Windows, 22, his opening partner Chris Clark, 71. McLaren failed to score but he was wicketkeeper for this game, taking a stumping as Durham restricted their opponents for 166 for 9 from their allotted overs.

By 1997 McLaren had found his way to Hampshire Second Eleven, playing a Second Eleven Championship fixture against Northants which started on 11th June. He batted at eight in the first innings, making 8 out of 314 all out. When Northants batted, he bowled seven overs for twenty-eight as they scored 251 all out. He didn't bat in the second innings, Hampshire 247 for 5 declared, but did take 2 for 44 from nine overs when they bowled again, 113 from Richard Warren, a future first class cricketer with Nottinghamshire and England Young Cricketer, saw the visitors home by five wickets.

He would play twice more for Hampshire Seconds, with a best score of 33 and he would also play three Second XI Championship games for Leicestershire, two in 1998 and one in 2002. Rain completely ruined the game with Essex on 29th, 30th and 31st July 1998, ending up as a one innings match, McLaren did take 3 for 24 from 14 overs as his side won by seven wickets in a surprisingly high scoring game.

It was September 2002 before McLaren featured again, another second team game for Leicestershire, Northamptonshire again the opposition. He scored 1 and 33 not out, batting eleven both times, and took 1 for 49 as Northants won by an innings.

McLaren made his NEPL debut on 8th July 2000 at Gateshead Fell for Chester le Street. He made 47 not out batting at eight, Ashley Thorpe had 60 earlier in the innings, as Chester made 203 for 8 declared. Graham Onions, among the Fell bowlers.

McLaren took the big wicket of future Aussie Test Player Marcus North, whom he bowled, for 4 and finished with 1 for 10 from an unknown number of overs. Fell were 124 for 9 to hang on for the draw, despite 5 for 56 from Durham player Ian Hunter and 3 for 23 from Thorpe.

Dan Shurben has fond memories of McLaren taking the last wicket of the 2001 season at Gateshead Fell on 8th September, recalling that Chester went into the game needing two batting points to win the league, under the existing rules they needed to get to 150. After losing Allan Worthy for 15, Shurben and Ashley Thorpe guided them past the 150 mark, Shurben scoring the run that brought up the 150. Shurben would fall for 60, Thorpe went on to make 115, his fifth hundred of the season, Chester scoring 261 for 3 declared from 51 overs. When Fell batted openers Stewart Hutton, 31, and Phil Taylor, 40, made a steady start. Birbeck used seven bowlers in his efforts to win the game, although Dodsley and Merrington finished wicketless, the other five all got at least one wicket each. Worthy 2 for 35, Thorpe 1 for 10, Chivers 1 for 17, and Hughes 3 for 30. McClaren had 5.5 overs, 1 maiden, 16 runs conceded and 3 wickets. The last of those wickets, Dan Shurben still remembers well, nearly 25 years later, the number eleven batsman R. Kidd bowled by Ross McLaren as Fell were all out for 165.

McLaren played 6 times for Chester in the title winning season, he batted on 2 occasions, with 1 not out, scoring 8 runs with a high score of 5 not out.

He also bowled 217 balls in the season, with 14 maidens, conceding 131 runs and taking 5 wickets at an average of 26.20, his best bowling was the 3 for 16 described above, he also took 2 NEPL catches this season.

The game on 8th September 2001 was his last for Chester in the NEPL, his career NEPL stats with Chester at the time were he played 14 matches, batting 7 times, with 3 not outs, scoring 106 runs at an average of 26.50 and a best of 47 not out which is described earlier.

He bowled 468 balls with 19 maidens, conceding 415 runs and took 16 wickets at an average of 25.93 and a best of 3 for 16.

McLaren joined Philadelphia when they became the 12th member of The NEPL in 2002, making his debut for them when the club debuted in the league on 27th April at home to Tynemouth. Philadelphia batted first, scoring an impressive 236 for 7 declared from 60 overs, opener Graham Hoben had 89 not out and McLaren 48. Tynemouth were bowled out for 128 in 47.2 overs, Ian Potter, right arm medium pace bowler, took 5 for 16. McLaren had 2 for 21. A strong start to the season for Philadelphia, a win by 108 runs. McLaren played his last game for Philadelphia on 7th September 2002 at home to Stockton, taking 1 for 43 and scoring 25 when he batted in a drawn game.

McLaren had played 17 games for Philadelphia, batting 15 times, with 4 not out's, he scored 263 runs at an average of 23.90 and 1 half century. That half century was his highest score, on 17th August 2002 he made 50 not out at Norton.

He bowled 1156 balls for the club, with 35 maidens, conceding 735 runs and taking 20 wickets at an average of 36.75, with a best of 3 for 15 away against Gateshead Fell on 1st June 2002. He also took 1 catch in the 2002 season.

On 29th April 2006 McLaren made his NEPL debut for Newcastle at Norton, he made 10 batting at number nine as Newcastle were dismissed for 120. He opened the bowling but finished with 0 for 25 as Norton won by 9 wickets.

His last game for Newcastle in The NEPL came on 10th September 2011 at Jesmond against Benwell Hill, he opened the bowling but bowled just one over, 0 for 5, he top scored with 33 not out when his side batted.

His Newcastle career had spanned 87 matches, with 62 innings, 12 not outs, scoring 908 runs at an average of 18.16, he had 4 half centuries with a high score of 75. The high score came on 25th June 2011 at Denton Bank against Benwell Hill.

He bowled 5188 NEPL balls for Newcastle, with 170 maidens, conceding 3298 runs and taking 129 wickets at an average of 25.56. His best bowling figures were 11 overs, 4 maidens, 32 runs conceded for 9 wickets taken against Tynemouth on 29th July 2006. He was on for all ten wickets when Jonathan Bailey, a slow left arm orthodox bowler, had the last man, John Callaghan caught by James Bailey for 15. He took 31 catches for Newcastle in the NEPL.

Ross McLaren's NEPL career had seen him play 118 matches, with 84 innings, 19 not outs, scoring 1277 runs at an average of 19.64, he had 5 half centuries with a high score of 75.

He bowled 6812 balls, with 224 maidens, conceding 4448 runs and taking 165 wickets at an average of 26.95. His best bowling figures were the 9 for 32 quoted earlier. He took 34 catches.

McLaren would also spend 5 years playing grade cricket in Australia and played for Whickham in 2024.

David N. Robson was largely a second team player in 2001 but as a stand in wicket keeper in the first team he had a role to play. He made his NEPL debut for Chester le Street on 6th May 2000 at Newcastle, playing 12 matches in the league that year.

In the title winning side of 2001 Robson played 4 matches, batting once, he scored 5, he also made catches and had 1 stumping. His last match for Chester in the NEPL was on 4th August 2007 at Blaydon, he had played

67 matches in the NEPL for Chester, batting 50 times with 9 not outs, he scored 503 runs at an average of 12.26. He scored 1 half century, 57 not out, on 1st June 2002 at home to Newcastle. He bowled 6 balls, 0 for 2 and took 28 catches and 3 stumpings.

So, returning to matters in hand, when the dust had settled on the 2001 season Chester Le Street were deserved champions by 30 points from Benwell Hill.

Quentin Hughes was top of the league batting averages with 493 runs at an incredible 92.60 and Ashley Thorpe was second with 1003 runs at 71.64. Allan Worthy was sixth in the league batting averages and Dan Shurben thirty fifth. Ashley Thorpe scored five centuries this season, 132 not out and 106 against Stockton, 128 against South North, 115 against Gateshead Fell, and 109 against Norton. In addition to Thorpe's efforts, Allan Worthy scored two centuries this season, 124 not out against Tynemouth and 104 not out against Blaydon.

Allan Worthy was also second in the league bowling averages, with 22 wickets at 14.64 each. Ashley Thorpe was fifth in the league bowling averages, 33 wickets at 33.88, and Paul Chivers featured at eleven and Chris Dodsley at seventeen. Dan Shurben was joint fourth in the list of fielders with 8 catches.

In addition to all of the above, Allan Worthy was deservedly named as The NEPL Player of the Year and The Banks Salver was won by Stockton this season.

Just as an aside, Mark Stoneman's name popped up earlier in this chapter, so I will now take a few words to reflect on his NEPL involvement.

Stoneman made his NEPL debut for Durham Academy on 26th July 2003 at Benwell Hill, scoring 6 batting at number three in a rain affected game. His last game for The Academy in The NEPL came on 9th September 2006 at Sunderland, opening the batting he scored 69 in a drawn game.

Mark Stoneman played 54 matches in The NEPL for The Academy, batting 54 times, with 2 not out's, he scored 1706 runs at an average of 32.80. He scored 13 half centuries and 2 centuries. His highest score was 129 on 20th August 2005 at Benwell Hill. The innings came from 143 balls and contained 20 fours and 2 sixes. He never bowled for The Academy but took 14 NEPL catches for them.

He played for Blaydon for the 2007 season, making his NEPL debut for them on 28th April 2007 at home to South Shields, he scored 22 opening the batting, bowled by Chris Nichol.

Mark Stoneman played 12 matches in The NEPL for Blaydon in 2007, batting 12 times, with 1 not out, he scored 506 runs at an average of 46.00. He scored 2 half centuries and 2 centuries. His highest score for Blaydon in 2007 was 150 on 11th August at Stockton. He bowled 12 deliveries for Blaydon, 0 for 21, he also took 2 NEPL catches for them in 2007.

Stoneman played a little of the 2008 season in the NEPL, this time at Newcastle, making his debut for them on 10th May against The Durham Academy at The Riverside. He opened the innings and started well, 130 with 18 fours and 3 sixes against his former side.

He played 6 matches in The NEPL for Newcastle in 2008, batting 6 times, with 0 not out's, he scored 388 runs at an average of 64.66. He scored 1 half centuries and 2 centuries. His highest score for the season in the NEPL was 147 on 23rd August at Jesmond against Sunderland. He bowled 24 deliveries for Newcastle, 0 for 32, he also took 4 NEPL catches for them in 2008.

Stoneman returned to Blaydon for the 2009 season, playing the first NEPL game of his return on 2nd May at home to Newcastle, he scored 64 opening the batting, falling leg before to Joe Austin, a right arm off spinner.

Mark Stoneman played 11 matches in The NEPL for Blaydon in 2009, batting 11 times, with 1 not out, he scored 444 runs at an average of 44.40. He scored 2 half centuries and 2 centuries. His highest score for Blaydon in 2009 was 110 on 4th July at Denefield Bank against Tynemouth. This innings came from 117 balls and contained 13 fours and four sixes. He didn't bowl for Blaydon in 2009, but he did take 6 NEPL catches for them.

Stoneman didn't play in The NEPL in 2010, but he returned to Blaydon for the 2011 season, his first appearance coming on 21st May at Blaydon against The Durham Academy as he scored 48 opening the batting, Blaydon won by 4 wickets.

He played 10 matches in The NEPL in 2011, batting 10 times, with 1 not out, scoring 547 runs at an average of 60.77. He didn't score a half century but did manage 4 centuries! His highest NEPL score of 2011 was 130 on 25th June at home to Hetton Lyons, he was dismissed by a catch from Gary Adey off the bowling of Graeme Martin. He bowled 6 deliveries for them in 2011, 0 for 6 and took 4 NEPL catches.

Stoneman returned to Newcastle for the 2012 season, unfortunately for them he once again played very little for them, just 4 times. This was long enough for him to bat 3 times, with 0 not outs, he scored 175 runs at an average of 58.33 with 1 century. The century, 114 on 8th September at Jesmond against Benwell Hill, came from 116 balls, with 17 fours and a six. He was caught by Ben O'Brien off the bowling of Peter Jones.

He bowled 54 deliveries in The NEPL in 2012, with no maidens, conceding 42 runs and taking 1 wicket. The wicket he took was Blaydon's Ben Raine, bowled for 21 on 23rd June 2012 at Denefield Bank. He didn't take a catch this season.

Stoneman played just one game in the 2013 season, for Blaydon at home to South North on 17th August, he was caught behind by Adam Cragg off the bowling of Jonny Wightman for 2. Despite fielding a strong side Blaydon were dismissed for just 57, Stephen Humble had 7 for 32. Stoneman bowled 4 balls when South North batted, conceding the winning runs as South North won by 7 wickets. This was his last NEPL appearance as he went on to better things, most notably playing 11 Test Matches for England!

Mark Stoneman played 98 matches in the NEPL, batting 97 times, he was not out 5 times, scoring 3768 runs at an average of 40.95. He scored 18 half centuries and 13 centuries. His highest score was 150 on 29th May 2004 at Benwell Hill. The innings came from 135 balls and contained 20 fours and 2 sixes. He bowled 100 deliveries in the NEPL, with 0 maidens, conceding 106 runs and taking 1 wicket. He took 30 NEPL career catches.

TABLE 8   NEPL Final Table 2001.

	Played	Won	Drawn/Aban	Lost	Bonus Points	Points
Chester le St	20	9	10	1	148	341
Benwell Hill	20	8	9	3	140	311
Blaydon	20	8	4	8	126	288
Newcastle	20	8	4	8	116	278
Durham CA	20	6	5	9	129	262
Sunderland	20	7	6	7	105	251
Stockton	20	5	7	8	112	223
South North	20	5	7	8	106	215
Norton	20	3	5	12	98	199
Tynemouth	20	3	8	9	96	188
Gateshead Fell	20	0	12	8	72	102

TABLE 9   NEPL Batting Averages 2001.

Qualification 300 Runs.

42 Batsmen Qualified this season.

Player	Club	Inns	N. O	H. S	Runs	Average
(1) Q.J Hughes	Chester le St	16	11	82 no	463	92.60
(2) A.M Thorpe	Chester le St	17	3	132 no	1003	71.64
(3) N.A Perry	Blaydon	17	4	141 no	811	62.38
(4) J. Miller	Tynemouth	17	3	132 no	771	55.07
(5) W. Falla	Tynemouth	17	5	160 no	655	54.58
(6) A. Worthy	Chester le St	17	2	124 no	740	49.33
(7) S.J Birtwisle	Benwell Hill	11	1	135 no	466	46.60
(8) G. Hallam	Tynemouth	13	3	116	458	45.80
(9) G.J Muchall	Durham CA	14	2	103 no	549	45.75
(10) S. Kay	Newcastle	17	1	150 no	728	45.50
(11) J.A Benn	Tynemouth	15	4	96 no	472	42.91
(12) C. Symington	Norton	17	5	80	507	42.25
(35) D.G Shurben	Chester le St	17	1	69	418	26.13

TABLE 10   NEPL Bowling Averages 2001.

Qualification 20 Wickets.

25 Bowlers Qualified this season.

Player	Club	Overs	Mdns	Runs	Wkts	Ave	Best
(1) B.R Evans	Benwell Hill	99.4	18	262	21	12.48	4-14
(2) A. Worthy	Chester Le St	120.4	35	322	22	14.64	8-12
(3) A. Walker	Stockton	140.4	38	352	23	15.30	5-20
(4) S. Humble	Blaydon	115.5	26	372	24	15.50	6-46
(5) A.M Thorpe	Chester Le St	219.4	71	524	33	15.88	7-14
(6) M.J Symington	Norton	123.4	23	403	25	16.12	5-38
(7) Shahid Nazir	Benwell Hill	214.3	41	642	39	16.46	6-63
(8) A. Brown	Newcastle	116.2	18	415	24	17.29	4-30
(9) I. Shah	South North	141.4	30	469	26	18.04	8-48
(10) D. Rutherford	Benwell Hill	162.2	50	420	23	18.26	6-24
(11) P. Chivers	Chester Le St	142.2	31	529	28	18.89	6-36
(12) D. Townsend	South North	259.1	60	779	41	19.00	8-19
(18) C.W Dodsley	Chester Le St	148	34	482	22	21.91	5-36

Chester le Street CC 2001.

Back Row Left to Right David N. Robson, Chris Dodsley, David B. Robson, Daniel Shurben, Steven Lee Merrington, Paul Chivers.

Front Row David Wilson, Allan Worthy, Tony Birbeck, Ashley Thorpe, Gary Hunter.

Quentin Hughes, seen here preparing to bat at Sunderland on 19th May 2001.

Dan Shurben, batting here on 29th May 2004 at Benwell Hill.

Top Left- Ross McLaren seen here on 29th July 2000 at Sunderland.

Top Right-Chris Dodsley seen here on 19th May 2001 at Sunderland.

Bottom Left- Gary Hunter on the left and David Wilson, seen here on 19th May 2001 at Sunderland.

Bottom Right- Allan Worthy seen here on 19th May 2001 at Sunderland.

CHAPTER THREE

Benwell Hill 2002

Benwell Hill had started life in The NEPL by finishing seventh in the inaugural season of 2000, they had four batsmen in the league batting averages that year, John Windows, Phil Nicholson, Simon Birtwisle and Richard Sellers. Nicholson had an unbeaten century to his name also.

They also had three bowlers in the league bowling averages, John Windows, Lee Crozier and Gary Gilder, their overseas pro from Zimbabwe and Phil Nicholson was third in the list of wicketkeepers with 15 catches and 6 stumpings.

They had fared much better in the second season, 2001, finishing as runners up to an excellent Chester le Street side by 30 points. In 2001 Simon Birtwisle, Richard Sellers, Phil Nicholson, John Windows and David Rutherford had all made the league batting averages. Simon Birtwisle had scored one century this season, 135 not out against Gateshead Fell, and Phil Nicholson had scored two, 121 against South North and 118 not out against Gateshead Fell.

John Windows had moved on to join The Durham Academy set up and Richard Sellers moved elsewhere.

Barry Evans had topped the league bowling averages, overseas pro Shahld Nazir, David Rutherford and Lee Crozier also featured.

Having improved across the first two seasons in both league position and performance, it was fair to say that Benwell Hill knew they had a good side in 2002, and the challenge was to go and prove it. Simon Birtwisle recalls that they had a strategy going in to the season, they wanted to win the toss and bowl first, they knew they had a strong opening bowling attack and so looked to dismiss the opposition cheaply, and they had a strong top order in the batting to chase scores down.

In December 2001 Philadelphia resigned from the Durham Senior League to a place in The North East First Division/Premier League and so for the 2002 season The NEPL had it's full and always intended composition of twelve teams.

Benwell Hill had opened their 2002 campaign on 27th April with an away fixture at Jesmond against Newcastle. Newcastle had batted first, 194 all out from 61.3 overs, all five Hill bowlers used got wickets, Nazir 1 for 47, Rutherford 1 for 43, Pollard 2 for 19, Sharland 3 for 43 and Crozier 3 for 28. Martin Hynd had 73 opening for Newcastle. Half centuries from openers Birtwisle and Miller plus 44 not out from wicketkeeper Phil Nicholson saw Hill home by seven wickets.

The side Benwell Hill side that day was as follows.

Simon Birtwisle is a right-handed batman and slow left arm orthodox bowler. When the 2002 season got underway, he scored 50 opening the batting in the first fixture at Newcastle. He is the son of Durham Senior League and Durham Minor Counties player Peter Birtwisle. Peter Birtwisle was very well known throughout the North East cricket scene as a prolific batsman and medium pace bowler for Sunderland and Durham City. Records from back in the day are sketchy to say the least so I asked Peter about his cricket and his list of achievements are remarkable.

He played in the Durham Senior League from 1962 to 1992 inclusive and scored over 13,000 runs. He was at Sunderland from 1962 to 1981 and won the Durham Senior League in 1965 to 1968 inclusive and 1971 moving to Durham City where he played from 1982 to 1992 and they were champions in 1982, 1984, 1986 and 1987.

He made his debut for Durham in 1965, playing for Durham until 1984, making 91 Minor Counties appearances, being awarded his Durham cap in 1968. During his time with Durham County, they were Minor Counties Champions in 1976, 1980,1981 and 1984 and between 1976 and 1982 the county went a record 65 consecutive matches without defeat.

He played ten "List A" matches for Durham, scoring 223 runs at an average of 24.77 and a high score of 59 against Northants in 1977 in The Gillette Cup.

He also played one match for The Minor Counties East, against Yorkshire also in 1977, he was bowled for 8 by Graham Stevenson.

Peter Birtwisle bowled off spin in the later days of his career and when he retired, in addition to Sunderland, Durham City and Durham County, he had also played for Worcestershire Second XI, Minor Counties East, The Durham Senior League and he was also selected for the Northumberland and Durham Select XI which took on an International Select XI at Jesmond as part of the Callers Pegasus Festival of matches.

Simon recalls that his father was "a right-handed middle order batsman, by the standard of the day he would have been described as aggressive or attacking, he particularly liked facing left arm spin so he could hit it straight. His bowling at Durham City would have been curtailed because of Brian Lander and Gary Hume bowling an unrestricted amount of overs before he could get on!"

Simon Birtwisle opened the batting today, 27th April 2002 and throughout the season.

He scored 50 against Newcastle, to open the season, from just 48 balls and with ten boundaries in an opening partnership with Jimmy Miller worth 92. He played 18 matches in the NEPL in 2002, batting 18 times with 4 not outs, he scored 595 runs at an average of 42.50. He scored 5 half centuries, with a highest score of 81, made on 11th May 2002 at Tynemouth. He didn't bowl but took 4 NEPL catches in 2002.

Simon Birtwisle first came to light on 23rd August 1995 playing for Durham Under 17's against Northumberland at East Boldon, opening the batting he scored 52 in a 50 over match. Ian Hunter was amongst his team mates that day and John Graham in the Northumberland side.

On 26th August 1996 Birtwisle played in a three-day match for Durham Second's, at home to Worcestershire at Heworth. Worcester batted first, 449 for 8 declared, Birtwisle had 0 for 8 from two overs, Steve Harmison 3 for 86 the most successful bowler. Birtwisle opened the batting with Michael Gough in both innings, but both had a game to forget with the bat. Melvyn Betts 70, Andrew Pratt 65 and Paul Collingwood 63 ensured respectability, Durham 289 all out, but they were a long way behind, having to follow on. Durham finished 50 for 2 and the match was drawn.

Birtwisle played 5 more times for Durham Second's in 1997, making 54 against Scotland in August. He played three more times for them in 1998 and once more in 1999, without ever scoring the runs he was capable of.

His NEPL debut came on 6th May 2000 for Benwell Hill at Stockton, he batted at four, making 24 as Hill scored 241 for 9 declared from 64.5 overs. Stockton replied with 157 for 7 as the match was drawn, Birtwisle bowled two overs 0 for 0! His first NEPL wicket came a week later on 13th May at Gateshead Fell, Mark Smith bowled for 23.

On 4th June 2000 Birtwisle, and John Graham, made their Minor Counties debut for Northumberland in a two-day game at Bedfordshire. They were in good Benwell Hill and NEPL company on that day, Adam Heather, Phil Nicholson, David Rutherford and Lee Crozier in the side, Graeme Hallam and Graeme Angus also playing. Birtwisle didn't bat in the first innings and scored 4 in the second. Wayne Larkins opened the batting for the opposition, he made 8 and 27, Birtwisle bowled one over, a maiden, in a drawn match.

He would go on to play 14 times for Northumberland, batting on 15 occasions, scoring 334 runs at an average of 25.69, and scoring two half centuries, a high score of 72.

He bowled 240 balls, with 2 maidens, conceding 185 runs and taking 5 wickets. at an average of 37.00 and a best of 2 for 22, he also took 6 catches. His last appearance for Northumberland came on 18th May 2008.

After the first two NEPL seasons, Birtwisle entered the 2002 season with 24 matches, 23 innings, scoring 852 runs at an average of 42.60, with five half centuries and one century, 135 not out, his first NEPL century, it took place on 23rd June 2001 at Gateshead Fell and was part of an unbroken opening partnership of 270 with Phil Nicholson, Nicholson also had 135 not out.

Birtwisle had also bowled 642 balls, with 24 maidens, conceding 411 runs and taking 8 wickets at an average of 51.37, his best bowling was 3 for 72 and he had 7 catches in the first two seasons.

James (Jimmy) Miller was a right-handed batsman and right arm medium pace bowler. He opened the batting with Simon Birtwisle in the 2002 season opener at Newcastle on 27th April and top scored in the inning with 59 from 66 balls. Simon Birtwisle recalls that Miller was "difficult to bowl to on his day, he had fast hands and an aggressive attitude to batting, he liked the ball in the slot and was equally adept off either front or back foot, he would play shots all around the wicket, he played the sweep shot well and we made a good pair running between the wickets."

The first recorded innings I could find for him was opening for King's School, Tynemouth against Dame Allan's School, Newcastle on 8th May 1993 and his first recorded senior appearance was just under a year later, 2nd May 1994 for Tynemouth first team at Benwell Hill. Miller, batting eight, made 28 out of 137 as Benwell won by 28 runs.

On 12th June 1994 Miller was selected for Northumberland Under 17's against their Durham counterparts, at High Heworth, Felling CC. Northumberland posted 199 for 6 wickets in their 55 overs, John Graham had opened and made 63, Miller batting at seven, 26 not out. Durham won with 2 overs and 5 wickets to spare, Harry Hubber and Dave Nevin, part of their side. Miller then progressed through the Northumberland Under 19 and Under 21 side.

On 23rd June 1996 he was selected for a 50 over Northumberland Cricket Association away game with Lincolnshire & Humberside Cricket Association. Northumberland included several names who would go on to become recognizable in North East cricket and beyond, Wayne Falla, John Graham, Mike Thewlis, Phil Nicholson, David Rutherford and Steve Harmison among them. Falla top scored for Northumberland, Miller making 5, as they made 195 all out and the hosts got the runs to win by 4 wickets.

On 16th June 1998 Miller made his Minor Counties debut for Northumberland at Cambridgeshire, what should have been a two-day match ended up a single innings. Northumberland batting first were 108 all out, lots of familiar names in the side including future club team mates, Adam Heather, John Windows and Lee Crozier. The hosts were dismissed for 64 as Northumberland won by 44 runs, Lee Crozier having the outstanding figures of 7.3-3-8-5. Several Northumberland appearances followed for Miller over the next two years.

On 29th April 2000 the NEPL played its first ever fixture list. Miller batted three as his Tynemouth side hosted Blaydon, scoring 4 as Tynemouth made 150 for 8 in their 65 overs. Blaydon replied with 139 for 7, opener Ian Somerville scoring 14, as the match was drawn.

He played 13 matches for Tynemouth in The NEPL that season, with a best of 75 on 29th July against Norton.

The 2001 season was more successful for Miller as he finished fourth in the league batting averages, with 771 runs from 17 innings at an average of 55.07 and a high score of 132 not out against Gateshead Fell.

In May 2001 Miller and opening partner Wayne Falla hit "a purple patch" for Tynemouth, with three huge successive opening partnerships.

On 19th May 2001 Wayne Falla and Miller had a big unbroken first wicket stand for Tynemouth against Newcastle at Preston Avenue, unfortunately Falla had to retire hurt having made 81, Miller had 118 not out and Graeme Hallam 18 not out, Tynemouth scoring 230 for no loss as they chased down 229.

On Saturday 26th May 2001 Wayne Falla and Miller put on an unbroken first wicket stand for Tynemouth against Stockton of 236 from just 48 overs in a ten-wicket win. Richard Waite had 104 of his own in a losing effort, three centuries in the match as Falla had 106 not out and Miller 118 not out.

Two days later on 28th May 2001 Wayne Falla and Miller put on an unbroken first wicket stand for Tynemouth against Gateshead Fell of 316 from just 53 overs. Falla had 160 not out and Miller 132 not out.

Jimmy Miller moved to Benwell Hill for the 2002 season and once again made the league batting averages. He played 20 matches in the NEPL that season, batting 20 times with 4 not outs, he scored 526 runs at an average of 32.87. He scored 5 half centuries with a high score of 95 not out, made on 1st June 2002 at Norton. He took 8 catches in the 2002 NEPL season. Miller later moved to South North and had some success there and will feature later in the book.

Marcus Turner was a right-handed batsman, he batted at three in the 2002 season opener, making 19. During the 2002 title winning season he played 19 matches in the NEPL, he batted 16 times with 1 not out, he scored 208 runs at an average of 13.86. His highest score was 30, made on 26th August 2002 at Sunderland. He bowled 1 ball for 4 runs in the 2002 NEPL season but took 6 NEPL catches.

Simon Birtwisle recalls that Turner was "a rugby player, he had gone to King's School and had a connection with Phil Nicholson, that's how he ended up at The Hill, he loved the battle, he never backed down, he was a solid lad rather than big, but he hit the ball hard, if the ball was in the slot, he just hit it, he was a composed, uncomplicated batsman, a good team mate. He later moved to play at Tynemouth."

When I was looking at Marcus Turner and his early cricket days, I came across him first playing for Tynemouth, on 17th August 1997 at home to Durham, it was a 12 a side match, only 11 to bat and field. The fixture was a 40 over match to mark the 150th Anniversary of Tynemouth Cricket Club. Benwell Hill team mate of 2002 Jimmy Miller was in the Tynemouth side that day along with Wayne Falla, Tony Lion, Barry Stewart and Richard Brook. Blaydon scored 139 for 7, for the draw, Barry Stewart taking 4 for 21, Turner didn't bowl.

After playing for Tynemouth in The Northumberland County League, he made his NEPL debut when Tynemouth made theirs, on 29th April 2000 with a home fixture against Blaydon.

Blaydon won the toss and elected to field, Tynemouth scoring 150 for 8 from 65 overs. Graeme Hallam top scored with 42, Turner batting at five, scored 11. Stephen Humble opened the bowling for Blaydon that day, taking 2 for 27, West Indian pro Warrington Phillip took 3 for 34, I did note that Ian Somerville bowled a single delivery as first change for Blaydon, a closer inspection reveals that opening bowler Colin Campbell had been unable to finish his eighth over, Somerville completing it.

Turner's two years in The NEPL leading up to winning the title show that he had played 26 matches, batting 24 times, with 5 not out's, he had scored 400 runs at an average of 21.05 and 2 half centuries and 1 century. The century, exactly 100, had come on 1st July 2000 for Tynemouth at home to Newcastle. As a bowler he had bowled just 6 balls, conceding 4 runs for 0 wickets but he did have 5 catches.

On 9th July 2000 Turner made his Minor Counties debut for Northumberland in a 2-day match at Gosforth against Staffordshire. Staffs batted first 153 all out, all four bowlers used taking a wicket, Lee Crozier, opened the bowling, taking 1 for 51, Benwell Hill's David Rutherford had 3 for 44, Barry Stewart 2 for 33 and James Harmison 2 for 20. When Northumberland batted, they made 77 for 5 when the game was stopped as a draw, I can only presume bad weather, Marcus Turner was 2 not and Graeme Hallam 20 not out.

Marcus Turner made his NEPL debut for Benwell Hill on 28th April 2001 against Durham Academy at Denton Bank. The Academy batted first, 111 all out, Phil Mustard top scored with 19, Lee Crozier had 7 for 44. When Hill batted, Turner opened the batting, and although he failed to score, fellow opener Joe Thompson, 33 not out, and John Windows, 67 not out, saw them home by 9 wickets.

Phil Nicholson is a right-handed batsman and wicketkeeper; he was also captain in the 2002 season, he kept wicket, taking one catch, and scored 44 not out batting at number four in Hill's 2002 season opener. He played 21 matches in the NEPL in the 2002 season, batting 18 times with 5 not outs, he scored 431 runs at an average of 33.15. He scored 2 half centuries with a highest score of 66, made on 24th August 2002 at home to Stockton. He took 18 catches and had 3 stumpings in the NEPL in 2002.

Simon Birtwisle recalls that "as a wicketkeeper Nicholson modelled himself on Jack Russell, he was a good all-round keeper who took a lot of pride in his keeping, he hated byes, he just went out and did it, the biggest compliment I can pay him is that as a keeper you often didn't notice he was there, he was clean, efficient. He was also a real competitor, this came through in his batting, he could be a gritty, determined batsman, he liked to nurdle his runs and accumulate, but he hit the ball very well square, if you were in trouble he was the guy you wanted to bat for you."

Nicholson first came to light as a teenager, on 7th May 1988 I found a record of him playing for Benwell Hill against Blyth in The Northumberland County League. He was keeping wicket that day in an experienced Hill side that also contained Mike Younger, Simon Lunn, Barry Evans, David McKay and Hugh Dyson. It was an experienced Blyth side that day too, Paul Cormack, who had 118 not out in the game, Neil Pont and Russell Perry also turned out for them. Once in the side he seems to have become a regular for them.

On 21st July 1991 he played for Northumberland Under 21's against The Alnwick and District League at Denton Bank. Northumberland batted first, Nicholson opening the batting, made 66, as they scored 197 for 6 from 45 overs. When Alnwick batted, they were dismissed for just 58, all seven bowlers used taking wickets, Nicholson had 1 for 8.

Just two days later he kept wicket for a Durham side in a game against Denmark at Norton. Geoff Cook captained the Durham side, winning the toss and batting first, opening batsman Stewart Hutton had 69, Darren Blenkiron at three, made 50, Nicholson, batting five, was run out for 10 as Durham made 238 for 5 from 55 overs. Denmark had no answers for Paul Henderson, 4 for 12, and John Christie, 3 for 17, Nicholson kept wicket, taking 3 catches as the visitors were bowled out for 95.

As well as playing for the league under 21's, on 30th April 1992 Nicholson was selected to play for Durham Seconds in a Bain Clarkson Trophy match at Leicestershire. Although he didn't bat, he did take one catch keeping wicket, off the bowling of another well-known NEPL name, Quentin Hughes.

On 17th May 1992 he made his Minor Counties debut for Northumberland at Cheshire in a 55 over Holt Cup match. Northumberland had a strong side that day, with many recognizable names, Jon Benn, Graeme Morris, Paul Burn, Peter Willey, Paul Dutton, Mike Younger, Steve Greensword, Ian Conn, Peter Graham, Craig Stanley, plus Nicholson himself! Cheshire had Ian Cockbain and Geoff Miller in their ranks, so they weren't too bad either! Despite or perhaps because of the quality of the players on show, there was only half century in the match, 57 from Graeme Morris, as Northumberland won by 43 runs, Nicholson contributing 8 and a catch.

He was also selected for The NCA Young Cricketers North on seven occasions in 1992, as well as an appearance for The English Schools Cricket Association in Dublin. Further appearances for both these teams and continued selection for Northumberland meant that 1992 and 1993 were very busy years for Nicholson.

He played a 3-day game for Glamorgan Seconds at Nottinghamshire, starting on 13th June 1994, he made 17 in his only innings, and he was then selected for English Universities on 8th July 1994 but didn't get the opportunity to bat in a winning effort against Irish Universities.

In 1995 Nicholson played 4 times or Gloucestershire Seconds, in his first game, against Lancashire at Great Crosby, starting on 31st July, he opened the batting in the second innings and scored 100, he also had 3 stumpings and took 2 catches in the match.

He was selected for The Minor Counties Under 25's on 23rd May 1996 for a game with Leicestershire, rain stopped the game after just 32 overs of the home side innings.

Whilst continuing to play for Northumberland, he had to wait until 28th April 1997 to make his full debut in List A matches, selected for Minor Counties in a Benson and Hedges game against Derbyshire. He didn't get a bat in a strong side which contained Wayne Larkins, Ian Cockbain and Neal Radford. The opening bowlers for Derbyshire were Phil Defreitas and Devon Malcolm, despite this Minor Counties posted 256 got 7 from their 50 overs. Richard Dalton had 76. Chris Adams hit 138 in the reply as Derbyshire won by 6 wickets with 11 balls to spare. Nicholson did have the satisfaction of catching Kim Barnett.

He played 10 matches in total for Minor Counties, batting 9 times, with 0 not out's, he scored 50 runs at an average of 5.55, taking 8 catches as he continued to play for Benwell Hill and Northumberland throughout the nineties.

In a 2-day match starting on 17th August 1997 he scored 100 not out opening the batting for Northumberland against Cumberland, this was his first ton in Minor Counties cricket. He already had several centuries in The County League by this time.

After making his debut on 12th August 1990 Nicholson played 175 matches for Northumberland, he batted 189 times, with 49 not outs, he scored 2938 runs at an average of 20.98, making 10 half centuries and 2 centuries, his highest score was 107 not out. He bowled 58 deliveries, with 0 maidens, conceding 108 runs and taking 1 wicket. He also took 265 catches and had 51 stumpings. His last game for Northumberland was on 10th June 2012.

He marked his NEPL debut on 6th May 2000 away at Stockton with 72 in a drawn game. In his opening two years in The NEPL he played 32 games, all for Benwell Hill, batting 29 times with 5 not outs, scoring 972 runs at an average of 40.50, with 5 half centuries and 3 centuries.

His highest score in that period was 121 on 2nd June 2001 at South North, he had also taken 31 catches and had 9 stumpings.

David Rutherford was a left-handed batsman and right arm fast medium bowler, he batted at number five on 27th April 2002, 23 not out. Rutherford played 21 matches in the NEPL in 2002, batting 16 times with 4 not outs, he scored 197 runs at an average of 16.41. His highest score was 30, made on 18th May 2002 at home to Durham Academy.

He bowled 1346 balls in the 2002 NEPL season, with 61 maidens, he conceded 566 runs and took 42 wickets at an average of 13.47. His best bowling figures were 4 for 17, taken on 8th June 2002 at Stockton. He took 8 catches in the NEPL that season.

Birtwisle's memories of Rutherford as a bowler are that "he hit the bat hard, he was always an accurate bowler, very tight lines, he got more skilful as he matured. He was a good foil for Nazir."

The first record for Rutherford was an appearance on 19th June 1993 for Morpeth at Benwell Hill in the Northumberland County League, he took 1 for 20 and didn't bat.

He is recorded in a handful of games for Morpeth over the next two years but can be found on 30th July 1995 playing for Northumberland Under 25's against Durham at Heworth in a 55 over match. Northumberland batted first, Ben Jones-Lee made 125, Jimmy Miller 68 and Michael Smalley 61, Rutherford didn't bat as they made 304 for 5 from their allotted overs. Steven Naylor made 120 when Durham replied but the next highest score was 24 as Durham were bowled out for 205. Rutherford had opened the bowling and took 3 for 33 and John Windows had 3 for 37 in a comfortable Northumberland win.

On 22nd August 1995 Rutherford played for The Northumberland Under 21's against The West Tyne League at Stocksfield in a 40 over match, Rutherford opened the bowling, taking 0 for 26. Despite him making 30 not out batting at number eight, his side fell 15 runs short.

On 6th September 1995 Rutherford was selected for Durham Seconds in a 3-day match at Worcestershire Seconds. In a rain-affected match he made 24 in his only innings and took 0 for 45 when he bowled. He was given a further opportunity with Durham Seconds at the start of the following season, a one-day match with Durham University at The Racecourse Ground on 26th April 1996. He opened the bowling, taking 2 for 50 but didn't get a bat.

It appears that he joined Benwell Hill from Morpeth for the 1997 season. Onn 26th April 1997, possibly in the Northumberland County League season opener, Morpeth batted first scoring 166 for 9 from 50 overs, Rutherford had 0 for 52 while Lee Crozier took 6 for 62. Phil Nicholson made 85 in the response, his opening partner, Lee Crozier made 12, Rutherford didn't bat as his side won by 6 wickets.

On 12th May 1998 Rutherford and team mate Lee Crozier were selected to play for The Minor Counties Under 25's against Middlesex Seconds at Totternhoe in Bedfordshire. Crozier made 9 not out and Rutherford 8 not out as their side posted 216 for 8 from their 50 overs. Rutherford took 1 for 41 and Crozier 1 for 25 as Middlesex won by 4 wickets.

Both Rutherford and Crozier, along with David Love from Shotley Bridge, were selected to represent The England and Wales Cricket Board in a fixture against Ireland on 18th July 1999 at The Hague in The Netherlands. Ireland batted first, making 203 for 5 from their 50 overs, Rutherford had 1 for 34, Crozier 2 for 36 and Love 0 for 30. When their side batted, they fell just 2 runs short, Rutherford was run out for 10, Crozier and Love were both 1 not out.

Rutherford would play several games for The Minor Counties, The England and Wales Cricket Board over the next few years.

His last game for Northumberland was at Swalwell against Lincolnshire in a 3-day match starting on 26th June 2011. He had played 131 matches for the county, batting 140 times with 42 not outs, he scored 2052 runs at an average of 20.93, with 1 half century, his highest score of 56. This took place on 6th June 2010 at Jesmond against Hertfordshire.

He bowled 12354 balls, with 428 maidens, conceding 6884 runs and taking 220 wickets at an average of 31.29. His best bowling was 7 for 58 on 14th June 1999 at Jesmond against Norfolk and he had 29 career catches for Northumberland.

Rutherford made his NEPL debut for Benwell Hill on 28th April 2001 at Denton Bank against Durham Academy. Rutherford opened the bowling, 0 for 26 as Lee Crozier took 7 for 44 and he didn't bat as John Windows hit 67 not out in a 9-wicket win. He took his first NEPL wicket a week later, 5th May 2001 when he bowled Norton's Lee Hutton.

Rutherford played his last NEPL fixture for Benwell Hill on 14th September 2013 at Hetton Lyons, one to forget for Rutherford as Hetton won by 60 runs with Ryan Pringle scoring 105 not out and taking 4 for 73. He had played 113 matches for Benwell Hill in the NEPL, batting 84 times with 24 not outs, he scored 1308 runs at an average of 21.80, with 3 half centuries. His highest score was 96 not out, it took place on 24th April 2010 at home against Newcastle.

He bowled 8737 balls for Benwell Hill in the NEPL, with 391 maidens, conceding 3665 runs and taking 223 wickets at an average of 16.43. His best bowling was 6 for 24 on 25th August 2001 at Jesmond against Newcastle. He took 20 NEPL catches for Benwell Hill.

Rutherford would go on to play for South North in 2014, 2015 and 2016 and he would later play for Ashington in The NEPL in 2023. His stats will be updated later in the book.

Joseph (Joe) Thompson was a right-handed batsman and leg break bowler, He was listed to bat at number six to open the 2002 season, but he didn't get to bat. Thompson played 6 matches in the NEPL in the 2002 season, batting 3 times with 0 not outs, he scored 17 runs at an average of 5.66. His highest score was 13. He didn't bowl but took 3 catches in the NEPL that season.

Thompson had made his NEPL debut for Benwell Hill in the season opener of the 2001 season, on 28th April at home to Durham Academy. After the Academy had been bowled out for 111, Lee Crozier taking 7 for 44, Thompson opened the batting and finished with 33 not out in a nine wicket Hill win.

Thompson played his last NEPL game on 27th June 2009, for Benwell Hill at home to Blaydon, he had played 81 NEPL matches for Benwell Hill, batting 70 times, with 8 not outs, he scored 937 runs at an average of 15.11, with 1 half century. The half century was his highest score, 64 not out on 7th July 2001 at Durham Academy. The Durham opening bowling attack that day was Graham Onions and Liam Plunkett! He bowled just 36 balls in the NEPL, conceding 45 runs, he didn't take a wicket, but he did take 24 NEPL career catches.

Ben Ramsay left-handed batsman and slow left arm orthodox bowler, listed to bat seven in the season opener, he wasn't required. He made his NEPL debut, and only NEPL appearance of the season, for Benwell Hill on 1st September 2001 at home against Gateshead Fell. He batted at three, scoring 26, David Rutherford top scored with 86 not out from 103 balls and included 14 boundaries, as Hill declared on 247 for 7 after 60 overs. Mark Smith had 3 for 68 for Fell. When they batted Fell were dismissed for 186 in 57.4 overs with Shahid Nazir taking 4 for 37.

Despite starting the 2002 season, Ramsey only played 5 games in The NEPL that season, his only contribution was to take a single catch. His last NEPL appearance came on 9th September 2006 at Gateshead Fell. Ramsay played 25 times in the NEPL, batting on 16 occasions, with 3 not outs, scoring 70 runs at an average of 5.38, his highest score was the 26 on debut.

He bowled 414 balls in his NEPL career, with 3 maidens, conceding 299 runs and taking 8 wickets at an average of 37.37 and a best of 3 for 65. His best bowling came on 15th July 2006 at home to Blaydon, he took 5 catches.

Shahid Nazir was a right-handed batsman and right arm fast -medium bowler, listed to bat at number eight on 27th April 2002 but not required. He played 21 matches in the NEPL in 2002, batting 10 times with 1 not out, he scored 185 runs at an average of 20.55. He scored 1 half century, 63, made on 17th August 2002 at Blaydon.

He bowled 1578 balls in the NEPL in 2002, with 71 maidens, he conceded 685 runs and took 58 wickets at an average of 11.81. His best bowling figures were 6 for 31, taken on 3rd June 2002 at home to Blaydon. He took 6 catches in the NEPL in 2002.

Birtwisle remembers Nazir as "a fantastic bowler, he had come to us with some test cricket behind him and he would later return to test cricket, he swung the ball away at pace in his first spell, then bowled reverse swing in his second, he came to us with an excellent reputation, and he didn't disappoint."

Rather than go through Nazir's entire record, in line with Simon Birtwisle's comments, I'm just going to concentrate on his test record.

He made his test debut for Pakistan on 17th October 1996 against Zimbabwe, taking his first test wicket, left hander, Alistair Campbell, L.B.W. and he went on to take 5 for 53 in the innings. He got a duck when batting at eleven in Pakistan's only innings and took 2 for 45 in the second innings as the match was drawn.

He was in and out of the side over the next 3 or 4 years, making the last appearance of this spell on 4th March 1999 against Sri Lanka in Lahore. He scored 10 in his only innings of the game and took 0 for 45 and 1 for 27 with the ball.

Nazir made his NEPL debut for Hill on 5th May 2001 at Norton with Hill batting first, 248 for 8 declared from 60 overs. John Windows had 79, Richard Sellers 47 not out, Nazir had batted at seven and scored 17. Marc Symington had 3 for 40 for Norton. When Norton batted Nazir quickly got his first NEPL wicket, bowling opener Simon Hawk for 2, Norton were 199 for 9 after 60 overs when their innings was closed, and the match drawn. Nazir had taken 3 for 56 on his debut.

His first season, 2001, had been a success. He had played 17 games, batting 12 times with 1 not out, he scored 156 runs at an average of 14.18. His highest score was 38 on 25th August 2001 at Newcastle.

He bowled 1291 balls in his first season, with 41 maidens, conceding 642 runs and taking 39 wickets at an average of 16.46. His best bowling figures in 2001 were 6 for 63 on 7th July at The Riverside against Durham Academy, Phil Mustard and Liam Plunkett his most well-known victims. He took 5 NEPL catches in 2001.

He played his last game for Benwell Hill in The NEPL on 4th September 2004 at Denton Bank against Stockton, taking 3 for 42, he did not bat.

He returned to test cricket on 5th August 2006 at Headingly for the third match of the series against England. England batted first and Nazir took the wicket of Andrew Strauss but conceded 101 runs. He made 13 not out and 17 with the bat and took 3 for 32 in the second innings, Paul Collingwood, Sajid Mahmood and Matthew Hoggard his victims but England won by 167 runs.

He also played in the 4th test at The Oval, starting on 4th August 2006, he took 1 for 44 in the first innings, Alistair Cook being the wicket, and 1 for 26 in the second innings, Kevin Pietersen out for 96. With the bat he made 17. This was the controversial test match when Pakistan refused to take the field after the tea interval on the fourth day, there had been five penalty runs awarded earlier in the match against them for ball tampering and this was a protest of that decision. England were awarded the match!

Nazir played in 5 more tests for Pakistan, the last starting on 26th January 2007 in Cape Town against South Africa. He scored 3 and 27 and took 1 for 37 in the first innings, Graeme Smith being the wicket. In the second innings he took 1 for 27, his last test wicket was Jaques Kallis, bowled for 51 as South Africa won by 5 wickets.

His test career now over, he had played 15 test matches, batting on 19 occasions, with 3 not outs, he scored 194 runs at an average of 12.12. His highest test score was 40, in the second innings of the first test against South Africa which started on 11th January 2007.

He had bowled 2234 balls in test cricket, with 71 maidens, conceding 1272 runs and taking 36 test wickets at an average of 35.33 each. His best bowling figures was the 5 for 53 he took in the first innings of his first test match. He took 5 catches in test cricket.

Nazir joined Sunderland for the 2007 season, making his NEPL debut for them on 28th April 2007 at Ashbrooke against Benwell Hill, he took 2 for 44 and did not bat in a drawn game.

Nazir played his last NEPL on 30th August 2008 at Tynemouth. In a low scoring game, he got a duck when he batted but he took the last 4 wickets to fall as Tynemouth went from 71 for 6 to 75 all out as Sunderland won by 42 runs and he finished with 4 for 30.

Across the four seasons and two clubs he played NEPL cricket, Nazir won one NEPL title, with Benwell Hill in 2002. He also topped the league bowling averages that year as he took 58 wickets at 11.54 each.

He played a total of 103 matches, batting on 68 occasions, with 9 not outs, he scored 892 runs at an average of 15.11, with 1 half century. The half century, 63, was for Benwell Hill, and took place on 17th August 2002 at Blaydon.

He bowled 7956 balls in his NEPL career, with 328 maidens, conceding 3583 runs and taking 260 wickets at an average of 13.78. His best bowling figures were 7 for 19 for Sunderland at home to Tynemouth on 5th May 2007 and he took 21 NEPL career catches.

Lee Crozier is a right-handed batsman and right arm off break bowler, he was listed to bat at nine for the 2002 season opener but did not bat. He played 21 matches in the NEPL in 2002, batting 13 times with 4 not outs, he scored 285 runs at an average of 31.66. He made 1 half century, 89, scored on 25th May 2002 at Philadelphia. The innings came from 134 balls and contained 14 fours and 1 six.

He also bowled 1254 balls in the NEPL in 2002, with 62 maidens, he conceded 545 runs and took 34 wickets at an average of 16.02. His best bowling figures were 4 for 8 taken on 8th June 2002 at Stockton. He took 3 catches in the NEPL in 2002.

John Graham, who is a good friend of Crozier, remembers that "as an opponent Crozier had great control of both his pace and his length, a batsman had to be very wary advancing down the track to him because he was excellent at varying his length if a batsman gave away his intention too early. He always seemed to work out what pace to bowl at on each wicket and although not a great spinner of the ball, he had a good arm ball, he presented the very best batsmen with a challenge." In short, he recalls "a brilliant bowler."

Simon Birtwisle recalls that "I didn't know Lee before Benwell Hill, he was an impressive bowler, even way back then, I think he had played at Ryton at some point, now I've played and spent a lot of time with him, I don't think he has ever really changed."

Crozier had started as a junior at South North, moving to Ryton to keep his availability for Durham Juniors, then joining Benwell Hill.

The first record I could find was for Durham Under 19s on 8th September 1991, at Denton Bank against Northumberland, he had 0 for 25 and didn't bat in a 9 wicket win for a Durham side for whom Neil Killeen took 2 for 35 and Allan Worthy had 75 not out.

Crozier, alongside Allan Worthy and Phil Nicholson, was selected for The Durham Cricket Association for a 55-over match with The Yorkshire Academy at Stockton. Crozier had 2 for 45 and Worthy 3 for 41 as Durham won by 4 runs.

His first notable appearance for Benwell Hill took place on 27th April 1996 at home to County Club. Phil Nicholson had 59, Crozier, batting at four, made 19 as Hill scored 208 for 7 for their 50 overs. Barry Evans took 5 for 49 and Crozier 1 for 17 as County Club managed a draw with 138 for 9.

Crozier made his Minor Counties debut for Northumberland on 26th May 1996 in a 2-day match at Jesmond against Hertfordshire. He took 1 for 23 as Herts made 220 for 7 declared from 50 overs. When Northumberland batted Tim Adcock had 133 not out and Graeme Morris 53 not out as they declared after 47 overs at 225 for 2. Only 19 more overs were bowled in the match and only one Herts wicket fell as the game was drawn.

He continued to play for Benwell Hill and Northumberland in the mid and late nineties and in July 1998 he was selected, as mentioned earlier, with David Rutherford for the English Cricket Board for a series of games against Ireland, Scotland, Denmark and Italy.

His last game for Northumberland was on 7th May 2006 at Hertfordshire in the MCCA Trophy. Northumberland batted first, Allan Worthy had 78, Marc Symington 52 and Crozier made 8 as Northumberland scored 252 all out in 49.1 overs. Hertfordshire won by 2 wickets with 4 balls to spare, their number nine scored 54 not out as Crozier had 2 for 27.

His Northumberland career saw him play 85 times for the county, batting 70 times with 26 not outs, he scored 716 runs at an average of 16.27, with 2 half centuries. His high score of 71 came on 14th July 2002 at Jesmond against Lincolnshire.

He bowled 9203 balls for Northumberland, with 320 maidens, conceding 5159 runs and taking 179 wickets at an average of 28.82. His best bowling figure were 6 for 44 on 9th June 1997 at Jesmond against Lincolnshire. He also took 24 career catches for Northumberland.

He made his NEPL debut on 6th May 2000 for Benwell Hill at Stockton. He failed to score batting at ten and took 1 for 49 with the ball. His first NEPL wicket was R. Thomas, leg before wicket for 21.

Crozier had made a mark in the first two years of the NEPL, playing 33 games for Hill, batting 20 times, with 7 not outs, he had scored 194 runs at an average of 14.92. His highest score was 35, coming on 1st September 2001 at home to Gateshead Fell.

He had bowled 2367 balls, with 95 maidens, conceding 1261 runs and taking 54 wickets at an average of 23.35, with a best of 7 for 44 against The Durham Academy on 28th April 2001. He had also taken 13 catches, more of Crozier later.

Anthony (Tony) Sharland was from Fremantle in Western Australia. David Rutherford had gone across to Australia and played at the same club Sharland played and Sharland ended up coming across to the UK. Phil Nicholson remembers him as "a left arm seamer, he struggled with a back injury for most of the season. He batted low down the order, left-handed, and I remember he used to give it a whack! Off the field he was tremendously well liked. The Premier League changed the rules on overseas players at the end of the season, limiting it to one per club, it was a shame really."

When Newcastle batted in the 2002 season opener he came on as the second change bowler, taking 3 for 45 from fifteen overs. His first NEPL wicket was Wayne Ritzema, who was caught and bowled for 24, he was listed to bat at ten but not required in a 7-wicket win.

The 2002 season was his only season in the NEPL. He played 20 games, batting 6 times, with 3 not outs, he scored 22 runs at an average of 7.33 with a high score of 13.

He bowled 642 balls, with 28 maidens, conceding 273 runs and taking 9 wickets at an average of 30.33. His best bowling figures were the 3 for 45 he took on debut and he took 7 NEPL catches.

Martin Pollard right-handed batsman and right arm medium fast bowler, he was listed to bat at eleven on the season opener of 2002. He played 21 matches in the NEPL in the 2002 season, batting 3 times with 2 not outs, he scored 14 runs at an average of 14.00.

He also bowled 1015 deliveries in the NEPL in the 2002 season, with 48 maidens, he conceded 426 runs and took 29 wickets at an average of 14.68. His best bowling figures were 5 for 21, taken on 31st August 2002 at Chester le Street. He took 3 catches in the NEPL that season.

Simon Birtwisle recalls that Pollard was "a strong lad, a fast bowler, who, without being express, was fast enough, he was unerringly accurate, he hit a length and did just enough with the ball to cause a batsman problems."

He first appeared in the records on 16th June 1997 for Gateshead Fell in an Abbot Ale Cup match at home to Benwell Hill. He took 1 for 34, Tim Ditchburn was the batsman, as Hill made 125 for 7 from their 20 overs. When Fell batted, they were dismissed for 97, Pollard, batting at seven, made 1, Hill winning by 28 runs.

Pollard appeared next in the records on 2nd August 1998, this time for Ashington at home to Benwell Hill in a Northumberland County League match. Hill batted first, 195 for 6 from their 50 overs, opener Paul Currie had 84 and John Windows 61. Pollard had opened the bowling with James Harmison, taking 1 for 28, Harmison had 4 for 47. When Ashington batted an opening stand of 83 between Mike Thewlis, 52, and Scott Kay 31, seemingly put them on the road to success, but only two more batsmen made double figures as Lee Crozier took 3 for 60 and the game ended in a draw, Ashington 182 for 9. Pollard, batting ten, was run out for a duck. He played several games for Ashington over the next few years, up to and including the 2000 season.

He made his NEPL debut on 28th April 2001 for Benwell Hill in a home fixture with The Durham Academy. The visitors batted first, 111 all out, Pollard taking his first NEPL wicket when he had Gordon Muchall leg before for a duck, as he opened the bowling and had nine overs 1 for 9. The star of the show that day though was undoubtedly Lee Crozier, his off breaks resulting in the figures of 14.2 overs, 3 maidens, 44 runs conceded for 7 wickets. Phil Mustard had top scored with 19 for The Academy with Liam Plunkett and Graham Onions also both playing for The Academy. When Hill batted John Windows hit 67 not out batting at three as they won by nine wickets.

Pollard was selected for Northumberland for a match starting on 20th June 2001 at Jesmond against Hertfordshire. He was in good company as Lee Crozier, John Windows, Phil Nicholson and David Rutherford were also playing and representing Benwell Hill. Pollard had 0 for 36 from twelve overs in the first innings and took his first Minor Counties wicket in the second innings, 1 for 53 from seventeen overs. The match was a high scoring draw, Herts having a centurion in each innings.

Pollard would play his last match for Northumberland on 25th June 2006, having played 39 times for them, batting on 27 occasions, with 16 not outs, he scored 159 runs at an average of 14.45. His highest score was 25 not out in his last innings for the County on 26th June 2006.

He bowled 3207 deliveries for Northumberland, with 119 maidens, conceding 1821 runs and taking 53 wickets at an average of 34.35. His best bowling figures were 4 for 24 on 15th August 2004 in The MCCA Knockout Trophy Semi Final win at Wiltshire. Wiltshire had batted first and were all out for just 91, as well as Pollard there was a strong NEPL presence, Marc Symington had 2 for 32, Stephen Humble 1 for 9 and Lee Crozier 3 for 10. Only John Windows didn't get a wicket, 0 for 9. When Northumberland batted, despite losing Allan Worthy for 4, and Dan Shurben for 46, Adam Heather, 34 not out and Bradley Parker 2 not out, saw them win by eight wickets. John Graham and Phil Nicholson had completed the Northumberland team that day.

The Final of the MCCA Knockout Trophy took place at Lord's on 6th September 2004, Northumberland selected the same team as they had in the semi final, including Martin Pollard. Northumberland lost the toss and were put into bat, despite 37 from opener Allan Worthy, and seven batsmen making double figures, they posted a respectable but not unreachable 237 all out in 49.3 overs. Pollard, batting at eleven, made 6 not out. When Berkshire batted, they put on 87 for the first wicket, and 91 for the third, as they went on to win by 7 wickets. Pollard had six overs, 0 for 33.

He remained at Benwell Hill until the end of the 2008 season, playing his last game for them on 30th August at South Shields. Shields batted first, scoring 152 for 9 wickets declared in 46.5 overs. Pollard had 5 for 37. His last Hill NEPL wicket was Matthew Muchall. 55 not out from Alistair Maiden and 62 not out from Graeme Race saw Hill win by 8 wickets.

Pollard had played on 151 occasions for Benwell Hill in the NEPL, batting 66 times with 33 not outs, he scored 292 runs at an average of 8.84 and a high score of 27, made on 27th August 2005 at Tynemouth.

He was an out and out bowler, he delivered 9687 balls for Hill in the NEPL, with 367 maidens, conceding 4825 runs and taking 205 wickets at an average of 23.53. His best bowling figures were 6 for 21 on 19th May 2007 at Tynemouth. He also took 41 NEPL catches.

On 25th April 2009 Pollard made his NEPL debut for Blaydon at Stockton, during his period at Blaydon, they finished as runners up twice, in 2009 and 2012 and third in 2011. He played his last NEPL game for Blaydon on 14th September 2013.

His career stats at Blaydon in The NEPL saw him play 88 matches, batting 31 times, with 17 not outs, he scored 78 runs for them at an average of 5.57 and a high score of 13.

He bowled 4774 balls, with 177 maidens, conceding 2303 runs and taking 117 wickets at an average of 19.68. His best bowling figures for Blaydon were 5 for 19 on 6th June 2009 at home to Sunderland. He took 25 NEPL catches for the club.

On 19th April 2014 Pollard made his NEPL debut for Hetton Lyons at Chester le Street, he played the 2014 and 2015 seasons there, playing his last game for them on 5th September 2015 at Whitburn.

Pollard played 39 times for Hetton Lyons in the NEPL, batting 15 times with 8 not out's, he scored 50 runs at an average of 7.14 and a high score of 39 not out. The high score had been on 16th May 2015 at home to Chester le Street.

He bowled 2035 balls for Hetton in the NEPL, with 83 maidens, conceding 983 runs and taking 52 wickets at an average of 18.90. His best bowling figures for Hetton in The NEPL were 5 for 33 on 21st June 2014 at Whitburn. He also took 8 NEPL catches for them.

On 30th April 2016 Pollard made his NEPL debut for Tynemouth at Gateshead Fell. He was still playing for them and was captain for them at the start of the 2024 season.

Up to the end of the 2023 season Pollard had played 103 NEPL matches for Tynemouth, batting 47 times with 29 not outs, he has scored 127 runs at an average of 7.05 with a high score of 16.

He has bowled 4504 balls, with 110 maidens, conceding 2734 runs and taking 137 wickets at an average of 19.95. His best bowling for Tynemouth, 7 for 27, came on 4th August 2018 at home to Felling. He has taken 36 NEPL catches for the club.

Since his NEPL debut for Benwell Hill on 28th April 2001 until his last game of the 2023 season on 9th September for Tynemouth at home to Burnmoor, Pollard has played 381 NEPL matches, he has batted 159 times, with 87 not outs, he has scored 547 runs at an average of 7.59. His highest score was 39 not out for Hetton Lyons in May 2015.

He has bowled 21000 balls in the NEPL, with 737 maidens, conceding 10845 runs and taking 511 wickets at an average of 21.22. His best was the 7 for 27 for Tynemouth in August 2018. He has taken 110 NEPL career catches. Update-He captained Tynemouth throughout the 2024 season and features in the weekly roundup.

Michael Gough was a right-handed batsman and right arm off break bowler. He didn't play in the season opener of 2002, but he was a huge influence in the outcome of the season, he came with a strong pedigree, first coming to my attention in an Under 17 match between Northumberland and Durham at Ashington on 2nd July 1995. Northumberland batted first, 143 all out, Jonathan Bailey took 5 for 21. Gough opening the batting, scoring 71 before Steve Harmison bowled him, fellow opener Chris Hewison scoring 54 not out as Durham won by 7 wickets.

On 5th May 1996 Gough appeared in a Second Eleven Championship game for Durham at The Oval against Surrey. Surrey batted first, 262 all out, Ian Ward made 10, Jason Searle 4 for 57. Gough, batting at number six made 3, Durham 135 all out, Shaun Birbeck top scored with 34. Alex Tudor was in the Surrey side, 0 for 31, Joey Benjamin had 5 for 28. Surrey 159 for 8 declared in their second innings, Ian Ward 22, David Cox 3 for 39. Gough got a duck in the second innings, Durham 287 for 6 in a drawn match, Darren Blenkiron 48.

Gough continued to play for Durham at different levels, then on 7th July 1997 he played for England Under 17's in an International Youth Tournament against Bermuda Under 19's at The Sea Breeze Oval, Bermuda. Bermuda batted first, 139 for 9 from 50 overs, Gough bowled ten overs for 22, Chris Hewison, had 3 for 28. Rob Key opened the batting and top scored with 55 not out as England won by eight wickets, neither Gough nor Hewison got a bat.

Gough continued to progress playing for England Under 17's and Durham Second Elevens in the rest of 1997, until on 11th December 1997 he was selected for England Under 19's against South Africa in a test match in Cape Town. Graeme Swann, Gary Schofield, Gary Napier and Rob Key also making their debuts at this level. South Africa batted first, 504 for 8 declared, Grant Elliott, 201 not out and Jaq Rudolph had 28, for England Paul Franks took 4 for 65 and Swann 3 for 139. When England batted only Swann had more than 50, 75 to be exact and Gough failed to score as England were 286 all out and had to follow on. They did no better in the second innings, Stephen Peters 92, Rob Key 51, and Gough had 32 not out but England were 256 all out went on to lose by 9 wickets.

Gough would go on to captain England Under 19's, playing 11 test matches for them, he batted 21 times, with 2 not outs, scoring 767 runs at an average of 40.36, he had 6 half centuries and 1 century, a high score of 116 against New Zealand in February 1999.

He also bowled 396 balls at this level, with 19 maidens, conceding 187 runs and taking 4 wickets at an average of 46.75, and a best of 2 for 15 and he took 7 catches.

Gough made his first-class debut for Durham on 13th May 1998 in a 4-day match against Essex at The Riverside. He made 62 in his first innings, opening the batting, in a Durham score of 276 all out and 16 in the second innings, Durham 247 all out. Essex had scored 185 all out in their first innings, and were dismissed for 243 in their seconds, Melvyn Betts had 6 for 83 as Durham won by 95 runs.

Gough played nine games for Benwell Hill in 2002, making his debut on 8th June 2002 at Stockton, he scored 6. In those 9 appearances he scored 2 hundreds, 2 half centuries and had 476 runs, topping the league batting averages, with an average of 158.67, with a high score of 118 not out. The high score of 118 not out came against Sunderland at Denton Bank on 15th June 2002, batting at four, it came from 146 balls and included 10 fours and a six. Shahid Nazir took 5 for 17 as Hill won by 120 runs, Sunderland were to finish third that year and were a strong side.

South North captain, John Graham, is of the opinion that Gough's contribution was key to Benwell Hill getting across the line to win the title this year.

After the 2002 season Gough didn't play again in the NEPL, he did, however, pursue a career in cricket. He played his last first-class game for Durham against Glamorgan at Cardiff, starting on 13th August 2003, he scored 30 and 25 and afterwards he quit playing.

He had played 67 first class matches, batting 119 times with 3 not out's, scoring 2952 runs at an average of 25.44, with a high score of 123 and 15 half centuries and 2 centuries to his name, his highest score was 123. He also played 49 List A matches for Durham, batting 45 times, with 4 not out's, scoring 974 runs at an average of 23.75, with a high score of 132.

He had sat his umpire's exams in 2006 and officiated his first game as an umpire in April 2006, in the Second Eleven Championship. Promotion was rapid, in umpire terms, officiating in his first game international game in 2013, he was one of the umpires in the 2015 Cricket World Cup and on 28th July 2016 he stood in his first test match, between Zimbabwe and New Zealand in Bulawayo.

From 2010 he was named ECB Umpire of the Year for eight years in a row and in 2019 he became a member of The Elite Panel of I.C.C Umpires, representing The E.C.B.

He was one of the on-field umpires for the 2021 I.C.C World Test Championship and in 2023 he was one of the 16 match officials for the Cricket World Cup of that year.

Simon Lunn was a left-handed batsman and right arm medium pace bowler, he is the current Benwell Hill chairman, and he played 3 matches in the NEPL in 2002, he batted just once, making 39 not out on 25th May 2002 at Philadelphia. He didn't bat or bowl in either of the other two games he played in the NEPL that season, but he did take 1 catch.

Lunn had made his NEPL debut on 29th May 2000 at home to Sunderland, he played one further match that season and one more match in 2001. His last NEPL appearance of that season, and to date, April 2024, was on 3rd August 2002 at home to Philadelphia.

He was playing seniors cricket, Over 50's for Northumberland up to his last game on 6th June 2012 at Gosforth against Lancashire over 50's.

Oliver Bellwood a right-handed batsman had also played in 2002, he had played for Northumberland Under 15's in July 1996 and Under 21's in September 1996. He didn't bat or bowl in a Northumberland County League game Hill played at Morpeth on 29th August 1999, but he was on the scorecard, listed at ten.

His NEPL debut came on 8th July 2000 at The Durham Academy, once again he didn't bat or bowl. His first NEPL run came on 15th July 2000 at home to Stockton, he made 17 not out in an innings in which Phil Nicholson had 100 not out.

During the title winning season of 2002, Bellwood played 8 times, batting on 3 occasions, with 2 not outs, he scored 18 runs with a high score of 12 not out. He took 2 catches.

Oliver Bellwood played 34 NEPL matches for Benwell Hill, batting 19 times, with 7 not outs, he scored 106 runs at an average of 8.83 with a high score of 19. He never bowled but took 6 catches at this level.

Mark Wright was a right-handed batsman and right arm medium pace bowler, he played 3 matches in the NEPL in the 2002 season, he batted once, making 2 not out on 17th August 2002 at Baydon. He had made his NEPL debut for Benwell Hill on 8th July 2000 at Maiden Castle against Durham Academy. His last NEPL game was for Benwell Hill on 13th June 2009 at South Shields.

In total he played 40 matches in the NEPL, he batted 26 times with 3 not outs, he scored 258 runs at an average of 11.21. He scored 1 half century, 53, which was scored on 4th August 2007 at Newcastle.

He bowled 546 balls in the NEPL with 13 maidens, conceding 285 runs and taking 11 wickets at an average of 25.90. His best bowling figures were 3 for 19, taken on 1st September 2007 at home to Chester le Street. He took 8 NEPL catches in his career.

Paul O'Leary, a right-handed batsman and right arm off break bowler also played 5 matches in the NEPL for Benwell Hill in the 2002 season. He batted 5 times with 0 not outs, he scored 85 runs at an average of 17.00. His highest score was 32, made on 31st August 2002 at Chester le Street. He didn't bowl or take any catches in the 2002 NEPL season. He had made his NEPL debut on 27th July 2002 at Durham Academy and his last NEPL game was on 5th August 2002 at home to Hetton Lyons.

In total O'Leary played 13 matches in the NEPL, batting 11 times with 1 not out, he scored 144 runs at an average of 14.40. His highest score was the 33 mentioned earlier. He bowled 18 balls, taking 0 for 25 in his NEPL career and took 1 catch.

Simon Birtwisle says that the tactics they started the season with served them well, Nazir and Rutherford were one and two in the league bowling averages, Pollard was sixth, Crozier eighth, batting wise, although Michael Gough didn't play many games, he clearly influenced most of the ones he did, topping the league batting averages, although he was the only Hill batsman to appear in the top ten, Birtwisle at thirteen, Nicholson at twenty three and Miller at twenty five scored over 1500 league runs between them, making a strong batting line up. Birtwisle says that "we hit a purple patch a few games into the season, after starting with a win at Newcastle, we lost to South North, our only loss of the season as it turned out, a win at Tynemouth bowling them out for 99, a low scoring draw in a weather affected game with The Academy, they were 93 for 6, after another draw with Philadelphia we won seven in a row, during this time our bowler's really shone, Norton 188, Blaydon 57, Stockton 61, Sunderland 102, Chester 90, Gateshead Fell 140 and Newcastle 97, 96 from Chris Hewison broke the run as we drew the next one but we had set ourselves up to win the league and we saw it out."

In addition to the batting and bowling statistics, Phil Nicholson was fourth in the list of wicketkeepers with 18 catches and 2 stumpings.

Chester le Street won The Banks Salver in the 2002 Season and John Graham of South North was named NEPL Player of the Year.

Graham had played 20 matches in the NEPL in 2002, batting 20 times, with 2 not outs, he had scored 799 runs at an average of 44.38. He scored 7 half centuries and 1 century, 103, made on 17th August 2002 at Chester le Street.

He also bowled 594 balls, with 28 maidens, conceding 269 runs and taking 16 wickets at an average of 16.81. His best bowling figures were 3 for 44, taken on 22nd June at Philadelphia. He also took 8 catches in the NEPL in 2002.

When I was looking at Marcus Turner and his early cricket days, I came across him first playing for Tynemouth, on 17th August 1997 at home to Durham, it was a 12 a side match, only 11 to bat and field, the fixture was a 40 over match to mark the 150th Anniversary of Tynemouth Cricket Club. Given the special occasion of the game I want to take a moment out to have a look at the game and also four of Tynemouth's stalwarts.

Durham sent a strong team and batted first, Martin Speight, Michael Roseberry, Melvyn Betts, Steve Harmison and Simon Brown among their ranks. They scored 218 for 7 from their 40 overs, Stewart Hutton top scoring with 44, Martin Leake took 3 for 37 for the hosts. When Tynemouth batted opener Matthew Kerr top scored with 36, Turner batted at number eight, scoring 16, Tynemouth finished on 144 for 9 from their 40 overs, Durham won by 74 runs.

Wayne Falla was primarily an opening batsman, he made his NEPL debut on 29th April 2000 when Tynemouth hosted Blaydon. He opened the batting scoring 9. His last NEPL game for them was on 14th June 2008 at home to South North, he opened the batting and scored 24.

He played 105 NEPL matches, all for Tynemouth, batting 103 times, with 6 not out's, he scored 2948 runs at an average of 30.39 and a best of 160 not out. The best score was on 28th May 2001 at home to Gateshead Fell. This was the occasion mentioned elsewhere when he and Jimmy Miller, 132 not out, put on an unbroken 316 for the first wicket. He also scored 13 half centuries and 5 centuries.

He bowled 1056 balls, with 20 maidens, conceding 687 runs and taking 19 wickets at an average of 36.15. His best bowling was 3 for 29 against The Durham Academy on 15th May 2004 at The Riverside. He also took 33 catches and had 1 stumping.

Falla made his debut for Northumberland on 20th May 1990 and played his last game for them on 25th July 2000 away against Norfolk, he scored 14 and 28.

In total he played 53 times for Northumberland, batting on 70 occasions, with 12 not out's, he scored 1425 runs for them at an average of 24.56. He had 1 century for them, 103 not out on 25th June 2000 at North Shields against Cumberland. He also scored 8 half centuries.

Falla bowled 887 deliveries for Northumberland, with 17 maidens, conceding 648 runs and taking 14 wickets at an average of 46.28. His best bowling figures were 2 for 27 on 16th June 1992 against Hertfordshire at Jesmond. He took 17 catches for the county.

Barry Stewart is primarily a middle order batsman and right arm medium pace bowler, he made his NEPL debut for Tynemouth on 29th April 2000 when Tynemouth hosted Blaydon. He batted at six, scoring 27. He also opened the bowling that day and took 4 for 27. His first NEPL wicket was Paul Underwood, leg before wicket. As a youngster Stewart had played for England at Under 15 and Under 17 level.

He played one game for the first eleven in The NEPL in 2023, away at Burnopfield on 26th August 2023. Rain only allowed 17 overs, and he didn't bat or bowl.

He has played 252 NEPL matches, all for Tynemouth, batting 216 times, with 33 not out's, he scored 4124 runs at an average of 22.53 and a best of 116 not out. The high score came on 31st May 2003 at Norton. He scored 16 half centuries and 2 centuries.

He has also bowled 11695 balls, with 385 maidens, conceding 6679 runs and taking 284 wickets at an average of 23.51. His best bowling figures were 8 for 17 on 26th April 2008 against Gateshead Fell. He also took 61 catches.

Stewart made his debut for Northumberland on 8th June 1999 against The Durham Cricket Board at Ropery Lane. He took 1 for 18 from three overs, his first county wicket was Nicky Peng. He didn't bat.

His last appearance for Northumberland was on 27th July 2003 at Bedfordshire in a 3-day match. He 1 for 16 in the first innings and didn't bowl in the second innings. He made 6 not out in the first innings and was absent hurt in the second innings.

He played 16 matches for Northumberland, batting 11 times with 3 not out's, he scored 93 runs at an average of 11.62 and a high score of 33, against Cumberland on 4th June 2002.

He bowled 855 balls, with 22 maidens, conceding 626 runs and taking 17 wickets at an average of 36.82. His best bowling figures were 3 for 51 on 11th June 2000 against Yorkshire Cricket Board at Jesmond. He took 6 catches for the county. Update- Stewart played 15 times for Tynemouth in the NEPL IN 2024, taking a further 11 wickets.

Anthony (Tony) Lion is a right-handed batsman and right arm medium pace bowler, he made his NEPL debut for Tynemouth along with a few other Tynemouth stalwarts, on 29th April 2000 at Blaydon. He opened the batting, scoring 3. His last NEPL game for Tynemouth on 23rd April 2016, at home to South North, he batted at eight, scoring 1.

He played 65 NEPL matches, all for Tynemouth, batting 55 times, with 3 not out's, he scored 968 runs at an average of 18.61 and a best of 91 not out. He has also bowled 20 balls, with 0 maidens, conceding 12 runs and taking 1 wicket. His best bowling is 1 for 3 and he also took 16 catches.

Graeme Hallam was a right-handed batsman and right arm medium pace bowler, he had one season as a professional at Seaton Burn in 1994, although relatively young and still a student, he scored 997 runs in The Tyneside Senior League that season, only a duck in his last innings preventing him from scoring 1,000 runs in a season.

He made his NEPL debut for Tynemouth along with one or two other long serving Tynemouth players, on 29th April 2000 at Blaydon. He batted at four and top scored with 42. His last NEPL game came on 7th August 2021 against Chester Le Street at Preston Avenue, he took 3 for 38 when Chester batted, and he made 30 batting at number eight.

He played 201 NEPL matches, all for Tynemouth, batting 181 times, with 19 not out's, he scored 4218 runs at an average of 26.03 and a best of 116. The high score came on 27th August 2001 away at Norton. He scored 26 half centuries and 2 centuries.

He has also bowled 1757 balls, with 46 maidens, conceding 1106 runs and taking 48 wickets. His best bowling is 3 for 31. The best bowling figures came on 3rd July 2010 at Blaydon, and he also took 60 catches.

Hallam made his debut for Northumberland on 26th June 1994 at Lincolnshire in a 2-day match. Northumberland batted first, Hallam batted at eight and scored 19 not out. Ollie Youll had earlier scored 103 and Jon Benn 57, in a score of 222 for 6 declared. The two Lincs openers had a good day, a very good day, in fact they had a very good game, Jonathan Wileman scored 142 not out and 102 not out, Russell Evans had 115 not out and 92 not out, Hallam o for 34. Both batters would go on to play first class cricket.

His last match for the county came on 28th August 2003 at Shropshire, he scored 14, he had played 65 matches for Northumberland, batting 98 times with 15 not out's, he scored 2064 runs at an average of 24.86. He had 13 half centuries and 1 century, his highest score of 123 coming on 11th July 1999 at Hertfordshire. He bowled 42 balls, with 0 maidens, conceding 71 runs and not taking a wicket and took 18 catches for the county.

He would go on to become Chairman of Tynemouth.

TABLE 11   NEPL Final Table 2002.

	Played	Won	Drawn/Aban	Lost	Bonus Points	Points
Benwell Hill	22	14	7	1	166	409
South North	22	11	7	4	170	378
Sunderland	22	9	8	5	149	324
Philadelphia	22	7	10	5	140	293
Chester le St	22	8	7	7	131	288
Gateshead Fell	22	7	10	5	113	268
Blaydon	22	5	12	5	124	263
Durham CA	22	4	12	6	126	242
Norton	22	5	7	10	98	204
Newcastle	22	3	11	8	106	204
Stockton	22	1	13	8	110	190
Tynemouth	22	2	8	12	104	174

TABLE 12   NEPL Batting Averages 2002.

Qualification 300 Runs.

52 Batsmen Qualified this season.

Player	Club	Inns	N. O	H. S	Runs	Average
(1) M.A Gough	Benwell Hill	9	6	118 no	476	158.67
(2) A.M Thorpe	Chester le St	9	4	98 no	390	78.00
(3) J. Allenby	Blaydon	19	4	130	818	54.53
(4) M.J North	Gateshead Fell	18	3	111	810	54.00
(5) A. Worthy	Chester le St	18	2	136	807	50.44
(6) G.M Scott	Durham CA	18	5	130 no	651	50.08
(7) P. Mustard	Durham CA	7	0	116	331	47.29
(8) M. Drake	Blaydon	18	6	89 no	540	45.00
(9) M.P Speight	South North	18	5	60	581	44.69
(10) J.A Graham	South North	20	2	103	799	44.39
(11) A.H Lion	Tynemouth	7	0	91	306	43.71
(12) C.J Hewison	South North	19	2	165 no	736	43.29
(13) S.J Birtwisle	Benwell Hill	18	4	81	604	43.14
(23) P.J Nicholson	Benwell Hill	18	5	66	431	33.15
(25) J.N Miller	Benwell Hill	20	4	95 no	520	32.50

TABLE 13   NEPL Bowling Averages 2002.

Qualification 20 Wickets.

28 Bowlers Qualified this season.

Player	Club	Overs	Mdns	Runs	Wkts	Average
(1) Shahid Nazir	Benwell Hill	262.5	72	669	58	11.54
(2) D.J Rutherford	Benwell Hill	220.4	59	561	42	13.36
(3) D. Pretorius	South North	313.1	83	778	56	13.89
(4) F.A Rose	Sunderland	266.3	38	852	61	13.97
(5) M.J North	Gateshead Fell	260.0	59	658	45	14.62
(6) M.L Pollard	Benwell Hill	169.1	38	426	29	14.69
(7) A. Walker	Stockton	249.0	58	645	42	15.36
(8) L.J Crozier	Benwell Hill	207.2	61	535	34	15.73
(9) A. Worthy	Chester le Street	179.2	53	513	31	16.55
(10) S. Pattison	Sunderland	199.2	41	558	33	16.91
(11) L. Plunkett	Durham CA	124.0	21	398	22	18.09
(12) G.G Swan	Philadelphia	317.0	70	954	52	18.35

Benwell Hill 2002 NEPL Champions.

Back Row L to R- J.N Miller, M.P Wright, P. A O'Leary, M.L Pollard, A.W Sharland, M.J Turner, O. Bellwood, S. Nazir.

Front Row L to R- L. J Crozier, D. J Rutherford, P. J Nicholson, S. J Birtwisle.

Benwell Hill's wicket keeper Phil Nicholson keeps a close eye on Adam Heather of South North.

Photo Courtesy of Martin Avery.

CHAPTER FOUR

South Northumberland 2003-2008

South North had a respectable start in the first three years of the NEPL, finishing fourth, eighth and runners up. John Graham summarized those three years as a good side, a poor side and a very good side! In 2002 Benwell Hill had won the title by 31 points from South North. Graham recalls "that Benwell were just that bit better than South North that year and were an outstanding side who were deserved champions. They had a very, very balanced side, full of talented local cricketers, such as Phil Nicholson, David Rutherford and Lee Crozier and a very good overseas pro in Shahid Nazir. Michael Gough was a huge player for Benwell Hill this season and that, ultimately, he may well have been the key to Hill winning the title."

For South North in 2002, Martin Speight, John Graham, Chris Hewison, Adam Heather and overseas pro Dewaald Pretorious had all featured in the League batting averages that year. Hewison and Heather had both scored two centuries and John Graham had scored one. Pretorius had come to South North this season almost straight from making his test debut for South Africa against Australia, Justin Langer was his first test wicket. Pretorious, who had 56 wickets, Richard Brook and Craig MacKellar featured in the league bowling averages. Pretorious was involved with Durham in 2003 and so was replaced by West Indian fast bowler Reon King as overseas pro. MacKellar had returned to Scotland and was to play for Penicuik in The Scottish National Cricket League.

Jimmy Miller had joined South North this season from the reigning champions Benwell Hill and John Graham took over as captain for the 2003 season from Adam Heather. Graham gives an enormous amount of credit to then Club Chairman, Ian Gilthorpe, as being the heartbeat and driving force of the club at this time and for the next 15 years or so.

He was Chairman from 2006 until 2012, but he played a big part in the administration of the club before taking on this role. Gilthorpe is widely acknowledged as being behind the decision to sell off the area of the ground on which the tennis courts had stood, approximately half of the money was used to upgrade the nets/indoor facilities at the club.

Gilthorpe was South North through and through, the first record of his playing cricket I could find was on 1st July 1972 for South North at home to Benwell Hill in a Northumberland League game, he batted at three, scoring 27. He scored 406 runs for the first team in 1988, in 1989 he had 503 runs at an average of 37. 85, 1990 he had 475 runs and was selected for both the league side and The Northumberland Cricket Association. His good form continued throughout the early 90's,1993 saw him score 503 runs, 1994 saw him make 506 runs. He was first team captain in 1996, 1997 saw him captain the side to a league title, they were also runners up in 1998 under his leadership.

Gilthorpe featured for almost the next thirty years and was still playing first team cricket when The NEPL came around, making his NEPL debut on 29th April 2000 at home to Stockton, he didn't bowl but did bat, making 5. His last NEPL game came on 10th May 2003, at home to Tynemouth, he made 19.

Gilthorpe played 38 NEPL matches for South North, batting 32 times, with 5 not out's, scoring 508 runs at an average of 18.81. He had no half centuries but 1 century, aged 48 on 13th May 2000 at Jesmond he scored 109. He also took 6 NEPL catches.

The last game of note I could find for him was on 12th June 2008 for Northumberland Over 50's away against Nottinghamshire Over 50's.

Returning to the 2003 season, John Graham recalls that they didn't have a scripted game plan as such, but they did have a methodology, plus a very strong top five batting order, in which Chris Hewison stood out by weight of runs, he had over 1,000 NEPL runs in 2003, and a pair of exceptional opening bowlers in Reon King and Ian Hunter. When Hunter couldn't play Jonny Gill did a job for the team. They didn't lose a game in The NEPL in 2003.

He says that as captain he had a very big part in player recruitment, that South North really operated a recruitment plan that was centred on three things.

Friendship, success and facilities.

Graham himself was very good friends with Imran Shah from their days in youth cricket and it was he who asked John to play at South North for the 2000 season. Graham in turn was very good friends with Jimmy Miller. This was repeated a number of times over the years, Lee Crozier coming to join his good friends Graham and Adam Heather at South North in 2004 being another notable example.

South Northumberland began a six-year domination of The NEPL with their first title in 2003. Graham says that every NEPL title his side won was hard won, and had to be earned, he says that the standard of the cricket in the first decade of the league in particular was incredible.

The style of cricket in the early years, with the first team having the option of batting up to 65 overs meant that a lot of teams played not to lose, given how good some of the batsmen and wickets were it was a tough ask to win a game with 10 overs less than your opponents.

Over his years South North had three occasions when they entered the last game of the season in second place and needed help from elsewhere. Graham also says that "it wouldn't have taken much for the distribution of those league titles to be a lot different and more evenly shared." He goes on to say that every year they won the league you could find a pivotal moment in the course of the season.

In 2003 that moment came on 21st June in a home game against Stockton. He said Stockton were "a good side, including players such as Richard Waite and Alan Walker."

Stockton batted first and scored 169 all out from 49.2 overs. Waite had top scored with 82, the next highest score being 22 as Richard Brook 3 for 43 and Michael Smalley 4 for 45 had kept them in check. When South North batted Graham recalls that they were in trouble, lot of trouble at "about 80 for 8." Records show they were 85 for 8! Graham himself was still at the crease having batted at four, he went on to make 95 not out and, in partnership with Jonny Gill, 26 not out, put on the highest scoring 9th wicket partnership, 88 unbroken, in the league that season, as South North won by two wickets.

Graham says this also typified the South North attitude throughout his years, they regularly had good contributions, often match winning contributions from the middle-lower order, batsmen at six, seven and eight, lads like Hall, Smalley or Seymour, in the 2003 side, in later years Stephen Humble would be added to that list. They won the title with two games to spare that season, taking the title on the Bank Holiday Monday, 25th August at home to Gateshead Fell.

They opened that campaign with a home fixture on 26th April 2003 against Newcastle, this season the first innings was again limited to 65 overs, the match total being 120 overs. Newcastle batted first and scored 278 for 6 declared from 64.4 overs. Jonathan Gill taking 2 for 50, new pro Reon King 2 for 71, Chris Hewison 1 for 56, Richard Brook 1 for 64 and Michael Smalley 0 for 28. Australian Pro Ryan Phillimore top scored with 74, Gordon Muchall 58 and Wayne Ritzema 54, all starting the season well for Newcastle. Chris Hewison, with 124 not out, ensured that South North got a draw to start their season, 203 for 5.

The South North side that day was as follows-

John Graham opened the batting that day, scoring 16. As well as being captain, he was a right-handed opening or middle order batsman and a right arm medium pace bowler. He was also an excellent fielder with a very safe pair of hands. He is the youngest son of Seaton Burn stalwart Bill Graham.

Bill Graham made his debut for Seaton Burn CC in 1961, whilst still a pupil at Gosforth Grammar School. A left-handed batsman he went on to score a century in 1963 and 1964.

He was a talented footballer as well as a cricketer, so much so that he played professional football at Aberdeen in 1964 as a centre forward. Despite scoring a hat trick in his last game for them, he was sold to Queen of the South in 1965. He would subsequently go on to play for South Shields for several years, the highlight of his football career coming when on 3rd January 1970 Shields played away at Queens Park Rangers. Rangers at the time were a big spending second division club, with George Graham and Terry Venables in their side, despite a 4-1 loss, the crowd of 16,811 gave Shields a standing ovation at the end! When he returned to his cricket, he added a further century in 1974. When his batting tailed off a bit, he developed himself into a useful left arm spinner, taking all 9 Shotley Bridge wickets that fell in a game in 1984. When he retired, he was one of the few batsmen to be credited with more than 10, 000 Tyneside Senior League runs.

He was also a fine administrator, acting for many, many years as Seaton Burn Club Secretary and acting as Team Manager for Northumberland, this included a final of The MCC Knockout Trophy in 2004.

The first record of any senior innings of note for John Graham at Seaton Burn occurred on 8th May 1993 when the First Team were at home to Lintz in the Tyneside Senior League. Batting first Seaton Burn made 141-6. John Graham scoring his maiden half century, 52, in a losing effort. Several valuable contributions in the high twenties to low forties followed that season as he set about learning his trade in senior cricket.

Graham had to wait until 28th May 1994 when Seaton Burn were at home to Sacriston to post his next senior half century, making 57 in a losing cause. Further half centuries that season followed against Consett home and away, Hebburn, Ryton and Sacriston.

On 12th June 1994 Graham played for Northumberland Under 17's at Felling against Durham Under 17s in a single innings match. He top scored with 63 in a score of 199 for 6 declared from 55 overs. The Durham bowlers included some familiar names in Colin Campbell, Harry Hubber and David Nevin. When Durham batted, they won with two overs and 5 wickets to spare,

His highest score of the season for Seaton Burn was on 13th August 1994, away at Sacriston. Sacriston scored 311-8, the second highest team score the club would concede in their Tyneside Senior League history. His father Bill, 4-81, was the best of the bowlers. Seaton Burn scored a respectable 213-6 in reply. John Graham leading the way with 76, Graeme Hallam, club pro and long-standing Tynemouth player and subsequently Chairman, had 62 and I, the author, Steve Graham had 55.

On 20th May 1995 Seaton Burn were away at Lintz. Lintz batted first, scoring 162-9, Andrew White 3-25 & David Felton 3-52. When Seaton Burn batted, they were soon in trouble, losing Cade Brown for 1 and then Kevin Corby first ball when David Smart came to the wicket on a Graeme Clennell hat trick. Clennell was heard to say to a teammate "He's the last **** you want to see on a hat trick!" Seaton Burn were 161 when Smart was dismissed for 106. A single for John Graham and another for Richie Allan meant Seaton Burn won by 7 wickets. John Graham was 53 not out and starting to show true maturity in his batting. Smart was a huge character in both the TSL and Seaton Burn Cricket Club. In his career he scored 23 centuries with a career best of 201 not out. On this occasion Graham, despite his young age, had been content to play the supporting role as he and Smart guided Seaton Burn to the win.

On 28th May 1995 Graham was selected for Durham Under 19's in a game against Durham second eleven at Crook. Durham Seconds batted first and scored 211 all out from 48.1 overs. Wicketkeeper Chris Scott had 68, David Cox 50 and Quentin Hughes 40, leg break bowler Chris Clark had 3 for 36. When the Under 19's batted, Graham batted at four, scoring 28, Chris Clark was the only other batsman who made double figures, 34, as the youngsters were dismissed for 107, Paul Collingwood among the wicket takers, Quentin Hughes the pick of them, with 3 for 25.

Over the next few weeks Graham turned what had been 20's and 30's the previous season into bigger scores, for example on 17th June 1995 Seaton Burn were away at Swalwell, Graham had 88, on 24th June 1995 Seaton Burn were at home to Consett, a maiden century, 106 not out from Cade Brown and another 72 from John Graham.

The following week, 1st July 1995 Seaton Burn were away at Greenside another 78 for Graham and 49 from Kevin Corby saw them post 164 all out.

On 9th July 1995 Seaton Burn were at Annfield Plain, Cade Brown 134 not out scored his highest individual score for the club and John Graham scored 53.

On 15th July 1995 Seaton Burn were away at Ryton. Batting first Seaton Burn, for the third innings in a row, scored more than 200, 204-5 to be exact. Cade Brown had 88 and John Graham 72.

Graham continued to represent Northumberland at Under 17 and Under 19 level this season, the highlight being 83 against Derbyshire Under 17's on 24th August 1995.

On 26th August 1995 Seaton Burn were away at South Moor, Graham scoring 79, as Seaton Burn chased down 202 to win by seven wickets.

The runs continued the following week, on 2nd September 1995 Seaton Burn were at home to Swalwell. Seaton Burn batted first, 215-7, Cade Brown 94 and John Graham 73.

Seaton Burn completed the 1995 season on 16th September at home to Greenside. Seaton Burn batted first, Cade Brown 94 and John Graham, with his maiden century for the club, 104, set a new club record for the first wicket in the TSL, 206. A total of 225-4 was posted.

John Graham fell just short of 1,000 league runs this season but did well enough to feature in the league averages with 912 runs at an average of 45.60.

The 1996 season, although still a good one for Graham, was more about consistently making runs rather than big scores. He made five half centuries, with a high score of 91 on the last day of the season, 7th September away at Swalwell.

On a higher stage than the Tyneside Senior League Graham continued to be selected, and score runs throughout 1996. On 23rd June 1996 he played for The Northumberland Cricket Association at Lincolnshire and South Humberside Cricket Association. Graham opened the batting with Wayne Falla, Falla making 44 and Graham 17, the Northumberland side also contained well-known names of the future in Michael Thewlis, Phil Nicholson, Jimmy Miller, David Rutherford and Steve Harmison. They were dismissed for 195 from 49 overs. Lincolnshire won by four wickets as a steady team performance saw them home, Graham had two overs for six runs.

On 29th July 1996 Graham was selected to play for Durham Seconds in a County Championship at Leicestershire. Durham batted first, Chris Clark 103, Simon Brinkley 53, Graham batting at four, made 16 as Durham were 278 all out. Leicestershire scored a formidable 171 for 1 when they batted before they declared. Durham responded with 143 for 3 declared, Graham top scoring with 55 not out. Leicestershire's batting proved too strong for Durham though as 253 for 8 saw them win by two wickets. The standout player had been Greg Macmillan who had 105 not out and 76 not out. He would play first class cricket for Leicestershire and Gloucestershire.

Graham continued to be selected for Durham Seconds, 91 against Kent, coming in a loss in August.

He was subsequently selected for an England Under 19 tour to Pakistan. His fellow tourists included Andrew Flintoff, Steve Harmison, Chris Read, Ben Hollioake, Alex Tudor and Gareth Batty. Future stars on the Pakistan side included Abdul Razzaq, Saeed Anwar, Hasan Raza, Shoaib Malik and Imran Tahir.

Both teams clearly had some very good players, Graham recalls that "it only struck me a while ago, years after the actual tour, how good some of those players were and how many went on to play for England."

On a personal level Graham says that he felt okay in the warmups and "I did pretty well, I didn't have a great first innings in the first test but felt comfortable, I got the dreaded Delhi Belly in the second innings and had to drop down the order. I had a couple of failures in the second test and was dropped for the third. I played only the last game of the one-day series and had a decent fifty."

He was selected to play a 3-day match starting on 29th November 1996 in Karachi against Karachi Under 19s. He did not bat in the first inning but scored 41 in the second.

The first test match between the two sides was played in Faisalabad and started on 8th December 1996, John Graham scored 13 and 11 not out.

In the second test match, played in Sheikupara, starting on 19th December, John Graham scored 2 and 0.

John Graham's last appearance was the third one day international in Karachi on 8th January 1997. He scored 51, opening the innings as England made 231-7. Pakistan 235-8 won by 2 wickets.

He recalls that "it was a tough place to go, it all felt a bit alien to us in respect of none of us had been anywhere like it and seen nothing like it, the culture was completely different to what we were used to, it was also mentally tough being away for six weeks over Christmas, Steve Harmison got homesick and returned home after a week. The cricket was a steep learning curve, when we returned, England then had no real infrastructure or continuity like they do now. All things considered though, it was a unique and rare opportunity which I enjoyed overall."

The 1997 season saw Graham continue to play for Durham Seconds, playing several games but failing to score any significant runs. A combination of an injury which led to scar tissue on his right index finger which caused discomfort when batting and then glandular fever meant that Graham barely played in 1998 nor 1999 and not getting a contract with Durham.

He also had his education and cricket running side by side, studying at Leeds University he recalls that he had plenty to concentrate on with his studies and that if he hadn't have had this, he may well have pursued cricket more vigorously, he did have offers, interestingly enough though, he also said that the lack of the Durham contract would later give him a huge desire and drive to succeed with South North, he thinks that some of his team mates there were similarly motivated in later years.

John Graham, as many did, including future title winners, Adam Heather and Chris Hewison, made his debut in The NEPL on 29th April 2000 as South North started life in the new league at home to Stockton. Stockton batted first, 118 for 9 dec, Nigel Campbell taking 5 for 27. When South North batted Graham 13, and Heather 5, opened the innings, Hewison was 49 not out as South North won by 5 wickets.

When the 2003 season started Graham had played 51 NEPL matches, batting 51 times with 5 not outs, he had scored 1945 runs at an average of 42.28. He had 17 half centuries and 2 centuries. His highest score was 108 on 8th July 2000 at Stockton.

He had bowled 1276 balls, with 45 maidens, conceding 663 runs and taking 22 wickets at an average of 30.13 each. His best bowling figures were 3 for 44 on 22nd June 2002 at Philadelphia. He had taken 22 NEPL catches.

He played 20 matches in the NEPL in the 2003 season, batting 19 times with 5 not outs, he scored 486 runs at an average of 34.71. He scored 3 half centuries with a high score of 95 not out, made on 21st July 2003 at home to Stockton. He did not bowl in the NEPL in 2003, but he did take 9 catches in the league that season.

James (Jimmy) Miller opened the batting with John Graham today. He had joined South North this season after a title winning year the previous season at Benwell Hill. He had previously played for Tynemouth in the NEPL, and his background is documented in the previous chapter.

He played 19 matches in the NEPL in the 2003 season, batting 19 times with 1 not out, he scored 390 runs at an average of 21.66. He scored 1 half century and 1 century. The century, 106 not out was scored on 19th July 2003 at Tynemouth. He did not bowl in the NEPL in 2003, but he did take 9 catches in the league that season.

John Graham describes him as a friend, as a cricketer he remembers "an exceptional batter, he was a destructive batsman, exciting to watch, he was very good off the back foot, playing the hook shot particularly well and an excellent sweeper and player of spin. He could be unorthodox and was hard to bowl at. He was also an incredible fielder, Geoff Cook is reputed to have said he rated him as one of the best in the country at one time," Graham agrees with that sentiment, saying that "Adam Cragg would also be in that category later in his career."

Suffice to say that Miller joined South North as a proven player in The NEPL and would prove so again this season and for several seasons to come, featuring in all of the six in a row title winning seasons and playing in the first eleven up to and including 2016. His last game for South North in The NEPL was on 24th August 2019 against Chester le Street when he made 35 not out.

Although he did further represent South North on 21st July 2021 in a one-day match at Roseworth Terrace against M.C.C, scoring 42 as South North won by 31 runs.

He played another match for South North against M.C.C a year later 20th July 2022, again at Roseworth Terrace, and he scored 41 as South North again emerged as victors, this time by 2 wickets.

Miller finished his NEPL career having played 294 matches, this comprised 250 innings, 42 of which were not out, he scored 5820 runs at an average of 27.98, with a highest score of 132 not out and 32 half centuries and 6 centuries to his name, as well as 97 catches. He is also credited with one wicket, Benwell Hill's, J.J Moore the unfortunate victim on 24th July 2004. He was part of ten title winning sides at South North and one at Benwell Hill.

Chris Hewison batted at three for the 2003 season opener, he was a right-handed batsman and a right arm medium pace bowler. His father, Neil, was a talented and well-respected league cricketer. He was a right-handed batsman who scored at least ten centuries and is credited with over 10,000 league runs. He was also an excellent fast bowler, taking over 500 Tyneside Senior League wickets. He regularly represented The League side. He also played for Chester Le Street in the Durham Senior League and as an amateur and professional at both Whickham and Burnopfield.

Chris Hewison came through the Durham Juniors set up, initially at Burnopfield and then onto Durham Under 17's. The earliest record for Hewison was on 2nd July 1995 when Durham and Northumberland Under 17's met at Ashington. The Northumberland side contained John Graham and Steve Harmison. Hewison scored 54 not out as Durham won by seven wickets.

He subsequently played for Durham Second Eleven. On 4th July 1996 they played a Durham Cricket Association team, Hewison scored 27 before the game was abandoned not long after the DCA started their innings. Some of the other cricketers playing that day were also of note, Michael Gough, Neil Killeen, Ian Jones, Ian Hunter, Paul Veitch, Ian Somerville, Quentin Hughes and Allan Worthy amongst them!

In 1997 Hewison was selected for England for an International Youth Tournament in Bermuda, he played his first game for England Under 17'S on 7th July 1997 against the hosts Under 19 side at the wonderfully named Sea Breeze Oval, although he didn't bat, he did take 3-28 as England won by 8 wickets. He played 5 games in the tournament in total.

Further games followed against Scotland Under 19's and then more games for Durham Seconds, throughout 1998 and 1999. On 7th April 2000 Hewison represented Nottinghamshire in a 50 over match against Derbyshire at Derby County Ground. Batting first it was clearly a difficult wicket as Derbyshire were dismissed for 74. Dominic Cork, 2-11, the pick off the bowlers. Hewison scored 9. Derbyshire won by 7 wickets, Hewison bowling two overs for twenty-three.

Hewison made his NEPL debut in the NEPL opening fixtures on 29th April 2000 for South North at home to Stockton. John Graham and Adam Heather were amongst others in the team. Stockton made 118-9 declared, South North 119-5 in reply, Hewison 49 not out, in a 5-wicket win.

He continued to play for Nottinghamshire Seconds and South North throughout 2000 and on 6th September 2000 he was selected for his first-class debut in Nottinghamshire's first eleven County Championship fixture at Trent Bridge against Glamorgan. Nottinghamshire won the toss and batted first, Jason Gallian top scoring with 150, Hewison scored 24, as they posted 371 all out. Glamorgan replied with 187 all out, forcing them to follow on, Robert Croft had top scored for them with 56. A better effort in the second innings saw Glamorgan make 246 all out, Mark Wallace 59 top score. Only 62 were required to win, batting at four, Hewison scored 6 before being dismissed as the home side reached 66 for the loss of three wickets.

Hewison was selected for a Nottingham pre-season tour to South Africa in March 2001, he played in seven games on the tour, making 105 not out against a Gauteng Invitation XI.

As he continued to pursue a cricket career with Nottinghamshire, he played a number of pre-season warm up games and regularly in the second XI, he also played for Clifton Village in The Nottingham Premier League, debuting on 5th May 2001 against Notts Unity Casuals.

Hewison made his List A debut this season also, on 8th July 2001 in a Norwich Union 45 over match at The County Ground, Taunton, against Somerset. Kevin Pietersen opened the batting for Nottinghamshire as they successfully chased down 248-8, Hewison scoring 20.

His time with Nottinghamshire ended with the close of the 2001 season, and a new chapter in his cricket career opened as he joined South North for the upcoming 2002 season.

John Graham is about a year older than Chris Hewison and played a lot of youth cricket with him. When Geoff Cook didn't play, Graham was his captain when they were at The Durham Academy together in 1997 playing in The Durham Senior League. He says that Hewison was an exceptional youngster, he had a very good technique and a wide range of shots. He also bowled seam up and bowled it well!

Graham also referenced Hewison's ability at first slip, he recalls an unbelievable catcher, Graham himself was no slouch at second slip, regularly featuring in the league fielding lists, he goes on to say that in every successful side he played in it shouldn't be underestimated the value of good slip catchers, especially first slip and especially if you have an overseas pro fast bowler.

Hewison played 20 matches in the NEPL in the 2003 season, batting 20 times with 2 not outs, he scored 1085 runs at an average of 60.27. He scored 4 half centuries and 5 centuries in the NEPL during the 2003 season.

His first century of the season, 124, was made in the season opener on 26th April at home to Newcastle.

The second century of the season, 106 not out, was made on 7th June 2003 at home to Norton.

The third century of the season 103, was made on 2nd August 2003 at home to Philadelphia.

The fourth century of the season, 127 not out, was Hewison's highest score of the season and was scored on 16th August 2003 at home to Chester le Street.

The fifth and last Hewison NEPL hundreds of the 2003 season, 124, was scored in the last game of the season on 30th August 2003 at Stockton.

Chris Hewison also bowled 484 balls in the NEPL in 2003, with 18 maidens, he conceded 286 runs and took 11 wickets at an average of 26.00. His best bowling figures were 3 for 35, taken on 14th June 2003 at Gateshead Fell. He also took 12 catches in the league that season.

Adam Heather batted at four in the 2003 season opener, he is a left-handed batsman, his first recorded innings was for Scotland Under 16's v Wales Under 15's on 26th July 1989 at The Graig, Glamorgan. He scored 61 in the first innings of a two-day match. The first senior sighting of Heather was on 4th May 1992 in a Northumberland County League game between Benwell Hill and Backworth. Heather batted at four for Backworth and scored a respectable 34 in a score of 182 all out. Benwell Hill fell short and were dismissed for 169.

Further appearances for Scotland Under 19's and Under 21's followed, where Heather was a consistent run scorer without getting a big score.

On 9th May 1993 Heather represented Newcastle University against York University at Heslington in a 60-over match. Opening the batting he scored 122 not out as Newcastle chased down 225.

The first record I found for Heather at South North was on 18th May 1996, at Benwell Hill in The Northumberland County League. Lee Crozier was playing for Benwell Hill, and batting three, making 9 in a score of 172 for 9 from their 50 overs. Heather made a duck batting at six in South North's reply, 148 for 8, match drawn.

On 22nd July 1996 Heather made his minor counties debut for Northumberland at Jesmond against Staffordshire in a two-day match. He made 3 in the first innings and 0 not out in the second innings as the match was drawn. Over the next three years Heather represented Minor Counties Under 25's, Scotland B, Northumberland and The Northumberland Cricket Board.

Adam Heather made his NEPL debut on 29th April 2000 for South North at home to Stockton in the opening NEPL fixtures. John Graham and Chris Hewison were in the same team. Stockton made 118-9 declared, South North 119-5 in reply, Heather made 5, Chris Hewison 49 not out, in a 5-wicket win.

John Graham and Adam Heather were good mates, such good mates that Heather was best man when Graham got married! As a batsman Graham remembers that at this time, the early 2000's, "Heather was the lynchpin around which South North built their innings. He would anchor one end, whilst still scoring at a decent pace keeping things ticking over, and this allowed the more expansive, quicker scoring players to be more aggressive at the other end."

That wasn't to say he only had one pace, Graham recalls himself getting out early, for 7, in a game at Philadelphia on 22nd June 2002. Heather 122 not out and Chris Hewison 165 not out took the score to 312 for 1 declared from just 58 overs. Graham continues "He had a very good defence, offensively he was very strong hitting straight, through the covers and off his legs. Mentally Heather knew what his strengths were and how to play to them, he wasn't as limited in range as Alistair Cook but he had that knowledge of his game which meant he got the most from his ability. He was a popular figure in the dressing room, bringing both morale and focus to the side."

Heather played 19 matches in the NEPL in the 2003 season, batting 19 times with 1 not out, he scored 553 runs at an average of 30.72. He scored 2 half centuries and 1 century. The century, 127, was scored 25th August 2003 at home to Gateshead Fell. He didn't bowl in the NEPL in 2003, but he did take 9 catches in the league that year.

Martin Speight kept wicket and batted at number five, scoring 3 on the season opener of 26th April 2003. He was a right-handed batsman and wicketkeeper who had previously played for Sussex and Durham. He had joined Sussex in 1986, playing two youth test matches the following year against Sri Lanka and representing Sussex at Under 25 and Second XI level before moving into the first team.

He made his County Championship debut on 20th August 1986 against Somerset at Taunton. Viv Richards and Joel Garner were both in the Somerset team. Speight took a couple of catches but didn't get to bat as the weather intervened.

Speight made his debut for The England Young Cricketers, under 19's by another name, on 1st February 1987 against Sri Lanka in Columbo. He wasn't the only debutant, Mark Ramprakash, Mike Atherton, Nasser Hussein, Martin Bicknell and Warren Hegg also appeared for the first time. Speight top scored with 33 as England scored 113 for 8 from their 45 over. Warren Hegg is listed as the wicket keeper although Speight did take one catch as Sri Lanka won by 2 wickets.

Speight would go on to represent Durham University, British Universities and Combined Universities in 1987 and 1988 as well as further appearances for Sussex Seconds. 1988 also saw him selected for Sussex First team on several occasions and across several formats, he was now playing a lot of cricket across first, second and University teams.

He also played cricket in New Zealand at the end of 1989 and into 1990 and 1990 also saw him a regular in the Sussex first team, in both Championship and Sunday League cricket.

Apart from wintering in New Zealand he pretty much stayed there until he joined Durham in 1997. He made his Durham debut in a one Day match with Sussex on 12th April 1997 at Hove, making 6 against his former side as Durham lost by 54 runs, he played at Durham until 2001.

He played 193 first class matches, scoring 9225 runs, with a high score of 184, with 13 centuries and 48 half centuries, at an average of 31.59. He took 292 catches and 5 stumpings. He also had over 5,000 one day runs.

He made his NEPL debut for South North on 27th April 2002 at home to The Durham Academy. The Academy batted first and scored 182 for 9 from 65 overs. John Graham 62 and Speight 44 saw South North home by six wickets.

He coached England player Harry Brook at Sedbergh School and is credited with a big role in Brook's success. John Graham recalls that he first came across Speight at Durham, he says Speight was a talented batsman who was "unbelievable" in this time. When he came to South North Graham said Speight was "ahead of his time, this is the days before the rise of T20 cricket and The Indian Premier League. Speight was playing the reverse sweep to spinners and sweeping fast bowlers for six, he gave you a chance to win every game he played in. As a wicketkeeper he was more Bairstow than Foakes but that shouldn't take anything away from his ability behind the stumps."

Graham talks a lot about pivotal moments, he clearly recalls one involving Speight at Chester le Street on 16th August 2003. South North batted first, Hewison 127 not out, 41 from Speight and good contributions from others, 293 for 5 declared from 60.5 overs. When Chester batted Allan Worthy was dismissed for 20 but Dan Shurben and Quentin Hughes were going well, very well, until "Speight pulled off an amazing catch to get rid of Dan Shurben, it was a key moment in the game, possibly the season, Shurben was quite capable of winning that game for them." Shurben was in fact out for 89, King being the successful bowler, Hughes had 61, Chester fell away though as the momentum changed with that catch, 214 all out from 54 overs, King and Ian Hunter both with five wickets.

Graham says that "Speight was a very talented artist, you can now buy his art, who brought something different to the dressing room. He was a bit of a different character in the dressing room."

Speight played 18 matches in the NEPL in 2003, batting 18 times with 1 not out, he scored 600 runs at an average of 35.29. He scored 2 half centuries and 2 centuries. The first century, 100 not out, was scored on 24th May 2003 at Philadelphia.

Speight's second century,117, in the 2003 NEPL season was scored on 7th June at home to Norton. He also bowled 18 balls in the NEPL in 2003, taking for 1 for 15 and he took 26 catches in the league that season.

Matthew Hall batted at number six on the season opener on 26th April 2003, he made 25 not out, he was a right-handed batsman and right arm medium pace bowler. He made his NEPL debut for South North on 28th April 2001 at home to Stockton. It was a debut and start to the season South North would probably rather forget as they were bowled out for 72 in 34.4 overs. Howard Sidney -Wilmot top scored with 19. Hall made 5. Former Northants and Durham bowler Alan Walker taking 5 for 20 and C. Burke 4 for 27 as Stockton won for the loss of two wickets, Hall didn't bowl.

He was selected for two games for Northumberland Under 19's against Scotland Under 19's on 15th and 16th August 2002. On the 15th, on home territory at Roseworth Terrace, he bowled four over 0 for 20, as Scotland made a hefty 293 for 8 from their 50 overs. Rana Hussain had 132 from just 139 balls. Hall opened the batting and top scored, scoring 42, before Kyle Coetzer trapped him L.B.W. Northumberland were 202 for 9 at the end of their 50 over, giving the Scots a 91-run win.

The next day cricket once again proved how fickle it is, Hall again opened the batting, this time getting a four-ball duck after his top score the previous day. Future teammate Neil Corby was in the Northumberland side, but he fared little better, making two. Northumberland 110 all out. Scotland 112 for 4 won comfortably by six wickets, Hall 0 for 19 from five overs.

In 2003 as well as playing for the title winning South North side, Hall played four games for Northumberland. He had seven innings and scored 31 runs with a high score of 20.

John Graham said that Hall was "just a young lad, around 16 or 17 when he joined South North, as a batsman he liked to hit straight and over the top, he didn't bowl much but was a very good outfielder and contributed a lot in the field. He was a nice lad who fitted well into the dressing room."

Hall played 18 matches in the NEPL in 2003, he batted 18 times with 2 not outs, he scored 312 runs at an average of 19.50. He scored 1 half century, his highest score of the season, 61, was made on 14th June 2003 at Gateshead Fell. He didn't bowl but took 7 catches in the NEPL in 2003.

Tom Seymour batted at number seven on the season opener of 2003, scoring one not out, he was a right-handed batsman and right arm bowler. John Graham remembers "a big hitter, he could and did change the outcome of games with his batting. Although generally a second team cricketer, he was a player who could be relied upon to contribute and do a job when he played for the first team."

He made his NEPL debut on 6th May 2002 for South North at Benwell Hill. He batted at seven and top scored with 41.

Seymour had played 6 NEPL games prior to the start of the 2003 season, batting 6 times, with 1 not out, scoring 94 runs at an average of 18.80 and 1 half century.

He played 4 matches in the title winning side of the 2003 season, he batted only 3 times, with 1 not out, scoring 5 runs. He didn't bowl or take any catches in the league that season.

His last NEPL appearance was on 1st August 2015 at Tynemouth.

He would go on to play 19 matches in The NEPL for South North, batting 17 times with 4 not outs, he scored 173 runs at an average of 13.30. He scored 1 half century. His best score was 58 not out on 1st June 2002 at Sunderland. He took 1 career catch in the NEPL.

Michael Smalley was listed to bat at eight on the season opener of 2003, he was a left-handed batsman and right arm off break bowler. He was first recorded on 5th May 1993 for in an away match against Dame Allan's School for The Royal Grammar School. Smalley took 4 for 15 from ten overs as Dame Allan's were 95 all out from 40 overs. Smalley opened the batting, scoring 6, his side however won comfortably by eight wickets.

Just a few weeks later, on 29th May 1993 the first sign of Smalley in senior cricket is found, playing for Benwell Hill in a Northumberland County League match at home to Percy Main. Both sides contained some very well-known names on the Northumberland Cricket scene, Main had Michael, Martin and Joe Thewlis, Blythe Duncan and Ron Balsillie in their side.

Balsillie would play 30 matches for Northumberland, with a high score of 78, he was one of the first people I started talking to on the sidelines when I started photographing the NEPL, I found him very welcoming and good company as we talked cricket for hours on end, his views on what we were watching and of days gone by, enjoyable in equal measure. Sadly, he passed away in 2023 and was missed on quite a few NEPL boundaries.

Hill's team that day contained Mike Younger, Simon Lunn and Barry Evans. Percy Main batted first and scored 70 all out. Evans 4 for 22, Younger 3 for 8 and Smalley, one over for one run. Smalley didn't bat as his side won by nine wickets, Duncan taking the only wicket to fall.

Smalley progressed through the Northumberland Junior set up through the early 90's, playing for the Under 19's several times, he made 43 not out and took 2 for 54 in a one-day loss to Durham Under 19's on 31st May 1994.

Later that year, 12th June, he played for Northumberland Under 17's against their Durham counterparts. Future South North captain John Graham opened with 63, future South North batsman, Jimmy Miller, had 26 not out, Smalley did not bat as his side scored 199 for 6 from their 55 overs. Smalley 0 for 29 from eleven overs as Durham won by five wickets.

Smalley played regular first team cricket for Benwell Hill in the County League from 1994 onwards, being selected for league under 21 sides and County Under 19's and 21's.

In 1995 he first appeared on the South North scorecards, featuring on a match on 16th September 1995 against Benwell Hill at Roseworth Terrace. He bowled four overs 0 for 26 as Hill scored 209 for 4 from 50 overs, South African Cristiaan Craven 85, Mike Younger 83 not out. Smalley did not bat as an opening partnership of 136 between Michael Anderson, 59, and Howard Sidney -Wilmot, 77, saw South North home by 4 wickets with a ball to spare.

Smalley made his NEPL debut on 19th August 2000 at home to Norton. Marc Symington top scored with 69, as Norton made 176 for 6 declared. South North, Chris Hewison 67 not out, 142 for 3 wickets in a drawn match. Smalley did not get a bat or bowl.

John Graham recalls "a really talented bowler, as a spinner he would hustle through his overs, often taking valuable wickets of key players and he would chip in with runs to get his team home."

Smalley played 18 matches in the NEPL in 2003, batting 12 times with 5 not outs, he scored 192 runs at an average of 27.42. he scored 1 half century, 55 not out, made on 10th May 2003 at home to Tynemouth.

He also bowled 350 balls in the NEPL in 2003, with 13 maidens, he conceded 192 runs and took 8 wickets at an average of 24.00. His best bowling figures were 4 for 45, taken on 21st June at home to Stockton. He took 5 catches in the NEPL in 2003.

Reon King was listed to bat at nine on the season opener of 2003, he was a right-handed batsman and right arm fast bowler. He was the oversea pro for South North for both the 2003 and 2004 seasons. He was an established test cricketer for the West Indies at this time, he had two spells in test cricket, either side of his time with South North.

He first came to notice on 2nd July 1993 playing for Guyana Under 19's against Jamaica Under 19's in a three-day match. He scored 5, batting at 11, Guyana 200 all out in their first innings. Jamaica were 162 all out, future Durham all-rounder, Gareth Breese was in their lineup. King opened the bowling 0 for 17 from four overs. He didn't bat in the second innings and took 1 for 12 from three overs as the game petered out into a draw.

He progressed from The Guyana Under 19's to The West Indies Under 19's, making his Under 19 test debut against England on 12th-15th July 1995 in Port of Spain. Marcus Trescothick, Anthony McGrath, Vikram Solanki and Andrew Flintoff among others all in the England side. King took 4 for 49 in the first innings as England were 317 all out. He scored 1 in the West Indies first innings as his side were dismissed for 168, Flintoff 5 for 39. When England batted again, they scored 199 for 4 before declaring, Trescothick 106 not out, King 2 for 57. West Indies lost seven wickets as the match was drawn, King didn't get a bat in the second innings.

He played the full series against England and was selected for an Under 19 tour to Pakistan in 95/96. Around the same time, he graduated to the full Guyana side and then subsequently West Indies "A" side.

He made his International One Day debut on 31st October 1998 against India in a Wills International Cup match in Dhaka. King had ten overs 0 for 26 against a strong Indian side containing Tendulkar and Dravid amongst others. He didn't bat as his side won by six wickets.

He would go on to make 50 ODI appearances for The West Indies, taking 76 wickets at 23.77 each and a best bowling of 4-25 against Pakistan on 23rd April 2000.

King made his test debut on 15th January 1999 against South Africa. He failed to take a wicket in the game but came back strongly and he went on to make 19 test appearances for The West Indies, taking 53 wickets at a cost of 32.69 and a best of 5-51 against Zimbabwe on 24-28th March 2000.

He made his South North debut on 26th April 2003 in a home match with Newcastle. John Graham states that speed wise he probably bowled in the low 80's, not an express bowler, but that he hit the bat hard and was a lot for most club cricketers to deal with.

When he played for the West Indies, he had Curtley Ambrose and Courtney Walsh opening the bowling in front of him, King and Franklyn Rose would bowl after those two, and whilst neither, and let's be honest here, not many were of that standard, both King and Rose were good enough to play international cricket. As a bowler, Graham recalls King had "the X factor", he was a captain's dream, he would always bowl, even after long spells, I would ask him if he could give me a few more, he always did. He had no ego whatsoever, if it's not too much of a contradiction, he was a workhorse who was also a thoroughbred!"

Newcastle batted first and batted well, Wayne Ritzma had 54, Gordon Muchall 58 and Aussie pro Ryan Phillimore 74, as they scored 278 for 6 declared from 64.4 overs. King had 2 for 71 from 20 overs. He didn't bat as Chris Hewison, with 124 not out, made sure South North got the draw, 203 for 5.

King played 19 matches in the NEPL in 2003, batting 10 times with 2 not outs, he scored 67 runs at an average of 8.37. His highest score was 21 not out, made on 5th July 2002 at Newcastle.

He bowled 1724 balls in the NEPL in 2003, with 64 maidens, he conceded 889 runs and taking 54 wickets at an average of 16.46. His best bowling figures were 6 for 60, taken on 19th July 2003 at Tynemouth. He took 1 NEPL catch in 2003.

Jonathan Gill was listed to bat at ten on the season opener of 2003, he was a right-handed batsman and right arm medium pace bowler. There is only a minimal record of him before the start of the NEPL, first was a game for Northumberland Under 21's against The West Tyne Cricket League on 6th September 1996 at Percy Main. Gill batted at nine and scored 11 not out in a total of 106 for 9 from their 40 overs. Gill took the first wicket as he bowled eight over, 1 for 26, but the visitors won by 7 wickets.

On 1st June 1999 he played for South North at Gateshead Fell in a National Club Championship game.

South North batted first, Adam Heather top scoring with 47 from a 20 over score of 108 for 7, Gill didn't get a bat. When Fell batted, they could only muster 80 for 7, South North winning by 27 runs. Gill bowled an unknown number of overs, 0 for 6. As an aside Adam Heather is listed as having a stumping in this game, so I presume he also kept wicket!

Gill also played for South North on 14th August 1999 in a Northumberland County League fixture at home to Benwell Hill. South North scored 160 for 8 from 50 overs when their innings closed. No batsman made 30, Gill batting at nine, 2 not out. David Rutherford had 5 for 46 and future South North teammate for Gill, 2 for 61. When Benwell Hill batted, captain, wicketkeeper and opening batsman, Phil Nicholson, had 64 as Hill won by 3 wickets with 5 balls to spare. Current Hill Chairman, Simon Lunn, seeing his team home with 3 not out! Gill 5-1-18-1.

Gill was another of those players who made their debut in The NEPL when The NEPL made its debut, 29th April 2000. The game, against Stockton, is featured in Adam Heather's bio earlier in this chapter, Gill didn't bat or bowl but did take a catch in a South North win.

He played a handful of NEPL games in the 2000 season and ten games in the 2001 season, during the 2002 season, when South North were league runners up Gill played in thirteen NEPL games.

In the previously mentioned opening fixture of 2003 against Newcastle, Gill opened the bowling and took 2 for 50. He played 20 matches in the NEPL in 2003, batting 11 times with 5 not outs, he scored 71 runs at an average of 11.83. His highest score was 26 not out, made on 21st June 2003 at home to Stockton.

He bowled 775 balls in the NEPL in 2003, with 25 maidens, he conceded 457 runs and took 20 wickets at an average of 22.85. His best bowling figures were 3 for 28, taken on 3rd May 2003 at The Racecourse against Durham Academy. He took 5 catches in the NEPL in 2003.

John Graham recalls that when Ian Hunter wasn't available "Gill was the replacement with the new ball. He was medium pace but swung the ball and that's where his wickets came from. He was another who accepted his role in the team and who contributed to the team success by doing his role well."

Richard Brook was listed to bat at eleven on the season opener of 2003, he was a right-handed batsman and slow left arm orthodox bowler. The first record I could find of him was for the wonderfully named Godmanchester Town Second Eleven against St Ives Second Eleven on 20th May 1995 in a 50 over Smith Barry Junior Cup match. St Ives batted first and were all out for 128, Brook taking 4 for 28 from ten overs. He didn't bat as his side won by 7 wickets.

On 22nd June 1996 he was selected for Northamptonshire County Colts for a single innings match against Wolverton Town at Wolverton. Northants batted first and were all out for 196, Brook did bat, but his score was not recorded! Teammates included Graeme Swann and Neil Foster. Wolverton were dismissed for 102, Brook had 1 for 27, Swann came on after him and had 4-1-7-1, Foster didn't bowl!

1997 and 1998 saw games for both Huntingdonshire Cricket Board and Godmanchester Town. On 22nd June 1998 Brook played a game for English Universities North against Irish Universities at Amblecote. He took 1 for 35 in a winning effort.

Brook popped up on a Northumberland County League scorecard on 8th May 1999 playing for Tynemouth in a home match with Benwell Hill. The game was abandoned after less than 10 overs because of the weather.

Through 1999 Brook was at Godmanchester Town, his NEPL debut was on 29th April 2000 for Tynemouth at home to Blaydon. Tynemouth batted first, 150 for 8 from 65 overs. Brook making 0 not out batting at ten, future South North teammate Jimmy Miller also in the side. The match was drawn, Blaydon 139 for 7 in 55 overs. Brook fifteen overs 0 for 36.

He would play just three games this season for Tynemouth, going back to Godmanchester Town in The East Anglian Premier League for the rest of 2000 and 2001.

He returned to The NEPL on 27th April 2002, now with South North, for a home game with Durham Academy. This game was covered earlier as part of Martin Speight's story.

That said, when I went through it again, I saw a familiar name on the South North score card, Ian Smart. I played with Ian and his father David at Seaton Burn; indeed, I wrote my first book on David Smart, he is mentioned elsewhere in this one. Ian, a leg spinner, would play just this game and one other in the NEPL, the next one, on 22nd June 2002 at Philadelphia. He didn't bat and bowled four overs 0 for 20.

He did also represent Northumberland on one occasion, 19th August 2001 against Cambridgeshire, taking 1 for 5 from five overs. He played for several other clubs, Seaton Burn, Shotley Bridge, Greenside and Ponteland.

Brook would go on to be a fixture in the South North side over the next few years, as he started the 2003 season, he had already played 21 NEPL matches, batting just 7 times, with 5 not out's, scoring 7 runs at an average of 3.50.

As a bowler, his record was much better, bowling 1142 balls, with 44 maidens, conceding 663 runs and taking 36 wickets at an average of 18.41. His best bowling figures at this time were 6 for 48 on 20th May 2000 for Tynemouth at Norton.

Brook played 18 matches in the NEPL in 2003, he hardly batted, but he did bowl 1422 balls, with 62 maidens, he conceded 661 runs and took 43 wickets at an average of 15.37. He took 1 catch in the 2003 NEPL season.

John Graham describes Brook as a very good spinner, he used flight well and could turn the ball on a flat wicket. He often took wickets in "clumps," not always getting his wickets in one's and two's but often in three's and four's and over his time at South North he dismissed a lot of good players. When Lee Crozier joined in 2004 the pair of them formed a great duo, they turned the ball in different directions which undoubtedly helped the partnership."

Ian Hunter was an integral part of the 2003 title winning side, despite his limited availability as he set about establishing himself with Durham. He was identified at a young age as being an outstanding cricketer and would play representative cricket for Durham at Under 15, Under 17, Under 19 and Second team level before he made his way to the first team.

He also played for ECB Schools North, and England Under 19's, his England debut coming against Australia on 17th -20th August 1999 at Edgbaston. The Aussie side included Michael Clarke, Adam Voges and Nathan Hauritz to name a few. Hunter's England side had Ian Bell, Michael Carberry and another Northeast name, Michael Gough amongst their ranks. Hunter didn't take a wicket in either innings but bowled economically, ten overs for twenty-three and seven overs for twenty-five. He scored 21 not out batting at eleven in the first innings in a drawn game.

His cricket career would encompass Durham and Derbyshire at first class level, and he played Minor Counties cricket for Cumberland and Northumberland.

He played a total of 63 first class matches; this brought him 81 innings with two fifties and a high score of 65. He is credited with 150 first class wickets at an average of 17.73, this included three five wickets hauls and a best of 5-46.

Hunter would originally play in the NEPL for Chester le Street in 2000, making his debut on 6th May of that season against Newcastle at Jesmond. He scored 29 with the bat, batting at seven as Chester made 158 all out and opened the bowling when the hosts batted, taking Chester's first wicket in the newly formed NEPL when he had Matthew Hynd caught by Tony Birbeck for a single. He finished with 2 for 37 as Newcastle were dismissed for 103. He would play only four NEPL games for Chester that season, finishing with 13 wickets.

Hunter didn't play in The NEPL in 2001 or 2002 as he was playing for Durham in both County Championship and One Day cricket as well as second team cricket for them. His South North NEPL debut came on 24th May 2003 at Philadelphia. Martin Speight had 100 not out as South North scored 187 for 9 declared from 50 overs, Philadelphia 115 for 6 in reply in a drawn game. Hunter had 1 for 43.

He played 8 matches in the 2003 NEPL season for South North, he batted 4 times with 0 not outs, he scored 38 runs at an average of 9.50. His highest score was 18.

He bowled 800 balls in the NEPL in 2003, with 27 maidens, he conceded 374 runs and took 24 wickets at an average of 15.58. He had two five wickets' hauls, the best of which was 6 for 35 away at Chester le Street on 31st May. He took 1 catch in the NEPL that season.

Neil Killeen played a small number of games in the NEPL, his career with Durham is well documented elsewhere, so a summary of his NEPL career, in keeping with the subject of this book! Killeen made his NEPL debut on 3rd May 2003 for South North at The Racecourse against The Durham Academy, he took 1 for 26, his first NEPL wicket was opener Paul Cummins, caught by John Graham for 16. When South North batted Killeen, batting at number seven, made 25.

He made three appearances for South North in the 2003 season, his top score was 63 and he took 3 wickets on two of his three appearances. His last game for South North was on 15th July 2006 at home to Sunderland, he took 1 for 37 when Sunderland batted first and scored 20 when he batted.

He then made his debut for The Durham Academy on 26th May 2007 at home to South Shields, scoring a single and then taking 1 for 26 with the ball. His second, and last, game for The Academy came on 21st July 2007 at The Racecourse against Tynemouth, he didn't bat but took what turned out to be an NEPL career best of 5 for 20 when Tynemouth batted.

Killeen next played in The NEPL on 4th May 2019, making his debut for Burnopfield at home to Hetton Lyons. He took 3 for 30 when Hetton batted first and scored 8 when they batted. His last NEPL appearance came on 27th August 2022, at home to Sunderland. He took 1 for 32 and scored 40 when Burnopfield batted.

All told, Neil Killeen played 14 matches in the NEPL, batting 10 times, he scored 194 runs at an average of 19.39, with 1 half century. The half century, 63, in fact, came on 28th June 2003 for South North at home to Blaydon.

He bowled 650 balls in The NEPL, with 25 maidens, conceding 305 runs and taking 19 wickets at an average of 16.05. His best bowling was the 5 for 20 mentioned earlier. He took 3 NEPL catches in his career.

His son, Mitchell, played the 2023 season at Ashington in the NEPL and the 2024 season at Burnmoor.

South North won their first NEPL title by 65 points from The Durham Academy.

The Banks Salver was won by Sunderland and Richard Waite of Stockton was The NEPL Player of the Year.

Waite had played 21 matches in the NEPL in 2003, batting 21 times with 0 not outs, he scored 919 runs at an average of 43.76. He scored 7 half centuries and 1 century. The century, 102, was scored on 14th June 2003 at home to Tynemouth.

He also bowled 1707 balls in the NEPL in 2003, with 65 maidens, conceding 867 runs and taking 43 wickets at an average of 20.16. His best bowling figures were 6 for 30, taken on 10th May 2003 at Norton. He took 3 catches in the NEPL in 2003.

TABLE 14   NEPL Final Table 2003.

	Played	Won	Draw	Lost	Aban	Points
South North	22	13	9	0	5	447
Durham CA	22	10	11	1	4	382
Stockton	22	10	7	5	4	352
Chester le St	22	9	7	6	4	323
Sunderland	22	9	6	7	6	321
Blaydon	22	8	7	7	4	275
Philadelphia	22	8	5	9	5	264
Newcastle	22	4	12	6	3	258
Benwell Hill	22	5	6	11	7	207
Norton	22	5	6	11	2	192
Tynemouth	22	2	10	10	3	184
Gateshead Fell	22	2	8	12	3	168

TABLE 15   NEPL Batting Averages 2003.

Qualification 300 Runs.

45 Batsmen Qualified this season.

Player	Club	Inns	N. O	H. S	Runs	Average
(1) C.J Hewison	South North	20	2	127 no	1085	60.28
(2) D. Barnes	Durham CA	17	4	177 no	695	53.46
(3) A. Worthy	Chester le St	21	5	143 no	797	49.81
(4) L.J Rushworth	Sunderland	19	2	133 no	839	49.35
(5) R.E Philimore	Newcastle	20	2	120 no	853	47.39
(6) M.J Symington	Norton	20	5	99 no	695	46.33
(7) A. Roberts	Durham CA	14	6	77	353	44.12
(8) R.P Waite	Stockton	21	0	102	919	43.76
(9) Q.J Hughes	Chester le St	20	5	97	624	41.60
(10) S. Hutton	Gateshead Fell	18	2	102 no	634	39.62
(11) A. Walker	Stockton	13	5	67	312	39.00
(12) T.C Stonock	Newcastle	11	1	110	389	38.90
(17) M.P Speight	South North	18	1	117	600	35.29
(19) J.A Graham	South North	19	5	95 no	486	34.71
(27) A.T Heather	South North	19	1	127	553	30.72
(38) J.N Miller	South North	19	1	106 no	390	21.67
(43) M. Hall	South North	18	2	61	312	19.50

TABLE 16   NEPL Bowling Averages 2003.

Qualification 20 Wickets.

28 Bowlers Qualified this season.

Player	Club	Overs	Mdns	Runs	Wkts	Average
(1) N.C McGarrell	Blaydon	343.1	117	658	60	10.97
(2) J. O'Neill	Blaydon	120.0	31	289	24	12.04
(3) M.L Creese	Stockton	103.4	20	319	26	12.27
(4) M. Iqbal	Durham CA	189.4	43	560	41	13.66
(5) S.J.E Brown	Sunderland	214.0	61	626	45	13.91
(6) I.D Potter	Philadelphia	223.3	51	638	42	15.19
(7) Shahid Nazir	Benwell Hill	286.5	70	826	54	15.30
(8) R. Brook	South North	237.1	62	661	43	15.37
(9) I.D Hunter	South North	134.2	27	374	24	15.58
(10) S. Gale	Chester le Street	178.4	30	622	39	15.95
(11) L.J Crozier	Benwell Hill	253.1	73	665	41	16.22
(12) R.D King	South North	287.2	64	889	54	16.46
(23) J. Gill	South North	129.1	25	458	20	22.90

PREMIER PASSION – South Northumberland captain John Graham proudly shows off the Foster's ECB North East Premier League trophy, watched by his triumphant team-mates   EVENING CHRONICLE, Wednesday, September 24, 2003

South North 2003 NEPL Champions.

Left to Right - M. Smalley, C.J Hewison, J.M Gill, M.J Hall, J.A Graham, R.D King, J.N Miller, R. M Brook, H.M Sidney-Wilmot, A.T Heather, M.P Speight.

Credit to the unknown Evening Chronicle Photographer.

John Graham seen here batting on 13th September 2017 at Derby.

Photo Courtesy of Ken Waller.

2004

After taking their first NEPL title in 2003 the South North team which started the following season had few changes to it, although spinner Lee Crozier had joined from 2002 Champions Benwell Hill and his addition was seen as a difference maker by many in the South North camp. Skipper John Graham says that they evolved their tactics as the season unfolded, but that they were remarkably consistent throughout the season. They didn't have a Durham player this season, but Graham felt that in Crozier and Reon King they had two of the best bowlers in the league. So much so they often opened the bowling with the pair of them. At this time bowlers were restricted to 20 overs maximum rather than the 15 of the present rules, Graham says that his tactic of the time was that if those two bowl 40 overs per game between them, then South North were more likely than not to be in a strong position at the end of it. It also helped that Crozier enjoyed bowling with the new ball. He also had Richard Brook, who was an excellent and proven spinner at this level, and Graham himself and Michael Smalley bowled some effective medium pace.

Batting wise Graham recalls that Adam Heather had an exceptional season this year, scoring a lot of runs, and that was another reason why they would look to insert the opposition, bowl King and Crozier 20 overs apiece, then, with Heather leading the batting charge, try and chase the score down. This was not necessarily the best tactic to amass bowling bonus points, but they felt that in a league where a lot of games were drawn, they would win enough games through their tactics. South North became the first team to retain the NEPL title, by 5 points from Sunderland, so it seems they were effective.

South North started the defence of their first NEPL title with an away game at Sunderland on 24th April 2004. Reon King hadn't joined up with the team and missed the first two games. South North had batted first, 221 for 5 from 60 overs declared, Adam Heather 75, Chris Hewison 84. Simon Brown had 3 for 37 for Sunderland. When Sunderland batted, they scored 144 for 9, Alan Mustard with 41 and Stuart Pattison 43 not out ensuring that Sunderland got the draw. Lee Crozier 3 for 39 had been the pick of the bowlers, although they all took at least one wicket to open the season.

Their team that day was.

John Graham captain and opened the batting in the 2004 season opener, scoring 1. He entered the season second to Chester le Street's Allan Worthy (2530 runs) on the all-time list of NEPL run scorers since its formation, he had played 71 matches, batting 70 times with 10 not outs, he had scored 2431 runs at an average of 40.52, with 20 half centuries and 2 centuries and a high score of 108. He also had 22 wickets at 30.13, with a best bowling of 3 for 44 and 31 NEPL catches.

Graham played 20 matches in the NEPL in 2004, batting 16 times with 4 not outs, he scored 330 runs at an average of 27.50. He scored 1 half century and 1 century. The century, 118 not out, was scored on 22nd May 2004 at home to Philadelphia.

He bowled 438 balls in the NEPL in 2004, with 16 maidens, conceding 224 runs and taking 9 wickets at an average of 24.88. His best bowling figures were 2 for 15, taken on 30th August 2004 at home to Tynemouth. He took 8 catches in the league in 2004.

Adam Heather opened the innings with Graham for that season opener, he scored 75. He entered the season with 1853 NEPL career runs to his name, at an average of 32.50 and a high score of 127, he also had 6 half centuries and 4 centuries. He had also taken 28 catches and 4 stumpings.

Heather played 20 matches in the NEPL in 2004, batting 19 times with 5 not outs, he scored 894 runs at an average of 63.85. He scored 8 half centuries and 2 centuries. The first century, 106, was scored at Jesmond against Newcastle on 14th August 2004. The second, 115, his highest score in the NEPL of the season, was scored at home to Tynemouth on 30th August 2004. He didn't bowl in the NEPL in 2004 but did take 10 catches.

Chris Hewison batted at three for the 2004 season opener, having started the previous season with 124, he made another strong start to the season with 84. Hewison started this season with 2291 runs in the bank, at an average of

52.06, with a high score of 165 not out, he also had 9 half centuries and 8 centuries. He was still bowling at this point and had 24 wickets at 35.87, with a best of 3 for 25, an excellent first slip fielder he also had 28 catches.

Hewison played 20 matches in the NEPL in 2004, batting 20 times with 5 not outs, he scored 742 runs at an average of 49.46. He scored 4 half centuries and 1 century, the century, 127 not out, was scored on 24th July 2004 at home to Benwell Hill. The innings came from 130 balls and contained 14 fours and 1 six.

He bowled 294 balls in the NEPL this season, with 4 maidens, conceding 168 runs and taking 5 wickets at an average of 33.60. His best bowling figures were 2 for 30, taken on 19th June 2004 at Tynemouth. He also made 4 catches in the league in 2004.

Martin Speight batted at four in the season opener, making 18. Going into the season he had 1181 NEPL runs at an average of 39.36 and a high score of 117, he had 4 half centuries and 2 centuries as well as 1 wicket for 15, coincidentally his best bowling performance also. Speight had 40 catches and 4 stumpings to his credit also.

He played 20 matches in the NEPL in 2004, he batted 17 times with 7 not outs, he scored 291 runs at an average of 29.10. He scored 2 half centuries with a highest score of 62 not out, made on 24th July 2004 at home to Benwell Hill. He took 15 catches and had 1 stumping.

Jimmy Miller batted five in the season opener, making 13. Miller had a proven NEPL track record, with 1856 NEPL runs to his name when the season started, he had an average of 31.45 and a high score of 132 not out, with 10 half centuries and 5 centuries. He had only bowled one over in the league in his career, 0 for 2, but had taken 28 catches so far.

During the 2004 NEPL season he played 20 matches in the league, batting 17 times with 1 not out, he scored 545 runs at an average of 34.06. He scored 3 half centuries, with a highest score of 78, made on 14th August at Newcastle.

He bowled 6 balls in the NEPL that season, taking 1 for 2 against Benwell Hill on 24th July at Roseworth Terrace. He took 4 catches in the league in 2004.

Michael Smalley batted six in the season opener; he was another returning from 2003. Career wise, he started the season with 270 NEPL runs at an average of 22.50 with a high score of 55 not out, that high score was his only career half century at this time. He also had 34 wickets at an average of 20.47 each and a best bowling of 5 for 30. He had 6 catches.

Smalley played 18 matches in the NEPL in 2004, batting 6 times with 2 not outs, he scored 27 runs at an average of 6.75.

He bowled 280 balls in the league in 2004, with 11 maidens, conceding 129 runs and taking 8 wickets at an average of 16.12. His best bowling figures were 4 for 11, taken on 31st July 2004 at Philadelphia. He took 1 catch in the NEPL that season.

Matthew Hall batted at seven in the season opener, scoring 4 not out. His NEPL career so far has brought him 565 NEPL runs at an average of 17.12 and a high score of 61, he had 2 half centuries. He had bowled 41 NEPL deliveries giving up 21 runs for 0 wickets, he did however also have 14 catches and 3 stumpings.

During the 2004 season Hall played 20 matches in the NEPL, batting 10 times with 5 not outs, he scored 168 runs at an average of 33.60. His highest score was 35 not out, made on 30th August 2004 at home to Tynemouth. He bowled 66 balls in the season, taking 0 for 45. He didn't take a catch in the league in 2004.

Lee Crozier is a right-handed batsman and right arm off break bowler. He made his South North NEPL debut in the 2004 season opener at Sunderland, he was listed to come in at eight but did not bat. He took 3 for 39 from 20 overs when bowling.

He made his NEPL debut on 6th May 2000 for Benwell Hill which is covered earlier in the book, and he had played the first four seasons of The NEPL at Benwell Hill. Before he had played a shot or bowled a ball for South North, Crozier had scored 598 NEPL runs at an average of 16.16 and a high score of 89. That was his sole half century at this point. More importantly, he also had 129 NEPL wickets at an average of 19.44 and a best bowling of 7 for 44.

He also had 21 catches and an NEPL League title to show for his time at Benwell Hill. John Graham recalls that Crozier was a "captain's dream, a go to bowler, he the unique ability of being able to bowl defensively whilst retaining the threat of taking a wicket."

Crozier played 19 matches in the NEPL in 2004, batting 7 times with 4 not outs, he scored 37 runs at an average of 12.33. His highest score was 20, made on 15th May 2004 at Benwell Hill.

He bowled 1497 balls in the NEPL in 2004, with 86 maidens, conceding 495 runs and taking 43 wickets at an average of 11.51. His best bowling figures were 5 for 21, taken on 28th August 2004 at Blaydon. He took 2 catches in the NEPL in 2004.

Neil Corby is a left-handed bat and wicketkeeper. He made his NEPL debut in the 2004 season opener at Sunderland, he was due to bat at number nine but didn't get to bat. His father is Kevin Corby, who is well known on the Northumberland Cricket scene, having played for Tynedale, County Club and Northumberland. Kevin started as a 15-year-old at Seaton Burn in 1974, after one game in the second team he was in the first team the following week. He left for Tynedale following the 1977 season to play in The Northumberland County League. He remained there for nine seasons, winning many league titles and cups along the way. 1977 also saw Kevin Corby make his Minor Counties debut for Northumberland, against Lancashire at Jesmond. He played for Northumberland from 1977 until 1991, making 55 Minor Counties appearances. He also played in 9 NCCA knockout matches and 4 List A matches.

An injury to Jeff Dujon also saw Kevin Corby appear as a last-minute replacement and feature in The Callers Matches at Jesmond in 1988.

During his time with County Club, Kevin Corby scored at least six centuries for them, during his two spells with Seaton Burn he scored 25 half centuries and 4 more centuries, with a high score of 116 not out. John Graham had known Neil Corby as a child, indeed they were children together, as their fathers played together at Seaton Burn where both started as juniors.

Neil Corby had come to South North for the 2004 season as a wicketkeeper/batsman and had come into the South North first team through his performances for their second eleven. He made his debut in the NEPL on 24th April 2004 at Sunderland. Although he played 5 games in the NEPL in 2004, he had little opportunity to contribute, batting only once, for a duck and not taking a catch.

John Graham, who had seen Kevin Corby keep at Seaton Burn, recalls that he saw a lot of his father's traits in Neil. He was very consistent as a wicket keeper, making important contributions to the side with both his batting and his keeping. He was very young when he came into the side, a side that Graham acknowledges had some big personalities but that although Corby took a little time to adjust, he fitted in well and was a popular figure in the dressing room.

Jonathan Gill was listed on the scorecard as ten but didn't get to bat in the season opener, another returning player from 2003. He entered the 2004 season he had 98 NEPL runs from 19 innings with 6 not outs and an average of 7.53, with a high score of 26 not out. His bowling had brought him 30 NEPL wickets at an average of 26.30 each and a best bowling of 3 for 24. He also had 10 NEPL career catches.

He played his last game for South North in The NEPL on 5th June 2004, he didn't get a bat and bowled seven overs 0 for 23. He played 7 matches in the title winning South North side of 2004, batting once and scoring 6 not out.

He bowled 228 balls for South North in 2004, with 6 maidens, he conceded 122 runs and took 3 wickets at an average of 40.66. His best bowling figures were 2 for 20, taken on 24th April at Sunderland.

He made his NEPL debut for Benwell Hill on 24th July 2004 at South North. He played 7 matches in the NEPL for Benwell Hill in 2004, batting 3 times with 1 not out, he scored 38 runs with a highest score of 32 not out, made on 7th August 2004 at Chester le Street.

He bowled 260 balls for Hill in the 2004 NEPL, with 9 maidens, conceding 147 runs and taking 4 wickets at an average of 36.75. His last NEPL game was for Benwell Hill on 3rd September 2005 at Stockton.

His final NEPL stats show he played 62 matches in the NEPL, batting 27 times with 8 not outs, he scored 177 runs at an average of 9.31 with a high score of 32 not out mentioned earlier.

He bowled 1993 balls, with 64 maidens, conceding 1183 runs and taking 39 wickets at an average of 30.33. His best bowling figures were 3 for 24 on 15th June 2002 at home to Newcastle. He took 14 NEPL catches.

Richard Brook was listed as number eleven for the season opener but did not bat. At this point he had 8 NEPL runs from 11 innings with 8 not out's, he had an average of 2.66 and a high score of 2 not out. A much different story with his bowling career, 79 NEPL wickets at 16.75 each and a best of 7 for 28. He also had 4 career NEPL catches.

Brook played 16 matches in the NEPL in 2004, he bowled 808 balls with 34 maidens, conceding 353 runs and taking 25 wickets at an average of 14.12. His best bowling figures of the season was 7 for 28, taken on 22nd May 2004 at home to Philadelphia. He took 5 catches in the NEPL in 2004.

Reon King missed the season opener, playing his first game of the 2004 NEPL season on 6th May at home to Chester le Street, the game was washed out after a few overs. He played his last game in The NEPL on 4th September 2004 at Gosforth against Norton.

During the 2004 season King played 19 matches in the NEPL, batting 5 times with 1 not out, he scored 22 runs at an average of 5.50.

He bowled 1469 balls in the NEPL in 2004, with 59 maidens, conceding 784 runs and taking 56 wickets at an average of 14.00. His best bowling figures of the 2024 NEPL season were 7 for 54, taken on 14th August 2004 at Jesmond against Newcastle. He took 3 catches in the NEPL in 2004.

At this point he had played 38 NEPL matches for South North, batting 15 times with 3 not outs, he had scored 89 runs at an average of 7.41 and a high score of 21 not out.

His NEPL bowling career saw him bowl 3193 balls, with 123 maidens, conceding 1673 runs and taking 110 wickets at an average of 15.20 each and a best of 7 for 54, mentioned earlier. He also had 4 career NEPL catches.

John Graham recalls a hard-fought season, with the league lead a bit back and forth between South North and Sunderland. South North started with a home draw against Sunderland. Their second game of the season was supposed to be away at Gateshead Fell on 1st May, it didn't get started due to a waterlogged pitch, everyone else played, including Sunderland, although they lost. The third game of the season also fell victim to the weather. After ten games South North had won three, drawn three and had two abandoned, they then played Blaydon.

Graham says that "Blaydon were a bit of a bogey side around this time for us, they always seemed to beat us, this season they did us home and away, in the home game we had them nine down and their last pair got them home, in the away game, on a bowler friendly wicket it was a very low scoring game." Records confirm both defeats.

On 12th June 2004 South North hosted Blaydon at Gosforth. South North batted first and were dismissed for 130, from 57.2 overs. Opener Adam Heather had 35 and was the top scorer. Graham Onions, who would go on to play first class cricket for Durham and Lancashire and test cricket for England, opened the bowling for Blaydon, taking 1 for 9.

Onions played 9 test matches, taking 32 wickets at an average of 29.90, and 4 one day internationals for England, he also had two spells at Gateshead Fell in the NEPL, and also played in the league for both Durham Academy and Blaydon.

He played a total of 85 NEPL matches, batting 58 times, with 18 not outs, scoring 792 runs at an average of 19.80. He scored 3 half centuries. He had a highest score of 92, on 23rd July 2016 for Gateshead Fell at home to Chester le Street.

As a bowler in the NEPL, Onions bowled 4824 deliveries, 156 maidens, conceding 2612 runs and taking 121 wickets at an average of 21.58. His best bowling figures were 5 for 27 on 24th April 2004 for Blaydon at home to Benwell Hill. He also took 19 catches. He is now a coach at Durham CCC.

The real damage on 12th June 2004 was done to South North by Neil McGarrell, Blaydon's overseas pro from The West Indies, his left arm orthodox spin taking 6 for 44. McGarrell played 4 test matches and 17 one day internationals for West Indies and followed in the Blaydon method of having a very good West Indian as pro. Wesley Thomas, Clyde Butts and Mark Harper immediately come to my mind if I think of Blaydon, very quickly followed by nightmares of our bowlers opening against Paul Veitch and Ian Somerville!

McGarrell played for 3 years for Blaydon in the NEPL, making his debut on 26th April 2003 at Philadelphia. He scored 10 and took 5 for 20 in a losing effort. His last game for Blaydon in The NEPL was on 3rd September 2005 at The Racecourse against Durham Academy. He scored 34 and took 1 for 49 in an Academy win.

He played in 55 NEPL matches, with 55 innings, he had 10 not out's and scored 1467 runs at an average of 32.60, his highest score was 105 not out. The highest score came on 24th July 2004 at home to Newcastle.

He bowled 5829 balls, with 268 maidens, conceding 2296 runs and taking 142 wickets, at an average of 16.16. His best bowling figures, 7 for 32, took place on 20th August 2005 at Jesmond against Newcastle. He took 31 catches in the NEPL.

When Blaydon batted, they were soon in trouble at 11 for 2, Reon King bowling Paul Underwood for 1 and John Graham trapping Ian Somerville L.B.W for 12. McGarrell, batting at four had shown his quality, making 43, the highest score of the game, before Crozier bowled him. As Graham remembered, Blaydon were indeed "nine down," 93 for 9 to be exact. Tobias Whitmarsh, batting at nine, scored 19 not out and Gary Stewart, batting at eleven, made 18 not out in a last wicket stand of 39 as Blaydon won by 1 wicket. Richard Brook had 4 for 25 and Lee Crozier 2 for 38.

In the return fixture, on 28th August 2004, Blaydon batted first, only two batsmen made double figures, skipper Mark Drake had 34 and David Steel scored 14. Reon King took 4 for 36, Lee Crozier 5 for 21 and John Graham 1 for 16. Blaydon 85 all out. South North's batsman fared no better when they batted, in fact they fared even worse! Only Tom Seymour made double figures, 14, as they were shot out for 41 in 19.3 overs. McGarrell took 1 for 24, Graham Onions 3 for 2, but it was Craig Simpson who had the remarkable figures of 9.3-5-10-7. Blaydon won by 44 runs!

There are now just two games left in the season.

A comfortable win over Tynemouth the following week, South North, 260 for 5 declared from 54 overs, Adam Heather 115, Chris Hewison 75. Tynemouth 133 all out, Reon King 6 for 71. Most importantly they picked up the maximum bonus points for a 30-point win.

Sunderland had picked up 28 points from their penultimate game of the season, away at Norton on 30th August 2004. Sunderland had batted first, scoring 208 for 8 declared from 60 overs, opener Simon Old 79 was the key batsman, 38 from Andrew Pratt also helping them along. When Norton batted, they had no answer to West Indian pro Marlon Black, 3 for 33, and Paul Goodwin, 4 for 40, as they were bowled out for 128. Black had played 6 test matches and 5 one day internationals for The West Indies before joining Sunderland. Adam Applegarth 1 for 34 and Simon Brown 1 for 16 both chipped in with wickets too.

With one game to play Sunderland had 331 points and South North 344 points.

Sunderland were due to play their last game of the 2004 season on 4th September at home to Durham Academy. The Durham side would contain Mark Stoneman, Kyle Coetzer, Ben Harmison and Chris Rushworth. Sunderland won the toss and decided to bat, Simon Old and Robin Weston put on 37 for the first wicket before Old was bowled by Mark Turner for 17. Weston and Alan Mustard put on 79 for the second wicket, Mustard was bowled by Moneeb Iqbal for 47. Sunderland 116 for 2 wickets.

Iqbal bowled Andrew Pratt for a duck and no addition to the score, Sunderland 116 for 3.

Number five batsman Simon M Brown scored 13 and he and Weston took the score to 137 when Brown was caught by Mark Stoneman off the bowling of Iqbal, Sunderland 137 for 4.

Stuart Pattison batted at six, he had made 2 when he was stumped by Karl Turner off the bowling of Iqbal, Sunderland 144 for 5.

Craig Burton was batting at seven, he had scored 9 when he was caught behind by Turner off the bowling of Chris Rushworth, Sunderland 168 for 6.

Weston was the next man to fall, caught by Stoneman off the bowling of Rushworth for 79, Sunderland 181 for 7. Overseas pro Marlon Black had come in at number eight, he and number nine, Paul Goodwin, had added 42 when Black was leg before to Luke Evans for 21, Sunderland 223 for 8.

Only 5 more were added when number ten, Simon J.E Brown was caught by Evans off the bowling of Iqbal for 4 from the fifth ball of the 58th over, Sunderland 228 for 9. At which point they declared. Iqbal had 5 for 74 and Chris Rushworth, 2 for 24 were the two best bowlers for The Academy, Sunderland collected 9 bonus points from their innings, this now put them on 340 points.

When The Academy batted, they regularly lost wickets, opener Mark Stoneman was stumped by Andrew Pratt for 49 and Steven Gale had 24 not out but The Academy were never in a position to threaten Sunderland, they finished the season being dismissed for 142. Marlon Black had 4 for 29, James Butler 1 for 29, Simon Brown 3 for 30 and Paul Goodwin 2 for 43. Sunderland had done what they could, taking 29 points from their last fixture to finish the season on 360 points.

South North, on 344 points, at home to Norton, South North won the toss and elected to field. Given that they if they won the match, they won the league, John Graham explained the decision, "we knew the weather forecast wasn't great, we felt the best option was to put them in and try and bowl them out cheaply, before the rain hit. We knew we didn't need maximum points, but early on, and I still have a vivid memory of this, their best player Marc Symington, before he had scored, shouldered arms to Reon King very early on, his off stump was uprooted!"

Norton were bowled out for 145 in 58.3 overs. Opener Nicky Beal had 42 but King 3 for 45 and Crozier 3 for 18 had broken the strength of the batting, Crozier had bowled 20 overs for his figures. John Graham 1 for 14, Richard Brook 2 for 25 and Michael Smalley 1 for 4, only Chris Hewison was wicketless.

South North gained the maximum bowling points, 5, but the best they could do batting wise, was 1 bonus point. They duly knocked the runs off, Adam Heather 55 not out and Martin Speight 50 not out, saw them home by eight wickets. They picked up 21 points for the win and finished the season with 365 points.

The Banks Salver was won by Chester le Street and Richard Waite was The NEPL Player of the Year for the second consecutive year. Waite had played 19 matches in the NEPL in 2004, batting 19 times with 1 not out, he scored 779 runs at an average of 43.27. He scored 4 half centuries and 3 centuries.

The first century, 107 was made in the season opener on 24th April 2004 at home to Philadelphia.

The second century, 101, was made on 29th May 2004 at home to Tynemouth.

The third century, another 101, was made on 12th June 2004 at Gateshead Fell.

He also bowled 1538 balls in the NEPL in 2004, with 41 maidens, conceding 842 runs and taking 34 wickets at an average of 24.76. His best bowling figures were 4 for 23, taken on 14th August 2004 at home to Norton. He took 7 catches in the NEPL in 2004.

TABLE 17   NEPL Final Table 2004.

	Played	Won	Drawn	Aban	Lost	Points
South North	22	10	5	5	2	365
Sunderland	22	11	3	4	4	360
Blaydon	22	10	6	4	2	337
Chester le St	22	10	3	4	5	328
Benwell Hill	22	8	3	6	5	279
Stockton	22	6	4	4	8	265
Durham CA	22	7	4	5	6	260
Newcastle	22	4	8	3	7	230
Gateshead Fell	22	4	3	7	8	216
Tynemouth	22	2	8	2	10	191
Norton	22	3	8	3	8	183
Philadelphia	22	2	5	3	12	141

TABLE 18   NEPL Batting Averages 2004.

Qualification 300 Runs.

39 Batsmen Qualified this season.

Player	Club	Inns	N. O	H. S	Runs	Average
(1) A.T Heather	South North	19	5	115	894	63.86
(2) C. Symington	Norton	18	7	95 no	555	50.45
(3) C.J Hewison	South North	20	5	127 no	742	49.47
(4) P. Mustard	Benwell Hill	17	3	97	648	46.29
(5) W. Falla	Tynemouth	20	2	111	654	43.60
(6) R.P Waite	Stockton	19	1	107	779	43.28
(7) N.C McGarrell	Blaydon	18	5	105 no	531	40.85
(8) A. Worthy	Chester le St	19	2	100	683	40.18
(9) D.G Shurben	Chester le St	18	0	138	716	39.78
(10) A. Roberts	Stockton	16	1	95	576	38.40
(11) K. Coetzer	Durham CA	14	3	86	417	37.91
(12) G. Darwin	Stockton	19	4	88	562	37.47
(17) J.N Miller	South North	17	1	78	545	34.06
(29) J.A Graham	South North	16	4	118 no	330	27.50

TABLE 19   NEPL Bowling Averages 2004.

Qualification 20 Wickets.

27 Bowlers Qualified this season.

Player	Club	Overs	Mdns	Runs	Wkts	Ave
(1) S.J.E Brown	Sunderland	216.2	62	516	47	10.98
(2) L.J Crozier	South North	249.3	86	495	43	11.51
(3) Shahid Nazir	Benwell Hill	258.3	56	682	51	13.37
(4) I.D Hunter	Chester le St	260.1	52	813	59	13.78
(5) R.D King	South North	244.5	59	784	56	14.00
(6) R. Brook	South North	134.4	34	353	25	14.12
(7) C. Rushworth	Durham CA	128.3	23	356	25	14.24
(8) Q.J Hughes	Chester le St	114.4	21	348	22	15.82
(9) N.C Phillips	Gateshead Fell	223.5	48	635	39	16.28
(10) C. Simpson	Blaydon	191.3	39	573	34	16.85
(11) J. O'Neill	Blaydon	121.3	21	380	21	18.10
(12) M.I Black	Sunderland	274.3	50	869	48	18.10

South North 2004 NEPL Champions.

Left to Right – M.J Harbottle, M.J Smalley, L.J Crozier, R.D King, M.J Hall, R. M Brook, M.W Shotton (Scorer).

J.N Miller, A.T Heather, J.A Graham, C.J Hewison, M.P Speight.

Jimmy Miller seen here on 21st July 2021 at South North.

Photo Courtesy of Ken Waller.

2005

South North won the NEPL for the third year in a row and added the Banks Salver for good measure.

John Graham recalls that entering this season their plans had been somewhat disrupted by problems engaging an overseas pro, first West Indian Corey Colleymore was supposed to be coming, that fell through, and then a young South African called Morne Morkel was supposed to be coming and that fell through. They went through the first few weeks without an overseas pro but eventually engaged a West Indian, Kerry Jeremy, who was only available for a few weeks.

Jeremy had played six one day internationals for The West Indies, in 2000-2001, but had failed to make any real impression, scoring a total of 17 runs and taking 4 wickets. He made his NEPL debut on 21st May 2005 at Gateshead Fell, he didn't bat as South North made 243 for 5, Matthew Hall had 101 not out, but he did bowl 11.5-4- 19-4. He would only play 6 matches for South North in the NEPL, with 4 innings and 1 not out, he scored 55 runs, at an average of 18.33 and with a high score of 27. His last match came on 18th June 2005 at Tynemouth when he scored 27 from 199 for 9 and took 4 for 25 as Tynemouth were bowled out for 97.

He bowled 508 balls, with 21 maidens, conceding 186 runs while taking 18 wickets. His best bowling was 4 for 19. He also took 1 NEPL catch.

Jeremy was replaced by Waqas Chughtai from Pakistan who made his NEPL debut on 25th June 2005 at home to Norton. South North batted first, 235 for 6 declared from 62 overs, John Graham top scorer with 85. Chughtai batted at seven, scoring 26 not out. He opened the bowling, taking 2 for 48 from twelve overs. His first NEPL wicket was Marc Symington. Norton were dismissed for 128, Stephen Humble with 5 for 27, the main cause.

Chughtai played just 5 games for South North, the last coming on 23rd July 2005 at home to Benwell Hill, injury then forced him to return home. His 5 games had encompassed 5 innings, 2 not out's, scoring 93 runs at an average of 31.00 and a high score of 46. The highest score was against Chester Le Street on 16th July 2005 at home. He bowled 275 balls, with 7 maidens, conceding 169 runs and taking 13 wickets, his best bowling was 5 for 30 which came on 9th July 2005 at Philadelphia. He took 1 NEPL catch.

It's fair to say that both overseas pros did contribute to this season's title success.

Martin Speight had moved on for this season, but that loss was offset, albeit in a different direction by the addition for season with the arrival of all-rounder Stephen Humble from Blaydon. Graham describes Humble as becoming "the ultimate big game player, he was guaranteed to perform on the big stage, taking everything in his stride, either way with bat or ball, as a batsman he could have batted anywhere from one to seven, he was that good, the strength of our batting meant he could go in a late as seven for us and still be a game changer, he hit the ball a long way. As a bowler he swung the ball both ways at a good pace, he also had a very good bouncer. He kept the slips occupied and he could run in all day. Humble and Lee Crozier were the two best local cricketers I played with or against who didn't have a first-class career."

They started this season with a home game against Philadelphia on 30th April 2005, their team that day was.

Adam Heather opened the batting, scoring 28. He was an established NEPL batsman at this time, he had played 89 NEPL matches, batting 85 times, 15 not out's and scoring 2747 runs at an average of 38.69, with 14 half centuries and 6 centuries. His highest score was 127. He had also taken 38 catches and 4 stumpings.

During the 2005 season Heather played matches in the NEPL, batting 20 times with 1 not out, he scored 519 runs at an average of 27.31. He scored 2 half centuries and 1 century, 107, scored on 3rd September 2005 at Norton. He didn't bowl in the NEPL in 2005, but he did take 6 catches.

Jimmy Miller was the other opening batsman for the 2005 opener, scoring 39. He was another established NEPL batsman at this time, he had played 90 NEPL matches, batting 86 times with 11 not out's and scoring 2401 runs at an average of 32.01, with 13 half centuries and 5 centuries. His highest score was 132 not out. He bowled 12 balls in the NEPL, with 0 maidens, conceding 4 runs and taking 1 wicket. He had also taken 32 catches.

Miller played 20 matches in the NEPL in 2005, batting 20 times with 1 not out, he scored 525 runs at an average of 27.63. He scored 3 half centuries. His highest score was 85, made on 3rd September 2005 at Norton. He didn't bowl in the NEPL in 2005, but he did take 9 catches.

Chris Hewison batted at three in the 2005 opener, scoring 17. Hewison was yet another established NEPL batsman at this time in a strong, experienced South North top order. Coming into the season he had played 73 NEPL matches, batting 72 times with 13 not outs and scoring 3033 runs at an average of 51.40, with 13 half centuries and 9 centuries. His highest score was 165 not out on 22nd June 2002 at Philadelphia.

He bowled 1737 balls in the NEPL, with 49 maidens, conceding 1029 runs and taking 29 wickets at an average of 35.48. His best bowling was 3 for 25 on 20th July 2002 at Norton. He had also taken 32 catches.

Hewison played 20 matches in the NEPL in 2005, batting 20 times with 1 not out, he scored 511 runs at an average of 26.89. He scored 4 half centuries with a highest score of 77, made on 30th May 2005 at home to Blaydon. He bowled 36 balls in the NEPL in 2005, with 0 maidens, taking 1 for 16. He took 8 catches in the NEPL in 2005.

John Graham batted at four in the season opener, scoring 57 and opening the bowling taking 1 for 32 from 6 overs. He came into the 2005 season with five years of NEPL captaincy and stats behind him, he had played 91 NEPL matches, batting 86 times, with 14 not outs and scoring 2761 runs at an average of 38.34, with 21 half centuries and 3 centuries. His highest score was 118 not out which came on 22nd May 2004 at home to Philadelphia.

He had also bowled 1714 balls, with 61 maidens, conceding 887 runs and taking 31 wickets at an average of 28.61. His best bowling was still the 3 for 44 mentioned earlier. He also had 39 NEPL catches.

During the 2005 NEPL season, Graham played 20 matches in the league, batting 19 times with 3 not outs, he scored 610 runs at an average of 38.12. He scored 6 half centuries with a highest score of 85, made on 25th June 2005 at home to Norton.

He bowled 366 balls in the NEPL in 2005, with 16 maidens, conceding 199 runs and taking 10 wickets at an average of 19.89. His best bowling figures were 3 for 11, taken on 18th June 2005 at Tynemouth. He took 11 catches in the NEPL in 2005.

Graham came to a major decision during the 2005 season, he says that he had "got a taste for the National Competitions and he decided to stop playing for Northumberland and concentrate on playing in those for South North," his dad, Bill was the Northumberland Team Manager at the time, so it wouldn't have been an easy decision, but John recalls that his father understood the rationale behind it.

Graham says that "over the next two or three years a number of my South North teammates did the same thing, it wasn't an organized or deliberate team decision, it was almost organic, I think it was a very natural process that each individual took."

He played his last game for them on 27th July 2005 at Jesmond against Norfolk, at the semifinal stage of The MCCA Knockout Trophy. He played 40 times for Northumberland, batting 51 times, with 4 not out's, scoring 1047 runs at an average of 22.27 and a high score of 85.

He had also bowled 954 balls for the county, with 31 maidens, conceding 569 runs and taking 21 wickets at an average of 27.09 and a best of 4 for 40. He also took 21 catches.

Matthew Hall batted at number five in the season opener, scoring 5. He had already played 70 times for South North in the NEPL, batting 54 times, with 16 not outs, scoring 733 runs at an average of 19.28 and a high score of 61 on 14th June 2003 at Gateshead Fell. He had scored 2 half centuries in his career at this point.

He had bowled 107 balls in the NEPL, with 3 maidens, conceding 66 runs although he had failed to take a wicket. He also had 14 catches and had 3 stumpings to his credit.

During the 2005 season Hall 19 times in the NEPL, batting 17 times, with 2 not outs, he scored 431 runs at an average of 28.73. He scored 3 half centuries and 1 century. His century, 101 not out, was scored on 21st May 2005 at Gateshead Fell. He didn't bowl in the NEPL in 2005, but he did take 12 catches.

Daniel Clark batted six in the 2005 opener, scoring 9. The only trace I could find of him was at Under 15 level, playing for Northumberland against Scotland on 8th July 2002 at Preston Avenue, North Shields. Northumberland batted first, Stuart Tiffin, 50, and Adam Cragg, 62, putting on 134 for the first wicket. Clark batted at five and scored 5, as Northumberland scored 190 for 6 from their 45 overs. Scotland fell just short in reply, 185 for 8 from their

45 overs. Clark opened the bowling, taking the first wicket to fall and finishing with 1 for 37. He made his NEPL debut for South North on 21st June 2003 at home to Stockton. This was the game that John Graham described earlier as a "pivotal moment" in the season. Clark didn't get a bowl as Stockton batted first, but he did take a catch. Clark, batting at nine, scored 2.

He played 6 matches for South North in 2005, batting on 4 occasions with 0 not outs, he scored 32 runs at an average of 8.00 and a high score of 20, made on 14th May at home to Benwell Hill. He didn't bowl in the NEPL in 2005 but took 1 catch.

Stephen Humble was a right-handed batsman and right arm fast medium bowler. The 2005 season opener was his NEPL debut for South North, he was run out for a duck but opened the bowling, taking his first South North wicket when he had Paul Riddle leg before wicket. He finished with 1 for 42. He had previously played for Blaydon in The NEPL and his stats at this point were all with Blaydon, he made his NEPL debut on 29th April 2000 in Blaydon's first ever NEPL fixture, at Tynemouth.

He bowled the first ball in the new league and finished with 2 for 27 from 16 overs. His first wicket in the NEPL was Jimmy Miller, who was caught by Gary Stewart for 4. Miller would be a teammate at South North for this and other seasons. Tynemouth went on to make 150 for 8 from 65 overs. Graeme Hallam had top scored with 42. When Blaydon batted, Humble went in at three, he failed to score as Blaydon were 139 for 7 wickets as the game was drawn.

On 18th June 2000 he played a 50-over game for The Durham Cricket Board against Northumberland at Stockton. Durham batted first and 103 from Gary Pratt and 53 from Gary Brown saw them to a score of 326 for 8 from their allotted overs. Humble, batting at nine, scored 14. Craig Stanley had 4 for 64 for Northumberland and future South North teammate Lee Crozier 2 for 40. When Northumberland batted opener Wayne Falla top scored with 27 as they struggled to chase such a big total, South North captain John Graham made 14. Northumberland were all out for 153 in 39.3 overs. Humble had 3 for 29, his wickets all had NEPL connections, Wayne Falla, Adam Heather and Graeme Hallam.

He would go on to play 13 matches for The Durham Cricket Board, with 9 innings, including 2 not outs, scoring 46 runs at an average of 6.57 and a high score of 14.

He bowled 620 balls for them, with 10 maidens and conceding 433 runs whilst taking 21 wickets at an average of 20.61 and a best bowling of 3 for 17. He also took 7 catches for them, playing his last game on 12 September 2002.

He made his debut for Northumberland in Minor Counties cricket on 18th May 2003 at Jesmond against Lincolnshire. Chris Hewison, John Graham, and Lee Crozier were in the same side. Lincolnshire batted first, 159 for 9 from 30 overs in a reduced over match. Humble took 2 for 22 from his six overs. When Northumberland batted an unbroken 6th wicket partnership between John Graham, 60 not out, and Humble, 20 not out, saw them win by five wickets.

When he arrived at South North, he had played 24 NEPL matches, with 22 innings, 2 not outs, scoring 249 runs at an average of 12.45, with a high score of 40.

As a bowler he had bowled 1984 balls, 85 maidens, conceding 887 runs and taking 57 wickets at an average of 15.56, with a best bowling of 6 for 46. He had taken 8 catches NEPL at this time.

During the 2005 season Humble played 20 matches in the NEPL, 18 batting times with 3 not outs, he scored 279 runs at an average of 18.60. His highest score of the season in the NEPL 45 not out, made on 20th August at home to Sunderland.

He also bowled 1438 balls in the 2005 NEPL, with 63 maidens, conceding 649 runs and taking 43 wickets at an average of 15.09. His best bowling figures were 5 for 27, taken on 25th June 2005 at home to Norton, he took 6 catches in the NEPL in 2005.

Lee Crozier batted at number eight in the season opener, scoring 35 not out. He took 2 for 68 with the ball. Crozier entered the 2005 season having played 94 NEPL matches, with 58 innings, 18 not out's, scoring 635 runs at an average of 15.87 and a high score of 89. That high score was his sole half century to this point.

As a bowler he bowled 6637 balls, with 316 maidens, conceding 2966 runs and taking 172 wickets at an average of 17.24, with a best bowling of 7 for 44. He had taken 23 catches in the NEPL at this time.

He played 20 matches in the NEPL in 2005, batting 17 times with 9 not outs, he scored 197 runs at an average of 24.62. His highest score of the season was 41, made on 30th May 2005 at home to Blaydon.

He bowled 1391 balls in the NEPL in 2005, with 75 maidens, conceding 546 runs and took 44 wickets at an average of 12.40. His best bowling figures were 5 for 21, taken on 29th August 2005 at home to Tynemouth. He took 2 catches in the 2005 NEPL season.

Michael Smalley batted at number nine in the 2005 season opener, scoring 11, he also took 1 for 23 from eight overs. Smalley was an established part of the South North set up at this time, he had played 54 times in The NEPL so far, batting 26 times, with 10 not outs, he had scored 297 runs at an average of 18.56. He had 1 half century to his name, 55 not out on 10th May 2003 at home to Tynemouth.

He had also bowled 1364 balls, with 40 maidens, conceding 825 runs and taking 42 wickets at an average of 19.64. His best bowling figures were 5 for 30 on 26th May 2001 at home to Norton. He had taken 7 NEPL catches.

Smalley played 18 matches in the NEPL in 2005, batting 10 times with 2 not outs, he scored 140 runs at an average of17.50. He scored 1 half century, 50 not out, made on 14th May 2005 at home to Benwell Hill.

He bowled 132 balls in the 2005 NEPL season, with 3 maidens, he conceded 84 runs and took 2 wickets at an average of 42.00. He took 2 NEPL catches in 2005.

Neil Corby kept wicket in the 2005 season opener and batted at ten, making nought not out. He had played a handful of games as part of the successful 2004 title winning side, making his NEPL debut on 24th April, he played 5 games that season but didn't get to bat nor take any catches.

Corby played 20 matches in the NEPL in 2005, batting 9 times with 8 not outs, he scored 52 runs at an average of 52.00. His highest score was 17 not out. He took 17 catches and had 6 stumpings in the NEPL in 2005.

Richard Brook was listed at number eleven for the 2005 opener, he didn't bat but took 5 for 49 with the ball. Brook was another who was now part of the fixtures and fittings in the South North dressing room.

Entering the 2005 season he had now played 55 NEPL matches, batting 12 times with 8 not outs, scoring 8 runs at an average of 2.00 and a high score of 2 not out.

He had, however, also bowled 3372 balls, with 140 maidens, conceding 1677 runs and taking 104 wickets at an average of 16.12. His best bowling figures 7 for 28 had been taken last season in 2004, on 22nd May at Roseworth Terrace against Philadelphia. He also took 9 catches.

During the 2005 season Brook played 18 matches in the NEPL, batting 3 times with 2 not outs, he scored 3 runs at an average of 5.00.

He bowled 761 balls in the NEPL in 2005, with 29 maidens, conceding 387 runs and taking 21 wickets at an average of 18.42. His best bowling figures were 5 for 33, taken on 3rd September 2005 at Norton. He took 4 catches in the NEPL in 2005.

John Graham remembers that although they won the league by 16 points it was another hard-fought season. What sticks out in his memory more than anything was that South North "lost two games in a row, something which rarely happened, the first was on a sporty wicket against Chester le Street, in a low scoring game, then Benwell Hill beat us, fortunately we were a reasonable amount in front at this point, and while it damaged us, we managed to re-focus and see the season out."

The first of the two games Graham is referring to took place at Gosforth on 16th July 2005. Chester le Street batted first and were dismissed for 106 from 33.5 overs. Opener Dan Shurben had top scored with 33, only two others made double figures as Stephen Humble 4 for 47 and Waqas Chughtai 3 for 31 caused all sorts of problems, they were supported by Richard Brook 2 for 15 and Lee Crozier 1 for 9. When South North batted the Chester bowlers caused their batsmen just as many, if not more problems than their own batters had faced. Waqas Chughtai had the highest score of the game, with 46, but Alex Brown, 9.1 overs, 1 maiden, took 6 for 41. He was well supported by the other Chester bowlers, each one who bowled took a wicket, Glen Read, 1 for 19, Liam Simpson 1 for 20, Andrew Bell 1 for 9 and C. Andrews 1 for 1. South North 90 all out as Chester won by 16 runs. The damage was limited somewhat with it being a low scoring game, South North took 5 points and Chester 20, but it only equated to a 15-point swing.

The second loss Graham spoke about came a week later, 23rd July 2005 at Denton Bank. South North batted first and despite three batsman making double figures, Matthew Hall was the innings top scorer with 17. Callum Thorp, who would go on to play first class cricket for Durham, was the chief architect of South North's troubles, bowling 14 overs and taking 7 for 53. Only one other bowler was used, Martin Pollard, who bowled 13.1 overs, taking 3 for 34. South North 87 all out. When Benwell Hill batted they lost opener Simon Birtwisle to the last ball of the first over, caught by John Graham off the bowling of Stephen Humble for a duck. An unbroken second wicket stand of 89 between opener and overseas pro Taufeeq Umar, 53 not out, and Graeme Race, 36 not out, saw Hill home by 9 wickets. South North failed to pick up a point in this game, a rarity.

Of their remaining six fixtures, South North won five and one was abandoned after a handful of overs, nearest rivals Chester le Street won five and drew one. As it turned out the draw, where they picked up 15 points, was probably the key fixture, it could easily have been a win, and a further 15 points.

It occurred in the second last game of the season, at home to Stockton on Monday 29th August. Chester batted first, 237 for 8 declared from 60 overs, Quentin Hughes leading the way with 72. Kevin Ward had 3 for 31 and Richard Waite 3 for 78 for Stockton. When Stockton batted their openers put on 79 for the first wicket, Guy Darwin going on to make 75 and they appeared to be doing well at 113 for 1.

At which point Hughes removed Chris Oliver, L.B.W for 11, 113 for 2.

The introduction of medium pace bowler Andrew Bell shook things up, taking all four wickets as Stockton slipped to 134 for 6, Darwin amongst the victims and the ever-dangerous Waite out for a duck. Bell would finish with ten overs and 4 for 25. Opening bowler Glen Read was brought back and he bowled Chris Hooker for 6, Stockton 141 for 7.

Read took two more wickets, Peter Howells, caught by Wayne Ritzema for 14, and Kevin Ward 12, Stockton 168 for 9.

Despite Read finishing with 3 for 51 and Hughes 2 for 28, plus the earlier efforts of Andrew Bell, Ian Still, who had come in at number eight, made 21 not out, and last man Tom Armstrong, 27 not out, as the last pair took the score to 208 when the 60 overs ran out on Chester. Match drawn.

John Graham reflects that "we had built up a decent lead before we lost those two games, and that the defeats, and the manner of the defeats hurt us, but we bounced back strongly and still had enough of a cushion to feel comfortable."

When I looked at the league throughout the season, in respect of South North and Chester in particular, Graham's words ring true, after three drawn games to open the season, including a draw between the two sides, South North were ten points clear of Chester.

Although Chester were still unbeaten by the time South North lost their first game, on 4th June, even after the loss, South North were still ten points clear of Chester.

It was the next five games which provided South North with the cushion Graham spoke of South North won four and drew one, picking up 127 points from them, Chester won one, drew one but lost three, picking up 59 points and South North opening up a 78-point gap.

South North finished the season with an away game against Norton, on 3rd September 2005. An opening stand of 125 between Adam Heather and Jimmy Miller set them up at least for the draw they needed to ensure the league title, Heather eventually dismissed for 108, Miller 85, Chris Hewison made 65 for good measure and they finished up 299 for 6 declared from 52 overs. Norton were bowled out for 121, Craig Symington 28, as Richard Brook 5 for 33, Stephen Humble 2 for 26, Brendan Ford 2 for 34 and Lee Crozier 1 for 25. South North finished the season with a maximum point win and won the league by 16 points.

The Banks Salver was won by Chester le Street this season and Simon Birtwisle of Benwell Hill was named NEPL Player of the Year.

Birtwisle played 19 matches in the NEPL in 2005, he batted 19 times with 1 not out, he scored 745 runs at an average of 41.38. He scored 6 half centuries with a highest score of 95 not out, made on 13th August 2005 at Sunderland.

He also bowled 606 balls in the NEPL in 2005, with 21 maidens, conceding 376 runs and taking 14 wickets at an average of 26.85. His best bowling figures were 3 for 30, taken on 16th July 2005 at home to Gateshead Fell. He took 2 catches in the NEPL in 2005.

TABLE 20   NEPL 2005.

	Played	Won	Drawn/Aban	Lost	Bonus Points	Points
South North	22	12	7	3	189	410
Chester le St	22	12	7	3	177	394
Gateshead Fell	22	9	7	6	141	317
Benwell Hill	22	6	14	2	129	297
Stockton	22	7	8	7	148	294
Durham CA	22	5	12	5	147	278
Sunderland	22	7	7	8	143	275
Tynemouth	22	6	7	9	131	255
Norton	22	7	7	8	114	253
Blaydon	22	5	10	7	116	235
Newcastle	22	3	8	11	102	179
Philadelphia	22	2	8	12	97	163

TABLE 21   NEPL Batting Averages 2005.

Qualification 300 Runs.

43 Batsmen Qualified this season.

Player	Club	Inns	N.O	H.S	Runs	Average
(1) Taufeeq Umar	Benwell Hill	13	2	164 no	765	69.55
(2) M.J Symington	Norton	19	7	118 no	634	52.83
(3) Q.J Hughes	Chester le St	18	4	136 no	718	51.29
(4) J.A Lowe	Stockton	18	2	118 no	705	44.06
(5) D.N.G Myers	Benwell Hill	15	5	58 no	438	43.80
(6) I. Pattison	Gateshead Fell	17	2	136 no	656	43.73
(7) C. Ferguson	Gateshead Fell	10	1	133	386	42.89
(8) S.J Birtwisle	Benwell Hill	19	1	95 no	745	41.39
(9) A. Worthy	Gateshead Fell	17	4	76	523	40.23
(10) M. Stoneman	Durham CA	18	0	129	706	39.22
(11) C. Symington	Norton	18	5	55 no	509	39.15
(12) J.A Graham	South North	19	3	85	610	38.13
(33) M.J Hall	South North	17	2	101 no	431	28.73
(34) J.N Miller	South North	20	1	85	525	27.63
(36) A.T Heather	South North	20	1	107	519	27.32
(37) C.J Hewison	South North	20	1	77	511	26.89

TABLE 22   NEPL Bowling Averages 2005.
Qualification 20 Wickets.
35 Bowlers Qualified this season.

Player	Club	Overs	Mdns	Runs	Wkts	Ave
(1) L.J Crozier	South North	231.5	75	546	44	12.41
(2) N.C Phillips	Gateshead Fell	299.2	68	807	57	14.16
(3) S. Humble	South North	239.4	66	649	43	15.09
(4) S. Puri	Norton	196.0	55	504	32	15.75
(5) G. Read	Chester le St	207.2	51	519	31	16.74
(6) R. Brook	South North	126.5	29	387	21	18.43
(7) L. Simpson	Chester Le St	126.4	30	392	21	18.67
(8) C.D Thorp	Benwell Hill	140.2	30	443	23	19.26
(9) B. Stewart	Tynemouth	183.4	47	549	28	19.61
(10) M. Cummins	Durham CA	181.5	46	494	25	19.76
(11) Gary Stewart	Blaydon	228.1	49	720	36	20.00
(12) N.C McGarrell	Blaydon	331.3	82	856	42	20.38

South North 2005 NEPL Champions.

Standing Left to Right – N. Corby, S. Humble, M.J Smalley, B.N.W Ford, C.J Hewison, L. J Crozier, M.J Hall, J.N Miller, M.W. Shotton (Scorer).

Sitting- A.T Heather, J.A Graham, R.M Brook.

Simon Birtwisle seen here batting on 13th September 2017 at Derby.

Photo Courtesy of Ken Waller.

2006

South North dominance continued with a fourth league title in a row, the League had a new sponsor this year, it was now to be known as The Northern Rock North East Premier League. It had also lost its first club, Philadelphia, relegated at the end of the 2005 season to be replaced by Hetton Lyons.

South North started their 2006 campaign with a home game against Chester le Street on 29th April. John Graham recalls "We played them on a used wicket at our place, they did okay with the bat then Graeme Bridge rolled us over cheaply." Wayne Ritzema had 47 opening the innings and Quentin Hughes 35 as Chester made 183 all out. Lee Crozier had 4 for 45, Brendan Ford 3 for 41 and Richard Brook 2 for 61. Despite an opening stand of 41 between Adam Heather and Jimmy Miller, South North were bowled out for 109. Graeme Bridge had 5 for 20.

Their team that day was.

Adam Heather opened the batting, scoring 30. His stats as this time stack up with the very best batters in the NEPL, making him one of the best in The League. He had played 109 matches in The NEPL entering the 2006 season, he had batted 106 times, with 16 not outs, scoring 3266 runs at an average of 36.28, he had scored 16 half centuries and 7 centuries. His highest score was 127 on 25th August 2003 at Gosforth against Gateshead Fell. He had never bowled in The NEPL but had taken 44 catches and 4 stumpings.

During the 2006 NEPL season Heather played 19 matches, batting 19 times with 0 not outs, he scored 3 half centuries and 1 century. The century, 100, was scored on 24th June 2006 at home to Newcastle. He bowled 12 balls in the NEPL in 2006, taking 0 for 2 and he took 4 catches.

Jimmy Miller opened the batting with Heather in the season opener, scoring 18. Miller was one of the established cornerstones of the South North top order at this time, coming in to the 2006 season starting he had played 110 NEPL matches, batting 106 times, with 12 not outs and scoring 2926 runs at an average of 31.12, with 16 half centuries and 5 centuries. His highest score was still 132 not out, which came on 28th May 2001 for Tynemouth at home to Gateshead Fell.

He had also bowled 12 balls, with 0 maidens, conceding 4 runs and taking 1 wicket at an average of 4.00. His best bowling was 1 for 2 on 24th July 2004 at home to Benwell Hill. He had also taken 41 NEPL catches.

During the 2006 season Miller played 20 matches in the NEPL, he batted 18 times with 1 not outs, he scored 210 runs at an average of 12.35. He scored 1 half century, 71 not out on 10th June 2006 at home to Tynemouth. He bowled 24 balls, taking 0 for 18 and took 9 catches in the NEPL in 2006.

Chris Hewison batted at three in the first game of 2006, scoring 6. Prior to this season starting he had played 93 NEPL matches, batting 92 times, with 14 not outs and scoring 3544 runs at an average of 45.43, with 17 half centuries and 9 centuries. His highest score was 165 not out which came on 22nd June 2002 at Philadelphia.

He had also bowled 1773 balls, with 49 maidens, conceding 1045 runs and taking 30 wickets at an average of 34.83. His best bowling was now 3 for 25 on 20th July 2002 at Norton. He had also taken 40 NEPL catches.

During the 2006 season Hewison played 20 matches in the NEPL, batting 20 times with 5 not outs, he scored 746 runs at an average of 49.73. He scored 5 half centuries and 1 century. The century, 116 not out, was scored on 29th July 2006 at home to Blaydon. John Graham scored a century that day as he and Hewison added 170 for the third wicket.

Hewison bowled 54 balls in the NEPL in 2006, with 1 maiden, conceding 14 runs and taking 2 wickets. He also took 12 catches in the league that season.

John Graham batted four against Chester in the 2006 season opener, scoring 6. He came into the 2006 season as the well-established leader of the most successful team in the Leagues short history, with three titles in a row. Prior to this season starting he had played 111 NEPL matches, batting 105 times, with 17 not outs and scoring 3371 runs at an average of 38.30, with 27 half centuries and 3 centuries. His highest score was 118 not out which came on 22nd May 2004 at home to Philadelphia.

He had bowled 2080 balls, with 77 maidens, conceding 1086 runs and taking 41 wickets at an average of 26.48. His best bowling was now 3 for 11 on 18th June 2005 at Tynemouth and he had also taken 50 NEPL catches.

Graham played 20 matches in the NEPL in 2006, batting 20 times with 3 not outs, he scored 840 runs at an average of 49.41. He scored 4 half centuries and 3 centuries. The first of the centuries, exactly 100, was scored on 27th May 2006 at home to Gateshead Fell.

The second century, 119, was made on 22nd July 2006 at Hetton Lyons.

The third century, 132, was his highest NEPL score of the season and was made the week after his second century of the season, it was scored at home to Blaydon and was mentioned earlier re the partnership with Chris Hewison.

Graham also bowled 330 balls in the NEPL in 2006, with 7 maidens, he conceded 220 runs and took 9 wickets at an average of 24.44. His best bowling figures were 4 for 51, taken on 3rd June 2006 at home to Benwell Hill. He took 14 catches in the NEPL in 2006.

Brendan Ford batted five in the season opener of 2006, scoring a single and took 3 for 41 with the ball when Chester batted. Ford had played 3 games in the 2005 title winning side, making his South North and NEPL debut on 27th August 2005 at The Racecourse against Durham Academy. He took 3 for 39 and scored 39 not out in that debut. His second game of the 2005 season went equally as well, if not better, on Monday 29th August at home to Tynemouth, he scored 46 and took 3 for 18. He also played the last game of the season, at Norton, scoring 8 and taking 2 for 34.

So, he entered the 2006 season having played in 3 NEPL matches, batting 3 times with 1 not out, scoring 93 runs at an average of 46.50.

He had also bowled 168 balls, with 6 maidens, taking 8 wickets at an average of 10.37. He had 1 NEPL catch.

He had come to South North from Scottish Cricket, the first recorded performance I could find on 1st May 2004 for Dundee High School Former Pupils at Dunfermline. He played 14 matches for them in 2004 and one in 2005, his last appearance being on 8th May.

In total he played 15 matches for them, batting 14 times, with 1 not out, he scored 547 runs at an average of 42.07 with 3 half centuries and 2 centuries. His highest score was 134 not out on 17th July 2004 at home to Stoneywood-Dyce.

He also bowled 807 balls, with 20 maidens, conceding 570 runs and taking 21 wickets at an average of 27.14. His best bowling was 4 for 30 on 14th August at home to St Modan's High School Former Pupils. He also took 6 catches for them. His last appearance for them, the one game of 2005 he played, saw him score 112.

Ford played 16 matches in the NEPL for South North in 2006, he batted 16 times with 4 not outs, he scored 618 runs at an average of 51.50. He scored 5 half centuries with a highest score of 96, made on 5th August 2006 at Gateshead Fell.

He also bowled 996 balls in the NEPL, with 28 maidens, conceding 562 runs and taking 24 wickets at an average of 23.41. His best bowling figures were 5 for 40, taken on 24th June 2006 at home to Newcastle. He took 5 catches in the NEPL in 2006.

Stephen Humble batted at number six against Chester in the opening game of 2006, made 18 with the bat and had taken 0 for 28 when Chester had batted. Humble was now in his second season with South North, he had played 44 NEPL games, batting 40 times with 5 not outs, he had scored 528 runs at an average of 15.08. His high score of 45 not out was made on 20th August 2005 for South North at home to Sunderland.

He had bowled 3422 career NEPL deliveries, with 148 maidens and conceding 1536 runs, he had taken 100 wickets at an average of 15.36, his best bowling was still the 6 for 46 mentioned earlier for Blaydon. He had taken 14 NEPL catches.

Humble played 19 matches in the NEPL in 2006, batting 12 times with 3 not outs, he scored 270 runs at an average of 30.00. He scored 2 half centuries, with a highest score of 78, made on 26th August 2006 at home to Stockton.

He bowled 1540 balls in the NEPL in 2006, with 60 maidens, he conceded 800 runs and took 43 wickets at an average of 18.60. His best bowling figures were 8 for 55, taken on 27th May 2006 at home to Gateshead Fell. He took 5 catches in the NEPL in 2006.

Tom Seymour batted at number seven in the season opener, he failed to trouble the scorers. Seymour was not a regular in the South North first team, he had played 13 NEPL matches up to the start of the 2006 season, batting 12 times, with 3 not outs. He had scored 133 runs at an average of 14.77 with 1 half century, 58 not out, made on 1st June 2002 at Sunderland. He hadn't bowled in The NEPL but had taken 1 catch. The season opener of 2006 was his only NEPL appearance of the 2006 season.

Daniel (Danny) Clark batted at number eight and scored 11 in the season opener. He was never a regular in the side. He had played 9 NEPL matches up to this point, batting 5 times, with 0 not outs, he had scored 34 runs at an average of 6.80, with a high score of 20. He did not bowl and took 2 NEPL catches.

Clark played 16 matches in the NEPL in 2006, batting 10 times with 2 not outs, he scored 111 runs at an average of 13.87. His highest score was 34, made on 1st July 2006 at Stockton. He took 4 catches in the NEPL in 2006.

After South North Clark would go on to play for Gateshead Fell and 1 game for Felling in the NEPL. He played 56 NEPL games, batting 43 times, with 2 not out's, he scored 500 runs at an average of 12.19. His highest score was the one-half century he made, 54, on 26th July 2008 against Sunderland. He took 11 NEPL career catches.

Lee Crozier batted at nine in the 2006 season opener, he scored 2 and took 4 for 45 when Chester had batted. Crozier had played 114 NEPL games, batting 75 times with 27 not out's, he had scored 832 runs at an average of 17.33, with 1 half century. His high score remained as the 89 discussed earlier.

He bowled 8028 career NEPL deliveries, with 391 maidens and conceding 3512 runs, he had taken 216 wickets at an average of 16.25, his best bowling was still the 7 for 44 mentioned earlier. He had taken 25 NEPL catches.

Crozier played 17 matches in the NEPL in 2006, batting 9 times with 4 not outs, he scored 101 runs at an average of 20.20. His highest score of the 2006 season was 25, made on 6th May 2006 at Sunderland.

He bowled 1606 balls in the NEPL in the 2006 season, with 83 maidens, conceding 630 runs and taking 45 wickets at an average of 14.00. His best bowling figures in the NEPL in 2006 were 6 for 47, taken on 26th August 2006 at home to Stockton. He took 1 catch in the NEPL in 2006.

Neil Corby batted at number ten in the season opener, making 5, he also kept wicket, taking 1 catch. He entered the 2006 season having played 20 NEPL matches, batting 9 times with 8 not outs, he had scored 52 runs at an average of 52.00! His highest score to this point was 17 not out. As a wicketkeeper he had taken 17 catches and 6 stumpings to his credit.

He made his debut for Northumberland on 4th June 2006 at Barrow in Furness against Cumberland in a 50 over match. He did not get a bat but took one catch. He would play a handful of games over the next few years, but very sporadically, his second appearance coming in 2011, one in 2013 and two in 2014.

His last appearance for the county came on 18th May 2014 at Lincolnshire in a 50 over match. He made 4. Corby had played 5 matches for Northumberland but in fairness had been given no opportunity to shine. He played 20 matches in the NEPL in 2006, batting 7 times with 2 not outs, he scored 24 runs at an average of 4.80. His highest score was 11 not out. He took 19 catches in the NEPL in 2006.

Richard Brook was number eleven for the season opener, he didn't score but was not out, he also took 2 for 61 with the ball. He had now played 73 NEPL games, all for South North, batting 15 times with 10 not outs, he had scored 13 runs at an average of 260 with a high score of 3.

Brook was selected as an "out and out bowler," as the 2006 season got underway, he had 4133 career NEPL deliveries, with 169 maidens and conceding 2064 runs, he had taken 125 wickets at an average of 16.51, his best bowling was still the 7 for 28 mentioned earlier. He had taken 13 NEPL catches.

During the 2006 NEPL season his batting was once again negligible, he did however bowl 1127 balls with 57 maidens, conceding 540 runs and taking 33 wickets at an average of 16.36. His bets bowling figures were 7 for 39, taken on 22nd July 2006 at Hetton Lyons. He took 2 catches in the 2006 NEPL season.

Michael Smalley missed the first few games of the season but still played 10 games in the NEPL in the 2006 season. He was now established in the South North side. Prior to the 2006 season starting he had played 72 NEPL games, batting 36 times with 12 not outs, he had scored 437 runs at an average of 18.20, with 2 half centuries. His high score was 55 not out on 10th May 2003 at home to Tynemouth.

He had 1496 career NEPL deliveries, with 43 maidens and conceding 909 runs, he had taken 44 wickets at an average of 20.65, his best bowling was still the 5 for 30 mentioned earlier. He had taken 9 NEPL catches.

In his 10 NEPL games of 2006 he batted 5 times with 1 not outs, he scored 23 runs at an average of 5.75.

He bowled 148 balls in the NEPL in 2006, with 7 maidens, he conceded 92 runs and taking 3 wickets at an average of 30.66. His best bowling figures were 1 for 9. He didn't take an NEPL catch in 2006.

Matthew Hall was another who missed the first game of the season, making his first appearance on 6th May 2006. Up to this point he had played 89 matches in the NEPL, batting 71 times with 18 not outs, he had scored 1164 runs at an average of 21.96. He had scored 5 half centuries and 1 century, 101 not out, made in May 2005 and mentioned earlier. He had taken 26 catches and made 3 stumpings in his NEPL career to this point.

During the 2006 season Hall played 16 matches in the NEPL, batting 14 times with 5 not outs, he scored 260 runs at an average of 28.88. He scored 1 half century, 70 not out, made on 20th May 2006 at Blaydon. He took 6 catches in the 2006 NEPL season.

John Graham says that "after the first week loss to Chester, we lost the second week as well, Marc Symington bowled well for Sunderland that day and we were bowled out cheaply again." As usual his memory is pretty good!

On 6th May 2006 South North travelled to Sunderland. South North batted first and were bowled out for 110, Lee Crozier top scored with 25. Marc Symington had 4 for 19, Simon Brown took 2 for 17, Chris Rushworth 2 for 28, Imran Shah 1 for 0 and Merv Dillon 1 for 36. When Sunderland batted Symington continued to plague South North, making 54 not out at three, opener Fred Napier made 44, Sunderland winning by 8 wickets.

Graham says that "we pulled ourselves round, so much so that by about the halfway mark of the season we were on top of the league, we lost to Chester Le Street, something we did pretty often to be fair to them, then put another run together."

That loss to Chester came on 8th July 2006, Chester batted first, half centuries from Dan Shurben, 53, and Quentin Hughes 68, helped them to 224 for 5 wickets declared in 60 overs. Brendan Ford top scored with 41 as Hughes took 4 for 9 and Glen Read 3 for 51 as South North were dismissed for 132, Chester winning by 92 runs.

Graham says there was still "one more pivotal game to come. The following week we were at home to Sunderland, they got 200 or so, Chris Hewison had ninety odd to see us home, we saw it out from there really and won the league with a couple of games to go."

Records show that on 15th July 2006 South North hosted Sunderland at Roseworth Terrace. Sunderland batted first, this time it was the other Symington, Craig who had a decent day against South North, scoring 72. Sunderland 199 all out in 60.2 overs. Stephen Humble had 5 for 59 and John Graham 3 for 50. When they batted South North were in a bit of trouble themselves at 52 for 5 but Chris Hewison batting at number four, scored 95 not out, Neil Killeen had made 20 and Dan Clark 18 not out as South North got the 200 for the loss of 6 wickets to take the win.

Chester le Street won the Banks Salver this season and Stephen Humble was named the 2006 NEPL Player of the Year.

Graham says that "we had matured together as a team this year, we also had a very balanced team, me, Hewison and Ford all had good years with the bat and with Humble and Crozier with the ball we were a good unit, it just all came together, and it spilled from the league into us winning The Cockspur Cup."

South North won The ECB National Club Championship, The Cockspur Cup, on 4th September 2006 at Lord's, beating Bromley by 84 runs in The Final. Bromley won the toss and asked South North to bat, opener Adam Heather top scored the innings with 68 and number six, Matthew Hall made 60, as they posted 227 for 6 from their 45 overs. When Bromley batted opener Nadeem Shahid scored 78 but only one other batter made double figures as they were bowled out for 143 in 39.2 overs. Stephen Humble had 3 for 16, Michael Smalley 2 for 6, Lee Crozier 2 for 26 and Richard Brook 2 for 28.

The NEPL representative side won The President's Trophy at Chester le Street against the North Staffordshire and South Cheshire Cricket League (N.S.S.C.C.L) on 3rd September 2006.

The side had no South North players in their side as they pursued National honours, but they did have a pair of brothers, Marc and Craig Symington. NEPL captain and wicketkeeper Peter Howells won the toss and elected to field. Norton bowler Jon Kean took an early caught and bowled but a solid partnership of 55 for the second wicket only ended with a run out. The visitors then slipped to 93 for 4 as Marc Symington picked up a couple of wickets. Former England batsman Kim Barnett held the innings together for the visitors, going on to make 69, he was well supported by Philip Cheadle with 52. Barnett was dismissed by a catch from Simon Birtwisle off the bowling of Newcastle slow left armer Jonny Bailey and Cheadle was bowled by Kean. The N.S.S.C.C.L scored 195 for 6 from their 45 overs. Kean had 2 for 45, Martin Pollard ten overs 0 for 14, Chris Rushworth 0 for 43, Marc Symington 2 for 49 and Bailey 1 for 38.

When the NEPL batted they lost opener Dan Shurben for 7, but a second wicket partnership of 45 put them in a good position, Paul Muchall was the second wicket to fall, out for 10. The score was 138 when opener Simon Birtwisle was dismissed for 73. Alan Mustard 76 not out and Marc Symington 21 not out then saw the NEPL home by 7 wickets with 11 balls to spare.

TABLE 23   NEPL 2006.

	Played	Won	Drawn/Aban	Lost	Bonus Points	Points
South North	22	13	6	3	194	423
Chester le St	22	11	6	5	176	371
Tynemouth	22	9	6	7	144	307
Blaydon	22	7	10	5	139	296
Benwell Hill	22	7	12	3	139	295
Durham CA	22	7	10	5	128	289
Sunderland	22	7	10	5	136	283
Gateshead Fell	22	5	10	7	141	268
Stockton	22	5	10	7	130	263
Norton	22	5	7	10	110	222
Newcastle	22	5	6	11	111	206
Hetton Lyons	22	1	7	14	102	152

TABLE 24   NEPL Batting Averages 2006.

Qualification 300 Runs.

45 Batsmen Qualified this season.

Player	Club	Inns	N. O	H. S	Runs	Average
(1) M. Bekker	Gateshead Fell	20	2	204 no	1027	57.06
(2) A. Worthy	Blaydon	19	4	105 no	812	54.13
(3) M.L Turner	Gateshead Fell	16	5	126 no	567	51.55
(4) B. Ford	South North	16	4	96	618	51.50
(5) G.T Park	Norton	13	2	137 no	560	50.91
(6) C.J Hewison	South North	20	5	116 no	746	49.73
(7) J.A Graham	South North	20	3	132	840	49.41
(8) S.J Birtwisle	Benwell Hill	18	1	110 no	818	48.12
(9) C. Symington	Sunderland	18	6	75 no	522	43.50
(10) S.D Birbeck	Hetton Lyons	19	2	116 no	709	41.71
(11) D.G Shurben	Chester le St	19	1	118	744	41.33
(12) P.B Muchall	Tynemouth	21	2	93 no	762	40.11
(28) A.T Heather	South North	19	0	100	574	30.21

TABLE 25   NEPL Bowling Averages 2006.

Qualification 20 Wickets.

36 Bowlers Qualified this season.

Player	Club	Overs	Mdns	Runs	Wkts	Ave
(1) G.D Bridge	Chester le St	146.0	30	365	30	12.17
(2) G.G Read	Chester le St	235.2	66	596	47	12.68
(3) A. Walker	Stockton	154.4	65	272	21	12.95
(4) L.J Crozier	South North	267.4	83	630	45	14.00
(5) M. Cummins	Durham CA	184.0	37	493	35	14.09
(6) C. Barr	Chester le St	142.0	30	479	30	15.97
(7) R.M Brook	South North	187.5	57	540	33	16.36
(8) J. Kean	Norton	206.4	52	657	40	16.43
(9) P. Armstrong	Norton	204.2	39	641	37	17.32
(10) S. Gale	Blaydon	202.1	27	748	42	17.81
(11) S.J.E Brown	Sunderland	144.5	36	416	23	18.09
(12) Yasir Ali	Benwell Hill	342.2	75	1013	56	18.09
(13) S. Humble	South North	256.4	60	800	43	18.60
(25) B. Ford	South North	166.0	27	562	24	23.42

South North 2006 NEPL Champions.

Left to Right – Back Row- J.N Miller, R. M Brook, M.J Hall, C.J Hewison, B.N.W Ford, S.D West, M.W Shotton (Scorer).

Front Row- D. Clark, L. J Crozier, J. A Graham, A.T Heather, N. Corby.

Stephen Humble seen here on 4th June 2017 at South North.

Photo Courtesy of Ken Waller.

2007

South North were champions once more and also won the Banks Salver, they opened the defence of their 2006 title with a home fixture against Gateshead Fell on 28th April.

Gateshead Fell batted first, Danny Clark, who had played for the previous season and others for South North was one of the opening batsmen, made 2. Fell scored 166 all out from 55.4 overs, Richard Smith top scoring with 33. Brendan Ford, 4 for 38, and Richard Brook, 4 for 48, the main wicket takers. When South North batted captain and opening bat John Graham had 76 not out, Chris Hewison batting at four weighed in with 44 and they won by seven wickets in 47.1 overs.

Their team that day was.

John Graham opened the batting, making 76 not out. Prior to the 2007 season starting he had played 131 NEPL matches, batting 125 times, with 20 not outs and scoring 4211 runs at an average of 40.10, with 31 half centuries and 6 centuries. His highest score was 132 not out, which came on 29th July 2006 at home to Blaydon.

He had also bowled 2410 balls, with 84 maidens, conceding 1306 runs and taking 50 wickets at an average of 26.12. His best bowling was now 4 for 51 on 3rd June 2006 at home to Benwell Hill. He had also taken 64 NEPL catches.

During the 2007 NEPL season, Graham played 18 matches in the league, batting 17 times with 3 not outs, he scored 601 runs at an average of 42.92. He scored 5 half centuries, his highest score was 77 not out, made on 4th August 2007 at home to Stockton.

He bowled 56 balls in the NEPL in 2007, with 1 maiden, he conceded 49 runs and didn't take a wicket. He took 7 catches in the league that season.

Neil Corby opened the batting after Adam Heather broke his collarbone taking a catch, he made 6. Corby also took three catches behind the stumps. Corby entered the 2007 season having played 45 NEPL matches, batting 17 times, with 10 not outs, he had scored 76 runs at an average of 10.85, his highest score was 17 not out. He had taken 36 catches and had 6 stumpings up to this point.

He played 18 matches in the NEPL in 2007, batting 9 times with 1 not out, he scored 99 runs at an average of 12.37. His highest score was 23, made on 2nd June 2007 at Durham Academy. He took 25 catches and made 4 stumpings in the NEPL in 2007.

Brendan Ford batted at three in the 2007 season opener, he made 6 when he batted but had taken 4 for 38 when Fell batted. Ford was now in his third season with the club after playing in Scotland, as the 2007 season started he had played 19 NEPL games, batting 19 times with 5 not outs, he had scored 711 runs at an average of 50.78, he had 5 half centuries at his time. His highest score was 96, on 5th August 2006 at Gateshead Fell.

He bowled 1164 balls, with 34 maidens, conceding 645 runs and taking 32 wickets at an average of 20.15. His best bowling figures were 5 for 40 on 24th June 2006 at home to Newcastle. He also took 6 catches.

Ford played 18 matches in the NEPL in 2007, batting 16 times with 0 not outs, he scored 280 runs at an average of 17.50. He scored 1 half century, 51, scored on 26th May 2007 at Stockton.

He bowled 796 balls in the NEPL in 2007, with 18 maidens, conceding 472 runs and taking 19 wickets at an average of 24.84. His best bowling figures were 4 for 38, taken on 28th April in the season opener. He took 3 catches in the NEPL in the season.

Chris Hewison batted at number four in the season opener, scoring 44. Going into the 2007 season Hewison had played 113 NEPL games, batting 112 times with 19 not outs, he had scored 4290 runs at an average of 46.12, he had 22 half centuries and 10 centuries. His highest score was 165 not out previously mentioned.

He bowled 1827 balls, with 50 maidens, conceding 1059 runs and taking 32 wickets at an average of 33.09. His best bowling figures were still the 3 for 25 mentioned earlier. He had now taken 52 catches.

Hewison played his last game for Northumberland on 7th May 2006, one to forget!

After making his Northumberland debut on 9th May 2002 at York against The Yorkshire Cricket Board he would play just 9 times for the county, batting on 9 occasions, with 0 not outs, he scored 280 runs at an average of 31.11. He scored 3 half centuries. His highest score was 78 on 16th June 2002 at Preston Grange against The Yorkshire Cricket Board.

He bowled 90 balls for Northumberland, with 0 maidens, conceding 94 runs and taking 1 wicket. He took 5 catches for the county.

During the 2007 NEPL season Hewison played 18 matches in the league, batting 16 times with 3 not outs, he scored 720 runs at an average of 55.38. He scored 2 half centuries and 3 centuries.

The first of his hundreds, 108, was scored on 26th May 2007 at Stockton, the second, 113 not out, was scored on 1st September 2007 at Newcastle. And the third, 118, was his highest NEPL score of the season and came the week after his second hundred, it was scored on 8th September 2007 at home to South Shields. Hewison also took 18 catches in the NEPL in 2007.

Adam Cragg is a left-handed batsman, he batted at number five on his South North NEPL debut, making 17 not out. Cragg first came to my attention playing for Northumberland Under 15's against Scotland Under 15's at Preston Avenue. He opened the batting and top scored with 62.

He progressed through to Northumberland Under 17's, playing a two-day game against Huntingdonshire Under 17's which started on 26th July 2004. In a drawn game Cragg only got to bat once, he top scored in the innings, making 54.

The first sign the records show of him in senior cricket, I suspect he played senior cricket a lot earlier than this, was on 15th May 2005 when Ashington played a Cockspur Cup match against Guisborough at Langwell Crescent. He was dismissed for a single.

Cragg left Ashington to join Tynemouth, making his NEPL debut on 6th May 2006 at home to Hetton Lyons. He batted at number seven and was run out for 45.

He played 16 games in the NEPL for Tynemouth in the 2006 season, batting 12 times, with 2 not outs, he scored 337 runs at an average of 33.70. He had 1 half century, his highest score of 57 not out on 15th July at Hetton Lyons. He had taken 6 catches for the club in the NEPL.

Cragg made his Northumberland debut in Minor Counties cricket in 2006, in a 3-day match starting on 20th August, against Buckinghamshire at Jesmond. He made 47 in the first innings as Northumberland made 216 all out, Allan Worthy was the top scorer with 82. Cragg got a duck in the second innings as Bucks went on to win by 5 wickets.

His last appearance for Northumberland came on 6th May 2018 at Jesmond against Lincolnshire in a one day match. Cragg made 13 as Phil Mustard hit 105 as Northumberland won by seven wickets.

He played 68 games for Northumberland, batting 86 times, with 10 not outs, he scored 2373 runs at an average of 31.22. He scored 11 half centuries and 3 centuries. His highest score of 164 came in a three-day match which started on 7th July 2013 at Jesmond against Bedfordshire. The 164 came from 183 balls and contained 20 boundaries. For the record, Karl Turner made 82 and 99, Tom Cant had 90 in the first innings and Jaques Du Toit had 138 in the second innings.

Cragg also bowled 238 balls for the county, with 2 maidens, conceding 196 runs and taking 8 wickets at an average of 24.50. His best bowling was 4 for 47, against Lincolnshire at Sleaford in a 3-day match which started on 10th June 2012. He also took 3 for 37 in the first innings! Cragg took 58 catches and had 9 stumpings for Northumberland.

Cragg played 18 matches for South North in the NEPL in 2007, batting 14 times with 4 not outs, he scored 361 runs at an average of 36.10. He scored 2 half centuries, with a highest score of 78 not out, made on 8th September 2007 at home to South Shields. He took 8 catches in the NEPL in 2007.

Jimmy Miller was listed to bat at number six in the 2007 opener, he didn't get to bat as South North won by 7 wickets. Going into the 2007 season Miller had played 130 NEPL games, batting 124 times with 13 not out's, he had scored 3136 runs at an average of 28.25, he had 17 half centuries and 5 centuries. His highest score was 132 not out previously mentioned.

He bowled 36 balls, with 0 maidens, conceding 22 runs and taking 1 wicket at an average of 22.00 and he had now taken 50 NEPL catches.

Miller played his last game for Northumberland on 6th August 2006 at Jesmond against Cumberland in a 3-day match, he scored 0 and 3.

He played 17 matches for Northumberland, batting 22 times with 0 not outs, he scored 216 runs at an average of 9.81. His highest score was 47, made in a 3-day match which started on 28th July 2002 at Staffordshire.

He bowled just 6 balls, conceding 16 runs for 0 wickets and took 5 catches.

During the 2007 NEPL season Miller played 18 matches in the league, batting 12 times, with 7 not outs, he scored 376 runs at an average of 75.20. He scored 4 half centuries with a highest score of 73 not out, made on 14th July 2007 at home to Norton. He took 4 catches in the NEPL in the 2007 season.

Stephen Humble was listed to bat at number seven in the 2007 opener, he didn't get to bat but did open the bowling, 0 for 14. Humble had now played 63 NEPL games, batting 52 times with 8 not out's, he had scored 798 runs at an average of 18.13, he had 2 half centuries. His highest score was now 78, made on 26th August 2006 at home to Stockton.

He had bowled 4962 balls, with 208 maidens, conceding 2336 runs and taking 143 wickets at an average of 16.33. His best bowling figures were now 8 for 55 on 27th May 2006 at home to Gateshead Fell. The best bowling also included a hat trick. He has now taken 19 NEPL catches.

Humble played 18 matches in the NEPL in 2007, batting 9 times with 5 not outs, he scored 221 runs at an average of 55.25. He scored 1 half century, 68 not out, made on 26th May 2007 at Stockton.

Humble also bowled 1385 balls in the NEPL in 2007, with 68 maidens, he conceded 598 runs and took 33 wickets at an average of 18.12. His best bowling figures were 6 for 49, taken on 9th June 2007 at home to Benwell Hill. He also took 5 NEPL catches in 2007.

Michael Smalley was listed to bat at number eight in the 2007 opener, he didn't get to bat. He had missed the early part of the title winning 2006 season, he made his first appearance of that season on 20th May, at Blaydon. He did play 10 NEPL matches in the 2006 season, batting 5 times, with 1 not out, he scored 23 runs at an average of 5.75. He also bowled 148 balls, with 7 maidens, conceding 92 runs and taking 3 wickets.

His career stats were much better than his 2006 season, he had now played 82 NEPL matches, batting 41 times, with 13 not outs, he had scored 460 runs at an average of 16.42. He had scored 2 half centuries. His highest score was still 55 not out from May 2003.

He had bowled 1644 balls, with 50 maidens, conceding 1001 runs and taking 47 wickets at an average of 21.29. His best bowling remained the 5 for 30 from 2001. He had 9 NEPL career catches at the start of 2007. During 2007 Smalley played just 2 matches in the NEPL, batting just once for a single, he didn't bowl or take a catch.

Craig Smith was listed to bat at number nine in the 2007 opener, he didn't get to bat. The season opener was his South North NEPL debut, he opened the bowling, Dan Clark his first South North NEPL wicket, caught by Adam Cragg for 2. Smith finished with 2 for 44.

Smith made his NEPL debut on 29th April 2006 for Gateshead Fell at Benwell Hill. He opened the bowling taking 2 for 50, his first NEPL wicket was David Myers caught by Martin Bekker for 4. Smith was bowled for a duck when his side batted. He played his last game for Fell on 9th September 2006 at home to Benwell Hill. He was 0 not out when his side batted and took 2 for 53 when they bowled.

Smith's Fell career, in effect the 2006 season, saw him play 17 matches, he batted 10 times, with 3 not outs, he scored 29 runs at an average of 4.14. His highest score was 13 not out.

As a bowler he bowled 1330 balls, with 43 maidens, conceding 775 runs and taking 31 wickets at an average of 25.00. His best bowling was 5 for 58 on 5th August at home to South North. He took 2 catches that season.

During the 2007 NEPL season Smith played 16 matches in the league for South North, batting 4 times with 3 not outs, he scored 21 runs at an average of 21.00.

He bowled 688 balls, with 19 maidens, conceding 450 runs and taking 14 wickets at an average of 32.14. His best bowling figures were 3 for 48, taken on 5th May 2007 at Norton. He took 1 catch in the NEPL in 2007.

Richard Brook was listed to bat at number ten in the 2007 opener, he didn't get to bat but he did take 4 for 48 when South North bowled. Brook had now played 90 NEPL matches, he had batted 18 times, with 13 not out's, he scored 18 runs at an average of 3.60. His highest score was 5 not out.

As a bowler he bowled 5260 balls, with 226 maidens, conceding 2604 runs and taking 158 wickets at an average of 16.48. His best bowling was still the 7 for 28 mentioned earlier. He had taken 15 NEPL career catches.

Brook played 17 matches in the 2007 NEPL season, his batting was minimal, as a bowler he delivered 1019 balls, with 39 maidens, he conceded 481 runs and took 35 wickets at an average of 13.74. His best bowling figures were 5 for 15, taken on 7th July 2007 at Gateshead Fell. He took 6 NEPL catches in 2007.

Adam Heather would normally have opened, he had suffered a broken collarbone taking a catch whilst fielding, therefore he is listed on the scorecard as number eleven. The scorecard show that Heather took 2 catches that day, the second was Nick Phillips, so I think that was probably the catch that did the damage!

Entering the season Heather had played 128 NEPL matches, batting 125 times, with 16 not outs, he had scored 3840 runs at an average of 35.22, he had 19 half centuries and 8 centuries. His highest score was still the 127 he made on 25th August 2003. Heather didn't bowl in 2006, so he still had no wickets to his name. He did, however, have 48 catches and 4 stumpings.

Despite the injury Heather still played 12 matches in the NEPL in 2007, batting 10 times with 2 not outs, he scored 348 runs at an average of 43.50. He scored 1 half century and 1 century, 128 not out, scored on 14th July 2007 at home to Norton. He took 7 catches in the NEPL in 2007.

Lee Crozier missed the season opener but still played 17 times in the 2007 season. Going into the 2007 season Crozier played 131 NEPL matches, batting 84 times, with 31 not outs, scoring 933 runs at an average of 17.60. His highest score was still the 89 mentioned earlier.

He had also bowled 9634 balls, with 474 maidens, conceding 4142 runs and taking 261 wickets at an average of 15.86. His best bowling in The NEPL remained 7 for 44 from his Benwell Hill days in 2001. He had 26 NEPL career catches.

During the 2007 season Crozier played 17 matches in the NEPL, batting 6 times with 1 not out, he scored 66 runs at an average of 13.20. His highest score was 29, made on 19th May 2007 at home to Chester le Street.

He bowled 1464 balls in the NEPL in 2007, with 82 maidens, he conceded 574 runs and took 47 wickets at an average of 12.21. His best bowling figures were 7 for 21, taken on 28th July 2007 at Chester e Street. He took 1 catch in the NEPL in 2007.

Before I go into the actual cricket played on the last day of the 2007 season, you, and I, need to understand the NEPL bonus point system, I was hoping to avoid this, but it was inevitable at some point.

Teams get 15 points for a win, 7 points for a tie and either 7 points or 3 points for a draw depending on which side had the highest scoring rate per over batted, an abandoned match is worth 5 points each.

When it comes to bonus points, the batting side gets 1 point each for reaching the following score within the first 60 overs of the innings, 120, 150, 180, 210 and 240. The key number in respect of the 2007 season was 210.

Bowling bonus points are 1 point for every two wickets, 2, 4, 6, 8 and 10, with 5 points awarded if a side is dismissed, irrespective of how many wickets have fallen.

Clear?

John Graham also reminded me that at this time there was no play cricket or internet streams of the NEPL, so you had to rely on phone calls or text messages to friends or acquaintances at different grounds if you needed a live score from anywhere.

On the morning of Saturday 8th September 2007 before a ball was bowled, Sunderland sat top of The NEPL table, with 362 points from South North who were in second position on 361 points. Sunderland had a home fixture with The Durham Academy, South North at home to South Shields.

Both Sunderland and South North won the toss and elected to bat. At Sunderland John Watson and Alan Mustard opened the batting, Ben Stokes was one of the opening bowlers for The Academy, putting on 40 for the first wicket before Mustard was caught by Richard Coughtrie off the bowling of Karl Turner for 14.

South North meanwhile were soon in trouble, at 11 for 2, losing Adam Heather for 1, L.B.W to Mark Woodhead, and Brendan Ford, also for 1, to a catch by Michael Dunn off the bowling of Matthew Muchall.

At Ashbrooke Watson was the next wicket to fall, caught by Paul Muchall off the bowling of Turner for 26, Sunderland 52 for 2.

This quickly became 56 for 3 when Gary Scott, who had come in at number three, was caught by Coughtrie off the bowling of Paul Muchall.

South North opener John Graham went next for 38, with the score on 82, caught by Woodhead off the bowling of Muchall. South North 82 for 3.

Marc Symington batted at four for Sunderland today, younger brother Craig was batting at five. The brothers then set the Sunderland innings up with a partnership of 85, Craig departing for 54, L.B.W to Scott Borthwick, Sunderland 141 for 4.

Greg Applegarth batted at five, he fell quickly for 2, caught by Ben Stokes off the bowling of Borthwick, Sunderland 145 for 5.

Shahid Nazir, Sunderland's overseas pro, came in at seven and he and Marc Symington took the score to 177 for 6 when Nazir was caught by Andrew Smith for 23.

Imran Shah was batting at eight for Sunderland today, he had previously played at South North and had several friends playing for them today. He scored 18, from a partnership of 21, taking the score to 198 when he was bowled by Uzair Mahomed. Sunderland 198 for 7.

Chris Youlden came and went quickly, run out for a single, Sunderland 199 for 8 wickets.

Simon Brown came in at ten, he would score 2 not out. The drama and arguably another of John Graham's "pivotal points" came from the last four balls of the 60th over.

Marc Symington, who was unbeaten on 54, was on strike, the 60th over fell to Karl Turner to bowl. Turner would later go on to play the 2014 season for South North, more of that later!

Now remember the bonus point rules for batting, Sunderland had three bonus points in the bag, they had to get to 210 from 60 overs or less, to pick up a fourth bonus point.

John Graham recalls that he was told what happened next later that night in a call from John Windows, The Durham Academy Head Coach, whom he had played many times with and knew well. Marc Symington was a good bat, he had played first class cricket for Durham, smacked each of the four balls firmly, very firmly by all accounts, into the covers, The Academy protecting the runs, had a ring of fielders, each of the four balls hit a fielder, for no run. Greg Applegarth remembers those four balls exactly as the story was relayed to John Graham.

Sunderland declared at the end of the over, 209 for 8 from 60 overs, Marc Symington was 54 not out. Michael Robson was the only Sunderland batsman who didn't get a knock during the Sunderland innings. Karl Turner had 2 for 37, Uzair Mahomed 1 for 34, Borthwick 3 for 61 and Paul Muchall 1 for 34, for the record Ben Stokes had 0 for 22.

Sunderland picked up 8 batting bonus points, meaning they now had 370 points in the battle for the title.

Meanwhile, at Roseworth Terrace, the fall of John Graham, at 82 don't forget, had brought Adam Cragg to the crease, he and Chris Hewison took the score to 238 before the next wicket fell, Hewison bowled by Muchall for 118. South North 238 for 4.

Cragg, who finished on 78 not out, and Jimmy Miller, 12 not out, took the score to 254 for 4 wickets when South Norh declared after 54 overs. Muchall had 3 for 102 from 19 overs.

By reaching 240 inside the first 60 overs South North had obtained their first goal of the maximum ten batting bonus points. South North now had 371 points as, at the halfway mark of the final game of the season, they overtook Sunderland by one point.

When The Academy batted at Sunderland they were quickly in trouble and never recovered. Scott Borthwick, who had opened the batting, went for 3, caught by Youldon off the bowling of Simon Brown, 9 for 1, this became 14 for 2 when Andrew Smith was bowled by Shahid Nazir for 4 and then 15 for 3 when Ben Stokes was L.B.W to Simon Brown for a duck. Without adding any runs, Paul Muchall was then bowled by Simon Brown for a duck, The Academy, 15 for 4.

Opener Karl Turner was the next to go, with the score at 44, L.B.W to Marc Symington for 17, Durham Academy 44 for 5 wickets.

A few miles up the road at Gosforth, when South Shields batted South North had opened the bowling with Stephen Humble and Lee Crozier. The decision to start with Crozier proved to be sound as he quickly dismissed Michael Fishwick, L.B.W, for a single. Shields 14 for 1.

Dan Shurben and Lee Whalley took the score to 41 when Shurben was bowled by Crozier for 27.

Number four batsman Oliver Stedman departed quickly, bowled by Richard Brook for a single, South Shields now 47 for 3.

Back at Ashbrooke, Uzair Mahomed and Michael Turns had added 22 when John Watson caught Mahomed for 28, the innings top score, off the bowling of Marc Symington. The Academy were now 56 for 6 wickets and going nowhere. Richard Coughtrie was next to go for a duck, L.B.W to Marc Symington, 69 for 8 wickets. The ninth Academy wicket to fall was Michael Turns, caught by John Watson off the bowling of Marc Symington for 15. Durham Academy 78 for 9.

At South North a 36-run partnership between Lee Whalley and Michael Dunn took Shields to 83 before Dunn was caught by Adam Heather off the bowling of Richard Brook for 24.

The tenth and final Academy wicket to fall was their number eleven, Scott Redhead, L.B.W to Shahid Nazir for 5. Durham Academy 83 all out, Sunderland won by 126 runs. Shaid Nazir 2 for 24, Simon Brown 3 for 17, and Marc Symington 5 for 14, the wicket takers.

They picked up the 5 bowling bonus points on offer, this plus their 15 points for winning the match and their 8 batting points, gave them 28 points for the afternoon and meant that they finished the season with 390 points.

At South North, Shields had just got past the hundred when the next wicket fell, Lee Whalley was caught by wicketkeeper Neil Corby off the bowling of Lee Crozier for 33, 101 for 5.

Number seven batsman Neil Dixon went next for 7, bowled by Crozier, 121 for 6.

Chris Dorothy, who had batted six, was next out, caught by Heather off Brook for 32. Shields now slipping to 133 for 7.

The tail couldn't wag, losing two wickets with the score 137, Matthew Muchall L.B.W to Crozier for a duck and James Goff, L.B.W to Brook for a single. Shields now 137 for 9.

Opening bowler Stephen Humble was brought back, he quickly bowled last man Chris Nichol for 2, Michael Woodhead 9 not out but Shields 152 all out. Humble finished with 1 for 5, Crozier 5 for 53 and Brook 4 for 36, Craig Smith 0 for 9 and Brendan Ford, 0 for 34, had also bowled.

A win by 102 runs, the margin of victory, less important than the taking of all ten Shields wickets, giving South North the maximum 5 bowling points, when added to their 10 batting points and 15 points for the win, South North took 30 points from the day. By doing so, they finished on 391 league points, to win the 2007 NEPL title by one point from Sunderland.

South North would also add The Banks Salver to their league title this year.

Marc Symington had, at least, the satisfaction of being named the NEPL Player of the Year, he had played 18 matches in the NEPL in 2007, batting 18 times with 8 not outs, he scored 513 runs at an average of 51.30. He scored 5 half centuries with a highest score of 70 not out, made on 4th August 2007 at Gateshead Fell. He also bowled 1503 balls in the NEPL in 2007, with 53 maidens, conceding 817 runs and taking 57 wickets at an average of 14.33. His best bowling figures were 6 for 43, taken on 28th May 2007 at South North. He also took 5 catches in the NEPL in 2007.

TABLE 26   NEPL 2007.

	Played	Won	Draw/Aban	Lost	Penalty Points	Bonus Points	Points
South North	22	10	11	1	1	175	391
Sunderland	22	14	7	1	1	150	390
Blaydon	22	6	6	7	0	134	275
Durham CA	22	4	13	5	0	139	266
Chester le St	22	5	12	5	0	125	260
Benwell Hill	22	4	15	3	1	118	254
South Shields	22	6	8	8	0	118	244
Tynemouth	22	6	7	9	0	115	240
Gateshead Fell	22	5	10	7	4	106	221
Newcastle	22	4	12	6	0	98	218
Norton	22	3	12	7	6	102	201
Stockton	22	3	8	11	3	110	184

TABLE 27   NEPL Batting Averages 2007.

Qualification 300 Runs.

34 Batsmen Qualified this season.

Player	Club	Inns	N. O	H. S	Runs	Average
(1) J.N Miller	South North	12	7	73 no	376	75.20
(2) G.T Park	Norton	7	1	115 no	407	67.83
(3) D.G Shurben	South Shields	17	5	74 no	666	55.42
(4) C.J Hewison	South North	16	3	118	720	55.38
(5) C.E Knox	Norton	18	6	109 no	622	51.83
(6) M.J Symington	Sunderland	18	8	70 no	513	51.30
(7) A. Worthy	Blaydon	17	2	156 no	702	46.80
(8) Q.J Hughes	Chester le St	15	1	110	647	46.21
(9) M.D Stoneman	Blaydon	12	1	150	506	46.00
(10) A.T Heather	South North	10	2	128 no	348	43.50
(11) J.A Graham	South North	17	3	77 no	601	42.93
(12) G.D Bridge	Blaydon	14	3	95	471	42.82
(18) A.D Cragg	South North	14	4	78 no	361	36.10

TABLE 28   NEPL Bowling Averages 2007.

Qualification 20 Wickets.

34 Bowlers Qualified this season.

Player	Club	Overs	Mdns	Runs	Wkts	Average
(1) L.J Crozier	South North	244.0	82	574	47	12.21
(2) P.B Muchall	Durham Academy	93.0	12	306	24	12.75
(3) M.J Muchall	South Shields	115.1	26	377	29	13.00
(4) Shahid Nazir	Sunderland	215.1	65	524	40	13.10
(5) P.R Hindmarch	Durham Academy	112.0	25	316	24	13.17
(6) R.M Brook	South North	169.5	39	481	35	13.74
(7) M.J Symington	Sunderland	250.3	53	817	57	14.33
(8) S.J.E Brown	Sunderland	113.4	24	338	21	16.10
(9) W.R.S Gidman	Gateshead Fell	191.2	49	600	34	17.65
(10) S. Humble	South North	230.5	68	598	33	18.12
(11) G.D Bridge	Blaydon	278.4	57	762	41	18.59
(12) R.P Waite	Stockton	266.3	59	888	47	18.89

South North 2007 NEPL Champions.

Back Row -Left to Right- N. Corby, B.N W Ford, C.R.D Smith, C.J Hewison, R. M Brook, S Humble, A. Cragg.

Front Row- A.T Heather, J. A Graham, L.J Crozier, J.N Miller, M.W Shotton (Scorer).

Chris Hewison seen here batting for South North at Philadelphia on 24th May 2003.

Credit to the unknown photographer.

2008

Going in to the 2008 season John Graham recalls that "we had a very good side, but we knew that South Shields had one too, with Jonny Wightman and Matthew and Paul Muchall they were a real threat with the ball, and they would take plenty of wickets, batting wise Dan Shurben and Paul Muchall were a strong opening pair. They also had a good overseas pro in Geoff Cullen from Western Australia."

The South North side for the season opener in 2008 was almost identical to the side which had opened the 2007 season, Lee Crozier had missed the first game of 2007 but was back in the lineup for the 2008 opener, replacing Michael Smalley. Smalley didn't play much for the first eleven in 2007 but had made valuable contributions in previous years.

They started the 2008 season with an away game at Sunderland on 26th April. Sunderland batted first and made 111 all out in 53.1 overs, Gary Scott top scoring with 30. Opening bowler Stephen Humble with 4 for 20 was the key bowler, although all five bowlers used got at least one wicket. When South North batted Brendan Ford had 79 from just 55 balls with 12 fours and 2 sixes, as South North won by eight wickets in just 19.2 overs.

Their team that day was.

Adam Heather opened the batting and made 16 not out. Heather had played 140 NEPL matches prior to the start of the 2008 season, he had batted 135 times, with 18 not out's, scoring 4188 runs at an average of 35.79. He had scored 20 half centuries and 9 centuries. His highest score was 128 not out on 14th July 2007 at home to Norton.

He had bowled just 12 balls, 0 maidens, conceding 2 runs for no wickets and had taken 55 catches and had 4 stumpings.

Heather would play his last match for Northumberland in the 2007 season, on 5th August at Jesmond against Hertfordshire. He made 23 and 93. His Northumberland debut, although not productive, had been on 22nd July 1996 at Jesmond against Staffordshire.

In his career Heather played 78 matches for Northumberland, he batted 116 times with 7 not out's, he scored 3046 runs at an average of 27.94, with 15 half centuries and 4 centuries. He bowled 60 balls, with 1 maiden, conceding 81 runs and 0 wickets and took 25 catches.

During the 2008 season Heather played 19 matches in the NEPL, batting 17 times with 2 not outs, he scored 358 runs at an average of 23.86. He scored 1 half century, 53, made on 14th June 2008 at Tynemouth. He didn't bowl in the NEPL in 2008, but he took 1 catch.

John Graham was captain and opened the batting in April 2008 and made a single. Prior to this season starting he had played 149 NEPL matches, batting 142 times, with 23 not outs and scoring 4812 runs at an average of 40.43, with 36 half centuries and 6 centuries. His highest score was still the 132 mentioned earlier.

He had bowled 2466 balls, with 85 maidens, conceding 1355 runs and taken 50 wickets at an average of 27.10. His best bowling was still the 4 for 51 mentioned earlier. He had also taken 71 NEPL catches.

During the 2008 NEPL season Graham played 19 matches, batting 17 times with 1 not out, he scored 469 runs at an average of 29.31. He scored 3 half centuries and 1 century, 106, made on 14th June 2008 at Tynemouth.

He bowled 146 balls in the NEPL in 2008, with 7 maidens, conceding 95 runs and taking 9 wickets at an average of 10.55. His best bowling figures were 4 for 15, taken on 31st May 2008 at Newcastle. He also took 18 catches in the NEPL in 2008.

Brendan Ford bowled eight overs and took 1 for 8 with the ball and scored 79 from just 55 balls when South North batted in the 2008 opener. Ford was now an established part of the South North batting line up. Coming into the 2008 season he played 37 NEPL matches, all for South North, he batted 35 times with 5 not outs, he scored 991 runs at an average of 33.03. He had scored 6 half centuries. His highest score remained the 96 from August 2006 mentioned earlier.

He had bowled 1960 balls, with 52 maidens, conceding 1117 runs and taking 51 wickets at an average of 21.90. His best bowling remained the 5 for 40 taken in 2006 mentioned earlier. He had taken 9 NEPL catches.

During the 2008 NEPL season, Ford played 12 matches, batting 10 times with 3 not outs, he scored 251 runs at an average of 35.85. he scored 1 half century,79, made on 26th April in the season opener.

He bowled 298 balls in the 2008 NEPL season, with 12 maidens, conceding 133 runs and taking 16 wickets at an average of 8.31. His best bowling figures were 6 for 44, taken on 14th June 2008 at Tynemouth. He took 2 NEPL catches in 2008.

Chris Hewison took the first catch of the season and scored 11 not out in the season opener. As he entered the 2008 season Hewison was widely acknowledged as one of the best batters in the league, he finished the 2007 season with successive hundreds.

He had now played 131 NEPL matches, all for South North, he had batted 128 times with 22 not outs, he had scored 5010 runs at an average of 47.26. He had 24 half centuries and 13 centuries. His highest score remained the 165 not out from June 2002 mentioned earlier.

He bowled 1827 balls, with 50 maidens, conceding 1059 runs and taking 32 wickets at an average of 33.09. His best bowling remained the 3 for 25 taken in July 2002 mentioned earlier. He took 62 NEPL catches.

Hewison played 19 matches in the NEPL in 2008, batting 16 times with 4 not outs, he scored 460 runs at an average of 38.33. He scored 1 half century and 1 century, 120 not out, scored on 31st May 2008 at Newcastle. He didn't bowl but did take 17 catches in the NEPL in the 2008 season.

Jimmy Miller didn't get to bat or bowl in the season opener. He had now played 148 NEPL matches, he batted 136 times with 20 not outs, he had scored 3512 runs at an average of 30.27. He had scored 21 half centuries and 5 centuries. His highest score remained 132 not out from May 2001 mentioned earlier.

He bowled 36 balls, with 0 maidens, conceding 22 runs and taking 1 wicket at an average of 22.00 and he had taken 55 NEPL catches.

During the 2008 season Miller played 17 matches in the NEPL, batting 12 times with 3 not outs, he scored 329 runs at an average of 36.55. He scored 4 half centuries with a highest score of 72, made on 26th May 2008 at home to South Shields. He bowled 6 balls in the NEPL in 2008, taking 0 for 1 and took 8 NEPL catches in 2008.

Adam Cragg didn't get to bat or bowl in the season opener. Entering the 2008 season he has now played 34 NEPL matches, he has batted 26 times with 6 not outs, he had scored 698 runs at an average of 34.90. He had scored 3 half centuries. His highest score was 78 not out on the last day of the 2007 season, 8th September at home to South Shields. He had yet to bowl in the NEPL, but he had taken 14 NEPL catches.

Cragg played 17 matches in the NEPL in 2008, batting 12 times with 1 not out, he scored 261 runs at an average of 23.72. he scored 1 half century, 85, made on 24th May 2008 at Blaydon. He didn't bowl in the NEPL in 2008, but he did keep wicket, taking 15 catches and making 3 stumpings.

Stephen Humble took 4 for 20 from fifteen overs when Sunderland batted in the season opener, he didn't bat. Humble had played 81 NEPL matches as entered the 2008 season, batting 61 times, with 13 not outs and scoring 1019 runs at an average of 21.22. He had scored 3 half centuries. His highest score was 78 on 26th April 2006 mentioned earlier.

He had bowled 6347 balls, with 276 maidens, conceding 2934 runs and taking 176 wickets at an average of 16.67. His best bowling remained 8 for 55 taken on 27th May 2006 mentioned earlier. He had also taken 24 NEPL catches.

Humble played 18 matches in the NEPL in 2008, batting 11 times with 3 not outs, he scored 103 runs at an average of 12.87. His highest score of the 2008 NEPL season was 24, made on 26th May 2008 at home to South Shields.

He bowled 1219 balls in the NEPL in 2008, with 61 maidens, conceding 413 runs and taking 46 wickets at an average of 8.97. His best bowling figures were 7 for 28, taken on 24th May 2008 at Blaydon, he also took 5 catches in the NEPL season.

He made his first appearance for Northumberland on 18th May 2003 at home to Lincolnshire in a 50 over match. He took 2 for 22, his first county wicket was opener James Clarke, caught by Chris Hewison for 17. Humble also scored 20 not out when he batted as Northumberland won by 5 wickets.

His last appearance for Northumberland came very early into the 2008 season, on 27th April at Roseworth Terrace against Suffolk. He took 0 for 20 and did not bat as they won on a faster scoring rate.

In total Humble played 27 matches for Northumberland, batting 31 times, with 8 not outs and scoring 726 runs at an average of 31.56, with 5 half centuries. His highest score was 88 not out, scored on 3rd May 2005 at Jesmond against Middlesex.

He bowled 2698 balls, with 95 maidens, conceding 1596 runs and taking 78 wickets at an average of 20.46. His best bowling now 6 for 37 taken in a 3-day game starting on 21st August 2005 at Jesmond against Suffolk. He has also taken 11 catches for the county.

The game where Humble made his highest score was a significant game in the county's history as the entire team played their last List A fixture in this game.

Dan Shurben, Adam Heather, Allan Worthy, Bradley Parker, Marc Symington, John Graham, John Windows, Stephen Humble, Phil Nicholson, Lee Crozier and Martin Pollard all retired from List A cricket, but as evidenced by Humble, some of them would continue to play other formats for the county.

I think this is an appropriate time to have a look at The NEPL career of John Windows, whilst researching, especially the early days of the league, his name came up repeatedly. Whilst he is widely recognized for the assistance he has given to many young players, what can be overlooked is that he was a decent player himself.

I'm going to have a look at his NEPL and Northumberland stats, he made his NEPL debut on 6th May 2000 for Benwell Hill at Stockton. Phil Nicholson made 72 and Windows 57 when Hill batted, Windows also took 3 for 39 when his side bowled in a drawn game, his first NEPL wicket was C. Harrison. caught by Barry Evans for 15. Windows played his last game for Benwell Hill on 8th September 2001 at Tynemouth, he scored 32 and took 2 for 18.

He played 30 NEPL matches for them, batting 28 times, with 3 not outs, he scored 961 runs at an average of 38.44. He scored 9 half centuries, with a highest score of 79 on 5th May 2001 at Norton.

He bowled 1229 balls in The NEPL for Hill, with 49 maidens, conceding 627 runs and taking 27 wickets at an average of 23.22. His best bowling was 4 for 52 on 24th June 2000 at home to South North. He took 16 NEPL catches.

John Windows made his NEPL debut for The Durham Academy on 27th April 2002 at Roseworth Terrace against South North, scoring 6 and taking 0 for 8 and his last appearance for The Academy came on 1st September 2018 at Whitburn, he made 0 not out and didn't bowl.

He played 105 NEPL matches for The Academy, batting 52 times, with 29 not out's, he scored 469 runs at an average of 20.39. He scored 1 half century, 51 not out on 24th July 2004 at Tynemouth.

He bowled 474 balls, with 13 maidens, conceding 251 runs and took 10 wickets at an average of 25.10. His best bowling was 2 for 1 and he also took 26 catches.

Across his NEPL career Windows played 135 NEPL matches, batting 80 times, with 32 not outs, he scored 1430 runs at an average of 29.79. He scored 10 half centuries. His highest score was 79 for Benwell Hill mentioned earlier.

He bowled 1703 balls, with 62 maidens, conceding 878 runs and took 37 wickets at an average of 23.72. His best bowling was the 4 for 52 for Benwell Hill mentioned earlier. He also took 42 NEPL catches.

Windows also played for Saltburn in the N.Y.S.D IN 2006, as well as playing for Northumberland.

He made his debut for Northumberland in a 2-day match which started on 28th July 1997 at Staffordshire. He made 13 and 22 and took 0 for 4 in the second innings. His last appearance for the county came on 6th May 2007 at Cheshire in a 50-over match, he scored 3 not out and didn't bowl.

All told Windows played 77 matches for Northumberland, he batted 96 times with 22 not out's, he scored 2054 runs at an average of 27.75. He scored 8 half centuries and 1 century, 188 not out on 14th July 2002 in a 3-day match against Lincolnshire at Jesmond.

He bowled 2928 balls, with 68 maidens, conceding 2096 runs and took 63 wickets at an average of 33.26. His best bowling was the 6 for 57 on 13th June at Suffolk. He also took 37 catches.

I don't know John Windows but having looked at his stats, he was clearly a player of NEPL standard, the numbers would also suggest that as a coach he has sacrificed his own opportunities to give those in his care their opportunities.

Lee Crozier took 2 for 29 when Sunderland batted but didn't get to bat himself on 26th April. He was now established as one of the NEPL's top bowlers. He had played 148 NEPL matches, batting 90 times, with 32 not outs and scoring 999 runs at an average of 17.22, with 1 half century. His highest score was still the 89 mentioned earlier.

He had bowled 11098 balls, with 556 maidens, conceding 4716 runs and taking 308 wickets at an average of 15.31. His best bowling now 7 for 21 taken on 14th July 2007 at home to Norton. He had also taken 27 NEPL catches.

Crozier played 19 matches in the NEPL in 2008, batting 8 times with 6 not outs, he scored 52 runs at an average of 26.00. His highest score was 18 not out.

He bowled 1435 balls in the 2008 NEPL season, with 76 maidens, conceding 505 runs at and taking 41 wickets at an average of 12.31. His best bowling figures were 6 for 15, taken on 25th August 2008 at home to Tynemouth. He took 3 NEPL catches in 2008.

Neil Corby kept wicket and didn't get to bat in the 2008 season opener, this was symptomatic of the season, as he played 13 matches in the NEPL, he had only 1 completed innings, although he did take 15 catches and had 1 stumping.

Corby would play his last NEPL match for South North on 12th September 2009 at Chester le Street, he scored 9 when they batted and took a catch and two stumpings in the field.

Corby had played 93 NEPL matches for South North, batting 36 times with 13 not out's, he scored 242 runs at an average of 10.52. His highest score was 23. As a wicketkeeper he took 90 catches and had 16 stumpings in The NEPL for South North.

He made his NEPL debut for Newcastle on 24th April 2000 at Benwell Hill, he took 2 catches and scored 39 not out, his highest NEPL score to date.

His last NEPL appearance came for Newcastle on 27th August 2016 at Jesmond against South Shields, he made 39 opening the batting, although he didn't keep wicket.

Corby played 130 NEPL matches for Newcastle, he batted 107 times with 11 not outs, he scored 1815 runs at an average of 18.90. He scored 6 half centuries and 1 century, 123 not out, on 19th April 2014 at Jesmond against Sunderland. It came from 151 balls and contained 19 fours and 2 sixes. He took 122 catches and had 23 stumpings for Newcastle in the NEPL.

His career NEPL stats are that he played 223 matches, batting 143 times, with 24 not outs, he scored 2057 runs at an average of 17.28. He scored 6 half centuries and 1 century. The century mentioned earlier was his highest NEPL score. He took 212 catches and had 39 stumpings in the NEPL.

He moved on to play for Swalwell after Newcastle where he won several T.S.L titles and still plays in 2024.

Craig Smith opened the bowling with Humble and took 1 for 25 to open the season. The 2008 season would be the third NEPL season Smith had undertaken after initially playing for Gateshead Fell. He had played 33 matches in The NEPL going into the season, he had batted 14 times with 6 not out's, he had scored 50 runs at an average of 6.25. His highest NEPL score was 13 not out on 24th June 2006 at Gateshead against The Durham Academy.

As a bowler in the NEPL, Smith bowled 2018 balls, with 625 maidens, conceding 1225 runs and taking 45 wickets at an average of 27.22. His best bowling figures were still the 5 for 58 taken in August 2006 and mentioned earlier. He had also taken 3 catches.

During the 2008 season Smith played 18 matches in the NEPL, his batting was negligible, he bowled 709 balls, with 27 maidens, conceding 368 runs and taking 22 wickets at an average of 16.72. His best bowling figures were 7 for 22, taken on 3rd May 2008 at home to Norton. He took 1 catch in the NEPL.

Richard Brook took 1 for 12 from nine overs and didn't bat in the season opener. Entering the 2008 season Brook played 107 matches in the NEPL, he batted 21 times with 13 not outs, he scored 37 runs at an average of 4.62. His highest NEPL score was 19 on 12th August 2007 at Roseworth Terrace against The Durham Academy.

As a bowler in the NEPL, Brook bowled 6279 balls, with 265 maidens, conceding 3085 runs and taking 193 wickets at an average of 15.98. His best bowling figures were still the 7 for 28 on 23rd August 2003 mentioned earlier. He had also taken 21 catches.

Brook played 17 matches in the NEPL in 2008, he bowled 650 balls, with 24 maidens, conceding 334 runs and taking 22 wickets at an average of 15.18. His best bowling figures were 6 for 32, taken on 23rd August 2008 at Stockton. He took 3 NEPL catches in 2008.

Nicky Peng was a right-handed batsman and a right arm off break bowler, he made his NEPL debut for The Durham Academy on 22nd July 2000 at The Riverside against Stockton, scoring 104 opening the batting. That was his only NEPL appearance of the season.

He made his South North NEPL debut on 28th April 2001 against Stockton, he failed to score in a low scoring 72 all out for his team. Alan Walker had 5 for 20 and C. Burke 4 for 27. He only played once more in 2001 and was rarely available in the years up to 2008.

Although he did make an NEPL debut for Tynemouth on 15th June 2002 at Gateshead Fell, scoring 54. He played just once more for them in 2002, once in 2003 and once in 2004 and his last Tynemouth appearance came on 28th August 2004 at home to Norton. He made 50 opening the batting.

Returning to Peng at South North, he didn't play in the season opener of 2008, his first appearance of the season coming on 10th May, when he got a duck! He did play 13 games that season in The NEPL for the club, batting 13 times with 1 not out, he scored 349 runs at an average of 29.08. He made 1 half century and 1 century, 107 not out, in his final appearance of the season at home to Tynemouth. He didn't bowl in 2008 and took 4 NEPL catches.

His career NEPL stats were that he played 21 matches, batting 21 times with 1 not out, he scored 641 runs at an average of 32.04. He scored 4 half centuries and 2 centuries. His highest score was 107 not out mentioned earlier. He never bowled in the league but took 7 catches.

John Graham describes Peng as "a very destructive player, an unbelievable player when he got in, like all of us batsman he could be vulnerable early on."

Graham remembers that 2008 was a comfortable margin in the end, by 62 points from South Shields.

"Shields had beaten us at South North in the first part of the season, Jonny Wightman had five and their Aussie pro seventy odd, but we were a strong confident side at this point, and we still felt that we were on track."

Records do show that South North hosted South Shields on 26th May that year, despite 72 from Jimmy Miller and 42 from Chris Hewison, they were dismissed for 198 and Jonny Wightman did have 5 for 47. When Shields batted Australian pro Geoff Cullen made 77 and Dan Shurben 38 as Shields won by 3 wickets.

That was the only NEPL game South North lost that season, as well as the league title, they also won the inaugural NEPL T20 competition 2008 Cockspur Club Twenty20 at Cardiff live on Sky Sports on 29th September 2008. They beat Stanmore from Middlesex in The Final.

South North won the toss and decided to bat, they made 142 for 6 wickets from their 20 overs, John Graham had 52 from just 41 deliveries and Adam Heather had 30 from 31 deliveries.

When Stanmore batted, they were soon in trouble and never recovered, their top score was just 27 as they were dismissed for 88 from 18.4 overs, John Graham took 3 for 11, Lee Crozier had 3 for 18, Stephen Humble had 2 for 22 and Craig Smith had 1 for 4. They won by 54 runs and John Graham was named man of the match.

A couple of things to round off the season, the League side won The President's Trophy, and a certain Benjamin Andrew Stokes of the Durham Academy kept popping up in games around this period, this now seems an appropriate time to have a look at his NEPL career.

He made his NEPL debut on 28th April 2007 for The Durham Academy at Maiden Castle against Norton, he was run out for 44 when Durham batted, and he took 1 for 44 when they bowled. His first NEPL wicket was Norton opening batsman Craig Knox, caught by Richard Coughtrie for 19.

In 2008 he was 22nd in the league batting averages with 272 runs at an average of 30.22 and a high score of 66.

His last NEPL wicket was Norton batsman Matthew Brown, caught by Ben Raine for 25, on 12th September 2009.

From 2009 onwards Stokes only appeared sporadically in the NEPL, making one appearance in both 2011 and 2014, he made two appearances in 2016. His last appearance in the league came on 9th July 2016 at The Emirates against Whitburn, he didn't bowl as Whitburn made 219 for 7 declared. The Whitburn openers both made half centuries, Dan Shurben had 65 and Lee Henderson 63. Two players who would both go on to good NEPL careers were among Durham's bowlers that day, Callum Harding had 2 for 52 and Liam Trevaskis had 2 for 41.

When The Academy batted, they lost both openers and their number four batsmen first ball, all to Kieran Waterson, they were 5 for 3. Stokes had come in at the fall of the first wicket, batting at number three, he and the wonderfully named Asher Hale-Bopp Joseph Arthur Hart, took the score to 149 before Hart fell for 34. Stokes would go on to make 107 from 108 balls, he hit 11 fours and 6 sixes. He was the fifth wicket to fall, bowled by Ian Elliot with the score on 160. The Academy were bowled out for 215, Waterson had 5 for 48 as Whitburn won by 4 runs.

Stokes had played 51 matches in the NEPL, all for Durham Academy, he batted 46 times with 5 not outs, he scored 1608 runs at an average of 39.21. He scored 6 half centuries and 3 centuries. His highest NEPL score was 142 on 25th April 2009 at Sunderland. This innings came from 136 balls and contained 19 fours and 5 sixes. He also took 1 for 11 that day!

As a bowler in the NEPL, Stokes bowled 673 balls, with 18 maidens, conceding 419 runs and taking 16 wickets at an average of 26.18. His best bowling figures were 2 for 10, on 16th May 2009 at Maiden Castle against Tynemouth. He also took 22 catches.

The 2008 Banks Salver was shared between Chester le Street and The Durham Academy and Stockton's Richard Waite picked up his third NEPL Player of the Year award.

Waite had played 20 matches in the NEPL in 2008, batting 18 times with 3 not outs, he scored 415 runs at an average of 27.66. He scored 2 half centuries and 1 century, 106 not out, scored on 26th July 2008 at Newcastle.

He also bowled 813 balls in the NEPL in 2008, with 40 maidens, conceding 351 runs and taking 28 wickets at an average of 12.53. His best bowling figures were 4 for 8, taken on 28th June 2008 at Norton. He took 8 catches in the 2008 NEPL season.

TABLE 29   NEPL 2008.

	Played	Won	Draw/Aban	Lost	Penalty Points	Bonus Points	Points
South North	22	12	9	1	0	151	384
South Shields	22	9	9	4	0	146	322
Chester le Street	22	8	12	4	0	129	295
Sunderland	22	7	9	6	0	117	271
Blaydon	22	5	15	2	0	106	260
Durham CA	22	5	15	5	0	121	254
Stockton	22	7	8	7	0	94	241
Norton	22	4	14	4	0	107	239
Gateshead Fell	22	6	9	7	1	98	228
Tynemouth	22	6	7	9	0	100	225
Benwell Hill	22	2	10	10	2	79	151
Newcastle	22	1	8	13	0	83	138

TABLE 30   NEPL Batting Averages 2008.
Qualification 300 Runs.

29 Batsmen Qualified this season.

Player	Club	Inns	N. O	H. S	Runs	Average
(1) M.D Stoneman	Newcastle	6	0	147	388	64.66
(2) M. Bekker	Gateshead Fell	17	5	114 no	700	58.33
(3) A. Worthy	Blaydon	16	4	101 no	590	49.16
(4) A.L Smith	Durham Academy	19	2	158	787	46.29
(5) G.I Cullen	South Shields	19	5	100 no	637	45.50
(6) P.B Muchall	South Shields	20	4	103 no	720	45.00
(7) R. Evans	Newcastle	12	2	130	396	39.60
(8) A.M Thorpe	Sunderland	14	2	105	464	38.66
(9) M.T Drake	Blaydon	15	3	61 no	462	38.50
(10) G.J Muchall	Newcastle	8	2	138 no	231	38.50
(11) C.J Hewison	South North	16	4	120 no	460	38.33
(12) U. Mahomed	Benwell Hill	15	1	118 no	533	38.07
(13) J.N Miller	South North	12	3	72	329	36.55
(14) B. Ford	South North	10	3	79	251	35.85
(23) J.A Graham	South North	17	1	106	469	29.31
(24) N. Peng	South North	13	13	107 no	349	29.08

TABLE 31   NEPL Bowling Averages 2008.
43 Bowlers Qualified this season.

Player	Club	Balls	Mdns	Runs	Wkts	Average
(1) B. Ford	South North	298	12	133	16	8.31
(2) S. Humble	South North	1219	61	413	46	8.97
(3) L. Evans	Chester Le Street	698	22	322	27	11.92
(4) Shahid Nazir	Sunderland	524	23	220	18	12.22
(5) L.J Crozier	South North	1435	76	505	41	12.31
(6) R.P Waite	Stockton	813	40	351	28	12.53
(7) M.J Muchall	South Shields	1139	51	554	44	12.59
(8) B. Stewart	Tynemouth	925	39	435	32	13.59
(9) J.J Kean	Norton	1157	35	603	43	14.02
(10) M. Akram	Sunderland	567	32	231	16	14.43
(11) R.M Brook	South North	650	24	334	22	15.18
(12) B.C Adams	Stockton	803	33	324	21	15.42
(15) C. Smith	South North	709	27	368	22	16.72

South North 2008 NEPL Champions.

Left to Right – Back Row- Dan Jaques (Sponsor), James Miller, Lee Crozier, John Graham, Adam Heather, Chris Hewison, Richard Brook, Stephen Humble, Frank Jaques (Sponsor).

Front Row- Adam Cragg, Craig Smith, John Harbottle, Brendan Ford, Neil Corby Absent Nicky Peng.

Adam Heather, batting on 13th September 2017.

Photo Courtesy of Ken Waller.

CHAPTER FIVE

Chester le Street 2009-2010

The League had a new sponsor in 2009, it was now to be known as The Dukes North East Premier League. Chester le Street had finished third in the 2008 season, South North winning their six title in a row. It seems Chester's response was to make a few changes from the side which had played the last game of the 2008 season, Simon Birtwisle, Tony Birbeck, Quentin Hughes, John Coxon, Liam Simpson and wicketkeeper David Wilson the players retaining their place in the side for the first game of 2009 and Quentin Hughes was to be captain.

Alan Mustard was brought in from Sunderland, Luke Evans, who had played for Chester le Street previously before playing for The Durham Academy and then first-class cricket for Durham, returned to Chester le Street, Richard Waite, who was the NEPL Player of the Year in 2003, 2004 and 2008 whilst at Stockton, was another new face and they also had engaged Andrew Tye, an Australian, as overseas pro. Andrew Bell and Liam Simpson had both missed the last game of 2008 but were available for the 2009 season opener.

Simon Birtwisle says that the attitude of the team was that "we should impose our will on the opposition, to go hard at them, make things happen."

Chester le Street opened their 2009 campaign at Tynemouth on 25th April. Chester batted first and scored 242 for 8 declared from 58 overs. Richard Waite, making his Chester debut after nine years at Stockton had 80 and overseas pro Andrew Tye, 39. When Tynemouth batted, they never really looked like chasing the score down but did succeed in batting for 55.5 overs to make 143 all out. Liam Simpson had been the key bowler with figures of 10.5 overs, 5 maidens, conceding 28 runs but picking up 6 wickets.

The Chester le Street side that day was as follows-

John Coxon opened the batting today; he was a right-handed batsman and right arm medium fast bowler. Coxon was just a youngster coming through at this point in his career, he normally batted a bit lower down, Simon Birtwisle, the normal opener missed this game, he says "possibly through a bad back!"

Birtwisle recalls that Coxon was "a good fit in the dressing room, he was a stylish batsman, equally good off his legs and driving, now years later he is simply a better version of his young self, he was then and remains so now, an accomplished cricketer."

Coxon had first come to attention on 6th July 2003 representing Durham Under 17's against Scotland at Edinburgh in a 50 over match. Scotland had batted first, scoring 165 all out in 46.3 overs. Coxon, the most effective bowler, had 2 for 18. When Durham batted, future England opener Mark Stoneman had 11, future NEPL title winning captain Kevin Ward was also in the side, making 6, and Coxon, batting at five, scored 14. Durham were 103 all out, Scotland winning by 63 runs.

Coxon made his NEPL debut for Chester on 23rd August 2003 at home to Philadelphia, he batted at five, scoring 11.

Coming in to the 2009 season Coxon had played 96 NEPL matches, all for Chester, with 85 innings, 8 not outs, scoring 1449 runs at an average of 18.81, he also had 7 half centuries and 1 century, 112, achieved on 8th August 2008 at Stockton.

He had also bowled 454 balls, 11 maidens, conceding 261 runs and taking 11 wickets at an average of 23.72. His best bowling figures were 5 for 36 on 30th August 2008 at home to South North. He had taken 34 NEPL catches at this point.

Coxon played 11 matches in the NEPL in 2009, batting 10 times with 1 not out, he scored 230 runs at an average of 25.55. He scored 1 century, 112, made on 8th August 2009 at Stockton. The innings came from 154 balls and contained 17 fours. He didn't bowl in the NEPL in 2009 but did take 11 catches in the NEPL. An update on Coxon's career will appear later in this book.

Alan Mustard also opened the batting today, scoring 21, he was a right-handed batsman and right arm off break bowler. He was also the brother of Durham and England wicketkeeper, Phil Mustard and cousin to Durham bowler, Chris Rushworth.

Simon Birtwisle recalls that Mustard was "a good opening bat, he liked to play off the front foot, he liked to drive in particular, he was a fast scorer."

Mustard had appeared for the Durham Coast League representative side on 25th June 2000 in a 45 over match against The North Yorkshire and South Durham League. He top scored with 79 in a losing cause.

This was his first season away from Sunderland in the NEPL, all his NEPL stats at this point therefore came from Sunderland. He had made his NEPL debut for Sunderland on 27th April 2002 at home to Stockton, taking 1 for 48 and scoring 48 in a drawn game.

Prior to the start of the 2009 season Mustard had played 130 matches, batting 121 times, with 14 not outs, scoring 2979 runs at an average of 27.84, he had 16 half centuries and a high score of 88. That high score came on 20th August 2005 at South North.

He had also bowled 663 balls, 11 maidens, conceding 494 runs and taking 22 wickets at an average of 22.45 and a best bowling of 6 for 69 against Blaydon on 26th August 2006. He had taken 58 catches and 1 stumping.

Mustard would continue to play for Chester in the NEPL until 8th September 2012, his last NEPL game being at home to Stockton. He didn't bat but took 3 for 13 with the ball. His last game for the club came the next day, Sunday 9th September 2012 in The Just Sport Trophy Final at Benwell Hill against Tynemouth. He took 1 for 50 but didn't bat as Quentin Hughes made 100 not out as Chester won by 6 wickets.

He had played 56 NEPL matches for Chester, batting 52 times, with 7 not outs, he had scored 1087 runs at an average of 24.15. He had scored 5 half centuries and 1 century, 121 not out, was made on 22nd August 2009 at Norton.

He bowled 118 balls in the NEPL for them, with 3 maidens, conceding 67 runs and taking 6 wickets at an average of 11.16. His best bowling figures were 3 for 13 in his last NEPL match for the club, as mentioned above. He took 15 NEPL catches for Chester.

Mustard made his debut for Hylton in The Durham Cricket League Division 1 on 27th April 2013and he played his last league game for them on 5th September 2015 at home to Dawdon Welfare.

He then made his debut on 30th April 2016 for Bill Quay at Philadelphia again in The Durham Cricket League Division 1, his last appearance in the league on 10th September 2016.

Mustard next appeared in the NEPL on 17th April 2021 for Felling at Washington. He didn't get the opportunity to bat or bowl as Felling won by 8 wickets as he was listed to come in at number five.

His latest Felling appearance coming on 9th September 2023 at home to Newcastle, although he has now played in the 2024 season.

At the time of writing, as we approach the 2024 season, Mustard had played a further 60 NEPL matches for the club, batting 55 times, with 5 not outs, he had scored 1140 runs at an average of 22.80. He has had 6 half centuries. His highest score for Felling, 95 not out, came on 11th September 2021 at home to Eppleton.

He has bowled 127 balls for Felling, with 1 maiden, he has conceded 139 runs and taken 4 wickets at an average of 34.75. His best bowling figures were 2 for 11. He had taken 22 catches.

In total, across his time with Sunderland, Chester le Street and Felling, Mustard won two NEPL title's in 2009 and 2010 with Chester le Street. He also won the National Club Championship with Chester in 2009.

He had played 246 NEPL matches, batting 228 times, with 26 not outs, he has scored 5206 runs at an average of 25.77. He scored 27 half centuries and 1 century, 121 not out, for Chester against Norton in 2009, remains his highest score.

He has bowled 908 balls, with 15 maidens, conceding 700 runs and taking 32 wickets at an average of 21.87. His best bowling figures remain the 6 for 69 for Sunderland in 2006. He has taken 95 catches and 1 NEPL stumping.

Alan Mustard played 17 matches in the NEPL in 2009, batting 17 times with 2 not outs, he scored 584 runs at an average of 38.93. He scored 3 half centuries and 1 century. The century, 121 not out, was scored on 22nd August 2009 at Norton. He didn't bowl in the NEPL in 2009 but did take 7 catches in the league.

Andrew Smith was a right-handed batsman, he batted at three today, scoring 9. He also bowled four overs, taking 1 for 5. Simon Birtwisle recalls that in his opinion Andrew Smith was "one of the best bats The NEPL has seen, he is so destructive, you simply can't bowl to him on his day, I've seen him hit the first ball of an innings for six on numerous occasions, he likes to take the spinners on, one of the very few I've seen take the very best of spinners down, although he prefers the front foot to the back, he could and did certainly play off the back foot. He was very loyal to Chester le Street, I'm sure he had offers, good offers, to go elsewhere but he chose to remain at Chester."

Smith first came to notice as an Under 13, playing for Durham against Scotland Under 13's on 10th July 2002. He made this 56 in this game and a further 53 not out in a second game against Scotland on 17th July 2002. He progressed to Under 15 level for Durham, playing a game on 17th June 2003 against Lancashire Under 15's. He opened the batting and made 9. Karl Turner top scored with 70 in the same innings.

On 25th April 2004 he played in a 50 over match for Durham Academy against Northern Universities Student Club Community Cricketers Elite at Maiden Castle. He made 20.

On 7th July 2004 Smith played for Durham Under 17's against Scotland at Longhirst in a 50 over match. He scored 8.

Smith made his NEPL debut for Chester le Street on 15th May 2004 at home to Gateshead Fell. He took 0 for 47 and scored 7.

He scored his first half NEPL half century and took his first NEPL wicket in the same game, for Chester le Street away at Newcastle on 14th May 2005. He scored 68 not out, batting at number eight, Dan Shurben had 83 in the same innings as Chester scored 254 for 8 declared. His first NEPL wicket was a good one, Andrew Pratt bowled for 23, as he finished with 3 for 26.

His last appearance for Chester in this spell came on 3rd September 2005 at Philadelphia. Dan Shurben made 109 as Chester scored 242 for 8 declared, Smith scored 10. Philadelphia were bowled out for 182, Quentin Hughes had 5 for 16, Smith had 0 for 10.

He had played 30 NEPL matches for Chester, batting 25 times with 5 not outs, he scored 442 runs at an average of 22.10. He had 1 half century and 1 century, 100 not out on 27th August 2005 at Norton.

He had bowled 307 balls with 3 maidens, he conceded 212 runs and took 6 wickets at an average of 35.33. His best bowling was the 3 for 26 mentioned earlier. He had taken 8 catches.

Smith then entered a new chapter in the NEPL as he played for The Durham Academy for three seasons, making his Academy debut on 29th April 2006 at Longhirst against Hetton Lyons, he scored 3 batting at three.

He scored his first half century for The Academy in just his second innings for them, 57, on 6th May 2006 at Maiden Castle against Newcastle.

He played his first game for Durham Second XI against Scotland A on 3rd May 2006 at Edinburgh. Durham batted first and Smith, batting at three, made 120, his innings took 99 balls and contained 14 fours and 3 sixes.

Andrew Smith would go on to play 21 times for Durham Second XI, he batted 25 times with 1 not out, he scored 683 runs at an average of 28.45. He scored 2 half centuries and 2 centuries. His highest score was the 120 mentioned earlier.

He bowled 48 balls, with 2 maidens, conceding 35 but failed to take a wicket. He also took 8 catches.

He took his first wicket for The Academy on 28th May 2007 at Gateshead Fell, Will Gidman caught by Richard Coughtrie for 11.

His last NEPL appearance for The Academy came on 30th August 2008 at Maiden Castle against Blaydon. He top scored with 61 in a side which contained Ben Stokes and Mark Wood.

Smith had played 60 matches in the NEPL for The Academy, he batted 56 times, with 7 not outs, he scored 1842 runs at an average of 37.59. He scored 13 half centuries and 3 centuries. His highest score was 158, which came on 10th May 2008 at The Riverside against Newcastle. Mark Stoneman had scored 130 when Newcastle batted and they posted 308 for 6 declared, largely due to Smith, The Academy chased it down in 50.1 overs to win by 5 wickets.

He had bowled 300 balls for them, with 8 maidens, conceding 171 runs and taking 7 wickets at an average of 24.42. His best bowling for The Academy was 3 for 29 on 27th August 2007 at Ropery Lane against Chester le Street. He also made 27 career catches in the NEPL for The Academy.

Prior to the start of the 2009 season Smith had played 90 NEPL matches, batting 81 times, with 12 not outs, scoring 2284 runs at an average of 33.10, he had 14 half centuries and 4 centuries. His highest NEPL score was the 158 mentioned earlier.

He had also bowled 607 balls, 11 maidens, conceding 383 runs and taking 13 wickets at an average of 29.46 and a best bowling of 3 for 26 against Newcastle for Chester le Street on 14th May 2005. He had taken 35 catches.

Smith played 20 matches in the NEPL for Chester le Street as they won the 2009 title, he batted 20 times, with 4 not outs, he scored 825 runs at an average of 51.56. He scored 6 half centuries and 1 century, 106 not out, scored on 16th May 2009 at home to Newcastle.

He also bowled 350 balls in the NEPL in 2009, with 13 maidens, conceding 166 runs and taking 13 wickets at an average of 12.76. His best bowling figures were 3 for 18, taken on 1st August 2009 at Newcastle. He took 7 catches in the NEPL in 2009.

Richard Waite he was a right-handed batsman and right arm off break bowler, he batted at four today, scoring 80, he also bowled eight overs, taking 0 for 20. His history up until this point was all achieved whilst at Stockton CC.

Simon Birtwisle describes Waite as "a very good cricketer, he could, and did, win games with bat or ball, he was good enough at both disciplines to be that match winner with either, as a batsman he was very good both straight or at facing short bowling in equal measure, despite all his achievements I still feel he was an under-rated spinner."

Waite first came to note in an Under 15 match for Cleveland against Scotland on 26th July 1995 at Ampleforth. Scotland batted first, scoring 181 for 7 from their 50 overs. Waite wasn't required to bowl. He did, however, bat at three, scoring a creditable 41, which included seven boundaries. Marc Symington was the one who really caught the eye that day, 75 not out, including ten boundaries as Cleveland won with over eight overs to spare.

He got a cricket scholarship to Worcester University, this led to him playing a game for Worcestershire Seconds against Durham Seconds at Hartlepool.

Waite next appeared on the radar a couple of times in 1999. On 17th May he played in the National Club Championship 45 over game for Stockton at Tynemouth. Waite opened the batting, top scoring with 47, as Stockton made 88 for 5 as rain cut their allotted overs to 20. Opener Barry Stewart, 32 not out, saw Tynemouth home for the loss of 2 wickets. Waite did bowl, 0 for 23 from an unspecified number of overs.

He featured for Durham Second XI against Surrey Second XI in a three day Second XI Championship game starting on 9th August 1999 at South Shields. It was a strong Durham side, featuring several future NEPL players, Michael Gough, Simon Birtwisle, Quentin Hughes, Andrew Pratt, Gordon Muchall and Graeme Bridge. Surrey's side contained Michael Carberry, Gareth Batty and Tim Murtagh. Waite batted at six, scoring 8, Simon Birtwisle top scored with 52 as Durham were dismissed for 162 in their first innings. Gary Butcher, younger brother of Mark Butcher, who would also go on to play first class cricket for Glamorgan and Surrey, was the pick of the bowlers, 4 for 48. When Surrey batted, they scored 229 all out, Gareth Batty top scoring with 59. Batty was a future England Test Cricketer. Waite didn't get a bowl, Graeme Bridge taking 6 for 50 was the best of the bowlers. Bridge would go on to an excellent first-class career with Durham and appear for several NEPL teams over the years, Norton, Stockton, Chester le Street, Blaydon, Sacriston and Burnmoor to be exact, more of him later! Waite scored 10 in Durham's second innings as they struggled to 150 all out, despite 76 from Andrew Pratt. Butcher took 4 for 46 to give him eight for the match. Kim Barnett 45 not out, and Michael Carberry 37 not out, saw Surrey home by ten wickets.

Barnett went on to play Minor Counties cricket with Devon, Carberry to play first class cricket for Surrey, Kent, Hampshire and Leicestershire and make six test appearances for England.

Richard Waite made his NEPL debut on 29th April 2000 for Stockton at South North, batting at three he scored 8 as Stockton declared on 118 for 9 after batting first. Long serving South North and Northumberland bowler Nigel Campbell taking 5 for 27. When South North batted, they got the required runs for the loss of 5 wickets, Chris Hewison seeing them home with 49 not out. Waite didn't get a bowl.

He didn't have to wait too long for his first NEPL wicket, on 13th May 2000 he had Tim Hughes of Durham Academy, caught by Hilton Wordsworth for a single.

On 29th May 2000 Waite scored his first NEPL half century, 53 against Newcastle although he had to wait for his first century, 104, coming a year later on 26th May 2001 at home to Tynemouth.

On 9th August 2001 Waite made his Minor Counties debut for The Durham Cricket Board at home to Norfolk. The game was played at Hartlepool. Durham fielded a strong side with NEPL connections, ten of the eleven playing in the league at some point. Despite batting at eight, Waite top scored in the Durham innings with 81 not out, Quentin Hughes with 33, the only other player in double figures, as Durham made 185 for 9 from their 50 overs. Norfolk lost just three wickets as they won comfortably with three overs to spare, Waite had 0 for 12 from three overs.

Waite played 8 times for the Durham Cricket Board between 2001 and 2003, he batted 8 times with 1 not out, scoring 216 runs at an average of 30.85, He scored one half century, the 81 not out on debut being his highest score.

He bowled 211 balls for The Durham Cricket Board, with 1 maiden, conceding 179 runs and taking 5 wickets at an average of 35.79 and best of 2 for 35.

Waite was selected for Durham Second XI for a three-day game with Yorkshire Second XI at Darlington starting on 5th September 2001. The NEPL was once again strongly represented, Dan Shurben, Ashley Thorpe, Gordon Muchall, Marc Symington just some of the players playing alongside Waite. Tim Bresnan, who would go on to play first class cricket for Yorkshire and test cricket for England, was the most notable name on the Yorkshire side. Durham batted first 139 from Thorpe, 101 from Muchall and 69 Hiran Marambe saw Durham post 410 for 5 declared, Waite made a single. When Yorkshire batted Joseph Sayers scored 149 not out as they responded with 333 for 7 declared, Waite bowling eight overs 0 for 43. Waite did not bat in the Durham second innings, Ashley Thorpe again top scoring with 85, as Durham made 199 for 6 declared. When Yorkshire batted again, they scored 219 for 8 wickets as the match was drawn. Waite bowled 22.5 overs, had 7 maidens and took 5 wickets for 50 runs.

On 27th June 2004 Waite made his Minor Counties debut for Cumberland against Cambridgeshire in a 3-day match at Barrow In Furness. The visitors batted first, scoring 248 all out Waite taking 1 for 57. When Cumberland batted, Waite batted at three and top scored with 51 as his side were dismissed for 201. Cambridgeshire 249 for 8 declared in the second innings, Waite 1 for 78.

Waite had 19 as Graham Lloyd, son of Lancashire, England and broadcast legend, amongst other things, David "Bumble" Lloyd, had 90 not out in a drawn match. Graham Lloyd would go on to play six one day internationals for England and a decent career with Lancashire.

Waite would play 14 matches for Cumberland, batting 24 times with 0 not outs, he scored 369 runs at an average of 15.37 and a high score of 51.

He bowled 1176 balls for them, with 35 maidens, conceding 788 runs and taking 15 wickets at an average of 52.53.

He picked up NEPL player of the Year awards four times leading up to the start of the 2013 season, the first three of which, 2003, 2004 and 2008, were whilst playing for Stockton, the fourth was for this season with Chester Le Street.

In 2003 Waite had played in 21 NEPL matches for Stockton, batting 21 times, 0 not outs, as he scored 919 runs at an average of 43.76, with 7 half centuries and 1 century, 102, against Tynemouth at Stockton on 14th June 2003.

He also bowled 1707 balls in The NEPL in 2003, including 65 maidens, conceding 867 runs and taking 43 wickets, at an average of 20.16, his best bowling of the season was 6 for 30, on 10th May 2003 at Norton. He also took 3 catches in the 2003 season.

In 2004 Waite had played in 19 NEPL matches for Stockton, batting 19 times, with 1 not out, as he scored 779 runs at an average of 43.27, with 4 half centuries and 3 centuries, his highest score was 107 against Philadelphia at Stockton on 24th April 2004 in the season opener.

He added two further centuries in 2004, 101 at home to Tynemouth on 29th May and 101 away at Gateshead Fell on 12th June.

He also bowled 1538 balls in The NEPL in 2004, including 41 maidens, conceding 842 runs and taking 34 wickets, at an average of 24.76. His best bowling of the season was 4 for 23 on 14th August 2004 at home to Norton. He also took 7 catches in the 2004 season.

In 2008 Waite had played in 20 NEPL matches for Stockton, batting 18 times, with 3 not outs, as he scored 4159 runs at an average of 27.66, with 2 half centuries and 1 century, 106 not out, against Newcastle at Jesmond on 26th July 2008.

He also bowled 813 balls in The NEPL in 2008, including 40 maidens, conceding 351 runs and taking 28 wickets, at an average of 12.53, his best bowling of the season was 4 for 8 at Norton on 28th June 2008. He also took 8 catches in the 2008 season.

Waite's career record going into the 2009 season with Chester Le Street was impressive to say the least, he had played 171 matches, all for Stockton, with 166 innings, scoring 4453 runs at an average of 28.91 and a high score of 135 on 23rd July 2005 at home to Sunderland, with 24 half centuries and 9 centuries.

He had also bowled 12340 balls, with 418 maidens, conceding 6545 runs and taking 294 wickets at an average of 22.26 and a best bowling of 8 for 28 on 10th June 2006 at home to Benwell Hill, 20-6-28-8. He also had 56 NEPL career catches at this point.

Waite played 19 matches in the NEPL in 2009, batting 17 times with 0 not outs, he scored 513 runs at an average of 30.17. He scored 4 half centuries, with a highest score of 82, made on 2nd May 2009 at home to Benwell Hill.

He bowled 1069 balls in the NEPL in 2009, with 61 maidens, he conceded 389 runs and took 36 wickets at an average of 10.80. His best bowling figures were 7 for 13, taken on 8th August 2009 at Stockton. He also took 7 catches in the NEPL in 2009. More of Waite to come later in the book.

Quentin Hughes batted at five today, scoring 20, he also bowled five overs, taking 1 for 27. Simon Birtwisle recalls of Hughes that "he is the man you want for a crisis, he is such a competitor, the sort of batsman that the longer he stays at the crease the more his team's chances of winning increase by multiples, as a batsman he seems to score in unusual areas at times, making him absolutely horrible to bowl at, as a captain he was a great thinker."

Th last career update I did for Hughes was up to the start of the 2001 season, going into the 2009 season, Hughes had now played 143 matches in the NEPL, he had batted 136 times, with 30 not outs, he had scored 4323 runs at an average of 40.78, with 28 half centuries and 4 centuries, his highest score was 136 not out on 9th July 2005 at home to Benwell Hill.

Hughes had delivered 4467 balls in the NEPL, with 135 maidens, conceding 2344 runs and taking 111 wickets at an average 21.11. His best bowling figures were 5 for 16 on 3rd September 2005 at Philadelphia. He had taken 55 NEPL catches.

Away from The NEPL Hughes had also been playing regularly for The Durham Cricket Board and The England Board XI. After making his debut in June 2000 for The Durham Board, Hughes played his last game for them on 21st June 2005 at Gateshead against Durham. Hughes didn't bowl when Durham batted, a strong Durham side were held to 127 for 7 from their 20 overs. Scott Kay led the response from The Board XI, making 40, Hughes scored 22 not out as his team won by 7 wickets.

In total Hughes played 16 matches for The Durham Cricket Board, batting 16 times, with 2 not outs, he scored 505 runs at an average of 36.07, with 4 half centuries. His highest score was 87 on 19th July 2000 at Cheshire.

He bowled 162 balls, with 1 maiden, conceding 109 runs and taking 4 wickets at an average of 27.25, his best bowling figures were 3 for 45 on 19th July 2001 at Darlington against Lincolnshire. He took 5 catches for them.

On 26th June 2002 he played for The England Board against the M.C.C. at The Dennis Compton Oval. He didn't bowl but opened the batting, making 54 not out as his side won by 9 wickets.

On 20th July 2002 Hughes played for The England and Wales Cricket Board against Scotland at Sandy Bay, Larne, Ireland. He opened the batting, making 56 before he was run out. He didn't bowl but his side squeezed home by 2 runs. His last match for The England and Wales Cricket Board came on 23rd July 2004 against Scotland in the wonderfully named Sportpark, Maarschalkerweerd, Utrecht, Holland. Hughes again opened the innings, top scoring with 58. Once again, he didn't bowl but his side won by 24 runs.

Hughes played 9 matches for The England and Wales Cricket Board, batting 9 times with 1 not out, he scored 398 runs at an average of 49.75. He scored 5 half centuries with a highest score of 70 on 10th July 2003 against Wales. He never bowled for them but took 2 catches.

On 27th July 2003 Hughes made his debut for Cumberland in a 3-day match at home to Hertfordshire at Carlisle. He took 4 for 53 in the first innings and 2 for 53 in the second innings and scored 26 in the one innings when he batted. The match was drawn.

He would play only twice more for Cumberland. The second match was a 3-day match against Northumberland on 3rd August 2003 at Jesmond. Hughes took 1 for 34 and 2 for 22 and made 1 and 17. Ashley Metcalfe scored 172 in the first innings, setting up a Cumberland win by 5 wickets. His third and final game for Cumberland came on 31st August 2003 at Edinburgh against Scotland. Hughes failed to score and took 1 for 53.

He batted 4 times for the county, with 0 not outs, he scored 44 runs at an average of 11.00 and a high score of 26.

He bowled 432 balls, with 23 maidens, conceding 215 runs and taking 10 wickets at an average of 21.50. His best bowling was 4 for 53.

Quentin Hughes played 17 matches in the NEPL in 2009, batting 15 times with 4 not outs, he scored 343 runs at an average of 31.18. He scored 2 half centuries with a highest score of 74 not out, made on 9th May 2009 at Blaydon.

He bowled 535 balls in the NEPL in 2009, with 26 maidens, he conceded 229 runs and took 23 wickets at an average of 9.95. His best bowling figures were 4 for 18, taken on 27th June 2009 at Chester le Street. He took 5 catches in the NEPL in 2009.

Tony Birbeck batted at six today being run out for 26. After captaining Chester le Street to The NEPL title in 2001 Birbeck continued to play for Chester first XI. Entering the 2009 season he had now played 126 NEPL matches, he had batted 90 times, with 21 not outs, scoring 1554 runs at an average of 22.52. He had scored 6 half centuries with a highest score of 90 not out on 14th July 2007 at home to South Shields.

He had also bowled 176 balls, with 6 maidens, conceding 103 runs and taking 7 wickets at an average of 14.71. His best bowling was 2 for 0 on 14th July 2007 at home to South Shields. He had taken 32 NEPL catches and had 4 stumpings.

He was a regular in the Chester side up to and including 2014, his last game of that season came on 23rd August 2014 at Sunderland. He did play once more for the firsts, on 20th May 2017 at home to South North.

His NEPL career so far, had encompassed 144 matches, batting 103 times, with 23 not out's, he had scored 1715 runs at an average of 21.43. He had scored 6 half centuries with the highest score of 90 not out mentioned earlier.

He had bowled 176 balls in the NEPL, with 6 maidens, conceding 103 runs and taking 7 wickets ay an average of 14.71. His best bowling figures were 2 for 0 on 14th July 2007 at home to South Shields. He had taken 33 catches and had 4 stumpings.

He continued to play for Chester Second XI and on 8th August 2021 he made his debut for Durham Over 50's at Bedfordshire.

He has now played 10 matches for the seniors, that includes the Over 60's as well, batting 10 times with 0 not outs, he has scored 136 runs at an average of 13.60. His highest score is 29. He has yet to bowl for them but has taken 2 catches.

On 5th August 2022 Tony Birbeck made his debut for England Over 60's against Wales at Dumbleton, Worcestershire. He opened the innings and scored a remarkable 151, the innings came from 119 balls and contained 25 fours and 1 six.

Unsurprisingly he was selected again for the side, playing another match on 25th May 2023 against England Over 60 Trialists, he made 20 on this occasion.

During the 2009 title winning season Birbeck played 12 matches in the NEPL, batting 10 times with 2 not outs, he scored 129 runs at an average of 16.12. His highest score of the season was 30, made on 27th June 2009 at home to South Shields. He also took 1 catch in the league in 2009.

Liam Simpson batted at seven today, making a single, as a bowler he had a much better day, bowling ten overs and five balls and taking 6 for 28. Simon Birtwisle recalls that "Simpson was a right arm opening bowler, he was a strong lad with a bustling action, he hit the bat hard. As a batsman he could whack it, he was powerful with the bat, he liked to play his shots and hit it straight, he was a very strong player off his legs and a good cutter. He was a genuine all-rounder. He still plays at Chester."

Simpson had made his NEPL debut on 7th July 2001 at Tynemouth for Chester le Street, he didn't bat or bowl.

He made his NEPL debut for The Durham Academy on 27th April 2002 at South North, Liam Plunkett was also in The Academy side that day. Simpson scored 12 but didn't bowl. He had to wait until 3rd June 2002 in a game at The Riverside for The Durham Academy to take his wicket, Stockton batsman Andrew Bowman caught by Mark Turner for 21.

His last appearance in the NEPL for The Academy came on 14th August 2004 at The Racecourse Ground against Gateshead Fell. He had played 45 matches in the league for The Academy, batting 30 times, with 7 not outs, scoring 280 runs at an average of 12.17. He scored 2 half centuries with a highest score, 63 not out, scored on 24th April 2004 at Newcastle.

He had bowled 294 balls, with 7 maidens, conceding 182 runs and taking 7 wickets at an average of 26.00. His best bowling figures was 3 for 41 on 1st May 2004 at The Riverside against Stockton. He had taken 15 catches.

Simpson resumed his Chester career on 30th April 2005 at Benwell Hill.

He was selected for Northumberland in 2006, making his debut in a 3-day match starting on 9th July at Bedfordshire. He made 19 in his solitary innings and took 1 for 40 and 2 for 33 as Bedfordshire won by 4 wickets.

He played a second game in another 3-day match starting on 23rd July at Hertfordshire, scoring 4 and 40 not out and taking 2 for 32 and 3 for 43 as Northumberland won by 115 runs.

His third and final appearance for the county came in a 3-day match starting on 6th August at Jesmond against Cumberland. He took 1 for 79 and 0 for 42, he also made 7 and 32 when batting in a drawn match.

As he entered the 2009 season, Simpson had played 119 NEPL matches, batting 89 times, with 15 not outs, he had scored 957 runs at an average of 12.93. He had scored 3 half centuries. His highest score was 63 not out on 24th April 2004 at Jesmond for The Durham Academy against Newcastle.

He bowled 3121 balls, with 98 maidens, conceding 1747 runs and taking 71 wickets at an average of 24.60. His best bowling was 5 for 25, taken for Chester le Street at home to Blaydon on 21st May 2005. He had taken 36 catches.

During the 2009 season, Simpson played 19 matches in the NEPL, batting 15 time with 6 not outs, he scored 237 runs at an average of 26.33. He scored 1 half century, 58 not out, made on 29th August 2009 at home to Chester le Street.

He bowled 737 balls in the NEPL in 2009, with 23 maidens, conceding 411 runs and taking 21 wickets at an average of 19.57. His best bowling figures were 6 for 28, taken in the season opener and mentioned earlier. He also took 4 catches in the NEPL in 2009.

Whilst looking at Liam Simpson the name of Liam Plunkett cropped up, as is the way of this book, if a future England player appears, I will have a quick look at his NEPL career.

Plunkett made his NEPL debut for The Durham Academy on 28th April 2001 at Benwell Hill, he scored 18, batting at four, he was caught by Joe Thompson off the bowling of Lee Crozier. He opened the bowling, 0 for 22 from six overs as Hill won by 9 wickets. John Windows had 67 not out.

He had to wait until 19th May 2001 for his first NEPL wicket, Adam Heather, bowled for 18 for The Academy at The Racecourse Ground against South North.

Plunkett's last NEPL appearance 30th May 2011 at Tynemouth, he took 5 for 46, his last NEPL wicket was Barry Stewart caught by Ben Raine for 15.

Plunkett had played 41 NEPL matches, all for The Academy, batting 32 times, with 4 not outs, he scored 618 runs at an average of 22.07, He scored 2 half centuries and 1 century, 116, in his last appearance against Tynemouth mentioned earlier.

He had also bowled 2044 balls, with 48 maidens, conceding 1112 runs and taking 51 wickets at an average of 21.80. His best bowling figures were 5 for 20 on 26th May 2003 at Maiden Castle against Norton. He also took 10 NEPL catches.

Plunkett would go on to play 13 Test Matches, 89 One Day Internationals and 22 T20 games for England.

As well as playing first-class cricket for Durham, Yorkshire, England Lions and Surrey, he was widely acknowledged as being an integral part of the England side which won the 50 over World Cup on 14th July 2019 at Lord's.

Andrew Tye was a right-handed batsman and right arm fast opening bowler, he was the club overseas pro this season and batted at eight today, scoring 39. He also opened the bowling, nine overs, 0 for 16. He had come to the Northeast from playing Perth First Grade cricket for Scarborough in Australia.

Simon Birtwisle remembers Tye as "more of a bowler than a batsman, he was certainly quick enough for league cricket, he came over here as little more than a kid, although a potential game winner, he was still young and raw at this point in time with us, he still needed time to develop in cricket terms, I think he trialled around a bit, but later in his career, Justin Langer got hold of him, he got him fit to start with and then Tye developed a knuckle ball and became a twenty over specialist. As a batsman he was a bit of a slogger back then."

Tye first played for Chester le Street in 2007, making his debut on 28th April at home to Newcastle, he made 2 when he batted and took 4 for 53 when he bowled.

Going into the 2009 season Tye had played 15 NEPL matches, batting 15 times with 2 not out's, he had scored 277 runs at an average of 21.30. He had 1 half century, his highest score of 82 not out on 9th June 2007 at home to Sunderland.

He bowled 936 balls, with 21 maidens, conceding 543 runs and taking 22 wickets at an average of 24.68. His best bowling figures were 4 for 50, taken on 8th September 2007 at home to Tynemouth. He had taken 4 NEPL catches.

Tye played 20 matches in the NEPL in 2009, batting 13 times with 5 not outs, he scored 271 runs at an average of 33.87. He scored 1 half century, 65, made on 31st August 2009 at home to Sunderland.

He bowled 882 balls in the NEPL in 2009, with 36 maidens, conceding 428 runs and taking 22 wickets at an average of 19.45. His best bowling figures 3 for 28, taken on 25th July 2009 at home to Blaydon. He took 8 catches in the league that season.

Andrew Bell was a right-handed batsman and right arm medium fast bowler, he batted at nine in the season opener, scoring 21 not out, he also bowled seven overs, 0 for 13. Simon Birtwisle says that Bell, "bowled off the wrong foot, he was medium-fast bowler, outswingers to the right hander, he was a scratch golfer and his batting style and shot selection reflected that, if it was pitched up, he drove it like a golfer, he did struggle a bit with the short stuff."

Bell made his debut for Chester le Street on 17th June 2000 at home to Benwell Hill, he took 0 for 24 and was 4 not out when he batted. He didn't play again for Chester in The NEPL until 26th My 2003 at Tynemouth.

He was a regular leading up to the 2009 season, by the end of 2008 he had played 82 NEPL matches, batting 47 times, with 16 not out's, scoring 356 runs at an average of 11.48. His highest score was 30 not out on 29th July 2006 at Sunderland.

He bowled 3459 balls, with 106 maidens, conceding 2025 runs and taking 86 wickets at an average of 23.54. His best bowling figures was 5 for 52 on 2nd September 2007 at home to Stockton. He had taken 12 catches.

During the 2009 season in the NEPL Bell played 19 matches, batting 10 times with 4 not outs, he scored 91 runs at an average of 15.16. His highest score was 22, made on 31st August 2009 at home to Sunderland.

Bell bowled 666 balls in the NEPL in 2009, with 35 maidens, conceding 280 runs and taking 14 wickets at an average of 20.00. His best bowling figures were 3 for 18, taken on 27th June 2009 at home to South Shields. He took 5 catches in the NEPL in 2009.

Luke Evans batted at ten in the 2009 season opener, making 2 not out, he also took 1 for 30 opening the bowling. As a bowler Simon Birtwisle says that he was "an out and out bowler, he was a bit of a wildcard in some respects, he was very tall, around six foot seven I think, this made him awkward to deal with as a batsman, he was quick, an absolute handful on his day, I remember two spells in particular, one game against Durham Academy when he had a hot spell and another when he blew South North away one day in a National game. He was a nice lad from Sunderland. He was on a Durham contract and would go to Northants later."

Evans first came to the notice of the record keepers playing for The English Schools Cricket Association North Under 15's against their Midlands counterparts at Billericay on 22nd July 2002 as part of The Bunbury Festival.

Adil Rashid and Paul Muchall were in the same side. The North side made it to The Final of the competition, only to lose by just 2 runs to the Midlands side, Evans made 7 not out and took 0 for 27.

Evans made his debut in The NEPL for Chester le Street on 7th September 2002 at Norton, he took 0 for 17 and didn't get to bat.

Evans played for Durham Under 17's against Scotland Under 17's at Edinburgh, he took 2 for 22 and made 6 as Scotland won by 63 runs.

He played only three more times in The NEPL in 2003 before making his debut for The Durham Academy on 22nd May 2004 at Norton. He didn't get a bat but took his first NEPL wicket, opener Nicky Beall caught by Paul Craig for 4.

He was selected to play for Durham Second XI in a 3-day game starting on 16th August 2004 at Stamford Bridge against Yorkshire Seconds. He would continue to play for Durham Seconds up to and including 2007.

He played a total of 83 matches for Durham Seconds, he bowled 7565 balls for them, with 268 maidens, conceding 4452 runs and taking 163 wickets at an average of 27.31. His best bowling figures was 5 for 25 on 29th July 2008 against the M.C.C Universities.

He played his last NEPL game for The Academy on 1st September 2007 at The Racecourse against Stockton and he then returned to play for Chester le Street in the NEPL, his first game of this spell coming on 3rd May 2008 at home to Gateshead Fell.

By the time the 2009 season opener came round, Evans had played 72 NEPL matches, batting 23 times, with 12 not outs, he had scored 88 runs at an average of 8.00. His highest score was 21.

He had bowled 4049 balls, with 139 maidens, conceding 2142 runs and taking 89 wickets at an average of 24.06. His best bowling figures were 6 for 52 on 31st May 2008 at Stockton for Chester. He had taken 9 catches.

His first-class career was restricted to 8 matches, 2 with Durham and 6 with Northants.

He bowled 1075 balls in first class cricket, with 35 maidens, conceding 666 runs and taking 26 wickets at an average of 25.61. His best bowling was 4 for 38 for Northants against Hampshire at The Ageas Bowl in a match starting on 15th August 2012.

He also played 9 List A matches, bowling 240 balls, with 0 maidens, conceding 273 runs and taking 7 wickets at an average of 39.00.

Evans also played 3 Twenty20 matches for Northants, taking a wicket in each.

He played 18 matches in the NEPL in 2009, batting 5 times with 4 not outs, he scored 13 runs at an average of 13.00. He bowled 1210 balls in the NEPL in 2009, with 44 maidens, conceding 597 runs and taking 34 wickets at an average of 17.55. His best bowling figures were 6 for 13, taken on 4th July 2009 at South North. He took 4 catches in the NEPL in 2009.

David Wilson listed to bat at eleven today, didn't get a bat but he did take 2 catches behind the stumps. Wilson was a "carry over" from the Chester side which had played in The Durham Senior League days, Simon Birtwisle says that now Wilson was "an out and out wicketkeeper, he was an old guard style of keeper, he a brilliant keeper, so tidy, as a lower order batsman he was another who would respond to a crisis, he loved competition. A club man through and through, the sort that every club needs and relies on."

Approaching the 2009 season, Wilson had played 118 NEPL matches, all for Chester Le Street.

He had batted 75 times, with 31 not outs, he had scored 666 runs at an average of 15.13. He had scored 1 half century, 60 on 26th May 2001 at home to Benwell Hill. As a wicketkeeper he had taken 126 catches and made 33 stumpings.

He played 20 matches in the NEPL in 2009, he batted just twice and had just one completed innings, as a wicketkeeper he took 24 catches and made 2 stumpings.

Graeme Cessford was a right arm fast bowler, an out and out bowler. Simon Birtwisle remembers him as "fast, express fast, for league cricket at the time, I think he possibly won a speed gun contest at some time, he was picked up by Worcester after playing T20 finals day at Essex. He had come to us from Tynedale." I did indeed find a solitary record of Cessford at Tynedale, on 23rd May 1999 at Percy Main, he scored 3 and took 0 for 1 with the ball.

He next appeared on my radar on 15th August 2002 in a 50 over match for Northumberland Under 19's against Scotland Under 19's at Roseworth Terrace. Kyle Coetzer was in the Scottish side that day. Cessford opened the bowling, 0 for 29 and was run out for 16 when he batted, Scotland won by 91 runs.

The two sides played again the following day, Cessford scoring 3 and taking 1 for 15 as Scotland won by 6 wickets this time.

Cessford made his NEPL debut for Gateshead Fell on 26th April 2003 at Chester le Street, his first NEPL wicket was a good one, Dan Shurben caught by Stewart Hutton for 31 as he finished with 1 for 51. He was 16 not out when he batted, Chester winning by 54 runs.

Cessford played his last NEPL game for Fell on 4th September 2004 at home to Tynemouth.

In total he played 21 matches in The NEPL for Gateshead Fell, batting 12 times, with 2 not outs, he scored 108 runs at an average of 10.80. His highest score was 25.

He also bowled 1058 balls, with 31 maidens, conceding 622 runs and taking 28 wickets at an average of 22.21. His best bowling figures was 5 for 31 on 7th August 2004 at home to Philadelphia. He took 2 catches.

He next appeared in The NEPL on 29th April 2006 for Chester le Street at South North, making 0 not out when his side batted and taking 2 for 27 when they bowled. His first Chester wicket was Jimmy Miller, caught by John Coxon for 18. Cessford played his last NEPL game for Chester on 1st August 2015 at Blaydon, he scored 6 and took 1 for 28.

In total he played 76 matches in The NEPL for Chester le Street, batting 33 times, with 11 not outs, he scored 392 runs at an average of 17.81. He made 1 half century, 67, made on 6th June 2015 at Benwell Hill. He also bowled 3645 balls, with 112 maidens, conceding 2120 runs and taking 85 wickets at an average of 24.94. His best bowling figures were 5 for 53 on 26th August 2006 at home to Hetton Lyons. He took 15 catches.

In his NEPL career Cessford played 97 matches, batting 45 times, with 13 not outs, he scored 500 runs at an average of 15.62. His highest score was the 67 mentioned earlier.

He also bowled 4703 balls, with 143 maidens, conceding 2742 runs and taking 113 wickets at an average of 24.26. His best bowling figures was 5 for 31 on 7th August 2004 at home to Philadelphia mentioned earlier. He took 17 catches.

Cessford was a regular for several years for The Combined Services, making his debut on 16th February 2009 against a Namibia Invitation XI. He played his last game for them on 17th May 2015.

He played 20 matches in total for Combined Services, batting 16 times, with 4 not outs, he scored 480 runs at an average of 40.00. He scored 3 half centuries with a high score of 99 not out, on 6th June 2011 against M.C.C in a 45-over match.

He bowled 841 balls, with 14 maidens, conceding 613 runs and taking 25 wickets at an average of 24.52.

His best bowling of 5 for 87 on 30th May 2010 against The Duke of Norfolk's XI at Arundel Castle, he also took 1 catch.

Cessford played 6 first class matches for Worcestershire in 2013.

He made his debut for them in a 3-day match starting on 1st May 2013 against Oxford M.C.C. University at The University Parks. He didn't get to bat in either innings but took 1 for 38 and 1 for 29 with the ball. His last match for the county came on 11th September 2013 at New Road against Hampshire. He took 1 for 139 and 1 for 29 with the ball and made 1 not out when he batted.

He batted 6 times in first class cricket, with 2 not outs, scoring 45 runs at an average of 11.25, his highest score was 20.

He also bowled 874 balls, with 26 maidens, conceding 591 runs and taking 17 wickets at an average of 34.76. His best bowling figures were 4 for 73 against Lancashire in August 2013, South African test player, Ashwell Prince was one of his wickets. He also took 1 catch in his first-class career.

Cessford also played 4 List A matches for Worcestershire, he took 6 wickets at an average of 29.33, this included 4 for 24 against Warwickshire on 19th August 2013.

He also played 41 matches for Worcestershire Second XI, batting 35 times, with 15 not out's, he scored 252 runs at an average of 12.60, his highest score was 24 not out.

He bowled 3161 balls, with 90 maidens, conceding 2184 runs and taking 71 wickets at an average of 30.76. His best bowling figures were 5 for 67, taken on 25th July 2014 against the M.C.C Young Cricketers. He took 7 catches for them.

Cessford also enjoyed a good cricket career representing The Royal Air Force, making his debut on 19th June 2008 against The British Police. He would go on to play 56 matches for the RAF, batting 51 times, with 7 not outs, he scored 1176 runs at an average of 26.72. He scored 8 half centuries for them; his highest score was 80 not out on 22nd April 2015 against The RAF Development XI at Uxbridge.

He bowled 2016 balls, with 35 maidens, conceding 1668 runs and taking 68 wickets at an average of 24.52. His best bowling figures were 5 for 31 on 14th May 2009 against Huntingdonshire. He took 10 catches for the RAF.

During the 2009 side Cessford played matches in the NEPL, he didn't bat but bowled 84 balls, without taking a wicket and conceding 54 runs. He took 1 catch in the NEPL in 2009.

Simon Birtwisle missed the first game of season, he thinks because of a bad back, he returned to the side for the next game of the season and opened the batting for the remainder of it. He played 18 matches in the NEPL in the 2009 season, batting 18 times with 1 not out, he scored 497 runs at an average of 29.23. He scored 4 half centuries with a highest score of 74, made on 16th May 2009 at home to Newcastle. He didn't bowl in the NEPL in 2009 but did take 7 catches in the league that season.

Birtwisle says that "Looking back, and talking to you, I now realize that we had at least four good young quick bowlers in Simpson, Tye, Evans and Cessford, but really the team just clicked this year, we also won The National Club Championship, we had a very strong bowling attack and some good solid batters. It was a real team effort this year."

Given that the side didn't lose a game that season and they won the NEPL by 74 points, that may sound like a bit of an understatement, they had six batsmen in the league averages this year and they had the top two bowlers in the League bowling averages that season, and three more well placed in the top 25 bowlers.

In respect of The ECB National Club Championship, Chester played the final on 19th September 2009 against Spencer CC, from The Surrey Premier League at Derby. Chester won the toss and elected to bat first. Quentin Hughes had 76 not out when Chester batted first, his innings coming from 99 balls, with a single boundary, Andrew Smith made 27 as they posted 175 for 9 from their 45 overs.

When Spencer batted, they were dismissed for 151 from 43 overs, Hughes had 3 for 15, Simon Birtwisle, 3 for 31 and wickets for Andrew Tye, 1 for 19 and Richard Waite 2 for 37. Five of the Spencer batsmen were bowled, and one was leg before wicket, this, plus the fact that there were only two overs left when they were all out, would suggest that the accuracy of The Chester bowlers had been a key part of their success, Hughes for example took his 3 for 15 from nine overs as Chester le Street won by 24 runs.

The Banks Salver of 2009 was won by South North; Chester le Street also added The NEPL T20 to their list of achievements in the year, and Richard Waite, whose 2009 stats were covered earlier, added to it further by picking up his fourth NEPL Player of the Year award.

TABLE 32   NEPL 2009.

	Played	Won	Draw/Aban	Lost	Pen Points	Bonus Points	Points
Chester le Street	22	14	8	0	0	227	485
Blaydon	22	13	7	2	0	175	409
South North	22	12	7	3	1	185	407
Benwell Hill	22	9	7	6	0	162	332
South Shields	22	8	6	8	0	137	289
Sunderland	22	7	8	7	1	130	274
Gateshead Fell	22	7	9	6	0	132	270
Durham CA	22	6	8	8	0	121	253
Stockton	22	5	6	11	1	140	242
Tynemouth	22	3	8	11	0	96	177
Newcastle	22	2	8	12	2	109	173
Norton	22	2	6	14	1	91	148

TABLE 33   NEPL Batting Averages 2009.

Qualification 300 Runs.

45 Batsmen Qualified this season.

Player	Club	Inns	N. O	H. S	Runs	Average
(1) W.R.S Gidman	Gateshead Fell	13	4	136	792	88.00
(2) R. May	South Shields	8	2	118	378	63.00
(3) C.E Knox	Blaydon	17	6	117 no	663	60.27
(4) S.G Borthwick	Tynemouth	11	2	118 no	523	58.11
(5) S.A Walker	Sunderland	19	5	101 no	758	54.14
(6) A.L Smith	Chester Le Street	20	4	106 no	825	51.56
(7) B.A Stokes	Durham Academy	15	1	142	677	48.36
(8) Zohaib Khan	Benwell Hill	17	5	105	554	46.17
(9) M.D Stoneman	Blaydon	11	1	118	444	44.40
(10) A.T Heather	South North	20	3	140 no	750	44.12
(11) K. Turner	Stockton	17	1	134	705	44.06
(12) P.B Muchall	South Shields	20	3	130	733	43.12
(13) A. Mustard	Chester Le Street	17	2	121 no	584	38.93
(25) Q.J Hughes	Chester Le Street	15	4	74 no	343	31.18
(27) R.P Waite	Chester Le Street	17	0	82	513	30.18
(30) S.J Birtwisle	Chester Le Street	18	1	74	497	29.24

TABLE 34   NEPL Bowling Averages 2009.

35 Bowlers Qualified this season.

Player	Club	Overs	Mdns	Runs	Wkts	Average
(1) Q.J Hughes	Chester le Street	89.1	26	229	23	9.96
(2) R.P Waite	Chester le Street	178.1	61	389	36	10.81
(3) G.D Bridge	Blaydon	211.3	55	528	44	12.00
(4) Gary Stewart	Blaydon	111.1	22	288	24	12.00
(5) S. Humble	South North	204.1	59	500	41	12.20
(6) L.J. Crozier	South North	225.0	65	501	39	12.85
(7) D.J Rutherford	Benwell Hill	278.5	68	712	52	13.69
(8) M.L Pollard	Blaydon	200.0	50	539	39	13.82
(9) R.M Brook	South North	128.5	25	415	30	13.83
(10) Zohaib Khan	Benwell Hill	232.3	62	585	42	13.93
(11) C.E Knox	Blaydon	205.5	41	612	42	14.57
(12) C.R.D Smith	South North	183.0	37	540	35	15.43
(15) L. Evans	Chester le Street	201.4	44	597	34	17.56
(20) A. Tye	Chester le Street	147.0	36	428	22	19.45
(21) L. Simpson	Chester le Street	122.5	23	411	21	19.57

Chester le Street CC 2009 NEPL Champions-seen here on 19th September 2009 at Derby prior to ECB National Championship.

Left to Right – Back Row- Catherine Coxon (Scorer), Tim Stonock, Wayne Ritzema, Andrew Bell, Andrew Tye, John Coxon, Alan Mustard, Richard Waite, Keith Robson (Chairman).

Front Row- Jack Harrison, David Wilson, Tony Birbeck, Quentin Hughes, Simon Birtwisle, Liam Simpson, Andrew Smith.

Richard Waite batting circa 2009/2010.

Photo Courtesy of an unknown photographer.

At the end of the 2009 Season the NEPL clubs voted for a "Team of the Decade."

The first name on the list was Dan Shurben, he shares his thoughts on his nominated teammates from that time.

Dan Shurben recalls that he had spent the first seven years at Chester le Street, winning the title in 2001. He says he scored a lot of runs in the decade that the team was selected from, his real "purple patch" came whilst at Chester le Street in May 2004.

The fifteenth of May was the start of it, Shurben hit 108 for Chester Le Street at home to Gateshead Fell, he then made 6 at home to Chester Le Steet on 22nd May, then came a Bank Holiday weekend.

Saturday the 29th May saw Chester le Street play an NEPL match at Benwell Hill, Shurben hit 138, Hill had Pakistan and outstanding NEPL wicket taker Shahid Nazir in their lineup.

On Sunday, 30th May 2004 Chester le Street played Blaydon in a Banks Bowl match, Shurben scored 119.

On Bank Holiday Monday, 31st May 2004, Chester le Street played Philadelphia at Chester in the NEPL, Shurben made 101.

I'm sure a handful of players have scored a century on each day of a double weekend, I can recall David Smart did it for Seaton Burn in the T.S.L in July 1984 for example, but I have never heard of anyone scoring three hundreds, against three different teams, in three consecutive days!

Shurben moved to newly promoted South Shields as captain for the 2007 season. He said he was "about 23 and Shields had a young, inexperienced team, I was the only one who had previously played in the NEPL. I didn't enjoy that first season too much, as a batting unit we were often in trouble, it was a wet summer and that didn't help as we often lost early wickets. 2008 was much better, I was a bit more experienced as a captain, we had Matty Muchall emerging as a fine bowler, and we had re-signed Jonny Wightman. They took a boat load of wickets as a pair. Paul Muchall was our Durham contracted player and he was a great batsman who scored a lot of runs for us. We also signed a really good overseas pro, an Australian, Geoff Cullen, he was only kept out of the Australian side because of the strength of their middle order, Damien Martyn, Mike Hussey and Adam Gilchrist were in front of him. This was probably my most enjoyable spell as a player, I was a better player and captain for the experiences of the previous season. I always had a high strike rate, and I think the volume of runs I had scored plus the rate I had scored them, got me into that team."

Dan Shurben in his NEPL career up to this point, the end of 2009, had seen him play 189 NEPL games, batting 183 times, with 16 not outs, scoring 5665 runs at an average of 33.92. He had scored 29 half centuries and 9 centuries, his highest score was 138 on 29th May 2004 at Benwell Hill.

He bowled 216 balls, with 3 maidens, conceding 175 runs and taking 3 wickets at an average of 58.33. His best bowling figures were 2 for 33. He had also taken 87 catches.

Allan Worthy was the other batsman selected to open the innings, NEPL Player of the Year and title winner in 2001. Dan Shurben recalls that Worthy was now "a better version of his original self, he had kept the same aggressive batting style, looking to dominate the bowlers from the off, if you were going against him, you had to get him early, if you didn't, he could really hurt you, he still looked to assert himself over the bowlers and then cash in, now though he had evolved to the point where he could quickly assess the playing conditions and was more adaptable because of it."

Allan Worthy in The NEPL up to this point, the end of 2009, had seen him play 184 NEPL games, batting 176 times, with 28 not outs, scoring 6402 runs at an average of 43.25. He had scored 38 half centuries and 14 centuries with a highest score of 156 not out, made on 26th May 2007 at home for Chester le Street against Blaydon.

He bowled 3899 balls, with 142 maidens, conceding 2075 runs and taking 98 wickets at an average of 21.17. His best bowling figures were 8 for 12 on 18th August 2001 at home for Chester le Street against Blaydon. He had also taken 100 catches.

Chris Hewison was listed at three in the team, he had won NEPL titles in 2003, 2004, 2005, 2006, 2007 and 2008 with South North. Shurben recalls that "Hewison was right up there with Worthy, John Graham, Quentin Hughes and Simon Birtwisle, he was another you had to get early, he usually batted at three or four, if he got thirty or forty, he would almost always convert it into eighty, ninety or beyond. He was a strong player down the ground, you couldn't bounce him, he could be dismissive of the short ball, the guy had no apparent weakness as a batsman."

His NEPL career up to this point, the end of 2009, had seen him play 170 NEPL games, batting 164 times, with 31 not outs, scoring 5913 runs at an average of 44.45. He had scored 26 half centuries and 15 centuries, his highest score was 165 not out, made on 22nd June 2002 at Philadelphia.

He bowled 1845 balls, with 50 maidens, conceding 1064 runs and taking 32 wickets at an average of 33.25. His best bowling figures were 3 for 25 on 20th July 2002 at Norton. He had also taken 101 catches.

John Graham was selected at number four and as captain of the side. He had captained South North to six successive NEPL titles, 2003 to 2008 inclusive, he was named as NEPL Player of the Year in 2002 and South North had also won The ECB National Championship in 2006 under his leadership.

Shurben describes Graham as "awkward to bowl or set a field to, he knew his own strengths and game so well, he liked to hit the ball square rather than straight, he had the knack of finding gaps in the field and he would hit the ball in weird areas, we started setting unusual fields to him at one point, two gullies, that sort of thing. It often took a bit of brilliance, a stunning catch or something to get rid of him, he complimented Hewison so well in the South North side."

Graham had played 189 NEPL games, batting 180 times, with 25 not outs, scoring 5807 runs at an average of 37.46. He had scored 42 half centuries and 7 centuries, his highest score was 132, scored on 29th July 2006 at Roseworth Terrace against Blaydon.

He had also bowled 2672 balls, with 93 maidens, conceding 1505 runs and taking 59 wickets at an average of 25.50. His best bowling figures were 4 for 15 on 31st May 2008 at Newcastle. He had also taken 98 catches.

Quentin Hughes was named at number five in The Team of the Decade, he had won the NEPL title in 2001 and in 2009 and The ECB National Club Championship in 2009. Shurben laughs when he says "Hughes was like a left-handed John Graham, another one who always seemed to hit the ball in weird areas, he used the pace of the ball so well, you had to get him out, he never gave it away, he was also a huge competitor, he loved competition. As a bowler he started as an off spinner, he's a bit more of a slow medium pacer now, he is very accurate, he uses a change of pace very well, bowling it straight, he has developed his style over the years."

Hughes' NEPL career up to this point, had seen him play 160 NEPL games, batting 151 times, with 34 not outs, scoring 4666 runs at an average of 39.88. He had scored 30 half centuries and 4 centuries, his highest score was 136 not out scored on 9th July 2005 at home to Benwell Hill.

He had bowled 5002 balls, with 161 maidens, conceding 2573 runs and taking 134 wickets at an average of 19.20. His best bowling figures were 5 for 16 on 3rd September 2005 at Philadelphia. He had also taken 60 catches.

Marc Symington was selected at number six. Shurben played a lot of cricket at Northumberland with Symington. He recalls "At this time, he was one of the top five or six batters around, he wasn't a big hitter of boundaries, more of an accumulator, he would always pace his innings beautifully, this made him a reliable finisher of games, he played spin very well, a superb sweeper of spinners. As a bowler he was a clever medium pace bowler, normally a first change bowler."

This is the first opportunity to look at Symington in The NEPL in any depth, he made his NEPL debut on 6th May 2000 for Norton at Blaydon. He made 17 when he batted and took 4 for 36 with the ball.

His last appearance for Norton in The NEPL came on 3rd September 2005 at home to South North, he took 0 for 13 and scored 16.

His time with Norton saw him play 88 times, batting on 88 occasions, with 15 not outs, he scored 2916 runs at an average of 39.94. He scored 24 half centuries and 1 century, 118 not out, on 6th August 2005 at Gateshead Fell.

He bowled 6058 balls, with 203 maidens, conceding 3576 runs and taking 171 wickets at an average of 20.91. His best bowling figures were 6 for 46 on 25th May 2002 at Maiden Castle against Durham Academy. He also took 30 NEPL catches for Norton.

Symington made his NEPL debut for Sunderland on 29th April 2006 at home to Stockton and his last NEPL game for them on 8th September 2007 at home to Durham Academy. His two seasons at Sunderland saw him play 36 NEPL games for them, batting 36 times, with 11 not outs, scoring 1066 runs at an average of 42.64. He scored 8 half centuries and 1 century, exactly 100, on 1st July 2006 at The Racecourse against The Durham Academy.

He bowled 2649 balls, with 88 maidens, conceding 1431 runs and taking 90 wickets at an average of 15.90. His best bowling figures for Sunderland were 6 for 43 on 28th May 2007 at South North. He also took 10 catches.

He was named NEPL Player of the Year whilst at Sunderland in 2007 and he returned to Norton for the 2008 season, playing his last game in this spell on 30th August 2008 at Stockton.

Symington played 20 NEPL games for them in 2008, batting 17 times, with 2 not out's, scoring 566 runs at an average of 37.73. He scored 4 half centuries and 1 century, 113 not out, on 2nd August at home to Gateshead Fell.

He bowled 1028 balls, with 30 maidens, conceding 587 runs and taking 25 wickets at an average of 23.58. His best bowling figures for Norton in 2008 were 6 for 51 on 26th April at home to Chester Le Street. He also took 9 catches.

He would next appear in The NEPL for Burnmoor in their title winning 2019 season and an update can be found there.

His NEPL career up to this point, the end of 2009, had seen him play 144 NEPL games, batting 141 times, with 28 not outs, scoring 4548 runs at an average of 40.24. He had scored 36 half centuries and 3 centuries. His highest score was 118 not out, mentioned earlier.

He had bowled 9735 balls, with 321 maidens, conceding 5594 runs and taking 286 wickets at an average of 19.55. His best bowling figures were 6 for 43 on 28th May 2007 at South North. He had also taken 49 catches.

Richard Waite was the number seven pick for The Team, he had been named The NEPL Player of the Year in 2003, 2004, 2008 and 2009. Shurben remembers that "as a batsman he was very similar to Allan Worthy, aggressive, he would punish the bad ball, hitting it hard and playing big shots, he also played the spinners very well. As a bowler, his off spin took a lot of wickets, he was probably the best all-rounder at this level in the North East around this period of time."

At the end of 2009, Waite had played 190 NEPL games, batting 183 times, with 12 not outs, scoring 4966 runs at an average of 29.04. He had scored 28 half centuries and 9 centuries, his highest score was 135, made on 23rd July 2005 at Stockton against Sunderland.

He had bowled 13409 balls, with 479 maidens, conceding 6934 runs and taking 330 wickets at an average of 21.01. His best bowling figures were 8 for 28 on 10th June 2006 at home to Benwell Hill, he had also taken 63 catches.

Phil Nicholson was to be the wicketkeeper; he had won The NEPL title with Benwell Hill in 2002. Shurben says Nicholson was his captain at Northumberland several times, he recalls "a great captain, he always played to win, he was another who was fiercely competitive and wanted to win, he was an exceptional wicketkeeper, truly outstanding, as a batsman he was a very good player of spin, a very busy batsman, looking to score quickly and fast between the wickets."

His NEPL career up to this point, the end of 2009, had seen him play 172 NEPL games, batting 152 times, with 23 not outs, scoring 3634 runs at an average of 28.17. He had scored 20 half centuries and 4 centuries, his highest score was 121 on 2nd June 2001 at South North. He bowled 23 balls, with 0 maidens, conceding 15 runs and taking 0 wickets and had also taken 151 catches and had 42 stumpings.

Stephen Humble was number nine in The Team, he had won NEPL titles in 2005, 2006, 2007 and 2008 with South North and had been named The NEPL Player of the Year in 2008. Shurben remembers Humble as "a very skilful bowler, he wasn't rapid but quick enough for this level, he presented the seam beautifully and could move the ball both ways, because of where we played, I often felt that it was me against him, I won some, he won some, it was always a challenge batting against him."

At the end of 2009, he had played 119 NEPL games, batting 84 times, with 20 not out's, scoring 1400 runs at an average of 21.87. He scored 4 half centuries with a highest score of 78, made on 26th August 2006 at home to Stockton.

He had bowled 8791 balls, with 396 maidens, conceding 3847 runs and taking 263 wickets at an average of 14.62. His best bowling figures were 8 for 55 on 27th May 2006 at home to Gateshead Fell and he had also taken 35 catches.

Lee Crozier was selected to bat at ten and as a front-line spinner in The Team of the Decade, he won his first NEPL title in 2002 with Benwell Hill, he won further titles in 2004, 2005, 2006, 2007 and 2008 with South North. Shurben's memories of Crozier are mixed at best, he says that "of his thousand wickets, I'm probably a hundred of them, he got me out every which way possible, bowled, leg before, stumped, caught all over the field, wherever you could be caught, Lee had me caught. I had some good days against him but overall, I think he won! He wasn't a massive spinner of the ball, but he was very accurate, and he had good control and varied his pace well. He would try and impose his will on you, he was exceptional at this level."

Crozier had played 186 NEPL games by the end of 2009, batting 106 times, with 41 not outs, scoring 1128 runs at an average of 17.35. He had scored 1 half century, 89, made on 23rd July 2005 for Benwell Hill at Philadelphia.

He bowled 13883 balls, with 679 maidens, conceding 5722 runs and taking 388 wickets at an average of 14.74. His best bowling figures were 7 for 21 on 28th July 2007 at Chester le Street for South North. He had also taken 32 catches.

Shahid Nazir was selected as the overseas pro and number eleven batsman, he won the NEPL title in 2002 with Benwell Hill. Shurben says "I remember playing against him for Chester, early on, I took guard, and he came running in from the sight screen, he glided in, with a beautiful action, he was pleasing on the eye when you watched him bowl, you could see the ball in his hand all the way and I think that helped me when I batted against him. He was fast, just fast. I remember one game when he hit me in the glove with a short one, it sort of popped up but fell safe and we ran a single, Tony Birbeck was at the other end and we met in the middle, before the next ball, Birbeck laughing at me, I think Nazir heard him, he wasn't one to say much, if anything, but the next ball was quicker, this one hit Tony in the glove and went straight in the air, he was caught, as he trudged off I remember saying to him "You're not laughing now mate, are you!"

Nazir played 103 matches in the NEPL, batting 68 times, with 9 not outs, he scored 892 runs at an average of 15.11, he made 1 half century, 63, made on 17th August 2002 for Benwell Hill at Blaydon. He bowled 7956 balls, with 328 maidens, conceding 3583 runs and taking 260 wickets at an average of 13.78. His best bowling figures were 7 for 19 on Sunderland at home to Tynemouth, he also took 21 NEPL catches.

Dan Shurben finished his observations on the "Team of the Decade" by saying, "the first ten years in particular, the quality of the cricket and the cricketers, playing in The NEPL was something else, if you take the fact that first of all South North, then Chester won The National Competition, that's a pretty good indicator of how good things were at the time."

If you were looking for another indicator of the quality of cricketers in the league at the time, the highest individual score of the 2009 season, 142, came on 25th April, it was scored by a certain Benjamin Andrew Stokes for The Durham Cricket Academy at Ashbrooke Sports Club against Sunderland, the innings came from 136 balls and contained 19 boundaries and 5 sixes. Mark Wood, whose NEPL career will be covered later, had 77 from 109 balls, with 11 boundaries in the same innings.

Stokes made his NEPL debut on 28th April 2007 for The Durham Academy at Maiden Castle against Norton. He was run out for 44 and took 1 for 19 when Norton batted, his first NEPL wicket being opener Craig Knox, caught by Richard Coughtrie for 19. Stokes played his last NEPL match on 9th July 2016 against Whitburn at The Riverside. He didn't bowl and batted at number three, making 107 from 108 deliveries with 11 fours and 6 sixes. He was bowled by Ian Elliot. As an aside, both Durham openers and their number four, were all out first ball, to Kieran Waterson.

Stokes played 51 matches in the NEPL, batting 46 times with 5 not outs, he scored 1608 runs at an average of 39.21, with 6 half centuries and 3 centuries, his highest score was the 142 mentioned earlier.

He bowled 673 deliveries in his NEPL career, with 18 maidens, conceding 419 runs and taking 16 wickets at an average of 26.18. His best bowling figures were 2 for 10 on 16th May 2009 at Maiden Castle against Tynemouth.

His last NEPL wicket was Matthew Brown of Norton on 12th September 2009, caught by Ben Raine for 25 and he took 22 catches in his NEPL career.

2010

After taking The NEPL title and winning the T20 Chester le Street made almost no changes for the upcoming 2010 season. The rules were still that the side batting first could bat for a maximum of 65 overs and that the match was limited to 120 overs.

Chester le Street opened the 2010 season on Saturday 24th April with an away fixture at Blaydon, the home side won the toss and decided to bat, batting their full allocation of overs and made 204 for 9 wickets when the innings was closed. They had been in trouble at 112 for 7 but number nine batsman Ian Hunter made 46 to top score the innings. Andrew Tye had 3 for 52 and Quentin Hughes had 3 for 37. When Chester batted, 49 from Liam Simpson and 43 from Andrew Smith got them close but after they had received their 55 overs, they were 193 for 8. Match drawn.

The Chester le Street side which opened the 2010 season was as follows-

Simon Birtwisle opened the batting, scoring 8. Birtwisle was now among the top batsmen in the NEPL at this time, he had now played 161 matches, batting 157 times, with 13 not outs, he had scored 5270 runs at an average of 36.59. He had scored 35 half centuries and 5 centuries, his highest score was 135 not out scored for Benwell Hill in 2001 mentioned earlier.

He had also bowled 3046 balls, with 103 maidens, conceding 1840 runs and taking 65 wickets at an average of 28.30. His best bowling remained the 6 for 32 taken in 2008 and mentioned earlier. He had now taken 46 catches.

Birtwisle played 20 matches in the NEPL in 2010, batting 20 times with 2 not outs, he scored 809 runs at an average of 44.94. He scored 4 half centuries and 2 centuries. The first century, 151 not out, was scored on 3rd July 2010 at home to Stockton, Andrew Smith scored 107 not out in the same game as Birtwisle and Smith added an unbeaten stand of 208 for the second wicket. His second century, 102 not out, was scored on 21st August 2010 at Gateshead Fell.

Birtwisle also bowled 69 balls in the NEPL in 2010, with 1 maiden, conceding 38 runs and taking 1 wicket and he also took 5 catches in the NEPL in 2010.

Alan Mustard had opened the innings with Birtwisle and scored 4. He was another experienced, established NEPL batsman at this point, he had played 147 NEPL matches, batting 138 times, with 16 not out's, he had scored 3563 runs at an average of 29.20. He had scored 19 half centuries and 1 century, his highest score was 121 not out, scored on the last day of the 2009 season, 22nd August at Norton.

Mustard had also bowled 663 balls, with 11 maidens, conceding 494 runs and taking 22 wickets at an average of 22.45. His best bowling figures remained the 6 for 69 taken in August 2006. He had also taken 65 catches and had 1 stumping.

He played 21 matches in the NEPL in 2010, batting 21 times with 2 not outs, he scored 333 runs at an average of 17.52. He scored 2 half centuries with a highest score of 70 not out, made on 4th September 2010 at home to Sunderland. He took 5 NEPL catches in 2010.

Andrew Smith batted at three and started the season with 45, he also bowled one over, a maiden. Smith entered the 2010 season as one of the best batsmen the league had, he had now played 110 matches in the NEPL, batting 101 times, with 16 not out's, he had scored 3109 runs at an average of 36.57. He had scored 20 half centuries and 5 centuries, his highest score remained the 158 he had scored in May 2008 against The Durham Academy.

He had also bowled 957 balls with 24 maidens, conceding 549 runs and taking 26 wickets at an average of 21.11. His best bowling figures were now 3 for 18, taken on 1st August 2009 at Newcastle. He had taken 42 NEPL catches.

Smith played 21 matches in the NEPL 2010 season, batting 21 times with 2 not outs, he scored 1052 runs at an average of 55.36. He scored 5 half centuries and 4 centuries.

His first century of the 2010 season, 173 not out, was scored on 15th May 2010 at home to Newcastle.

His second century, 100, was also scored at home, on 19th June 2010 to Sunderland, the innings contained 11 fours.

The third century, 107 not out, was scored on 3rd July 2010 at home to Blaydon and was mentioned earlier in respect of Simon Birtwisle.

His fourth century of the 2010 NEPL season, 123, was scored on 30th August at Sunderland.

Smith also bowled 301 balls in the NEPL in 2010, with 9 maidens, he conceded 152 runs and took 13 wickets at an average of 11.69. His best bowling figures were 8 for 43, taken on 7th August 2010 at South Shields. He took 7 NEPL catches in 2010.

Richard Waite, batting at number four on April 26th, scored 18, he had also bowled sixteen overs, taking 1 for 41 when Blaydon batted. Waite had initially played Minor Counties for Cumberland, he went on to also play Minor Counties for Northumberland, his debut coming at home to Staffordshire on 25th April 2010 at Roseworth Terrace, Gosforth. Staffs batted first, scoring 292 for 8 from their 50 overs, Marc Symington 3 for 52 the best of the bowlers, Waite had 0 for 49 from ten overs. When Northumberland batted, despite nine players making double figures, they were all out for 169 as Staffs won by 123 runs. Waite scored 14.

Waite played his last match for Northumberland on 14th June 2015. He had played 15 matches for them, batting 19 times, with 3 not outs, he scored 592 runs at an average of 37.00. He had 4 half centuries and 1 century, 103 not out, which came during a 3-day match which started on 4th July 2010 against Bedfordshire at Denton Bank. The innings took 137 balls and contained 12 fours and 2 sixes.

As a bowler for Northumberland Waite bowled 1663 balls, with 50 maidens, conceding 986 runs and taking 35 wickets at an average of 28.17. His best bowling was 5 for 38 against Lincolnshire at Swalwell in a 3-day match starting on 26th June 2011. He also took 5 catches for Northumberland.

During the 2010 NEPL season Waite played 20 matches in the league for Chester le Street, batting 19 times with 3 not outs, he scored 742 runs at an average of 46.37. He scored 3 half centuries and 2 centuries.

His first century of the 2010 season, 150 not out, was scored on 22nd May at home to South Shields and the second century of the season, 109 not out, was scored on 5th June at home to Gateshead Fell, containing 17 fours and 1 six.

He also bowled 1394 balls in the NEPL in 2010, with 73 maidens, conceding 588 runs and taking 33 wickets at an average of 17.81. His best bowling figures were 5 for 23, taken 15th May 2010 at home to Newcastle. He took 3 catches in the NEPL in 2010.

By the end of the 2010 season Waite had played 39 matches in The NEPL for Chester, he had batted 36 times, with 3 not out's, he had scored 1255 runs at an average of 38.03. He scored 7 half centuries and 2 centuries. His highest score during this period was 150 not out on 22nd May 2010 at home to South Shields.

He had also bowled 2463 balls, with 134 maidens, conceding 977 runs and taken 69 wickets at an average of 14.15. His best bowling figures were 7 for 13 on 8th August 2009 at Stockton. He made 10 catches in The NEPL in that 2-year period.

He played his last NEPL game for Chester le Street on 10th September 2011 at home to The Durham Academy.

His four years at Chester Le Street had seen him play 73 games for them in the NEPL, he batted 66 times with 6 not outs, he scored 2184 runs at an average of 36.40. He scored 11 half centuries and 4 centuries for them, his highest score for Chester was 150 not out on 22nd May 2010 at home to South Shields.

He bowled 4829 balls for Chester in the NEPL, with 220 maidens, conceding 2251 runs and taking 150 wickets at an average of 15.00. His best bowling figures of his time with Chester was 7 for 13 on 8th August 2009 at Stockton. Waite also took 22 catches for Chester.

Quentin Hughes had batted at five to open the season, he scored 4 and bowled thirteen overs when Blaydon batted, taking 3 for 37. Entering the 2010 season Hughes was now widely regarded as one of the best all-rounders in the NEPL. Having played 160 matches, he batted 151 times, with 34 not outs, he had scored 4666 runs at an average of 39.88. He had scored 30 half centuries and 4 centuries, his highest score remained the 136 not out made in July 2005 mentioned earlier.

He had also bowled 5002 balls in the NEPL, with 161 maidens, conceding 2573 runs and taking 134 wickets at an average of 19.20. His best bowling figures remained the 5 for 16 taken in 2005 mentioned earlier. Hughes also had 60 NEPL catches to his credit.

During the 2010 NEPL season Hughes played 18 matches in the league, batting 15 times with 3 not outs, he scored 187 runs at an average of 15.58. His highest score was 39 not out, made on 8th May 2010 at Tynemouth.

He bowled 730 balls in the NEPL in 2010, with 33 maidens, conceding 320 runs and taking 24 wickets at an average of 13.33. His best bowling figures were 6 for 38, taken on 12th June 2010 at The Emirates against Durham Academy. He also took 3 catches in the 2010 NEPL season.

John Coxon batted at number six to start the season, scoring 13. As Chester looked to retain their 2009 title and entered 2010, Coxon was a key part of their side, he had now played 96 NEPL matches, batting 85 times, with 8 not outs, he had scored 1449 runs at an average of 18.81. He had scored 7 half centuries and 1 century, 112, on 8th August 2009 at Stockton.

Coxon had also bowled 454 balls, with 11 maidens, conceding 261 runs and taking 11 wickets at an average of 23.72. His best bowling remained the 5 for 36 was taken on 30th August 2008. He had 34 NEPL catches to his name.

Coxon played 21 matches in the NEPL in 2010, batting 20 times with 2 not outs, he scored 484 runs at an average of 26.88. He scored 3 half centuries and 1 century, 112, scored on 4th September 2010 at Stockton.

Coxon also bowled 102 balls in the NEPL in 2010, with 5 maidens, conceding 37 runs and taking 5 wickets at an average of 7.40. His best bowling figures were 2 for 1, taken on 5th June 2010 at home to Gateshead Fell. He took 7 catches in the NEPL in 2010.

Liam Simpson batted at number seven, starting the season with the innings top score of 49 and taking 2 for 35 from thirteen overs when Blaydon batted. Prior to the 2010 season Simpson had now played 138 matches in the NEPL, batting 104 times, with 21 not outs, he had scored 1194 runs at an average of 14.38. He scored 4 half centuries; his highest score remained the 63 not out scored for Durham Academy in April 2004.

As a bowler, Simpson had delivered 3858 balls in the NEPL, with 121 maidens, conceding 2158 runs and taking 92 wickets at an average of 23.45. His best bowling figures were now 6 for 28 taken on 25th April 2009 at Tynemouth. He had also taken 40 NEPL catches.

During the 2010 NEPL season Simpson played 19 matches in the league, batting 16 times with 4 not outs, he scored 290 runs at an average of 24.16. He scored 1 half century, 50 not out, made on 19th June 2010 at home to Sunderland.

He bowled 974 balls in the NEPL in 2010, with 35 maidens, conceding 577 runs and taking 28 wickets at an average of 20.60. His best bowling figures were 3 for 23, taken on 26th June 2010 at Hetton Lyons. He also took 5 catches in the NEPL in 2010.

Andrew Tye batted at number eight on the season opener, scoring 10, he also opened the bowling, taking 3 for 52 from his thirteen overs. During the 2010 season Tye played 19 NEPL matches for Chester, batting 14 times, with 3 not outs, he scored 164 runs at an average of 14.90. His highest score was 29.

He also bowled 1323 balls, with 45 maidens, conceding 686 runs and taking 41 wickets at an average of 16.73. His best bowling figures were 8 for 34, taken on 30th August at Sunderland. He also took 5 catches in the NEPL that season.

Tye would continue to play for Chester throughout 2011 and 2012, his last game coming on 1st September 2012 at Tynemouth. He marked the occasion by taking 5 for 10!

Or was it his last game......he made one more NEPL appearance on 25th June 2022 for Chester at Benwell Hill. He took 3 for 53 and scored 17.

When all was done on his NEPL career he had played 84 matches, batting 63 times with 13 not outs, he scored 1099 runs at an average of 21.98. He scored 4 half centuries, his highest score was 84, made on 4th June 2011 at home to Blaydon.

Tye also bowled 4894 balls in the NEPL, with 168 maidens, conceding 2507 runs and taking 147 wickets at an average of 17.05. His best bowling figures remained the 8 for 34 on 30th August 2010 at Sunderland. He made 29 NEPL catches.

Upon his return to Australia Tye went on to have a very good professional career, playing for Western Australia, Sydney Thunder and Perth Scorchers amongst others.

He would also play T20 and 50 over cricket for the Australian National Side, as well as T20 cricket for Durham, Northants and Gloucestershire in the UK, The Rajasthan Royals, The Lucknow Super Kings and The Karachi Kings in The Indian Premier League. He would also play for Team Abu Dhabi in The Abu Dhabi T10 Competition.

At the time of writing, his last appearance had come on 30th July 2023 at The Grand Prairie Stadium, Texas in the Final of Major League Cricket. He was playing for MI New York against The Seattle Orcas. The MI is pronounced as MY and they are owned by the same people who own The Mumbai Indians in The Indian Premier League. Despite having Quinton de Kock in the Orcas line up, Tye and his New York side won by 7 wickets!

Andrew Bell batted at number nine to open the 2010 season, he scored 29 not out and he had 0 for 22 from six overs when Chester bowled. Going into the 2010 season Bell had played 101 NEPL matches, batting 57 times, with 20 not outs, he had scored 447 runs at an average of 12.08. His highest score was still the 30 not out on 29th July 2006 mentioned earlier.

He bowled 4125 balls, with 141 maidens, conceding 2305 runs and taking 100 wickets at an average of 23.05. His best bowling was still the 5 for 52 taken on 2nd September 2007 mentioned earlier. He had taken 17 catches.

During the 2010 NEPL season he played 19 matches in the league, batting 11 times with 4 not outs, he scored 130 runs at an average of 18.57. His highest score was 29 not out in the season opener at Blaydon. He bowled 744 balls in the NEPL in 2010, with 33 maidens, conceding 388 runs and taking 16 wickets at an average of 24.25. His best bowling figures were 3 for 30, taken on 1st May 2010 at home to Benwell Hill. He took 7 catches in the NEPL in 2010.

Graeme Cessford batted at number ten, he only faced half a dozen balls, making 0 not out, he also bowled three overs, 0 for 6, when Blaydon batted. Cessford was also playing for The RAF and The Combined Services during the 2010 season, and he would only play 6 NEPL matches for Chester in the 2010 season, taking a total of 4 wickets for 117 runs.

During the 2010 NEPL season he played 6 matches in the league, his batting opportunities were so limited he completed only one innings and didn't score any runs across the three times he batted.

He bowled 192 balls in the 2010 NEPL season, with 5 maidens, conceding 117 runs and taking 4 wickets at an average of 29.25. His best bowling was 2 for 27. He took 3 catches in the NEPL in 2010.

Cessford would play his last NEPL match on 1st August 2015 at Blaydon. He had played 97 NEPL matches, he had batted 45 times, with 13 not outs, scoring 500 runs at an average of 15.62. He had one half century, his highest score of 67 on 6th June 2015 at Benwell Hill.

He bowled 4703 balls, with 143 maidens, conceding 2742 runs and taking 113 wickets at an average of 24.36. His best bowling figures were 5 for 31, taken on 7th August 2004 for Gateshead Fell at home to Philadelphia. He had taken 17 catches in his NEPL career.

David Wilson was listed to bat at number eleven but didn't get the opportunity to bat, he kept wicket and took one catch. Wilson entered this season having played 138 NEPL matches, he had batted 77 times, with 32 not outs, scoring 673 runs at an average of 14.95. As a wicketkeeper he took 150 catches and had 35 stumpings.

During the 2010 NEPL season Wilson played 19 matches in the league, batting 7 times with 6 not outs, he scored 21 runs at an average of 21.00. He took 23 catches and made 4 stumpings in the NEPL in 2010.

Wilson would play his last NEPL match on 1st September 2012 at Tynemouth, he took 3 catches when the hosts batted. He had played 190 NEPL matches, all for Chester, he had batted 95 times, with 42 not outs, scoring 780 runs at an average of 14.71. He had one half century, his highest score of 60 in May 2001 mentioned earlier. As a wicketkeeper he took 201 catches and had 46 stumpings.

He also won NEPL titles in 2001, 2009 and 2010.

Luke Evans had been a key part of the 2009 title winning side but this appearances in 2010 were limited as he moved into a professional career with Durham and Northamptonshire. He entered the 2010 season having played 90 matches in the NEPL, batting 28 times with 16 not outs, he scored 101 runs at an average of 8.41. His highest score was 21.

Up to the end of the 2009 season he had bowled 5259 balls in the NEPL, with 183 maidens, conceding 2739 runs and taking 123 wickets at an average of 22.26. His best bowling figures were 6 for 13, taken in May 2009 against South North and mentioned earlier, he had taken 13 NEPL catches to this point.

He played 5 matches in the NEPL in 2010, he didn't bat but bowled 306 balls, with 12 maidens, he conceded 171 runs and took 8 wickets at an average of 21.37. He took 3 NEPL catches in 2010.

The Banks Salver this season was also won by Chester le Street and the T20 won by South North.

Andrew Smith of Chester le Street was named NEPL Player of the Year.

In addition to his total of runs scored, 1052, Smith had also scored the highest individual score of the season, 173 not out on 15th May 2010 at Chester against Newcastle.

One name that kept cropping up around this period of the NEPL was Scott Borthwick, a left-handed batsman and leg break bowler, as he went on to play for England, I think it appropriate to include his time in the NEPL.

Borthwick made his NEPL debut on 13th August 2005 for Philadelphia at Tynemouth, rain ruined the game after just 34 overs before he could bat or bowl.

He took his first NEPL wicket for Philadelphia on 29th August 2005 when he bowled Gateshead Fell all-rounder, Ian Pattison for 43. This game was notable for a bowling feat by Nick Phillips of Gateshead Fell, he took five wickets in five balls, something I've never heard of at this level of cricket!

So, I'm going to digress a bit further, Nick Phillips was a right-handed batsman and right arm off break bowler, he had played first class cricket for both Sussex and Durham, as well as Minor Counties for Northumberland. He also played for England at Under 19 level.

On the day he took his "five in five" Philadelphia's openers had started well with an opening stand of 115. South African pro Brett Pelser would go on to make 74, his opening partner, Paul Riddle was on 56 when he was caught at first slip by Allan Worthy off the bowling of Phillips. Stuart Walker was then bowled, Mark Turner was also caught by Worthy at first slip to complete the hattrick, James Davidson was bowled, and then Scott Borthwick was the last of the five, also bowled! Phillips finished with 20 overs, 6 maidens, 7 for 34! Allan Worthy had 57 and Ian Pattison 43 as Philadelphia won by 7 wickets.

Returning to Scott Borthwick, he played his last NEPL game for Philadelphia on 3rd September 2005 at home to Chester le Street.

His next NEPL appearance came when he debuted for The Durham Academy on 30th June 2007 at The Racecourse against Sunderland, this debut was also washed out, this time after 16.5 overs. His last appearance in the NEPL for The Academy was on 30th August 2008 at Maiden Castle against Blaydon.

Borthwick then debuted for Tynemouth on 25th April 2009 for Tynemouth at home to Chester le Street, his first Tynemouth wicket was Liam Simpson, caught by Iain Purdy for 1. He also scored 26 opening the batting.

His last game for Tynemouth was on 11th June 2011 at home to Newcastle, only 2.4 overs were possible before the game was abandoned.

He then played 1 game for Chester le Street on 26th May 2012 at home to Hetton Lyons, he scored 61 and had 0 for 20.

Two more NEPL appearances, both for Whitburn, the first on 27th May 2023 and the second, and last NEPL appearance to date, was on 26th August 2023 for Whitburn at home to Felling. His last NEPL wicket, was Daniel Donaldson, caught by Matthew Muchall for 9.

Scott Borthwick played 54 matches in the NEPL, batting 47 times with 4 not outs, he scored 1417 runs at an average of 32.95. He scored 9 half centuries and 1 century, 118 not out on 11th July 2009 for Tynemouth at Chester le Street. The innings came from 148 balls and contained 17 fours.

He also bowled 3179 balls in the NEPL, with 88 maidens, conceding 1893 runs and taking 90 wickets at an average of 21.03. His best bowling figures were 6 for 30 taken for Durham Academy on 26th April 2006 at The Racecourse against South Shields. He made 15 NEPL catches.

Scott Borthwick played 1 test match for England, at The Sydney Cricket Ground starting on 3rd January 2013 against Australia. He took 1 for 49 in the first innings, his first test wicket was Mitchell Johnson, caught by the sub fielder, Joe Root for 12. In the second innings he had 3 for 33, his wickets being Chris Rogers, caught and bowled for 119, Brad Haddin, bowled for 28 and Ryan Harris, caught by Michael Carberry for 13. He made 1 and 4 when he batted, and he also took 2 catches.

He played 2 one-day internationals for England, the first on 25th August 2011 in Dublin against Ireland was reduced by rain to 42 overs rather than the 50 scheduled, he scored 15 when he batted and had 0 for 13 when he bowled. The second, and last, was on 23rd October 2011 against India at Mumbai, he made 3 and had 0 for 59.

Borthwick played 1 Twenty20 International on 25th September 2011 at The Kia Oval, Kennington, against the West Indies. He took 1 for 15 from his 4 overs, the wicket was opener Johnson Charles, bowled for 21. He was run out for 14 when he batted.

After making his first-class debut for Durham on 15th September 2009 at The Rose Bowl against Hampshire, Borthwick played 211 first class matches for Durham, Surrey and England, batting 351 times with 31 not outs, he scored 11322 runs at an average of 35.38. He scored 64 half centuries and 22 centuries. His highest score was 216, scored at The Emirates for Durham in a County Championship match against Middlesex which started on 1st June 2014. His innings came from 415 balls and contained 25 fours and a six. Mark Stoneman had 187 in the same game and almost the entire Durham side had played at some point in the NEPL.

He bowled 13914 balls in first class cricket, with 269 maidens, conceding 9120 runs and taking 229 wickets at an average of 39.82. His best bowling figures were 6 for 70, taken in a County Championship match at The Emirates against Middlesex., he also scored 82 not out in the same game! He made 264 catches at this level.

He also played 89 List A matches for Durham, Wellington and Surrey, batting 67 times with 10 not outs, he scored 1488 runs at an average of 26.10. He scored 12 half centuries with a highest score of 88 made on 10th August 2022 for Durham at Taunton against Somerset.

He bowled 2768 balls in List A cricket for Durham, with 2 maidens, conceding 2895 runs and taking 69 wickets at an average of 41.95. His best bowling figures were 5 for 38 on 6th August 2015 for Durham at Leicestershire. He took 43 catches at this level.

Scott Borthwick also played 116 Twenty20 matches for Durham, Surrey and England, batting 61 times with 20 not outs, he scored 729 runs at an average of 17.78. He scored 1 half century, 62, on 14th July 2013 for Durham at Old Trafford against Lancashire.

He bowled 1538 balls at this level, 0 maidens, conceding 2107 runs and taking 82 wickets at an average of 25.69. His best bowling figures were 4 for 18, taken for Durham on 10th July 2016 at The Riverside against Leicestershire. He took 55 catches in Twenty20 cricket.

TABLE 35   NEPL 2010.

	Played	Won	Draw/Aban	Lost	Pen Points	Bonus Points	Points
Chester le Street	22	14	7	1	0	223	474
South North	22	14	7	3	3	227	465
Benwell Hill	22	8	11	3	0	170	355
Durham CA	22	8	8	6	0	166	328
Blaydon	22	7	9	6	0	170	320
Newcastle	22	6	7	9	1	144	268
Stockton	22	5	10	7	0	125	244
Gateshead Fell	22	6	8	8	1	121	244
Sunderland	22	5	8	9	0	121	230
Hetton Lyons	22	4	7	11	0	123	226
South Shields	22	5	5	12	0	95	195
Tynemouth	22	3	9	10	2	108	182

TABLE 36   NEPL Batting Averages 2010.

Qualification 300 Runs.

34 Batsmen Qualified this season.

Player	Club	Inns	N. O	H. S	Runs	Average
(1) G. Muchall	South Shields	7	3	174 no	471	117.75
(2) T.W.M Latham	Gateshead Fell	20	3	122	1102	64.82
(3) A.L Smith	Chester Le Street	21	2	173 no	1052	55.37
(4) M.J Richardson	Newcastle	17	3	141	755	53.93
(5) K. Turner	Gateshead Fell	20	6	137 no	734	52.43
(6) J. Rickard	Stockton	18	1	111	889	52.29
(7) G. Clark	Durham CA	17	4	78	638	49.08
(8) C.J Hewison	South North	18	2	121 no	752	47.00
(9) R.P Waite	Chester Le Street	19	3	150 no	742	46.38
(10) S.J Birtwisle	Chester Le Street	20	2	151 no	809	44.94
(11) Rameez Shazhad	Sunderland	18	2	109 no	702	43.88
(12) Zohaib Khan	Benwell Hill	17	3	120	606	43.29

TABLE 37   NEPL Bowling Averages 2010.

Qualification 20 Wickets.

32 Bowlers Qualified this season.

Player	Club	Overs	Mdns	Runs	Wkts	Average
(1) S. Humble	South North	157.0	41	372	28	13.29
(2) Q.J Hughes	Chester le Street	121.4	33	320	24	13.33
(3) G.D Bridge	Blaydon	253.5	54	737	49	15.04
(4) Zohaib Khan	Benwell Hill	313.2	81	882	58	15.21
(5) M.A Wood	Durham CA	114.1	30	351	23	15.26
(6) D.J Rutherford	Benwell Hill	312.0	91	757	47	16.11
(7) L.J Crozier	South North	243.0	62	596	37	16.11
(8) A. Tye	Chester le Street	220.3	45	686	41	16.73
(9) J.R Wightman	South North	246.2	25	987	56	17.63
(10) Shahid Nazir	Tynemouth	247.3	58	712	40	17.80
(11) R.P Waite	Chester le Street	233.2	73	588	33	17.82
(12) P. Jones	Benwell Hill	132.1	14	479	26	18.42
(17) L. Simpson	Chester le Street	162.2	35	577	28	20.61

Chester le Street CC 2010.

Andrew Smith seen here batting on 12th May 2018 at Tynemouth.

Photo Courtesy of Ken Waller.

CHAPTER SIX

South North 2011-2012

South North had finished third in 2009 and as runners up in 2010, Chester le Street taking the title by 9 points in 2010. They had also finished as runners up in The ECB National Club Twenty20 of 2010, losing out to Swardeston by 11 runs at The Rose Bowl, Southampton. The spine of the team that won the title in 2008 was still intact for the 2011 season, but there had been one or two changes along the way. At the end of the 2009 season wicketkeeper Neil Corby moved to Newcastle, Adam Cragg had been doing some wicketkeeping and the feeling at South North was that Cragg keeping wicket meant that they could strengthen the side elsewhere. Looking back John Graham thinks this may have been harsh on Corby but that the teams around them were strengthening and South North had to also. Chester le Street going on to win the NEPL in 2009 and 2010 was evidence of this. Fast bowler Jonny Wightman had joined them from South Shields for the 2010 season. After the 2010 season, Jack Jessop had gone to Ashington, John Graham recalls that he was "very young at the time, only 15 or 16, he clearly had something about him, to be playing in our first team was enough evidence of that, he obviously fulfilled his early potential later in his career, surprising no-one really."

South North started the 2011 season at Stockton on 30th April and made a rocky start, losing both openers cheaply, they recovered well to make 228 for 9 declared from 50.2 overs. Chris Hewison, as he seemed to do often, started the season well with 55, Sam Jobson also had 55 and Stephen Humble made 47. Andrew Parr had 3 for 36 and Jonathan Rickard 3 for 30 as the pick of the Stockton bowlers. When Stockton batted, despite 54 from Matthew Brown and 43 from James Ward, they never really got started, losing wickets early and then at regular intervals, 163 all out. Lee Crozier and Richard Brook both had three wickets each as they won by 65 runs.

The South North team that started the first game of the season was as follows-

John Graham opened the batting, making 7, he was now entering his 12th season as South North captain and had now played 210 NEPL matches, batting 200 times, with 26 not outs, he had scored 6598 runs at an average of 37.91. He had scored 48 half centuries and 9 centuries, his highest score was still the 132 from 2006 mentioned earlier.

He had also bowled 2690 balls in The NEPL to this point, with 94 maidens, conceding 1509 runs and taking 60 wickets at an average of 25.15. His best bowling was still the 4 for 15 from 2008 mentioned earlier and he had taken 112 catches.

Graham played 17 matches in the NEPL in 2011, he batted 17 times with 2 not outs, he scored 362 runs at an average of 24.13. He scored 3 half centuries. His highest score of the season was 69 not out, scored on 7th May 2011 at home to Hetton Lyons.

He bowled 48 balls in the NEPL that season, with 2 maidens, he conceded 29 runs and took 2 wickets at an average of 14.50. His best bowling figures were 2 for 29 taken on 30th May 2011 at home to Gateshead Fell and he took 10 catches in the NEPL in 2011.

Adam Heather opened the batting with Graham and scored 1. Heather had now played 198 NEPL matches, batting 189 times, with 24 not outs, he had scored 5857 runs at an average of 35.49. He had scored 28 half centuries and 11 centuries. His highest score was still the 140 not out from July 2009 mentioned earlier. His bowling record hadn't changed from the 12 balls mentioned earlier but he had now taken 69 catches and had 4 stumpings.

Heather played 15 matches in the NEPL in 2011, batting 14 times with 2 not outs, he scored 504 runs at an average of 42.00. He scored 5 half centuries with a highest score of 90, scored on 28th May 2011 at Newcastle. He didn't bowl but took 4 NEPL catches in 2011.

Chris Hewison batted at three in the season opener, scoring 55. He had now played 190 NEPL matches, batting 182 times, with 33 not outs, he had scored 6673 runs at an average of 44.78. He had scored 29 half centuries and 18 centuries. His highest score was still the 165 not out from June 2002 mentioned earlier.

He had now bowled 1893 balls in the NEPL, with 51 maidens, conceding 1107 runs and taking 32 wickets at an average of 34.59. His best bowling was still the 3 for 25 from 2007 mentioned earlier and he had taken 109 catches.

Hewison played 17 matches in the NEPL in 2011, batting 16 times with 0 not outs, he scored 557 runs at an average of 34.81. He scored 7 half centuries with a highest score of 90, scored on 4th June 2011 at South Shields. He didn't bowl but took 5 NEPL catches in 2011.

Adam Cragg batted at four in the season opener of 2011, he scored 23. He had now played 92 NEPL matches, batting 73 times, with 14 not outs, he had scored 1705 runs at an average of 28.89. He had scored 6 half centuries and 1 century, his highest score was now 102, this came during the 2010 season, scored on 15th May at home to Blaydon. He had never bowled in the NEPL to this point, but he had kept wicket, taking 67 catches and 10 stumpings.

Cragg played 16 NEPL matches in the 2011 season, batting 15 times, with 2 not outs, he scored 346 runs at an average of 26.61. He scored 2 half centuries with a highest score of 65, made on 20th August 2011 at home to South Shields. He did not bowl in The NEPL in 2011 but took 7 catches and had 1 stumping that season.

Sam Jobson a right-handed batsman, batted at five and kept wicket in the season opener of 2011, he scored 55 and took 2 catches and had a stumping in the game. John Graham recalls that he was" just a young lad, around 16 at the time he started playing regularly for our firsts, but he was an eye-catching batsman, unorthodox, very destructive on his day. I think he scored a hundred before lunch in a game for Northumberland at Norfolk, he was a talented wicketkeeper, natural soft hands, he was one of those good all round sportsman types."

The first record of any note for Jobson came on 27th May 2005 when he made an appearance for Northumberland Under 13's against Cumbria at Hexham. He progressed through the county age groups, playing at Under 14, Under 15 and Under 17 levels.

He made his debut in The NEPL in the same season he was representing the Under 15's, his debut came on 26th May 2007 at Stockton, he made 6 when he batted.

He would also go on to play for Manchester University, making his debut for them on 27th April 2011 at Hulme against Loughborough University. He would play 4 matches for them, and despite starting and finishing with a duck, he also had a century and a half century in the middle of them!

He batted 4 times, with 0 not outs, scoring 188 runs at an average of 47.00. His highest score was 122 on 1st May 2011 at Northumbria University. He also took 1 catch and had 1 stumping for The University.

Up to the start of the 2011 season Jobson had played 7 NEPL matches, batting 6 times, with 2 not outs, he had scored 210 runs at an average of 52.50, with 2 half centuries, his highest NEPL score at this point was 70 not out on 11th September 2010 at Newcastle. He had taken 2 catches.

Jobson played 16 matches in the NEPL in 2011, batting 14 times with 0 not outs, he scored 301 runs at an average of 21.50. He scored 2 half centuries with a highest score of 68, scored on 28th May 2011 at Newcastle. He didn't bowl but took 19 catches and had 4 stumpings in the NEPL in 2011.

Stephen Humble batted at number six to open the 2011 season, scoring 47, he also opened the bowling, taking 2 for 13. He had now played 139 NEPL matches, batting 96 times, with 25 not outs, he had scored 1581 runs at an average of 22.26. He had scored 4 half centuries with the highest score of 78, scored in August 2006 and mentioned earlier.

He had bowled 9733 balls in The NEPL to this point, with 437 maidens, conceding 4219 runs and taking 291 wickets at an average of 14.49. His best bowling was still the 8 for 55 mentioned earlier and he had taken 41 catches.

Humble played 16 matches in the NEPL in 2011, batting 13 times with 3 not outs, he scored 430 runs at an average of 43.00. He scored 3 half centuries, with a highest score of 63 not out, made on 3rd September 2011 at home to Durham Academy.

He also bowled 983 balls in the NEPL in the 2011 season, with 40 maidens, he conceded 450 runs and took 39 wickets at an average of 11.53. His best bowling figures were 7 for 38, taken on 30th May 2011 at home to Gateshead Fell. He took 10 catches in the NEPL in 2011.

Ben Jones-Lee, a right-handed batsman and wicketkeeper, batted at number seven on 30th April to start the season, scoring 19. John Graham remembers him as being "a very good junior player, he was a really determined batsman, he was hard hitting and very destructive on his day, as a keeper, he was a natural, it came pretty easy to him. He went to work in the City of London and didn't play as much as cricket as he could have done."

He first came to the attention of the record keepers on 5th May 1993 playing for The Royal Grammar School at Dame Allan's School in a 40-over match. He didn't bowl but scored 30 not out. Within a few weeks he was playing for Northumberland Under 19's against Durham Under 19's at Backworth. Unfortunately, he didn't get to bat. He played several times for The Under 19's, progressing to The Northumberland Under 21 side, on 22nd August 1995 he played against The West Tyne Cricket League at Stocksfield. He had a catch and a stumping when his side bowled and scored 19 when they batted.

He appeared for South North first eleven on 27th July 1996 at home to Benwell Hill, he had 2 stumpings when his side bowled and scored 3 when they batted.

He had to wait until the season opener on 30th April 2011 against Stockton to make his NEPL debut, he made 19. He would play 3 more NEPL games in 2011, making a high score of 28 on 4th June at South Shields. He played 1 more NEPL game in 2012 and 2 more in 2013, his seventh and last NEPL appearance came on 4th May 2013 at home to Hetton Lyons.

In total he scored 89 runs in his 5 NEPL innings, scoring 89 runs at an average of 17.80.

Jonny Wightman a right-handed batsman and right arm fast bowler, he batted at eight to open the season, scoring a single, he opened the bowling and took 1 for 28. John Graham recalls that when he arrived at South North from South Shields he was "a tearaway fast bowler, he was fast, he could leak a lot of runs but he also took a lot of wickets, he has a bit of a slingy action, moving the ball away from the right hander, as a batsman this made him hard to line up, he had a good bouncer and the habit of getting good players early on, very early on, often first or second ball with a good yorker or a full ball bowling them. He complimented Stephen Humble well as our opening bowler's. He would evolve to become a very good bowler, using a change of pace well, and showing control and accuracy as he got more experienced. Like Humble, he was also a big game player, often outstanding when it mattered most."

The first thing I could find for Wightman was he was selected for The Bradford/Leeds University Centre of Cricketing Excellence for a 2-day game against Northamptonshire starting on 9th April 2005. It wasn't a memorable debut as his side lost by an innings and 62 runs. His last appearance for The University side came on 6th June 2007 against Warwickshire at Leeds. He took 5 for 102 but was absent hurt when his side batted.

He played 23 matches for the side, batting 23 times, he was not out 7 times, scoring 260 runs at an average of 16.25 with a highest score of 36.

He bowled 1828 balls, with 28 maidens, conceding 1432 runs and taking 26 wickets at an average of 55.07. His best bowling was the 5 for 102 mentioned earlier. He took 5 catches.

He made his NEPL debut on 26th April 2008 for South Shields at The Racecourse against The Durham Academy, taking his first NEPL wicket, Michael Turns, leg before for 10 as he finished with 2 for 45.

He played his last match for South Shields on 30th August 2008 at home to Benwell Hill, he scored 3 and took 0 for 26. At this point he had played 20 NEPL matches, batting on 9 occasions, with 1 not out, scoring 59 runs at an average of 7.37 and a high score of 13.

He had bowled 1209 balls, with 24 maidens, conceding 823 runs and taking 43 wickets at an average of 19.13. His best bowling figures were 6 for 75 on 7th June 2008 at Norton. He had taken 1 NEPL catch.

Wightman played in The Lancashire League as pro for Burnley in 2009, making his debut on 26th April, at Turf Moor against Rawtenstall. He took 6 for 44 and didn't bat as his side won by 10 wickets.

It looks like he only played three matches for Burnley, he next appeared in the 2009 season, when he made his Minor Counties debut for Northumberland on 31st May at Suffolk. He made 10 when he batted and took 4 for 44 when he bowled.

He played his last Northumberland on 27th May 2018 at Jesmond against Staffordshire; he didn't bat and took 0 for 49.

He played 17 times for the county, batting 8 times, with 3 not outs, he scored 62 runs at an average of 12.40 and a high score of 18 not out.

He bowled 933 balls, with 7 maidens, conceding 980 runs and taking 25 wickets at an average of 39.20. His best bowling figures were 4 for 44 against Suffolk on 31st May 2009. He took 2 catches.

On 5th July 2009 Wightman represented The Durham Senior Cricket League against North Staffordshire in a 45 over match. He took 4 for 52 but failed to score with the bat in a heavy loss.

He made his South North NEPL debut on the season opener of 2010 on 24th April against Durham Academy at Gosforth, he took 2 for 71, Ryan Pringle his first NEPL wicket for South North.

In the 2011 NEPL season Wightman played 16 matches, batting 11 times with 0 not outs, he scored 127 runs at an average of 11.54. his highest score was 37, made on 14th May 2011 at home to Blaydon.

He also bowled 1065 balls in the NEPL in 2011, with 25 maidens, conceding 683 runs and taking 27 wickets at an average of 25.29. His best bowling figures were 4 for 38, taken on 21st May 2011 at Tynemouth. He took 3 catches in the NEPL in 2011.

Wightman is by all accounts a decent non-league footballer, playing as a centre forward for a number of clubs including South Shields, Jarrow, Chester Le Street, Sunderland RCA and Boldon CA.

Lee Crozier batted at nine to start the season, he failed to score but he did take 3 for 48 when South North bowled. He had now played 206 matches, batting 112 times, with 45 not outs, he had scored 1176 runs at an average of 17.55. His highest score and still only half century remained the 89 from his days at Benwell Hill mentioned earlier.

He had also bowled 15341 balls, with 759 maidens, conceding 6318 runs and taking 425 wickets at an average of 14.86. His best bowling was 7 for 21 from 2007 mentioned earlier. He had taken 33 catches.

Crozier played 17 matches in the NEPL in 2011, batting 11 times with 8 not outs, he scored 37 runs at an average of 12.33. His highest score was 14 not out.

He bowled 1311 balls in the NEPL in 2011, with 48 maidens, he conceded 596 runs and took 39 wickets at an average of 15.28. His best bowling figures were 6 for 25, taken on 25th June 2011 at home to Sunderland. He took 3 catches in the NEPL in 2011.

Mayank Banerjee, a right arm medium pace bowler, batted at number 10 to open the 2011 season, he was 0 not out and took 1 for 19. Banerjee was just a young lad of around 16 or 17 at this time, John Graham describes him as "tall, medium pace, he showed great promise, but he didn't play much cricket, I think he sort of drifted away."

Banerjee played for Northumberland Under 13's on 20th June 2006 at Benwell Hill against Cumbria Under 13's. He played for the county at every age group up to and including Under 17 level. His last county appearance coming in a 2-day match starting on 10th August 2010 at Roseworth Terrace for the Under 17's against Cumbria Under 17's.

Up to this point he had played only 2 NEPL matches, making his debut on 15th August 2009 at Tynemouth. He didn't bat but took 2 for 9 when he bowled, his first NEPL wicket was a good one, Andrew Smith, leg before wicket for 3. He did bat in his second game, making 4 on 12th September 2009 but didn't bat in a rain affected game at Chester le Street.

The season opener of 2011 was his only NEPL appearance of the season, in fact it was his last NEPL appearance.

Richard Brook didn't get to bat on 30th April 2011 but took 3 for 42 when his side bowled. Brook had now played 162 NEPL matches, batting 35 times, with 21 not outs, he had scored 64 runs at an average of 4.57. His highest score was 19. He had bowled 8781 balls, with 352 maidens, conceding 4428 runs and taking 276 wickets at an average of 16.04. His best bowling remained the 7 for 28 taken in May 2004 mentioned earlier. He had taken 31 catches.

Brook played 15 matches in the NEPL in 2011, batting 5 times with 3 not outs, he scored 19 runs at an average of 9.50. His highest score was 14 not out.

He bowled 588 balls in the NEPL in 2011, with 17 maidens, conceding 350 runs and taking 15 wickets at an average of 23.33. His best bowling figures were 4 for 7, taken on 13th August 2011 at Gateshead Fell. He didn't take a catch in the NEPL in 2011.

Michael Craigs was a right-handed batsman and left arm seam bowler. John Graham says that "he joined us halfway through the 2011 season, he bowled inswingers to the right hander, when he got it swinging, he would take wickets in clumps for us, he was a captain's dream as he would run in all day when asked, he was a good team player and great in the dressing room. As a batsman he was unorthodox, lots of scoop's, sweep's and paddle's, he was a situational batsman, he understood what needed to be done for the team and would bat accordingly. he was just a good club cricketer; he still plays at Morpeth."

Craigs played just 7 matches in The NEPL in 2011 for South North, batting 7 times with 1 not out, he scored 66 runs at an average of 11.00 and a high score of 24 not out.

He also bowled 181 balls, with 4 maidens, conceding 116 runs and taking 6 wickets, his best bowling figures, 3 for 37 came on 2nd July 2011 at home to the Durham Academy. He also took 7 catches.

Jimmy Miller didn't play in the NEPL in 2011 until 7th May but entering the season he had played 191 matches in the NEPL, batting 169 times with 32 not outs, he had scored 4272 runs at an average of 31.18. He had scored 27 half centuries and 5 centuries. His highest score was 132 not out made for Tynemouth and mentioned earlier.

He had bowled 42 balls in the NEPL, with 0 maidens, conceding 23 runs and taking 1 wicket at an average of 23.00. His best bowling figures was 1 for 2. He had taken 70 NEPL catches up to the end of 2010.

During the 2011 season Miller played 14 matches in the NEPL, batting 13 times with 3 not outs, he scored 237 runs at an average of 23.70. He scored 1 half century, 74 not out on 3rd September 2011 at home to Durham Academy. He didn't bowl in the NEPL in 2011, but he did take 2 catches.

Mark Wood missed the first game of the 2011 season, his South North debut coming a week later, 7th May at home to Hetton Lyons. He took 1 for 26, his first NEPL wicket for South North was opener Paul Riddle, caught by Lee Crozier for 10. He made 26 when he batted, bowled by Jonny Malkin.

Wood played 7 games for South North in 2011, batting 5 times, scoring 54 runs at an average of 10.80, with a high score of 28.

He bowled 344 balls this season, with 7 maidens, conceding 217 runs and taking 13 wickets at an average of 16.69, with a best of 3 for 33.

His last game for them was the game at Sunderland to finish the 2011 season and win or lose the league title. John Graham describes Wood as being "around 18 or 19 at this time, he came to us as more of an all-rounder than an out and out bowler, the lad could bat, he wasn't as aggressive as you see him now but even back then he was a good batsman at our level. In terms of his bowling, we had to be careful with his workload, depending on what he had done in the week Durham would sometimes place limitations on him, he was quick, quick enough for our level, we had really good slip catchers though and I think that helped us and him, he had a slippery bouncer, quick, and he could swing the ball, he was exceptionally good at bowling at left handers. Around the dressing room he was a lovely lad, a good lad, best described as a down to earth Ashington lad with no ego or airs and graces about him."

There was strong rumours that Wood was going to turn out for Ashington during the 2023 season as he built his fitness up prior to The Ashes series, I suspect that the batsmen of Tynemouth and South North who he was supposed to play against were pleased The ECB had a change of heart and didn't let him play!

Wood made his NEPL debut on 12th July 2008 for The Durham Academy against Sunderland at Maiden Castle. He bowled six overs, taking 1 for 25, his first NEPL wicket was Ashley Thorpe, leg before, for 32 and he made 5 when The Academy batted. He was a regular in The Academy side in The NEPL from his debut until 4th September 2010, when he played the last game of this period, away at Sunderland. He didn't bowl in the game but did score 88 when he batted. This spell with The Academy had seen Wood play 43 games, he batted 39 times with 4 not outs, he scored 837 runs at an average of 23.91, his highest score was 88 at Sunderland.

After spending the 2011 season with South North he next appeared in The NEPL in the 2012 season, 12th May to be exact, playing for Tynemouth at home to Sunderland. He played 11 matches for Tynemouth that season, batting 11 times, with 2 not outs, he scored 242 runs at an average of 26.88. He made 1 half century, exactly 50, made on 19th May 2012 at home to Newcastle.

He also bowled 173 balls for them, with 9 maidens, conceding 65 runs and taking 3 wickets at an average of 21.66. His best bowling was 3 for 23 on 28th July 2012 at Sunderland.

He would play one more NEPL match, for Durham Academy on 28th June 2014 at home to Blaydon, he didn't bowl in the game and scored 13.

His NEPL career covered 59 matches, with 53 innings, 6 not outs, scoring 1062 runs at an average of 22.59, with a high score of 88. He had 4 half centuries to his credit.

He also bowled a bit, 2435 balls to be precise, 72 maidens, conceding 1378 runs and taking 79 wickets at an average of 17.44 and a best of 7 for 43, taken on 1st May 2010 for Durham Academy at Hetton Lyons. He took 8 NEPL career catches.

Mark Wood, to the date of writing this, April 2024, and he is by no means done, as well as being a key part of England's 2019 World Cup winning side, has now played 34 Test Matches, 66 One Day Internationals and 28 International T20 games for England.

Right, back to the matter in hand, the 2011 season had started badly for South North, losing three games in a row early on, to Blaydon, Newcastle, and Tynemouth.

The Blaydon game on 14th May 2011 was "worthy" of closer inspection, South North's bowling attack that day comprised of Stephen Humble, Jonny Wightman, Mark Wood, Lee Crozier and Richard Brook. Blaydon batted first and scored 250 for 8 wickets declared, Allan Worthy had scored exactly 100 when Mark Wood bowled him. The next highest score was 38 from Henry Nicholls. Wood had 3 for 49, Crozier 3 for 69 and Humble 2 for 39. When South North batted, wicketkeeper Sam Jobson had 47 but they were dismissed for 196, Gary Stewart 3 for 35 as Blaydon won by 54 runs.

John Graham recalls that "reigning champions Chester le Street were about eighty, possibly ninety points ahead with only six or seven games left, but we had gone on a strong winning run in the second half of the season, including beating them at Gosforth by one wicket. It all came down to the last game of the season."

That win against Chester took place on 29th August 2011, Chester batted first and were 174 all out in 58.1 overs. Quentin Hughes opened, and top scored with 30. Seven batsmen were in double figures. All four South North bowlers that day took wickets, Humble had 1 for 23, Wightman 4 for 71, Brook 1 for 35 and Crozier 3 for 42. When South North batted, only three batsmen plus extras made double figures, they had lost John Graham second ball, caught by Andrew Smith off the bowling of Andrew Tye. The middle order got them close, Chris Hewison at three, making the top score in the match with 75, Sam Jobson at four, scored 17 and Adam Cragg at five, had 35. The bowling combination of Andrew Tye and Richard Waite however almost got Chester home, South North slipped from 136 for 3 to 136 for 4 when Hewison was caught by Andrew Bell of the bowling of Tye, number six Jimmy Miller went next, caught by Hughes off Waite for 4, 145 for 5. Cragg and Humble took the score to 157 when the sixth wicket, Cragg, fell, caught by Simon Birtwisle off Tye. At 167 Humble, batting seven, was caught by Waite, again off Tye. 167 for 7.

Michael Craigs went next, caught by John Coxon off the bowling of Waite for 3, South North 168 for 8, when the scores were level, number nine, Jonny Wightman was bowled by Tye for 2, South North 174 for 9. Lee Crozier 5 not out and Richard Brook 0 not out, got the required run. Tye had 5 for 52 and Waite 4 for 49.

South North got 26 points, Chester 6 points, a 20-point swing with only two games left.

In the penultimate game of the season, South North drew with Durham Academy, taking 11 points. Chester le Street also drew, with South Shields, they had Shields 47 for 8 from 25 overs, chasing 244 to win when the weather intervened, Chester picked up 16 points.

The League table with one game to go would show Chester le Street on top, with 382 points, South North second on 377 points. Advantage Chester le Street for the final day of the season, Saturday 10th September 2011.

Chester le Street were at home to The Durham Academy for their final game, both teams had strong sides out, Keaton Jennings among the Academy players. South North's final game was away at Sunderland, both teams had strong sides out, Chris Rushworth in the Sunderland line up, Mark Wood playing for South North. Both Chester le Street and South North won the toss and elected to bat, both sides with an eye on bonus points?

Chris Rushworth soon had South North in trouble at 6 for 2 after removing John Graham for a duck and Chris Hewison for a single.

Chester were also in trouble early on, Simon Birtwisle leg before to Jamie Harrison, a left arm fast bowler. Chester 2 for 1. This became 14 for 2 when fellow opener Quentin Hughes was run out for 2.

Four-time NEPL Player of the Year Richard Waite came in at number four and he and Andrew Smith calmed Chester nerves as they added 34 for the third wicket before Waite was caught by Cole Pearce off the medium pace bowling of Usman Arshad for 17. Chester 48 for 3.

South North opener Adam Heather and number four Adam Cragg, 37, steadied their ship, taking the score to 71 before Cragg was out, caught off the bowling of Jaspreet Singh. South North 71 for 3.

Over at Chester, Smith and John Coxon had taken the score to 72 when Coxon was caught by skipper Ben Raine off the bowling of Arshad for 13. Chester 72 for 4. This became 87 for 5 when Smith was caught by Ramanpreet Singh off the bowling of Harrison for 44.

South North meanwhile fell to 91 for 4 when number five batsman, Sam Jobson was caught and bowled by Jaspreet Singh for 17.

Alan Mustard was batting six for Chester and he and number seven Liam Simpson put on 48 for the sixth wicket, Mustard next out for 18, caught by Josh Bousfield off the bowling of Ryan Buckley. Chester 135 for 5. When Chester number eight Ian Hunter was caught by Cole Pearce off the bowling of Arshad for just 2, Chester were now 138 for 7.

Jimmy Miller and Adam Cragg added 50 for the fifth South North wicket, Miller making 20 when he was caught by Chris Youldon off the bowling of Kieran Waterson. South North 141 for 5. South North's Mark Wood copped a duck with only one run added to their score, bowled by Jaspreet Singh. South North 142 for 6. Stephen Humble batted at eight today, he fell next, caught by Chris Rushworth off the bowling of Waterson for 5. South North 148 for 7. Opener Adam Heather was out next for 62, caught by Youldon off Chris Rushworth as South North were now 158 for 8.

Meanwhile, elsewhere, Liam Simpson was out next, for 48, caught and bowled by Keaton Jennings, Chester 185 for 8.

South North number nine, Michael Craigs and number ten, Jonny Wightman, 19 had taken their score to 192 for 9 when Wightman was dismissed, caught by Jaspreet Singh off Waterson.

Chester's Aussie pro Andrew Tye, who was predominately a bowler, batted at number nine today, he was 47 not out, Andrew Bell was 9 not out, when Chester declared on 210 for 8 from 60 overs. Only David Wilson did not bat. Arshad had 3 for 46, Jamie Harrison 2 for 38, Buckley had 1 for 52 and Jennings 1 for 13. This got them 4 batting points, Chester now had 386 points.

South North's number eleven Lee Crozier was 4 not out and Craigs 24 not out when South North declared after 57 overs with their score on 203 for 9. Kieran Watson was the pick of the bowlers, 3 for 36, Rushworth had 2 for 41 and Jaspreet Singh 3 for 78. This got them 8 batting points, South North now had 385 points.

The weather was also threatening to play a part, The Academy innings was reduced to 48 overs, making a draw the most likely outcome.

When Sunderland batted, they too found the new ball difficult, losing both openers, Joe Coyne for a duck and Dan Shurben for a single, both to Stephen Humble, they were 15 for 2.

Number three Michael Turns and Chris Hooker took the score to 42 before Hooker was caught by Adam Heather off the bowling of Mark Wood for 7. Sunderland 42 for 3. Ashley Thorpe came in next, he scored 12, L.B.W to Humble, Sunderland now 57 for 4.

Over at Ropery Lane, Chester were finding the Academy a bit tougher to crack, their openers had put on 53 for the first wicket before Usman Arshad was caught by Andrew Smith off the bowling of Richard Waite for 28. Durham Academy 53 for 1.

At Sunderland the hosts slipped to 85 for 5 when number six batsman Greg Applegarth was caught by Craigs off the bowling of Wightman for 7. Next batsman up was number seven, Tom Skillbeck, he made 6, caught by Cragg off Lee Crozier. Sunderland now 95 for 6. Michael Turns was the main point of resistance in the Sunderland side, scoring 65, when the score was 114, he was caught by Cragg off the bowling of Craigs. Sunderland now 114 for 7.

Ramanpreet Singh was batting at three for The Academy, he had scored 44 and the second wicket added 94 when he was dismissed by Andrew Bell, caught by Quentin Hughes. Durham Academy 147 for 2.

Sunderland number nine Jaspreet Singh added just 5, caught by wicketkeeper Jobson off Craigs, they were now 121 for 8......storm clouds gathering in more ways than one for both Chester and South North.

Ben Raine was the third and final Durham Academy wicket to fall, caught by Hughes off Waite for 83, Durham 167 for 3. Keaton Jennings, batting five, was on 11 not out, number six Graham Clark was 19 not out when Durham's innings was closed at 190 for 3 from their 48 overs. Match drawn, Chester le Street picked up 1 bowling point and 3 points for a "losing draw." This gave them 8 for the match and meant they closed the season on 390 points.

At Ashbrooke Chris Youldon and Chris Rushworth then put together the second highest partnership of the Sunderland innings, 32, taking the score to 153 when Youldon was caught by Adam Cragg off the bowling of Humble for 17. Sunderland nine down, plenty of overs left but the clouds looking even less promising if you're South North.

They hadn't added a run when, with the second ball of the 42nd over, Mark Wood tempted Chris Rushworth to hit one straight up in the air, Lee Crozier obliged with the catch, Sunderland 153 all out, South North won by 50 runs. Rushworth had scored 23, last man Kieran Waterson was 0 not out. All five bowlers used took at least one wicket, Stephen Humble had 4 for 30, Jonny Wightman 1 for 28, Mark Wood 2 for 36, Lee Crozier 1 for 32 and Michael Craigs 2 for 24. Adam Cragg took 4 catches in the field.

John Graham recalls that "as we were walking off the field, it started to rain, it poured down, we wouldn't have got one more ball in, never mind one more over."

Nearly fifteen years later I asked Mark Wood about these events, he recalled, right down to which ball of the over it was, what had happened "It was the second ball of the over and I bowled a slower ball, and even though they weren't going to win, Sunderland were still coming hard at us, "Rushy" hit it straight to Lee Crozier at long on. We hadn't even left the field when it started pouring!"

South North picked up 28 points from the game to finish the season on 405 points, they had won the 2011 title on the last day of the season by 15 points from Chester le Street.

I also asked Wood about his memories of this season, he said" Funny enough, I don't remember much about the cricket, I remember more about the lads, the shared dressing room experiences, I do remember what a good cricketer Jimmy Miller was, and I used to love bowling with Stephen Humble, he was a great lad and bowler, we had a brilliant left arm spinner in Richard Brook who was great craic in the dressing room, we were really strong across the side.

Originally, I wasn't sure how I would fit in, me being an Ashington lad and South North had this posh boy's reputation, but it couldn't have been further from the truth. I knew Adam Cragg as he had been at Ashington and I had played for Northumberland with him and Michael Craigs, Bill Graham had been the Northumberland Team Manager at that time as well, I had a meeting with Bill and John Windows and they, and I, felt it was the right place for that time in my career.

I was still at college at this time, and they got me some coaching work at their indoor nets which helped me out, when I met John Graham, I was convinced that they wanted to win things and that if I felt that if I wasn't doing the business they had plenty of other good cricketers who could replace me, and I felt that would spur me on as well.

When I first started playing for South North, I found a dressing room full of guys I used to look up to, I was a Northumberland lad, my uncle Neil had played for the county with some of these guys, lads like Adam Heather, Lee Crozier, John Graham, I had the connection with Bill Graham from the county too and one of my Ashington coaches, Steve Williams was a Northumberland coach.

I enjoyed playing for John Graham, as a captain he was always calm, I never saw him flustered, he was very competitive, but it came through in a positive way, good body language, he had a good perspective on cricket and on life, so much so that he wanted us to enjoy ourselves on the field, he wanted us to enjoy our achievements, and he got a lot of respect from us because of his attitude to us. As a team we enjoyed each other's company as well and that helps around a cricket dressing room."

The 2011 Banks Salver was won by The Durham Academy, Chester le Street collected the T20 trophy and Ryan Pringle of Hetton Lyons was the NEPL Player of the Year.

Pringle had played 19 matches in the NEPL in 2011, batting 19 times with 3 not outs, he had scored 523 runs at an average of 32.68. He scored 3 half centuries with a highest score of 90 not out, made on 14th May 2011 at home to Gateshead Fell.

He also bowled 1375 balls in the NEPL in 2011, with 48 maidens, conceding 729 runs and taking 50 wickets at an average of 14.58. His best bowling figures were 6 for 30, taken on 29th August 2011 at home to Tynemouth. He also took 6 catches in the NEPL in 2011.

South North made it to the final of The Twenty20 Cockspur Cup at The Rose Bowl, Southampton on 23rd September 2010 where they played Swardeston CC from Norwich and The East Anglian Premier League. Swardeston won the toss and batted first, making 129 for 8 from their 20 overs. Their first four batmen scored just four between them, with three ducks, 72 not out from number five, Peter Lambert, the main reason they posted a score. Stephen Humble had 3 for 12, Jonny Wightman 2 for 27, Lee Crozier 2 for 22 and Richard Brook 1 for 14 the wicket takers. When South North batted, they fell just short, John Graham had 34, Chris Hewison 24 and Chris Hooker 22, 118 for 6 from their 20 overs.

TABLE 38   NEPL 2011.

	Played	Won	Draw/Aban	Lost	Pen Points	Bonus Points	Points
South North	22	13	6	3	0	180	405
Chester le Street	22	11	8	3	0	185	390
Blaydon	22	11	6	5	0	172	367
Benwell Hill	22	8	11	3	0	131	310
Hetton Lyons	22	8	9	5	0	141	306
Durham CA	22	6	11	5	2	137	286
Sunderland	22	7	8	7	0	132	279
Newcastle	22	5	11	6	1	109	236
Tynemouth	22	3	9	10	0	104	192
Stockton	22	3	7	12	0	102	184
South Shields	22	3	9	10	0	84	174
Gateshead Fell	22	2	9	11	0	70	139

TABLE 39   NEPL Batting Averages 2011.

Qualification 350 Runs.

23 Batsmen Qualified this season.

Player	Club	Inns	N. O	H. S	Runs	Average
(1) M.D Stoneman	Blaydon	10	1	130	547	60.78
(2) K.K Jennings	Durham CA	12	4	88	471	58.88
(3) M.J Richardson	Newcastle	14	3	162 no	618	56.18
(4) S.D Birbeck	Hetton Lyons	16	2	141 no	730	52.14
(5) Zohaib Khan	Benwell Hill	15	1	132 no	641	45.79
(6) G.M Scott	Hetton Lyons	18	2	131	723	45.19
(7) Rameez Shazhad	Tynemouth	16	1	109	673	44.87
(8) S. Humble	South North	13	3	63 no	430	43.00
(9) J.W Coxon	Chester le Street	16	5	102 no	469	42.64
(10) A.T Heather	South North	14	2	90	504	42.00
(11) A.J Maiden	Benwell Hill	15	1	105	585	41.79
(12) G.D Bridge	Blaydon	15	5	69	406	40.60
(20) C.J Hewison	South North	16	0	90	557	34.81

TABLE 40   NEPL Bowling Averages 2011.

Qualification 20 Wickets.

23 Bowlers Qualified this season.

Player	Club	Overs	Mdns	Runs	Wkts	Average
(1) S. Humble	South North	163.5	40	450	39	11.54
(2) Kamran Hussain	Hetton Lyons	99.5	23	321	27	11.89
(3) J. Kilpatrick	Benwell Hill	133.2	22	431	35	12.31
(4) G.D Bridge	Blaydon	313.2	81	882	58	12.68
(5) D.J Hymers	Tynemouth	175.2	42	529	38	13.92
(6) R.D Pringle	Hetton Lyons	228.1	51	729	50	14.58
(7) C. Rushworth	Sunderland	116.3	25	368	25	14.72
(8) R.P Waite	Chester le Street	220.5	55	683	45	15.18
(9) L.J Crozier	South North	218.3	48	593	39	15.21
(10) Zohaib Khan	Benwell Hill	214.2	41	688	41	16.78
(11) C. Varley	Blaydon	174.2	27	641	36	17.81
(12) L. Simpson	Chester le Street	122.0	35	363	20	18.15
(17) J.R Wightman	South North	177.3	25	683	27	25.30

South North 2011 NEPL Champions.

Left to Right – Back Row- J.N Miller, M.A Wood, S. Humble, C.J Hewison, M.A Craigs

Front Row- S.O Jobson, A.T Heather, J.A Graham, L.J Crozier, R.M Brook.

Ryan Pringle, Player of the Year in 2011, seen here on 27th April 2024 bowling at Tynedale.

Photo by Steve Graham.

2012

South North would start the 2012 season without one of the mainstays of their batting line up, Chris Hewison had gone to play for Swalwell for family reasons. They started the season at home to Gateshead Fell on Saturday 21st April, only 26 overs play was possible before the game was abandoned with South North 60 for 1.

The South North team that started the first game of the season was as follows-

John Graham opened the batting on 21st April, he was the unlucky batsman dismissed before the rain came, leg before for 9. Graham was still South North captain, he had now played 227 NEPL matches, batting 217 times, with 28 not outs, he had scored 6960 runs at an average of 36.82. He had scored 51 half centuries and 9 centuries, his highest score was still the 132 from 2006 mentioned earlier.

He had also bowled 2738 balls in The NEPL to this point, with 96 maidens, conceding 15389 runs and taking 62 wickets at an average of 24.80. His best bowling was still the 4 for 15 from 2008 mentioned earlier. He had taken 122 catches.

During the 2012 season Graham played 18 matches in the NEPL, he batted 18 times with 1 not out, he scored 550 runs at an average of 32.35. he scored 4 half centuries and 1 century, 100 not out, scored on 9th June 2012 at home to Newcastle. He bowled just one over in the NEPL in 2012, 0 for 2, he also took 18 catches in the NEPL in the 2012 season.

Adam Heather opened the batting on 21st April, he was 27 not out when the game was abandoned. Heather had now played 213 NEPL matches, batting 203 times, with 26 not outs, he had scored 6361 runs at an average of 35.93. He had scored 33 half centuries and 11 centuries, his highest score was still 140 not out from July 2009 mentioned earlier. His bowling record hadn't changed from the 12 balls mentioned earlier and he had now taken 73 catches and had 4 stumpings.

During the 2012 season Heather played 18 matches in the NEPL, batting 18 times with 1 not out, he scored 383 runs at an average of 22.52. He scored 2 half centuries, with a highest score of 68, made on 30th June 2012 at South Shields. He took 3 NEPL catches in 2012.

Joe Coyne, a right-handed batsman and off spin bowler, batted at three to start the 2012 season; he was 9 not out when the game was abandoned. This was his South North debut. John Graham recalls "He had been at The Durham Academy, then he went to Sunderland as their Durham Contracted player, then signed for us and played 2012 and a bit of 2013. He was a very good player of spin, he had a very good technique and would make big scores for us, as a bowler he developed himself nicely."

The first trace of Coyne in representative cricket came on 5th June 2007 for Durham Under 15's against Northumberland Under 15's at Percy Main. He scored 114, opening the batting. He progressed through the County Junior levels, playing at Under 17 level as well.

On 7th May 2008 Coyne appeared for The Durham Academy against Scotland Under 19's at Bothwell Castle. Ben Stokes and Mark Wood were in the same Academy side.

Coyne continued to progress at Durham, playing for The Second XI in a 3-day match starting on 20th May 2009 at Worcestershire. Mark Wood and Mark Stoneman among his team mates this time as he made 11 in his solitary innings. He would go on to play 34 matches for Durham Seconds, batting 29 times, with 9 not outs, he scored 607 runs at an average of 30.35. He scored 2 half centuries and 1 century, 181, made in a 3-day match starting on 23rd August 2010 at The Rose Bowl against Hampshire.

He bowled 546 balls for Durham Seconds, with 1 maiden, conceding 497 runs and taking 17 wickets at an average of 29.23. His best bowling figures were 3 for 23 on 27th May 2011 at Brandon against Nottinghamshire Second XI. He took 27 catches.

Coyne had made his NEPL debut on 24th April 2010 for The Durham Academy at South North, he was run out for 40 when he batted, his last NEPL game for The Academy came on 4th September 2010 at Sunderland.

Coyne played 18 matches in The NEPL for The Durham Academy, batting 18 times, with 0 not outs, he scored 419 runs at an average of 23.27. He had scored 2 half centuries and 1 century, 107, made on 31st July at Tynemouth.

He also bowled 212 balls in The NEPL for The Academy, with 3 maidens, conceding 156 runs and took 8 wickets at an average of 19.50. His best bowling figures were 2 for 18, taken on 8th May at Stockton. He took 9 catches in The NEPL in the 2010 season.

He made his NEPL debut for Sunderland at the start of the 2011 season, on 30th April, to be precise, at South Shields with his last NEPL game for Sunderland on 10th September 2011 at home to South North.

Coyne played 18 matches in The NEPL for Sunderland, batting 17 times, with 1 not out, he scored 389 runs at an average of 24.31. He had scored 3 half centuries, his highest NEPL score for them was 88 not out on 11th June at Hetton Lyons.

He bowled 350 balls, with 13 maidens, conceding 169 runs and took 8 wickets at an average of 21.12. His best bowling figures were 5 for 30, taken on 29th August at Stockton. He took 6 catches in The NEPL in the 2011 season.

When the 2012 season started Coyne had already played 36 matches in the NEPL, batting 35 times, with 1 not out, he had scored 808 runs at an average of 23.76. He had scored 5 half centuries and 1 century, 107 mentioned earlier.

He had also bowled 562 balls in the NEPL, with 16 maidens, conceding 325 runs and taking 16 wickets at an average of 20.31. His best bowling was the 5 for 30 mentioned earlier. He had taken 15 NEPL catches.

Having made his debut for South North in the washed out 2012 season opener, Coyne would go on to play 19 matches in the title winning side, batting 17 times, with 4 not outs, he scored 266 runs at an average of 20.46, with 1 half century, 56, scored on 18th August 2012 at home to Sunderland.

He bowled 305 balls in the season, with 10 maidens, conceding 136 runs and taking 14 wickets at an average of 9.71. His best bowling figures were 4 for 11, taken on 4th August at home to Hetton Lyons. He took 13 NEPL catches in 2013.

Coyne played his last NEPL match for South North on 7th September 2013 at Benwell Hill. He played 39 matches in The NEPL for South North, batting 37 times, with 7 not outs, he scored 559 runs at an average of 18.63. He had scored 2 half centuries, his highest NEPL score for them was 63 on 20th July at Hetton Lyons.

He bowled 1208 balls, with 52 maidens, conceding 545 runs and took 43 wickets at an average of 12.67. His best bowling figures were 5 for 30, taken on 25th May 2013 at Sunderland. He took 27 catches in The NEPL for South North.

Coyne made his NEPL debut for Whitburn on 23rd April 2013 at home to The Durham Academy. Batting at number four, he scored 71 not out, adding 118 in an unbroken 3rd wicket partnership with opener Dan Shurben, Shurben was 106 not out as Whitburn won by 8 wickets. Matthew Potts was in The Academy side that day.

Joe Coyne played his last NEPL game for Whitburn on 10th September 2016 at home to Tynemouth. He had played 20 matches in The NEPL for them, batting 19 times, with 4 not outs, he scored 615 runs at an average of 41.00. He had scored 4 half centuries and 1 century, 126 not out scored on 21st May 2016 at home to South Shields.

He bowled 121 balls in The NEPL for Whitburn, with 7 maidens, conceding 99 runs and took 2 wickets at an average of 49.50. His best bowling figures were 1 for 16, taken on 4th June 2016 at home to Chester le Street. He took 6 catches in The NEPL for Whitburn.

Coyne made his NEPL debut for Eppleton on 15th April 2017 at Newcastle, the hosts batted first, scoring 235 for 9 declared, Ben McGee had 91. When Eppleton batted Coyne top scored the innings with 53 as Eppleton won by two wickets.

Coyne played his last game for Eppleton, and last game to date, in the NEPL, on 1st September 2018 at Chester le Street.

He had played 41 matches in The NEPL for Eppleton, batting 41 times, with 6 not outs, he scored 864 runs at an average of 24.68. He had scored 5 half centuries. His highest NEPL score for them was 62 not out on 6th May 2017 at home to Hetton Lyons.

He bowled 2383 balls in The NEPL for Eppleton, with 74 maidens, conceding 1374 runs and took 62 wickets at an average of 22.16. His best bowling figures were 5 for 40, taken on 26th May 2018 at Whitburn. He took 16 catches in The NEPL for Eppleton.

Matthew Potts popped up during Joe Coyne's bio, so now seems to be an appropriate time to have a look at him in the NEPL. Potts made his NEPL debut for The Durham Academy on 23rd April 2016 at Whitburn, he opened the batting, scoring 12, and took 0 for 7 when he bowled. He had to wait until 21st May at The Riverside against Hetton Lyons for his first NEPL wicket, Jonny Malkin caught by Jack McCarthy for 20.

His last NEPL appearance for The Academy came on 19th August 2017 at home to Chester le Street.

Potts played 31 matches in The NEPL for The Academy, batting 26 times, with 3 not out's, he scored 310 runs at an average of 13.47. His highest score was 38, came at The Riverside on 30th July 2016.

He had bowled 1329 balls, with 32 maidens, conceding 700 runs and taking 31 wickets at an average of 22.58. His best bowling figures were 4 for 35 on 3rd June 2017 at Chester le Street. He took 10 NEPL catches.

He made his debut for Sacriston in The NEPL on 12th May 2018 at Stockton, he didn't bowl but batted at number three, making 94 not out as Sacriston won by 6 wickets. He played his last NEPL game for Sacriston and in the league, on 13th July 2019 at home to Burnmoor. The game was abandoned after 32 overs, Potts had neither batted nor bowled.

Potts played 38 matches in the NEPL, batting 32 times, with 4 not outs, he scored 655 runs at an average of 23.39. He scored 2 half centuries and 1 century, 110, came at Eppleton on 25th May 2019. And came from 118 balls and contained 13 fours and 2 sixes.

He bowled 1441 balls, with 36 maidens, conceding 738 runs and taking 31 wickets at an average of 23.80. His best bowling figures were 4 for 35 on 3rd June 2017 at Chester le Street. He took 11 NEPL catches.

At the time of writing, April 2024, Matthew Potts had represented England in 6 Test Matches and 4 One Day Internationals. He has played 48 first class matches for Durham and The England Lions; he had also played 10 List A matches for Durham and 44 Twenty 20 games for Durham and The Northern Superchargers.

Returning to the South North line up for 2012.

Adam Cragg was listed to bat at four to start the season. He entered the 2012 season having played 108 NEPL matches, batting 88 times, with 16 not out's, he had scored 2051 runs at an average of 28.48. He had scored 8 half centuries and 1 century, 102, his first in the NEPL, had come on 15th May 2010 at Roseworth Terrace against Blaydon. He had never bowled in The NEPL but had taken 74 catches and had 11 stumpings.

Cragg played 19 NEPL matches in the 2012 season, batting 17 times, with 1 not out, he had scored 380 runs at an average of 23.75. He scored 3 half centuries with a highest score of 79, made on 2nd June 2012 at Sunderland. He did not bowl in The NEPL in 2012 but took 21 catches and had 4 stumpings that season.

Paul Coughlin, a right -handed batsman and right arm medium pace bowler, was listed to bat at five to start the season, this was his South North debut. John Graham says that "he came to us for 2012 and a bit of 2013, he was a young lad, around 18 or 19 but he was breaking into the Durham set up at this time, you could see he was good enough to go on and play first class cricket, he bowled at a good pace, when he batted, he was a clean striker of the ball, and he was an absolutely unbelievable fielder. He was a nice lad around the dressing room too."

There is very little of Coughlin in the records for junior cricket, the first note coming on 24th June 2007 for Durham Under 14's against Cumbria. There was only one more recorded appearance, another under 14 one in 2007 and the next thing was his appearance in the NEPL. Coughlin made his NEPL debut on 24th April 2010 for The Durham Academy against South North at Roseworth Terrace. He scored 31 and took 0 for 24.

He took his first NEPL wicket on 8th May 2010 at Stockton, opener Jonathan Rickard, caught and bowled for 56.

His last game for The Academy in The NEPL came on 10th September 2011 at Chester le Street.

He had played 36 matches in The NEPL for The Academy, batting 30 times, with 6 not outs, he scored 812 runs at an average of 33.83. He scored 4 half centuries; his highest score was 84 not out on 30th April 2011 at Newcastle.

He bowled 930 balls in the NEPL, with 22 maidens, conceding 627 runs and taking 16 wickets at an average of 39.18. His best bowling figures were 4 for 24, taken on 30th August 2010 at Gateshead Fell. He had taken 10 NEPL catches to this point.

After making his debut in the washed out first game of the 2012 season, Coughlin played 14 times for South North in the NEPL that season, batting 11 times, with 0 not out's, he scored 260 runs at an average of 23.63. He scored 1 half century, 84, on 30th June at South Shields.

He bowled 558 balls in The NEPL for South North, with 18 maidens, conceding 292 runs and taking 21 wickets at an average of 13.90. His best bowling figures were 4 for 50, taken on 23rd June at home to Stockton. He took 4 NEPL catches in 2012.

Coughlin would also play the 2013 season in The NEPL at South North, his last game for them coming on 7th September 2013 at Benwell Hill.

He had represented South North 22 times in the NEPL, he batted 18 times with 1 not out, he scored 471 runs at an average of 27.70. He had scored 3 half centuries; his highest score remained the 84 mentioned earlier.

With the ball he bowled 576 balls in The NEPL for them, with 18 maidens, conceding 299 runs and taking 21 wickets. His best bowling figures remained the 4 for 50 mentioned earlier. He took a total of 4 NEPL catches for the club.

Coughlin was to appear for Whitburn in the NEPL in 2014, making his debut on 19th April at Stockton. His first wicket for the club in The NEPL was opening batsman David Seymour who was caught by Michael Turns for 17.

His last appearance for Whitburn came in the season opener of 2015, 25th April at Chester le Street.

He had played 12 matches in The NEPL for Whitburn, batting 9 times, with 1 not out, he had scored 291 runs at an average of 36.37. He scored 2 half centuries with a high score of 98, made on 31st May 2014 at Blaydon.

He bowled 378 balls, with 17 maidens, conceding 158 runs and taking 5 wickets at an average of 31.60. His best bowling figures was 3 for 21 on 5th July 2014 at home to Stockton. He took 3 NEPL catches.

Coughlin made his NEPL debut for Eppleton on 23rd April 2016 at home to Newcastle, his last game for them, and last NEPL game to date, April 2024, came on 6th August 2022 at home to Felling.

He had played 12 matches in The NEPL for Eppleton, batting 12 times, with 2 not outs, he had scored 185 runs at an average of 18.50. His highest score was 42.

He also bowled 294 balls in The NEPL for them, with 9 maidens, conceding 155 runs and taking 4 wickets at an average of 38.75. He took 5 catches.

In his NEPL career Paul Coughlin played 82 matches, batting 69 times, with 10 not outs, he had scored 1759 runs at an average of 29.81. He scored 9 half centuries with a high score of 98, mentioned earlier.

He bowled 2178 balls, with 66 maidens, conceding 1239 runs and taking 46 wickets at an average of 26.93. His best bowling figures were 4 for 24 mentioned earlier. He took 22 NEPL catches.

After making his debut for Durham Second XI on 5th May 2010 Coughlin has continued to play for them up to and including 11th September 2023.

He has played 114 matches for Durham Seconds, batting 106 times, with 25 not outs, he has scored 2554 runs at an average of 31.53. He has scored 14 half centuries and 1 century, 231, against Middlesex Second XI in a match starting on 6th September 2016.

He has also bowled 4129 balls for Durham Seconds, with 116 maidens, conceding 2901 runs and taking 131 wickets at an average of 22.14. His best bowling figures are 5 for 33 on 10th April 2012 against Durham M.C.C. He has taken 35 catches for Durham Seconds.

Paul Coughlin played 49 first class matches for Durham, batting 69 times, with 11 not outs, he has scored 1560 runs at an average of 26.89. He scored 9 half centuries and 1 century, 100 not out, in a 4-day match starting on 12th June 2022 at The Riverside against Worcestershire.

He has also bowled 6243 balls in first class cricket, with 218 maidens, conceding 3513 runs and taking 111 wickets at an average of 31.64. His best bowling figures are 5 for 49 on 2nd June 2017 against Northamptonshire in June 2017. He has taken 24 catches.

He has also played 31 List A matches, batting 23 times, with 3 not outs, he has scored 330 runs at an average of 16.50. He scored 1 half century, his highest score in this format being 77 on 12th August 2022 at The Riverside against Gloucestershire.

He has bowled 1042 balls at this level, with 4 maidens, conceding 999 runs and taking 21 wickets at an average of 47.57. His best bowling figures is 3 for 36, taken on 14th May 2017 at Worcestershire. He has taken 9 catches.

Coughlin has also played 59 Twenty20 matches for Durham, batting 41 times, with 9 not outs, he has scored 724 runs at an average of 22.62. He has 1 half century, his highest score of 53.

He has bowled 961 balls in Twenty20 cricket for Durham, with 2 maidens, conceding 1532 runs and taking 63 wickets at an average of 24.31. His best bowling figures is 5 for 42. He has also taken 13 catches.

Jimmy Miller was listed to bat at six to start the season, he had now played 205 NEPL matches, batting 182 times, with 35 not outs, he had scored 4509 runs at an average of 30.67. He had scored 28 half centuries and 5 centuries. His highest score was still 132 not out from May 2001 for Tynemouth mentioned earlier. He hadn't bowled in The NEPL since 2008, so his bowling record hadn't changed from then, but he had now taken 72 catches.

Miller played 19 matches in the NEPL in 2012, batting 15 times with 2 not outs, he scored 363 runs at an average of 27.92. He scored 1 half century and 1 century, the century, 102 not out, was scored on 12th May 2012 at home to Benwell Hill and came from 84 balls and contained 10 fours and 5 sixes. He didn't bowl in 2012 but took 3 NEPL catches.

Sam Jobson was listed to bat at seven to start the season and keep wicket. Up to the end of the 2011 season Jobson had played 23 NEPL matches, batting 20 times, with 2 not outs, he had scored 511 runs at an average of 28.38. He now had scored 4 half centuries and his highest NEPL score at this point remained the 70 not out on 11th September 2010 at Newcastle mentioned earlier. He had now taken 21 and catches and 4 stumpings.

He played 19 matches in the NEPL in 2012, batting 18 times with 4 not outs, he scored 332 runs at an average of 23.71. He scored 1 half century and 1 century. The century, 118 not out was scored on 28th July 2012 at Benwell Hill. The innings came from 130 balls and contained 17 fours and 2 sixes. He didn't bowl in 2012 but took 3 NEPL catches.

Stephen Humble was listed to bat at eight to start the season, he had now played 155 NEPL matches, batting 109 times, with 28 not outs, he had scored 2011 runs at an average of 24.82. He had now scored 7 half centuries with a highest score of 78, scored in August 2006 mentioned earlier.

He had bowled 10716 balls in The NEPL to this point, with 477 maidens, conceding 4669 runs and taking 330 wickets at an average of 14.14. His best bowling was still the 8 for 55 mentioned earlier. He had taken 51 catches.

Humble played 18 matches in the NEPL in 2012, batting 12 times with 2 not outs, he scored 296 runs at an average of 29.60. He scored 2 half centuries, with a highest score of 89, made on 8th September 2012 at home to South Shields.

He bowled 1031 balls in the NEPL in 2012, with 36 maidens, conceding 425 runs and taking 37 wickets at an average of 11.48. His best bowling figures were 6 for 27, taken on 19th May 2012 at Hetton Lyons. He took 4 catches in the NEPL in the 2012 season.

Michael Craigs was listed to bat at nine to start the 2012 season, he had joined part way through the 2011 season and his stats from that season were already stated. The first record and it's a very limited record at that, was that on 27th July 2003 he played a game for Northumberland Under 13's against Cumbria at Sedberg School, Mark Wood was also in the Northumberland side that day, but they lost heavily to Cumbria, by 141 runs.

By 2005 he had progressed through to The County Under 15 set up, playing a match on 26th June at Preston Avenue against Yorkshire, he scored 15 and took 0 for 18 as Yorkshire won by 7 wickets. Craigs moved to Under 17 level for Northumberland, playing a 2-day game against Worcestershire Under 17's starting on 18th July 2006. He scored 9 not out in his one innings and took 2 for 43 when he bowled in a drawn game.

Craigs was selected for a Northumberland Development XI fixture against Durham Academy on 5th May 2009 at Winlaton. He took 0 for 23 and scored 13 as his side won by 3 wickets.

He made an appearance for Northumberland Second XI before he made his Northumberland debut in a 3-day match at Jesmond starting on 6th June 2010 against Hertfordshire. He took 2 for 29 and 0 for 23 and scored 9 in his only innings of a drawn match. His last match for Northumberland would be on 19th May 2019 in a T20 match against Cumberland.

He had played 10 Minor Counties Trophy matches for Northumberland, batting 9 times, with 4 not outs, he had scored 60 runs at an average of 12.00. His highest score was 18.

He had also bowled 415 balls, with 2 maidens, conceding 360 runs and taking 15 wickets at an average of 24.00. His best bowling figures were 3 for 31 taken on 5th May 2013 at home to Herefordshire. He took 2 catches.

Michael Craigs played 19 matches in the NEPL in 2012, batting 13 times with 8 not outs, he scored 154 runs at an average of 30.80. His highest score was 39.

He bowled 509 balls in the NEPL in 2012, with 14 maidens, conceding 317 runs and taking 19 wickets at an average of 16.68. His best bowling figures were 3 for 21, taken on 1st September 2012 at Stockton. He took 3 NEPL catches in 2012.

Lee Crozier was listed to bat at ten to start the 2012 season, he had now played 223 matches, batting 123 times, with 53 not outs, he had scored 1213 runs at an average of 17.32. His highest score and still only half century remained the 89 from his days at Benwell Hill mentioned earlier.

He had also now bowled 16652 balls, with 807 maidens, conceding 6914 runs and taking 464 wickets at an average of 14.90. His best bowling was 7 for 21 from 2007 mentioned earlier. He had taken 36 catches.

Crozier played 19 matches in the NEPL in 2012, batting 6 times with 11 not outs, he scored 11 runs at an average of 3.66. His highest score was 9.

He bowled 1240 balls in the NEPL in 2012, with 51 maidens, conceding 527 runs and taking 36 wickets at an average of 14.63. His best bowling was 5 for 28, taken on 18th August 2012 at home to Sunderland. He didn't take a catch in the NEPL in 2012.

Thomas Hodnett is a right-handed batsman and left arm medium fast bowler; he was listed to bat at eleven to start the season. John Graham remembers that "he was young when he was playing for us, as a batsman he was a tail ender, but he was quick and when it was his day he bowled at a good pace, I recall him going through Benwell Hill one day in 2015, he picked up six or seven wickets, as with a lot of young bowlers he was a little inconsistent, but he had lots of promise, I don't think he played for very long though."

He first came to attention on 4th June 2010 playing for Northumberland Under 14's against Lincolnshire Under 14's in The ECB Under 14 County Cup at Percy Main. He progressed to the county under 15's then made his NEPL debut in the season opener of 2012 against Gateshead Fell.

Hodnett played for The Durham Academy on 9th May 2012 at Winlaton against Northumberland Development XI. He didn't bat but he did take 1 for 18 when he bowled, Neil Corby the victim, bowled for 10.

He played a 2-day game for Northumberland Under 17's starting on 17th July 2012 at Roseworth Terrace, against Norfolk Under 17's. He made 4 in his solitary innings and took 1 for 26 when he bowled in a drawn match. He would play 13 times for Northumberland Under 17's, as an out and out bowler, bowling 744 balls, with 23 maidens, conceding 431 runs and taking 11 wickets at an average of 39.18.

Hodnett made his NEPL debut on 21st April 2012 for South North at home to Gateshead Fell, the game was washed out with South North 60 for 1 after 26 overs. This was his only game in the NEPL during the 2012 season.

He had to wait until 19th April 2014 for his next NEPL game, this game was notable for a double hundred by Karl Turner against Gateshead Fell. Hodnett bowled five overs but didn't take a wicket.

His first NEPL wicket came on 14th June 2014 at Sunderland, middle order batsman, David Hill caught by Jonny Miller for 17. This was his second, and last appearance of the 2014 season for South North.

He also played for Durham Academy during the 2014 season, making his debut on 9th August at The Emirates against Gateshead Fell.

He played 6 matches for The Academy, his best bowling figures being 3 for 33 on 30th August at Chester le Street and his last game for The Academy in 2014 was on 13th September at Blaydon.

He played once more for The Academy in 2015, the opening game of the season at The Emirates against Benwell Hill and he then resumed playing for South North on 30th May 2015 at Hetton Lyons.

His last game for South North in The NEPL came on 14th July 2018 at home to Benwell Hill, he had played 19 matches for the club in the NEPL, bowling 573 balls, with 12 maidens, conceding 374 runs and taking 17 wickets at an average of 22.00.

His best bowling figures were 5 for 16 taken on 20th June 2015 at home to Benwell Hill, this would be the occasion John Graham mentioned earlier when talking about Hodnett.

Hodnett next appeared in The NEPL on 9th August 2014 for Durham Academy at The Emirates against Gateshead Fell. He bowled four overs 0 for 20.

He would play 7 matches in The NEPL for The Academy, again as an out and out bowler, he bowled 246 balls, with 9 maidens, conceding 155 runs and taking 6 wickets at an average of 25.83. His best bowling figures were 3 for 33 on 30th August 2014 at Chester le Street.

Hodnett also played 4 NEPL games for Newcastle in The NEPL in 2016.

His overall career NEPL stats were that he played 30 matches, as a bowler, he bowled 849 balls, with 22 maidens, conceding 537 runs and taking 23 wickets at an average of 23.34, his best bowling figures remained that 5 for 16.

Jonny Wightman missed the first game of the 2012 season. He entered the season having played 57 matches in the NEPL, batting 28 times with 5 not outs, he had scored 205 runs at an average of 8.91. His highest score was 37, mentioned earlier.

He had bowled 3752 balls in the NEPL to the end of the 2011 season, with 74 maidens, he had conceded 2493 runs and took 126 wickets at an average of 19.78. His best bowling figures were 7 for 44, taken on 12th June 2010 and mentioned earlier. He had taken 6 NEPL catches to the end of 2011.

He played 18 matches in the NEPL in 2012, batting 10 times with 5 not outs, he scored 36 runs at an average of 7.20. His highest score was 10.

He also bowled 1092 balls in the NEPL in 2012, with 30 maidens, conceding 588 runs and taking 27 wickets at an average of 21.77. His best bowling figures were 4 for 35, taken on 23rd June 2012 at home to Stockton. He took 2 NEPL catches in 2012.

I want to take a moment to have a look at something in connection with Blaydon, and something that Durham had in place around this time.

Allan Worthy drew my attention to an arrangement between Durham CCC and Canterbury Cricket Club in New Zealand. It was basically an exchange program, it resulted in Cole McConchie playing for Blaydon in the 2012 season.

McConchie played 16 matches in The NEPL in 2012, batting 15 times, with 0 not outs scoring 483 runs at an average of 32.30. He scored 3 half centuries, with a highest score of 86, made on 27th August at Denefield Bank against Sunderland.

He also bowled 413 balls in The NEPL for the club, with 10 maidens, conceding 224 runs and taking 14 wickets at an average of 16.00. His best bowling figures were 5 for 43 on 28th July again at Denefield Bank, this time against Chester le Street. He took 7 NEPL catches.

At the time of writing, before the start of the English 2024 season, McConchie had played 6 ODI's for New Zealand, batting 5 times, with 2 not out's, he has scored 126 runs at an average of 42.00, with 1 half century. His highest score is 64 not out, made on debut, on 3rd May 2023 in Karachi against Pakistan.

He has also bowled 168 balls, with 1 maiden, conceding 135 runs and taking 4 wickets at an average of 33.75. He has taken 3 catches at this level.

He has also played 9 Twenty20 International matches for New Zealand, batting 7 times, with 3 not outs, he has scored 84 runs at an average of 21.00. His highest score is 31 not out.

He has bowled 133 balls, with 0 maidens, conceding 159 runs and taken 7 wickets at an average of 22.71 and a best bowling of 3 for 15. He has taken 1 catch.

Tom Latham was amongst the other players who came to play in The NEPL under the exchange scheme.

Latham made his NEPL debut on 24th April 2010 for Gateshead Fell at home to South Shields, he made 40, caught by Chris Dorothy off the bowling of Nick Quinn.

His last appearance for Fell came on 4th September 2010 at South North, he scored 4, caught by Stephen Humble off the bowling of Lee Crozier.

He played 20 matches in The NEPL for Fell, batting 20 times, with 3 not out's, he scored 1102 runs at an average of 64.82. He scored 7 half centuries and 3 centuries, his highest score was 122 made on 21st August 2010 for Gateshead Fell at home to Chester le Street. He never bowled in The NEPL but took 10 catches for Fell.

He returned to the league again for the 2013 season, making his debut in The NEPL for South Shields on 8th June at home to Chester le Street. He scored 118 before he was stumped by Chris Youldon off the bowling of Quentin Hughes.

His last appearance for Shields and indeed in the NEPL, came on 6th July 2013 at home against The Durham Academy. He made 9 before he was caught by Adam Hickey off the bowling of Charlie Parker.

Latham played only 4 matches in The NEPL for South Shields, batting 4 times, with 0 not outs, he scored 236 runs at an average of 59.00. He scored 0 half centuries and 2 centuries, his highest score was the 118 he made on debut mentioned earlier. He never bowled in The NEPL but took 4 catches for Shields.

He played 24 matches in the NEPL, batting 24 times, with 3 not outs, he scored 1338 runs at an average of 63.71. He scored 7 half centuries and 5 centuries, his highest score was 122 made on 21st August 2010 for Gateshead Fell at home to Chester le Street. He never bowled in The NEPL but took 14 catches.

To date, the end of the English 2023 season, Latham has played 79 Test matches, 147 One Day Internationals and 26 Twenty20 International matches for New Zealand.

He was part of the New Zealand side which lost the 2019 World Cup Final to England.

Henry Nicholls was another New Zealand youngster who benefitted from the Durham and Canterbury exchange. He made his NEPL debut on 30th April 2011 for Blaydon at Tynemouth, batting at four he scored 29.

His last NEPL appearance came on 10th September 2011 at Hetton Lyons, he scored 1, caught by Jack McBeth off the bowling of Kamran Hussain.

He played 17 matches in The NEPL for Blaydon, batting 17 times, with 2 not outs, he scored 407 runs at an average of 27.13. He scored 2 half centuries; his highest score was 53 made on 20th August 2011 for Blaydon at home to Chester le Street.

He bowled 24 balls in the NEPL, with 0 maidens, he conceded 26 runs and didn't take a wicket. He took 7 NEPL catches for Blaydon.

To date, the end of the English 2023 season, Latham has played 56 Test matches, 75 One Day Internationals and 10 Twenty20 International matches for New Zealand.

He was part of the New Zealand side which lost the 2019 World Cup Final to England.

The final player to benefit from the Durham and Canterbury exchange and go on to bigger and better things but also play in The NEPL was Theo van Woerkom.

He made his NEPL debut for Blaydon on 27th April 2013 at home to Newcastle, he took 0 for 32 and scored 20, he was out leg before to Ben Stevens.

His first NEPL wicket was Matthew Muchall, leg before wicket for 5 for South Shields on 4th May 2013.

His last game for Blaydon and in The NEPL came on 14th September 2013 at Gateshead Fell, he took 1 for 17 and scored 13.

Theo van Woerkom played 19 matches in the NEPL for Blaydon, batting 16 times, with 3 not outs, he scored 140 runs at an average of 10.76. His highest score was 23 not out on 31st August at home to the Academy.

He bowled 915 balls in the NEPL, with 23 maidens, he conceded 549 runs and took 31 wickets at an average of 17.70. His best bowling figures were 6 for 11 taken on 8th June 2013 at home to Hetton Lyons. He took 8 NEPL catches for Blaydon.

Theo van Woerkom made his Test debut for Ireland on 28th February 2024 against Afghanistan in Abu Dhabi. He took 0 for 12 and 1 for 43 when he bowled and scored 1 in his only innings.

To date, the end of April 2024, he has played 2 One Day Internationals for Ireland, his debut coming against England on 26th September 2023 at Bristol. His first wicket at this level was Zac Crawley.

He has played 1 Twenty20 International for Ireland, against Zimbabwe on 9thDecember 2023 in Harare, he took 0 for 10 and didn't bat.

Returning to the 2012 season, John Graham recalls that "Blaydon had started the season strongly, beating us as part of that strong start, they led the league for a long time, they drew with us in the return match." Once again, the records confirm John Graham's memory!

On 5th May 2012 at Denefield Bank Blaydon hosted South North, the rules were still that the team batting first could bat 65 overs and the total in the match was 120.

South North won the toss and put Blaydon in to bat and they were soon in trouble at 6 for 2, both openers falling to Stephen Humble. Allan Worthy and New Zealand overseas pro Cole McConchie took the score to 65 before the third wicket fell, Worthy L.B.W to Paul Coughlin for 22. Graeme Bridge at four made 6, 83 for 4, which quickly became 84 for 5 when McConchie was caught by Joe Coyne for 45 off Michael Craigs.

Peter Howells provided some resistance with 14, but they fell away and were bowled out for 129. Lee Crozier taking 4 for 33, two wickets each for Humble, Coughlin and Craigs.

What happened when South North batted was nothing less than remarkable, John Graham was out fifth ball of the innings, 0 for 1, the fall of wickets then went as follows, 8 for 2, 8 for 3, 11 for 4, 11 for 5, 14 for 6, 14 for 7, it took a partnership between Michael Craigs and Stephen Humble to get them to 32 for 8, Humble dismissed for 9, Wightman and Craigs got the score to 43 before Wightman fell for 10. When Peter Howells stumped last man Lee Crozier for a duck, South North were 49 all out! Craigs was 16 not out. The four bowlers used all took wickets, Gary Stewart 3 for 10, Martin Pollard 4 for 25, Ben Raine 1 for 4 and Graeme Bridge 2 for 7.

Blaydon picked up 21 points, South North 5 points.

The return match was called off before a ball was bowled, 5 points each.

With three games to go Blaydon were top of the league with 316 points from South North with 285 points.

John Graham recalls "late in the season we were at Tynemouth, we knew the weather forecast was very poor, rain coming at some point in the afternoon, we planned to bat and just tee off and go for it." We declared after 25 or 30 overs, then bowled them out before it rained, next week we beat a strong Stockton side, containing Keaton Jennings amongst others, and then the title headed to the last game of the season."

Once again putting Graham's memory to the test, South North played Tynemouth at home on the Bank Holiday Monday, the fact it was a bank holiday probably explains the poor weather forecast for 27th August 2012. Records show South North did win the toss, they did indeed go for it, and they did declare, 160 for 6 from 27 overs. Jimmy Miller top scored with 33 from 22 balls, Adam Cragg had 31 from 32 balls, Joe Coyne 13 from 11. When Tynemouth batted, they were quickly 10 for 2, openers Dan Candlish 1, and Ben Debnam 5, both falling to Stephen Humble. The South African pair of Chad Koen, 18 and overseas pro Patrick Botha took the score to 40 when Botha fell to a catch by Craigs off Wightman for 20. Tynemouth slipped to 79 all out as a steady procession of wickets fell, only Anthony Turner with 14 showing any real resistance. Humble finished with 4 for 18, Wightman 1 for 18, Crozier 4 for 20 and Joe Coyne 1 for 8. South North got the win before the rain came, and it did come and got 27 points for their efforts.

South North would also beat Tynemouth a few days later, on 2nd September to take The Banks Salver this year as well.

On the same Bank Holiday Monday Blaydon were at home to Sunderland, Blaydon batted first and scored 216 for 6 when they declared after 45 overs. Cole McConchie hit 86 from 92 balls setting the innings up, with good support from Ben Raine 37, Mark Drake 33 and Allan Worthy 25. Sunderland started steadily when they batted, Mark Dale 17 and Dan Shurben 41, with an opening partnership of 41.

They lost wickets at regular intervals though, despite six batsmen making double figures, Shurben's 41 was the highest score. Craig Simpson took 5 for 51 but Blaydon couldn't force the issue, the innings was closed on 160 for 8 after 38 overs, the inference being rain cut it short. Although Blaydon picked up 15 points from the draw, South North had closed the gap by 12 points on the Monday.

Blaydon had 331 points, South North 312 points.

With two games to go both sides won comfortably, Blaydon picking up 29 points from their game with Newcastle, 360 points, South North picking up 30 points from their game with Stockton, 342 points. So, Blaydon had an 18-point lead as they took to the field against Tynemouth.

On Saturday 8th September 2012 Blaydon were at home to Tynemouth, South North were at home to South Shields. On paper not a lot between the two sides the two potential Champions were playing. South Shields entered the game on 203 league points, they did have overseas pro Rameez Shahzad in their line up as well as the Muchall brothers, Gordon being a very dangerous player with the bat, Matthew very reliable with the ball!

Tynemouth entered the game with 171 league points, they had skipper Matthew Brown in their side, he was a capable batsman who could turn a game, and their Durham player was available for the season finale, Mark Wood! Blaydon won the toss and elected to bat first. A solid opening partnership of 25 between Ben Raine and Paul Freary before Raine was caught by Phil Morse off the bowling of Patrick Botha for 15. Allan Worthy came in at three, and he and Freary took the score to 100 when the latter was caught by Matthew Brown off the bowling of David Hymers for 46. They were 138 when the third wicket fell, Worthy caught by Sam Robson off the bowling of Morse for 31. Graeme Bridge was the next to go, run out for 4. Blaydon 151 for 4. A partnership of 40 for the fifth wicket between Cole McConchie and Mark Drake took Blaydon to 191 when Drake was caught by Morse off the bowling of Koen. 191 for 5 soon became 200 for 6, McConchie also caught by Morse off the bowling of Koen for 56, his innings had taken 56 balls and included 7 fours and 1 six. They were 223 when the seventh wicket fell, Peter Howells caught by Sam Robson off Hymers. Blaydon would declare on 233 for 7 after 60 overs, Ross Nicholson 21 not out, Chris Varley 0 not out. Joshua Koen had the best bowling figures, 2 for 40, for the record Mark Wood had twelve overs 0 for 33. Blaydon had picked up four batting points from their innings, meaning they now had 364, 22 points ahead of South North before they batted.

Across the River Tyne at Roseworth Terrace South North were batting first, John Graham bowled by Chris Watson for a single wasn't a great start! When Sam Jobson fell for 5 a short time later, caught by Kris McShane off Matthew Muchall, they were 6 for 2 and in a bit of bother. Opener Adam Heather and Jimmy Miller calmed things down a little, taking the score to 43 when Heather was also caught by Kris McShane off Matthew Muchall for 14, South North were 43 for 3. Number five batsman Joe Coyne made a single when he was L.B.W to Chris Watson, South North now 44 for 4. This quickly became 47 for 5 when Miller was also L.B.W to Watson, for 19. Adam Cragg, batting at six, and Paul Coughlin batting at seven took the score to 96 when Coughlin was out for 27, caught by Adam Shaw off Shahzad. South North six wickets down. This brought Stephen Humble to the crease to join Cragg.

They were 204 when the next wicket fell, a seventh wicket stand of 108, Cragg out for 60, caught by Shazhad off the bowling of McShane, South North 204 for 7. Humble would go on to make 89, he was caught by wicketkeeper Chris Rainbow off the bowling of Shazhad when the score was 249. This was the highest NEPL score of his career at this point, although he did have 8 half centuries under his belt before this innings. South North declared shortly after,258 for 8 from 54.2 overs, Michael Craigs was 21 not out, Jonny Wightman 4 not out, only Lee Crozier did not bat. Chris Watson had 3 for 23, the pick of the bowlers. South North did pick up 10 batting points for their efforts and had 65 overs to dismiss Shields.

This now meant that at the change of innings in both games, Blaydon had 364 points and South North 352 points. John Graham vividly remembers "when we heard the half time scores at Blaydon, without being disrespectful, we didn't fancy our chances too much!"

When Shields batted, they got off to a steady start, 18 for the first wicket before Jonny Wightman trapped Andrew Elliott for 8. A partnership of 49 for the second wicket between opener Chris Watson and Gareth Dunn took the score to 67 before Dunn was bowled by Lee Crozier for 20, Shields 67 for 2. This brought Gordon Muchall to the crease at four, his reputation as a run scorer around the league was well known and well justified. Fortunately for South North, today was not his day, Paul Coughlin bowled him for 7, Shields were now 76 for 3 and opener Watson fell soon after, caught by Humble off Crozier for 24, Shields 78 for 4. At 93 for 4 the pendulum took a swing in South North's favor, first Shazhad was caught by Humble off Crozier for 9, at the same score Chris Dorothy was caught by wicketkeeper Adam Cragg off the bowling off Coughlin for 5, Shields now 93 for 6. When Lee Crozier bowled Chris Rainbow for 7, Shields were 100 for 7. Adam Shaw, batting at number seven, showed some resistance, with 21, but he fell next, caught by Cragg off the bowling of Michael Craigs, Shields now 126 for 8. Number ten, Kris McShane next in and next out, caught by Joe Coyne off Crozier for a duck, Shields 127 for 9. With the fifth ball of the 44th over, and the score on 136, Michael Craigs bowled last man Chris Stewart for 4, South Shields all out, South North win by 122 runs and pick up 30 points, they finish the season on 372 points.

Blaydon currently sit on 364 points, dismiss Tynemouth for 233 or less and they win the game and the league title. And so, on to matters at Blaydon.

Ben Raine opened the bowling, with the fifth ball of the first over he had Richard Straughan L.B.W for a duck, Tynemouth 0 for 1. Phil Morse and Matthew Brown had put on 56 for the second wicket when Brown was caught behind by Peter Howells off the bowling of Ben Raine for 20, Tynemouth 56 for 2. Morse and Botha then added 86 for the third wicket before Morse was run out for 68 by Craig Simpson, his innings had come from 83 balls and contained 7 fours and a six and Tynemouth were now 140 for 3. Mark Andrew Wood came to the crease at this point, ex South North, see last season's title winning tale, and future star of the game at international level......as a bowler! If you remember his career NEPL batting stats, he did score 4 half centuries with a best of 88, that wasn't today but he did contribute. The score was 205 when the next wicket fell, Botha out for 76, caught by Martin Pollard off the bowling of Raine, his innings had taken 107 balls and contained 6 fours and 2 sixes and Tynemouth 205 for 4. Wood and new batsman Sam Robson had an unbroken partnership of 30 for the fifth wicket, Wood finished on 41 not out from 61 deliveries, including 4 boundaries, Robson was 18 not out from 15 balls with 2 boundaries. Ben Raine had 3 for 53 but Tynemouth had won by 6 wickets. With no points for the win and only 2 bowling points, Blaydon finished the season with 366 points, South North had won the league by just 6 points.

I asked Mark Wood if he had any memories of this season and this game in particular, he recalls "I felt a bit bad about this one, I knew a lot of the Blaydon lads, guys like Graeme Bridge and Allan Worthy and they were solid guys. I had played for Northumberland with Worthy, and he had sort of mentored me a bit, I recall a cracking night out in Macclesfield with him when we were away with the county, just daft singing songs and cracking on really. They were a very strong team that Blaydon side, they had boatloads of experience, and they would come across as very friendly, then before you knew it your "friends" had you 40 for 5 and heading for a beating, John Windows would even warn us at the Academy about it, "they suck you in and then beat you up!"

Wood says that he recalls some of the Blaydon lads asking him what he was doing helping South North win the league again as he batted on that day, but he was "there to do a job for Tynemouth, not South North."

Wood continues "Once again Steve Williams and Ashington had helped me with the direction of my career, I couldn't play for Ashington as I was on a 6-month contract with Durham and teams in Ashington's league were only allowed one pro.

Steve and I had met with a guy called "Fanta," Steven Mordue, and Tynemouth just felt right, it had the same sort of feel that Northumberland had, it was a little different to what I had expected because they had a bit of edge about their cricket, and I wasn't expecting that for some reason. I knew their captain, Ben Debnam, through Northumberland and I thought he also made them into a good fit for me."

Talking to Mark Wood the pride he feels in the teams he represents shines through, "England, Durham, Northumberland and Ashington, they're my teams, but I also respect my time at Tynedale, Tynemouth, South North and Lanchester, even though I only played one game for them. I am a life member of Ashington Cricket Club, and I go there regularly, to socialize, to train sometimes, it's my club. It's my family club too, my dad, my uncle Neil and I are all regulars there, I imagine my son will be one day as well. The Harmison's, Mel, Jimmy, Steve, Ben and their families are all regulars, and you could add the Storey family and others to that list as well. In the short term if I need to get fit or some match practice in, I can definitely see myself playing a game or two for Ashington, I love the idea of playing cricket for Ashington with my son one day in the future if my body allows."

More of Mark Wood in the final chapter.

As stated earlier South North also won The Banks Salver and Chester le Street won the T20.

Kieran Waterson of Sunderland was named Player of the Year, he had played 18 matches in the NEPL in 2012, he only batted 6 times with 3 not outs, and therefore his contribution with the bat was negligible.

He did, however, bowl 1299 balls in the NEPL in 2012, with 61 maidens, conceding 592 runs and taking 51 wickets at an average of 11.60. His best bowling figures were 6 for 27, taken on 5th May 2012 at home to Newcastle. He took 4 catches in the NEPL in 2012.

TABLE 41   NEPL 2012.

	Played	Won	Draw/Aban	Lost	Penalty Points	Bonus Points	Points
South North	22	10	11	1	1	164	373
Blaydon	22	11	10	1	0	149	366
Chester le St	22	9	11	2	0	149	347
Sunderland	22	9	10	3	0	125	310
Durham CA	22	6	12	4	0	109	259
Stockton	22	6	9	7	0	100	239
Hetton Lyons	22	5	9	8	0	100	216
South Shields	22	5	9	8	0	88	208
Tynemouth	22	4	9	9	0	96	199
Newcastle	22	3	12	7	2	85	188
Benwell Hill	22	2	10	10	0	71	145
Gateshead Fell	22	2	8	12	0	63	127

TABLE 42   NEPL Batting Averages 2012.

Qualification 300 Runs.

28 Batsmen Qualified this season.

Player	Club	Inns	N. O	H. S	Runs	Average
(1) M.J Richardson	Newcastle	9	2	171 no	453	64.71
(2) Q.J Hughes	Chester le Street	12	4	81	383	47.88
(3) A. Worthy	Blaydon	14	2	105 no	420	35.00
(4) R.P Waite	Stockton	15	0	112	523	34.87
(5) A.L Smith	Chester le Street	15	3	94	418	34.83
(6) J. Clark	Durham CA	17	2	110	491	32.73
(7) J.A Graham	South North	18	1	100 no	550	32.35
(8) C.E McConchie	Blaydon	15	0	86	483	32.20
(9) K.K Jennings	Durham CA	14	0	100	444	31.71
(10) D. Shurben	Sunderland	17	2	144 no	475	31.67
(11) M.A.P Dale	Blaydon	17	1	76	496	31.00
(12) C.J Pearce	Durham CA	14	1	109 no	380	29.23
(14) J.N Miller	South North	15	2	102 no	363	27.92
(22) A.D Cragg	South North	17	1	79	380	23.75
(23) S. Jobson	South North	18	4	118 no	332	23.71
(25) A.T Heather	South North	18	1	68	383	22.53

TABLE 43   NEPL Bowling Averages 2012.
Qualification 20 Wickets.
31 Bowlers Qualified this season.

Player	Club	Overs	Mdns	Runs	Wkts	Average
(1) A. Tye	Chester le Street	143.2	38	368	39	9.44
(2) C. Rushworth	Sunderland	78.0	23	201	20	10.05
(3) M.J Muchall	South Shields	235.4	81	608	55	11.05
(4) S. Humble	South North	171.5	36	426	37	11.51
(5) K. Waterson	Sunderland	216.3	61	592	51	11.61
(6) A. Watson	Hetton Lyons	122.4	21	397	34	11.68
(7) G.D Bridge	Blaydon	140.1	21	367	31	11.84
(8) B.A Raine	Blaydon	146.1	28	452	36	12.56
(9) L. Simpson	Chester le Street	139.0	26	469	34	13.79
(10) P. Coughlin	South North	93.0	18	292	21	13.90
(11) W.J Weighall	Durham CA	108.0	26	290	20	14.50
(12) L.J Crozier	South North	206.4	52	526	36	14.61
(24) J.R Wightman	South North	182.1	30	587	27	21.74

South North 2012 NEPL Champions.

Left to Right – Back Row- S.O Jobson, J.J Coyne, P. Coughlin, J. R Wightman, S. Humble.

Front Row- J.N Miller, L.J Crozier, J.A Graham, A.T Heather, A.D Cragg, M. A Craigs.

Lee Crozier seen here bowling on 6th May 2017 at Newcastle.

Photo Courtesy of Ken Waller.

CHAPTER SEVEN

Stockton 2013

The League was re-named as The Premier League and expanded into two divisions, (Premier and Division 1) following a restructure of North East Cricket Leagues at the end of the 2012 season, subsequently the Durham & North East Cricket League and also the Northumberland and Tyneside Cricket League began to feed into the revised pyramid with promotion and relegation. The rules were still that the team batting first could bat up to 65 overs and that the match could be 120 overs in total.

Stockton were among the original eleven members of The NEPL and had finished third in 2003, which up until this season had been their best performance although they had remained in the league throughout the years since it was formed and finished 6th in 2012.

They did have Richard Waite in their ranks, he had been named NEPL Player of the Year in 2003, 2004, 2008 and 2009. A remarkable feat. Waite had entered the 2013 season with 6637 NEPL runs and 444 NEPL wickets to his credit, across two spells with Stockton and a title winning spell at Chester le Street.

From the side that finished the 2012 season they also had David Seymour, Matthew Brown, Kevin Ward, James Ward, Joe Hewison and Simon Davison returning for the 2013 opener. In addition, they also had Keaton Jennings returning from the previous two seasons. Jennings would go on to play first class cricket for Durham and Lancashire and test cricket for England. Kevin Ward, the Stockton captain of 2013 has recalled some of his memories of that title winning season.

Stockton opened the campaign with an away fixture at Benwell Hill, the home side batted first, making 212 all out from 64.4 overs, opener Sameet Brar top scored with 44. Stockton used six bowlers, five of them taking wickets, Kevin Ward 4 for 53 was the best of them. When Stockton batted a fine knock of 91 by opener David Seymour, 32 from Andrew Parr, 37 from Malcolm Brown and 39 not out from Richard Waite saw them home by seven wickets. A statement win to open the season, especially with Keaton Jennings coming back into the side in the upcoming weeks.

The Stockton side that day was as follows-

David Seymour opened the season and the batting in style in the first game of the 2013 season, making 91. Kevin Ward recall that Seymour was "a right-handed batsman, just a young lad of around 18 at this time, he had a very good technique, he was very good defensively."

He made his NEPL debut for Stockton on 8th August 2009 at home to Chester Le Street, he made 22 not out batting at number nine. This was the first of six NEPL appearances that season.

He made his debut for Durham Academy on 11th May 2010 at Uddington in an away match against The Scotland Academy. It wasn't a memorable debut as he failed to register a run or wicket.

He made his first NEPL half century on 12th June 2010 at South Shields, 52 from 72 balls with 8 boundaries.

On 29th June 2010 Seymour played for Durham Under 17's at Hartlepool against Yorkshire Under 17's. He didn't get a bowl and scored 6.

He played a 2-day match for Durham Academy against Cheshire Development Squad starting on 13th July 2010. After a duck in the first innings, he made 35 in the second innings.

On 28th June 2011 Seymour started a 2-day match for Durham Under 17's against Scotland Under 17s at Uddingston. He made 33 in his only innings and took 0 for 5 and 0 for 2 with the ball.

Seymour played 14 games for Durham Under 17's, batting 14 times, with 2 not out's, he scored 360 runs at an average of 30.00. He scored 2 half centuries; his highest score was 71 on 26th July 2011 against Derbyshire at Norton

He had to wait until 23rd July 2011 to pick up his first NEPL wicket, in an away game at Newcastle, he dismissed Michael Richardson for 4, caught by Kevin Ward.

Seymour made a valuable contribution to the title success of 2013, he played 21 NEPL matches, batting 18 times with 0 not outs, he scored 326 runs at an average of 18.11, with 2 half centuries, that 91 he opened the season with was his highest NEPL score of the season. He didn't bowl in 2013 in The NEPL, but he did take 4 catches.

He played his last game in The NEPL for Stockton on 6th September 2014 at Gateshead Fell, he made 11 opening the batting. In total he played 85 NEPL matches for Stockton, batting 75 times with 5 not outs, he scored 1301 runs at an average of 18.58, with 6 half centuries. His highest score for Stockton in The NEPL was 96, made on 28th May 2011 at home to Tynemouth.

He did bowl in The NEPL for Stockton, 153 balls, with 5 maidens, conceding 120 runs and taking 5 wickets at an average of 24.00. His best bowling was 3 for 16 on 23rd July 2011 at Jesmond against Newcastle. He also took 25 catches.

He made his NEPL debut for Burnopfield at South North on 16th April 2022, scoring 25 batting at three. He was still playing in The NEPL IN 2023, his last appearance coming on the last game of the season on 8th September at Whitburn for Burnopfield. He made 50 in that game.

In total he played 116 NEPL matches, batting 104 times with 9 not out's, he scored 2130 runs at an average of 22.42, with 13 half centuries. His highest score remained the 96 for Stockton mentioned earlier. He bowled 198 balls, with 5 maidens, conceding 188 runs and taking 6 wickets at an average of 31.33. His best bowling remained the 3 for 16 mentioned earlier. He also took 34 catches.

Andrew Parr, a right-handed batsman, opened the batting in the season opener of 2013, scoring 32. He was a Stockton lad, his older brother Chris, also played for the club. Ward says that "Andrew was unfortunate in this season, he played and opened the first game, then Keaton Jennings came back and replaced him, also we didn't use many players that season so opportunities for him, and others, were limited. He was a really talented young lad, he used to play in the V, with a straight bat, he would do nothing extravagant, best described as an old school opening bat. He still plays, he was second team captain last season."

Parr made his NEPL debut for Stockton on 19th August 2006 at home to Newcastle, he batted eleven and failed to score. He didn't get a bowl so a debut he would rather forget. He had to wait until 5th May 2007 for his next NEPL game, again at home to Newcastle, he took 0 for 7 with the ball and made 9 with the bat.

It was 17th May 2008 before he collected his first NEPL wicket, a home fixture with Newcastle saw Parr remove both Newcastle openers to finish with 2 for 21. That first NEPL wicket was Matthew Hynd, leg before wicket for a duck.

By the end of the 2012 season Parr had played 85 NEPL matches, batting 55 times with 20 not outs, he had scored 347 runs at an average of 9.91, with 1 half century, exactly 50, was his highest NEPL score at this time, and it would remain so in his NEPL career, came on 30th May 2011 at Blaydon.

He bowled 2582 balls, with 80 maidens, conceding 1573 runs and taking 46 wickets at an average of 34.19. His best bowling figures, 5 for 27 came on 1st August 2009 at home to South North. He had taken 16 catches at this point.

He played 4 matches in the 2013 side, batting 4 times with 0 not out's, he scored 60 runs at an average of 15.00. His highest score was 32 in the season opener at Benwell Hill. He didn't bowl in The NEPL in 2013 but did take 2 catches.

The stats about Parr are a little confusing and make little difference after 2013, rather than assign him stats I can't be sure he made, I shall leave him as a 2103 title winner!

Matthew Brown batted at number three in the season opener of 2013, scoring 37 and taking 1 for 5 when bowling. He was a left-handed batsman, he was from Cockermouth and a cousin to Richard Waite, that's how he came to play for Stockton. He came through Stockton Juniors and went through all the junior age groups at county level with Cumbria as captain, two players under his charge were fellow Stockton player Jamie Harrison and Ben Stokes.

As a batsman Ward says that Brown "loved scoring runs through backward point off the seamers, he was strong through there and gully, probably horrible as a seam bowler to bowl at, that said, he was also a very good sweeper of the spinners, he was a very effective batsman who knew his own game."

He had originally made his NEPL debut for Norton at South North on 25th April 2009 and his last NEPL game for Norton was on 12th September 2009 at home to Durham Academy. He made his NEPL debut for Stockton on 24th April 2010 at Tynemouth and his first NEPL wicket was South Shields opener James Hill, stumped by Dean Williams on 25th June 2011 at Stockton for 38.

Brown's contribution to the title win in 2013 was to play in 20 NEPL matches, he batted 18 times with 1 not out's, he scored 349 runs at an average of 20.52, with 2 half centuries, his highest NEPL score of the season was 85 not out on 10th August at home to Hetton Lyons.

He bowled 54 balls in the 2013 season, with 1 maiden, conceding 22 runs and taking 1 wicket and he took 12 catches.

He would go onto play 138 matches in the NEPL, batting 130 times with 10 not outs, he scored 2514 runs at an average of 20.95. He scored 13 half centuries, his highest score was 99 not out, made on 5th September 2009 for Norton at Sunderland.

He bowled 234 balls in the NEPL in his career, with 2 maidens, he conceded 164 runs and took 4 wickets at an average of 41.00 His best bowling figures was 1 for 5. He made 65 catches and had 2 stumpings in the NEPL.

Richard Waite is a right-handed batsman and right arm off break bowler, he batted at number four in the season opener for 2013, scoring 39 not out and taking 2 for 51 with the ball. This game marked his return to Stockton after spending four seasons at Chester le Street, during which he won an NEPL title and was NEPL Player of the Year in 2009.

Kevin Ward describes Waite as "a lot better than many I've seen who have played in county cricket, he was, as a batsman he was just class, he could and did score in any situation, he had this knack of controlling his innings and a game, he seemed to have this sense of what to do and how to do it, he was also very patient when circumstances dictated, and he could grind an innings out. He was very strong off his hip; he knew how to manipulate a field and get a run. As a bowler he was aggressive in that he looked to take wickets, he spun the ball a lot, he could go for runs but he also got a lot of wickets, he would bowl a really dangerous, potential wicket taking ball every one or two overs."

Up until this point in his NEPL career Waite had played 224 games in The NEPL, he had batted 232 times with 18 not outs, he had scored 6637 runs at an average of 31.01. He had scored 35 half centuries and 13 centuries. His highest score was still the 150 not out for Chester le Street in May 2010.

He bowled 17169 balls, with 638 maidens, conceding 8796 runs and taking 444 wickets at an average of 19.81. The best bowling figures of his career so far were 8 for 28 on 10th June 2006 for Stockton at Benwell Hill. Waite had also taken 78 career catches in the NEPL.

Waite played 21 games in the title winning side of 2013, he batted 19 times with 3 not outs, he scored 509 runs at an average of 31.81. He scored 3 half centuries. His top score of the season was 66 on 1st June at home against The Durham Academy.

He bowled 1705 balls in the 2013 season, with 61 maidens, conceding 787 runs and taking 54 wickets at an average of 14.57. His best bowling figures of the season was 5 for 41 on 8th June at Sunderland. Waite also took 9 catches in the season.

He was awarded his fifth and final NEPL Player of the Year award at the end of the 2013 season.

He played his last NEPL game on 7th July 2018 at home to South North, he took 3 for 45, when South North batted, his last NEPL wicket was Rob Peyton, bowled for a duck.

When he batted, he opened the innings, he was dismissed for 32, caught by Sean Tindale off the bowling of Lee Crozier as South North won the game by 53 runs.

When his NEPL career was done Richard Waite had won titles in 2009, 2010 and 2013, he had been Player of the Year in 2003, 2004, 2008, 2009 and 2013.

He had played 321 games in his NEPL career, batting 302 times with 26 not outs, he scored 8857 runs at an average of 332.09. He scored 48 NEPL half centuries and 15 centuries. His highest score was 150 not out mentioned earlier.

He bowled 22061 balls, with 783 maidens, conceding 11514 runs and taking 575 wickets at an average of 20.02. His career best NEPL bowling were the 8 for 28 mentioned earlier. Waite took 98 career NEPL catches.

Waite had been named in The Team of the Decade in 2009 and also in the NEPL Team of 20 Years in 2020.

Kevin Ward batted at number five for the season opener in 2013, scoring 3 not out, he also bowled 9.4 overs taking 4 for 53, removing 4 of the top 5 batsman. His father, also Kevin Ward, was still playing at the time the NEPL started, he played in three games in 2000 and one game in 2002.

Kevin Ward the 2013 version, describes himself as "an aggressive, proactive batsman, I tried to captain the same way, always trying to look ahead", he made his NEPL debut on 27th April 2002 at Sunderland. He didn't get a bat or bowl as Chris Hooker hit 116 not out in the Stockton innings of 268 for 6 declared. Franklyn Rose had 4 for 72. When Sunderland batted 48 from Alan Mustard got them a draw, despite 5 for 33 from Alan Walker.

On 13th July 2004 Ward started a two-day game for Durham Under 17's against Worcestershire at Darlington. He made 19 not out in the first innings when Durham batted but didn't get an opportunity in the second as Durham made 161 for 0 in a drawn game. A couple of familiar names in the Durham side, Mark Stoneman had 90 not out in the second innings, John Coxon had 42 in the first and 59 not out in the second, there is no scorecard for the Worcester innings.

On 23rd July 2006 Ward was selected for The NEPL side against Derbyshire Premier League at Stavely, he made 14 and opened the bowling as The NEPL won by two runs.

On 16th August 2006 Ward was selected to play for the NEPL Select Eleven against a Lashings World Eleven at Benwell Hill. Lashings batted first, their openers had a good day, Tatenda Taibu scored 150 and Grant Flower had 100, putting on 200 for the first wicket. Unfortunately, rain caused the day to end after just 36.3 overs of the innings.

In the title winning season of 2013 Ward played 19 games, he batted 17 times with 2 not outs, he scored 543 runs at an average of 36.20. He scored 7 half centuries. His top score of the season was 80 on 14th September at home against Tynemouth.

He bowled 404 balls in the 2013 season, with 5 maidens, conceding 278 runs and taking 16 wickets at an average of 17.37. His best bowling figures of the season was 5 for 18 on 14th September, in the same game against Tynemouth that he made his highest score of the season! Ward also took 9 catches in the season.

Ward was selected to play for Northumberland on 31st May 2015 in a 20 over match at Cheshire, not a memorable debut. He was also selected for a 3-day game for the county starting on 7th June 2015 at Roseworth Terrace against Cumberland. He made 2 and 36 and took 1 for 39 in the Cumberland second innings. He played a third time for Northumberland in a 50 over match on 14th June 2015 at Oxfordshire, he took 2 for 25 and scored 39 as Northumberland won by 2 wickets.

His last appearance in The NEPL was on 8th September 2018 at Jesmond against Newcastle, he didn't bowl but scored 20 when Stockton batted, they were relegated at the end of this season.

Kevin Ward has played 300 matches in The NEPL, batting 262 times, with 32 not out's, he has scored 4719 runs at an average of 20.51. He has made 24 half centuries and 1 century, 136, on 29th August 2009 at Tynemouth.

He has bowled 8014 balls in The NEPL, with 164 maidens, conceding 5830 runs and taking 165 wickets at an average of 35.33. His best bowling figures were 5 for 8 on 20th August 2005 at Gateshead Fell. He has taken 81 catches in The NEPL.

Ward is still playing up to 2nd September 2023 and when I got in touch with him in February 2024, he delayed talking to me as he was off for a net!

Peter Howells was the wicketkeeper and a right-handed batsman; he was listed to bat at number six for the season opener in 2013. He didn't bat in the game, but he did take three catches. Kevin Ward recalls that "as a keeper he was one of the best I've seen, as good as any, probably him and Phil Nicholson were right up there, Peter was a big lad, about 6 foot 4, with huge hands. As a batsman he was very creative, he would sweep, reverse sweep, hit it inside out, hit it over cover in the air, he would try and manipulate the field, I sometimes thought his creativity outstretched his ability, but he was entertaining to watch, and he scored plenty of runs."

He made his NEPL debut when Stockton did, on 29th April 2000 at South North, he scored 5 and took a catch behind the stumps, his first NEPL catch being South North skipper, John Graham for 13.

He was selected for Durham Under 19's in a 2-day game starting on 11th July 2000 at Norton against Derbyshire. He scored 8 when Durham batted, the match was restricted by the weather to one innings.

Howells was then picked for Durham Seconds, for a 3-day game against Yorkshire Seconds starting on 5th September 2001. He didn't get to bat in the first innings as Ashley Thorpe hit 139 and Gordon Muchall 101 not out, Durham declaring on 410 for 5. He took a catch and had a stumping when Yorkshire batted, they made 333 for 7 declared, Joe Sayers had 149 not out. Howells didn't get to bat in the second innings either, as Thorpe, 85, and Muchall 45, continued to play well. Durham 199 for 6 declared. Incidentally, Tim Bresnan was in the Yorkshire side, he had 1 for 80 in the Durham first innings and 1 for 22 in their second. Despite 5 for 50 from Stockton team mate Richard Waite, Yorkshire got the draw with 2 wickets remaining, Howells got another stumping in their second innings.

Howells played 7 games for Durham Seconds XI, batting 3 times, with 0 not outs, he scored 48 runs at an average of 16.00. His highest score was 20 and he took 8 catches and had 5 stumpings.

Howells was selected for a 3-day game starting on 10th April 2004 to play for Durham University Centre of Cricketing Excellence in a game against Durham at The Riverside. He took 3 catches when Durham batted first, John Lewis, Marcus North and Graham Onions the batsmen. He scored 2 when his side batted. He had no action in the second innings but made 20 not out when he batted again as the match was drawn.

Howells played 12 matches for the side over two seasons, batting 14 times with 5 not outs, he scored 194 runs at an average of 21.55. He had 1 half century, 51 not out against Durham in May 2005. He took 16 catches for the Durham University side.

On 14th August 2005 Howells was selected for a President's Trophy Semi Final match against The Derbyshire Premier League at Ockbrook. He took a catch when Derbyshire batted and made 4 when his side batted as Derbyshire won by 7 runs.

Howells was part of the successful NEPL side which won The President's Trophy on 3rd September 2006, this is covered elsewhere.

He played his last game of his first spell with Stockton on 3rd September 2005 at home to Benwell Hill, he had 3 catches and a stumping and scored 3. His NEPL stats for Stockton up to this point were that he had played 106 NEPL matches, batting 98 times, with 18 not out's, he had scored 1622 runs at an average of 20.27. He had 4 half centuries. His highest score, 64, came on 14th June 2003 at home to Tynemouth. He had taken 94 catches and had 21 stumpings up to this point of his NEPL career.

Howells made his NEPL debut for Blaydon on 29th April 2006 at Tynemouth, he scored 56 and took 2 catches in a Blaydon win. Blaydon twice finished as runners up during Howell's time with them, in 2009 and 2012. He played his last NEPL game for them on 8th September 2012 at home to Tynemouth, he made 20 and took a catch as Tynemouth won by 6 wickets.

He played 126 NEPL matches for Blaydon, batting 100 times, with 24 not outs, he had scored 1557 runs at an average of 20.48. He had 6 half centuries. His highest score, 89 not out, came on 10th June 2006 at Sunderland. He had taken 134 catches and had 30 stumpings in the NEPL for Blaydon.

By the time the 2012 season had ended Howells had played 232 NEPL matches, batting 198 times, with 42 not outs, he had scored 3179 runs at an average of 20.37. He had 10 half centuries, his highest score, 89 not out, came on 10th June 2006 for Blaydon at Sunderland. He had taken 228 catches and had 51 stumpings up to this point of his NEPL career.

The first game of Howell's second stint at Stockton came on 27th April 2013 at Benwell Hill, the season opener covered earlier. His contribution to the 2013 title success was that he played 20 NEPL matches that season, batting 16 times, with 6 not outs, he scored 173 runs at an average of 17.30. He made 1 half century that season, 65 not out, scored on 22nd June at home to Newcastle. He took 28 catches and had 4 stumpings that season, putting him second by 1 victim to Phil Nicholson of Benwell Hill.

He continued to play for Stockton in The NEPL, his last appearance coming on 30th July 2016 at Gateshead Fell, his last NEPL catch was Graham Onions, out for 60, off the bowling of Ryan Buckley. His last stumping and indeed last wicket behind the stumps was Sam Roseby for 43 off the bowling of Ryan Buckley.

He played 174 times for Stockton, batting 157 times with 30 not outs, he scored 2378 runs at an average of 18.72. He had 8 half centuries and a high score of 65 not out. He took 160 career NEPL catches and had 34 career stumpings in The NEPL for Stockton.

At the end of his NEPL career, Peter Howells had won the title in 2013 and been runner up twice with Blaydon. He had played 300 NEPL matches, batting 257 times with 54 not outs, he scored 3935 runs at an average of 19.38, with 14 half centuries. His highest score was 89 not out for Blaydon. He took 294 catches with 64 stumpings.

James Ward was listed to bat at number seven for the season opener in 2013, he didn't bat in the game, but he did bowl eight overs, 1 for 51. He was the skipper's younger brother, a right-handed batsman who Kevin describes as "a nurdler, he was brilliant at batting with the tail or lower middle order, he was better than where he batted in our lineup but that was down to the quality of our top six. As a bowler he was a right arm medium pacer, Kevin says that he "had a square on action, bowling big inswingers to the right hander."

James Ward made his NEPL debut on 9th July 2005 for Stockton at home to Newcastle, he opened the bowling taking 3 for 68, his first NEPL wicket was Matthew Hynd, caught by Joel Thwaites for 75. He made 0 not out when he batted.

During the title winning season, he played 20 matches, batting 16 times with 4 not outs, he scored 342 runs at an average of 28.50, he scored 2 half centuries. His highest score was 52 not out on 6th July at Tynemouth.

He also bowled 720 balls that season, with 23 maidens, conceding 360 runs and taking 25 wickets at an average of 14.40. His best bowling figures of the season were 7 for 27 on 7th September at home to South Shields. He took 5 catches this season.

He played 2 games for Northumberland, making his debut in a 3-day match against Cambridgeshire which started on 3rd August 2014. He made 41 and 9 with the bat and took 2 for 60 and 0 for 19 with the ball.

His second and final game for the county came in a 50 over match on 19th April 2015 against Durham Second XI at The Emirates. When Durham batted, Ryan Pringle with 167 and Stuart Poynter with 107, helped them to a massive 397 for 4 from their 50 overs. Ward had 0 for 70 as all the bowlers suffered, Sean Tindale had 2 for 49. Northumberland were dismissed for 132, Ward made 2, as Durham won by 261 runs.

So, his Northumberland career was brief, he played those 2 matches, batting 3 times with 0 not out's, he scored 52 runs at an average of 17.33, his highest score was 41 on debut.

He bowled 168 balls, with 4 maidens, conceding 149 runs and taking 2 wickets at an average of 74.50. He didn't take a catch in either game.

Ward played his last NEPL game on 27th August 2018 at home to Felling, he scored 2 and took 0 for 9.

Ward's NEPL career saw him play 142 matches, batting 132 times with 25 not outs, he scored 2455 runs at an average of 22.94, he scored 10 half centuries. His highest score was 75 on 23rd July 2011 at Jesmond against Newcastle.

He also bowled 4671 balls in the NEPL, with 147 maidens, conceding 2807 runs and taking 117 wickets at an average of 23.99. His best bowling figures of the season were the 7 for 27 mentioned earlier. He took 38 career catches in The NEPL.

Joshua Bousefield was listed to bat at number eight for the season opener in 2013, he didn't bat in the game, but he did open the bowling taking 1 for 35 from eighteen overs. Kevin Ward remembers "a right arm medium fast bowler, he could move the ball both ways. When he played for The Academy his bowling partner was Ben Stokes. As a batsman he was an aggressive player, a potential match winner, I do remember him hitting fifty against Blaydon going in at eight or nine for us. He would take on the short ball and was a good player of fast bowling."

Bousefield first shows up in the records on 3rd August 2006 playing for Durham Under 12's against Scotland Under 12's, he bowled four overs, 0 for 10 and scored 20 not out. He played through the age groups with Durham, representing them at Uner13, Under 14 and Under 15 level.

He also played for Barnard Castle along the way, on 14th May 2009 he played a 20 over match for them against Bishop Auckland, Gary Pratt was in the opposition to give you some idea of the level of cricket the teenage Bousefield was going up against, he took 1 for 22 and scored 7.

On 28th July 2009 Bousefield was selected to play for The English Schools Association North Under 15s against their London and East counterparts. Reece Topley and Ollie Robinson were among the opposition. Bousefield made 0 not out when his side batted, he took 3 for 38 when they bowled. He represented The North 3 more times that season.

On 10th August 2009 he played for Durham Under 17's away at Nottingham Under 17's, Bousefield took 0 for 24 opening the bowling, he scored 2 when his side batted. Less than two weeks later, on 20th August 2009 Bousefield started a two-day game for Durham Under 19's at home against Scotland Under 19's at Longhirst. He took 1 for 49 with the ball and made 10 when his side batted.

By 2010 Bousefield had progressed to Durham Second team, playing a 20 over match at Cardiff Marylebone Cricket Club on 22nd June, he took 4 for 21 with the ball and didn't bat as Will Gidman hit 59 in a Durham win.

He played for Durham Academy in a 2-day match starting on 13th July 2010 at Boldon Colliery against Cheshire Development Squad. He made 4 in his only bat of the game; he took 0 for 11 in the one innings he bowled in.

Bousefield made his NEPL debut on 24th April 2010 for The Durham Academy at South North, he made 18 not out, Mark Wood top scored for The Academy with 40 and Stephen Humble had 5 for 42 for South North. When South North batted, Chris Hewison had 118 and Adam Heather 70 as South North won by 6 wickets, Bousefield had 1 for 15, his first NEPL wicket was South North's John Graham, bowled for 4.

His last game for Durham Academy came on 8th September 2012 at Gateshead Fell, Bousefield took 1 for 12 when his side bowled but didn't get to bat as Durham won by 7 wickets.

He played 22 matches in The NEPL for The Academy, batting on 16 occasions with 1 not out, he scored 185 runs at an average of 12.33. He had 1 half century, 51 not out on 23rd July 2011 at Benwell Hill.

He bowled 827 balls for The Academy in the NEPL, with 27 maidens, he conceded 457 runs and took 22 wickets at an average of 20.77. His best bowling figures was 4 for 4 on 29th August 2011 at Gateshead Fell. He took 5 catches.

Bousefield made his NEPL debut for Stockton on 27th April 2013 at Benwell Hill. He opened the bowling, taking 1 for 35, his first Stockton NEPL wicket was David Rutherford who he caught and bowled for a single.

He played 16 matches in the 2013 title winning side, batting 10 times with 2 not outs, he scored 199 runs at an average of 24.87. He had 2 half centuries; his highest score was 56 not out on at home to South Shields on 7th September.

With the ball Bousefield bowled 664 deliveries in the NEPL in 2013, with 30 maidens, conceding 269 runs and taking 16 wickets at an average of 16.81. His best bowling of the season was 4 for 67 on 15th June at home to Blaydon. He took 2 catches in 2013.

Bousefield played his last game in The NEPL on 13th September 2014 at home to Hetton Lyons, he took 2 for 67 and scored 20.

His NEPL career had seen him play 53 matches, batting 39 times with 7 not out's, he scored 703 runs at an average of 21.96. He scored 4 half centuries. His highest score was the 56 not out covered earlier.

He bowled 2066 balls in The NEPL, with 72 maidens, conceding 1110 runs and taking 48 wickets at an average of 23.12. His best bowling figures was the 4 for 4 mentioned earlier. He took 13 catches in The NEPL.

Joe Hewison was listed to bat at number nine for the season opener in 2013, he didn't bat or bowl in the game, nor did he take any catches. Ward remembers Hewison as "just a kid at this time, he was a quiet individual and quiet at the crease, he was a fidgety batsman, giving the impression he was nervous, although, funny enough I never thought he was, at this time he was limited in his range of shots and lacked power, he has developed well over the years, he knows his strengths now, he's a very good player on the off side now. He has been first team captain since 2019."

He made his NEPL debut on 25th May 2012 at Tynemouth, he made 1 batting at number nine and didn't get a bowl.

During the 2013 season Hewison played 14 matches in The NEPL, batting 5 times with 1 not out, he scored 24 runs at an average of 6.00 and a high score of 12.

He bowled 108 balls in the league that season, with 2 maidens, he conceded 94 runs and took 3 wickets at an average of 31.33. His best bowling figures were 3 for 61 on 25th May at home to Gateshead Fell. He took 5 catches that season.

Hewison played his last NEPL match on 8th September 2018 at Jesmond against Newcastle, he finished his NEPL career with 53 when Stockton batted.

Hewison's NEPL career had seen him play 78 matches, batting 61 times, with 7 not outs, he scored 1250 runs at an average of 23.14. He scored 9 half centuries. His highest score was 68 on 19th August 2017 at Stockton against Newcastle.

With the ball, he bowled 502 balls, with 6 maidens, conceding 374 runs and taking 7 wickets at an average of 53.42. His best bowling figures were the 3 for 61 mentioned earlier. He took 22 career NEPL catches.

Simon Davison was listed to bat at number ten for the season opener in 2013, he didn't bat in the game, but he did bowl five overs, 0 for 10. Ward recalls that Davison was a right-handed batsman and right arm medium pace bowler, "he was an intelligent cricketer, very adaptable, he was a team player, a club man, he would do anything and everything that the club needed him to do. he loved the game and the cricket club. He was a talented youngster, bowling medium pace seam up. These days he is third team captain and coaches the kids."

Davison made his NEPL debut on 15th July 2000 at Benwell Hill, he didn't bat or bowl in the game. It was his only appearance of the 2000 season, and he had to wait until August 2003 for his next appearance.

He played 5 matches in the 2013 season, batting 2 times, with 1 not out, he scored 3 runs with a high score of 2 not out. He bowled 78 balls in The 2013 season in The NEPL, with 1 maiden, conceding 41 runs but failing to take a wicket.

Davison played his last NEPL match on 4th August 2018 at Benwell Hill, he scored 12 not out batting at number ten and didn't get a bowl.

He played 40 matches in his NEPL career, batting 25 times, with 11 not outs, he scored 118 runs at an average of 8.42 and the high score of 12 not out that was mentioned earlier.

He bowled 306 balls in The NEPL, with 1 maiden, conceding 271 runs and taking 4 wickets at an average of 67.75. His best bowling figures were 2 for 56. He took 6 catches in The NEPL.

Ian Richards was listed to bat at number eleven for the season opener in 2013, he didn't bat or bowl nor did he take any catches, playing in this match was his only contribution to The NEPL. Ward says that "he was known as Rocky, he was another good club member, he was a fill in player in the first team really, as a left arm seamer he could swing it, he was a good prospect as a youngster, persistent shoulder problems stopped him from bowling, so he started keeping wicket. He was a good keeper, he kept wicket for the firsts in 2023."

Keaton Jennings is a left-handed batsman and right arm medium pace bowler. Kevin Ward says the club got lucky when they got Jennings, he recalls getting a call from John Windows at Durham, saying they "had a real prospect but already had an overseas pro, could we do him a favour and have Stockton take him, Durham picked up most of the cost and we got Keaton Jennings, he had 600 runs in his first season! He was tall, but he didn't look like a classical or finesse type of player, he just went about his business, accumulating runs, he knew how to score runs efficiently, I knew watching him he would go on to a good career. As a bowler he was a right arm medium pacer, he would nibble the ball about a bit and change his pace really well, his talent as a bowler though was that he could read the game and more importantly he could read batsmen, I remember chatting to him about it one day, he was talking about a batsman who couldn't play the short ball well, Keaton said that it wasn't the pace that caused him the trouble but the height of the bounce, anything at his chest or above, he couldn't handle. That was the key to his bowling understanding batsman and working out how to dismiss them."

Keaton Jennings made his NEPL debut on 30th April 2011 for Durham Academy at Jesmond against Newcastle, he had scored 49 batting at number four when he was bowled by Indian pro Prateek Kar, he also bowled nine overs and took 1 for 18, his first NEPL wicket was Richard Fearon, bowled for 53.

He played his NEPL game for The Academy on 10th September 2011 at Chester Le Street, he took 1 for 13 when Chester batted, Liam Simpson being his last wicket for the Academy, caught and bowled for 48.

Jennings had played 13 NEPL games for The Academy, he had batted 12 times, with 4 not outs, he scored 471 runs at an average of 58.87, with 4 half centuries. His highest score was 88, on 21st May at Blaydon, leg break bowler Chris Varley had him stumped by Peter Howells to dismiss him.

Jennings bowled 384 balls in The NEPL for The Academy, with 10 maidens, conceding 224 runs and taking 15 wickets at an average of 14.93. His best bowling figures were 4 for 32 on 13th August 2011 at Tynemouth. He took 6 catches.

Jennings joined Stockton for the 2012 season, making his debut on 28th April 2012 at Benwell Hill, he scored 2, batting at number five when Stockton batted and took 1 for 25 when they bowled, Phil Nicholson was his first Stockton wicket, leg before for 17.

Jennings played 15 times for the club in 2012, batting 14 times, with 0 not outs, he scored 446 runs at an average of 31.85, with 3 half centuries and 1 century, 100, on 28th July at The Emirates, against Durham Academy. His innings had come from 175 balls and contained 10 fours and a six.

Jennings bowled 968 balls in The NEPL in the 2012 season, with 36 maidens, conceding 499 runs and taking 26 wickets at an average of 19.19. His best bowling figures were 6 for 42 on 12th June at Tynemouth. Mark Wood was one of his victims that day. He took 12 NEPL catches that season.

Jennings returned to Stockton for the successful 2013 season, playing 11 times for the club in The NEPL, he batted 10 times, with 1 not out, he scored 493 runs at an average of 54.77, with 2 half centuries and 2 centuries. His highest score of the season was 111, on 4th May at Chester Le Street. His innings came from 169 balls and contained 14 fours and a six.

Jennings bowled 865 balls in The NEPL in the 2013 season, with 44 maidens, conceding 351 runs and taking 19 wickets at an average of 18.47. His best bowling figures were 4 for 23 on 26th August at Blaydon. He took 7 NEPL catches that season.

Jennings would play a few more games in The NEPL, all for Stockton, he played four games in 2014, three in 2015 and one in 2016. The game on 7th May 2016 was his last NEPL appearance. He had played 47 matches in his NEPL career, batting 44 times, with 7 not outs, he had scored 1648 runs at an average of 44.54. He had 9 half centuries and 4 centuries, his highest score was the 111 mentioned earlier.

Jennings bowled 2701 balls in The NEPL, with 102 maidens, conceding 1300 runs and taking 81 wickets at an average of 16.04. His best bowling was the 6 for 36 mentioned earlier. He took 31 career catches in The NEPL.

Umar Shafiq didn't play in the early part of 2013, but he did play enough to contribute to the title win, he was around 15 at this time. Ward recalls "he was a leggie, a good one, he put fast spin or lots of revs on the ball and bowled a lot of wicket taking deliveries, as a batsman he was right handed, he was very technically correct, even at this young age he would have batted in the top four of our second team, he was doing very well for Durham too, he excelled with both bat and ball, he had a lovely supportive family too, but he was also very intelligent and he sort of moved away from cricket to study and he became a doctor."

He played his first NEPL game for Stockton on 10th September 2011 at South Shields, the last game of the season, he was 2 not out batting at eleven and he had 0 for 35 with the ball.

He played 11 NEPL games for the club in 2012, although he made no contributions with the bat, he did have a couple of bowling performances when he got three wickets, his first NEPL wicket was Jonny Malkin of Hetton Lyons on 5th May 2012, out leg before wicket.

He played his first NEPL game of the 2013 season on 6th July at Tynemouth, he took 5 for 48 when the hosts batted and made a single in a narrow Stockton loss. He would play 8 matches in 2013, batting 3 times with 0 not outs, he scored 9 runs with a high score of 8.

He also bowled 216 balls in the NEPL in 2013, with 2 maidens, conceding 114 runs and taking 10 wickets at an average of 11.40. His best bowling figures for the season were the 5 for 48 mentioned earlier. He took 2 catches in the season.

Shafiq played his last NEPL game on 30th April 2016 at Benwell Hill. He took 1 for 49 and did not bat. In total he played 30 NEPL matches, batting 14 times with 7 not outs, he scored 78 runs at an average of 11.14 and with a high score of 33 not out, made on 3rd May 2014 at South North, he batted for 75 balls and hit 3 boundaries.

He bowled 683 balls in The NEPL, with 11 maidens, conceding 445 runs and taking 21 wickets at an average of 21.19. The 5 for 48 remained his best bowling figures. He took 4 NEPL catches.

Jamie Harrison, a right-handed batsman and left arm medium fast bowler was another who contributed to the success of 2013. Ward recalls that "as a left arm medium fast bowler he bowled a lot of inswingers and hit the pads a lot, he and Josh Bousefield were a good foil for each other, similar in pace but different in what they did with the ball."

He first came to note in an Under 13 game for Cumbria against Lancashire on 8th June 2004 at St Annes, he took 0 for 33 and did not bat. He progressed to the Under 15's, playing a fixture on 5th June 2005 against Northumberland at Cleator, Mark Wood was in the Northumberland side. Harrison made 5 not out and took 1 for 12 as Cumberland won by 107 runs.

On 26th July 2006 Harrison was selected alongside Joe Root, Ben Stokes and Chirs Read to play for The English Schools Cricket Association North against their counterparts from The Midlands as part of The Bunbury Festival. Harrison took 0 for 2 and did not get a bat.

On 28th August 2006 Harrison played for Cleator against Keswick in The Higson Cup Final at Workington, he didn't bowl and scored 10 as Keswick won by 16 runs.

On 25th May 2007 Harrison played a 30 over match for Sedbergh School against a Lashings World XI, Graham Lloyd, Nathan Astle, Collis King, Chris Cairns and Henry Olonga among the opposition. Harrison took one wicket, he bowled Devon Malcolm, he took 1 for 24.

On 11th July 2007 Harrison started a 2-day match for Cumbria Under 17's against Derbyshire Under 17's at Whitehaven, he took 1 for 61 and did not bat as the game was abandoned on the second day.

He played a Second Eleven Championship match for Gloucestershire against The M.C.C Young Cricketers which started on 16th September 2008 at The County Ground, Bristol. Centuries from future first-class cricketers Ian Cockbain and Michael Richardson saw the visitors post a big total. Harrison had 1 for 92. He did not bat in the game but in the second innings he bowled Cockbain and took 1 for 3.

A game for Durham Second XI followed on 12th April 2009 against The North Yorkshire and South Durham League at Middlesbrough, Marc Symington had 47 not out for the hosts, Harrison took 1 for 10 and did not bat as his side won by 8 wickets.

He played his first NEPL game on 23rd May 2009 for The Durham Academy at Benwell Hill. Benwell Hill batted first, scoring 231 for 3 wickets declared, Phil Nicholson had 61, Alistair Maiden 68 and Mark Dale had 50. Harrison took 0 for 46 when Durham bowled and scored 8 when they batted. Ben Stokes top scored with 56 but 5 for 34 from David Rutherford saw Hill win by 63 runs.

Harrison took his first NEPL wicket on 30th May 2009 at Maiden Castle against Blaydon, Steven Gale trapped leg before wicket.

He played his last NEPL game for The Durham Academy on 10th September 2011 at Chester Le Street, he took 2 for 38 but didn't bat.

In total he played 21 NEPL matches for The Durham Academy, batting 12 times with 7 not outs, he scored 143 runs at an average of 28.60. He had a high score of 37 not out, away against South Shields on 26th June 2010.

He bowled 1188 balls in The NEPL for The Academy, with 33 maidens, conceding 650 runs and taking 33 wickets at an average of 19.69. His best bowling figures was 7 for 26 on 12th June 2010 at The Emirates against Chester le Street. He took 5 NEPL catches for The Academy.

As well as playing for the Durham Academy, he would play very regularly for Durham Second XI up to and including 2012. He made his first-class debut for Durham on 22nd May 2012 at Taunton against Somerset. He made 15 in his first innings and took 4 for 112 when Somerset had their first innings, his first wicket was Anil Suppiah who was leg before wicket for 4. Harrison made 20 in the second innings and took 1 for 19 as Somerset and won by 5 wickets.

In the title winning Stockton side of 2013 he played 11 NEPL matches, batting 7 times with 4 not outs, he scored 127 runs at an average of 42.33. He had a high score of 41, made on 29th June at South Shields.

He bowled 724 balls in The NEPL that season, with 36 maidens, conceding 311 runs and taking 35 wickets at an average of 8.88. His best bowling figures was 8 for 35 on 13th July at home to Benwell Hill. He took 5 NEPL catches in 2013.

His last NEPL game came on 8th September 2018 for Stockton at Jesmond against Newcastle. In total he played 78 NEPL matches, batting 63 times with 17 not outs, he scored 845 runs at an average of 18.36. He had 1 half century with a high score of 54, made on 1st August 2015 at Gateshead Fell.

He bowled 4158 balls in the NEPL, with 142 maidens, conceding 2017 runs and taking 110 wickets at an average of 18.33. The 8 for 35 from 2013 remained his best bowling figures and he took 21 NEPL catches.

Harrison went on to play 18 first class matches for Durham, he batted 30 times with 5 not out's, he scored 436 runs at an average of 17.44. He had 2 half centuries with a highest score of 65 in a match starting on 13th April 2014 at Northants.

He bowled 2518 balls in first class cricket, with 69 maidens, conceding 1573 runs and taking 52 wickets at an average of 30.25. His best bowling was 5 for 31 in a match starting on 22nd August 2013 at The Emirates against Surrey. Surprisingly, he never took a catch at this level.

Kevin Ward recalls that "early in the season we started well, we won the first game, we beat South North and beat them well, a few weeks in we beat The Academy, and we beat them well, things kind of snowballed from there, I think after few games I, and one or two of the senior players, realized that with our three main bowlers, Jamie Harrison, Josh Bousefield and Richard Waite, we were going to bowl a lot of sides out cheaply, we knew we had a solid batting line up too, Keaton Jennings was always going to score runs and we had solid players around him. We got on a roll and winning became a habit.

Looking back though we had a top five or six who all scored a good amount of runs, and three or four wicket taking bowlers, I think it was a squad win, lots of good contributions from a lot of areas. A couple of things stick in my mind, first of all, a game against South Shields, they had Tom Latham as their Durham contracted player, he was a good player, he was caught at slip by our overseas pro, Keaton Jennings off the bowling of our Senior Durham Academy player, Jamie Harrison. We won the title with about four games to go, we were at Blaydon and had bowled them out cheaply and won the game before tea, we were sitting around waiting for the South North result to come through, they had to win and get maximum points to keep the title open."

Richard Waite echoes the words of his captain "we had four really tough fixtures to start the season, after the last of those games there were a few of us sitting around the dressing room, someone said "we can win this thing, we can win the league this year," there was a dissenting voice saying the season was only a few weeks old, but the older hands agreed, we could win it, we had competed and proved it, we sort of gained some belief from this, when required throughout the season someone stood up when required, we just kept winning."

Records show that the South Shields game Ward referred to took place at Shields on 29th June, Stockton batted first and made 255 for 9 declared from 53 overs. John Hutton had 4 for 60 and Matthew Muchall 4 for 99. When Shields batted, they were soon in all sorts of trouble, they were 2 for 2 when Latham had been dismissed, caught by Jennings off Harrison for 2. No player made double figures, and they were shot out for 27. Jennings had 3 for 2, Harrison 5 for 13, Waite 1 for 11 and James Ward 1 for 0.

The Blaydon fixture Ward refers to was the fourth last game of the season, at Denefied Bank on Monday 26th August. Blaydon batted first and scored 121 all out from 43.3 overs, Graeme Bridge had top scored the innings with 41. Jennings had 4 for 23, Shafiq 3 for 22, Waite 2 for 24 and Kevin Ward 1 for 23, only Bousefield didn't take a wicket, 0 for 22. When Stockton batted despite a poor start, they were 2 for 2, 58 not out from Kevin Ward, 22 from Richard Waite and 21 from James Ward saw them home by 5 wickets in just 23.1 overs. They picked up 29 points and that was enough, South North were at South Shields on this day and although they did win, they only picked up 20 points in a very low scoring game.

At the season end, Stockton had won the NEPL title by an incredible 121 points and Richard Waite picked up his fifth NEPL Player of the Year award. His stats for the 2013 season were covered earlier in this chapter. The 2013 Banks Salver was won by Benwell Hill and the Twenty20 by Chester le Street.

TABLE 44   NEPL 2013.

	Played	Won	Draw/Aban	Lost	Penalty Points	Bonus Points	Points
Stockton	22	16	5	1	1	218	486
South North	22	10	7	5	2	178	365
Hetton Lyons	22	9	5	8	0	179	345
Newcastle	22	9	6	7	2	167	332
Chester le St	22	8	10	4	0	158	326
Blaydon	22	9	6	7	0	159	326
Benwell Hill	22	8	7	6	0	139	305
Tynemouth	22	7	6	9	0	138	271
Sunderland	22	7	7	8	0	128	260
Durham CA	22	6	8	8	0	132	256
Gateshead Fell	22	3	6	13	0	88	159
South Shields	22	0	6	16	0	92	120

TABLE 45   NEPL Batting Averages 2013.

Qualification 300 Runs.

25 Batsmen Qualified this season.

Player	Club	Inns	N. O	H. S	Runs	Average
(1) R.D Pringle	Hetton Lyons	10	3	156 no	606	86.57
(2) M.J Richardson	Newcastle	8	1	106 no	412	58.86
(3) B.A Raine	Newcastle	15	5	86 no	587	58.70
(4) J. du Toit	Newcastle	19	4	105 no	828	55.20
(5) K.K Jennings	Stockton	10	1	111	493	54.78
(6) Zohaib Khan	Benwell Hill	18	7	100 no	570	51.82
(7) G.J Muchall	South Shields	9	2	124	348	49.71
(8) D.G Shurben	Sunderland	18	4	126 no	678	48.43
(9) J.A Graham	South North	16	4	131 no	536	44.67
(10) S.J Birtwisle	Chester le Street	18	1	137	707	41.59
(11) J. Clark	Durham CA	20	3	153 no	700	41.18
(12) A.L Smith	Chester le Street	18	0	132	734	40.78
(15) K.L Ward	Stockton	17	2	80	543	36.20
(20) R.P Waite	Stockton	19	3	66	509	31.81

TABLE 46   NEPL Bowling Averages 2013.

Qualification 20 Wickets.

26 Bowlers Qualified this season.

Player	Club	Overs	Mdns	Runs	Wkts	Average
(1) J. Harrison	Stockton	120.4	36	311	35	8.89
(2) S. Humble	South North	177.1	41	462	39	11.85
(3) D.W Foster	Chester le Street	173.1	45	494	38	13.00
(4) D.J Hymers	Tynemouth	240.0	55	679	49	13.86
(5) J.J Coyne	South North	150.3	42	409	29	14.10
(6) J. Ward	Stockton	120.0	23	360	25	14.40
(7) R.P Waite	Stockton	284.1	61	787	54	14.57
(8) L.J Crozier	South North	200.2	43	610	39	15.64
(9) D. Evans	Blaydon	161.5	32	480	30	16.00
(10) G.D Bridge	Blaydon	196.1	28	609	38	16.03
(11) T.F Van Woerkom	Blaydon	150.5	23	549	31	17.71
(12) Gary Stewart	Blaydon	127.0	33	393	22	17.86

Stockton CC 2013 NEPL Champions.

Back Row left to right -Adam Warnes, Dan Barton (scorer), Peter Howells, Lee Ward, David Seymour, Keaton Jennings, Jamie Harrison.

Front Row- James Ward, Kevin Ward, Richard Waite, Mathew brown.

Photo Credit Mark Fletcher.

Keith Robson hands the NEPL trophy to Kevin Ward.

Photo Credit Mark Fletcher.

CHAPTER EIGHT

South North 2014-2015

Stockton won the league in 2013 by 121 points from South North, South Shields had finished bottom in 2013 and been relegated, they were replaced by Whitburn.

South North started the season with a home game against Gateshead Fell, the visitors won the toss and decided to field. South North made 306 for 2 wickets declared from 57 overs, opener Karl Turner made 209 not out and fellow opener Adam Heather had 43. When Fell batted, they were all out for 145, Andrew Porter, batting at nine, made 47 not out and Adam Whatley had 44, Lee Crozier took 5 for 41.

The South North team that day was as follows-

Karl Turner was a left-handed batsman, John Graham says of him "he had been on Durham's books, but he was never really given a fair crack at it, Notts then picked him up and he played there for a while. He could hit it all round the wicket and he seemed to adapt quickly to different match conditions, he was hungry for runs. As a bowler he was right arm, medium paced, a decent bowler, he had that ability to take big wickets, to get good players out."

Turner was clearly a talented youngster, the first record I found for him was on 17th June 2003 playing for Durham Under 15's against Lancashire Under 15's. He opened the batting, scoring 70 not out and took 2 for 19.

On 25th April 2004 he played for Durham Academy against Northern Universities Student Club Community Cricketers Elite at Maiden Castle. He top scored the innings with 59, future NEPL players John Coxon, Andrew Lee Smith, Paul Muchall and Scott Borthwick were among his teammates that day.

On 7th July 2004 Turner played for Durham Under 17's at Longhirst Hall against Scotland Under 17's, he top scored the innings with 68 and took 1 for 16.

He made his NEPL debut for Durham Academy on 24th July 2004 at Tynemouth and he played for Durham Second XIs in a 3-day match at Stamford Bridge against Yorkshire Second XI starting 25th April 2006, making 45 not out in the second innings. His last game for The Academy in the NEPL was on 8th September 2007 at Sunderland.

He played 68 NEPL matches for them, batting 60 times with 9 not outs, he scored 1459 runs at an average of 28.60. He scored 7 half centuries and 2 centuries, his highest score was 124 not out, made on 15th July 2006 at Newcastle.

He bowled 1201 balls in the NEPL for Durham Academy, with 29 maidens, conceding 795 runs and taking 33 wickets at an average of 24.09. His best bowling figures were 4 for 38, taken on 28th July 2007 at Newcastle. He took 33 NEPL catches and 1 stumping in the NEPL for The Durham Academy.

He made his NEPL debut for Stockton on 26th April 2008 at Benwell Hill and he played his last NEPL game for them on 12th September 2009, also at Benwell Hill.

Turner played 36 NEPL matches for Stockton, batting 35 times with 2 not outs, he scored 957 runs at an average of 29.00. He scored 2 half centuries and 3 centuries, his highest score was 134, made on 22nd August 2009 at home to Gateshead Fell.

He bowled 2015 balls in the NEPL for Stockton, with 58 maidens, conceding 1228 runs and taking 66 wickets at an average of 18.60. His best bowling figures were 7 for 43, taken on 15th August 2009 at South Shields. He took 3 NEPL catches in the NEPL for Stockton.

He made his NEPL debut for Gateshead Fell on 24th April 2010 at home to South Shields and his last NEPL game for them was on 4th September 2010 at South North.

He played 20 matches in the NEPL for Fell, batting 20 times with 6 not outs, he scored 734 runs at an average of 52.42. He scored 4 half centuries and 2 centuries. His highest score was 137 not out, scored on 28th August at Newcastle.

He bowled 1279 balls in the NEPL for Fell, with 30 maidens, conceding 837 runs and taking 37 wickets at an average of 22.62. His best bowling figures were 8 for 78, taken on 31st July at Hetton Lyons. He took 9 NEPL catches for the club.

His last game for Durham Second XI was on 3rd September 2010 at Derbyshire, he then made his debut for Hampshire Second XI on 11th April 2011 at The Rose Bowl against Southampton Solent University.

His last game for Hampshire Second XI was in a 3-day match starting on 17th May 2011 against Middlesex Second XI. He then moved to play for Derbyshire Second XI on 13th June 2011 against Yorkshire at Marske. The game was abandoned after just a few overs, Joe Root was 12 not out at the time. After just two games for Derbyshire Seconds Turner then played for Nottinghamshire Seconds on 20th June 2011 at Wellingborough against Northamptonshire.

He made his first-class debut for Nottinghamshire in a County Championship Division 1 match on 2nd August 2011, he scored 9 and 40 in a drawn match. He went on to play 5 first class matches for Nottinghamshire, batting 9 times with 0 not outs, he scored 227 runs at an average of 25.22. He scored 1 half century, 64, it came in his last appearance in first class cricket, in a 4-day match at Trent Bridge against Sussex. He also played 2 List A matches for Notts, scoring 22 runs at an average of 11.00.

Turner made his debut for Northumberland on 16th June 2013 at Jesmond against Norfolk, his last appearance for the county came in a 3-day match starting on 3rd August 2014 at Cambridgeshire.

He played 9 matches for Northumberland, batting 14 times with 1 not out, he scored 765 runs at an average of 58.84, with 5 half centuries and 1 century, 175, scored in a 3-day match starting on 22nd June 2014 at Roseworth Terrace against Lincolnshire. It took 295 minutes, and was scored from 236 balls, with 23 fours and 2 sixes.

He bowled 474 balls with 8 maidens, conceding 367 runs and taking 8 wickets at an average of 45.87, his best bowling figures were 2 for 25 and he took 3 catches.

Turner made his debut in the Derbyshire Premier League on 21st April 2012 for Dunstall at Ticknell, he made 47 and took 2 for 29 and played his last game for them on 9th September 2012 at home to Quarndon.

He appeared for Brandon in the 2013 season in NEPL Division 1, as well as playing Second Team cricket for Leicestershire.

The game to open the 2014 season was his NEPL debut for South North. He went on to play 22 matches in the 2014 season in the NEPL for South North, he batted 19 times with 3 not outs, he scored 919 runs at an average of 57.43. He scored 4 half centuries and 2 centuries. His highest score came on his NEPL debut on 19th April at home to Gateshead Fell in the season opener described earlier, he made 209 not out off just 180 balls, the innings contained 23 boundaries and 9 sixes. John Graham remembers it well, "the boundary on one side of the ground was very short, Karl just kept hitting sixes into the gardens at Roseworth Terrace, they couldn't bowl to him, he was playing that well. He started the season with two hundred and he finished it with a hundred!"

Turner played just this season for South North, he next appeared in the league making his NEPL debut for Hetton Lyons on 20th April 2019 at home to South North, he played his last NEPL game for Hetton Lyons on 11th September 2021 at home to Sacriston.

He played 37 NEPL matches for them, batting 37 times with 0 not outs, he scored 1185 runs at an average of 32.02. He scored 7 half centuries and 2 centuries with the highest score of 111, made on 24th July 2021 at Sacriston and was scored from 120 balls and contained 13 fours and 3 sixes.

He bowled 1649 balls in the NEPL for Hetton, with 40 maidens, conceding 1089 runs and taking 54 wickets at an average of 20.16. His best bowling figures were 7 for 15, taken on 31st August 2019 at Sacriston. He took 10 NEPL catches for Hetton.

Turner then made his NEPL debut for Burnmoor on 29th April 2023 at home to Benwell Hill. He played the entire 2023 NEPL season at Burnmoor, playing 18 NEPL matches for them, batting 18 times with 4 not outs, he scored 515 runs at an average of 36.78. He scored 3 half centuries and 1 century, 100 not out, made on 27th May at home to Burnopfield and was scored from 137 balls and contained 13 fours.

He bowled 548 balls in the NEPL in 2023 for Burnmoor, with 8 maidens, conceding 394 runs and taking 16 wickets at an average of 24.62. His best bowling figures were 6 for 37, taken on 8th July at home to South North. He took 3 NEPL catches in 2023.

To date, the last game of the 2023 season, he has played 201 matches in the NEPL, batting 189 times, with 24 not outs, he has scored 5769 runs at an average of 34.96. He has scored 27 half centuries and 12 centuries. His highest score is 209 not out mentioned earlier.

He has bowled 6900 deliveries in the NEPL, with 169 maidens, conceding 4469 runs and taking 212 wickets at an average of 21.08. His best bowling figures are 8 for 78, taken on 31st July 2010 for Gateshead Fell at Hetton Lyons. He has taken 69 NEP catches and has 1 stumping.

Adam Heather made 43 opening the batting in the season opener. Coming into the season he had played 250 matches in the NEPL, batting 240 times with 28 not outs, he had scored 7304 runs at an average of 34.45. He had 41 half centuries and 11 centuries. His highest score remained 140 not out scored on 25th July 2009 at Sunderland. He bowled 12 deliveries, conceding 2 runs and he had taken 77 catches and had 4 stumpings.

Heather played 20 matches in the NEPL in 2014, batting 18 times with 1 not out, he scored 297 runs at an average of 17.47. He scored 1 half century, 51, on 30th August 2014 at home to Sunderland. He took 7 NEPL catches in 2014.

Andrew Doig was a right-hand batsman; he scored a single to open the 2014 season, he scored 26 runs in the NEPL in 2014, he never bowled but did take 2 catches and 1 stumping. John Graham recalls Doig being "a talented, stylish batsman, he would have been a first team player elsewhere, but our top order was so strong he was in and out of the team, he always did a job for us when he played in the firsts, he was reliable. He was an excellent fielder; he was good around the dressing room."

Andrew Doig first came to my attention in a 2-day match for Northumberland Under 17's against Leicestershire and Rutland Under 17's starting on 13th July 2010. He played 13 times for Northumberland at this level, his highest score was 46. He also played 3 games for a Northumberland Development XI, the first occasion being on 6th June 2013 against The British Fire Service at Swalwell.

Doig had made his NEPL debut on 30th July 2011 for South North at home to Tynemouth and to date, his last game in the NEPL was on 24th August 2019 at home to Chester le Street.

He has played 28 matches in the NEPL, all for South North, batting 21 times with 8 not outs, he scored 170 runs at an average of 13.07. His highest score was 27, scored on 11th August 2012 at home to Durham Academy. He took 4 catches and had 1 stumping in his NEPL career.

John Graham was once again captain, and he scored 32 not out batting at number four to start the 2014 season. He entered the 2014 season having played 263 matches in the NEPL, batting 251 times with 33 not outs, he had scored 8046 runs at an average of 36.90. He has scored 58 half centuries and 11 centuries. His highest score was 132, made in July 2006 against Blaydon mentioned earlier.

He bowled 2834 balls, with 98 maidens, conceding 1601 runs and taking 66 wickets at an average of 24.25. His best bowling was 4 for 15, taken in May 2008 and discussed earlier. He had taken 145 NEPL catches.

Graham played in 22 matches in the NEPL title winning season of 2014, batting 18 times with 7 not outs, he scored 699 runs at an average of 63.54. He scored 6 half centuries with the highest score of 94, made on 31st May at Tynemouth and is discussed later when Graham talks about Rob Peyton. He took 7 catches in the NEPL in 2014.

Adam Cragg kept wicket in the season opener of 2014 but didn't get to bat. Cragg had played 144 matches in the NEPL up to the end of 2013, batting 120 times with 19 not outs, he had scored 2746 runs at an average of 27.18. He had scored 13 half centuries and 1 century, his highest score was 102, made in May 2010 and mentioned earlier. He had bowled 30 balls, taking 1 for 16 and he had taken 106 catches and made 18 stumpings in the NEPL.

Cragg played 21 matches in the NEPL in 2014, batting 14 times with 3 not outs, he scored 353 runs at an average of 32.09. He scored 2 half centuries and 1 century, 101, was scored on 9th August at Blaydon and came from 136 balls with 8 fours and a six. He took 23 NEPL catches and had 3 stumpings in 2014.

Jimmy Miller was listed to bat at five to start 2014 but didn't bat. Miller had played 242 matches in the NEPL as he started the 2014 season, batting 211 times with 39 not outs, he had scored 5070 runs at an average of 29.47. He had scored 30 half centuries and 6 centuries. His highest score was 132 not out made for Tynemouth in May 2001 and discussed earlier. He had bowled 60 balls and taken 1 wicket for 32 runs, and he had 83 NEPL catches up to this point.

Miller played in 19 matches in the NEPL title winning season of 2014, batting 11 times with 1 not out, he scored 160 runs at an average of 16.00. His highest score was 38 on 10th May at Hetton Lyons. He didn't bowl in the NEPL in 2014, but he did take 4 catches.

Stephen Humble was listed to bat at number seven in the 2014 opening game, he didn't bat but did open the bowling, taking 1 for 24. He entered the 2014 season having played 193 matches in the NEPL, batting 137 times with 34 not outs, he had scored 2575 runs at an average of 25.00. He has scored 10 half centuries, his highest score was 89, made on 8th September 2012 against South Shields at Roseworth Terrace.

He had bowled 12810 balls, with 554 maidens, conceding 5556 runs and taking 406 wickets at an average of 13.68. His best bowling figures were 8 for 55, taken in May 2006 and discussed earlier and he had taken 63 NEPL catches.

Humble played in 22 matches in the NEPL title winning season of 2014, batting 14 times with 4 not outs, he scored 335 runs at an average of 33.50. He scored 2 half centuries with the highest score of 92, made on 12th July at home to Chester le Street.

He bowled 1015 balls, with 35 maidens, conceding 537 runs and taking 30 wickets at an average of 17.89. His best bowling figures were 3 for 6, taken on 5th July at Gateshead Fell. He took 3 catches in the NEPL in 2014.

David Rutherford was a left-handed batsman and right arm medium fast bowler. He was listed to bat at number eight on 19th April 2014 but didn't get the opportunity, he did bowl, taking 2 for 29, the season opener of 2014 was his NEPL debut for South North.

John Graham says "I played a lot of representative youth cricket with him, he was medium fast in his youth, when he got a little older, he slowed his pace down a little. He was a tall lad, he was a high calibre bowler as an adult, he was skilful with excellent control and variety, in 2014 he would come on as first change for us and he was unbelievably economic, he went for under two an over across the premier league season, despite how good he was for us I don't think we had him in his prime, he would go on to play for Swalwell and Benwell Hill and he was still playing for Ashington in 2023."

Rutherford had played 113 matches in the NEPL, all for Benwell Hill. As he entered the 2014 season, he had batted 84 times, with 24 not outs, he had scored 1308 runs at an average of 21.80. He had scored 3 half centuries, his highest score was 96 not out, scored for Benwell Hill on 24th April 2010 at home to Newcastle.

He bowled 8737 balls, with 391 maidens, conceding 3665 runs and taking 223 wickets at an average of 16.43. His best bowling figures were 6 for 24, taken on 25th August 2001 at Newcastle. He had taken 20 NEPL catches.

During the 2104 season Rutherford played 19 matches in the NEPL for South North, he scored 64 runs at an average of 16.00. His highest score was 35 not out on 10th May at Hetton Lyons.

He bowled 1323 balls, with 61 maidens, conceding 438 runs and taking 35 wickets at an average of 12.51. His best bowling figures were 6 for 23 taken on 26th July at home to Hetton Lyons. He made 1 NEPL catch in 2014.

Jonny Wightman was listed to bat nine to start 2014 but didn't bat, he opened the bowling taking 2 for 29. Entering the season Wightman had played 90 matches in the NEPL, batting 49 times with 14 not outs, he had scored 297 runs at an average of 8.48 and a high score of 37.

He had bowled 5490 balls, with 124 maidens, conceding 3443 runs and taking 168 wickets at an average of 20.49. His best bowling figures were 7 for 44, taken on 12 June 2010 for South North at Hetton Lyons. He had taken 9 NEPL catches by the end of 2013.

He played 22 NEPL matches in 2014, batting 10 times with 5 not outs, he scored 51 runs at an average of 10.19 with the highest score of 17.

He bowled 1324 balls, with 28 maidens, conceding 878 runs and taking 59 wickets at an average of 14.88. His best bowling figures of the season were now 6 for 27, taken 31st May 2014 at Tynemouth. He made 4 NEPL catches in 2014.

Wightman was named NEPL Player of the Year for his work in 2014.

Lee Crozier was listed to bat at number ten in the 2014 opener, he didn't bat but took 5 for 41 when he bowled. Going into 2014 Crozier had played 259 matches in the NEPL, batting 136 times with 62 not outs, he had scored 1240 runs at an average of 16.75. He had 1 half century, 89 for Benwell Hill mentioned earlier.

He had bowled 19094 balls, with 901 maidens, conceding 8051 runs and taking 539 wickets at an average of 14.93. His best bowling figures were 7 for 21 mentioned earlier. He had taken 41 NEPL catches by the end of 2013.

In the 2014 season Crozier played 22 NEPL matches for South North, batting 4 times with 1 not out, he scored 19 runs at an average of 6.33.

He bowled 1425 balls, with 51 maidens, conceding 691 runs and took 41 wickets at an average of 16.85. His best bowling figures were 5 for 41 taken on 19th April in the season opener. He took 4 catches in the 2014 season.

Tom Hodnett was listed on the scorecard to bat at number eleven to start the 2014 season, he didn't bat. He did bowl, 0 for 21. Hodnett is covered when he made his NEPL debut for South North on 21st April 2012 in that earlier chapter.

He played 8 matches in the NEPL in the 2014 season, only two of them were for South North as he also played 6 matches for the Durham Academy. He made little impression with the bat, but he did bowl 282 balls, with 9 maidens, conceding 191 runs and taking 7 wickets at an average of 27.28. His best bowling figures were 3 for 33 taken on 30th August for Durham at Chester le Street.

Richard Brook missed the first game of the 2014 season. He entered the season as an established NEPL player. He had played 279 matches in the league at this point, batting 73 times with 43 not outs, he scored 152 runs at an average of 5.06. His highest score was 19.

He bowled 14879 balls with 498 maidens, conceding 8355 runs and taking 421 wickets at an average of 19.98. His best bowling figures were 7 for 28 on 22nd May 2004 at home to Philadelphia. He had taken 45 NEPL catches.

During the 2014 season Brook played 13 times in the NEPL for South North, batting 3 times with 3 not outs, he scored 6 runs. He bowled 344 balls with 3 maidens, conceding 266 runs and taking 19 wickets at an average of 14.00 and his best bowling figures were 4 for 17 on 13th June at Stockton. He took 4 catches that season.

Jonathan Craigs was a left-handed batsman; he missed the first game of the 2014 season. Craigs had made his NEPL debut for Benwell Hill on 4th May 2013 at home to The Durham Academy, he batted three and scored 33.

He played 19 matches for Benwell Hill that season, batting 18 times with 1 not out, he scored 561 runs at an average of 33.00. He scored 4 half centuries and had a highest score of 86, scored on 26th August 2013 at home to Gateshead Fell. He bowled 144 balls in the NEPL for Hill, with 1 maiden, conceding 120 runs and taking 1 wicket, he took 11 catches in 2013.

He made his NEPL debut for South North on 26th April 2014 at Chester le Street, this game is covered in a bit more detail later in this chapter.

He played 20 NEPL matches in 2014, batting 16 times with 1 not out, he scored 2 half centuries and 1 century. The century, 112 not out was scored on 14th June 2014 at Sunderland, it came from 156 balls and contained 17 fours. He bowled just 6 balls in the season, 0 for 2 but took 12 catches and had 1 stumping.

Rob Peyton is a right-handed batsman and wicketkeeper; he didn't play in the season opener of 2014. He made his NEPL debut for South North on 3rd May 2014 at home to Stockton, he didn't get to bat but he did keep wicket, taking 4 catches.

He played 12 matches in the NEPL title winning side, although he didn't get much opportunity to bat, he had just 4 innings, scoring 37 runs. He did contribute with the gloves, taking 9 catches.

John Graham says that "Rob started as our scorer as a kid, he was a good junior. I remember his debut at Tynemouth, we were 2 for 2 when he joined me at the crease on a green sporty wicket against an experienced bowling attack, Rob didn't get many, but he hung around and looked okay, he showed plenty of character, Adam Cragg came in at five and got a score and we recovered.

The same year we played a game against Chester le Street in a National competition, we lost by 1 run, but Rob played brilliantly. His batting kicked on from there, he was a very clean hitter and became a good bat. He was another good character in the dressing room. As a keeper he was very good at standing up to the seamers, he would regularly take leg side stumpings off Jonny Wightman in particular."

Putting John Graham's memory to the test once again, Peyton played for South North on 31st May 2014 at Tynemouth, they were 4 for 3, Peyton came in at four and John Graham at five, Peyton made 8, from 40 balls, they were still in a lot of trouble at 29 for 4 but Graham himself made 94 and Adam Cragg 66 and they reached 198 for 8, declaring after 60 overs. When Tynemouth batted, they were 86 all out, Jonny Wightman taking 6 for 27 was the chief destroyer.

Rob Peyton had first come to notice of the record keepers playing for Northumberland Under 13's, playing a 40 over match at Hipsburn against Durham Under 13's on 9th June 2011.

The following season he was playing for Northumberland Under 15's, his first appearance, as a wicketkeeper/batsman, coming on 31st July 2012 at Urmston against Lancashire Under 15's.

He continued to progress through the junior system, playing for Northumberland Under 17's on 13th August 2013, again at Hipsburn, this time against Leicestershire and Rutland Under 17's.

He then progressed to South North's first XI as described above.

John Graham recalls that "Hetton had a good side this year, Allan Worthy, Martin Pollard, obvious stand outs who were proven players, they also had an overseas pro, Lal Kumar from Pakistan, he came over as a left arm medium pacer but turned to left arm orthodox spin when he played on the Hetton wickets. We lost to Chester Le Street early on but put a run together then beat them well at Gosforth, Jonny Wightman had a good day, I think. Probably the pivotal game of the season came five or six from the end of the season, we got a winning draw against them and that kept them at arm's length, we eventually won the league with two or three games to go."

Before I look at South North, I found a truly remarkable scorecard involving Hetton Lyons from this season, on 31st May 2014 Hetton Lyons played The Durham Academy at The Emirates. Hetton won the toss and decided to bat, nothing unusual there, 180 for 9, a reasonable score, from 57.5 overs, eight players made double figures, Jonny Malkin top scored with 27. Adam Hickey, an off spinner, was the best of the bowlers, 3 for 31. Nothing unusual so far.

Durham were on 9 when they lost their first wicket, opener Reece Carr, caught by Gary Scott off Lal Kumar for 3, still nothing unusual there. They then lost the next 9 wickets for 7 runs, Martin Pollard finished with 7.2 overs and took 2 for 8, Kumar bowled 7 overs and had the truly remarkable figures of 8 for 4, just to clarify, eight wickets for four runs. There were 8 ducks on the Academy side, extras top scored with 6, 16 all out!

Returning to South North, once again, I put John's memory to the test, Chester le Street did indeed beat South North early on, the game being on 26th April 2014 at Ropery Lane. Chester had batted first and 53 from John Coxon and 50 from Callum Thorp saw them reach 208 for 9 declared from 61.5 overs. Jonny Wightman took 4 for 53. When South North batted, Liam Simpson had 4 for 27, Thorp 3 for 8, Stephen Cantwell 2 for 14 and Andrew Bell 1 for 12, as they were dismissed for 64.

The game at Gosforth Graham refers to was on 12th July 2014, South North batted first after winning the toss and scored 218 all out in 62.1 overs, Stephen Humble had scored 92 and Jonathan Craigs 58. Callum Thorp had 4 for 43 and Quentin Hughes 4 for 24.

When Chester batted, Andrew Smith scored 86 but their middle order and tail fell away, and they were bowled out for 201 in 50.2 overs. Smith was the last wicket to fall, caught by Richard Brook off the bowling of Jonny Wightman. Wightman, as John Graham thought, did have a good day, taking 6 for 37.

In respect of Hetton and South North, the fixture between the two sides was very early in the season, taking place at Hetton on 10th May, rain had caused a 12.45 start and reduced the match to 108 overs and a further reduction of 17 overs was put in place after further rain at 3 o'clock. South North won the toss and batted, 191 for 7 declared from 49 overs, Stephen Humble had 60 and David Rutherford 35 not out. When Hetton batted they lost wickets at regular intervals and were unable to build any momentum, they finished on 100 for 7 from 38.2 overs. Humble had 3 for 34. South North, with the winning draw, picked up 13 points and Hetton 6.

The return fixture at Gosforth, the one Graham refers to as "probably a pivotal moment," took place on 26th July 2014, South North won the toss and batted first, they scored 214 for 8 from 65 overs when their innings was closed. In a rather unusual statistic, three South North batsmen made 49, opener Karl Turner, number four John Graham, and number 7, David Edwards was unbeaten on 49 when the innings closed. Left arm fast bowler and overseas pro, Lal Kumar had 5 for 71.

An opening stand of 54 between Gary Scott and Allan Worthy saw Hetton start well, but once Scott was dismissed for 22 and Worthy for the top score of the innings, 36, they struggled a bit, David Rutherford with 6 for 23 the main reason why, they finished on 151 for 8 from their 55 overs. Match drawn. South North 13 points, Hetton 9.

The game with Chester le Street which was described earlier was South North's only loss of the season, Hetton had lost two games, one early on to Blaydon by 1 wicket and the other was also to Chester le Street, in July.

That second loss was also probably a pivotal moment, but a 33-point title win would once again suggest that John Graham's memory is good, and the title won with at least one game to go.

Chester le Street won the Banks Salver in 2014, and the Twenty20 Cup was won by Durham Academy.

Jonny Wightman of South North was named NEPL Player of the Year, his stats were covered earlier in this chapter.

TABLE 47   NEPL 2014.

	Played	Won	Draw/Aban	Lost	Penalty Points	Bonus Points	Points
South North	22	13	8	1	1	203	445
Hetton Lyons	22	12	8	2	3	197	412
Chester le Street	22	8	11	3	0	171	352
Blaydon	22	9	6	7	2	139	329
Benwell Hill	22	8	10	4	0	120	288
Newcastle	22	6	8	8	0	134	266
Stockton	22	6	7	9	0	127	248
Tynemouth	22	4	9	9	1	133	241
Whitburn	22	5	9	8	1	85	200
Durham CA	22	1	13	8	2	95	175
Gateshead Fell	22	3	6	13	0	88	162
Sunderland	22	2	11	9	0	81	158

TABLE 48   NEPL Batting Averages 2013.

Qualification 300 Runs.

25 Batsmen Qualified this season.

Player	Club	Inns	N. O	H. S	Runs	Average
(1) Zohaib Khan	Benwell Hill	16	6	116 no	848	84.80
(2) J.A Graham	South North	18	7	94	699	63.55
(3) J. du Toit	Newcastle	18	3	119	926	61.73
(4) K. Turner	South North	19	3	209 no	919	57.44
(5) G. Clark	Newcastle	19	5	134 no	786	56.14
(6) Q.J Hughes	Chester le Street	15	4	98 no	563	51.18
(7) R.P Waite	Stockton	19	3	140	773	48.31
(8) A.L Smith	Chester le Street	19	1	136	862	47.89
(9) R. Singh	Benwell Hill	15	5	96 no	453	45.30
(10) J.A Thompson	Durham CA	16	3	111 no	503	38.69
(11) A. Whatley	Gateshead Fell	19	1	92	689	38.28
(12) J.J McClure	Blaydon	15	3	118	452	37.67
(17) S. Humble	South North	14	4	92	335	33.50
(18) A.D Cragg	South North	14	3	101	353	32.09
(24) J.D Craigs	South North	16	1	112 no	391	26.07

TABLE 49   NEPL Bowling Averages 2014.

Qualification 20 Wickets.

25 Bowlers Qualified this season.

Player	Club	Overs	Mdns	Runs	Wkts	Average
(1) Lal Kumar	Hetton Lyons	210.5	63	517	48	10.77
(2) D.J Rutherford	South North	220.3	61	438	35	12.51
(3) M. Elliott	Whitburn	129.0	37	358	26	13.77
(4) Zohaib Khan	Benwell Hill	223.4	51	725	52	13.94
(5) C.D Thorp	Chester le Street	226.2	72	576	40	14.40
(6) J.R Wightman	South North	220.4	28	878	59	14.88
(7) M.L Pollard	Hetton Lyons	149.3	43	417	28	14.89
(8) R.D Pringle	Hetton Lyons	146.4	23	477	32	14.91
(9) A.J.J.A Hart	Durham CA	110.5	25	335	22	15.23
(10) D.J Hymers	Tynemouth	268.3	75	784	51	15.37
(11) Gary Stewart	Blaydon	235.4	60	675	43	15.70
(12) A.P Smith	Tynemouth	102.4	11	435	26	16.73
(13) L.J Crozier	South North	237.3	51	691	41	16.85
(16) S. Humble	South North	169.1	35	537	30	17.90

South North CC 2014 NEPL Champions.

Left to Right – Back Row- A.J Doig, A.D Cragg, J.D Craigs, S. Humble, D.J Rutherford, J.R Wightman, K. Turner, R. Peyton.

Front Row- J.N Miller, L.J Crozier, J.A Graham, A.T Heather.

Jonny Wightman, seen here bowling for South North on 29th July 2023 at home to Burnopfield.

2015

South North started the 2015 season with at least one major change, Karl Turner, despite a very successful first season had moved on, he was replaced by Australian Test Player Marcus North. They opened the season on 18th April 2015 at Jesmond against Newcastle, South North won the toss and elected to field. Seven Newcastle players made double figures but only James Carding made a half century, 55 to be exact. Richard Brook had 4 for 24 as Newcastle were dismissed for 193 all out from 61.5 overs.

When South North batted the also struggled for the big match winning score, Adam Cragg was 43 not out and Marcus North had 43, but they were unable to force the win, South North 175 for 8 when the innings was closed after 58 overs. Charlie Stobo, a right arm medium fast bowler had 4 for 58.

The South North side which started the 2015 season was as follows-

Jimmy Miller opened the batting but made just a single. During the 2015 season Miller played 16 NEPL matches for South North, batting 15 times with 0 not outs, he scored 308 runs at an average of 20.53. He scored 1 half century, 84, on 30th May 2015 at Hetton Lyons. He took 5 catches in the NEPL in 2015.

He played his last NEPL match for South North on 24th August 2019 at home to Chester le Street, he scored 35 not out, this was his first appearance in the NEPL since September 2016 and appears to have been a one-off.

After initially playing for Tynemouth, since his debut for South North in 2003 he played 243 matches in the NEPL for them, batting 200 times with 33 not outs, he scored 4354 runs at an average of 26.07. He scored 23 half centuries and 2 centuries. His highest score for South North in the NEPL was 106 not out, scored on 19th July 2003 at Tynemouth. He bowled 54 balls in the NEPL for them, taking 1 wicket at a cost of 30 runs and he took 78 NEPL catches for South North.

In his NEPL career Jimmy Miller played 294 matches, batting 250 times with 42 not outs, he scored 5820 runs at an average of 27.98. He scored 32 half centuries and 6 centuries. His highest score was 132 not out, scored for Tynemouth on 28th May 2001 at home to Gateshead Fell. He bowled 60 balls with 0 maidens, conceding 32 runs and taking 1 NEPL wicket, he also took 97 catches in the NEPL.

Miller won NEPL titles in 2003 to 2008 inclusive, 2011 and 2012, 2014 and 2015.

Adam Heather also opened the batting, scoring 33. Heather entered the 2015 season having played 270 matches in the NEPL, he had batted 258 times with 29 not outs, he has scored 7601 runs at an average of 33.19. He had scored 42 half centuries and 11 centuries, his highest score was 140 not out, scored on 25th July 2009 at Sunderland. He had bowled 12 balls, 0 for 2 and taken 84 catches and 4 stumpings.

His contribution to the 2015 season was that he played 18 matches, batting 18 times with 2 not outs, he scored 319 runs at an average of 19.93. He scored 1 half century, 74, which was scored on 2nd May 2015 at Gateshead Fell. He took 5 NEPL catches.

Heather would play the 2016 season at South North before moving to Benwell Hill for the 2017 season.

In total he had played 299 NEPL matches for South North, batting 286 times with 33 not outs, he scored 8144 runs at an average of 32.18. He scored 44 half centuries and 11 centuries in the NEPL for South North, his highest score was 140 not out mentioned earlier. His bowling hadn't changed from the 12 balls mentioned earlier but he had now taken 91 catches and had 4 stumpings for South North in the league.

He made his debut for Benwell Hill at home to Tynemouth on 15th April 2017. To date, the end of 2024, Heather was still playing for Hill, appearing in the last game of the season on 14th September at Burnopfield and he featured a number of times during the 2024 weekly round ups.

At the end of 2024 he has played 82 NEPL matches for Benwell Hill, batting 77 times with 6 not outs, he has scored 1769 runs at an average of 24.91. He has scored 9 half centuries and has the highest score of 92, made on 9th July 2022 at home to Tynemouth. He hasn't bowled for Hill, but he has taken 14 NEPL catches.

To the end of the 2023 season, Adam Heather has played 368 matches in the NEPL, he has batted 350 times with 38 not outs, scoring 9531 runs at an average of 30.54. He has scored 49 half centuries and 11 centuries, the 140 not out mentioned earlier is his highest score. He has taken 100 catches and made 4 stumpings.

Heather won NEPL titles from 2003 to 2008 inclusive, 2011 and 2012, 2014 and 2015, all with South North.

Marcus North was a left-handed batsman and right arm off break bowler, he batted at number three to start the 2015 season, he scored 43 and bowled six overs 0 for 13. North had arrived in the NEPL as an overseas pro, having come through the Western Australia and Australian Cricket Academy system.

He made his debut in List A cricket in England on 2nd May 2000 for The Durham Cricket Board against Leicestershire Cricket Board at Gateshead. Allan Worthy, Ian Pattison and Phil Mustard made their List A debuts in the same match.

North made his NEPL debut for Gateshead Fell on 6th May 2000 at home to South North, he opened the batting and scored 10, he was caught by Ian Gilthorpe off the bowling of Stephen Boyd.

He played 14 matches for Fell in the inaugural NEPL season of 2000, batting 14 times with 3 not outs, he scored 770 runs at an average of 70.00. He scored 4 half centuries and 3 centuries, his highest score was 163 not out, made on 22nd July 2000 at Benwell Hill, his innings came from 204 balls and contained 21 fours and 4 sixes.

North bowled 437 balls in the NEPL for Fell in 2000, with 13 maidens, conceding 539 runs and taking 22 wickets at an average of 24.50. His best bowling figures were 4 for 47, taken on 22nd July at Benwell Hill in the game where he scored his highest score. He made 9 catches that season.

He played the 2001 season at Colne in the Lancashire League, returning to Gateshead Fell for 2002 and 2003. He was selected for Australia A in 2002 and continued to play for Western Australia up to and beyond his debut for Durham in a County Championship match at Hampshire starting on 16th April 2004.

His last game in the NEPL for Gateshead Fell was on 30th August 2003 at home to Philadelphia. He played 51 matches in the NEPL for Gateshead Fell, batting 50 times with 7 not outs, he scored 2198 runs at an average of 51.11. He scored 12 half centuries and 6 centuries, his highest score was 163 not out mentioned earlier at Benwell Hill.

He bowled 3678 balls, with 131 maidens, conceding 1985 runs and taking 96 wickets at an average of 20.67. His best bowling figures were 8 for 42, taken on 15th June 2002 at Tynemouth. He took 27 NEPL catches for Fell.

He would also play first class cricket for Lancashire, Derbyshire, Gloucestershire and Glamorgan amongst others before he made it to the full Australian Side.

He played 21 test matches for Australia, batting 35 times with 2 not outs, he scored 1171 runs at an average of 35.48. He scored 4 half centuries and 5 centuries. His highest score in test cricket was 128, made in a match in Bangalore starting on 9th October 2012 against India.

He bowled 1258 balls in test cricket, with 37 maidens, conceding 591 runs and taking 14 wickets at an average of 42.21. His best bowling figures were 6 for 55 in a match starting on 13th July 2010 at Lord's against Pakistan. He took 17 test match catches for Australia.

North played 2 List A matches for Australia, batting 2 times with 0 not outs, he scored 6 runs with the highest score of 5. He bowled 18 balls, conceding 16 runs, he didn't take a wicket but took 1 catch, he also played 1 Twenty20 for Australia, scoring 20.

His next appearance in the NEPL was his debut for South North on 18th April 2015 at Newcastle, the game described earlier. Marcus North played 16 matches in the NEPL for South North in 2015, he batted 15 times with 2 not outs, he scored 616 runs at an average of 47.38. He scored 2 half centuries and 2 centuries, his highest score was 133, made on 25th July 2015 at home to South Shields and the innings came from 154 balls, with 19 fours and 2 sixes.

He bowled 363 balls, with 14 maidens, conceding 185 runs and taking 8 wickets at an average of 23.12. His best bowling figures were 4 for 22, taken on 6th June 2015 at home to Blaydon, he made 14 catches in the 2015 NEPL season.

More on Marcus North during the chapter on 2017.

John Graham captained the side which started 2015 and also batted at number four, he made 4. Lee Crozier said of John Graham that "as a captain I think his ability with the bat meant that his captaincy was overlooked sometimes, he had such a good knowledge of the game and was incredibly thoughtful about the game, he was very attacking, he would risk a losing a game if he thought it gave us more chance to win it, his captaincy was a major factor in our success and winning titles, it's probably best summed up as the fact that his captaincy was a difference maker for us. As an individual he is very easy to talk to and it shouldn't be underestimated how hard it can be to keep a dressing room of very good players all content with their role in the team. As a batsman he is one of the best the league has had, his volume of runs support this, he was technically very good, but he was also at the next level when it came to playing situational innings, at reading the scoreboard and working out what the team required and then delivering that innings. He was also a very determined cricketer, a driven cricketer and that was key to our team success."

He had played 285 matches in the NEPL by the end of 2014, batting 269 times with 40 not outs, he had scored 8745 runs at an average of 38.18. He had scored 64 half centuries and 11 centuries, his highest score was 132, scored July 2006 and mentioned earlier.

He had bowled 2840 balls with 98 maidens, conceding 1606 runs and taking 66 wickets at an average of 24.33. His best bowling figures were 4 for 15, taken in May 2008 and mentioned earlier. He had taken 152 NEPL catches.

His contribution to the 2015 season was to play 19 matches in the NEPL, batting 16 times with 1 not out, he scored 505 runs at an average of 33.66. He scored 4 half centuries, with a highest score of 89, made on 8th August 2015 at home to Hetton Lyons. He didn't bowl in 2015 but took 5 catches.

Adam Cragg batted at five to open the season and made 43 not out. Entering the 2015 season, Cragg had played 165 NEPL matches, batting 134 times with 22 not outs, he had scored 3099 runs at an average of 27.66, He had scored 15 half centuries and 2 centuries, his highest score was 102 in May 2010 mentioned earlier. His bowling figures hadn't changed since the start of 2013, but he now had 129 NEPL catches and 21 stumpings.

He played 18 matches in the NEPL in 2015, batting 15 times with 4 not outs, he scored 344 runs at an average of 31.27. He scored 2 half centuries, with a highest score of 54 not out scored on 8th August at home to Hetton Lyons. He made 28 catches and had 1 stumping in the NEPL in 2015.

Jonathan Craigs was a left-handed batsman, he batted six to start 2015, scoring 7. John Graham says that "everyone knew him as "Burgers," he was the older brother of Michael Craigs who had played for us, he was a Morpeth lad and I think he started playing there, he had a season at Benwell Hill and impressed us, he came to us in 2014. He was strong through the covers and point, anywhere on the offside really, if he got in, he would generally go on and get a score. He was a bit of an enigma, there were times when you were wondering where his next run was coming from and times when he looked like a fine player. I remember a game at South Shields where he and Marcus North put on 200."

He played 18 matches in the NEPL for South North in 2015, batting 18 times with 3 not outs, he scored 383 runs at an average of 25.53. He scored 1 half century and 1 century, he had a highest score of 114 not out, scored on 16th May 2015 at South Shields.

He bowled 6 balls in the NEPL in 2015, conceding 7 runs and taking 1 wicket, his best bowling figures were 1 for 7, taken on 27th June 2015, Chris Hooker, the unlucky Stockton batsman, caught by Adam Cragg for 53 on 27th June 2015. He took 1 catch in 2015.

Brendan Ford batted at number seven on 18th April, he scored 19, he also took 3 for 32 when Newcastle had batted, this was his only appearance of the 2015 season. It appears that Ford then moved to Scotland as just one week later he made his debut for Arbroath United at home to Carlton in The Cricket Scotland League Eastern Premiership. He played there for the remainder of the 2015 season, having a good year, playing 21 times, scoring 538 runs at an average of 28.31 and the highest score of 145. He also took 28 wickets at an average of 17.25.

He had played 85 matches in the NEPL for South North, he batted 73 times with 12 not outs, he scored 1737 runs at an average of 28.47. He scored 9 half centuries and 1 century, 103 not out, scored on 16th May 2009 at home to Stockton, the innings came from 138 balls, with 11 fours and 1 six.

He bowled 3440 balls, with 108 maidens, conceding 1859 runs and taking 105 wickets at an average of 17.70. His best bowling figures were 6 for 44 taken on 14th June 2008 at Tynemouth. He took 19 catches in the NEPL.

Rob Peyton is a right-handed batsman and wicketkeeper, he batted at number eight, failing to score, he kept wicket taking a catch and a stumping during the Newcastle innings. Peyton played 13 matches in the NEPL in 2015, batting 10 times with 2 not outs, he scored 113 runs at an average of 14.12. He made 1 half century, 59, made on 5th September 2015 at Stockton, opening the batting, the innings had come from 68 balls with 7 fours and 2 sixes. He made 10 catches and had 1 stumping in the NEPL during the 2015 season.

Jonny Wightman had batted at number nine to start 2015, scoring 3. He opened the bowling, taking 1 for 87. Wightman entered the 2015 season having played 112 matches in the NEPL, batting 59 times with 19 not outs, he had scored 348 runs at an average of 8.69. His highest score was 37, made in May 2011 and mentioned earlier.

He had bowled 6814 balls with 152 maidens, conceding 4321 runs and taking 227 wickets at an average of 19.03. His best bowling figures were 7 for 44 taken in June 2010 and mentioned earlier. He had taken 13 NEPL catches.

In the 2015 season Wightman played 17 NEPL matches, his batting contribution was limited so we will stick with the bowling, he bowled 1027 balls, with 26 maidens, conceding 611 runs and taking 36 wickets. His best bowling of the season was 5 for 22 taken on 4th July at The Emirates against The Durham Academy. He took 2 catches in the NEPL in 2015.

Lee Crozier was 13 not out batting at number ten when the game was over, he had taken 2 for 30 after opening the bowling. Crozier had played 281 NEPL matches, batting 140 times, with 63 not outs, he had scored 1259 runs at an average of 16.35. He had 1 half century, 89 for Benwell Hill in 2002.

He had bowled 20519 balls, with 952 maidens, conceding 8742 runs and taking 580 wickets at an average of 15.07. His best bowling figures were 7 for 21 mentioned earlier. He had taken 45 NEPL catches to this point.

In 2015 he played 20 NEPL matches as South North retained their league title. His batting contribution was negligible, but he bowled 1190 balls, with 42 maidens, conceding 617 runs and taking 38 wickets at an average of 16.23. His best bowling figures were 5 for 36 taken on 2nd May at Gateshead Fell. He took 1 NEPL catch this season.

Richard Brook was number eleven to start the season off and was the only batsman on either side not to get a bat. He took 4 for 58 when he bowled. Brook had played 189 matches in the NEPL as he entered the 2105 season, he had batted 44 times with 28 not outs, he had scored 94 runs with a high score of 19.

With the ball he had now bowled 9874 balls, with 384 maidens, conceding 5041 runs and taking 304 wickets at an average of 16.58. His best bowling figures were 7 for 28, taken in May 2004. He had 32 catches.

In 2015 he played just 3 games in the NEPL, he bowled 173 balls, with 6 maidens, conceding 80 runs and taking 7 wickets at an average of 11.42. His best bowling figures were 4 for 24, taken in the season opener as mentioned earlier. After his last game of 2105 Brook would play just one more game in the NEPL, on 15th April 2017 at home to Stockton, his career stats will feature as part of the 2017 chapter.

As I was going through the two sides, I saw Callum Harding's name appear, he has regularly popped up when I have been doing my research, so I think it's appropriate to have a look at his NEPL career.

Harding is a left arm medium fast bowler and lower order batsman, he made his NEPL debut for The Durham Academy on 3rd May 2008 at Sunderland. He had to wait until the following week at The Riverside, 10th May, to pick up his first NEPL wicket, Newcastle opener Matthew Hynd, caught by Ramanpreet Singh for 12, his second NEPL wicket was Mark Stoneman, caught and bowled for 130.

Harding played his last NEPL game for The Academy on 3rd September 2011 at South North. He played 46 matches in the NEPL for Durham Academy, batting 26 times with 10 not outs, he scored 83 runs. His highest score was 19.

He bowled 2122 balls in the NEPL for The Academy, with 58 maidens, conceding 1350 runs and taking 50 wickets at an average of 27.00. His best bowling was 4 for 28 on 12th July 2008 at Maiden Castle against Sunderland. He made 14 NEPL catches for The Durham Academy.

He then made his NEPL debut for Newcastle on 5th May 2012 at Sunderland, his first NEPL wicket for them was Dan Shurben, caught by Michael Richardson for a single. His last NEPL game for Newcastle was on 8th September 2018 at Jesmond against Stockton.

He played 116 matches in the NEPL for Newcastle, batting 61 times with 22 not outs, he scored 512 runs at an average of 13.12. His highest score was 48, scored at Jesmond against Blaydon.

He bowled 6723 deliveries in the NEPL for Newcastle, with 229 maidens, conceding 3683 runs and taking 186 wickets at an average of 19.80. His best bowling was 8 for 17 on 5th September 2015 at Jesmond against Blaydon. He made 27 NEPL catches for Newcastle.

Harding then made his NEPL debut for Benwell Hill on 27th April 2019 at Eppleton, his first NEPL wicket for Hill was opener Luke Henderson caught behind the wicket by Peter Halliday for a duck.

By the end of 2023 he has played 61 NEPL matches for Benwell Hill, batting 32 times with 13 not outs, he has scored 93 runs with the highest score of 22.

He has bowled 3056 balls in the NEPL for Hill, with 82 maidens, conceding 1729 runs and taking 97 wickets at an average of 17.82. His best bowling figures are 4 for 30, taken on 18th June 2022 at Burnmoor. He has taken 14 catches for Hill in the NEPL.

To date, March 2024, Callum Harding has played 223 matches in the NEPL, batting 119 times with 45 not outs, he has scored 688 runs at an average of 9.29. His highest score is 48, scored on 22nd August 2015 at Jesmond for Newcastle against Blaydon.

He has bowled 11901 balls in the NEPL, with 369 maidens, conceding 6762 runs and taking 333 wickets at an average of 20.30. His best NEPL bowling figures are 8 for 17 on 5th September 2015 at Jesmond for Newcastle against Benwell Hill. He has taken 55 NEPL catches.

Harding played for Benwell Hill throughout the 2024 season and featured on the weekly round ups.

Returning to South North and the 2015 title win, John Graham's memory of the season was that it was "a season where we felt in control, Marcus North had joined us and he was a very good player, there was one game at Chester le Street, a controversial game, where they got plenty and had us under the cosh when we batted, we came off and never got back on, obviously they were keen to get back on, a win might have put extra pressure on us, but that's cricket."

The game John Graham is referring to took place on 13th June at Ropery Lane, Chester had batted first and, after losing George Harrison early on for 8, bowled by Jonny Wightman, Simon Birtwisle 43, and Andrew Smith took the score to 99 when Birtwisle was caught by Adam Cragg off the bowling of Tom Hodnett. Solid contributions from Quentin Hughes, 19, Chris Martin 12, Cole Pearce 36 not out, Mark Turner 7 and Graeme Cessford 17 all helped but the undoubted star of the show was Andrew Smith, he struck 131 from 130 balls, with 11 fours and 3 sixes. Chester scored plenty as Graham suggested, 308 for 8 declared from 60 overs to be exact!

When South North batted, Marcus North made 46 not out, for Chester, Andrew Bell took 2 for 16, Hughes had 1 for 16 and Birtwisle 1 for 1 when the match was abandoned, South North were 128 for 4 from 39.2 overs.

The 2015 Banks Salver was won by Eppleton and the Twenty20 by Chester le Street.

The NEPL Player of the Year for 2015 jointly awarded to Jaques du Toit of Newcastle and Simon Birtwisle of Chester le Street.

Jaques du Toit had played 19 matches in the NEPL in 2015, batting 18 times with 1 not out, he scored 915 runs at an average of 53.82. He scored 3 half centuries and 3 centuries.

His first century, 183, was scored on 16th May 2015 at Whitburn. The innings came from 128 balls and contained 21 fours and 11 sixes.

The second century, 102, was scored on 30th May 2015 at Tynemouth.

The third century, 108 not out, a week after the second, was scored on 6th June 2015 at home to Hetton Lyons. The innings came from 84 balls and contained 11 fours and 5 sixes.

He also bowled 1141 balls in the NEPL in 2015, with 24 maidens, conceding 684 runs and taking 23 wickets at an average of 29.73. His best bowling figures were 5 for 72, taken on 11th July 2015 at home to Durham Academy. He also took 13 catches in the NEPL in 2015.

Simon Birtwisle had played 20 matches in the NEPL in 2015, batting 20 times with 3 not outs, he scored 805 runs at an average of 47.35. He scored 4 half centuries and 1 century, 150 not out, was scored on 30th May 2015 at home to Stockton. The innings came from 157 balls and contained 14 fours and 4 sixes.

He also bowled 763 balls in the NEPL in 2015, with 22 maidens, conceding 388 runs and taking 28 wickets at an average of 13.85. His best bowling figures were 4 for 1, taken on 2nd July 2015 at South Shields. He also took 9 catches in the NEPL in 2015.

TABLE 50   NEPL 2015.

	Played	Won	Draw/Aban	Lost	Penalty Points	Bonus Points	Points
South North	22	14	8	0	1	191	440
Chester le Street	22	8	11	3	0	193	382
Newcastle	22	11	7	4	2	165	365
Durham CA	22	7	12	3	2	188	359
Benwell Hill	22	7	7	8	1	136	273
Hetton Lyons	22	5	8	9	0	150	271
Tynemouth	22	6	7	9	0	149	270
Whitburn	22	6	7	9	1	136	257
South Shields	22	5	9	9	1	126	237
Stockton	22	3	12	7	2	132	233
Gateshead Fell	22	6	6	10	0	116	232
Blaydon	22	3	9	10	0	120	208

TABLE 51   NEPL Batting Averages 2015.

Qualification 400 Runs.

25 Batsmen Qualified this season.

Player	Club	Inns	N. O	H. S	Runs	Average
(1) J. du Toit	Newcastle	18	1	183	915	53.82
(2) T. David	South Shields	21	3	149 no	963	53.50
(3) D. Budge	Durham CA	19	3	101 no	777	48.56
(4) M. North	South North	15	2	133	616	47.38
(5) S.J Birtwisle	Chester le Street	20	3	150 no	805	47.35
(6) J. Burnham	Durham CA	19	1	105	841	46.72
(7) A. Worthy	Hetton Lyons	19	2	119 no	735	43.24
(8) D. Shurben	Whitburn	18	3	180 no	635	42.33
(9) Zohaib Khan	Benwell Hill	19	3	109	650	40.63
(10) R. Singh	Stockton	19	2	104 no	671	39.47
(11) Q.J Hughes	Chester le Street	18	2	88 no	624	39.00
(12) J. Clark	Benwell Hill	14	1	124 no	461	35.46
(15) J.A Graham	South North	16	1	89	505	33.67

TABLE 52   NEPL Bowling Averages 2015.

Qualification 20 Wickets.

25 Bowlers Qualified this season

Player	Club	Overs	Mdns	Runs	Wkts	Average
(1) C. Harding	Newcastle	128.5	30	383	39	9.82
(2) S. Humble	South North	118.2	32	338	31	10.90
(3) S.J Birtwisle	Chester le Street	127.1	22	388	28	13.86
(4) M. Muchall	Benwell Hill	207.5	33	778	51	15.25
(5) G.D Bridge	Blaydon	189.5	28	627	41	15.29
(6) O. F McGee	Newcastle	172.3	35	506	33	15.33
(7) D.J Rutherford	South North	219.0	52	602	38	15.84
(8) L.J Crozier	South North	198.2	42	617	38	16.24
(9) B. McCarthy	Gateshead Fell	136.2	33	440	26	16.92
(10) J.R Wightman	South North	171.1	26	611	36	16.97
(11) K. Waterson	Whitburn	146.2	28	486	28	17.36
(12) Q.J Hughes	Chester le Street	164.0	35	510	29	17.59

South North CC NEPL Champions 2015.

Left to Right- Back Row-Rob Peyton, Tom Hodnett, Marcus North, David Rutherford, Stephen Humble, Jonny Wightman, Jonny Craigs.

Front Row-James Miller, Lee Crozier, John Graham, Adam Heather, Adam Cragg.

Jaques du Toit, seen here batting on 9th June 2018 for Newcastle.

Photo courtesy of Ken Waller.

CHAPTER NINE

Chester le Street 2016

The rules were still that the team batting first could bat up to 65 overs and that the match could be 120 overs in total. Chester le Street were one of the original eleven founder members of the NEPL, they won their first title in 2001, taking further titles in 2009 and 2010 and were runners up in 2015, finishing 58 points behind South North.

Chester all-rounder Simon Birtwisle had been named as one of the joint Player of the Years for 2015, alongside Jaques du Toit, but he had left Chester for South North at the end of the 2015 season. Birtwisle had joined Chester for the 2008 season and had been a big part in their successes of 2009 and 2010. He left with outstanding career statistics, having won the league title in 2002 with Benwell Hill as well as twice with Chester.At this point in his career he had played 273 matches, with 266 innings, 22 not out's, scoring 8803 runs at an average of 36.07, with a high score of 151 not out, the highest score came on 3rd July 2010 against Stockton for Chester. He had 50 NEPL half centuries and 12 NEPL centuries to his credit at this time also.

As a slow left arm orthodox bowler he bowled 4292 NEPL deliveries, with 132 maidens, conceding 2552 runs and taking 110 wickets at an average of 23.20 and best bowling of 6 for 32, taken for Chester on 25th August 2008 at home to The Durham Academy.

His contribution to Chester was that he played in 149 matches, batting 146 times, with 12 not out's, scoring 4599 runs at an average of 34.32, he had 23 half centuries and 8 centuries with a high score of 151 not out. As a Chester bowler in The NEPL he bowled 1570 balls, with 42 maidens, conceding 844 runs and taking 59 wickets at 14.30 each, and a best bowling of 6 for 32. He had also taken 51 NEPL catches for them.

Chester did bring in another slow left arm orthodox bowler, Gurman Singh Randhawa from India, no doubt to help offset the loss of Birtwisle. They started their 2016 NEPL campaign on 23rd April at home to Benwell Hill, Chester won the toss and decided to bat. They were all out for 196 from 61.1 overs, skipper John Coxon was the only batsman to get past 30, top scoring the innings with 36. Sameet Brar had been Hill's most successful bowler, taking 4 for 56. When Hill batted, 78 from Kyle Coetzer and 52 not out from Brar and 40 from opener Jack Clark saw them home by 5 wickets.

The team that day was as follows-

James Thompson is a right-hand batsman and right arm off spin bowler, he opened the batting for the 2016 season opener, making 13. Quentin Hughes recalls Thompson as "he came to us from the M.C.C Young Cricketers, he had also played for Durham Academy, he had done well for Washington the previous year and he had come to us for 2016. He was very strong through the off side, he had strong, quick hands which he used well to push through the line of the ball, he was very good through the covers off the front foot, and he used to like to punch it through the off side off the back foot, I don't think he had the year he hoped he would for us, but he was a valued team member who contributed. He didn't bowl as much as he could have, but that was down to the fact that we had three good slow bowlers in the side already. He is returning to Chester for 2024."

Thompson had started in the Durham Under 14 set up, playing a one-day match on 17th June 2010 against Derbyshire Under 14's. He scored 45.

On 5th August 2010 he was selected by Durham Under 15's, playing at Darlington against Derbyshire, Jack Burnham and Sean Tindale were amongst his teammates.

Thompson made his debut in the NEPL for The Durham Academy on 21st April 2012 at The Emirates against Sunderland. He started well, scoring 45 before Chris Rushworth bowled him. He also played for a Durham Academy side on 9th May 2012 at Winlaton against a Northumberland Development XI, scoring 56 not out.

Thompson also played for Northumberland, making his debut on 2nd June 2013 at Cheshire. He played 45 matches for the county across different formats, batting 63 times with 6 not outs, he scored 1472 runs at an average of 25.82. He scored 10 half centuries and 1 century, 105 not out, in a 3-day match starting on 22nd July 2018 at Bedfordshire, he had made 78 in the first innings.

He bowled 503 balls for Northumberland, with 7 maidens, conceding 356 runs and taking 5 wickets at an average of 71.20. He made 23 catches for them.

He played his last NEPL game for the Academy on 13th September 2014 at Blaydon.

He played 57 matches in the NEPL for The Durham Academy, batting 53 times with 6 not outs, he scored 1202 runs at an average of 25.57. He scored 6 half centuries and 1 century, 111 not out, scored on 3rd May 2014 at Sunderland. He bowled 165 balls, with 2 maidens, conceding 133 runs and took 3 wickets at an average of 44.33. He also took 19 catches.

On 14th April 2015 Thompson played for the M.C.C Young Cricketers against The Chris Gayle Academy at The Denis Compton Oval, he scored 19 and took 0 for 9.

His last game for the M.C.C Young Cricketers was a 3 -day match starting on 1st August 2016 at The Denis Compton Oval against Gloucestershire Second XI, he scored 83 opening the innings.

He played 50 matches for them, batting 55 times with 11 not outs, he scored 989 runs at an average of 22.47. He scored 6 half centuries and 1 century, 103, scored in a game starting on 22nd July 2015 Newport against Hampshire Second XI. The innings came from 208 balls and contained 8 fours. He bowled 283 balls, with 3 maidens, conceding 253 runs and taking 7 wickets at an average of 36.14. He made 18 catches and 2 stumpings.

On 18th April 2015, Thompson made his debut for Washington in NEPL Division 1 at South Hetton, he played 8 times for Washington in NEPL Division 1 in 2015.

Thompson made his NEPL debut for Chester le Street on 23rd April 2016 at home to Benwell Hill.

He played 16 times in the NEPL for Chester as they won the NEPL in 2016, batting 16 times with 1 not out, he scored 364 runs at an average of 24.26. He scored 2 half centuries, with a highest score of 92 not out on 9th July at Benwell Hill. He didn't bowl in 2016 but made 12 catches and 1 stumping.

He made his debut for Whitburn in the NEPL on 15th April 2017 at Chester le Street and his last game in the NEPL for Whitburn was on 9th September 2017 at Eppleton, he scored 128 not out, from 191 balls with 16 fours and a six.

He played 19 times in the NEPL for Whitburn, batting 19 times with 1 not out, he scored 464 runs at an average of 25.77. He scored 1 half century and 1 century, the highest score obviously the 128 mentioned earlier.

Thompson made his NEPL debut for Sacriston on 28th April 2018 at Eppleton and he played his last NEPL game for them on 8th September 2018 at home to Durham Academy.

He played 19 times in the NEPL for Sacriston, batting 19 times with 2 not outs, he scored 490 runs at an average of 28.82. He scored 4 half centuries. His highest score was the 80 he scored on 9th June at Whitburn.

He bowled 249 balls for Sacriston in the NEPL, with 4 maidens, conceding 171 runs and taking 12 wickets at an average of 14.25. His best bowling was 3 for 17 on 11th August 2018. He took 8 NEPL catches for them in the NEPL.

He then made his second NEPL debut for Whitburn on 20th April 2019 at Benwell Hill, his last NEPL game for Whitburn was on 14th September 2019 at Whitburn, although he did play for Whitburn in the Banks Salver as part of the covid season of 2020.

He returned to Washington on 17th April 2021, this time in the NEPL at home to Felling.

At the end of 2023 he was still playing for Washington in NEPL Division 1 but he returned to Chester le Street for the 2024 season and features in the weekly round up.

James Thompson, to date, the end of 2023, has played 151 matches in the NEPL, batting 141 times with 15 not outs, he has scored 3438 runs at an average of 27.28. He scored 18 half centuries and 4 centuries, his highest score is 128 not out mentioned earlier.

He has bowled 1123 balls, with 17 maidens, conceding 940 runs and taking 50 wickets at an average of 18.80. His best bowling figures were 5 for 45 mentioned earlier. He has made 57 catches and 1 stumping.

George Harrison was a right-handed batsman, he opened the batting with Thompson to start the 2016 season off, he scored 9. Quentin Hughes describes Harrison as" another young lad, we liked the idea of having a couple of younger players having the opportunity to open the batting for us. Harrison was a nuggety, gritty determined opening batsman, he loved the battle and challenge of opening the batting, he was strong off the back foot, a good cutter and puller of the short ball."

He first came to note as a junior for Durham Under 12's on 11th June 2006 in a match at Edinburgh against Scotland Under 12's, he scored 26 when he batted. He progressed through the county junior set up, playing for the Under 13's, 14's and 15's, on 25th June 2009 he scored 95 for Durham Under 15's at Darlington against Lancashire Under 15's. By 2010 he was playing for Durham Under 17's, in a 2-day game starting on 3rd August at Norton against Cheshire Under 17's he scored 74 not out in his only innings of the game.

Harrison made his NEPL debut on 13 August 2011 at home to Newcastle, he didn't bat nor bowl in a comfortable 9 wicket win for Chester.

Up to the end of the 2015 season Harrison had played 48 matches in the NEPL, batting 42 times with 4 not outs, he scored 1008 runs at an average of 26.52. He has scored 6 half centuries and 2 centuries, his highest score 123, was scored on 26th July 2014 at home to Stockton. The innings had come from 165 balls and contained 21 fours. He has never bowled in the NEPL, but he has taken 12 catches.

Harrison played 18 matches in the NEPL in the title winning season of 2016, batting 15 times with 1 not out, he scored 556 runs at an average of 39.71. He scored 5 half centuries and 1 century, 101, scored on 23rd July 2016 at Gateshead Fell. The innings had come from 151 balls and contained 13 fours and a six. He has never bowled in the NEPL, but he has taken 4 catches in 2016.

Harrison was still playing with Chester in the NEPL as late as 29th July 2023, appearing in a home game with Tynemouth and he appeared once again on 7th September 2024 for Chester at Tynemouth.

Up to the end of 2023 he had played 150 NEPL matches, batting 134 times with 12 not outs, he scored 3312 runs at an average of 27.14. He scored 22 half centuries and 3 centuries, his highest score to this point is 123, made in July 2014 and mentioned earlier. He has taken 27 NEPL catches.

Andrew Smith batted at number three to get 2016 underway, he made a single. Quentin Hughes has nothing but the highest praise for the ability of Andrew Smith, he says" his father, Keith, had come to us from Langley Park to captain the second team and proved to be the ultimate club man, he deserves a lot of credit for the way Chester have become an established Premier League club, he was such a positive influence on younger players, and it is great to see that he is still involved in the NEPL, having recently become an umpire. When he arrived with us, Andrew came with him. Andrew was playing in the first team at 14, I remember a game in the NEPL at Norton, who had a good side then, and Andrew and I put on around 200, Andrew got a 100. I feel he was unlucky at The Academy and should have probably been given another go. As a batsman he hits the ball as cleanly as anyone I have ever seen, he has been a fantastic player for Chester le Street. He always seems to show up against South North and it seems the bigger the challenge the more it motivates him."

The game at Norton that Hughes referred to was on 27th August 2005, Smith would have been 15 and Hughes was 30, Chester le Street batted first and made 262 for 3 declared from 54 overs. Hughes, batting at three, scored 102 not out and Smith, batting at five, had exactly 100 not out, they put on an unbroken 192 for the 4th wicket.

Smith entered the 2016 season having played 226 matches in the NEPL, batting 211 times with 24 not outs, he scored 7421 runs at an average of 39.68. He scored 46 half centuries and 16 centuries, his highest score was 173 not out on 15th May 2010 at home to Newcastle.

He bowled 1914 balls, with 43 maidens, conceding 1152 runs and taking 63 wickets at an average of 18.28. His best bowling figures were 8 for 43 on 7th August 2010 at South Shields. He had 85 NEPL catches at the end of 2015.

During the 2016 season he played 19 matches, batting 14 times with 1 not out, he scored 436 runs at an average of 29.06. He scored 2 half centuries and 1 century, 104, scored on 13th August 2016 at Eppleton, it came from 100 balls and contained 13 fours and 2 sixes.

He bowled 183 balls in the 2016 NEPL season, with 8 maidens, conceding 100 runs and taking 9 wickets at an average of 11.11. His best bowling figures were 3 for 0, taken on 7th May 2016 at Ropery Lane against Gateshead Fell. He made 3 NEPL catches in 2016.

His NEPL career to date, the end of the 2023 season, had seen him play 353 matches, batting 324 times with 31 not outs, he has scored 10876 runs at an average of 37.11. He has scored 64 half centuries and 22 centuries, with a highest score of 180 not out made on 2nd July 2022 at Sunderland, the innings came from 155 balls and contained 14 fours and 12 sixes.

Smith has bowled 3280 balls in his NEPL career, with 74 maidens, conceding 2071 runs and taking 111 wickets at an average of 18.65. His best bowling figures are the 8 for 43 mentioned earlier. He has taken 112 NEPL catches.

Richard Waite batted at number four on 23rd April, making 25, he also took 0 for 47 when his side bowled. Quentin Hughes played in both spells Waite had at Chester le Street, he was captain during the first spell and says of Waite "he was the best signing we made of 2009 and 2010 when he joined the club then and he was the best signing we made when he joined us again in 2016. He was a huge influence on the club, he was the best amateur cricketer I played with, he was a good off spinner, he was a big spinner of the ball, I recall him taking 8 for 30 against Whitburn, he was very, very good.

As a batsman he was very hard hitting, he scored 120 off 60 balls against South North in a T20 against South North. In the year we won the National Knockout 45 over competition he scored 90 off 82 balls in the Regional Final against South North, 152 off 143 balls in the last 16 game against Bootle and 110 off 73 balls in the semi-final against Shrewsbury. We always felt that if we got past South North, we had a real chance of going all the way. Richard proved that theory that year!

He also had an absolute determination to win, he must have been very close to being a professional cricketer, he was a handful to play against, with bat or ball and I found it much better to play with him than against him! He was a pleasure around the dressing room and club and his parents were very supportive and bought into the club ethos of Chester le Street."

After winning his fifth Player of the Year award and the NEPL title with Stockton in 2013 Waite re-joined Chester le Street for the 2016 season, making his NEPL debut for the club on 23rd April at home to Benwell Hill.

He played 20 NEPL matches in the 2016 season, batting 17 times with 2 not outs, he scored 558 runs at an average of 37.20. He scored 4 half centuries, his highest score of the 2016 season was 60, scored on 30th April at South Shields.

He bowled 998 balls, with 29 maidens, conceding 644 runs and taking 23 wickets at an average of 28.00. His best bowling figures were 8 for 42 taken on 4th June at Whitburn. He took 1 NEPL catch that season.

He had now played 320 matches in the NEPL, batting 301 times with 26 not outs, he scored 8825 runs at an average of 32.09. He scored 48 half centuries and 15 centuries, his highest score was 150 not out scored on 22nd May 2010 for Chester le Street at home to South Shields.

He bowled 21971 balls in the NEPL to this point with 780 maidens, conceding 11469 runs and taking 572 wickets at an average of 20.05. His best bowling figures were 8 for 28 taken on 10th June 2006 at Stockton against Benwell Hill. He took 98 NEPL catches to this point.

A full update of Waite's NEPL career can be found in the Chapter which contains the Team of the Decade.

Quentin Hughes batted at five, making 10, and took 1 for 26 to start the 2016 season off. Quentin Hughes had joined Chester from Durham City when the NEPL was formed back in 2000 after being at University, he is well documented at various points of the book. The one thing that isn't covered elsewhere is where his drive and competitiveness comes from, Hughes told me that one of his coaches once asked him why he played cricket. Hughes replied, "I love competition, I also love the sense of achieving something as part of a team, a dressing room doing well and as a captain that sense of helping others to do well, I think if you can enjoy your teammates successes, if you want others to do well then you are well on the way to achieving something as a team. It's also a standing joke with some of my long-term team mates that I have more not outs than anyone in the league, I value my wicket, I can't influence a game if I am out and back in the pavilion, I don't deny I enjoy being not out, it means I am there when it matters, I can help determine the outcome of the game."

We also spoke about his attitude to captaincy and his longevity and drive to keep playing cricket. Hughes response was fascinating" I love the influence of captaincy, I struggle to think of any other sport where a captain has such influence on the outcome of the game, I was captain at University and of the British Universities as well as Chester from 2005 until 2013, as captain you control everything about the flow of the game, from batting order, to field placings to bowling changes as you do your best to control the game and get your side home."

In respect of his continued drive and longevity Hughes says that "I wanted the chance to play with my son, Sebastian, he has a double barrelled surname, Hughes-Pinan because my wife is from Majorca and that's how they do it, and I wanted to watch him develop as a cricketer on the field and as a young man off it, he first played in the Covid year and I have loved watching him grow around the various characters which make up the dressing room, as well as grow physically, he is 6 foot 1 now! I think I have learned and developed with him, I think initially I may have been too hard on him and also too harsh on the umpires when he was bowling, I have learned to reign myself in over the last two or three years, I will say this, he is better at his age than I was. He recently got the chance to play for Spain, he ended up having a weekend of cricket in Barcelona and he really enjoyed it, it gives me enormous pleasure to see him getting opportunities like this through cricket."

Sebastian Hughes-Pinan was actually man of the match for his 3 for 13 on 18th February 2024 when Spain played The Czech Republic in a T10 match. He is a slow left arm orthodox bowler and left-handed batsman, he first came to attention when he played for Chester le Street Under 15's on 30th April 2018 at Hetton Lyons, he took 3 for 7 when he bowled.

On 22nd August 2019 he played for Durham Under 14's against Lancashire Under 14's at Sacriston.

On 9th August 2020 during the covid season he played for Durham Academy at Willington in the NEPL Banks Salver.

On 13th May 2021 he played for Durham Under 15's against Cumbria Under 15's at Norton, taking 2 for 3 when he bowled.

Hughes-Pinan made his NEPL debut for Chester le Street on 5th June 2021 at home to Eppleton, his first NEPL wicket was Eppleton batsman Jake Pratt, caught by John Coxon for 19.

On 1st August 2021 he played in an ECB fixture for the North Under 15's against the South and West Under 15's. Benwell Hill's Haydon Mustard was in the same side.

On 31st May 2022 Hughes-Pinan played for Durham Under 18's against Lancashire Under 15's at Billingham in a 20 over match, rain ruined the game.

After playing numerous times for different youth sides for Durham he made his debut for Durham Second XI on 6th June 2023 at Belper against Derbyshire. He took 1 for 11 and scored 8.

On 17th June 2023 he played in an ECB Elite Player Development game for the North Under 18's against London and East Under 18's at Loughborough, he took 3 for 53 when he bowled.

To the end of the 2023 season Sebastian Hughes-Pinan had played 40 matches in the NEPL, batting 19 times with 10 not outs, he has scored 76 runs at an average of 8.44. His highest score is 13 not out.

He has bowled 1953 balls, with 40 maidens, conceding 1184 runs and taking 48 wickets at an average of 24.66. His best bowling figures are 5 for 14, taken on 9th September 2023 at home to Castle Eden. He has taken 8 NEPL catches.

He played regularly for both Chester le Street and Spain during the 2024 season and further details can be found in the weekly roundup for 2024.

Up to the start of the 2016 season Quentin Hughes had played 262 NEPL matches, batting 242 times with 52 not outs, he had scored 7144 runs at an average of 37.60. He scored 48 half centuries and 4 centuries, his highest score was 136 not out on 9th July 2005 at home to Benwell Hill.

He has bowled 8834 balls, with 312 maidens, conceding 4365 runs and taking 241 wickets at an average of 18.11. His best bowling figures were 6 for 38 taken on 12th June 2010 at The Emirates against Durham Academy. He has taken 84 catches.

Quentin Hughes' contribution to the 2016 season was that he played 20 matches in the NEPL that year, batting 16 times with 5 not outs, he scored 367 runs at an average of 33.36. He scored 3 half centuries with a highest score of 91, made on 30th April at South Shields.

He bowled 655 balls, with 25 maidens, conceding 346 runs and taking 13 wickets at an average of 26.61. His best bowling figures were 3 for 20 taken on 23rd July at Gateshead Fell. He took 14 catches in the NEPL in 2016.

Quentin Hughes updated career stats feature later in the book, in the chapter on the Team of the 20 Years.

John Coxon had taken over the captaincy from Quentin Hughes on 2013, he batted at number six on 23rd April 2016 and top scored the innings with 36. Hughes says of Coxon" John has a real desire to win as a captain, he goes into a game prepared to take chances to win the game, when he speaks to the team in the dressing room you can feel the passion coming from him, that inner fire comes across well, one of our players left in 2015 and it was said that he wanted the chance to win something, that really fired John up for 2016 and was a motivating factor for us all. He liked to put the opposition into bat then use his three spinners to tie teams up and bowl them out.

John is normally an opening batsman, but he will show leadership by batting himself down at six or seven if he feels it will help the team, I really admire that, he will sacrifice his own day of cricket to give the team the best chance to achieve something. John liked to say that in 2016 we often had 8 or so players who had come through the junior system at the club playing regularly in the first eleven, he was proud that the club was now nurturing its own talent.

When the club had first joined the NEPL Keith Robson had been the driving force of the club, he upset a few when he and Alec Birbeck had brought a lot of new faces to the club back in the day, so the wheel had gone full circle, Keith's son David is President now and organized an old players reunion last year and I think this emphasizes the changes that the club has undergone and also John Coxon's pride in the number of homegrown player's we had then.

Coxon is a good club man and team mate, as a batsman he is a very good player through the offside, over extra cover, he has good, fast hands and is a very tough determined character. I remember Mark Wood playing for The Academy against us once, I think there may have been a little history in the past, and Wood was bowling rapid this day, probably the fastest spell I saw in club cricket, and John stood up to it."

Coming into the 2016 season Coxon had played 210 matches in the NEPL, all for Chester le Street, he had batted 190 times, with 28 not outs, he had scored 3934 run s at an average of 24.28. He had scored 21 half centuries and 5 centuries. His highest score was 112, on 4th September 2010 at Stockton.

He had bowled 580 balls, with 16 maidens, conceding 328 runs and taking 16 wickets at an average of 20.50. His best bowling figures were 5 for 36 taken 30th August 2008 at home to South North. He had taken 77 catches up to the end of the 2015 season.

His contribution to the 2016 title winning season was that he played in 21 matches, batting 13 times with 3 not outs, he scored 362 runs at an average of 36.20. He scored 1 half century, 55 not out on 14th May at home to Tynemouth. He bowled 36 balls, with 3 maidens, conceding 16 runs for no wickets and he had taken 8 catches.

To date, by the end of the 2023 season, John Coxon had played 343 NEPL matches, batting 306 times with 47 not outs, he has scored 6900 NEPL runs at an average of 26.64. He has scored 36 half centuries and 7 centuries. His highest score is 125 scored on 28th August 2021 at home to Felling, the innings took 117 balls and contained 16 fours and a six.

He has bowled 700 balls, with 20 maidens, conceding 415 runs and taking 19 wickets at an average of 21.84. His best bowling remained the 5 for 36 mentioned earlier. He has taken 130 catches.

He featured regularly during the 2024 season and updates can be found in the 2024 weekly roundup.

Cole Pearce was a right-handed batsman and wicket keeper. He batted at number seven to start the season off, making 29, he also took 1 catch and had 1 stumping. Quentin Hughes says of Pearce "he had come through our juniors then gone to Durham Academy for a bit, he got injured part way through the 2016 season, and we tried a couple of options to replace him as a keeper, a lad called Sharif did it and we brought in Andrew Fothergill, ex Durham keeper.

Pearce was a typical keeper, he never shut up, chatting away behind the stumps, he was great fun around the dressing room, a smashing lad, he loved playing cricket, he was a really good keeper, with three slow bowlers in the side he had to be very good standing up to spin, and he was, he was a very tidy looking keeper. He is an Academy coach now."

Pearce came to notice at a very early age, playing for Durham Under 12's in June 2006. He would go on to play at all age groups for the county as well as for The Academy, looking at it, it looks as though he was always playing above his own age group. He made his NEPL debut keeping wicket for The Durham Academy in the NEPL on 25th April 2009 at Sunderland. Ben Stokes and Mark Wood were among the Durham bowlers that day.

His last game in the NEPL for The Academy came on 7th September 2013 at Newcastle. He played 72 games in the NEPL for them, batting 59 times, with 8 not outs, he scored 824 runs at an average of 16.15. He scored 3 half centuries and 1 century, 109 not out, scored on 19th May 2012 at The Emirates against South Shields, the innings came from 144 balls and contained 9 fours and 2 sixes.

He made his NEPL debut for Chester le Street on 18th April 2015 at Gateshead Fell and his last appearance for Chester in the NEPL was on 3rd September 2016 at Ropery Lane against The Durham Academy.

During the 2016 season Pearce played 14 times in the NEPL, batting 8 times with 1 not out, he scored 112 runs at an average of 16.00. His highest score was 29 and he took 4 catches and had 3 stumpings.

Including the title winning 2016 season Pearce played 35 times in the NEPL for them, batting 25 times, with 6 not outs, he scored 429 runs at an average of 22.57. His highest score was 47, on 4th July at Whitburn. He made 27 catches and 7 stumpings for Chester le Street in the NEPL.

He made his NEPL Division 1 debut for Burnopfield on 15th April 2017 at Gateshead Fell and was part of the side which won the Division 1 title in 2018 and promotion to the NEPL. He subsequently made his NEPL debut for Burnopfield on 20th April 2019 at home to Felling.

In total and up to 9th September 2023 he had played 28 times in the NEPL, batting 26 times, with 7 not outs, he scored 834 runs at an average of 43.89. He has scored 4 half centuries and 2 centuries, his highest score was 117 not out on his Burnopfield debut. He has bowled 60 balls but not taking a wicket, he has made 30 catches and 10 stumpings for Burnopfield in the NEPL.

At the time of writing, the end of the 2023 season going into 2024, Cole Pearce has played a total of 135 times in the NEPL, he has batted 110 times, with 21 not outs, he has scored 2087 runs at an average of 23.44. He has scored 7 half centuries and 3 centuries. His highest score is the 117 not out, mentioned earlier and he has made 129 catches and 24 stumpings in the NEPL.

Just to complete Cole Pearce he also played 3 times for Northumberland, making his debut on 5th June 2011 at Staffordshire. He played twice more, both in 2014, as a wicket keeper he had 5 catches and 1 stumping for the county but failed to make an impression with the bat.

Update-Pearce was a regular during the 2024 season and features in the weekly roundup.

Liam Simpson batted at eight on 23rd April, making 7, he opened the bowling and took 2 for 43. Quentin Hughes recalls that Simpson "was a right arm seamer, he bowled at a decent pace, I remember the Nationals on Sky television in 2009, they had the speed gun out and Graeme Cessford was clocked at 87 mph, Simpson was clocked at 85, at least that's what he tells everyone! He used to hit the wicket when he bowled, the seam would hit the wicket hard, and he got a lot of wickets leg before and bowled."

Simpson had been part of title winning sides at Chester le Street in 2001, albeit he only played two games, in 2009 and 2010 he played a major role in their success.

He spent the 2015 season at Felling in the NEPL Division 1. He played 22 matches at this level for Felling, batting 21 times, with 6 not outs, he scored 391 runs at an average of 26.06. He scored 2 half centuries; his highest score was 66 made on 25th May at Chester le Street in the Banks Salver.

He bowled 1184 balls, with 24 maidens, conceding 878 runs and taking 43 wickets at an average of 20.41. His best bowling figures were 6 for 20 on 2nd May 2015 at home to South Hetton. He took 5 catches.

Liam Simpson's contribution to the title winning 2016 season was that he played 20 matches, batting 14 times, with 7 not outs, he scored 305 runs at an average of 43.57. He scored 1 half century, 52 not out on 6th August at home to Stockton.

He bowled 1108 balls, with 41 maidens, conceding 530 runs and took 23 wickets at an average of 23.04. His best bowling figures were 5 for 26 on 28th May 2016 at home to Eppleton. He took 4 catches this season.

He was still playing in the NEPL for Chester le Street up to the end of the 2023 season and up to this point he had played 341 matches in the NEPL, batting 260 times, with 55 not outs, he has scored 4408 runs at an average of 21.50. He has scored 20 half centuries and 1 century, 107, came on 15th June 2013 at home to Tynemouth, the innings came from 118 balls, he struck 16 fours and 2 sixes.

He bowled 12551 balls, with 432 maidens, conceding 6961 runs and took 326 wickets at an average of 21.35. His best bowling figures were 8 for 40 on 10th August 2013 at Sunderland. He has made 110 catches.

Update- Simpson continued playing for the club in the 2024 season and updates can be found in the weekly roundup.

Gurman Singh Randhawa was a left-handed batsman and slow left arm orthodox bowler. He batted at number nine, he made 24, he also took 2 for 18 when his side bowled. This was his only season in the NEPL. Hughes recalls "Randhawa was a Durham contracted player; he was perfect for club cricket as he never bowled a bad ball. He had unbelievable control, also in my experience the higher standard of cricket you play the faster the spinners tend to bowl, Randhawa was like that, he bowled quicker than most spinners in the league, however this often meant that a lot of his deliveries went past the edge of the bat, and he didn't always get the wickets he deserved. He was very reliable because of his control. He would bat up the order if others were missing and he was a decent bat."

This game was his NEPL debut, his first NEPL wicket was Hill opening batsman, James Schofield, leg before wicket for 12. His last wicket in the NEPL was South North middle order batsman, Sam Dale, leg before wicket for 9 at Roseworth Terrace on 27th August 2016.

He had come through the Yorkshire Junior system, starting off in their Under 13 set up and progressing through the Under 14's, 15's, 17's and 19's into their Academy side. He debuted in the Yorkshire Premier League on 3rd May 2008 for The Yorkshire Academy at Harrogate. His last game for Yorkshire Academy was on 5th September 2010 at Sheffield.

After playing for Yorkshire Seconds, he made his debut for England Under 19's in test matches at Galle against Sri Lanka on 14th January 2011. He played 4 matches for England Under 19's, scoring 43 runs and taking 3 wickets.

He then made his debut for Rotherham Town at home to Barnsley in the Yorkshire Premier League, his last game in the league came on 9th September 2012 for Rotherham Town.

In total he played 102 matches in the league, batting 81 times, with 12 not outs, he scored 1359 runs at an average of 19.69. He scored 8 half centuries. His highest score was 85, made on 4th August 2012 at Cleethorpes for Rotherham Town.

He bowled 7231 balls, with 185 maidens, he conceded 4008 runs and took 228 wickets at an average of 17.57. His best bowling figures were 8 for 49 on 27th June 2009 for Yorkshire Academy at Hull and YPI.

He spent the 2013 season playing for Yorkshire Second 's and Kirkburton in the Huddersfield Cricket League Premiership and the 2014 season playing for Worcestershire Second's and Shropshire.

In the early part of 2015, he was playing for Ossett in the Central Yorkshire Cricket League Premier Division and continued playing Minor Counties for Shropshire.

He made his debut for Durham Seconds on 8th July 2015 in a 3-day match and played there for the remainder of the 2015 season.

In the title winning 2016 side Randhawa had played 17 matches in the league for Chester, batting 8 times, with 4 not outs, he scored 92 runs at an average of 23.00. His highest score was 24 not out scored on 6th August at home to Stockton.

He bowled 1303 balls, with 54 maidens, he conceded 585 runs and took 39 wickets at an average of 15.00. His best bowling figures were 6 for 38 on 21st May at home to Stockton. He made 3 NEPL catches.

He also played twice for Northumberland, making his debut on 24th April 2016 at Lincolnshire. His second and last game for the county came on 8th May 2016 at Benwell Hill against Norfolk, he scored 36 runs in total and took 1 wicket across those two games.

After the 2016 season it's unclear where he went but he reappeared on 17th April 2021 playing for New Farnley in the Bradford Premier League and he was still playing there at the end of 2023.

Andrew Bell batted at number ten, he scored 21, he also bowled ten overs, taking 0 for 28. Quentin Hughes describes Bell as "a right-handed batsman and right arm away swing bowler. He had an unusual action and used to bowl off the wrong foot, usually a bowler with this type of bowling action brings it back into the right hander but he didn't, he would pitch it up and bowl out swingers! He was a scratch golfer and at one time had been a professional at Celtic Manor and he was also a good goalkeeper by all accounts. As a batsman he hit it a long way, he would hit it for miles, into car parks, out of grounds, he scored some useful runs for us."

Bell had been part of the title winning sides of 2009 and 2010. By the time 2016 came round he had now played 202 NEPL matches, all for Chester, batting 112 times, with 44 not outs, he had scored 997 runs at an average of 14.66. He had scored 1 half century. That half century, 62, was his highest NEPL score to this point, it came on 30th August 2014 against Durham Academy.

He had bowled 8296 balls, with 319 maidens, conceding 4407 runs and taking 197 wickets at an average of 22.37. His best bowling figures were 5 for 32, taken on 5th May 2012 at home to Gateshead Fell. He had taken 46 NEPL catches up to this point.

He played his last NEPL game on 6th August 2022 at home to Burnopfield. Bell had now played 287 NEPL matches, all for Chester, batting 160 times, with 60 not outs, he had scored 1384 runs at an average of 13.84. He still had 1 half century, and it remained his highest NEPL score, 62, as was mentioned earlier.

He had bowled 11201 balls, with 408 maidens, conceding 6023 runs and taking 251 wickets at an average of 23.99. His best bowling figures were now 7 for 30, taken on 11th August 2018 at Felling. He made 66 NEPL catches in his career. Bell played one game in the NEPL in 2024 but didn't bat or bowl so very little has changed in his stats!

Stephen Cantwell was a right-handed batsman and right arm fast medium bowler, he batted at eleven to start the season, scoring 12 not out. Hughes says that Cantwell was "young, fast and raw, he used to hit the pitch when he bowled, he was another of our home-grown players and I enjoyed watching him develop into a very effective opening bowler."

He made his NEPL debut for Chester le Street on 3rd August 2013 at home to Blaydon, he opened the bowling, ten overs 0 for 38. He didn't get to bat as the match was drawn.

He had to wait until 26th April 2014 when South North visited Ropery Lane, to take his first NEPL wicket, Stephen Humble, caught by Callum Thorp for 9, he finished with 2 for 14, as Chester won by 144 runs.

Cantwell was a regular in Chester's first team until he played his last NEPL game for them on 14th September 2019 at home to Burnmoor.

He had played 68 NEPL games, all for Chester, batting 23 times, with 13 not outs, he had scored 96 runs at an average of 9.60. His highest score was 21 on 10th September 2016 at Newcastle.

He bowled 3011 balls in the NEPL, with 94 maidens, conceding 1573 runs and taking 90 wickets at an average of 17.47. His best bowling figure were 7 for 24 on 3rd August 2019 at Felling. He had taken 10 NEPL career catches.

Quentin Hughes says that "the makeup of the side was very different to our title winning sides of 2009 and 2010, this one was more about everyone pulling together so that your sum was greater than your parts, we had no massive names, if you look at the averages no-one stood out, it was a season with lots of contributions from lots of players. I do recall one game at Tynemouth that I missed, Andy Fothergill played, and we chased down 230 odd."

The game Hughes refers to was on 30th July 2016, Tynemouth did indeed post 230 odd, 236 for 6 declared from 60 overs. Ben Debnam had scored 111 and Nick Armstrong 80, they put on 190 for the first wicket when Chris Metcalfe got Debnam, caught by Andrew Bell. They were 221 for 1 when Fothergill stumped Armstrong off the bowling of Chris Metcalfe and Jack Harrison and Metcalfe then pulled them back to 235 for 6 and they declared just one run later. Harrison finished with 3 for 42 and Metcalfe 3 for 38.

When Chester batted seven players made double figures, George Harrison had 24, James Thompson 50, Richard Waite 53, John Coxon 24, Liam Simpson 42, Matthew Haswell 15 and Andrew Bell 14. Despite 4 for 43 from Martin Pollard we won with 7 wickets down and 11 balls to spare.

Andy Fothergill played only 3 games for Chester in the NEPL in 2016, Cole Pearce the regular wicketkeeper picked up an injury and they used several players to try and fill the gap, Fothergill was one of them. This game with Tynemouth was his NEPL debut, he only played 4 more games the following season and that was his NEPL career done. He batted just twice, scoring 9 runs and took 4 catches and had 4 stumpings in those 7 matches.

James Wilson was another who filled in for the injured Cole Pearce, he was a pupil of Quentin Hughes and only 15 or 16 when he played his one NEPL game, at South North on 11th June 2016. He didn't bat but did keep wicket and although he didn't take any catches, he gave up just one bye.

Chris Metcalfe was actually the second team captain at Chester, he had played one game in the NEPL prior to the match with Tynemouth, on 2nd September 2007 at home to Stockton. The Tynemouth game was his second and final game in the NEPL!

Jack Harrison was a right-handed batsman and right arm medium fast bowler; he had made his NEPL debut for Chester le Street on 25th August 2008 at home to Durham Academy. He took his first NEPL wicket on 28th May 2016 at home to Eppleton when he bowled Dean Musther for 45.

Harrison played 18 matches in the 2016 season for Chester le Street, batting 3 times with 2 not outs, he scored 51 runs at an average of 51.00. His highest score was 35 not out, made on 10th September 2016 at Newcastle.

He bowled 473 balls in the NEPL during the 2016 season, with 7 maidens, conceding 340 runs and taking 14 wickets at an average of 24.28. His best bowling figures were 3 for 42 against Tynemouth and described earlier. He took 2 catches in the season in the NEPL.

Harrison played his last NEPL game on 27th August 2018 at Benwell Hill. In total he had played 56 matches in the NEPL, batting 19 times with 3 not outs, he scored 152 runs at an average of 9.50 and a top score of 35 not out mentioned earlier.

He bowled 1487 balls with 26 maidens, conceding 1041 runs and taking 42 wickets at an average of 24.78. His best bowling figures were 4 for 8, taken on 9th September 2017 at home to South Shields. He took 10 catches in the NEPL.

Matthew Haswell was another who stepped in and helped the first team out when they were short of numbers. He played 8 matches in the NEPL in 2016, batting 3 times with 1 not out, he scored 38 runs at an average of 19.00. His highest score was 15 in the game against Tynemouth mentioned earlier. He took 1 catch, and these stats are his entire NEPL career. Quentin Hughes recalls that Haswell was "a batsman who hit the ball cleanly, he was a lovely striker of the ball, he liked to hit it over mid-wicket and to leg. He was a great fielder; he was a great character who loved a challenge and never worried about the consequences of playing his shots!"

Returning to the 2016 season Hughes says "Whenever we played South North, we always felt that whoever won the games would have a good chance of winning the league, we played them on 27th August at Gosforth, it was the third last game of the season, they batted first and got 200, Marcus North had 46 and John Graham 69 not out but we felt that we had kept them to a reasonable score, and we were on top of it. When we batted Andrew Smith had 80 not out and I had 30 not out and we won comfortably, I can still recall now how good it felt to be there at the end of that one."

Hughes is pretty much accurate with his recollections, South North won the toss and batted, they scored 207 for 7 declared from 60 overs, Marcus North had 46, John Graham had 69 not out, made from 92 balls with 5 fours and 3 sixes. Randhawa had 3 for 58 as the best of the bowlers. When Chester batted George Harrison and James Thompson put on 30 for the first wicket before Thompson was dismissed for 22. Harrison and Andrew Smith took the score to 113 when Harrison was out for 32. Richard Waite came in at four and scored 26, 150 for 3. Hughes and Smith then added an unbeaten 58 for the fourth wicket and saw Chester home by 7 wickets with 7 overs to spare. Smith was indeed 80 not out, made from 130 balls with 8 fours and a six. Hughes was 34 not out from 35 balls with 3 fours.

Hughes goes on "We were at home to The Academy the following week and it rained and that meant we had won with a week to spare, because we were rained off, I do remember the celebrations were good and went on long into the night!"

The records show that on 3rd September Chester hosted The Durham Academy, they were rained off after 8 overs with Durham 34 for 0.

Hughes says, "We should have lost the last game at Newcastle to finish the season, and they had a really good side but again rain intervened."

Newcastle were runners up when the day was done, they did indeed have a good side and as Hughes alluded to, they were well on their way to winning the last game of the season, but such was the points difference it would have made no difference to the outcome of the title race.

Chester had batted first, 232 all out from 64.2 overs, John Coxon had top scored with 49. Richard Stanyon, Oli McGee and Jaques du Toit each had two wickets and Calum Harding and Sean Tindale one each. When Newcastle batted Oli McGee had opened and was 47 not out and Jaques du Toit, batting at six, was 109 not out from just 63 balls with 7 fours and 8 sixes when the game was abandoned with Newcastle on 213 for 4 from 47.2 overs. Match drawn.

The 2016 Banks Salver was won by Chester le Street and the Twenty20 by The Durham Academy.

Jaques du Toit of Newcastle was named the 2016 NEPL Player of the Year.

Jaques du Toit had played 20 matches in the NEPL in 2016, batting 16 times with 4 not outs, he scored 920 runs at an average of 76.66. He scored 2 half centuries and 4 centuries.

His first century, 102 not out, was scored on 7th May 2016 at South North, the innings contained 10 fours and 2 sixes.

The second century, 167 not out, was scored on 4th June 2016 at home to Benwell Hill, the innings came from 115 balls and contained 11 fours and 13 sixes.

The third century, 122, was scored on 30th July 2016 at The Riverside against Durham Academy, the innings came from 133 balls and contained 13 fours and 4 sixes.

His fourth century of the season, 109 not out, was scored on 10th September 2016 at home to Chester le Street, the innings came from 63 balls and contained 7 fours and 8 sixes.

He also bowled 1436 balls in the NEPL in 2016, with 35 maidens, conceding 768 runs and taking 41 wickets at an average of 18.73. His best bowling figures were 5 for 68, taken on 4th June 2016 at home to Benwell Hill. He also took 11 catches in the NEPL in 2015.

TABLE 53   NEPL 2016.

	Played	Won	Draw/Aban	Lost	Penalty Points	Bonus Points	Points
Chester le Street	22	11	8	3	1	180	384
Newcastle	22	8	12	2	0	161	351
Tynemouth	22	10	9	3	0	139	340
South North	22	8	10	4	2	161	327
Durham CA	22	7	8	7	1	146	287
South Shields	22	8	8	6	0	124	286
Hetton Lyons	22	7	10	5	0	128	285
Whitburn	22	7	8	7	0	120	255
Stockton	22	5	8	9	0	118	235
Benwell Hill	22	1	13	8	1	120	201
Eppleton	22	2	10	10	0	104	178
Gateshead Fell	22	2	8	12	2	86	156

TABLE 54   NEPL Batting Averages 2016.
Qualification 400 Runs.

Player	Club	Inns	N. O	H. S	Runs	Average
(1) G.J Muchall	South Shields	14	7	137 no	820	117.14
(2) J. du Toit	Newcastle	16	4	167 no	920	76.67
(3) K.J Coetzer	Benwell Hill	17	5	134 no	902	75.17
(4) T. David	South Shields	19	4	126 no	1073	71.53
(5) N.R Hobson	Newcastle	17	3	124	739	52.79
(6) M.J North	South North	19	5	101 no	667	47.64
(7) S.W Poynter	Tynemouth	11	1	112	448	44.80
(8) S.J Birtwisle	South North	16	2	121 no	616	44.00
(9) J.J Coyne	Whitburn	19	4	126 no	615	41.00
(10) G.W Harrison	Chester le Street	15	1	101	556	39.71
(11) R.L Greenwell	Durham CA	15	2	105	500	38.46
(12) R.P Waite	Chester le Street	17	2	60	558	37.20
(20) A.L Smith	Chester le Street	16	1	104	436	29.07

TABLE 55   NEPL Bowling Averages 2016.
Qualification 20 Wickets.

Player	Club	Overs	Mdns	Runs	Wkts	Average
(1) Tahir Khan	Tynemouth	249.5	82	572	40	14.30
(2) O.F McGee	Newcastle	247.3	47	690	46	15.00
(3) G.S Randhawa	Chester le Street	217.1	54	585	39	15.00
(4) C.J Grimwood	Hetton Lyons	102.5	15	353	23	15.35
(5) A.J.H.A Hart	Durham CA	109.1	25	341	22	15.50
(6) M.L Pollard	Tynemouth	129.1	36	425	27	15.33
(7) M. Gardner	Stockton	206.5	49	597	37	15.74
(8) G.J Muchall	South Shields	90.0	16	343	21	16.14
(9) B.G Whitehead	Hetton Lyons	223.1	41	676	41	16.33
(10) K. Waterson	Whitburn	250.1	55	886	53	16.49
(11) S. Humble	South North	174.5	37	538	32	16.72
(12) A.P Smith	Tynemouth	194.3	40	623	37	16.81
(25) L. Simpson	Chester le Street	184.4	41	530	23	23.04

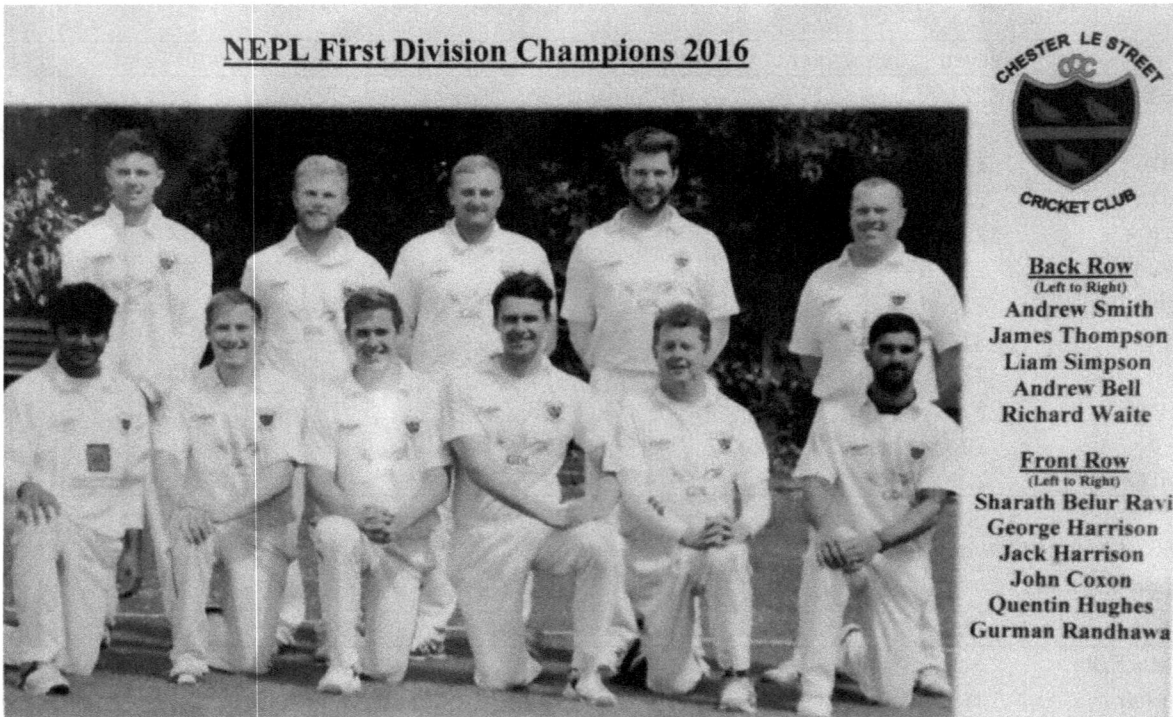

NEPL First Division Champions 2016

Back Row
(Left to Right)
Andrew Smith
James Thompson
Liam Simpson
Andrew Bell
Richard Waite

Front Row
(Left to Right)
Sharath Belur Ravi
George Harrison
Jack Harrison
John Coxon
Quentin Hughes
Gurman Randhawa

Chester le Street CC 2016.

John Coxon seen here batting at Benwell Hill on 20th July 2024

CHAPTER TEN

South North 2017-2018

Chester le Street had won the 2016 NEPL by 33 points from Newcastle, South North had finished fourth, 57 points behind Chester. South North did however win the 2016 Royal London Club Championship against Swardeston at Northampton's County round on 18th September. Swardeston were from The East Anglian Premier League, they had won this competition in 2010 when it was known as The Cockspur Club Twenty20, beating South North in the final, and they won it again in 2016 when it was The NatWest Club Twenty20. Mike Gatting's nephew, Joe Gatting was amongst their ranks as South North won the toss and elected to bat. Marcus North, batting at four top scored with 41 and opener Adam Heather had 30, despite seven batsmen making double figures, they were bowled out for 159 in 44.5 overs. Swardeston were soon in trouble against Stephen Humble and Jonny Wightman, falling to 8 for 3, change bowlers David Rutherford and Lee Crozier proved no easier to handle as they were shot out for just 84 in 23.4 overs. Humble had 2 for 10, Wightman 2 for 32, Rutherford 4 for 17 and Crozier 2 for 24, a convincing 75 run victory.

This was Adam Cragg's first season as the South North captain following John Graham's resignation in July 2016; Marcus North had seen the season out at captain and then Cragg was appointed for 2017. Amongst the changes for 2017 was the loss of Adam Heather to Benwell Hill, David Rutherford had also moved to pastures new, going to play first for Morpeth then later moving on to Ashington although they did have the arrival of professional Calum MacLeod, a Scottish International.

South North opened the 2017 NEPL season on 15th April with a home fixture against Stockton, who won the toss and elected to bat. At one stage they were 122 for 2 with Ryan Wallace, who would top score the innings with 67, and 28 from skipper Kevin Ward, having them set for a big score. When these two fell within 7 runs of each other, both bowled by Simon Birtwisle, Stockton stuttered and never really picked up their momentum, as they were dismissed for 180 from 48 overs. Birtwisle had 4 for 42 and Lee Crozier 3 for 29. When South North batted, they lost Marcus North early, but an unbeaten 111 from Calum MacLeod saw them win by eight wickets.

The South North side which started the game and thereby the 2017 season was as follows-

Simon Birtwisle took 4 for 42 with the ball and made 21 opening the batting. Birtwisle had joined South North from Chester le Street at the end of the 2015 season, playing his last game for Chester on 5th September 2015 at The Emirates against the Durham Academy.

He had joined Chester le Street for the 2008 NEPL season, he played 149 NEPL matches for them, batting 146 times with 12 not outs, he scored 4599 runs at an average of 34.32. He scored 23 half centuries and 8 centuries for Chester, his highest score of 151 not out was scored on 3rd July 2010 at home to Stockton.

He bowled 1570 balls in the NEPL for Chester, with 42 maidens, conceding 844 runs and taking 59 wickets at an average of 14.30. His best bowling figures were 6 for 32, taken on 25th August 2008 at home to Durham Academy. He took 51 NEPL catches for Chester.

Birtwisle won NEPL titles with Chester le Street in 2009 and 2010 and had been Player of the Year in 2005 and joint NEPL Player of the Year in 2015. He made his South North debut on 23rd April 2016 at Tynemouth, he scored 121 not out opening the batting and took 1 for 20.

When the 2016 season ended Birtwisle had played 290 NEPL matches, batting 282 times with 24 not outs, he had scored 9419 runs at an average of 36.50. He had scored 53 half centuries and 13 centuries. His highest score was the 151 mentioned earlier.

He had bowled 4508 balls, with 136 maidens, conceding 2674 runs and taking 115 wickets at an average of 23.25. His best bowling figures were the 6 for 32 mentioned earlier. He had taken 91 NEPL catches.

Birtwisle played 21 NEPL matches in 2017, batting 21 times with 2 not outs, he scored 667 runs at an average of 35.10. He scored 5 half centuries and 1 century. The century, 116 not out, was scored on 26th August 2017 at home to Benwell Hill. The innings came from 136 balls and contained 16 fours and 1 six.

He also bowled 623 balls, with 18 maidens, conceding 317 runs and taking 24 wickets at an average of 13.20. His best bowling figures were 5 for 29, taken on 1st July at Stockton. He took 9 NEPL catches in 2017.

Marcus North opened the batting on 15th April 2017, he made 2. Following his successful 2015 season he returned to for 2016, after John Graham had resigned the captaincy on 2nd July 2016 after a match at Whitburn, North took up the reigns for the rest of the season.

He returned as overseas pro for the 2017 season, playing 20 matches, batting 20 times with 2 not outs, he scored 633 runs at an average of 35.16. He scored 3 half centuries and 2 centuries. His highest score was 122, scored on 5th August 2017 at home to Chester le Street. The innings came from 167 balls and contained 11 fours and 2 sixes.

He bowled 138 balls in the NEPL in 2017, with 2 maidens, conceding 85 runs and taking 2 wickets and he also took 7 catches.

His last game in the NEPL for South North on 9th September 2017 at Tynemouth although he did return to Gateshead Fell for 1 more match, in NEPL Division 1 on 14th September 2019 at home to Ashington, he scored 39 and took for 4 for 3! In total he played 107 matches in the NEPL, batting 104 times with 16 not outs, he scored 4114 runs at an average of 46.75. He scored 21 half centuries and 11 centuries. His highest score was 163 not out, scored for Gateshead Fell on 22nd July 2000 at Benwell Hill.

He bowled 4552 balls, with 158 maidens, conceding 2467 runs and taking 116 wickets at an average of 21.26. His best bowling figures were 8 for 42, taken for Gateshead Fell on 15th June 2002 at Tynemouth. He made 58 catches in his NEPL career.

Calum MacLeod made his NEPL debut in this fixture, batting at number three to start the season, scoring 111 not out, his innings came from 87 balls, he struck 22 fours in his innings. He also opened the bowling, taking 1 for 36. His first NEPL wicket was opener Matthew Gill, caught by Adam Cragg for 30.

John Graham recalls that Macleod was "a skilful bowler, fast medium in pace, he could swing it, over the years I found with those who had played top level cricket was that when they bowled, they hit the bat harder and higher up than most out and out club cricketers. He had started as a seamer at Warwickshire but there was an issue with the angle of his bowling arm, so he re-invented himself as a batsman, he did such a good job he scored a ton against England for Scotland! As a batsman he could be unorthodox, he scored runs all-round the wicket, he was a great player of spin, playing lots of scoops and sweeps. I think because of his skill set, three or four teams hired him as a T20 specialist. He was a clever cricketer, he could work people out, he was also excellent in the dressing room, he used to take our training, and he had a great influence over our fitness, attitude and performance, he was a driving force. His wife was from Kent, and he moved down there."

MacLeod's contribution to the 2017 title success was that he played 17 matches in the NEPL, batting 16 times with 4 not outs, he scored 661 runs at an average of 55.08. He scored 2 half centuries and 2 centuries. His highest score was 111 not out, made on debut and mentioned earlier.

He also bowled 738 balls with 28 maidens, he conceded 364 runs and took 24 wickets at an average of 15.16. His best bowling figures were 5 for 16, taken 3rd June 2017 at Felling. He took 8 NEPL catches.

His last game for South North in the NEPL and indeed in the NEPL was the last game of the season on 2nd September 2017. He signed off with 107, scored from 109 balls and containing 16 fours.

MacLeod had first come to attention as a youngster, I don't think I have this wrong, but it looks like MacLeod and Kyle Coetzer were playing as young boys, aged around 12 or 13 in a Scotland National Cricket League Division 1 match on 23rd July 2000! Coetzer had 5 for 29 and scored 4 for Stoneywood-Dyce and MacLeod 0 not out for Drumpellier. By 8th July 2002 MacLeod was playing for Scotland Under 13's against Northumberland Under 13's.

Whist continuing to play for Drumpellier he was also playing for Scotland Under 15's and then into Scotland Under 17's, Under 19's and Under 21's. He went on to play for the under 19's at Warwickshire and then on to their Second XI in 2006. He was also playing club cricket for Moseley in the Birmingham and District Premier League around this time.

He made his first-class debut for Scotland in a 4-day match starting on 27th June 2007 at Alloway against The U.A.E. Whilst in Scotland it appears that by 2011 Macleod was playing for Uddingston in the Scottish national Cricket League as well as playing for Warwickshire Seconds.

Calum MacLeod would go on to play 88 One Day Internationals for Scotland, batting 86 times with 7 not outs, he scored 3026 runs at an average of 38.30. He scored 13 half centuries and 10 centuries. His highest score was 175, made on 23rd January 2014 in Christchurch against Canada.

He also bowled 968 balls at this level for Scotland, with 4 maidens, he conceded 836 runs and took 11 wickets at an average of 76.00 each. His best bowling figures were 2 for 26, taken on 2nd July 2013 in Aberdeen against Kenya. He took 53 catches at this level for Scotland.

The highlight of his ODI career I would imagine was that he and Kyle Coetzer were both part of the Scotland team which beat England in Edinburgh on 10th June 2018. Scotland had batted first, Coetzer made 58 and MacLeod 140 not out. MacLeod batted for 143 minutes, facing 94 balls, he struck 16 fours and 3 sixes as Scotland scored 371 for 5 from their 50 overs.

When England batted, neither Coetzer nor MacLeod bowled but Scotland dismissed England for 365 from 48.5 overs to win by 6 runs with 7 balls to spare. The England side that day was a strong one, Roy, Bairstow, Root, Morgan, Ali and Rashid amongst them and two NEPL players, Mark Wood and Liam Plunkett all played that day. They all played at Lord's in 2019 when England won the World Cup Final too!

MacLeod also played 64 Twenty20 matches for Scotland, batting 61 times with 9 not outs, he scored 1238 runs at an average of 23.80. He scored 7 half centuries. His highest score was 74, made on 24th October 2019 in Dubai.

He also bowled 180 balls at this level for Scotland, with 0 maidens, conceding 220 runs and taking 5 wickets at an average of 44.00. His best bowling was 2 for 17. He took 38 catches at this level.

He played first class cricket for Scotland, Warwickshire and Durham, playing 28 matches in total, he batted 41 times in first class cricket, with 6 not outs, he scored 904 runs at an average of 25.82. He scored 5 half centuries, with a highest score of 84, made in a 4-day match starting on 15th August 2014 for Durham at Old Trafford against Lancashire.

He bowled 767 balls in first-class cricket, with 19 maidens, conceding 444 runs and taking 16 wickets at an average of 27.75. His best bowling figures were 4 for 66, taken for Scotland against Canada in a 4-day match starting on 2nd July 2009. He took 20 catches at first class level.

MacLeod played List A cricket for Scotland, Warwickshire and Durham, playing 161 matches in total, he batted 152 times with 12 not outs, he scored 4330 runs at an average of 30.92. He scored 19 half centuries and 11 centuries. His highest score was the 175 mentioned earlier.

He bowled 1498 balls at this level, with 10 maidens, conceding 1337 runs and taking 23 wickets at an average of 58.13. His best bowling figures were 3 for 37, taken for Scotland against The U.A.E ON 19th January 2014. He took 83 catches in List A cricket.

As John Graham alluded to, MacLeod played Twenty20 cricket for a number of teams, Scotland, Durham, Derbyshire, Paktia Royals (Afghanistan Premier League), Sussex and Kent.

He played a total of 137 Twenty20 matches, batting 133 times with 16 not outs, he scored 3172 runs at an average of 27.11. He scored 15 half centuries and 2 centuries. His highest score was 104 not out, made for Derbyshire at Northamptonshire on 19th July 2018. Incidentally, Kyle Coetzer was playing for Northants in the game.

MacLeod also bowled 204 deliveries at this level, with 0 maidens, he conceded 236 runs and took 5 wickets at an average of 47.20. He took 80 catches in this format of cricket.

As John Graham suggested, MacLeod did indeed move to Kent, after the pandemic he was playing for Lordswood in the Kent Cricket League Premier Division. He was still there at the time of writing, at the end of the 2023 season, he played on 2nd September at Holmesdale in the same league.

John Graham batted at number four; he scored 39 not out. This was his first full season back in the ranks after resigning the captaincy during the 2016 season. He had played 324 NEPL matches as the 2017 season got underway, batting 302 times with 45 not outs, he had scored 9705 runs at an average of 37.76. He had scored 70 half centuries and 12 centuries. His highest score remained 132 scored in July 2006 and mentioned earlier. His bowling figures in the NEPL had remained unchanged since 2014 and up to the end of 2016, he had taken 162 catches in the NEPL.

Graham played 19 matches in the NEPL in 2017, batting 16 times with 3 not outs, he scored 366 runs at an average of 28.15. He scored 3 half centuries with a highest score of 69 on 17th June at home to Durham Academy. He didn't bowl in the NEPL in 2017 but took 3 catches.

Adam Cragg was listed to bat at five to open the 2017 season, he didn't get to bat as his side won by 8 wickets. This was his first season as captain. He entered the season having played 183 matches in the NEPL, batting 149 times with 26 not outs, he had scored 3443 runs at an average of 27.99. He had scored 17 half centuries and 2 centuries, his highest NEPL score at this time was 102, scored in May 2010 and mentioned earlier. He hadn't bowled in the NEPL since 2013 so change in his 1 wicket or bowling stats, but he has taken 157 catches and 22 stumpings.

Cragg played 20 matches in the NEPL in the 2017 season, batting 15 times with 1 not out, he scored 318 runs at an average of 22.71. He scored 1 half century, 53, on 29th July 2017 at Eppleton. He bowled 2 more balls in the season, conceding 4 runs and also took 9 catches.

Rob Peyton kept wicket in the Stockton innings, taking 3 catches, he was listed to bat at six but didn't get the opportunity. He started the 2017 season having played 41 matches in the NEPL, he had batted 29 times with 2 not outs, he had scored 348 runs at an average of 12.88. He had scored 2 half centuries with a highest score of 59, made on 5th September 2015 at Stockton. He had also taken 37 catches and made 4 stumpings in the NEPL.

During the 2017 season he played 20 matches in the NEPL, batting 14 times with 2 not outs, he scored 314 runs at an average of 26.16. His highest score was 80, made on 2nd September 2017 at The Durham Academy. He took 31 catches in the 2017 NEPL season.

Stephen Humble opened the bowling against Stockton, taking 1 for 24, he was down to bat at seven but not required. He played his last game for South North in the NEPL on 2nd September 2017 at home to Durham Academy, moving to Brandon in NEPL Division 1 for the 2018 season.

His last season for South North had seen him play 20 matches, batting 14 times with 3 not outs, he scored 118 runs at an average of 1072. His highest score was 24. He bowled 1066 balls, with 36 maidens, conceding 521 runs and taking 31 wickets at an average of 16.80. His best bowling figures were 6 for 29, taken on 15th July 2017 at Whitburn. He made 2 catches.

Since his debut for South North in the NEPL in April 2005 Humble had played 243 matches in the league, batting 166 times, with 43 not outs, he scored 3313 runs at an average of 26.93. He scored 15 half centuries. His highest score was 92 on 12th July 2014 at home to Chester le Street.

He bowled 14666 balls, with 609 maidens, conceding 6603 runs and taking 473 wickets at an average of 13.95. His best bowling figures were 8 for 55 taken on 27th May 2006 at home to Gateshead Fell.

He made 68 catches for South North in the NEPL, and his career statistics will be updated as part of the Team of 20 Years.

Sam Dale was listed to bat at number eight, he didn't bat. John Graham recalls "he was a right-handed batsman, he came through the second team at South North, he showed glimpses of his talent in the first team, he played some useful innings but never fulfilled his potential, he played football as well."

Dale made his NEPL debut for South North on 4th June 2016 at home to Gateshead Fell. Jonny Wightman took 8 for 31 when Fell batted first so whilst it was a memorable debut in some respects for Dale, he got no opportunity to bat. Dale played 5 matches in the NEPL in 2016 but had very little opportunity to contribute.

In the 2017 season he played 15 matches in the NEPL for South North, batting 10 times with 1 not out, he scored 60 runs at an average of 6.66. His highest score was 19, made on 6th May at Newcastle but he didn't bowl and took 4 catches in the season.

Lee Crozier bowled thirteen overs and took 3 for 29 when Stockton batted in the 2017 opener, he was listed to bat at nine but not required. As he entered the 2017 season Crozier had played 315 matches in the NEPL, batting 147 times with 68 not outs, he had scored 1299 runs at an average of 16.44. He had scored 1 half century, 89 for Benwell Hill in 2002.

He had bowled 22563 balls, with 1015 maidens, conceding 9863 runs and taking 642 wickets at an average of 15.36. His best bowling was 7 for 21 taken for South North in 2007. He had taken 47 NEPL catches.

He played 21 matches in the NEPL in 2017, batting 6 times with 4 not outs, he scored 13 runs at an average of 6.50. His highest score of the 2017 NEPL season was 8.

He bowled a bit as well though, delivering 1110 balls, with 43 maidens, conceding 530 runs and taking 37 wickets at an average of 14.32. His best bowling figures of the season were 4 for 41, taken on 1st July 2017 at Stockton. He took 4 catches in the NEPL in 2017.

Richard Brook was down to bat at ten, but he neither batted nor bowled. This fixture marked the last appearance in the NEPL by Brook. He had played 193 matches in the NEPL, batting 44 times with 28 not outs, he scored 94 runs at an average of 5.87. His highest score was 19, made on 12th August 2007 at home to Durham Academy. The Academy bowlers that day had included Ben Stokes and Scott Borthwick.

He had bowled 10047 balls in his NEPL career, with 390 maidens, conceding 5121 runs and taking 311 NEPL wickets at an average of 16.46. His best bowling figures were 7 for 28 mentioned earlier. He took 34 NEPL catches.

Jonny Wightman had come on as first change with the ball, 0 for 49 to start the 2017 season, he was listed to bat at eleven, but he also didn't bat. Coming into the 2017 season Wightman had played 150 NEPL matches in the NEPL, batting 75 times with 26 not outs, he had scored 423 runs at an average of 8.63. His highest score was 37, made in May 2011 and mentioned earlier.

He had bowled 8990 balls in his NEPL career, with 201 maidens, conceding 5683 runs and taking 299 wickets at an average of 19.00. His best bowling figures were now 8 for 31 from 4th June 2016 in a home game with Gateshead Fell. He had taken 18 NEPL catches.

During the 2017 season Wightman played 20 matches in the NEPL, batting 11 times with 5 not outs, he scored 102 runs at an average of 17.00. His highest score was 25, made on 29th July at Eppleton.

He bowled 1102 balls with 23 maidens, conceding 669 runs and taking 39 wickets at an average of 17.15. His best bowling figures were 5 for 15, taken on 22nd April at South Shields. His first wicket in this game, Sam Taylor-Gell, caught by Calum MacLeod, was his 300th NEPL wicket. He took 1 catch in the NEPL in 2017.

Michael Craigs made his first appearance of the 2017 NEPL season on 22nd April at South Shields. Prior to the season starting Craigs had played 67 NEPL matches for South North, batting 48 times with 16 not outs, he had scored 578 runs at an average of 18.06. He had scored 1 half century, 56, made on 6th June 2015 at home to Blaydon.

He had bowled 1562 balls with 40 maidens, conceding 933 runs and taking 45 wickets at an average of 20.73. His best bowling figures were 5 for 42, taken on 4th May 2013 at home to Hetton Lyons. He had taken 24 catches in the NEPL up to the end of 2016.

He played 10 matches in the NEPL in 2017. His batting contribution was negligible, but he did bowl 294 balls, with 14 maidens, he conceded 133 runs and took 10 wickets at an average of 13.33. His best bowling figures were 5 for 26, taken on 19th August at home to Felling. He took 3 NEPL catches in 2017.

Jonny Craigs was a left-handed batsman who didn't play in the 2017 season opener, but he did play 10 NEPL matches for South North in the season, batting 8 times with 2 not outs, he scored 53 runs at an average of 8.83. His highest score was 20 not out. He didn't bowl but took 2 catches.

In his NEPL career at South North he played 65 times for them, batting 57 times with 6 not outs, he scored 1072 runs at an average of 21.01. He scored 5 half centuries and 2 centuries. His highest score was 114 not out, scored on 16th May 2015 for South North at South Shields. The innings contained 12 fours and 2 sixes and Craigs and Marcus North added 246 for the third wicket in an unbroken stand. North had 127 not out. He bowled 48 balls, conceding 29 runs and taking 1 wicket and he also took 24 catches and had 1 stumping.

In his NEPL career, including 1 season at Benwell Hill, he played 84 matches, batting 75 times with 7 not outs, he scored 1633 runs at an average of 24.01. He scored 9 half centuries and 2 centuries, the highest score was 114 not out, mentioned earlier.

He bowled 192 balls, with 1 maiden, conceding 192 runs and taking 2 wickets and also had 35 catches and had 1 stumping.

David Edwards was a right-handed batsman. John Graham remembers that he was "an uncomplicated batsman, he was unorthodox, he had a wonderful eye, and he seemed to hit a lot of boundaries, meaning he scored quickly as well, he was training to be a medic, a doctor I think, so his availability wasn't great."

Edwards had made his NEPL debut on 28th June 2014 at Roseworth Terrace against Benwell Hill. He played 4 matches in the NEPL in 2014, 2 in 2015, 2 in 2017, 2 in 2018 and his last match on 14th September 2019, at Felling. Edwards played just 2 games in the NEPL in 2017, he neither batted nor bowled nor took a single catch!

In total he played 13 matches in the NEPL, batting 10 times and scoring 240 runs at an average of 34.28. He scored 2 half centuries with a highest score of 68. The highest score was made on 14th July 2018 at home to Benwell Hill. To date, March 2024, he has never bowled nor took a catch in the NEPL.

I have no idea how I came across him nor why I have included him, but once he was researched, I figured he might as well stay in, he clearly had ability, as well as his 2 half centuries he also had a 49 not out, so he could clearly bat.

I think he represents all those cricketers who managed a game or two here and there in the NEPL, but his availability may have meant he never fulfilled the promise he showed.

Andrew Doig was a left-handed batsman. John Graham recalls "he was a fairly orthodox batsman, he was strong through the covers and would whip it off his legs, he was stylish to watch. He did a job when he played in our first team, at a lot of clubs he would have been a first team regular but because of the strength of our side he only had limited opportunities. He was a good team man."

Entering the 2017 season Doig had played 15 matches in the NEPL, batting 11 times with 3 not outs, he had scored 80 runs at an average of 10.00. His highest score was 27, made on 11th August 2012 at home to The Durham Academy. He never bowled in the NEPL, but he had taken 2 catches and 1 stumping in the league to this point. Doig played just one game in the NEPL in 2017, at Tynemouth on 9th September, he scored 21 not out.

John Graham says that going into the season "we knew we had a strong side, it was Adam Cragg's first year as captain, we had both Marcus North and Calum MacLeod, and although we had lost David Rutherford, MacLeod filled his shoes as first change very well. Of the years I played in the league, this was the best side I played in, we had everything. The League was pretty much nip and tuck all year, I can't remember exactly when the points deduction was but we played a game against Newcastle in July and when I look back at it, at the players on both sides, in terms of quality of the players who took part, it was probably the game I played in with the highest calibre of players, we had Marcus North and Calum MacLeod on our side plus the top quality local players we had, they had Jaques du Toit, Cameron Steele, who went on to play first -class for Hampshire and Surrey, and also Josh Philippe who went on to play for Australia."

The game John Graham is referring to took place on 22nd July 2017 at Gosforth, South North won the toss and elected to field; the first innings was restricted to a maximum of 58 overs.

The Newcastle side that day was Alasdair Appleby, Ben McGee, Cameron Steel, Josh Philippe, Jaques du Toit, Sean Tindale, Sam Roseby, Oli McGee, Steven Allen, Callum Harding and Ben Quirk.

South North fielded the following XI-Simon Birtwisle, Marcus North, Calum MacLeod, John Graham, Adam Cragg, Rob Peyton, Stephen Humble, Jonathan Craigs, Sam Dale, Jonny Wightman and Lee Crozier.

Seven Newcastle players reached double figures, without one making the half century or bigger score that could win the game for them, Philippe top scored with 31, the next highest score was 22 from Ben McGee. Lee Crozier had 3 for 43, Calum MacLeod 2 for 28, Jonny Wightman had 1 for 55 and Stephen Humble 0 for 20, although Humble was wicketless he bowled 10 overs for the 20 runs he conceded. Newcastle declared on 150 for 6 after just 40 overs.

When South North batted three batsman got into the thirties, Calum MacLeod had 37, John Graham 39 and Rob Peyton was 39 not out, as they made the 151 required for the loss of 6 wickets from 35.4 overs. Jaques du Toit took 3 for 43, Callum Harding 2 for 33 and Alasdair Appleby 1 for 25. South North had won by 4 wickets.

I shall return to the league a little later, as John Graham reflects on other matters in respect of the 2017 season" If you win a National and your own league you know you have done well. We could have won two Nationals to be honest, the only disappointment is that Calum MacLeod couldn't play in the nationals. We had beaten York in the later rounds of the National 45 over competition, Calum had played in the game, afterwards they complained about him, some technicality, they got a lawyer involved, the result was reversed, not wanting to risk the same thing in the Twenty20 we didn't play him."

South North also added another national Competition to round off 2017, taking the ECB Vitality T20, defeating Wimbledon at The County Ground, Derby on 11th September. Wimbledon CC, who play in The Surrey Premier League, had won this competition in 2012 and 2013 when it was known as The NatWest Club Twenty20. Wimbledon won the toss and elected to bat and were going along steadily at 97 for 5 at one point, they then lost their last five wickets for just 20 runs to be bowled out for 117 in 18.1 overs. Stephen Humble had 1 for 17, Jonny Wightman 3 for 17, Michael Craigs 0 for 14, Lee Crozier 1 for 20, Marcus North 2 for 20 and Simon Birtwisle 3 for 23.

When South North batted, opener Simon Birtwisle had 47 from 46 balls, with 7 fours and wicketkeeper Rob Peyton, batting at three, had 37 not out from 37 balls, with 2 fours, as they reached 118 for 3 from 19.2 overs to win by 7 wickets.

When the 2017 season is discussed, reference must be made to Paul Leonard of Felling, he is a left-handed batsman and right arm medium pace bowler. His father, David, was well known as a wicketkeeper/opening batsman when Felling played in The Tyneside Senior League, in the days of Madan Lal.

Following a short spell at Boldon in NEPL Division 1 Paul Leonard returned to Felling in the week leading up to his NEPL debut on 29th July 2017 at home to Stockton. He went on to have the remarkable bowling figures of 9.4 overs, 2 maidens, conceding 24 runs and taking 10 wickets!

It must have been a fascinating watch, Felling had batted first and were bowled out for 86 from 34.2 overs, Joe Carroll top scoring with 16 not out, Leonard with 11, was the only other batsman in double figures. Brett Roberts took 4 for 37, Hassan Raza 3 for 2, Ryan Wallace 2 for 19 and George Harding 1 for 17.

When Stockton batted, Raza made 18 not out and Joe Hewison 17, the next highest scoring batsman had 6. Leonard removed both openers leg before wicket, his last wicket was also leg before, of the rest, one was caught, by Joe Carroll, and Leonard bowled the other six as Stockton were bowled out for 58 from 18.4 overs. Despite being bowled out themselves for 86, Felling had won by 28 runs.

To date, the end of 2023, Paul Leonard's latest NEPL game came on 9th September 2023 at home to Newcastle, to update, he played throughout the 2024 season and continued to pose problems to a lot of batsmen as he added to his wicket haul, he is now just a couple of wickets short of 200.

Paul Leonard has now played 104 matches, all for Felling, in the NEPL, he has batted 82 times, with 14 not outs, he has scored 1031 runs at an average of 15.16. He has 2 half centuries, his highest score is 80, made on 14th August 2021 at home to Burnmoor.

He has bowled 5708 balls, with 182 maidens, conceding 3291 runs and taking 174 wickets at an average of 18.91. His best bowling, obviously, is the 10 for 24 mentioned earlier. He has also taken 18 NEPL catches.

Returning now to the league table and therefore the 2017 NEPL title. When I was pulling the stats together for the 2017 season, I saw the amount of penalty points that some teams had accrued and thought it was a printer's error, I contacted league historian David McKay and was told the circumstances of events. It appears poor on field discipline had led to South Shields being penalized thirty points.

The case of Newcastle and Chester le Street were linked to visas and a change in Home Office rules for pro cricketers. If you hadn't played first-class or professional cricket in the last eighteen months, then you wouldn't get a visa, unless, maybe, there was a British parent in the equation. If you were across here on holiday and wanted to play, you couldn't play as a professional.

Without wanting to rekindle old fires I will simply say this, two young Australian's, Josh Philippe and Chris Carter, had come across to play in the league. Both they and their clubs fell foul of the new legislation and both players returned home early, but not before Philippe had scored 162 in The Banks Salver Final against Benwell Hill and played 18 NEPL games, scoring 900 runs at an average of 60, with 5 half centuries and 3 centuries.

Hill were subsequently awarded the Banks Salver and Newcastle hit with a 120-point penalty and Chester le Street 90 points.

Given that the points deduction came after the game John Graham described earlier in which Josh Philippe had, played on 22nd July and that his last game of the season was on 22nd August, I think John Graham's "nip and tuck" was accurate up to this point.

So, Benwell Hill won The 2017 Banks Salver and South North the Twenty20 competition.

Kyle Coetzer of Benwell Hill was named the 2017 NEPL Player of the Year. He had first come to light playing for Scotland Under 15's, he progressed through the junior set up, playing at Under 17 and Under 19 level as well. He was also playing club cricket for Stoney-Wood Dyce in Scotland and would go on to play for Cape Town in South Africa.

He made his NEPL debut for The Durham Academy on 26th April 2003 at Tynemouth and four days later he made his debut for Durham Seconds at The Racecourse against The Durham University Centre of Cricketing Excellence.

As well as playing for The Academy in The NEPL in 2003, Coetzer played for Durham Under 21's and made his debut for the full Scotland side on 7th June 2003 at home to Pakistanis.

He was also selected numerous times in 2003 for The Scotland A side. The pattern of playing for The Academy, Scotland Under 21's and Scotland A side carried on throughout 2003 and into 2004 until Coetzer was selected to make his County Championship debut for Durham in a match starting on 23rd June at Sophia Gardens against Glamorgan. Durham's first innings was notable for 219 from Marcus North but Coetzer contributed 67 in his first innings in first class cricket. He didn't bowl and the entire last day was washed out, so the match was drawn.

His first-class career would encompass Durham, Northants and Scotland. He played 94 first class matches, batting 156 times, with 11 not outs, he scored 4404 runs at an average of 30.37. He scored 19 half centuries and 8 centuries. His highest score was 219 in a County Championship match for Northants at Grace Road against Leicestershire. His innings came from 402 balls with 36 fours and 1 six and took 503 minutes!

He also bowled 678 balls, with 13 maidens, conceding 414 runs and taking 7 wickets at an average of 59.14. His best bowling was 2 for 46. He took 46 first class catches.

To date, Coetzer has played 199 List A matches, for Durham, Northants and Scotland.

He has batted 192 times, with 19 not outs, scoring 6296 runs at an average of 36.39. He has scored 38 half centuries and 11 centuries. His highest score is 156 in a World Cup Pool Match for Scotland against Bangladesh on 5th March 2015. He was named man of the match for the innings. At the time this was the highest score ever made by a batsman from an associate nation.

He has also bowled 516 balls at this level, with 4 maidens, conceding 508 runs and taking 5 wickets and he has 68 catches at this level.

Coetzer has also represented Durham, Northants and Scotland at Twenty 20 cricket, playing 134 matches in total, batting 127 times with 9 not outs, he scored 2790 runs at an average of 23.64.

He scored 11 half centuries with a high score of 89 on 16th September 2019 against The Netherlands for Scotland. This innings came from 50 balls and contained 11 fours and 5 sixes.

He also bowled 156 balls, 0 maidens, conceding 202 runs and taking 7 wickets at an average of 28.65 and he has taken 40 catches.

He also captained Scotland and in 2019 he was made a Member of the Order of the British Empire for services to cricket.

After making his debut in The NEPL for the Durham Academy in 2003, he played regularly for them until 4th September 2004. He played his last NEPL game for them, a one-off game it appeared for them on 14th June 2008.

In total he played 31 matches for the side, batting 29 times, scoring 862 runs at an average of 34.47. He scored 7 half centuries and 1 century. The century, 120 not out, came on 19th July at The Riverside against Philadelphia.

He had also bowled 326 balls, with 12 maidens, conceding 174 runs and taking 11 wickets at an average of 15.81. His best bowling figures were 3 for 5 on 30th August 2004 at Philadelphia he took 13 catches.

Coetzer made his NEPL debut for Benwell Hill on 13th May 2006 at home to Tynemouth with his last NEPL game for Benwell Hill came on 2nd September 2023 at home to Burnopfield.

He has played 122 matches for The NEPL for the club, batting 114 times, with 21 not outs, he scored 4878 runs at an average of 52.45. He scored 31 half centuries and 14 centuries. His highest score for Hill in The NEPL was 136 not out at Jesmond against Newcastle on 29th June 2019.

He also bowled 3698 balls, with 78 maidens, conceding 2299 runs and taking 96 wickets at an average of 23.94. His best bowling was 4 for 16 on 24th August 2019 at Burnopfield. He also took 55 catches.

In his NEPL career so far Coetzer has played 166 matches, batting 156 times with 29 not outs, scoring 6225 runs at an average of 49.01. He has scored 41 half centuries and 16 centuries. His highest score was 136 not out mentioned earlier.

He has bowled 4562 balls, with 110 maidens, conceding 2787 runs and taking 123 wickets at an average of 22.65. His best bowling was the 5 for 17 mentioned earlier. He has taken 71 NEPL catches.

Coetzer will play for Chester le Street in the upcoming 2024 season when coaching commitments with The Northern Diamonds Women's Team allows. Footnote- He played a number of times during the 2024 season for Chester and features in the 2024 weekly updates later in the book.

Kyle Coetzer seen here bowling on 23rd July 2022 for Benwell Hill

TABLE 56   NEPL 2017.

	Played	Won	Draw/Aban	Lost	Penalty Points	Bonus Points	Points
South North	22	14	6	2	6	158	444
Benwell Hill	22	8	9	5	4	116	309
Newcastle	22	13	4	5	121	170	305
Durham CA	22	7	10	5	0	118	294
Hetton Lyons	22	6	10	6	1	124	271
Eppleton	22	6	9	7	1	117	271
Tynemouth	22	7	8	7	3	100	269
Chester le Street	22	7	8	7	90	127	226
Stockton	22	5	5	12	0	99	212
Whitburn	22	4	10	8	0	95	205
Felling	22	4	7	11	0	82	191
South Shields	22	4	5	13	31	75	143

TABLE 57   NEPL Batting Averages 2017.
Qualification 450 Runs.

Player	Club	Inns	N. O	H. S	Runs	Average
(1) K.J Coetzer	Benwell Hill	18	6	121 no	741	61.75
(2) J.R Philippe	Newcastle	17	2	900	139	60.00
(3) C.S MacLeod	South North	16	4	111 no	661	55.08
(4) S.J Tindale	Newcastle	18	8	108 no	491	49.10
(5) J.N Clay	Hetton Lyons	20	3	94	795	46.76
(6) K. Davis	Chester le Street	17	2	106	693	46.20
(7) Salman Ahmed	South Shields	18	2	147 no	728	45.50
(8) J. du Toit	Newcastle	17	1	132 no	610	38.13
(9) J.G Erasmus	Eppleton	20	5	88	550	36.67
(10) M.J North	South North	20	2	122	633	35.17
(11) S.J Birtwisle	South North	21	2	116 no	667	35.11
(12) P.J Nicholson	Benwell Hill	16	2	138	469	33.50

TABLE 58   NEPL Bowling Averages 2017.
Qualification 25 Wickets.

Player	Club	Overs	Mdns	Runs	Wkts	Average
(1) L.J Crozier	South North	185.0	43	530	37	14.32
(2) Q.J Hughes	Chester le Street	166.2	40	466	30	15.53
(3) C.T Harding	Newcastle	202.2	44	580	36	16.11
(4) H. Shafiq	Durham CA	146.3	24	479	29	16.52
(5) Tahir Khan	Tynemouth	267.5	74	713	43	16.58
(6) S. Humble	South North	177.4	36	521	31	16.81
(7) Haseeb Azam	Benwell Hill	214.3	48	596	35	17.03
(8) J.R Wightman	South North	183.4	23	669	39	17.15
(9) M.J Muchall	South Shields	220.4	44	790	46	17.17
(10) D.J Hymers	Tynemouth	172.4	38	522	30	17.40
(11) J.A Thompson	Whitburn	106.0	9	541	30	18.03
(12) O.F McGee	Newcastle	203.4	44	627	34	18.44

South North 2017 NEPL Champions and Nat West T20 Winners.

Left to Right- Back Row- David Edwards, Tom Hodnett, Andrew Doig, Stephen Humble, Jonny Wightman, Rob Peyton, Sam Dale, Michael Craigs, Calum MacLeod.

Front Row- Lee Crozier, Marcus North, Adam Cragg, John Graham, Simon Birtwisle, Jonny Craigs.

Adam Cragg batting for South North at Derby on 13th September 2017.

Photo Courtesy of Ken Waller.

Paul Leonard, bowling for Felling at Newcastle on 9th July 2017.

Photo Courtesy of Ken Waller.

2018

South North opened the 2018 season on Saturday 21st April with a home game against Stockton, winning the toss and elected to field. George Harding scored 51 for the visitors as they scored 164 all out in 45.4 overs, four South North bowlers took 2 wickets each and there were two run outs. When they batted, despite losing two early wickets, 79 from John Graham and 32 from Adam Cragg, saw them win by 4 wickets in 43.4 overs.

The South North side that started the season was as follows-

Simon Birtwisle opened the batting to start the 2018 season, scoring 7 and bowling one over, 0 for 1. Entering the 2018 season Birtwisle had played 311 matches in the NEPL, batting 303 times with 26 not outs, he had scored 10086 runs at an average of 36.41. He had scored 58 half centuries and 14 centuries. His highest score remained 151 not out for Chester le Street mentioned earlier. When he reached 10,000 NEPL runs he was the first player to reach that landmark in the NEPL.

He had also bowled 5131 balls with 154 maidens, conceding 2991 runs and taking 139 wickets at an average of 21.51. His best bowling was still the 6 for 32 mentioned earlier. He had taken 100 NEPL catches.

During the 2018 season Birtwisle played 21 matches, batting 21 times with 0 not outs, he scored 613 runs at an average of 29.19. He scored 4 half centuries with a highest score of 71, made on 30th June 2018 at home to Eppleton.

He also bowled 378 balls, with 17 maidens, conceding 168 runs and taking 11 wickets at an average of 15.27. His best bowling figures were 3 for 16, taken on 27th August 2018 at Eppleton. He took 9 catches.

Rob Peyton opened the batting with Birtwisle to get 2018 underway, he failed to score but he did keep wicket taking 1 catch. Peyton started the 2018 season having already played 61 matches in the NEPL, he had batted 43 times with 4 not outs, he had scored 662 runs at an average of 16.97. He had scored 3 half centuries with a highest score of 80, scored on 2nd September 2017 at The Riverside against Durham Academy. He had also taken 68 catches and made 4 stumpings in the NEPL.

During the 2018 season he played 21 matches in the NEPL, batting 18 times with 1 not out, he scored 213 runs at an average of 12.52. His highest score was 36, made on 5th May 2018 at home to Durham Academy. He took 26 catches and made 6 stumpings in 2018.

John Graham batted at number three and made an excellent start to the 2018 season, scoring 79. At the close of the 2017 season Graham had played 343 matches in the NEPL, batting 318 times with 48 not outs, he had scored 10071 runs at an average of 37.29. He had scored 73 half centuries and 12 centuries. His highest score remained the 132 mentioned earlier. His bowling figures remain unchanged since 2014 and he had now taken 165 NEPL catches.

He played 20 matches in the NEPL in 2018, batting 19 times with 1 not out, he scored 570 runs at an average of 31.66. He scored 2 half centuries with a highest score of 79, made on the opening match of the season and mentioned earlier. He didn't bowl in the NEPL in 2018 but took 4 catches.

Liam Trevaskis is a left-handed batsman and a slow left arm orthodox spinner. The opening game of 2018 was his NEPL debut for South North, batting at four he made 6 and took 2 for 35 when he bowled. His first NEPL wicket for South North was Stockton wicketkeeper Gary Burgum, leg before for 2.

John Graham says of Trevaskis "he was playing a lot for Durham at this time, a lot of T20, he would often come to us on a Saturday having played Friday night for them. He was around 19 at this time, his bowling, as with many young spinners, lacked consistency and he didn't have a great 2018 for us with the ball, but as a batsman he was physically strong, and he hit the ball a long way. I could see why Durham used him in T20."

Trevaskis had first come to note playing for Cumbria Under 13's against Durham Under 13's at Penrith on 30th May 2012. Ryan Greenwell and Matthew Potts were in the Durham side that day, both making half centuries and Trevaskis made 39. By 22nd May 2013 he was playing for Cumbria Under 15's against Northumberland Under 15's at Great Salkeld.

He played a Northern Premier League fixture for Penrith at home to Kendal on 19th April 2014 before going on to make his NEPL debut for Durham Academy on 24th May 2014 at Gateshead Fell. He had to wait until his eighth appearance for the Academy to take his first NEPL wicket, Benwell Hill's Alasdair Appleby caught by Adam Hickey for 41 on 18th April 2015.

Over 2014 and 2015 Trevaskis played a lot of representative cricket for Cumbria at different age groups, as well as The English Cricket Association North and a Cumberland Development XI and he also continued to play in the NEPL for The Durham Academy.

He played for Durham Second XI in a 3-day match starting on 24th August 2015 at South North against M.C.C Universities and his first game for Durham Under 17's on 29th March 2016 at Lancashire.

He played an ECB Elite Player Development North v London Under 17 fixture on 23rd August 2017, he gave a good account of himself, scoring 36 and taking 1 for 14. This was the first of a number of games at this level for Trevaskis.

He played his last NEPL game for The Academy on 9th September 2017 at The Riverside against Benwell Hill. He had played 62 matches in the NEPL for Durham Academy, batting 55 times with 8 not outs, he scored 1069 runs at an average of 22.74. He scored 4 half centuries. His highest score was 92, made on 30th July 2016 at The Riverside against Newcastle.

He bowled 2728 balls in the NEPL for The Academy, with 83 maidens, he conceded 1505 runs and taking 64 wickets at an average of 23.51. His best bowling figures were 6 for 47, taken on 1st August 2015 at Whitburn. He took 29 catches.

Trevaskis had continued to play for Durham Seconds during 2017, in addition to this he was selected to play in a 2-day match for an ECB Invitation XI against India Under 19's which started on 20th July 2017.

He made his debut for England Under 19's on 7th August 2017 at Cardiff against India Under 19's, he opened the batting, making 33.

Due to the amount of cricket for various teams that Trevaskis was now playing I am now returning to his time in the NEPL, a more detailed summary of his professional career will come a bit later!

Trevaskis played 14 NEPL matches for South North in 2018, he batted 14 times with 2 not outs, he scored 323 runs at an average of 26.91. He scored 1 half century, the half century, 77, was made on 19th May 2018 at home to Newcastle,

He bowled 532 balls with 16 maidens, conceding 273 runs and taking 12 wickets at an average of 22.75. His best bowling figures were 4 for 34, taken on 1st September at home to Sacriston and he also took 6 catches in the 2018 season.

His last game for South North in the NEPL was on 8th September 2018 at home to Felling.

Trevaskis made his NEPL debut for Newcastle on 20th April 2019 at Chester le Street and he played 5 times for Newcastle in the NEPL in 2019, his last game was on 22nd June 2019.

He made his NEPL debut for Burnopfield on 6th May 2023 at Newcastle. His last NEPL game, to date, the end of the 2023 season, was on 9th September 2023 for Burnopfield at Whitburn.

Trevaskis has now played 88 matches in the NEPL, batting 79 times with 12 not outs, he has scored 1645 runs at an average of 24.55. He has scored 7 half centuries with a highest score of 92 mentioned earlier.

He has bowled 3762 balls with 116 maidens, he conceded 1975 runs and taken 86 wickets at an average of 22.96. His best bowling figures were 6 for 47 mentioned earlier. He has taken 39 NEPL catches.

Trevaskis made his first-class debut for Durham on 25th September 2017 at Worcestershire in a County Championship Division 2 match. He would go on to play 27 first-class matches, all for Durham.

He batted 41 times with 8 not outs, he scored 992 runs at an average of 30.06. He scored 7 half centuries with a highest score of 88, made on 28th April 2022 at Sussex.

He bowled 3317 balls in first-class cricket, with 120 maidens, he conceded 1655 runs and took 34 wickets at an average of 48.67. His best bowling figures were 5 for 78, taken on 21st September 2021 at Gloucestershire. He took 10 catches at this level.

He played 32 List A matches for Durham, batting 26 times with 4 not outs, he scored 507 runs at an average of 23.04. He scored 3 half centuries, with a highest score of 76 not out on 11th August 2023 at The Riverside against Derbyshire.

He has bowled 1447 balls at this level to date, with 9 maidens, conceding 1262 runs and taking 35 wickets at an average of 36.05. His best bowling figures are 4 for 50, taken on 1st August 2023 at The Riverside against Worcestershire. He has taken 7 catches at this level.

He has also played 68 Twenty20 matches for Durham, batting 45 times with 19 not outs, he has scored 379 runs at an average of 14.57. His highest score is 31 not out, made on 20th September 2020 at Nottinghamshire.

He has bowled 1252 balls in Twenty20 for Durham, with 1 maiden, conceding 1659 runs and taking 56 wickets at an average of 29.62. His best bowling figures are 4 for 16, taken on 7th August 2018 at Lancashire. He has 41 catches at this level.

Adam Cragg was now in his second season as skipper after winning the title in his first, he batted at number five to start 2018, making 32. He entered the 2018 season with 203 matches in the NEPL to his credit, he had batted 164 times with 27 not outs, he had scored 3761 runs at an average of 27.45. He had scored 18 half centuries and 2 centuries. His highest score remained the 102 mentioned earlier.

Adding the 2 balls he bowled in 2017 to his bowling record he had now bowled 32 balls in the NEPL, with 0 maidens, conceding 20 runs and taking 1 wicket, his best bowling was 1 for 16 mentioned earlier. He had now taken 166 catches and made 22 stumpings in his NEPL career.

During the 2018 season Cragg played 22 matches in the NEPL, batting 21 times with 7 not outs, he scored 657 runs at an average of 46.92. He scored 6 half centuries. His highest score was 72 not out, made on 1st September 2018 at home to Sacriston and he also took 12 catches in the NEPL this season.

Sean Tindale is a right-handed batsman and right arm fast bowler, he batted at number six to start the season, making 4 and opened the bowling taking 2 for 60. John Graham describes Tindale as "a good signing for the club, he has a good batting technique and temperament for batting, he could, and did bat anywhere he was needed, from one to six. He can go from first gear to fifth without any warning, he could just bat a while, nothing extravagant and then suddenly explode with a couple of sixes. He is quick between the wickets and a good partner to have with you at the crease, he understands cricket.

As a bowler he generates good pace, he wasn't express, but he was fast enough for league cricket, I would use the word slippery, I remember seeing one of our other bowlers, Craig Smith, on the speed gun on Sky during the televised T20 final, he clocked 85 mph, Sean was at least equal to that on his day. He could swing it, but I would say he was more of a seam bowler, he bowled an excellent length, top of off stump, this meant a lot of his wickets were what I call bowler's wicket's, bowled, leg before or nicking off and caught behind or in the slips. He would run in all day."

Sean Tindale is the son of former Durham cricketer John Tindale, a right-handed batsman and right arm medium pace bowler, he had a good career before the advent of the NEPL.

As a club cricketer John played junior and then senior cricket at Burnmoor until 1990 and then moved to Chester le Street as professional for five seasons. He then moved to Felling for four seasons, including a title win in 1997, before returning to Burnmoor for another ten years, finishing his playing career aged 44 with Hetton Lyons.

He played for Durham Under 19's, and Minor Counties for Durham from 1987 to 1991 before they became a first-class county in 1992, making his debut on 10th May 1987 at The Racecourse against Durham University. His last game for Durham was on 21st May 1991 at Bishop Auckland against Gloucestershire.

He played 26 matches for Durham, batting 33 times with 8 not outs, he scored 428 runs at an average of 17.12. This included one game for the Second XI. His highest score was 44 not out, made on 29th April 1990 at The Racecourse against Durham University.

He also bowled 858 balls for Durham, with 24 maidens, he conceded 587 runs and took 14 wickets at an average of 41.92. His best bowling figures were 3 for 32, taken on 18th July 1988 at Stockton against Cambridgeshire. He took 5 catches for Durham.

He made his NEPL debut on 24th April 2010 for Hetton Lyons at Sunderland, he made 27 batting at three, his last NEPL game was also for Hetton Lyons on 14th September 2013 at home to Benwell Hill.

John Tindale had played 51 matches in the NEPL, all for Hetton Lyons, batting 41 times with 7 not outs, he scored 707 runs at an average of 20.79. He scored 4 half centuries, with a highest score of 68, made on 1st May 2010 at home to Durham Academy.

He bowled 78 balls in the NEPL, with 4 maidens, he conceded 19 runs and took 1 wicket at an average of 19.00. His only wicket was taken on 31st July 2010 at home to Gateshead Fell, his only wicket was future New Zealand player Tom Latham, leg before wicket for 47. He took 5 NEPL catches.

John Tindale was also a respected coach and mentor with Hetton Lyons, Burnmoor, Newcastle and South North and also assistant manager and manager of Northumberland CCC.

Sean Tindale had first come to attention as a junior, playing for Durham Under 13's on 29th May 2009 at Swalwell against Cumbria Under 13's. He appears to have a batsman only in his junior days.

He played several matches at under 13 level, progressing to Durham Under 14's on 17th June 2010 against Derbyshire Under 14's and made his debut for Durham Under 15's on 1st August 2010 at Baxenden against Lancashire Under 15's.

He appeared in a T20 match for Hetton Lyons at Stockton on 17th June 2011, again as a batsman only.

Sean Tindale made his NEPL debut for Hetton Lyons at home to Newcastle on 20th August 2011, making 3 not out and didn't bowl, his father John was still playing and was also in the Hetton side that day.

He made his debut for Durham Under 17's on 3rd July 2012 at Edinburgh against Scotland Under 17's scoring 22 and taking 1 for 16.

He took his first NEPL wicket on 21st July 2012 at Stockton, Jonathan Rickard caught by Jarvis Clay for 31 and he played for Hetton Lyons and Durham Under 17's throughout 2013.

On 8th May 2014 he played for a Northumberland Development XI against Durham Academy at Winlaton, he made 13 and took 0 for 20, although I did note that he was now opening the bowling.

On 14th May 2014 he played a 2-day match for Durham Academy at Uddington against Scotland Development XI, he took 2 for 16 and scored 3.

Sean Tindale made his debut in Minor Counties matches for Northumberland in a 3-day match starting on 6th July 2014 at West Bromwich against Staffordshire.

He played for Durham Second XI in a 3-day match starting on 12th August 2014 at Stockton against Lancashire Seconds.

He played his last NEPL match for Hetton Lyons on 13th September 2014 at Stockton. He had played 56 NEPL matches for them, batting 43 times with 8 not outs, he scored 521 runs at an average of 14.88. He scored 1 half century, 76, made on 9th August 2014 at Sunderland.

He had bowled 1553 balls in the NEPL for Hetton, with 44 maidens, conceding 937 runs and taking 33 wickets at an average of 28.39. His best bowling figures were 5 for 34, taken on 27th August 2012 at Gateshead Fell. He took 12 NEPL catches for Hetton Lyons.

On 18th April 2015 Tindale was playing for Burnmoor at Felling in the NEPL Division 1, batting at three he made 8 and coming on first change he took 0 for 15.

He continued to play for Northumberland and Burnmoor, playing his last NEPL Division 1 game for them on 5th September 2015 at Eppleton. Tindale scored 3 half centuries that season, with a best of 85, made on 13th June 2015 at home to South Hetton, the same day he took his best bowling figures of the season.

He made the NEPL Division 1 bowling averages that season, bowling 144.3 overs, with 26 maidens, he conceded 584 runs and took 28 wickets at an average of 19.19. His best bowling figures were 7 for 58 taken on 13th June 2015 at home to South Hetton.

He made his NEPL debut for Newcastle on 23rd April 2016 at Eppleton, his first half century for them, 59 not out, opening the batting on 30th April 2016 at home to Whitburn. He took his first NEPL wicket for Newcastle on 28th May 2016 at Hetton Lyons when he had Jack McBeth caught by Ben McGee for 7. Newcastle had a good side this season and finished as runners up in the NEPL. Tindale played his last NEPL game for Newcastle on 9th September 2017 at Jesmond against Felling.

He had played 41 times for Newcastle in the NEPL, he batted 35 times with 11 not outs, he scored 723 runs at an average of 30.12. He scored 3 half centuries and 1 century. The century, 108 not out, was scored on 29th April 2017 at Hetton Lyons, the innings came from 136 balls and contained 14 fours and 2 sixes.

He bowled 2168 balls in the NEPL for Newcastle, with 56 maidens, conceding 1270 runs and taking 49 wickets at an average of 25.91. His best bowling figures were 5 for 50, taken on 19th August 2017 and mentioned earlier and he took 8 catches for them in the NEPL.

He moved to South North for the 2018 season and played 21 matches in the NEPL that season, batting 21 times with 2 not outs, he scored 479 runs at an average of 25.21. He scored 3 half centuries, his highest score was 83, made on 2nd June 2018 at home to Chester le Street.

He bowled 1295 balls, with 39 maidens, conceding 628 runs and taking 38 wickets at an average of 16.52. His best bowling figures were 5 for 16, taken on 8th September at home to Felling. He took 6 NEPL catches in 2018.

Up to the end of 2018 Sean Tindale had played 118 NEPL matches, batting 99 times with 21 not outs, he has scored 1723 runs at an average of 22.08. He has scored 7 half centuries and 1 century. His highest score was the 108 not out mentioned earlier.

He had bowled 5016 balls with 139 maidens, he has conceded 2835 runs and taken 120 wickets at an average of 23.62. His best bowling is the 5 for 16 mentioned earlier. He has taken 26 NEPL catches.

Sam Dale batted at number seven in the season opener, he scored 11 not out. Despite the fact that he had now played 20 NEPL games Dale had still to make a mark in the league. He played 17 matches in the NEPL in 2018, batting 16 times with 2 not outs, he scored 172 runs at an average of 12.28. His highest score was 40, made on 12th May at Whitburn. He didn't bowl but took 2 catches that season.

He played 3 more games in the NEPL in 2019, his last game was on 13th July 2019, at home to Whitburn.

Sam Dale played 40 matches in the NEPL, all for South North, he batted 31 times with 3 not outs, he scored 264 runs at an average of 9.42. His highest score was 40, mentioned earlier.

He bowled 12 balls, conceding 19 runs and not taking a wicket, he did take 7 catches in the NEPL.

Dale did pick up title wins in 2017 and 2018 despite his disappointing statistics. I think it would be unfair to Dale to leave his stats there, he was clearly a talented batsman at second team level, he played 35 times for the Second XI, batting 35 times with 5 not outs, he scored 656 runs at an average of 28.52. He scored 5 half centuries with a highest score of 97, made on 9th July 2016 against Tynemouth Second XI.

As an interesting aside, John Graham mentions in the 2017 bio of Dale that he was a good footballer, ironically, on the day he scored 97 he was caught and bowled by Sean David Longstaff.

Longstaff made his competitive debut for Newcastle United Football Club on 29th August 2018 in The Carabao Cup against Nottingham Forest, making his Premier League debut as a second half substitute at Liverpool on Boxing Day the same year.

To date, 30th March 2024 Longstaff has now played 173 matches for Newcastle United as a midfielder, he has 14 goals, played in a League Cup final, played 5 matches in the Champions League and beaten local rivals Sunderland 3 nil at The Stadium of Light. He has also captained Newcastle United.

Sean Longstaff still turns out, and he did so four times during the 2024 season, taking 9 wickets at 16.77, when he can for Tynemouth in the NEPL, he is a left-handed batsman and right arm medium fast bowler.

He made his NEPL debut on 6th June 2015 at The Emirates against Durham Academy. That was the only game he played in the NEPL that season, so he had to wait until his next game, 4th June 2016 at home to Hetton Lyons for his first NEPL wicket, Chris Martin leg before wicket for 24. He played only 1 more NEPL match in 2016 and 2 more in 2017.

The first game he played in 2017, on 1st July was at home to Benwell Hill. He took his best bowling figures taking 4 for 30 from nine overs.

He played 3 NEPL games in 2018, the second one, on 26th May at South North saw him make his only 50 to date, 57 not out to be exact.

Longstaff played 3 more NEPL games in 2021, 2 more in 2022 and 4 more in 2023, his last appearance to the end of 2023, was on 1st July 2023 at Benwell Hill.

Given his commitments elsewhere it's difficult to judge Longstaff the cricketer, but he clearly has natural talent, up to the end of 2023, he has now played 17 matches in the NEPL, batting 13 times with 4 not outs, he has scored

176 runs at an average of 19.55. He has 1 half century, the 57 not out mentioned earlier. He has bowled 877 balls with 25 maidens, he has conceded 427 runs and taken 25 wickets at an average of 17.07. His best bowling is the 4 for 30 mentioned earlier. He has taken 4 catches in the NEPL.

If you look at his stats as a season's work rather than random appearances here and there, then 17 matches is about right for most individuals in a season, a high score of 57 not out and an average of 19.55 and 25 wickets at 17.07 would represent a good season's work and 25 wickets in a season would be good enough to get him into the bowling averages most seasons, and some seasons, in the top ten.

Andrew Doig batted at number eight in the season opener, he was 0 not out when the game was won. As with much of his NEPL career, Doig seems to have been used as a filler when the regular first team players were unavailable. During the 2018 season he played 8 matches in the NEPL, batting 7 times with 3 not outs, he scored 54 runs at an average of 13.50. His highest score was 19, made on 14th July at home to Benwell Hill. He made 2 catches that season. His last NEPL game was on 24th August 2019 at home to Chester le Street.

He played 28 matches in the NEPL in his career, batting 21 times with 8 not outs, he scored 170 runs at an average of 13.07. His highest score was 27 made on 11th August 2012 and mentioned earlier. He never bowled but took 4 catches and had 1 stumping in the NEPL.

Richard Stanyon was listed to bat at number nine to get 2018 underway, this was his NEPL debut, he didn't get the opportunity to bat as South North won by 4 wickets. He did bowl five overs, taking 0 for 20. John Graham describes Stanyon as having "all the attributes to be a top bowler, he was tall and did just enough with the ball, when he gets it right, he would angle the ball into the right hander then just move it a fraction away, because of his height batsman would hang back in their crease and this caused them no ends of problems. He got good players out. Pace wise he was fast medium; he was an important piece of our team in 2018. As a batsman he scored some useful runs, he liked to hit straight or to cow corner."

Stanyon had originally come from the Merseyside area, first coming to the attention of the record keepers playing for Ainsdale Second XI on 22nd May 2004 against Prestatyn Second XI in the Merseyside Cricket Competition Division 1.

He would play for Ainsdale Firsts and Merseyside Under 16's in 2007 before playing for Northern in the Liverpool and District League in 2010. He was selected to play for Lancashire Under 19's in 2010.

Stanyon had originally made his NEPL debut for Newcastle on 7th May 2011 at Gateshead Fell. He had to wait until the following week, 14th May at Stockton to take his first NEPL wicket, Stockton skipper and opener Kevin Ward, caught behind by Neil Corby for 10. He returned to Northern in June 2011, playing there until the end of the 2011 season.

He made his Northumberland debut in Minor Counties Championship matches in a 3-day match at Buckinghamshire which started on 23rd June 2013.

He would go on to play 6 matches for Northumberland, scoring 53 runs and taking 10 wickets at an average of 44.60, he played his last game for Northumberland on 18th August 2013 at home to Cambridgeshire.

He played one 3-day game for Durham Second XI starting on 3rd September 2013 at Sussex, he took 1 for 38 and 1 for 31.

He played his first game for Ainsdale in the Liverpool and District League on 2nd August 2014, seeing the 2014 season out there and playing there until June 2016 when he returned to play for Newcastle in the NEPL.

He played his last NEPL game for Newcastle on 13th May 2017 at Benwell Hill. He had played 48 NEPL matches for Newcastle, batting 24 times with 6 not outs, he scored 211 runs at an average of 11.72. His highest score was 32, made on 6th July 2013 at home to Sunderland.

He bowled 2420 balls with 53 maidens, conceding 1521 runs and taking 61 wickets at an average of 24.93. His best bowling figures were 6 for 89, taken on 31st August 2013 at home to Stockton. He made 3 catches in the NEPL for Newcastle.

Stanyon played 12 matches for South North in the NEPL in 2018, this was his entire South North career, batting 7 times with 2 not outs, he scored 101 runs at an average of 20.20. His highest score was 32 not out, made on 19th May at home to Newcastle.

He bowled 293 balls with 5 maidens, conceding 191 runs and taking 11 wickets at an average of 17.36. His best bowling figures were 3 for 19, taken on 4th August at Newcastle. He didn't take a catch in the NEPL in 2018.

He played his last NEPL game for South North on 4th August 2018 at Jesmond against Newcastle.

He next appeared in the NEPL for Tynemouth on 9th July 2022 at Benwell Hill and he was still playing for Tynemouth at the end of the 2023 season, his last appearance coming on 12th August at South North.

Until the end of 2023 Stanyon had played 71 matches in the NEPL, batting 40 times with 11 not outs, he has scored 403 runs at an average of 13.89. His highest score is 36, made for Tynemouth on 27th August 2022.

He has bowled 3059 balls in the NEPL, with 62 maidens, conceding 2016 runs and taking 82 wickets at an average of 24.58. His best bowling remains the 6 for 89 mentioned earlier. He has taken 5 NEPL catches in his career.

Jonny Wightman was listed to bat at number ten in the season opener of 2018 but didn't get to bat, he did open the bowling, taking 2 for 20. At the close of the 2017 season Wightman had now played 170 matches in the NEPL, he had batted 86 times with 31 not outs, scoring 525 runs at an average of 9.54. His highest score was 37, made in May 2011 and mentioned earlier.

He had bowled 10092 balls in his NEPL career up to the end of 2017, with 224 maidens, conceding 6352 runs and taking 338 wickets at an average of 18.79. His best bowling figures were 8 for 31, taken in June 2016 and mentioned earlier. He had taken 19 NEPL catches to this point.

Wightman played 21 matches in the NEPL in 2018, batting 11 times with 4 not outs, he scored 107 runs at an average of 15.28. His highest score was 30 not out, made on 2nd June at home to Chester le Street.

He bowled 1363 balls in 2018 in the NEPL, with 47 maidens, he conceded 726 runs and took 43 wickets at an average of 16.88. His best bowling figures were 5 for 21, taken on 25th August 2018 at Hetton Lyons. He took 4 catches in the NEPL in 2018.

Lee Crozier was listed to bat at number eleven to start 2018, he didn't bat but took 2 for 22 when he bowled. Crozier had played 336 matches in the NEPL before the start of the 2018 season, batting 153 times with 72 not outs, he had scored 1312 runs at an average of 16.19. He had scored 1 half century, 89 for Benwell Hill in May 2002.

He had bowled 23673 balls, that's 3945.5 overs, with 1058 maidens, conceding 10393 runs and taking 679 wickets at an average of 15.30. His best bowling figures were 7 for 21 taken for South North in July 2007. He had taken 51 NEPL catches.

During the 2018 season he played 22 matches in the NEPL, batting 6 times with 5 not outs, he scored 32 runs at an average of 32.00. His highest score was 14 not out.

He bowled 1258 balls with 49 maidens, conceding 578 runs and taking 42 wickets at an average of 13.76. His best bowling figures were 5 for 26, taken on 27th August at Eppleton. He took 3 catches in the NEPL in 2018.

Michael Craigs didn't play in the NEPL in 2018 until the second week of the season. He entered the season having played 77 NEPL matches for South North, batting 54 times with 19 not outs, he scored 601 runs at an average of 17.17. He had scored 1 half century, 56, made in June 2015 and mentioned earlier.

He had bowled 1856 balls with 54 maidens, conceding 1066 runs and taking 55 wickets at an average of 19.38. His best bowling figures were 5 for 26, taken on 19th August 2017 at home to Felling. He had taken 27 catches in the NEPL to the end of 2017.

He would go on to play 17 matches in the NEPL in 2018, batting 12 times with 4 not outs, he scored 129 runs at an average of 16.12. His highest score was 21, made on 19th May at home to Newcastle.

He bowled 600 balls with 21 maidens in the NEPL in 2018, conceding 260 runs and taking 28 wickets at an average of 9.28. His best bowling figures were 4 for 36, taken on 21st July at The Riverside against Durham Academy. He took 4 catches in the 2018 season in the NEPL.

Michael Craigs would play his last NEPL game for South North on 13th July 2019 at home to Whitburn. He had played 105 matches in the NEPL, all for South North, batting 73 times with 27 not outs, he had scored 773 runs at an average of 16.80. he scored 1 half century, 56 mentioned earlier.

He had bowled 2768 balls with 87 maidens, conceding 1480 runs and taking 92 wickets at an average of 16.08. His best bowling figures were 5 for 26 mentioned earlier. He took 36 NEPL catches.

John Graham says that "we didn't have a strong side going into 2018, we certainly weren't the best team on paper, but we sort of gelled and everyone pulled together, when we needed someone to put their hand up and do something, someone did, and it wasn't always the same people, I think Sean Tindale was a significant signing from Newcastle, we managed to get our noses in front and just sort of stayed there, there was one game at home to Chester le Street where we were very fortunate, we were in trouble when it rained and got away with a draw, but that aside it was a great team season."

The game that he is referring to took place on 2nd June 2018 at Roseworth Terrace, the match was reduced, and the first innings was limited to a maximum of 58 overs.

Chester le Street won the toss and elected to bowl and South North were soon in trouble, 8 for 1, 15 for 2, 20 for 3, 20 for 4, a partnership of 50 between John Graham and Sean Tindale got them to respectability when Graham was caught by Quentin Hughes off the bowling of Alex McGrath for 31, they were now 70 for 5.

This quickly became 71 for 6 and then 77 for 7 as slow left armer Liam Burgess picked up a couple of wickets. Opening bowler, the left arm medium pacer McGrath, then took another wicket Michael Craigs caught by Jacob McCann, 84 for 8.

Number ten batsman Jonny Wightman and Tindale then added 78 for the ninth wicket, the score was 162 when Tindale was dismissed, caught by McGrath off the bowling of Quentin Hughes for 83, his innings had come from 141 balls and contained 11 fours.

South North were 162 for 9 from their 58 overs with three of the five bowlers used taking wickets, McGrath had 4 for 22, Hughes 2 for 43 and Burgess 2 for 36.

When Chester batted, they lost opener George Harrison for 6, caught by Simon Birtwisle off the bowling of Sean Tindale, but they were making good progress at 52 for 1 from 10 overs when rain halted proceedings. Opener Kyle Davis was 21 not out and Jacob McCann was 16 not out when the match was declared a draw.

I think John Graham is being modest, South North didn't lose a game in the NEPL in 2018, winning the league by 68 points, by the narrow standard of some of their previous title wins, that seems like a decent margin to me!

The 2018 Banks Salver was won by Chester le Street and the Twenty20 by South North., Kieran Waterson of Whitburn was named the 2018 NEPL Player of the Year.

Waterson had played 20 matches in the NEPL in 2018, batting 8 times with 3 not outs, he scored 34 runs at an average of 6.80. His highest score was 14 not out.

It was for his bowling efforts that he received the award. He bowled 1499 balls in the NEPL in 2018, with 46 maidens, conceding 832 runs and taking 63 wickets at an average of 13.20. His best bowling figures were 8 for 53, taken on 16th June 2018 at Durham Academy. He also took 10 catches in the NEPL in 2018.

He had started as a junior playing for Durham at Under 13 level, he also played at Under 15 and Under 17 level for Durham.

Waterson had made his NEPL debut on 8th September 2007 for Chester le Street at home to Tynemouth, this was his only NEPL appearance or the club, taking 1 for 18, his first NEPL wicket was John Callaghan, caught by Graeme Cessford for 12.

He next appeared in the NEPL making his debut for Hetton Lyons on 24th April 2010 at Sunderland.

He played his last NEPL match for Hetton Lyons on 11th September 2010 at Chester le Street.

Waterson then made his NEPL debut for Sunderland on 30th April 2011 at South Shields and he played his last game of this spell with Sunderland on 14th September 2013 at home to Newcastle.

He made his NEPL debut for Whitburn on 20th June 2015 at home to Tynemouth and he played his last NEPL game for Whitburn on 11th September 2021 at home to Tynemouth.

Waterson then made a second debut for Sunderland in the NEPL on 16th April 2022 at Tynemouth. To date, the end of March 2024, he played his last NEPL game for Sunderland on 10th September 2022 at Burnmoor. Update,

Waterson took a further 17 wickets at an average of 22.23 during 13 appearances for Sunderland in the NEPL in 2024. To this point Waterson had played 197 matches in the NEPL, batting 119 times with 44 not outs, he had scored 583 runs at an average of 7.77. His highest score was 41 not out, scored on 28th August 2021 for Whitburn at Eppleton.

He had bowled 13495 balls in the NEPL, with 462 maidens, conceding 7579 runs and taking 422 wickets at an average of 17.95. His best bowling figures were 8 for 53 taken for Whitburn and mentioned earlier.

In his NEPL career to the end of 2023, Waterson had taken 51 catches.

Update -Kieran Waterson played regularly for Sunderland in the NEPL throughout 2024 adding a further 17 wickets to his haul at an average of 22.23 each.

TABLE 59   NEPL 2018.

	Played	Won	Draw/Aban	Lost	Penalty Points	Bonus Points	Points
South North	22	16	6	0	3	146	471
Chester le Street	22	11	8	3	0	157	403
Hetton Lyons	22	11	5	6	0	137	362
Tynemouth	22	10	6	6	5	146	349
Newcastle	22	9	4	9	0	115	299
Whitburn	22	9	6	7	1	111	294
Benwell Hill	22	6	7	9	2	120	261
Eppleton	22	5	6	11	0	98	222
Durham CA	22	4	9	9	1	113	221
Felling	22	5	7	10	2	89	206
Sacriston	22	5	5	12	1	81	195
Stockton	22	5	3	14	5	91	189

TABLE 60   NEPL Batting Averages 2018.

Qualification 450 Runs.

Player	Club	Inns	N. O	H. S	Runs	Average
(1) K. Davis	Chester le Street	19	5	118	859	61.36
(2) G.J Snyman	Benwell Hill	13	1	643	173	53.58
(3) A.D Cragg	South North	21	7	72 no	657	46.93
(4) J. du Toit	Newcastle	19	4	124	646	43.07
(5) M.A Jones	Tynemouth	19	3	120	682	42.63
(6) K.J Coetzer	Benwell Hill	16	2	113 no	596	42.57
(7) R.L Greenwell	Durham CA	20	3	131 no	717	42.18
(8) S.A Walker	Hetton Lyons	22	2	96 no	696	34.80
(9) J.W Coxon	Chester le Street	18	2	102 no	533	33.31
(10) A.C Simpson	Newcastle	18	2	84	512	32.00
(11) J.A Graham	South North	19	1	79	570	31.67
(12) J. Hewison	Stockton	21	1	60 no	631	31.55
(18) S.J Birtwisle	South North	21	0	71	613	29.19
(25) S.J Tindale	South North	21	2	83	479	25.21

TABLE 61   NEPL Bowling Averages 2018.

Qualification 25 Wickets.

Player	Club	Overs	Mdns	Runs	Wkts	Average
(1) M.A Craigs	South North	100.0	21	260	28	9.29
(2) M.R.J Watt	Tynemouth	164.1	51	422	35	12.06
(3) J. Malkin	Hetton Lyons	143.2	22	468	37	12.65
(4) K. Waterson	Whitburn	249.5	46	832	63	13.21
(5) W. Bedja	Tynemouth	219.1	38	697	52	13.40
(6) S. Cantwell	Chester le Street	177.0	36	524	39	13.44
(7) L.J Crozier	South North	209.5	49	578	42	13.76
(8) O.F McGee	Newcastle	245.2	53	704	51	13.80
(9) G.J Snyman	Benwell Hill	168.3	40	475	31	15.32
(10) C. Ralston	Hetton Lyons	188.1	53	704	51	15.50
(11) M.L Pollard	Tynemouth	160.4	26	547	34	16.09
(12) S.J Tindale	South North	215.5	39	628	38	16.53
(15) J.R Wightman	South North	227.1	47	726	43	16.88

South North CC 2018 NEPL Winners and T20 Winners.

Left to Right-Back Row- Bobby Green, Calum Fletcher, Liam Trevaskis, Sean Tindale, Rob Peyton, Sam Dale, Alex Weetman, Peter Borran, John Tindale (Coach).

Front Row-Michael Craigs, Lee Crozier, John Graham, Adam Cragg, Jonny Wightman, Simon Birtwisle.

Inset- Richard Stanyon.

Kieran Waterson, seen here bowling on 16th April 2022 at Tynemouth.

Chapter Eleven

Burnmoor 2019

The NEPL saw one of its original members depart before the start of the 2019 season as The Durham Cricket Academy withdrew from the League, another one of the original eleven teams, Stockton had returned to the N.Y.S.D. At the start of the season only one team was supposed to be promoted to The NEPL from Division 1, because of the unusual circumstances of losing two teams, Burnmoor, who had been runners up were therefore promoted to The NEPL from Division 1 at the end of the 2018 season. Allan Worthy remembers that it was a bit of a joke at the time as they continued to do well that "we shouldn't even be here."

They opened their first NEPL campaign with an away game at Eppleton on 20th April 2019, Burnmoor won the toss and decided to bat. They scored 264 for 4 declared from 52 overs, Worthy top scored with 96. When Eppleton batted they made 195 for 6 from 58 overs, Marcus Brown made 80, when the innings was closed, and the match drawn.

The Burnmoor side which played that day was as follows-

Allan Worthy opened the batting and the season in style on 20th April, making 96 from 120 balls and contained 18 fours, he also bowled an over, a maiden over, to see out the game.

Worthy had dropped into Division 1 of The NEPL when he had made his debut for Burnmoor on 15th April 2017. Over the next two seasons, going into the 2019 season he played 44 matches in NEPL Division 1, batting 44 times, with 4 not out's, he had scored 1073 runs at an average of 26.82. He had made 4 half centuries and 1 century, 107, on 16th June 2018 at home to Washington, the innings came from 128 balls and contained 15 fours and 2 sixes.

He had also bowled 615 balls, with 19 maidens, conceding 406 runs and taking 18 wickets at an average of 22.55. His best bowling figures were 5 for 22 on 28th April 2018 at home to Sunderland. He also had 17 catches.

Quentin Hughes says of Worthy "He likes to attack a bowler from the start, from the first ball he is looking to get after you, I have seen him hit the first ball of an innings for six. I have had a lot of battles with him over the years, but I would say this, he is far better to play with than against, that aggressive attitude to batting elevated him to a different level."

Allan Worthy's up to date statistics can be found later in this chapter which looks at the Team of 20 Years.

Martin Hubber is a left-handed batsman and right arm medium pace bowler, he opened the batting with Worthy on 20th April 2019, scoring 23 and he also opened the bowling, four overs, 0 for 9. Allan Worthy describes him as follows "Martin was born and raised with cricket, his uncle, Harry, and father both spent a lot of time at Sacriston, when I was pro there, I knew them very well, as a small child Martin would always be playing on the boundary there. He played for Shotley Bridge for a while, but he had a couple of injuries as a youngster and he knew Graeme Bridge and I and we asked him to come to Burnmoor, I think he needed a bit of a change, and he came across.

On and off the field he is as tough as nails, away from cricket he was a boxer, and, on the field, he never gave an inch, a proper hardnosed cricketer. He had a quiet presence about him, as a team he gave us all an air of confidence, a don't mess with us kind of attitude, he was a good addition and a good fit for that 2019 team. He was a good fielder and as a batsman he knew his role in the team, he would accumulate runs and was a good partnership builder, he was a very good player through the offside, he loved width on the ball."

Hubber came to attention on 1st July 2002 playing for Durham Under 17's against Scotland Under 17's at Gosforth in a match badly affected by rain. Hubber would also play Perth Second Grade cricket in Australia in 2005/06 for Fremantle Second XI. He next appeared on the radar playing for Shotley Bridge at Benwell Hill in The Just Sport Trophy on 6th June 2011.

On 22nd July 2012 Hubber was selected as part of a strong Northumberland and Tyneside Senior League side to play The Nottinghamshire Premier League at Sutton Coldfield. Melvyn Betts, Paul Burn and Neil Killeen were amongst his teammates.

By 17th May 2014 Hubber was playing for Sacriston against Felling in The NEPL Division 1, he remained there until the start of the 2015 season when he played for Washington in the same league, NEPL Division 1. Hubber returned to Sacriston for 2016, still in NEPL Division 1, where he remained until the end of 2017 when the record went blank for a year.

The season opener of 2019 was his first appearance in the NEPL after playing at Sacriston, his last Burnmoor appearance would come in the last game of this season, at Chester le Street. He would play just this season before moving back to Sacriston. He played 18 matches in the 2019 season in the NEPL, batting 18 times, with 1 not out, he scored 384 runs at an average of 22.58. He scored 2 half centuries, his highest score was 69 not out, on 31st August at Newcastle.

He also bowled 270 balls, with 8 maidens, he conceded 154 runs and took 6 wickets at an average of 25.66. His best bowling figures were 3 for 39 on 18th May at South North. He took 5 NEPL catches in 2019.

Hubber made his NEPL debut for Sacriston on 17th April 2021 at home to Eppleton and his last NEPL appearance to date came on 4th September 2021 at Benwell Hill as Sacriston were relegated to NEPL Division 1. He played 15 NEPL matches for the club, batting 15 times, with 1 not out, he scored 332 runs at an average of 23.71. He scored 3 half centuries, his highest score, 53, came on 7th August at home to Burnopfield.

He also bowled 838 balls, with 23 maidens, conceding 521 runs and taking 17 wickets at an average of 30.64. His best bowling figures were 3 for 47, taken on 5th June 2021 at Felling. He didn't take a catch this season in the NEPL.

In total, to date, Hubber has played 33 matches in the NEPL, batting 33 times, with 2 not outs, he has scored 716 runs at an average of 23.09. He has scored 5 half centuries; his highest score was 69 not out mentioned earlier.

He has also bowled 1108 balls, with 31 maidens, he has conceded 675 runs and taken 23 wickets at an average of 29.34. His best bowling figures were the 3 for 39 mentioned earlier. He has taken 5 NEPL catches.

Paul Craig is a right-handed batsman, he batted at number three on the first day of the 2019 season, he made 70 not out. In effect he has had two NEPL careers, the first came in the early days with The Durham Academy, the second with Burnmoor a year or two later!

Allan Worthy recalls a "tall lad, around six two, he had broad shoulders on an athletic body, and he looked imposing at the crease, ironically he was a tiny youngster! He was another one who I feel Durham discarded too early. He won the D.C.L about six times with Kimblesworth then won the D.S.L with Burnmoor. He would fill in at wicketkeeper when required, as a batsman I think he could have batted higher, but he seemed content in to bat in the middle order, he could take you apart when he batted, he liked to hit inside out, over extra cover, he liked to sweep and take the spinners on, he was a brilliant hooker, a compulsive hooker, I have seen him take on the fast overseas pro's and he would really go for it. Paul knew his own game, he was one of those who went quietly about his business at the crease, a bit of a gentle giant type."

Before I get to Craig in The NEPL it's worth noting that he also played representative cricket as a youngster. He played for The English Schools Cricket Association North Under 15's on 23rd July 2002 against their counterparts from The South as part of the Bunbury Festival at Billericay. Paul Muchall and Adil Rashid were in the same side with Craig that day, Muchall scoring 105 not out. There was no opportunity for Craig to bat. He did play a second game in the festival against The Midlands Side, three days later, he scored 6 when he batted. Craig went on to play for Durham Under 17's against Scotland Under 17's on 6th July 2003 at Edinburgh.

He made his NEPL debut for The Durham Academy on 27th April 2002 at Roseworth Terrace against South North, he top scored the innings with 39 not out and kept wicket, Liam Plunkett and Chris Rushworth were among his team mates on that day. His last appearance in The NEPL for The Academy came on 9th July 2005, once again he top scored the innings, with 49, away at Gateshead Fell.

He played 65 NEPL matches for The Academy, he batted 50 times, with 13 not outs, he scored 886 runs at an average 23.94. He scored 3 half centuries. His highest score was 74 not out, made on 30th August 2003 at Newcastle. He took 66 catches and 11 stumpings in The NEPL for The Academy.

Given the nature of cricket records online, there is a gap in Craig's career, he next appeared for Kimblesworth at Marsden on 27th April 2013.

The first record for him at Burnmoor came on 26th May 2014 at home to Philadelphia in The Durham Cricket League. He remained in Burnmoor's first team until the game to start the 2019 season against Eppleton marked the start of his second NEPL career. To date, his last NEPL appearance came on 28th August 2023 for Burnmoor at Hetton Lyons. He has played 67 NEPL matches for Burnmoor, batting 58 times, with 5 not outs, he has scored 1127 runs at an average of 21.26. He has scored 7 half centuries, his highest score is 86 not out, made on 27th April 2019 at Felling. He has never bowled in The NEPL but has taken 25 catches in this spell with Burnmoor.

His overall NEPL stats, to date, are that he has played 132 NEPL matches, batting 108 times, with 18 not outs, he has scored 2013 runs at an average of 22.36. He has scored 10 half centuries; his highest score is 86 not out described earlier. He has taken 91 catches and had 11 stumpings in his NEPL career.

Update, he played 2 more matches for Burnmoor in the NEPL in 2024, adding 31 runs to his total.

Ryan Pringle is a right-handed batsman and right arm off break bowler. He batted at number four to open the season, scoring 19 and was the most successful bowler of the day, taking 3 for 31 from fifteen overs. Allan Worthy says of Pringle "he's related to me, he is my cousin's son, so I will try not to be biased, his mother used to babysit me! He first played as a youngster at Hetton Lyons, he was almost a child prodigy as a batsman, at 15 he was opening the batting for The Durham Senior League representative side and doing well. His captain, Chris Ellison said to me one day that he thought Ryan had something special about his batting. He went on to play for The Durham Academy, initially as a batsman but he developed his off-spin bowling there, he captained their side in the NEPL, Ben Stokes was in the same team.

Before one day cricket developed into what it is now, Ryan liked to hit it over the top early in the innings in the first five overs, off the faster bowlers. He had a wide stance and stood tall; he could take a bowler to bits. Over his time at The Academy, he went from belligerent batsman to stifling spinner. As a bowler he could dry you up, stifle you to such an extent that you weren't sure where you were going to score. The last game of the 2019 season against Chester was probably the best example of it and probably won us the game and the league with it! He had a good career at Durham, but he was probably a little inconsistent for them, I personally thought they gave up on him a little early."

Pringle was playing representative cricket at an early age, first coming to the attention of the record keepers on 3rd June 2005 for Durham Under 13's against Cumbria Under 13's.

Ryan Pringle made his NEPL debut for Hetton Lyons on 8th July 2006 at Gateshead Fell. He neither batted nor bowled. He progressed through the Durham Under 14's, 15's and 17's, then playing for The Durham Academy on 2nd September 2008 in a game against Yorkshire Academy. Joe Root, Gary Ballance and Jonny Bairstow were playing for Yorkshire and Ben Stokes and Mark Wood were in the Durham side with Pringle.

He next appeared in the NEPL for Durham Academy at Sunderland on 25th April 2009, Pringle was run out for 18, Ben Stokes made the highest individual score of the season that day, 142, and Mark Wood had 77. Pringle didn't bowl as the match was drawn.

He had to wait until 27th June 2009 to take his first NEPL wicket, Stockton middle order batsman Chris Hooker caught and bowled for 4.

He was selected to represent an ECB North Under 17 side against opposition from the South and West, and another against the Midlands in August 2009.

He made his debut for Durham Second XI in June 2010 and he would go on to play 162 times for Durham Seconds, scoring over 5,000 runs and taking 149 wickets. His last appearance in the NEPL for The Academy was on 4th September 2010 at Sunderland.

Ryan Pringle had played 38 matches in the NEPL for them, batting 36 times, with 3 not outs, he had scored 668 runs at an average of 20.24. He scored 4 half centuries, his highest score was 80, scored at Tynemouth on 1st August 2009.

He bowled 1241 balls in the NEPL for the Academy, with 21 maidens, conceding 659 runs and taking 23 wickets at an average of 28.65. His best bowling figures were 5 for 12 on 10th July 2010 at Hetton Lyons. He has caught 10 catches in the NEPL for The Academy.

In addition to playing for The Durham Academy Pringle also represented Northumberland, making his debut on 7th August 2011 in a 3 -day match at Cambridgeshire. He played twice more in 2012, once more in 2019, and twice more in 2021.

In total his Northumberland career, spanning eleven years, was that he played 6 times, batting 9 times, with 0 not outs, he scored 159 runs at an average of 17.66. His highest score was 93, his only half century, it came in a 3-day match starting 19th August 2012 at Jesmond against Buckinghamshire.

He also bowled 623 balls for Northumberland, with 17 maidens, conceding 365 runs and taking 7 wickets at an average of 52.14. His best bowling was 2 for 56. He made 3 catches.

Pringle made his "second" debut for Hetton Lyons on 30th April 2011 at home to Benwell Hill and he was named NEPL Player of the Year in 2011 for his performance at Hetton. His last NEPL appearance for them was on 13th September 2014 at Stockton.

He had played 60 matches in the NEPL for Hetton, batting 59 times, with 7 not outs, he had scored 1740 runs at an average of 33.46. He scored 7 half centuries and 4 centuries. His highest score was 156 not out on 1st June 2013 at home to Sunderland, the innings came from 141 balls and contained 15 fours and 4 sixes.

He bowled 4263 balls in the NEPL for Hetton, with 136 maidens, conceding 2188 runs and taking 134 wickets at an average of 16.32. His best bowling figures were 9 for 31 on 11th May 2012 at home to Gateshead Fell. His bowling figures on the day were 13.4 overs, 4 maidens, 31 runs conceded for 9 wickets taken. He also caught 22 catches in the NEPL for the club.

Ryan Pringle made his first-class debut for Durham in a County Championship game starting on 19th May 2014 at Taunton against Somerset. His last first-class game came for Durham in a match which started on 13th July 2019 at The Riverside against Worcestershire.

He played 40 first class matches for Durham, batting 63 times, with 8 not outs, he scored 1336 runs at an average of 24.29. He scored 8 half centuries, his highest score was 99, scored on 1st September at The Riverside against Hampshire.

He bowled 4020 balls, with 119 maidens, conceding 2401 runs and taking 63 wickets at an average of 38.11. His best bowling figures were 7 for 107, taken in September 2016 at Hampshire. He took 24 catches at this level.

He continued to play List A and Twenty20 cricket for Durham until June 2018, at List A level he played 40 matches for the club, batting 31 times, with 0 not outs, he scored 492 runs at an average of 15.87. He didn't score a half century but did have 1 century, 125, on 7th June 2016 at Derbyshire.

He bowled 987 balls, with 1 maiden, conceding 919 runs and taking 14 wickets at an average of 65.64, his best bowling figures were 2 for 14. He took 12 catches.

At Twenty20 for Durham he played 70 matches, batting 49 times, with 6 not outs, he scored 463 runs at an average of 10.76. His highest score was 35.

He bowled 744 balls, with 0 maidens, conceding 1061 runs and taking 29 wickets at an average of 36.58. His best bowling figures were 3 for 36. He made 24 catches.

In addition to appearing for Durham, he played in the NEPL Division 1 for Brandon, debuting on 7th May 2016 at Washington. He played 4 games in 2016 for them, 3 games in 2017 and 12 games in 2018.

In total he played 19 NEPL Division1 games for Brandon, batting 15 times with 1 not out, he scored 499 runs at an average of 35.64. He scored 2 half centuries with a high score of 85.

He bowled 1272 balls in NEPL Division 1, with 47 maidens, conceding 569 runs and taking 44 wickets at an average of 12.93. His best bowling figures were 5 for 36. He made 6 catches at this level.

He made his Burnmoor NEPL debut in the season opener of 2019, 20th April at Eppleton, he captained Burnmoor throughout the 2024 season.

Up to 9th September 2023 he has played 70 matches in the NEPL for Burnmoor, batting 64 times, with 9 not outs, he has scored 1947 runs at an average of 35.40. He has scored 13 half centuries and 4 centuries, his highest score is 124 on 25th June 2022 at Sunderland.

He has bowled 3298 balls, with 85 maidens, conceding 1794 runs and taking 95 wickets at an average of 18.88. His best bowling figures are 5 for 28 on 25th June 2022, just in case you missed it, that's the same day he had his current highest score for Burnmoor! He has taken 25 catches in the NEPL for them.

Ryan Pringle has played 169 matches in the NEPL, batting 159 times, with 19 not outs, he has scored 4355 runs at an average of 31.10. He has scored 24 half centuries and 8 centuries. His highest score is 156 not out, scored for Hetton Lyons on 1st June 2013.

He has bowled 8802 balls, with 242 maidens, conceding 4641 runs and taking 252 wickets at an average of 18.41. His best bowling figures are 9 for 41 taken for Hetton Lyons on 11th May 2013. He has made 57 catches in the NEPL.

His stats will be updated as captain of the 2024 title winning side.

Marc Symington is a right-handed batsman and right arm medium faster. He batted at five on 20th April, scoring 6 and he came on first change to bowl; he took 0 for 15 from five overs. Allan Worthy recalls that "Symington was brilliant as a youngster, he started off as Norton, the funny thing was that he was very proud to have been born "north of the water," he was a proud Geordie, but his family had moved to Teesside when he was just a small child, so he grew up on Teesside. He came from a cricket family; I will get round to his brother, but his father Keith still plays, and he must be around seventy! He was nicknamed "Skids," physically he was around five foot nine tall, slightly built, when he bowled a bouncer, it was always throat high and would skid on to you, hence the nickname. He was brisk without getting to fast bowler in terms of his pace, but he swung it both ways and that was his skill.

As a batsman he was the rock around which we all batted, I wouldn't say he was the best batsman on our team, but he was the most important, he was a stopper, stoic in his attitude and how he applied himself, he would accumulate rather than smash his runs, he played spin very well, he was a good sweeper and fast between the wickets.

As he developed as a cricketer and certainly when he came to Burnmoor, he cut his pace when he bowled, running in off around eight paces with the keeper standing up and bowling very accurately, he was awful to bat against, especially on slow wickets, we had a lot of low scoring games in 2019, and Marc was a key part in our success in those games. He had a very astute cricket brain, he would contribute in the field and read the game very well, he was a thinker and that helped the team enormously as well. He was a fiery character and another hard-nosed cricketer, another good fit for our dressing room."

Marc Symington first came to notice on 26th July 1995 when he was selected to play for Cleveland Under 15's against Scotland Under 15's at Ampleforth, he made 75 not out and future multiple NEPL Player of the Year, Richard Waite had 41.

He next appeared on the radar on 7th July 1996 when he was playing for Durham Under 19's against Northumberland Under 19's at Roseworth Terrace. The following year he was selected by Durham, playing a Second XI fixture on 10th June 1997 at Worksop against Nottinghamshire's Seconds. He made his List A debut for Durham on 7th September 1997 at Leicestershire, his last List A appearance for them came on 4th September 2002 at Nottinghamshire.

He played 20 List A games for Durham, batting 15 times, with 1 not out, he scored 167 runs at an average of 11.92. His highest score was 34.

He bowled 534 balls with 2 maidens, conceding 528 runs and taking 9 wickets at an average of 58.66. His best bowling figures were 2 for 11. He made 7 catches.

Symington also played 2 List A games for Northumberland, his debut was on 28th August 2003 at Shropshire, the second, and last, was on 3rd May 2005 at Jesmond against Middlesex. He scored 18 runs at an average of 9.00 and bowled 36 balls for 39 runs and no wickets.

He also represented Northumberland in Minor Counites and Minor Counties Trophy matches, playing a further 75 times for them, batting 99 times, with18 not outs, he scored 2992 runs at an average of 36.93. He scored 17 half centuries and 5 centuries, his highest score was 122, scored in a 3-day match starting on 20th June 2003 at Buckinghamshire.

He bowled 7583 balls, with 218 maidens, conceding 4933 runs and taking 157 wickets at an average of 31.42. His best bowling figures were 6 for 61, taken in a 3-day match starting on 18th July 2010 at Norfolk. He made 46 catches.

Marc Symington made his first-class debut for Durham on 18th May 1998 in a 3-day match with Cambridge University, Quentin Hughes was among the University side. His last first-class game came in a 4-day match starting on 6th September 2002 at Trent Bridge against Nottinghamshire.

He played 13 matches at first-class level, batting 19 times, with 4 not outs, he scored 276 runs at an average of 18.39. His highest score was 42, scored in July 2002 against Northamptonshire.

He bowled 1202 balls, with 38 maidens, conceding 805 runs and taking 24 wickets at an average of 33.54. His best bowling was 4 for 27 in a 4-day game against Sri Lanka at The Riverside. He took 7 catches.

He was selected by ECB Schools North for a 2-day match starting on 14th July 1998 at The Denis Compton Oval against ECB Schools South. He top scored the innings with 35 as his side won by 18 runs.

He was selected to play for England Under 19's against Lancashire Second XI at Ramsbottom in a 4-day match. He played 8 times for England Under 19's, batting 12 times, with 1 not out, he scored 232 runs at an average of 21.09. He scored 1 half century, 66, which came on 25th May 1999 against Northamptonshire Second XI.

He bowled 569 balls, with 16 maidens, conceding 357 runs and taking 7 wickets at an average of 51.00. His best bowling figures were 1 for 26 and he took 3 catches.

Moving on to his NEPL career, Marc Symington made his NEPL debut for Norton on 6th May 2000 at Blaydon, he scored 17 and took 4 for 36, his first NEPL wicket was opener Ian Somerville, bowled for 4. His last game in the NEPL in this spell was on 3rd September 2005 at home to South North.

He played 88 matches for Norton in the NEPL during this period with them, he batted 88 times, with 15 not outs, he scored 2916 runs at an average of 39.94. He scored 24 half centuries and 1 century, 118 not out, made on 6th August 2005 at Gateshead Fell.

He bowled 6058 balls, with 203 maidens, conceding 3576 runs and taking 171 wickets at an average of 20.91. His best bowling figures were 6 for 46, taken on 25th May 2002 at South North. He made 30 catches.

He made his NEPL debut for Sunderland on 29th April 2006 at home to Stockton and his last NEPL game for Sunderland came on 8th September 2007 at home to The Durham Academy.

He played 36 matches in the NEPL for Sunderland, batting 36 times, with 11 not outs, he scored 1066 runs at an average of 42.64. He scored 8 half centuries and 1 century, 100, scored on 1st July 2006 at The Racecourse against Durham Academy.

He bowled 2649 balls, with 88 maidens, conceding 1431 runs and taking 90 wickets at an average of 15.90. His best bowling figures were 6 for 43, taken on 28th May 2007 at South North. He made 10 catches.

Marc and brother Craig were part of the NEPL representative side which won The President's Trophy in 2006, and which is covered earlier, and Marc was named NEPL Player of the Year in 2007.

He returned to Norton for the 2008 season, his first game being on 26th April at home to Chester le Street. In this spell he played there for this season only, his last appearance coming on 30th August 2008 at Stockton.

He played 20 matches for Norton in 2008, batting 17 times, with 2 not outs, he scored 566 runs at an average of 37.73. He scored 4 half centuries and 1 century, 113 not out, scored on 2nd August 2008 at home to Gateshead Fell.

He bowled 1028 balls, with 30 maidens, conceding 587 runs and taking 25 wickets at an average of 23.48. His best bowling figures were 6 for 51, taken on 26th April 2008 at home to Chester le Street. He made 9 catches.

He was named in the NEPL Team of the Decade in 2009.

He made his debut for Hartlepool in the N.Y.S.D League on 18th April 2009 and The N.Y.S.D League became a Premier League in 2012. His last game for Hartlepool in the N.Y.S.D Premier League was on 20th September 2014 at home to Marske.

He returned to Norton for the 2015 season, although now in the N.Y.S.D Premier League and remained there until June 2017.

He then debuted for Seaham Harbour at home to Willington on 1st July 2017 in the NEPL Division 1. He played his last game for them in NEPL Division 1 on 2nd September 2017 at Brandon.

He played his first game for Burnmoor in NEPL Division 1 on 21st April 2018 at Boldon, his last game for them was on 14th September 2019 at Chester le Street.

In the title winning season he played 19 matches, batting 16 times, with 4 not outs, he scored 243 runs at an average of 20.25. He scored 1 half century, 53 not out, on 15th June 2019 at home to Newcastle.

He bowled 678 balls, with 24 maidens, conceding 335 runs and taking 18 wickets at an average of 18.61. His best bowling figures were 4 for 21, taken on 27th April 2019 at Felling. He took 4 catches.

His NEPL career saw him play 163 matches, batting 157 times, with 32 not outs, he scored 4791 runs at an average of 38.32. He scored 37 half centuries and 3 centuries. His highest score was 118 not out, made for Norton at Gateshead Fell in 2005.

He bowled 10413 balls, with 345 maidens, conceding 5929 runs and taking 304 wickets at an average of 19.50. His best bowling figures were 6 for 43, taken in May 2007 for Sunderland at South North. He made 53 catches.

Craig Symington is the younger brother of Marc Symington, he was a right-handed batsman who batted at number six to start the 2019 season and made 25 not out, he also bowled five overs, taking 2 for 17. Allan Worthy recalls that "we all called him Junior; he had a stocky build; he became the ultimate all-rounder. He started as a wicketkeeper, in fact initially he showed more promise as a keeper than he did as a bowler, but he developed into a brisk medium pacer, yorkers and bouncers were his stock balls, he was a partnership breaker, he was a good fielder with a great throw. As a batsman he could drop anchor if needed but he liked to belt it, he liked to take on the spinner, sweep's, reverse sweep's and slog sweep's, he could drive spinners mad.

As an individual he was fiery, more so than Marc, he would get in your face, when he batted if you came at him with verbal's he gave you it back with more, he was one of those you didn't want to fire up, it made him bat much better. I think for both Craig and Marc they were the right people in the right place at the right time in respect of Burnmoor and the 2019 season."

Marc Symington first appeared on the record keepers' radar on 16th July 1998 when he opened the batting for Cleveland Under 15's against Scotland Under 15's at Middlesbrough, he scored 39 and took 1 for 9. Kyle Coetzer was in the Scotland side that day.

He made his NEPL debut for Norton on 6th May 2000 at Blaydon and marked the occasion with 82.

On 10th July 2000 Craig Symington played for Durham Under 17's in a 2-day match at Edinburgh against Scotland Under 17's. Once again Kyle Coetzer was playing for Scotland, future NEPL players Dan Shurben, Phil Mustard, Phil Bell, and Graeme Race among the Durham side. Symington continued to play for Norton in the NEPL.

On 2nd July 2001 he was selected and played for Durham Under 19's in a 50-over match against Scotland Under 17's at Longhirst, he scored 58. Kyle Coetzer continued his progress with the Scotland side and Liam Plunkett became the latest NEPL name to play alongside Craig Symington.

He continued to play for Norton in the NEPL until he his last game for them in the NEPL on 3rd September 2005 at home to South North. He played 105 times for them in the NEPL, batting 105 times with 20 not outs, he scored 2793 runs at an average of 32.85. He scored 17 half centuries with a highest score of 95 not out on 12th June 2004 at home to Tynemouth.

He bowled 324 balls, with 7 maidens, conceding 379 runs and taking 11 wickets at an average of 34.45. His best bowling figures were 4 for 80, taken on 8th July 2000 at Newcastle. He made 111 catches and 25 stumpings.

He made his NEPL debut for Sunderland on 29th April 2006 at home to Stockton.

As mentioned earlier in September 2006 Craig Symington played for the successful NEPL representative side in The President's Trophy.

He played his last NEPL game for Sunderland on 8th September 2007 at home against The Durham Academy. He made 54 against a strong Durham side.

He played 37 times for Sunderland in the NEPL, batting 31 times with 10 not outs, he scored 822 runs at an average of 39.14. He scored 9 half centuries with a highest score of 79 not out on 28th June 2007 at home to South Shields.

He bowled 162 balls, with 6 maidens, conceding 84 runs and taking 5 wickets at an average of 16.80. His best bowling figures were 5 for 37, taken on 12th August 2007 at Blaydon. He made 42 catches and 6 stumpings.

He made his debut for Billingham Synthonia in the North Yorkshire and South Durham Premier Division on 26th April 2008, he played there until 15th September 2012.

On 20th April 2013 he debuted for Hartlepool in the same league, playing his last game for them on 20th September 2014. He then returned to Norton, now playing in the same N.Y.S.D league, his last game for them was on 2nd September 2017.

He played 109 matches in the N.Y.S.D league, batting 100 times with 19 not outs, he scored 2911 runs at an average of 35.93. He scored 17 half centuries and 2 centuries, his highest score of 116 not out for Norton on 2nd July 2016 at Middlesbrough.

He bowled 14809 balls, with 126 maidens, conceding 3118 runs and taking 156 wickets at an average of 19.98. His best bowling figures were 7 for 14, taken on 25th August 2014 for Hartlepool at home to Great Ayton. He made 55 catches and 8 stumpings.

He then joined Burnmoor in NEPL Division 1, playing his first game on 5th May 2018 at Brandon. He played 19 times in NEPL Division 1 in 2018, batting 16 times with 3 not outs, he scored 285 runs at an average of 21.92. He scored 1 half century, 52, on 7th July 2018 at home to Boldon.

He bowled 242 balls, with 10 maidens, conceding 143 runs and taking 10 wickets at an average of 14.30. His best bowling figures were 4 for 21 on 7th May 2018 at home to Castle Eden. He made 8 catches and 1 stumping.

It was the first game of the 2019 season when Craig Symington next appeared in the NEPL, the season opener for Burnmoor. His contribution to the title winning season was that he played 15 matches, batting 10 times with 3 not outs, he scored 157 runs at an average of 22.42. His highest score was 26 not out on 20th July 2019 at home to Felling. He bowled 96 balls, with 3 maidens, conceding 107 runs and taking 3 wickets at an average of 35.66. His best bowling figures were 2 for 17 on the season opener at Eppleton. He took 12 catches.

His NEPL career saw him play 157 matches, batting 146 times with 33 not outs, he scored 3772 runs at an average of 33.38. He scored 26 half centuries with his highest score 95 not out for Norton in 2004 mentioned earlier.

He bowled 582 balls, with 16 maidens, conceding 570 runs and taking 19 wickets at an average of 30.00. His best bowling figures were 5 for 37 taken for Sunderland in 2007 mentioned earlier. He made 165 catches and 31 stumpings.

Alec Linsley is a left-handed batsman; he was also captain and wicketkeeper for the 2019 season. He was listed to bat at number seven to open the season but didn't get to bat, he did take a stumping in the game. Allan Worthy calls Linsley "Mr. Burnmoor, his father was first team captain and chairman and is now grounds man, Alec is now chairman and works behind the bar two nights a week. He runs the whole club. He will probably die in his club shirt; he is so dedicated he moved his office into the club house so he can do little jobs during the week.

He was initially against The Premier League, I think Burnmoor and Swalwell both had opportunities to join over the years after winning leagues and for their own reasons chose not to take them up, he eventually changed his mind and gave it a go. As a wicketkeeper I think he is underrated, he has good hands and loves to stand up to the seamers. He's a proper wicketkeeper in that he has a sharp wit, and he loves to wind batsman up. He bats at eleven these days, he is a good blocker, if you need to hold out for a draw, he's your man."

Records for Linsley show that he was playing for Burnmoor first team at least as far back as 29th June 2001 when he played in a JustSport Trophy match against Benwell Hill. Another JustSport Trophy appearance was recorded on 9th August 2007, again at Benwell Hill.

I suspect the reason these two fixtures cropped up is that a lot of the cricket archive records that I use have been updated by David McKay of Benwell Hill and when he has updated his club with competitions other than the NEPL, other clubs and players occasionally pop up!

By 2013 Burnmoor were playing in The Durham Cricket League for Burnmoor, and that league has much better online records. In 2015 Linsley and Burnmoor were playing in The NEPL Division 1, and both remained there until their promotion at the end of 2018.

His NEPL debut therefore came in the season opener of 2019 against Eppleton. He has now played 66 NEPL matches, batting 26 times with 18 not outs, he has scored 49 runs at an average of 6.12. His highest score is 11 not out. He has taken 54 NEPL catches and has 21 stumpings. He played throughout the 2024 season; an update will follow there!

Kevin Dixon is a right-handed batsman occasional off spin bowler; he was listed to bat at number eight to start the season but didn't get to bat or bowl. Allan Worthy describes Dixon as "a counter attacking batsman, he was a useful weapon if we were in trouble as he would come in and give it a go, he liked to whack it, hitting inside out over cover, he liked width when he was batting. As a bowler he was a handy fifth or sixth bowler, he started as an off spinner but became more of an away swing bowler, no pace just floating it up there. He also played non-league football to a good standard, Northern League, I know he was at Chester le Street for a while. He was a good lad around the team."

Dixon represented Durham Under 17's on 6th July 2003 against Scotland Under 17's at Edinburgh, he took 2 for 38.

He played for Kimblesworth in The Durham Cricket League before joining Burnmoor, playing in The NEPL Division 1 for them from 2015. His highest score at Division 1 level was 88 not out on 16th June 2016 at Burnmoor against Washington, his innings came from 120 balls and contained 12 fours. He and Allan Worthy, 107, added 169 for the fifth wicket on that day.

The season opener at Eppleton was his NEPL debut, his last NEPL game came on 13th July 2019 at Sacriston. He had played 8 matches in The NEPL for the club, batting 4 times, with 1 not out, he had scored 21 runs at an average of 7.00. His highest score was 11. He didn't bowl or take a catch in the NEPL.

Craig Stephenson is a right-handed batsman and right arm off break bowler. He was listed to bat at number nine to start his Burnmoor career in 2019 but didn't get to bat, he did bowl six overs, taking 0 for 24. Allan Worthy says that Stephenson "was about 5 foot 6 tall, stocky, powerful build, as a batsman he was a nurdler and nudger, he was another handy lad down the order, he would get you 20 when you needed it, he didn't get much chance to bat with our side, I'm sure he would have had more opportunities elsewhere, as a bowler he was old school off spin, he would bowl it slowly, give it plenty of air and then beat you with flight, he got a lot of stumpings and people caught in the infield ring when he bowled."

Stephenson was clearly a promising cricketer at a very young age, playing for Durham Under 12's on 29th July 2004 against Scotland Under 12's. On 3rd June 2005 he played for Durham Under 13's against Cumbria Under 13's at Lanchester. By 6th June 2006 Stephenson had progressed through to Durham Under 14s, playing a fixture at Horden against Cumbria Under 14's. Durham Under 15's came next, playing against Northumberland Under 15's at Percy Main.

The first recorded appearance I found for him in senior cricket was for Seaham Harbour in The Banks Salver Final on 4th May 2014 at Jesmond against Newcastle, he scored 7 and took 1 for 20 as Newcastle won by 5 wickets. The last appearance I found for Seaham Harbour was on 10th September 2016 at home to Blaydon in The NEPL Division 1.

Stephenson made his NEPL debut for Felling on 15th April 2017 at home to The Durham Academy. He took 3 for 47 when The Academy batted first, his first NEPL wicket was Ross Greenwell, future England player Matthew Potts was among his other two wickets. His last NEPL appearance for Felling came on 5th May 2018 at home to Whitburn.

He had played 20 matches in The NEPL for the club, batting 18 times, with 5 not out's, he had scored 89 runs at an average of 6.84. His highest score was 17 not out. He had also bowled 1203 balls, with 40 maidens, conceding 748 runs and taking 31 wickets at an average of 24.12. His best bowling figures were 5 for 14 on 17th June 2017 at home to Benwell Hill. He took 3 NEPL catches for Felling.

He has now played 71 matches for them, batting 40 times, with 18 not outs, he had scored 291 runs at an average of 13.22. His highest score was 45 not out, this came on 27th August 2022 at home to Eppleton.

He bowled 2858 balls for Burnmoor in the NEPL, with 74 maidens, conceding 1524 runs and taking 92 wickets at an average of 16.56. His best bowling figures were 6 for 12 on 20th July 2019 at home to Felling. He had taken 12 catches.

Stephenson had now played 91 matches in total in the NEPL, batting 58 times, with 23 not outs, he had scored 380 runs at an average of 10.85. His best score was 45 not out mentioned earlier.

He had bowled 4061 balls, with 114 maidens, conceding 2272 runs and taking 123 wickets at an average of 18.47. His best bowling was the 6 for 12 mentioned earlier. He has taken 15 NEPL catches.

Stephenson played for Burnmoor throughout the 2024 season, an update will follow later in the book!

Samiullah Khan is a right-handed batsman and left arm medium fast bowler, he was listed to bat at number ten at Eppleton in the first game of the season but didn't get to bat. He opened the bowling and took 1 for 49 from fourteen overs. This was his NEPL debut, he was the overseas pro for the season. He had played 2 One Day Internationals for Pakistan in 2007/08 and also played first class cricket in Pakistan, for Sargodha and Faisalabad, he would finish his first-class career in Pakistan with over 500 wickets.

Allan Worthy describes him in detail "Sami was brisk, he wasn't express like some of the West Indians who played in the league or like Ian Hunter, but he was quick enough. The thing is he was so skilful with the ball, he was a wizard around the wicket, if the ball didn't swing in the first over, he would go around the wicket, contradicting everything we thought about the game, left arm over the wicket bowl inswingers to right handers, he would make the ball swing into right handers from round the wicket, the number of batsmen who would shoulder arms to him and get bowled was incredible. He was tall, strongly built, with a long loping run up, but he had absolute control of the seam, Cameron Cuffy was the best bowler, of any type, I had seen in my time in the league, up to the point I played with Sami, he was the best bowler I saw in league cricket, that's how highly I rate him. He would also work out batsmen very quickly, after an over or so, his bouncer was quick enough to dump you on your backside and if he thought you weren't technically up to it as a batsman, he would bowl full, straight and fast at you. He would also ask us about the opposition, who they're best batsman was, he would then go after them, trying that bit harder at him to get us the wicket and an advantage.

I can tell you a couple of stories about him, he was loved in the dressing room and outside as well, he was a very modest man but I can recall one day in the dressing room and the lads were taking the mickey out of him, he said he knew Imran Khan, who was at the time Prime Minister of Pakistan, the mickey taking got worse, so he took out his phone, in front of the lads and rang Imran Khan, Khan answered and they chatted happily for ten minutes!

I remember another story, when he first came over, he had a flat in Washington, across the road was a corner shop, it was run by someone from the same village in Pakistan as Sami, he recognized him, knew who he was and wouldn't let him pay for things!

On a personal note, when I was batting, he used to like to go and pray behind the sightscreen when I was batting, especially if I was batting well!

Over the course of the season, and 2019 was a wet season, our batsmen often struggled on green wickets, and we were bowled out for 120 or less four or five times, Sami produced to win us the game, we would always fancy our chances in games because of Sami, we didn't win the league because of Sami, it was more complex than that, but we didn't win the league without him, such was his contribution. As a batsman Sami liked to hit sixes, he would attack spinners, he now coaches' bowlers in Pakistan, everywhere he goes he wins, he took over a provincial side in Pakistan and they won, he then took over a much smaller side and got them to a state final."

He had first played for Burnmoor in 2017, initially a couple of T20 games before appearing in NEPL Division 1 on 17th June 2017 at home to Burnopfield. He would complete the 2017 season and then return for 2018 in the same league achieving promotion with them as they finished runners up. His last game for Burnmoor in The NEPL came on 14th September 2019 at Chester le Street.

He had played 19 matches in The NEPL for the club, batting 11 times, with 3 not outs, he had scored 240 runs at an average of 30.00. He had scored 1 half century, his highest score, 55 not out, in his last NEPL game on 14th September mentioned earlier.

He had also bowled 1274 balls, with 76 maidens, conceding 463 runs and taking 46 wickets at an average of 10.06, his best bowling figures were 9 for 33 taken on 7th September 2019 at home to Benwell Hill. Just for the record, Ryan Pringle got the other wicket that day! He also took 4 NEPL catches in 2019.

Graeme Bridge is a right-handed batsman and slow left arm orthodox bowler, he was number eleven on the scorecard for 20th April 2019 to start the season, he didn't bat but he bowled eight overs and took 0 for 37. Bridge had played for England at Under 15, Under 17 and Under 19 level, he also had a successful first-class career with Durham, as a bowler. He played 40 first class matches from 1999 to 2006, batting 66 times, with 12 not outs, he scored 966 runs at an average of 17.88. He made 3 half centuries.

He bowled 6257 balls, with 252 maidens, conceding 3141 runs and taking 89 wickets at an average of 35.29. His best bowling figures were 6 for 84. He also took 20 catches.

He also played 49 List A matches for the county, batting 35 times, with 13 not out's, he scored 332 runs at an average of 15.09. His highest score was 50 not out. He also took 8 catches.

He also played 11 matches in the Twenty20 Blast, batting 7 times, with 1 not out, he scored 41 runs at an average of 6.83. He bowled 205 balls in the competition, with 0 maidens, conceding 214 runs and taking 10 wickets at an average of 21.40. His best bowling was 2 for 16.

Bridge made his NEPL debut on 6th May 2000 for Norton at Blaydon. He scored 25 when Norton batted first and took 0 for 27 with the ball. His first NEPL wicket came on 20th May 2000 at home to Tynemouth, Graeme Hallam being his victim, caught by Stephen Ball for 17. He took another wicket that day, finishing with 2 for 28.

Bridge played the entire season for Norton, his last game for them coming on 9th September at Gateshead Fell. He played 15 games in The NEPL for Norton, batting 15 times, with 2 not out's, he scored 337 runs at an average of 25.92. He scored 1 half century, 59 not out on 20th May at home to Tynemouth.

He bowled 638 balls, with 35 maidens, conceding 511 runs and taking 29 wickets at an average of 17.62. His best bowling figures were 5 for 45 taken on 29th July at Tynemouth. He also took 7 catches.

Bridge joined Stockton for the 2001 NEPL season, making his debut on 28th April at South North, he took 1 for 0 when South North batted, his first wicket for his new club was Michael Hall, bowled for 5. He played 10 games in The NEPL for Stockton, batting 9 times, with 2 not out's, he scored 212 runs at an average of 30.28. He scored 2 half centuries; his highest score was now 67 on 7th July at home to South North.

He bowled 764 balls for the club in the NEPL, with 29 maidens, conceding 366 runs and taking 12 wickets at an average of 30.50. His best bowling figures were 4 for 35 taken on 30th June at Blaydon. He also took 5 catches.

Bridge didn't appear in The NEPL at all in 2002, he next appeared making his debut for Chester le Street on 3rd May 2003 at Stockton. He marked his debut with 5 for 50. He only played 6 NEPL matches for Chester that season, he did return for 2004, 2005 and 2006 but his appearances were limited due to commitments with Durham. He played his last NEPL game for Chester on 9th September 2006 at home to Tynemouth.

In total he played 32 games in The NEPL for Chester, batting 26 times, with 7 not outs, he scored 528 runs at an average of 27.78. He scored 3 half centuries; his highest score was now 75 not out on 23rd July 2005 at home to Newcastle. He bowled 2111 balls for the club in the NEPL, with 75 maidens, conceding 883 runs and taking 71 wickets at an average of 12.43. His best bowling figures were 6 for 51 taken on 22nd May 2004 at home to Sunderland. He also took 8 catches.

Bridge signed to play for Blaydon for the 2007 season, making his NEPL debut for them on 28th April 2007 at home to South Shields and he played his last game for Blaydon in The NEPL on 5th September 2015 at Gateshead Fell. He had played 160 matches in The NEPL for them, batting 133 times, with 29 not outs, he had scored 3038 runs at an average of 29.21, with 17 half centuries and 1 century, 108, scored on 19th June 2010 at Newcastle, it came from 119 balls and contained 17 fours and 1 six.

He also bowled 11232 balls for Blaydon in the NEPL, with 403 maidens, conceding 5192 runs and taking 342 wickets at an average of 15.18. His best bowling figures for them was 6 for 21 on 31st August 2009 at home to South Shields. He also took 55 catches.

Bridge then signed for Sacriston for the 2017 season, making his debut on 23rd April at home to Sunderland in a NEPL Division 1 match. Bridge and Sacriston played their last match of the 2017 season on 2nd September at Boldon. His one season in Division 1 had seen him play 24 matches, batting 15 times, with 3 not outs, he scored 218 runs at an average of 18.16 and had a high score of 43.

He had also bowled 937 balls, with 26 maidens, conceding 544 runs and taking 35 wickets at an average of 15.54. His best bowling figures were 5 for 11. He also took 6 catches.

Sacriston was then promoted to The NEPL for the 2018 season, Bridge making his NEPL debut for them on 28th April at Eppleton. His last game for Sacriston in The NEPL came on 8th September 2018 at home to the Durham Academy. In total he played 17 matches in The NEPL for Sacriston, batting 12 times, with 3 not outs, he scored 186 runs at an average of 20.66. His highest score was 47 which came on 5th May at home to Tynemouth.

He bowled 1095 balls, with 21 maidens, conceding 731 runs and taking 33 wickets at an average of 22.15. His best bowling figures were 5 for 24 on 28th April at Eppleton.

Bridge then played for Burnmoor in the 2019 season, making his debut on 20th April at Eppleton. During the title winning season he played 19 NEPL matches for them, batting 5 times, with 0 not outs, he has scored 13 runs at an average of 2.60.

As a bowler he delivered 882 balls, with 39 maidens, conceding 413 runs and taking 35 wickets at an average of 11.80. His best bowling figures were 5 for 24 on 17th August at home to Tynemouth. He also had 5 catches.

He has now played 72 NEPL matches for the club, batting 35 times, with 10 not outs, he has scored 220 runs at an average of 8.80. His highest score is 35 not out, made on 8th July 2023 at home to South North.

As a bowler he has delivered 882 balls in The NEPL for Burnmoor, with 99 maidens, conceding 1654 runs and taking 117 wickets at an average of 14.13. His best bowling figures are now 6 for 22 taken on 17th April 2021 at Tynemouth. He also had 12 catches.

Bridge remains at Burnmoor, he played throughout the 2024 season and a further update will follow later in the book.

In his NEPL career to date, not counting the year in Division 1, he has now played 305 matches, batting 229 times, with 53 not out's, scoring 4518 runs at an average of 25.67. He has scored 23 half centuries and 1 century. The century made for Blaydon in 2010, 108 remains his highest score.

He has now bowled 19134 balls, that's 3189 overs.... With 662 maidens, he has conceded 9298 runs and taken 602 wickets at an average of 15.44. His best bowling figures are 6 for 21 taken for Blaydon in August 2009. He also had 88 NEPL career catches.

In addition to playing for Durham, Bridge also played 18 matches for Northumberland, batting 21 times, with 3 not outs, he scored 599 runs at an average of 33.27. He scored 4 half centuries and 1 century. The century, 120, came in a 3-day match which started on 19th August 2007 at Jesmond against Bedfordshire.

He also bowled 1584 balls, with 45 maidens, conceding 956 runs and taking 33 wickets at an average of 28.96. His best bowling figures were 5 for 58, taken on his debut, 29th April 2007 at Roseworth Terrace against Cumberland. He also took 5 catches.

His last game for Northumberland came on 26th April 2009 at Roseworth Terrace against Hertfordshire.

In respect of the season overall Allan Worthy recalls that "we got momentum going and we went with it, we had some good characters in the side, plenty of fighters and competitors in the side and when it came down to it, that stood us in good stead. As the season came to its end, there were three teams who could win the NEPL title that year, Burnmoor were in pole position, if we won, we won the league, South North needed to win and us to lose, Chester le Street were second, but they were playing us, they had to beat us and then hope South North got beat. Both Chester and South North had been there before, in South North's case more than once, I played for Blaydon and remember too well South North's history."

Burnmoor had 349 points, Chester le Street 326 and South North 324.

On the weekend of 14th September 2019 Burnmoor had to go to Chester le Street. Chester were a strong side at this time, with some experienced, quality players at this level, players such as John Coxon, Andrew Smith and Quentin Hughes.

South North were at Felling. The Felling side contained Paul Leonard; Leonard was the bowler who had taken ten wickets in an innings in an NEPL match in 2017 which is covered elsewhere in this book. Lee Crozier was missing for South North today, they won the toss and decided to bat.

Both games were cut to a maximum of 58 overs to the side batting first and 110 over in total, presumably through poor weather.

South North quickly lost their first wicket, Simon Birtwisle leg before to Leonard, 4 for 1.

They had opened with Sean Tindale, he and Chris Hewison took the score to 73 when Tindale was caught by Eddie Hurst off the bowling of Chris Nicholls for 30, South North 73 for 2.

Number four batsmen for South North was Adam Cragg, he was dismissed for 1, bowled by Nicholls, South North 75 for 3.

Hewison and number five Jaques du Toit put together a partnership of 81 when Hewison was bowled by Nicholls for 55, South North 156 for 4.

John Graham batted at six today for South North, he scored 3 when he was leg before, to Leonard, South North 161 for 5.

David Edwards batted at seven for South North, he was run out for 4 as they slipped to 167 for 6.

Oli McGee had come in at number eight, he and du Toit added 31, McGee had scored 4 when he was bowled by Leonard. I can only assume that du Toit was "teeing off" at this point, although South North were now 199 for 7.

The eighth wicket added 44, number nine batsman Alex Weetman scored 1 not out as du Toit was the next man out, he had scored 125 from 87 balls, with 14 fours and 6 sixes and South North were now 234 for 8.

They would declare on 243 for 8 from 49 overs, Weetman was 1 not out and James Ruddick was 9 not out. Jonny Wightman was the only batsman who didn't get to the crease. Paul Leonard took 4 for 82 and Chris Nicholls 3 for 50.

When Felling batted, they made a steady start, Alan Robson and joe Carroll putting on 27 for the first wicket, when Robson was caught behind by Adam Cragg off the bowling of Jonny Wightman for 11. Felling 27 for 1.

Nihil Shilar, Felling's overseas pro, came in next, he was bowled first ball by Wightman, Felling 27 for 2.

Dale Shaw came in at four, he scored a single when he was caught by Simon Birtwisle off the bowling of Sean Tindale, Felling 38 for 3.

Wicketkeeper Eddie Hurst came in at five, he next wicket to fall for 38, caught by John Graham off the bowling of Oli McGee, Felling 117 for 4.

Opener Joe Carroll was the next wicket to fall, he had scored 54 when he was caught and bowled by Jonny Wightman, Felling 126 for 5.

South North then picked up two wickets quickly, number six, Sam Witherspoon, was caught by Sean Tindale off Wightman for 2 and then Graham Wright, number seven, was caught and bowled by Oli McGee, he also made 2 and Felling were now 133 for 7.

At this point the Felling tail started to "wag," Paul Leonard batting at eight and Gavin Paton at nine, both made runs before Leonard was caught by Wightman off McGee for 14, Felling 172 for 8.

Anthony Trotter batting at ten then showed he was no mug with the bat as he and Paton added 23 for the ninth wicket, Paton next out for 38, caught by Chris Hewison off Simon Birtwisle, Felling 205 for 9.

This became 216 all out from 51.5 overs when Sean Tindale bowled number eleven Chris Nicholls for 2. Trotter was 32 not out. Only James Ruddick of the South North bowlers did not take a wicket, Wightman had 4 for 50, McGee 3 for 54, Tindale 2 for 33 and Birtwisle 1 for 30.

South North won by 27 runs and got 30 points for their efforts, This now put them on 354 points.

Chester le Street had won the toss and elected to bat, making a rocky start, losing skipper Coxon for 5, bowled by Sami Khan, Chester 5 for 1.

Andrew Smith had come in at three, he and opener Jacob McCann had added 70 for the second wicket when Smith was caught by Craig Symington off the bowling of Graeme Bridge for 47, Chester 75 for 2.

Quentin Hughes was next batting at four, but McCann was the next to go, caught by Alec Linsley behind the stumps off the bowling of Ryan Pringle for 23, Chester 91 for 3.

Liam Simpson came in at five, he was the next wicket to fall, bowled by Pringle for 11, Chester 123 for 4.

George Harrison came in at six and he had made 4 when he was stumped by Linsley off the bowling of Pringle, Chester were now 145 for 5.

Liam Burgess was batting at seven, he was leg before to Pringle for 17, Chester 171 for 6.

John Harrison came in at eight and was leg before first ball to Pringle, 171 for 7.

Ben Whitehead batted at number nine, he was 1 not out and Quentin Hughes was 54 not out, from 75 balls, with 6 boundaries, when Chester declared on 172 for 7 from 50 overs. Ryan Pringle had 5 for 49 from 14 overs, this is the spell Allan Worthy described earlier as the one which won the league! Graeme Bridge had 1 for 35 and Sami Khan 1 for 47 were the other wicket takers, Marc Symington had bowled seven overs 0 for 20 and Craig Stephenson 0 for 11 from four overs.

Burnmoor were now sitting on 352 points, South North at their halfway point 332 and Chester le Street 328.

The maximum points Chester could get was now 354, mathematically possible but not realistic, South North could obtain 356, so Burnmoor were very much in the driving seat.

When they batted Martin Hubber and Allan Worthy put on 54 for the first wicket, Hubber first out for 21, leg before to Ben Whitehead. Burnmoor 54 for 1.

Paul Craig had come in at three, he had scored 4 when he was caught by John Coxon off the bowling of Liam Burgess, Burnmoor 71 for 2.

Ryan Pringle came in at four, he had scored 7 when he was caught by Coxon off Whitehead, Burnmoor 82 for 3.

Allan Worthy recalls "The game had been chippy, lots of needle going both ways, The Chester lads kept saying we were bottlers, that we were blowing it, that we weren't good enough, we put Sami up the order, and he went after the spinners, I was still there at the other end."

Worthy finished 80 not out from 170 balls, he hit 9 fours and a six, Sami Khan was 55 not out from 87 balls with 6 fours and a six. Burnmoor 175 for 3 from 55.4 overs, they had won by seven wickets and the NEPL crown of 2019 with it.

The final points total saw them 22 points in front of South North with 376 points to South North's 354.

The 2019 Banks Salver was won by Washington, Burnmoor added the Twenty20 to their league title and Karl Turner of Hetton Lyons was named Player of the Year.

During the 2019 NEPL season Turner played 18 matches in the league, batting 18 times with 0 not outs, he scored 725 runs at an average of 40.27. He scored 6 half centuries and 1 century, 101, was scored on 18th May 2019 at home to Newcastle, the innings came from 135 balls and contained 9 fours and 2 sixes. Turner and Stuart Walker had put on 224 for the first wicket, Walker made 108 from 166 balls with 11 fours and 1 six.

He also bowled 867 balls in the NEPL in 2019, with 27 maidens, he conceded 491 runs and took 31 wickets at an average of 15.83. His best bowling figures were 7 for 15, taken on 31st August at Sacriston. He took 6 catches in the NEPL in 2019.

Karl Turner's career is covered elsewhere so here is a brief recap of his numbers up to the end of 2023.

He had played 201 matches in the NEPL, batting 189 times with 24 not outs, he had scored 5769 runs at an average of 34.96. He has scored 27 half centuries and 12 centuries, with a highest score of 209 not out, which is covered earlier in the book.

He has also bowled 6900 balls in the NEPL with 169 maidens and conceding 4469 runs and taking 212 wickets at an average of 21.08. His best bowling figures were 8 for 78, taken for Gateshead Fell in July 2010 and covered earlier. He has taken 69 catches and made 1 stumping.

TABLE 62 NEPL 2019.

	Played	Won	Draw/Aban	Lost	Penalty Points	Bonus Points	Points
Burnmoor	22	12	7	3	3	123	376
South North	22	10	9	3	1	122	354
Chester le Street	22	10	9	3	0	100	329
Eppleton	22	8	9	5	0	94	275
Hetton Lyons	22	7	8	7	0	101	265
Tynemouth	22	6	9	7	0	91	246
Benwell Hill	22	5	11	6	0	94	237
Burnopfield	22	5	10	7	0	91	230
Sacriston	22	5	11	6	0	81	226
Whitburn	22	4	11	7	1	76	194
Felling	22	3	9	10	1	73	171
Newcastle	22	2	7	13	2	53	124

TABLE 63 NEPL Batting Averages 2019.
Qualification 300 Runs.

Player	Club	Inns	N. O	H. S	Runs	Average
(1) Q.J Hughes	Chester le Street	12	6	116 no	441	73.50
(2) A.L Smith	Chester le Street	15	2	141 no	610	46.92
(3) K.J Coetzer	Benwell Hill	12	1	136 no	485	44.09
(4) C.J Pearce	Burnopfield	15	3	117 no	517	43.08
(5) J. McCann	Chester le Street	15	2	120	539	41.46
(6) K. Turner	Hetton Lyons	18	0	101	725	40.28
(7) T. Easton	Eppleton	17	4	59	506	38.92
(8) A. Worthy	Burnmoor	18	2	96	600	37.50
(9) R.D Pringle	Burnmoor	12	2	87	344	34.40
(10) M.A Jones	Tynemouth	16	0	82	521	32.56
(11) P.J Halliday	Benwell Hill	14	3	104 no	334	30.36
(12) J. du Toit	South North	19	1	125	544	30.22

TABLE 64 NEPL Bowling Averages 2019.
Qualification 20 Wickets.

Player	Club	Overs	Mdns	Runs	Wkts	Average
(1) Sami Khan	Burnmoor	212.2	76	463	46	10.07
(2) C. Stephenson	Burnmoor	79.2	18	232	22	10.55
(3) W.R.S Gidman	Sacriston	131.1	32	368	32	11.50
(4) G.D Bridge	Burnmoor	147.0	39	413	35	11.80
(5) L.J Crozier	South North	148.5	38	382	29	13.17
(6) A. Ebdale	Eppleton	105.0	21	296	22	13.45
(7) F. Lonnberg	Tynemouth	120.0	19	359	26	13.81
(8) L.O Mussett	Benwell Hill	121.1	24	390	28	13.93
(9) S.J Tindale	South North	197.4	40	653	43	15.19
(10) M.L Pollard	Tynemouth	124.4	20	431	28	15.39
(11) C.T Harding	Benwell Hill	162.0	38	463	30	15.43
(12) C Winn	Hetton Lyons	138.3	29	468	30	15.60
(19) R.D Pringle	Burnmoor	128.1	22	404	23	17.57

Burnmoor CC 2019 NEPL Champions.

Left to Right- Back Row- Ian Linsley, Gary Brown, Sami Nazir, Craig Stephenson, Paul Craig, Allan Worthy, Ryan Pringle, Kevin Dixon, Mckenzie Wright, Ross Hodgson, Martin Hubber, Martin Thursfield.

Front Row- Connor Wright, Riley Blunt, Graeme Bridge, Alec Linsley, Craig Symington, Marc Symington.

Allan Worthy, seen here going to bat for Burnmoor at Tynemouth on 13th August 2016.

Photo Courtesy of Ken Waller.

Karl Turner, seen here bowling for Barnard Castle at South North on 4th June 2017.

Photo Courtesy of Ken Waller.

At the end of the 2019 season the clubs selected their NEPL Team of 20 Years.

Eight of the team had been part of the 2009 Team of the Decade, now seems to be a good time to update the statistics of those individuals and discuss the new additions, Richard Waite has shared his memories of the team. All the players will have statistics updated to at least the end of 2019, in the case of the South North players who went on to win additional titles, they will be updated beyond 2019 in the relevant section to their title win.

The team listed by The NEPL was as follows.

Simon Birtwisle had been named NEPL Player of the Year in 2005 and jointly in 2015. He won NEPL titles with Benwell Hill in 2002, Chester le Street in 2009 and 2010, South North in 2017 and 2018, 2021 to 2023 inclusive.

Richard Waite played with Birtwisle at Chester le Street, he remembers Birtwisle well, saying he first came across him in the N.Y.S.D playing a game for Stockton against Darlington R.C.A. Waite goes on "in the dressing room Simon was always neat and tidy, everything had its place, he used to like the dressing room door shut as he sat with the pads on, waiting to go out to bat, some of the lads picked up on this and, as is the way of cricket dressing rooms the world over, they would deliberately leave the door open, Simon would have to get up and close it, it wasn't done with malice this just sums up both Simon and dressing rooms really. Simon was always the first at the ground on a match day, he paired up with Alan Mustard and they would hit dozens and dozens of balls to get ready for the game. When he was at Benwell Hill we noticed he liked to walk towards square leg after every ball, we put a man there and told him not to move to try and disrupt his routine!

As a batsman he used to smash anything short of a length, he was an unbelievable player of the short ball, he also had a tough, gritty side to him, and he could tough it out when necessary.

His spin bowling, I think was under rated, he had a very simple technique, he practically tip toes to the wicket, uncomplicated but effective. I feel he could definitely have bowled more; I think the strength of the teams he has played for probably prevented him from doing so."

Up to 2019 Simon Birtwisle had played 350 NEPL matches, batting 342 times with 27 not outs, he had scored 11026 runs at an average of 35.00. He had scored 63 half centuries and 14 centuries, his highest score was 151 not out, scored on 3rd July 2010 for Chester le Street at home to Stockton.

He had bowled 5716 balls, with 177 maidens, conceding 3271 runs and taking 159 wickets at an average of 20.57. His best bowling figures were 6 for 18, taken on 7th September 2019 at home to Sacriston.

He has taken 116 catches in the NEP up to the end of 2019.

Allan Worthy had been named NEPL Player of the Year in 2001. He had won an NEPL title in 2001 with Chester Le Street and then again in 2019 with Burnmoor in the season just completed. Up until the 2019 season Worthy had played his last NEPL match on 10 September 2016 at The Riverside against The Durham Academy.

Richard Waite describes him as "he would have been perfect for Bazball, he was so aggressive, if the ball was pitched up it was going for six. I clearly remember a game for The NEPL side at Philadelphia, he hit the first ball over cover, over the boundary, over the adjacent car park and into the street, it was a huge hit. He tried to do it again with the next ball and got bowled but that was Allan. He was such a good player that teams were frightened of him, you could see sides go defensive against him from the off, they knew the damage he could do to them. He was a contradiction when batting, in between balls he would walk around, chat a bit to the other batsman, totally relaxed, at his own pace and then he would explode smashing the ball to all parts. Around the dressing room he was a very dry man, he had a great sense of humour, he is a very easy man to be around and brilliant to spend time with, especially at cricket."

By this time, he had played in The NEPL for Chester le Street, Gateshead Fell, Blaydon, Hetton Lyons and Stockton. In total he had played 312 NEPL matches, batting 303 times with 38 not outs, he had scored 10451 NEPL runs at an average of 39.43. He had scored 65 half centuries and 19 centuries, his highest score was 156 not out on 26th May 2007 for Blaydon at Chester le Street. He had also bowled 4974 balls, with 165 maidens, conceding 2757 runs and taking 111 wickets at an average of 24.83. Not surprisingly, the 8 for 12 mentioned earlier remained his best bowling figures. He had also taken 164 catches.

As stated earlier, he had joined Burnmoor in NEPL Division 1 for the 2017 season. At the time of writing, the end of the 2023 season, Allan Worthy has now played 385 NEPL matches, batting 371 times with 44 not outs, he has scored 12062 runs at an average of 36.88. He has scored 73 half centuries and 20 centuries, his highest score is 156 not out, mentioned earlier. He has bowled 5123 balls, with 169 maidens, conceding 2865 runs and taking 114 wickets at an average of 25.13. His best bowling figures remain 8 for 12 mentioned earlier. He has taken 196 NEPL catches. Worthy would go on to be part of the 2024 title winning side and an update will follow there.

Chris Hewison has won NEPL titles in 2003 to 2008 inclusive, 2011, 2021 to 2023, all with South North. Richard Waite says of Hewison "I wouldn't want to stand in front of him when he's batting, at under sixteen, under seventeen level he and Michael Gough were the best two youngsters around. Initially he hit the ball hard through timing and technique, as he developed physically the power came along with it as he matured. He could and would score everywhere, there were times I would ask myself, where do I bowl to him? He hit it off his legs, he could drive the ball, he was a violent puller of the short ball, an unbelievable player. He also had a presence about him at the crease, he was dominant, and he had all the shots, I would look at his score and think, to be the highest run scorer of the season, I had to outpace him. As a youngster he had been a good bowler too, he got it through at a decent pace and used to have a nice away swinger. Off the field he was a great lad, quiet in the dressing room, on reflection he would be in the top three of batters I played with or against in the NEPL."

Chris Hewison effectively has had 2 spells with South North in the NEPL, at the risk of duplicating some stats I'm going to break it into two or three parts. He made his debut in the NEPL on 29th April 2000 for South North at Stockton, his last game of this period was on 10th September 2011 at Sunderland.

He played 207 matches, batting 198 times, with 33 not outs, he scored 7230 runs at an average of 43.81. He scored 36 half centuries and 18 centuries. His highest score was 165 not out, made on 22nd June 2002 at Philadelphia.

He bowled 1893 balls, with 51 maidens, conceding 1107 runs and taking 32 wickets at an average of 34.59. His best bowling figures were 3 for 25, on 20th July 2002 at Norton. He made 114 catches in this period.

He spent the next few years at Swalwell and next appeared in the NEPL on 20th April 2019, for South North, at Hetton Lyons. The 2019 season saw him play 19 matches, batting 19 times, with 0 not outs, he scored 465 runs at an average of 24.47. He scored 4 half centuries, his highest score was 87, scored on 11th May 2019 at Tynemouth. He didn't bowl during 2019 but took 13 catches.

In respect of the Team of the Decade, up to the end of 2019, Chris Hewison had played 226 matches, batting 217 times with 33 not outs, he scored 7695 runs at an average of 41.82. He had scored 40 half centuries and 18 centuries, his highest score was 165 not out mentioned earlier.

He bowled 1893 balls, with 51 maidens, conceding 1107 runs and taking 32 wickets at an average of 34.59. His best bowling remained the 3 for 25 mentioned earlier. He had taken 127 catches in the NEPL to this point. Chris Hewison's stats will be updated later as part of the South North title years in 2023.

Jaques du Toit had been named NEPL Player of the Year jointly in 2015 and individually in 2016. Richard Waite recalls "I didn't play much against him, he came to the league from County Cricket, he was a bit of an unknown initially, but we quickly learnt that he was a powerful, aggressive batsman, he was very strong off his legs, and you couldn't give him any width. At Jesmond on their wickets, he would score heavily. As a bowler he would just chip away at you with his spin, he was always talking to the batsman, always at you, he could be in your face if the situation arose!"

He had indeed played first class cricket, playing for Easterns in South Africa and Colombo in Sri Lanka, as well as Leicestershire in England. He played 37 first-class matches for Leicestershire, batting 60 times with 2 not outs, he scored 1784 runs at an average of 30.75. He scored 8 half centuries and 4 centuries, his highest score was 154 on 21st April 2010 at Fenner's, Cambridge against Cambridge M.C.C University.

He bowled 384 balls for the county, with 5 maidens, conceding 273 runs and taking 5 wickets at an average of 54.60. His best bowling figures were 3 for 31 taken in a County Championship Division 2 match at Grace Road against Gloucestershire. He took 31 catches.

He played 50 List A matches for Leicestershire, batting 48 times with 2 not outs, he scored 1238 runs at an average of 26.91. He scored 4 half centuries and 2 centuries, his highest score was 144, made on 10th August 2008 at Glamorgan. He didn't bowl at this level but made 19 catches.

He played 55 Twenty20 matches for Leicestershire, batting 49 times with 6 not outs, he scored 646 runs at an average of 15.02. He scored 1 half century, 69, scored on 25th June 2010 at Grace Road against Lancashire. He bowled 32 balls at this level, 0 maidens, conceding 41 runs and taking 2 wickets, he also took 29 catches.

In addition to playing for Leicestershire, du Toit would also play minor counties cricket for Northumberland and Cumbria. Although not in datal order, I'm going to deal with his Northumberland career first, he made his debut for them on 19th May 2013 at Cambridgeshire.

Across all formats he played 50 times for Northumberland, batting 71 times with 3 not outs, he scored 3041 runs at an average of 44.72. He scored 3041 runs at ana average of 44.72. He scored 18 half centuries and 10 centuries. His highest score was 150, scored in a 3-day Championship starting on 13th August 2013 at Jesmond against Norfolk.

He bowled 1853 balls, with 27 maidens, conceding 1337 runs and taking 45 wickets at an average of 29.71. His best bowling figures were 6 for 64, taken in a 3-day match starting on 16th August 2015 at Bedfordshire. He made 35 catches for Northumberland.

He played 1 match for Cumbria, a 3-day match starting on 3rd July 2022 at Preston Avenue, North Shields against Northumberland, he scored 1 in his only innings and took 0 for 30.

Jaques du Toit made his NEPL debut on 27th April 2013 for Newcastle at Blaydon, he marked the occasion with 84 and took 5 for 30! His first NEPL wicket was Blaydon opener Craig Burke, bowled for 67. He played his last game for Newcastle in this spell on 8th September 2018 at home to Stockton.

During this period with Newcastle, he played 121 matches, batting 107 times with 17 not outs, he scored 4845 runs at an average of 53.83. He scored 25 half centuries and 13 centuries. His highest score was 183, scored on 16th May 2015 at Whitburn. The innings came from 128 balls and contained 21 fours and 11 sixes.

He bowled 7351 balls for Newcastle in the NEPL, 162 maidens, conceding 4296 runs and taking 186 wickets at an average of 23.09. His best bowling figures were 6 for 25, taken on 13th July 2013 at Jesmond against Blaydon. He took 80 NEPL catches for Newcastle.

He made his NEPL debut for South North on 20th April 2019 at Hetton Lyons. He played 20 matches for South North in the 2019 season, batting 19 times with 1 not out, he scored 544 runs at an average of 30.22. He scored 4 half centuries and 1 century, 125, scored on 14th September 2019 at Felling, the innings came from 87 balls and contained 14 fours and 6 sixes.

He bowled 156 balls, with 4 maidens, conceding 66 runs and taking 4 wickets at an average of 16.50. His best bowling figures were 2 for 25, taken on 24th August at home to Chester le Street. He made 9 catches.

By the end of the 2019 season du Toit had played 141 matches in the NEPL, batting 126 times with 18 not outs, he had scored 5389 runs at an average of 49.89. He had scored 29 half centuries and 14 centuries, his highest score was the 183 mentioned earlier.

He had bowled 7507 balls, with 165 maidens, conceding 4362 runs and taking 190 wickets at an average of 22.95. His best bowling was the 6 for 25 mentioned earlier. He had taken 89 NEPL catches to this point.

After the 2020 Covid Season he made his NEPL debut for Burnopfield on 17th April 2021 at Benwell Hill, his last NEPL game for Burnopfield was on 11th September 2021 at Chester le Street.

He played 18 matches in the NEPL for Burnopfield, batting 18 times with 3 not outs, he scored 582 runs at an average of 38.79. He scored 4 half centuries and 1 century, 107, made on 21st August 2021 at home to Felling, it came from 65 balls and contained 6 fours and 9 sixes.

He bowled 846 balls in the NEPL for the club, with 12 maidens, conceding 489 runs and taking 20 wickets at an average of 24.45. His best bowling figures were 5 for 25, taken on 4th September 2021 at Whitburn. He took 9 NEPL catches for Burnopfield.

He then returned to Newcastle for the 2022 season, his first game of the second spell being at Jesmond against South North. At the time of writing, April 2024 he remains at Newcastle, his stats to this point are that he has played another 38 matches for Newcastle, batting 37 times with 6 not outs, he scored 1312 runs at an average of 42.32. He has scored 11 half centuries and 1 century, 101 not out, scored on 14th May 2022 at Eppleton, the innings came from 94 balls and contained 7 fours and 8 sixes.

He bowled 1709 balls, with 29 maidens, conceding 1044 runs and taking 44 wickets at an average of 23.72. His best bowling figures were 5 for 32, taken on 3rd June 2023 at Jesmond against Burnmoor. He has taken 19 catches for Newcastle in this period.

At the time of writing, the end of the 2023 season, Jaques du Toit has now played 197 matches in the NEPL, batting 181 times with 27 not outs, he has scored 7283 runs at an average of 47.29. He has scored 44 half centuries and 16 centuries, his highest score is 183, mentioned earlier for Newcastle at Whitburn. He has bowled 10062 balls in the NEPL, with 207 maidens, conceding 5895 runs and taking 254 wickets at an average of 23.20. His best bowling figures were 6 for 25 mentioned above for Burnopfield at Whitburn. He has taken 117 NEPL catches. He played for Newcastle throughout the 2024 season, adding 5 half centuries and 567 runs at an average of 35.43 and a further 18 wickets at an average of 29.16 to his career totals.

John Graham was named captain of the Team of the Decade. He had been named NEPL Player of the Year in 2002 and had won NEPL titles with South North in 2003 to 2008 inclusive, 2011 and 2012, 2014 and 2015, 2017 and 2018, finishing off in 2021. He was captain of the side up until mid-way through the 2016 season. Richard Waite says of Graham "John knew his own game very, very well. He was very strong on the offside, especially through cover point, he would play with an open face, and you used to think this gave you a chance, it didn't, it was his way of manipulating fields and accumulating runs, he had a gritty, determined feel to his batting, if he got to thirty, as a bowler you knew you had a problem. He just knew how to get the job done, if there was a battle, John is the guy I would send out. I tried to bowl as straight as possible to him. As a captain he wasn't afraid to make changes, it's all very well saying that he had great resources to call upon, but they need managing and taking off and talking to, South North had some strong characters and good cricketers but it's to his credit that he moulded them into a unit. John sort of typifies the South North attitude of the period, he sort of put his DNA into them all and they were all competitors, they were all fighters in the cricketing sense, I believe it's probably still there at the club now."

By the end of the 2019 season he had played 380 NEPL matches, all for South North, batting 353 times, with 51 not outs, he scored 11016 runs at an average of 36.47. He scored 78 half centuries and 12 centuries, his highest score was 132, made on 29th July 2006 at South North against Blaydon.

He bowled 2840 balls, with 98 maidens, conceding 1606 runs and taking 66 wickets at an average of 24.33. His best bowling figures were 4 for 15 taken on 31st May 2008 at Jesmond against Newcastle. He had taken 176 NEPL catches up to the end of 2019.

Graham would play 7 matches in the Covid season of 2020 in the Banks Salver competition that was put in place instead of the conventional NEPL and a further 4 NEPL games in 2021.

He didn't play in the NEPL in 2022 but did make his debut for Tynemouth on 10th June 2023 at home to Burnopfield, he didn't bat or bowl. He played another game on 17th June for Tynemouth at home to Hetton Lyons, he scored 7 and, to date, these are the only runs he has scored in the NEPL which are not for South North.

By the end of the 2023 season, Graham has played 386 matches in the NEPL, batting 358 times with 51 not outs, he has scored 11069 runs at an average of 36.05. He scored 78 half centuries and 12 centuries, his highest score remains the 132 mentioned earlier. His bowling figures remain unchanged from 2019, and he has now taken 183 catches in the NEPL.

Jonny Wightman had been named NEPL Player of the Year in 2014 and won NEPL titles with South North in 2011 and 2012, 2014 and 2015, 2017 and 2018, 2021 to 2023 inclusive. Richard Waite describes Wightman as "the most awkward bowler I faced in The NEPL, he would hustle in at pace and then he had a slightly different action, a bit slingy, he picked his length very well, he had an effective bouncer and an unbelievable yorker, for a bowler of his pace he had great control of the ball, he was tough to face, I used to tell myself just get through his first ten balls, he was an aggressive bowler who set aggressive fields, short legs and the like, and he would bowl well to those fields. He was a relatively quiet man off the field but put the ball in his hand and his persona changed, if you got one away, he would be at you, verbally and with the ball, the next one was always a bit quicker, he also kept you looking out for his bouncer."

By the end of the 2019 season Wightman had played 207 matches in the NEPL, he had batted 103 times, with 37 not outs, he had scored 680 runs at an average of 10.30. His highest score was 37, made on 14th May 2011 at Roseworth Terrace for South North against Blaydon.

He had bowled 12357 balls, with 297 maidens, conceding 7544 runs and taking 407 wickets at an average of 18.53. His best bowling figures were 8 for 31, taken on 4th June 2016 at Roseworth Terrace for South North at home to Gateshead Fell. He had taken 26 NEPL catches by the end of 2019.

Further updates on Wightman will appear in the later chapters of the book.

Quentin Hughes won NEPL titles in 2001, 2009, 2010 and 2016, all with Chester le Street. Richard Waite says that "Hughes, along with Alan Walker, probably shaped my cricket career more than anyone, I learnt so much from my time at Chester le Street. He was a real leader of the team, he always had a plan, he would encourage and back his players to the hilt, Quentin had this huge drive to win, he wanted to win, and he knew how to win, he was so competitive, he was an excellent communicator within the team environment, he always wanted to bat.

As a batsman he was a true nurdler, he would accumulate, runs by playing awkward shots and hitting it to awkward places. At Chester when I was there, he was surrounded by more aggressive players than he was, but he realized someone had to be the glue which held the innings together, that was his role, he was clever at taking singles, rotating or giving up the strike, he was exceptional at batting with the tail, it was like he knew what had to be done and he knew exactly how he was going to achieve it. He was the constant in our team.

As a bowler Quentin was a non-spinning off spinner! He would set his fields as if he was an off spinner then bowl away swingers, he would leave mid-on open, and I would stand at slip and watch all these batsmen try and push him through mid-on and then wonder why I had caught them at slip! He was also very accurate and got a lot of leg before's."

Up to the end of the 2019 season Hughes had played 338 matches in the NEPL, batting 300 times, with 74 not outs, he has scored 8791 runs at an average of 38.89. He has scored 61 half centuries and 5 centuries, his highest score is 136 not out, scored on 9th July 2005 at home to Benwell Hill. The innings came from 160 balls and contained 15 fours and a six.

He has bowled 12108 balls, with 443 maidens, conceding 5939 runs and taking 317 wickets at an average of 18.73. His best bowling figures were 6 for 38 on 12th June 2010 at The Riverside against Durham Academy. He has taken 118 catches in the NEPL up to this point.

To date, by the end of the 2023 season, Hughes has played 386 matches in the NEPL, batting 342 times, with 82 not outs, he has scored 10111 runs at an average of 38.88. He has scored 68 half centuries and 6 centuries. His highest score remains 136 not out, scored on 9th July 2005 at home to Benwell Hill.

He has bowled 14585 balls, with 523 maidens, conceding 7067 runs and taking 374 wickets at an average of 18.89. His best bowling figures remain the 6 for 38 on 12th June 2010 at The Riverside against Durham Academy. He has taken 133 catches in the NEPL up to this point.

He continued to play throughout 2024, adding 101 runs and 22 wickets at an average of 20.40 to his totals.

Phil Nicholson was selected as the wicketkeeper; he had won the NEPL title in 2002 with Benwell Hill and played all his NEPL cricket for them. Richard Waite says "I played a lot for Northumberland when he was captain. As captain he was excellent, his character is jovial, chatty, upbeat and that came through into his cricket, he was a great one for telling stories. He created a good team spirit and atmosphere for the county, he understood cricket, and this led to him helping his bowlers by giving them fields which helped them out. As a batsman he liked to sweep the spinners, he reminded me of John Graham in the way he would accumulate his runs. As a keeper he was old school, he loved to stand up to everybody, he was brilliant to bowl to."

By the end of the 2019 season, he had played 339 matches in the NEPL, all for Benwell Hill, batting 284 times, with 43 not outs, he scored 6361 runs at an average of 26.39. He scored 29 half centuries and 5 centuries. His highest score was 138, scored on 3rd June 2017 at Hetton Lyons. The innings came from 155 balls and contained 17 fours and a six. He took 245 catches and had 71 stumpings.

To date, Phil Nicholson played his last NEPL fixture on 7th May 2022 at Eppleton. He played 358 matches in the NEPL, all for Benwell Hill, batting 294 times, with 46 not outs, he scored 6535 runs at an average of 26.35. He scored 30 half centuries and 5 centuries, his highest NEPL score was 138, made on 3rd June 2017 at Hetton Lyons, the innings came from 138 balls and contained 17 fours and a six. He bowled 41 balls in his NEPL career, 0 for 37! He made 246 catches and 71 stumpings.

He also captained Northumberland, playing 175 matches, batting 189 times, with 49 not outs, he scored 2938 runs at an average of 20.98. He scored 10 half centuries and 2 centuries, his highest Northumberland score remains 107 not out, scored on 6th June 2010 at Jesmond against Hertfordshire.

He bowled 58 balls, with 0 maidens and took 1 wicket for 108 and he took 265 catches and had 51 stumpings for Northumberland.

Stephen Humble had been named NEPL Player of the Year in 2006 and he won NEPL titles in 2005, 2006, 2007, 2008, 2010, 2011, 2014, 2014, 2015 and 2017 with South North. Richard Waite calls Humble "an absolute nightmare to bowl against, we would get South North five or six down for not many then Humble would come out to bat, he would invariably get forty or fifty and you were chasing a score. He was certainly no mug with the bat, he never got flustered, although he wasn't a great driver of the ball. He was an intelligent cricketer, he could be very patient to start, he would have a look, weigh things up, and then he would use the long handle, you didn't want him there at the end of an innings especially the last three overs or so, you had to get him early.

As a bowler he swung it round corners, he had a smooth run up and would bowl a good length, swinging it away from the right hander, he had an inswinger as well and great control over both. He was incredible at setting a batsman up, he would bowl repeatedly on off stump and then just put one down a bit wider, sixth stump sort of line, he got a lot of wickets bowled, leg before and caught behind, either by keeper or slips."

After spending 2018 in NEPL Division 1 with Brandon Humble spent the 2019 season at Burnopfield. He played his last game in the NEPL on 14th September 2019 for Burnopfield at Sacriston, he made 52 not out and took 1 for 39. The wicket, his last in the NEPL, was opener Ross Williams, bowled for 13.

He played 16 matches for Burnopfield in the NEPL in 2019, batting 14 times with 3 not outs, he scored 319 runs at an average of 29.00. He scored 2 half centuries, his highest score, 56, was made on 27th April at South North.

He bowled 679 balls, with 32 maidens, conceding 354 runs and taking 17 wickets at an average of 20.82. His best bowling figures were 3 for 16, taken on 3rd August at home to Burnmoor. He took 4 catches.

In total, Stephen Humble played 283 matches in the NEPL, he batted 202 times, with 48 not outs, he scored 3881 at an average of 25.20. He scored 17 half centuries with the highest score of 92 mentioned earlier.

He bowled 17329 balls, that's 2886.1 overs, with 726 maidens, conceding 7844 runs and taking 547 wickets at an average of 14.34. His best bowling figures were 8 for 55 mentioned earlier. He made 80 catches.

Kieran Waterson had been named NEPL Player of the Year in 2012 and 2018. Richard Waite says that "I didn't play against him much, I remember that he wasn't express in terms of pace, but he was accurate, he kept the ball in and around the danger area. He had good control over his line and length and although he tended to bowl away swing, he could bring it back in at you. He was a wicket taking bowler."

Waterson had now played 158 games in the NEPL, batting 88 times, with 39 not outs, he scored 389 runs at an average of 7.93. His highest score was 28 not out.

He bowled 11065 balls, with 380 maidens, conceding 6209 runs and taking 347 wickets at an average of 17.89. His best bowling figures was 8 for 53 on 16th June 2018 for Whitburn against The Durham Academy. He also took 37 catches.

Waterson continued to appear in The NEPL until his last appearance on 10th September 2022 for Sunderland at home to South North, although he has re-appeared in the NEPL in 2024 following Sunderland's promotion.

At this point, the end of 2022, he had played in 197 NEPL matches, batting 119 times, with 44 not outs, scoring 583 runs at an average of 7.77. His highest score was now 41 not out, made on 28th August 2021 for Whitburn at Eppleton. He had now bowled 13495 balls, with 462 maidens, conceding 7579 runs and taking 422 wickets at an average of 17.95. His best bowling figures remained the 8 for 53 mentioned earlier. He also took 51 catches.

After the 2020 pandemic season Waterson resumed his NEPL career with Whitburn, playing his last NEPL game for the club on 11th September 2021 at home to Tynemouth.

He made his NEPL debut for Sunderland on 16th April 2022 at Tynemouth, he played his last game in the NEPL for Sunderland on 10th September 2022 at Burnmoor, although he has re-appeared as stated above!

He had played 197 matches in the NEPL, batting 119 times, with 44 not outs, he scored 583 runs at an average of 7.77. His highest score was 41 not out, scored on 28th August 2021 for Whitburn at Eppleton.

He bowled 13495 balls in the NEPL, with 462 maidens, conceding 7579 runs and took 422 wickets at an average of 17.95. His best bowling figures were 8 for 53, mentioned earlier taken in June 2018 for Whitburn at Benwell Hill. He took 51 career catches.

He continues to play, following Sunderland's relegation at the end of 2022, Waterson played 17 times for them in NEPL Division 1 in 2023 and returned to the NEPL with the club in 2024, adding 17 wickets at an average of 22.23 to his career NEPL stats.

Richard Waite had been named NEPL Player of the Year in 2003, 2004, 2008, 2009 and 2013 and he had won NEPL titles in 2009 and 2010 with Chester Le Street and 2013 with Stockton. Waite says of his own cricket career "I was privileged to have the opportunities and experiences I did through cricket, cricket has given me everything, I left school with not great results but got a cricket scholarship to Worcester University, you could say I got my education through cricket, in later years Geoff Cook offered me the chance to become a cricket development officer and cricket has now been in every part of my life, I now look at my children playing cricket and I love the fact that they're playing cricket and I can share my passion for it with them."

Waite played his last NEPL game on 7th July 2018 at Stockton against South North. He had played 321 NEPL games, batting 302 times, with 26 not outs, he had scored 8857 runs at an average of 32.09, he had scored 48 half centuries and 15 centuries. His highest score was 150 not out on 22nd May 2010 for Chester Le Street at home to South Shields.

He had bowled 22061 balls, with 783 maidens, conceding 11514 runs and taking 575 NEPL wickets at an average of 20.02. His best bowling figures remained the 8 for 28 taken on 10th June 2006. He had also taken 98 catches.

Lee Crozier won NEPL titles in 2002 with Benwell Hill, then further titles with South North in 2004 to 2008 inclusive, 2011 and 2012, 2014 and 2015, 2017 and 2018, 2021, to 2023 inclusive. Richard Waite says of Crozier "I enjoyed playing against Lee, it was always a challenge and a battle, off the field, as a fellow spinner, I enjoyed chatting to him about our shared experiences. As a bowler he was skilful, he could certainly spin the ball, but he also had a really good arm ball that went away from you. Despite his gentlemanly demeanour he could get in your face, if you hit him for four and he bowled you a good one next ball he would always tell you it was the same ball, trying to get you to do something you didn't want to do to the next one. He is a good character, a tough opponent, facing him I knew I had to be on top of my game, in my time he was very well captained by John Graham, they understood each other, and John got the best out of him."

Crozier had now played 376 NEPL games, batting 164 times, with 81 not out's, he had scored 1361 runs at an average of 16.39. He had scored 1 half century, his highest score remained 89 for Benwell Hill in May 2002.

He had now bowled 25824 balls, just for the sake of context, that is 4304 overs, with 1145 maidens, conceding 11353 runs and taking 750 NEPL wickets at an average of 15.13. His best bowling figures remained the 7 for 21 taken on 28th July 2007. He had also taken 55 catches.

An outstanding group of cricketers and clearly all worthy of recognition.

Simon Birtwisle
Allan Worthy
Jaques du Toit
John Graham
Jonny Wightman
Quentin Hughes
Phil Nicholson
Stephen Humble
Kieran Waterson
Richard Waite
Lee Crozier

Personally, I would like to see a Champions v NEPL Select XI game to finish off every season, as a way of recognising those players who have had outstanding seasons.

CHAPTER TWELVE

Covid 2020

The 2020 covid season, where to start?

I wasn't sure how to approach this season, obviously some cricket was played but not The NEPL in the format around which this book is geared. It was cricket but not as we know it! Scorers sitting outside, players changing outside or coming dressed in whites, hand sanitizing every 5 or 6 overs, players sitting in their cars eating sandwiches, spectators not allowed in some places, where they were allowed in, they couldn't field the ball if it went over the boundary. Benwell Hill served beer through a hatch in the front of the pavilion so at least one good idea came from it!

The NEPL decided to go with three regional leagues over six weekends.

The Banks Salver North featured Benwell Hill, South North, Tynemouth, Newcastle, Felling, Ashington, Blaydon and Gateshead Fell.

The Banks Salver East featured Burnmoor, Eppleton, Hetton Lyons, Sunderland, Castle Eden, Whitburn, Philadelphia and Boldon.

The Banks Salver West featured Chester le Street, Durham Cricket Academy, Washington, Willington,

This resulted in teams moving on to quarterfinals, semifinals and then a final for the Banks Salver.

In the Quarter finals, Benwell Hill defeated Eppleton, Chester le Street defeated Hetton Lyons, Burnmoor defeated Tynemouth, South North defeated Washington.

In the semifinals, Chester le Street defeated Benwell Hill and Burnmoor defeated South North.

The Banks Salver Final was played at Ropery Lane, Chester le Street on 19th September 2020, it was a 40 over aside match. Burnmoor won the toss and decided to bat, Paul Craig scored 58 not out from 97 balls with 5 fours and a six and Allan Worthy, with 27, was the next highest scorer as Burnmoor made 149 for 8 from their allotted overs. Quentin Hughes had 0 for 27, Jack Campbell1 for 39, Amaan Ulhaq 1 for 19, Liam Burgess 2 for 26, John Harrison 1 for 16 and Andrew Bell 2 for 16.

When Chester le Street batted, they put together a polished team performance, all five batsmen used got to double figures, openers Jacob McCann 43, and George Harrison, 22, put on 90 for the first wicket, helped by an unusually high number of extras, Andrew Smith at number three, made 18, and although there was a little stutter to 112 for three, John Coxon, batting at four, scored 21 not out and Quentin Hughes 16 not out, saw them home by 7 wickets with 26 balls to spare. Ryan Pringle 1 for 22, Craig Stephenson 1 for 38 and Graeme Bridge 1 for 22, were the wicket takers for Burnmoor.

When I spoke to various players about the covid season I detected very little enthusiasm for any of this, despite the excitement of having some cricket to play. Having given the matter some thought, I decided that rather than reflect upon COVID and the problems of the world in general, I would find half a dozen photos of some of the people I have met on the sidelines whilst photographing the league or who have supported my research for this book. Each one of these people provide support to the NEPL in one way or another and each represents a group of people, and they are in no particular order.

In the case of Peter Birtwisle and Neil Hewison strolling the boundary at South North in 2023 they represent the family support that every player needs not just to be a successful cricketer but to be any kind of cricketer. Cricket is a unique sport in that the actual playing of it on a Saturday may take up to eight hours, plus travelling time, plus a sociable pint in the bar with the opposition afterwards, that is time spent away from the family. The photo could easily have been one of the many family groups of a mum with small children running around the outfield while dad plays cricket, or a grandparent letting their grandkids have a drive of the groundman's tractor while dad plays, I haven't got any of those photos so your stuck with Messrs. Hewison and Birtwisle!

When I started photographing the NEPL I spoke to a few people on the boundary edge, when Pete Young and I struck up a conversation I realized that he was an umpire, albeit an injured one, the first time I spoke to him. He is now back on umpire duties and it's worth remembering that without the umpire there is no game of cricket. He also gave me an enormous amount of advice and proof read the book, this helped me enormously and in respect of saving money on a proof reader!

Brian Bennett is the guy on Pete's left, I can only describe Brian as a media guru! He approached me at Ashington one day, we struck up a conversation and before I knew it, he was putting my photos in the local paper! Every club should have a Brian Bennett!

I'm sure many of you recognize the man behind the camera, Ken Waller. I bumped into Ken at Tynemouth initially, a lovely man who is great company and happy to help with my photographic education. As you go through the book, many of the photos will have come from Ken.

The trio of Hugh Dyson, David McKay and Martin Avery at Benwell Hill covers a number of things. Hugh Dyson is an ex-player and ex-work colleague of mine, the sort of cricket supporter you find up and down the land watching their old club. David McKay is the NEPL historian, and an absolute godsend to me with the writing of this book, he never refused a question and had the answer to everything I threw at him, the NEPL is fortunate to have such a man behind them. Martin Avery is another photographer, a professional photographer, he too has been happy to help my education and provide me with photos for the book. He is also the official NEPL photographer.

Duncan Stephen was an enormous help when I first started researching the book, for those who don't know he is a scorer and cricket historian and has written his own book on cricket, South Northumberland 150 Not Out, like David McKay, I leant heavily on Duncan on a lot of issues in respect of this book.

David McLaren was another I bumped into on the sidelines, he represents the casual spectator with no favourite in respect of who wins the game, I enjoy his company whilst photographing, he also made a very generous and totally unexpected donation to help with the production costs of the book.

Simon Lunn and Phil Haves are the Chairman and committee member that every club needs, the life blood of all amateur sport.

A huge thank you to all of the above and if you recognise yourself in any of the roles described above then thank you for supporting the NEPL and cricket in general.

Peter Birtwisle and Neil Hewison stroll the boundary at South North 30th July 2023.

Pete Young on the left and Brian Bennett on the right at Benwell Hill 3rd September 2023.

Ken Waller at Tynemouth 28th August 2023.

Hugh Dyson, David McKay and Martin Avery at Benwell Hill on 20th July 2024.

Duncan Stephen presenting his beloved
South North side with the NEPL Trophy,
11th September 2022.

David McLaren at Tynemouth in 2024.

Simon Lunn and Phil Haves at Newcastle, 21st July 2024.

CHAPTER THIRTEEN

South North 2021-2023

Following the 2020 covid pandemic the NEPL moved to a split season, playing the first 6 matches in a 50 over win or lose format, with coloured clothing and an orange ball, the middle eleven matches were traditional NEPL cricket, 120 overs in a day, winning and losing draws, traditional white clothing and red ball. The final 5 matches reverted to the same format as the first half dozen.

I wish I had the imagination and literary skills to come up with an apt or witty title for each of the chapters in this book, the 2021 season is a classic example of a chapter screaming out for a title, so, given my own limitations, and the fact that the last real NEPL cricket had been played in 2019, I decided to borrow a phrase from that season and just say this, the only way to describe the 2021 season is to say it was won by "the barest of margins!"

South North opened the 2021 season with a visit to Hetton Lyons on Saturday 17th April, they won the toss and decided to bat first, making 229 all out from their 50 overs. Michael Richardson had the only half-century of the match, scoring 71 and Chris Ralston had 3 for 56 for Hetton.

When Hetton batted, despite a steady start and opening partnership of 33, they were dismissed for 86, leaving South North to win by 143 runs. Lee Crozier had 5 for 19 and Oli McGee 4 for 19.

The South North starting eleven was as follows-

Simon Birtwisle opened the batting today, making 36. Birtwisle had played 350 matches in the NEPL going into the 2021 season, he has batted 342 times with 27 not outs, he has scored 11026 runs at an average of 35.00. He has scored 63 half centuries and 14 centuries. His highest score is 151 not out, made for Chester le Street in July 2010 and mentioned earlier.

He has bowled 5716 balls in the NEPL with 177 maidens, conceding 3271 runs and taking 159 wickets at an average of 20.57. His best bowling figures are 6 for 18 taken for South North on 7th September 2019 at home to Sacriston. He has taken 116 catches in the NEPL.

Lee Crozier says of Birtwisle "I had played at Benwell Hill with him and was delighted when he came to South North, his mental approach to the game of cricket is phenomenal, he understands the game so well, he is technically gifted, and this shows itself in his aggressive stroke play, he sets the tone for our innings, he deals with pressure very well, he transfers pressure from himself and puts it back on the bowler. He is someone who performs on big occasions, I remember him winning player of the match at Derby in the National T20 Final."

During the 2021 season Simon Birtwisle played 17 NEPL matches, batting 17 times with 2 not outs, he scored 576 runs at an average of 38.40. He scored 3 half centuries and 1 century, 102 not out, made on 4th September 2021 at home to Felling, the innings came from 137 balls and contained 10 fours.

He bowled 310 balls in the NEPL in 2021 with 14 maidens, conceding 151 runs and taking 12 wickets at an average of 12.58. His best bowling figures were 3 for 13, taken on 19th June at Chester le Street. He took 13 catches in the NEPL in 2021.

John Graham opened the batting with Birtwisle, scoring 27. Graham played just 4 matches in the NEPL in 2021, batting 4 times with 0 not outs, he scored 46 runs at an average of 11.50. His highest score was 27, described earlier in the first game of the season, he took 4 catches in those games. His last NEPL game of 2021, and for South North in the NEPL was on 7th August at Eppleton, he scored 8 and took a catch.

John Graham and his South North stats are recorded up to the end of the 2019 season as part of the Team of 20 Years.

His final South North stats are that he had played 384 matches in the NEPL for them, batting 357 times, with 51 not outs, he scored 11062 runs at an average of 36.15. He scored 78 half centuries and 12 centuries. His highest score was 132, scored in July 2006 and mentioned earlier.

He bowled 2840 balls in the NEPL, with 98 maidens, he conceded 1606 runs and took 66 wickets at an average of 24.33. His best bowling figures were 4 for 15 taken in May 2008 and mentioned earlier. He took 180 catches in the NEPL for South North.

John Graham did play 2 further NEPL games, in 2023 he made his NEPL debut for Tynemouth on 10th June at Preston Avenue against Burnopfield, he didn't bat or bowl but took 2 catches. He also played the following week, also at home, to Hetton Lyons on 17th June, he scored 7 and took 1 catch.

Quentin Hughes says of John Graham "When we played South North, he was the one we wanted, he was often the rock around which they built their innings, we felt when we got him our chances went up significantly. He used to hit the ball in unusual areas, therefore he was hard to set a field for, he was a very, very good player, he was especially strong square on the off side, but he would also hit you inside out and play you very late, as well as being a very strong sweeper. He was also an intelligent cricketer; he was a situational player who could adjust his innings to fit with the position in the game."

Michael Richardson batted at three to start the season, scoring 71, the only half century and top score from either side in the game. By the time Richardson came to play for South North in the NEPL in 2021 he had an excellent first-class career behind him, having made his first-class debut for Durham on 5th May 2010 in a 3-day match against Durham M.C.C University and his last first-class match was on 5th April 2019 at Derbyshire in a Division 2 County Championship match.

He has played 103 first-class matches, batting 176 times with 11 not outs, he scored 4828 runs at an average of 29.26. he scored 26 half centuries and 6 centuries. His highest score was 148, made in a 4-day Division 1 County Championship match against Yorkshire at The Emirates, Chester le Street. He bowled just 24 balls, 0 for 13, but took 186 catches and had 5 stumpings in first-class cricket for Durham.

Richardson also played 31 List A matches for Durham, batting 27 times with 4 not outs, he scored 1304 runs at an average of 56.69. He scored 10 half centuries and 3 centuries. His highest score was 111, made on 1st June 2018 at home to Warwickshire. He also took 12 catches at this level.

Richardson had also played 46 Twenty20 matches for Durham, batting 34 times with 10 not outs and scoring 514 runs at ana average of 21.41. He scored 1 half century, 53, made on 5th August 2017 at Nottinghamshire. He took 23 catches at this level for Durham.

Richardson had made his NEPL debut on 24th April 2010 for Newcastle at Benwell Hill, he scored 44. Although his number of NEPL appearances was limited due to his first -class career Richardson played his last NEPL game for Newcastle on 1st September 2018 at home to Benwell Hill, he made 55 not out.

He had played 62 NEPL matches for Newcastle, batting 57 times with 12 not outs, he scored 2626 runs at an average of 58.35. he scored 16 half centuries and 7 centuries. His highest score was 171 not out, made on 26th May 2012 at Stockton. The innings came from 169 balls with 11 fours and 6 sixes.

He also bowled 384 balls, with 5 maidens, conceding 283 runs and taking 12 wickets at an average of 23.58. His best bowling figures were 5 for 70, taken on 7th September 2013 at Jesmond against Durham Academy. He took 39 catches in the NEPL for Newcastle.

Lee Crozier recalls" Michael had come to us with a good first -class career under his belt, he was an incredibly talented cricketer, he loved scoring runs, he was an excellent accumulator of runs but he also had the ability to score runs quickly when required."

The season opener of 2021 was Richardson's NEPL debut for South North, he played 15 matches in the NEPL for South North in 2021, he batted 14 times with 2 not outs, he scored 596 runs at an average of 49.66. He scored 6 half centuries and 1 century, 111 not out, scored on 4th September 2021 at home to Felling, it came from 104 balls and contained 12 fours and a six. Richardson didn't bowl in the NEPL in 2021, but he took 16 catches and had 4 stumpings.

In total he played 77 matches in the NEPL, batting 71 times with 14 not outs, he scored 3222 runs at an average of 56.52. He scored 22 half centuries and 8 centuries. His highest score was the 171 not out mentioned earlier.

He bowled 384 balls in the NEPL, all for Newcastle, with 5 maidens, conceding 283 runs and taking 12 wickets at an average of 23.58. His best bowling figures were 5 for 70, taken on 7th September 2013 at Jesmond against Durham Academy. He took 55 catches and had 4 stumpings in his NEPL career.

Michael Richardson qualifies through relations on his mother's side for German citizenship, although he was born in South Africa and his father, David played test cricket for South Africa, Michael Richardson made his International debut for Germany on 19th June 2019 in Twenty20 in the ICC World Cup Finals against Denmark at Castel in Guernsey.

After the 2021 season finished Richardson began playing for Germany in the ICC T20 World Cup Qualifiers. He has played as recently as 25th July 2023 for Germany, on this occasion against Jersey at Edinburgh. He has now played 25 Twenty20 matches for Germany, batting 24 times with 7 not outs, he has scored 513 runs at an average of 30.17. He has scored 2 half centuries with a highest score of 61 not out, made on 20th October 2021 against Denmark. He has taken 15 catches and has 10 stumpings at this level.

Chris Hewison batted at number four to start the 2021 season; he made a single. Hewison had returned to the NEPL for the 2019 season after a six years at Swalwell, his first NEPL appearance of that return was on 20th April at Hetton Lyons.

He entered the 2021 season having played 226 matches in the NEPL, he had batted 217 times with 33 not outs, he had scored 7695 runs at an average of 41.82. He had scored 40 half centuries and 18 centuries, his highest score was 165 not out, made in June 2002 at Philadelphia. He had not bowled since 2010, so he still has 32 wickets at an average of 34.59, he had taken 127 catches in his NEPL career so far.

Hewison played 18 matches in the NEPL in 2021, batting 16 times with 3 not outs, he scored 387 runs at an average of 29.76. He scored 2 half centuries. His highest score was 92, made on 21st May at home to Eppleton. He took 7 catches in the NEPL in the season.

Sol Bell is a right-handed batsman, he batted at number five on 17th April, making 27. Lee Crozier says of Bell "he is a really laid-back character in the dressing room, a really nice lad, I am both surprised and disappointed that he hasn't got a first-class contract somewhere, he is that good. A very talented batsman, he just churns out runs. He has come back to us for 2024, and it is great having him and Nik Gorantla, who is in an almost identical situation, bat together."

Bell first came to my attention on 17th May 2015 when he played for Durham Under 14's at Boldon against Yorkshire Under 14's.

On 12th June 2015 he featured for Sacriston at Blaydon in a 20 over match. He played for Durham Under 14's throughout 2015, making his debut for Durham Under 15's on 1st May 2016 at Nottinghamshire Under 15's. He played regularly for Sacriston Second XI during 2016, as well as Durham Under 15's. He made 113 for Sacriston Seconds on 5th June 2016 at home to Felling.

His performances led to him making his NEPL debut on 6th August 2016 for Durham Academy at Hetton Lyons, he played only twice more in 2016 for The Academy before becoming a regular in 2017.

He also played his first match for Durham Second XI on 6th April 2017 at The Racecourse against Durham M.C.C University Second XI. He would go on to play 40 matches for Durham Second XI, batting 49 times with 0 not outs, he scored 1120 runs at an average of 22.85. He made 6 half centuries and 1 century, 109, scored at Scarborough against Yorkshire in a 3-day match starting on 16th September 2019. His last game for Durham Seconds was on 17th September 2021 at Lancashire. He also played regularly for Durham Under 17's in 2017 and 2018. As he continued to play for The Academy, he took a wicket for them in the NEPL, a good one as it happens, on 5th May 2018 they played at South North, Bell had South North's John Graham caught by Jamie Dass for 38.

In a 3-day match starting on 10th July 2018 for Durham Under 17's at Hartlepool against Cheshire Under 17's he scored 189 in the first innings, the innings came from 252 balls and contained 28 fours.

2018 saw him play four games for The ECB Elite Player development North Under 17's, the first of which was on 21st August at Loughborough against the London and East equivalent, he made 32.

His last game in the NEPL for The Academy was on 8th September 2018 at Sacriston.

Bell played 38 matches in the NEPL for Durham Academy, he had batted 36 times with 3 not outs, he scored 583 runs at an average of 17.66. He had scored 2 half centuries, his highest score was 66 not out, made 23rd June 2018 at The Riverside against Sacriston. He bowled 76 balls in the NEPL for The Academy, with 0 maidens, he conceded 65 runs for 1 wicket he also took 19 NEPL catches for The Academy.

He made his NEPL debut for Sacriston on 20th April 2019 at home to Tynemouth and his last NEPL game for Sacriston was on 14th September 2019 at home to Burnopfield.

He had played 18 NEPL matches for Sacriston, batting 17 times with 1 not out, he scored 464 runs at an average of 29.00. He scored 3 half centuries, his highest score was 86, made on 24th August 2019 at Felling. He bowled 18 balls, with 0 maidens, conceding 16 runs and failing to take a wicket, he took 3 NEPL catches in 2019.

Sol Bell played a 3-day match for Durham starting on 21st July 2020 against a Durham Second XI and he also played for Durham Second XI on 18th August 2020 at Gosforth against Scotland A in a T20 match.

He played 4 matches in total in 2020 for Durham Seconds, as well as playing for Sacriston and a game for Durham Academy.

The season opener of 17th April 2021 was his South North NEPL debut. With his NEPL experience at Durham Academy and Sacriston, Bell entered the 2021 season with South North having played 56 matches in the league, batting 53 times with 4 not outs, he had scored 1047 runs at an average of 21.36. He had scored 5 half centuries, his highest score was 86, made for Sacriston in 2019 and mentioned earlier. He had bowled 94 balls, with 0 maidens and had his 1 wicket for 81 runs and he had taken 22 NEPL catches as he entered 2021.

During the 2021 season Sol Bell played 17 matches in the NEPL for South North, batting 17 times with 4 not outs, he scored 779 runs at an average of 59.92. He scored 3 half centuries and 3 centuries.

His first century of the season, 116 not out, and his first in the NEPL, was scored on 5th June 2021 at home to Whitburn. It came from 140 balls and contained 19 fours.

His second century of the season, 118, was scored on 12th June 2021 at Burnopfield, the innings came from 136 balls and contained 14 fours.

His highest score of the season and third century in three consecutive NEPL innings was 129 not out, made on 19th June 2021 at Chester le Street. The innings came from 153 balls and contained 14 fours and 1 six. Bell also bowled 2 balls in the 2021 season, going for 2 runs and he took 3 catches in the NEPL in 2021.

Bell also made his debut for Northumberland on 30th May 2021 at Shropshire, to date, April 2024, he played his last game for Northumberland on 3rd July 2022.

He has now played 6 matches for Northumberland, batting 9 times, with 0 not outs, he has scored 134 runs at an average of 14.88. He has scored 1 half century, 54, made on 20th July 2021 at Yorkshire. He has taken 5 catches for Northumberland.

Adam Cragg captained the side and batted at six when the season got underway, making 39. Lee Crozier says of Cragg "he has the best hand/eye co-ordination of anyone I have played with. He is a fantastic striker of the ball and brilliant fielder. As a captain he is tactically very good, he is another who is not afraid to take chances to win games. He is very focussed on winning and has this immense desire to win, this is passed onto the team."

Cragg entered the 2021 season having played 242 matches in the NEPL, he had batted 201 times with 38 not outs, he had scored 4771 runs at an average of 29.26. He had scored 26 half centuries and 2 centuries, his highest score was 102, made in May 2010 at home to Blaydon. He had not bowled since 2017 so still had 1 wicket to his name and he had taken 188 catches and had 23 stumpings in his NEPL career so far.

Cragg played 18 matches in the NEPL in 2021, batting 14 times with 6 not outs, he scored 475 runs at an average of 59.37. He scored 3 half centuries. His highest score was 78, made on 24th July at Burnmoor. He took 3 catches and 1 stumping in the NEPL in the season.

Sean Tindale batted at number seven, scoring 5. He also opened the bowling taking 0 for 11 from two overs. Lee Crozier says of Tindale "Sean is the ultimate 3d cricketer. He is a very capable, aggressive batsman, a hugely impressive bowler and very athletic in the field. As a batsman he could bat in the top 4 in most teams in our league, he has a very sound technique and is capable of explosive, clean hitting and scoring quickly. As a bowler he is impressive, he is capable of genuine pace, but he achieves a consistency of performance that many older cricketers strive for and one that can be difficult for fast bowlers in particular to maintain. As an all-rounder with his skill set, I consider him unlucky not to have played at a higher level. he is the best all round cricketer in our league."

Tindale entered the 2021 season having played 137 matches in the NEPL, he had batted 117 times with 22 not outs, he had scored 2038 runs at an average of 21.45. He had scored 8 half centuries and 1 century, 108 not out mentioned earlier.

He had bowled 6202 balls with 179 maidens, conceding 3488 runs and taking 163 wickets at an average of 21.39. His best bowling figures were 6 for 67, taken on 27th April 2019 at home to Burnopfield. He had taken 31 catches.

During the 2021 season Tindale played 18 matches, batting 12 times with 3 not outs, he scored 231 runs at an average of 25.66. He scored 1 half century, 66 not out on 11th September at home to Burnmoor.

He bowled 954 balls with 37 maidens, conceding 521 runs and took 33 wickets at an average of 15.78. His best bowling figures were 6 for 18, taken on 15th May at Whitburn. He took 5 catches in the NEPL in 2021.

Oli McGee batted at number eight and failed to trouble the scorers when South North batted, he did however take 4 for 19 from six overs and one ball. He is a left-handed batsman and slow left arm orthodox bowler. He first came to attention on 11th May 2010 for Northumberland Under 13's against Lincolnshire Under 13's at Stocksfield. He played for Northumberland Under 13's throughout 2010 and made his debut for the Under 15's in 2011 as well as playing Under 14 at county level that season.

Oli McGee made his NEPL debut for Tynemouth on 13th August 2011 at home to Durham Academy. He took his first NEPL wicket in the game when Durham batted, Sameet Brar caught by Greg Hollins for 3. He finished with 1 for 43 from eleven overs and four balls.

McGee was selected for a 2-day match for Northumberland Under 17's starting on 17th July 2012 at Gosforth against Norfolk Under 17's. In 2013 he also played a couple of games for a Northumberland Development XI as well as continuing to play for the county Under 17's. He was also selected to play for Northern Universities Student Club Community Cricketers Elite in a couple of games against The Western Warriors Under 18's.

He played his last NEPL match for Tynemouth on 14th September 2013 at Stockton as he moved to Newcastle for the 2014 season, making his debut at Jesmond on 19th April 2014 against Sunderland. It was a memorable game to make a debut in with over 650 runs scored in 118 overs!

Newcastle had batted first and opener Neil Corby, 123 not out, and Graham Clark, batting at three, 134 not out added an unbroken 231 for the second wicket as Newcastle declared on 328 for 1 after 45 overs.

Incredibly Sunderland chased the score down, opener Dan Shurben hit 84, Simon Brown had 61, Greg Applegarth 51 and three others made 20 or over! Sunderland had scored 330 for 8 in 73 overs to take an unlikely win! McGee had taken a respectable 2 for 65 from eighteen overs, his first Newcastle NEPL wicket was Mark Dale, leg before wicket for 6.

Oli McGee made his Minor Counties Championship debut in a 3-day match starting on 6th July 2014 at Staffordshire, future teammate Sean Tindale made his debut in the same match. In 2014 McGee was playing for both Northumberland Under 17's and the senior side!

On 26th August 2014 he made his debut for Durham Under 19's at The Emirates against Middlesex Under 19's in a 2-day match and on 15th September 2014 he made his debut for Durham Second XI at Sussex in a 3-day match. He played a further match for Durham Under 19's in a 2-day match which started on 24th August 2016 against Lancashire Under 19's, he opened the bowling, taking 3 for 24.

McGee played his last NEPL game for Newcastle on 8th September 2018 at home to Stockton.

Lee Crozier says of McGee "he was young as a spinner when he came to us, although he had a good record. He has matured as a bowler, developed good variation and changes of pace in his bowling. I think he has a lot more confidence in his bowling than he did when he first came to us. He has a hunger for taking wickets and has become one of the premium bowlers in the league."

He made his NEPL debut for South North on 20th April 2019 at Hetton Lyons, he took 2 for 3, his first South North NEPL wicket was Robert Talbot, caught by Sam Dale for 1.

As he entered the 2021 season Oli McGee had played 150 NEPL matches, batting 89 times with 36 not outs, he had scored 900 runs at an average of 16.98 and scored 3 half centuries. His highest score was 99, made for Newcastle against Durham Academy on 9th June 2018 at The Riverside.

He had also bowled 8633 balls, with 259 maidens, conceding 4736 runs and taking 254 wickets at an average of 18.64. His best bowling figures were 7 for 54 taken on Newcastle on 27th August 2016 at Jesmond against South Shields.

He played for South North in the covid competition of 2020, and he has taken 34 catches in the NEPL up to the end of 2020.

During the 2021 season McGee played 18 matches, batting 9 times with 3 not outs, he scored 67 runs at an average of 11.16. His highest score was 15.

He bowled 808 balls, with 25 maidens, he conceded 406 runs and took 27 wickets at an average of 15.03. His best bowling figures were 4 for 19, taken in the season opener of 17th April at Hetton Lyons. He took 6 catches in the NEPL in 2021.

Jonny Wightman batted at number nine, scoring 9 not out, he also opened the bowling taking 1 for 11 from six overs. Lee Crozier recalls that Wightman was "an out and out quick bowler when he came to South North and as he has got older, he has developed himself into one of the most skilful bowlers in the league. A bowler single handedly capable of bowling teams out. He has been a fantastic asset to our team, with his bowling and character he brings a lot to us, and he has been instrumental in our success."

Wightman entered the 2021 season having played 207 matches in the NEPL, he had batted 103 times with 37 not outs, he had scored 680 runs at an average of 10.30. His highest score was 37 scored for South North in May 2011 and mentioned earlier.

He had bowled 12357 balls with 297 maidens, conceding 7544 runs and taking 407 wickets at an average of 18.53. His best bowling figures were 8 for 31, taken on 4th June 2016 for South North at home to Gateshead Fell. He had taken 26 catches.

During the 2021 season Wightman played 17 matches, batting 7 times with 4 not outs, he scored 22 runs at an average of 7.33. His highest score was 9 not out. He bowled 969 balls with 34 maidens, conceding 539 runs and took 31 wickets at an average of 17.38. His best bowling figures were 5 for 27, taken on 24th April at Washington. He took 2 catches in the NEPL in 2021.

Calum Fletcher batted at number ten in the season opener, he failed to score, he bowled six overs, taking 0 for 25. He first came to my attention on 24th May 2017 when he played for Northumberland Under 15's at Lincolnshire Under 15's, he took 2 for 9 from five overs. A few days later he played a Banks Salver game for South North First XI at home to Eppleton, he scored 1 not out and had figures of 0 for 29 from six overs. He represented Northumberland Under 15's throughout the 2017 season and made his NEPL debut for South North on 9th September 2017 at home to Tynemouth, he scored 3 and didn't bowl.

In 2018 Fletcher progressed to the Northumberland Under 15's side, playing his first match for them on 5th June at Gateshead against Durham. He played a representative game for South North on 27th July 2018 when they hosted a M.C.C side. As well as playing his second NEPL game, he didn't contribute, he also played for Northumberland Under 17's in 2018 and throughout 2019.

He played for South North first team during the covid competition of 2020 and he entered the 2021 season having played just 2 matches in the NEPL, once each in 2017 and 2018, he had batted once, as mentioned earlier, he had yet to bowl or take a catch in the NEPL. He took his first NEPL wicket on 24th April 2021 at Washington when Simon Birtwisle caught Ashley Thorpe for 16.

During the 2021 season Fletcher played 18 matches, batting 4 times with 2 not outs, he scored 8 runs at an average of 4.00. His highest score was 5 not out.

He bowled 670 balls in the NEPL in 2021, with 18 maidens, conceding 376 runs and took 17 wickets at an average of 22.11. His best bowling figures of 2021 were 2 for 21, taken on 31st July at home to Hetton Lyons. He took 2 catches in the NEPL in 2021.

Calum Fletcher also made his debut for Northumberland in 2021, on 13th June at Jesmond against Cheshire. He took 2 for 44 and made 4 not out. To date, 4th April 2024, Fletcher has now played 19 matches for Northumberland, batting 16 times, with 12 not outs, he has scored 81 runs at an average of 20.25. His highest score is 14.

He has bowled 1154 balls with 31 maidens, conceding 863 runs and taking 39 wickets at an average of 22.12. His best bowling figures are 6 for 19 Fletcher taking 6 for 19 on 4th June 2023 at Jesmond against Herefordshire. He has taken 10 catches for Northumberland.

Lee Crozier batted at number eleven to start the season off, he was another who got a duck today, he did take 5 for 19 from nine overs and was instrumental in bowling Hetton out so cheaply.

Quentin Hughes says of Crozier "Lee has such an excellent knowledge of his own game, he is also very good at working a batsman out, he controlled his pace very well and was so consistent, he had the knack of getting you to do something you didn't want to, through that control and consistency he would force you to try and hit the ball where you didn't want to go. He isn't a great spinner of the ball, but he has been at such a high level for such a long time. He is another one who likes the one-on-one challenge and likes to make it a battle."

As he entered the 2021 season Crozier had played 376 matches in the NEPL, batting 164 times with 81 not outs, he had scored 1361 runs at an average of 16.39. He had scored 1 half century, 89 for Benwell Hill in 2002.

He had bowled 25824 balls, with 1145 maidens, conceding 11353 runs and taking 750 wickets at an average of 15.13. His best bowling was 7 for 21 taken for South North in 2007. He had taken 55 NEPL catches.

He played 18 matches in the NEPL in 2021, batting 2 times with 0 not outs, he scored 10 runs at an average of 5.00. His highest score of the 2021 NEPL season was 10.

He bowled 1002 balls in the NEPL in 2021, with 34 maidens, conceding 530 runs and taking 34 wickets at an average of 15.58. His best bowling figures of the season were 5 for 19, taken on 17th April in the season opener and mentioned earlier. He made 4 catches in the NEPL in 2021.

Rob Peyton missed the first game of the 2021 season. He did, however, go on to play 17 matches in the NEPL that year, batting 11 times with 3 not outs, he scored 128 runs at an average of 16.00. His highest score was 34 not out, made on 7th August at Eppleton. He took 8 catches in the season.

Coming into the season he had played 98 matches in the NEPL, batting 73 times with 10 not outs, he had scored 1078 runs at an average of 17.11. He had scored 4 half centuries with a highest score of 80 made on 2nd September 2017 at The Riverside against Durham Academy. He had made 98 catches and had 17 stumpings so far in the NEPL.

And so, we come to the ongoing problems caused by Covid, after badly affecting the 2020 NEPL season, Covid related issues arose again during the 2021 NEPL season and the League Table of that year has an odd look to it because of that. The table looks as it does because of two matches, both involving Sacriston, over an eight-day period in July.

Sacriston were due to play a home fixture with South North on Saturday 3rd July 2021, a South North player had tested positive for Covid a few days before the match. South North said he was fit to play, and he was selected.

As the players took the field, a South North official mentioned this fact to the umpires, they were happy to play, if the captains agreed, they didn't, Sacriston disagreed, as was their right, and elected not to play, game cancelled.

Unfortunately, in the week that followed Covid struck again and Sacriston were unable to raise any teams for the weekend of Saturday, 10th July, the First XI were due to play a home match against Benwell Hill. They had no option other than to cancel the fixture.

The League Management Committee acted swiftly and decided that no points should be awarded and both matches should be voided, the fixtures removed from play cricket and that the League positions would be decided on average points per game.

Whilst there was obviously more to the story than that, it's easy to forget the problems that Covid presented, the wide range of views held at the time, and as more emerges and with the benefit of hindsight, the utter shambles our government made of it. Without attaching blame, all parties were treated equally by the league and I, personally, don't see what other options they had. Not wishing to open old wounds I think it's best to leave the matter there.

As the 2021 season was winding down the title race had become a two-horse race, Burnmoor and South North. When the teams played their matches on the weekend of 28th August 2021, Marcus Brown, 66, and Paul Craig 49, got Burnmoor to a healthy score of 224 for 8 from their 50 overs at home to Hetton Lyons. Despite 80 from Robbie Talbot, Lyons were dismissed for 198, Josh Coughlin 3 for 21 and Ryan Greenwell, 3 for 25. Burnmoor picked up the maximum 20 points and were now on 354, with a net points average of 17.70.

South North were at Benwell Hill on 28th August 2021, Hill were having a good season and would go on to finish third, South North batted first and made 222 all out from 49.5 overs, Chris Hewison had 59.

For Hill, Callum Harding took 4 for 46.

When Hill batted Kyle Coetzer, opening the batting, hit 71, he was well supported by fellow opener Mohsin Mukhtar with 49 and Adam Heather with 30, Hill won by 2 wickets off the last ball of the game.

South North collected 7 points for the loss and had now played 19 matches and got 311 points with a net points average of 16.36.

On the weekend of 4th September 2021 Burnmoor were at Washington, South North were at home to Felling. South North batted first and posted 278 for 1 from their 50 overs, Sol Bell had 47, but it was Simon Birtwisle 102 not out and Michael Richardson 111 not out who had got them to such a big score.

When Felling batted Alasdair Appleby 69, and Alan Mustard, 17, put on 95 for the first wicket but when Lee Crozier had Appleby stumped Felling slipped quickly to 153 all out, Crozier finished with 5 for 32.

South North picked up 20 points and now had 331 points for a net points average of 16.55 from their 20 matches.

Washington were already relegated by the time they took the field against Burnmoor. As is the British way, the weather played a part in proceedings, as well as the cricket gods who like to stir the pot occasionally, and the game was cut from 50 overs a side to 35 overs a side.

Washington batted first and made 152 for 4 from their 35 overs, Josh Wilson had 49 and James Thompson 55. After a steady start to 37 for 1 Burnmoor were unable to build a match winning partnership and lost wickets at a steady rate without making the inroads they needed to chase the score down. When opener Ross Greenwell was bowled by Graham Pickering for 44, they were 76 for 6, despite 25 from Josh Coughlin they fell short, they were 130 for 9 from their 35 overs and picked up just 2 points from the game. They now had 356 points from 21 games with a net points average of 16.95.

And so, as the season reached its finale, the title was still open to both Burnmoor and South North when they met on 11th September 2021 at Roseworth Terrace. The league would be decided on average points won per match played, if a team had played 20 matches and collected 200 points, their average would be 10 points.

Going into the last game of 2021 Burnmoor had played 21 matches and amassed 356 points, for a net points rate of 16.95, South North had played 20 matches and collected 331 points, giving them a net points rate of 16.55. Advantage Burnmoor, win the game and win the title, remember the teams are now playing the 50 over a side format with a draw only possible if caused by the weather.

South North won the toss and decided to bat, with the score on 5 they lost opener Sol Bell, caught by Ryan Pringle off the bowling of Chaminda Bandara, the overseas pro and left arm fast bowler, for 3.

Opener Simon Birtwisle and number three Michael Richardson then added 69 for the second wicket before Birtwisle was bowled by Craig Stephenson for 43. South North 74 for 2, soon became 88 for 3 when Stephenson bowled Chris Hewison for 6. This became 88 for 4 when Richardson was caught by Alec Linsley behind the wicket for 31 off the bowling of Graeme Bridge.

South North captain Adam Cragg had come in at five and all-rounder Sean Tindale at number six, the game was in the balance and could have gone either way, although Cragg and Tindale took the score to 140 before Cragg was leg before to Ryan Pringle. South North 140 for 5, game still in the balance.

The next three South North batsmen, Rob Peyton, Oli McGee and Jonny Wightman, all made single figures in the pursuit of a good total and quick runs as Burnmoor took wickets at regular intervals to keep them in check, Bandara accounting for Peyton, McGee was run out and Ryan Pringle bowled Wightman.

It turned out that Sean Tindale was the rock around which the innings was built, he finished on 66 not out, with 2 fours and 2 sixes from 91 balls faced as South North had their innings closed with the score on 190 for 8 wickets from 50 overs. Craig Stephenson was the pick of the bowlers, 2 for 32, Bandara had 2 for 34, Ryan Pringle 2 for 47 and Graeme Bridge 1 for 24.

I suspect both teams were relatively happy at tea, South North at 88 for 5 could easily have been bowled out for a low score, they weren't, Burnmoor probably felt they had let them off the hook a bit, but they had kept them to less than four an over and got themselves a reasonable score to chase down.

At tea, the game and the title were therefore nicely balanced.

When Burnmoor batted Allan Worthy took the attack to the bowlers, making 16 off 22 balls with 3 boundaries until he was bowled by Jonny Wightman with the score on 20. Marcus Brown had come in at three, wicketkeeper Michael Richardson caught him off the bowling of Calum Fletcher for 8.

Burnmoor 38 for 2, this soon became 45 for 3 when number four, Ryan Pringle was caught by Simon Birtwisle off the bowling of Lee Crozier for 2. Paul Craig had come in at five; after scoring 2 he was leg before wicket to Calum Fletcher, Burnmoor 50 for 4 and their innings was now in the balance.

With the score on 54, opener Ross Greenwell was run out by Rob Peyton for 23, Burnmoor 54 for 5, game and title still in the balance. Alex Simpson, batting at six, and Josh Coughlin batting seven, then set about getting Burnmoor back on track, they had added 30 when Oli McGee had Simpson leg before for 14 Burnmoor were now 84 for 6.

Craig Stephenson had come in at eight and he and Coughlin continued to put up a fight, adding 39 for the seventh wicket before Stephenson was caught and bowled by McGee for 17. Burnmoor 123 for 7 and now firmly in trouble.

With the score on 130, Coughlin was caught by Peyton off the bowling of McGee for 31, he had faced 61 balls and hit 1 boundary, 130 for 8 then became 134 for 9 when number nine Bandara was bowled by Jonny Wightman for 7.

When Wightman bowled Graeme Bridge for 12, Burnmoor were 150 all out from 44.3 overs, Alec Linsley was left on 3 not out. Wightman had 3 for 25, McGee 3 for 38, Fletcher 2 for 23 and Crozier 1 for 33.

South North picked up 20 points, they now had 351 points and a net point average of 16.71, Burnmoor had 361 points and a net point average of 16.41. Without the need for a "super over" South North were therefore the NEPL Champions of 2021 by the "barest if margins" or in mathematical terms by 0.3 of a point!

Chester le Street won The Banks Salver, South North won The Twenty20 and Sol Bell of South North was The NEPL Player of the Year,

TABLE 65   NEPL 2021.

	Played	Won	Draw/Aban	Lost	Penalty Points	Bonus Points	Points	Average
South North	21	12	8	1	0	67	351	16.71
Burnmoor	22	12	6	4	0	103	361	16.41
Benwell Hill	21	7	12	2	0	66	316	15.05
Chester le Street	22	7	11	4	0	71	322	14.64
Hetton Lyons	22	3	10	9	0	82	250	11.36
Tynemouth	22	4	10	8	5	73	246	11.18
Eppleton	22	1	12	9	0	92	246	11.18
Felling	22	6	5	11	0	50	206	9.36
Whitburn	22	2	9	11	0	74	194	8.82
Burnopfield	22	5	7	10	0	52	187	8.50
Washington	22	2	8	12	0	72	174	7.91
Sacriston	20	3	5	12	5	53	144	7.20

TABLE 66   NEPL Batting Averages 2021.
Qualification 400 Runs.

Player	Club	Inns	N. O	H. S	Runs	Average
(1) K.J Coetzer	Benwell Hill	14	2	132	756	63.00
(2) S.J.D Bell	South North	17	4	129 no	779	59.92
(3 A.D Cragg	South North	14	6	78	475	59.38
(4) J.A Schofield	Benwell Hill	8	1	87	405	57.86
(5) M.J Richardson	South North	14	2	111 no	596	49.67
(6) J.R Oswell	Burnopfield	19	3	148	783	48.94
(7) M. Brown	Tynemouth	16	4	70 no	587	48.92
(8) Q.J Hughes	Chester le Street	15	2	89	578	44.31
(9) R.D Pringle	Burnmoor	18	3	111 no	654	43.60
(10) K. Davis	Eppleton	12	1	80	467	42.45
(11) R.L Greenwell	Burnmoor	18	3	125 no	616	41.07
(12) J. du Toit	Burnopfield	18	3	107	582	38.80
(13) S.J Birtwisle	South North	17	2	102 no	576	38.40

TABLE 67   NEPL Bowling Averages 2021.
Qualification 20 Wickets.

Player	Club	Overs	Mdns	Runs	Wkts	Average
(1) S. Hussain	Eppleton	145.5	37	461	41	11.24
(2) G.D Bridge	Burnmoor	118.5	29	298	22	13.55
(3) J. Coughlin	Burnmoor	173.5	32	531	36	14.75
(4) J.R Harrison	Chester le Street	116.5	6	473	32	14.78
(5) O.F McGee	South North	134.4	25	406	27	15.04
(6) M. Saad	Tynemouth	120.0	26	399	26	15.35
(7) L.J Crozier	South North	167.0	34	530	34	15.59
(8) S.J Tindale	South North	159.0	37	521	33	15.79
(9) R.D Pringle	Burnmoor	178.4	37	549	34	16.15
(10) M. Mukhtar	Benwell Hill	129.4	16	500	30	16.67
(11) C. Ralston	Hetton Lyons	123.4	25	370	22	16.82
(12) J.R Wightman	South North	161.3	34	539	31	17.39

South North CC 2021.

Left to Right- Back Row John Tindale (Coach), Sol Bell, Rob Peyton, Chris Hewison, Jonny Wightman, Lee Crozier, John Ruddick (Scorer).

Front Row- Calum Fletcher, Michael Richardson, Oli McGee, Sean Tindale, Adam Cragg, Simon Birtwisle.

Sol Bell batting for South North v Newcastle on 9th July 2022.

2022

South North opened the season with an away fixture at Burnopfield on 16th April, they were without John Graham, who had retired at the end of 2021, and Adam Cragg who missed the first two games of the season, so Sean Tindale captained the side. South North won the toss and decided to bat, it proved to be a good decision, although opener Simon Birtwisle had to retire hurt after 9.5 overs with his score 25 and the team on 37 for 0. Sol Bell and Rob Peyton took the score to 66 for the first wicket, Peyton and Chris Hewison then added 49 for the second wicket, number four Sean Tindale, 41, and Hewison then put on 104, South North reaching 230 for 7 from their 50 overs, Hewison was run out for 97. Matthew Oswell took 3 for 45 and was the pick of the Burnopfield bowlers. When Burnopfield batted, Brydon Carse, batting at number four, hit 127 not out from 131 balls, he hit 9 fours and 7 sixes and Burnopfield got home by 4 wickets with five balls to spare.

As is the way of the book, now is a good time to have a look at Brydon Carse in the NEPL, he made his NEPL debut for The Durham Academy on 25th April 2015 at South North, he scored 26, he was out leg before wicket to Lee Crozier and he took 0 for 12 when he bowled.

His first NEPL wicket was Ben McGee of Newcastle on 2nd May 2015, caught by Jack Burnham for 1 at The Emirates.

He played his last NEPL game for The Academy on 5th September 2015 at Chester le Street.

He had played 6 games in The NEPL for The Academy, batting 6 times, with 2 not outs, he scored 199 runs at an average of 49.75. He scored 1 half century, his highest score of 77 not out on 30th May at South Shields.

He had bowled 264 balls, with 10 maidens, he conceded 165 runs and took 7 wickets at an average of 23.57. His best bowling figures were 2 for 27. He took 3 catches.

He made his debut for Hetton Lyons in The NEPL on 7th May 2016 at Whitburn, he made 59 not out and took 1 for 36. His first Hetton Lyons wicket was Dan Shurben, who was caught by Jarvis Clay. Carse played his last game for Hetton Lyons on 27th August 2016 at home to Benwell Hill.

He had played 5 games in The NEPL for Hetton, batting 4 times, with 2 not out's, he scored 166 runs at an average of 83.00. He scored 1 half century, his highest score of 59 not out on 7th May mentioned earlier. He had bowled 78 balls, with 2 maidens, he conceded 61 runs and took 1 wicket at an average of 61.00. His best bowling figures were 1 for 36. He took 1 NEPL catch for Hetton.

Carse then made his debut for Whitburn in The NEPL on 17th June 2017 at Newcastle, he made 25 and didn't bowl. Because of his Durham and England commitments Carse hardly played in The NEPL in 2017 and 2018. He played his last NEPL game for Whitburn on 7th July 2018 at home to Tynemouth, he didn't bowl and made 80 not out when batting.

He had played 12 games in The NEPL for Whitburn, batting 12 times, with 3 not out's, he scored 470 runs at an average of 52.22. He scored 3 half centuries; his highest score was 84 not out on 26th August 2017. He had bowled 54 balls, with 2 maidens, he conceded 22 runs and didn't take a wicket, he took 8 NEPL catches for Whitburn.

Carse next appeared in The NEPL on 20th April 2019, debuting for Felling at Burnopfield, he didn't bowl and scored 57 when he batted, he was caught by Scott Steel off the bowling of Harry Adair.

He would play five times in The NEPL for Felling in 2019, batting 5 times, he scored 123 runs at an average of 30.75, he scored 1 half century, the score he made on debut. He didn't bowl for them and took 2 NEPL catches.

Carse would then make his debut for Burnopfield in The NEPL on 16th April 2022 at home to South North, this was the game mentioned earlier as the start of the 2022 season for South North.

He played just one more game in the NEPL, the following week at Felling, he took 2 for 33 and scored 26.

To date, Brydon Carse has played 30 matches in the NEPL, batting 29 times, with 9 not outs, he has scored 1111 runs at an average of 55.55, he has scored 6 half centuries and 1 century, the century mentioned earlier to start the 2022 season, was his highest score.

He has also bowled 480 balls in the NEPL, with 14 maidens, conceding 304 runs and taking 11 wickets at an average of 27.63. His best bowling was 2 for 27, taken for Durham Academy against South Shields on 30th May 2015. He has taken 15 catches in the NEPL.

Originally born in Port Elizabeth in South Africa, Carse initially played his cricket for Eastern Province, up to Under 19 level, he then progressed through the Durham set up, starting in The Second XI, then into the first team.

At the time of writing, March 2024, Carse has played 12 One Day Internationals for England, he has also played 3 Twenty20 Internationals for them.

He has also played 41 first class matches for Durham, as well as 21 List A matches and, for Durham, Sunrisers Eastern Cape and The Northern Superchargers, 76 Twenty20 games.

Returning now to South North and their opening fixture of 2022, their lineup was as follows-

Simon Birtwisle opened the batting today, making 25 before he retired hurt. Birtwisle had played 367 matches in the NEPL going into the 2022 season, he has batted 359 times with 29 not outs, he has scored 11602 runs at an average of 35.15. He has scored 66 half centuries and 15 centuries. His highest score is 151 not out, made for Chester le Street in July 2010 and mentioned earlier.

He has bowled 6026 balls in the NEPL with 191 maidens, conceding 3422 runs and taking 171 wickets at an average of 20.01. His best bowling figures are 6 for 18 taken for South North on 7th September 2019 at home to Sacriston. He has taken 129 catches in the NEPL.

During the 2022 season Simon Birtwisle played 17 NEPL matches, batting 17 times with 3 not outs, he scored 402 runs at an average of 28.71. He scored 0 half centuries and 2 centuries.

The first century, 114 not out, was made on 2nd July 2022 at Whitburn, the innings came from 142 balls and contained 16 fours.

The second century, 108 not out, was scored on 16th July 2022 at Felling. It came from 139 balls with 18 fours.

He bowled 278 balls in the NEPL in 2022 with 2 maidens, conceding 190 runs and taking 11 wickets at an average of 17.27. His best bowling figures were 4 for 17, taken on 11th June at home to Benwell Hill. He took 4 catches in the NEPL in 2022.

Sol Bell opened the batting with Birtwisle, scoring 24. Bell entered the 2021 season having played 73 matches in the NEPL, batting 70 times with 8 not outs, he had scored 1826 runs at an average of 29.45. He had scored 8 half centuries and 3 centuries. His highest score was the 129 not out mentioned earlier. He had bowled 96 balls with 0 maidens, conceding 83 runs and taking 1 wicket, he had taken 25 NEPL catches.

In the 2022 season Bell played 21 matches in the NEPL for South North batting 21 times with 2 not outs, he scored 799 runs at an average of 42.05. He scored 7 half centuries and 1 century, 106 not out, scored on 18th June 2022 at home to Sunderland. It came from 90 balls and contained 16 fours and 2 sixes. He didn't bowl in the NEPL in 2022 but took 4 catches. For his efforts he was named The 2022 NEPL Player of the Year.

He has now played 94 NEPL matches, he has batted 91 times, with 10 not out's, scoring 2625 runs at an average of 32.40. He has scored 15 half centuries and 4 centuries, his highest score is 129 not out on 19th June 2021 at Chester Le Street.

He has bowled 96 balls in The NEPL, with 0 maidens, conceding 83 runs and taking one wicket. He has taken 29 NEPL catches.

Sol Bell spent the 2023 season at Sacriston and is returning to South North for 2024 after that one year away. During the 2023 season Bell played 16 times in NEPL Division 1, batting 15 times with 1 not out, he scored 1 half century and 3 centuries, with a highest score of 119, made on 17th June at home to Sunderland. He also bowled on four different occasions and added 1 wicket to his existing haul.

He also played 1 game for Warwickshire Second XI at Glamorgan in July 2023, he made 20 and 2. Having watched Bell quite a bit during 2022 I suspect that he is another North East young cricketer on whom first class cricket has given up too early.

Chris Hewison batted at number three to start the 2022 season, he made the highest score of the innings, 97. He entered the 2022 season having played 244 matches in the NEPL, he had batted 233 times with 36 not outs, he had scored 8082 runs at an average of 41.02. He had scored 42 half centuries and 18 centuries. His highest score was 165 not out, made in June 2002 at Philadelphia.

He had not bowled since 2010, so he still has 32 wickets at an average of 34.59 and he had taken 134 catches in his NEPL career so far.

Hewison played 21 matches in the NEPL in 2022, batting 18 times with 3 not outs, he scored 677 runs at an average of 45.13. He scored 4 half centuries and 2 centuries. His highest score was 107 not out, made on 2nd July 2022 at Whitburn, the innings came from 111 balls and contained 13 fours and 3 sixes.

His second century,100 not out was scored on 4th June 2022 at home to Eppleton, it came from 123 balls and contained 8 fours and 5 sixes. He took 7 catches in the NEPL in the season.

Rob Peyton batted at number four on 16th April, making 23, he also kept wicket. Coming into the season he had played 115 matches in the NEPL, batting 84 times with 13 not outs, he had scored 1206 runs at an average of 16.98. He had scored 4 half centuries with a highest score of 80 made on 2nd September 2017 at The Riverside against Durham Academy. He had made 114 catches and had 17 stumpings so far in the NEPL.

He played 20 matches in the NEPL in 2022, batting 20 times with 3 not outs, he scored 554 runs at an average of 32.58. He scored 1 half century, 50 not out on 7th May 2022 at home to Whitburn. He took 12 catches and made 3 stumpings in the season.

Sean Tindale captained the side in the absence of Adam Cragg, he batted at number five, he made 41. He also opened the bowling taking 1 for 47. Tindale entered the 2022 season having played 155 matches in the NEPL, batting 129 times with 25 not outs, he had scored 2269 runs at an average of 21.81. He had scored 9 half centuries and 1 century, 108 not out mentioned earlier.

He had bowled 7156 balls with 216 maidens, conceding 4009 runs and taking 196 wickets at an average of 20.45. His best bowling figures are 6 for 18 and were mentioned earlier. He had taken 36 NEPL catches.

During the 2022 season Tindale played 21 matches in the NEPL, batting 16 times with 3 not outs, he scored 361 runs at an average of 27.76. He scored 1 century, 101 not out on 14th May 2022 at home to Tynemouth, the innings came from 115 balls and contained 5 fours and 4 sixes.

He bowled 1143 balls with 26 maidens, conceding 720 runs and taking 33 wickets at an average of 21.81. His best bowling figures were 5 for 33 taken on 18th June 2022 at home to Sunderland. He also took 8 catches in the NEPL in 2022.

Oli McGee batted at number six to start the season; he made a single. He also took 2 for 29 with the ball. Entering the 2022 season McGee had played 168 matches in the NEPL, batting 98 times with 39 not outs, he has scored 967 runs at ana average of 16.38. He has made 3 half centuries with the highest score of 99 mentioned earlier.

He has bowled 9441 balls, with 284 maidens, conceding 5142 runs and taking 281 wickets at an average of 18.29. His best bowling figures are 7 for 54, taken for Newcastle in August 2016 and mentioned earlier. He had taken 40 catches.

In 2022 he played 22 matches In the NEPL, batting 16 times with 5 not outs, he scored 229 runs at an average of 20.81, he scored 1 half century, 58, on 23rd April 2022 at Newcastle.

He bowled 1142 balls in the NEPL in 2022, with 13 maidens, he conceded 717 runs and took 44 wickets at an average of 16.29. His best bowling figures were 5 for 36, taken on 2nd July 2022 at Whitburn. He took 11 catches that season.

Parth Mannikar, batted at number seven, not much opportunity to bat though, scoring 2 not out from three balls. Mannikar first came to my attention on 21st May 2012 when he was selected for Northumberland Under 13's against Cumbria Under 13's. He progressed to the Northumberland Under 15's, playing a match on 30th June 2014 at Cumbria and he continued throughout 2015 to play for Northumberland Under 15's.

He had made his NEPL debut for South North at Tynemouth on 23rd April 2016, going on to play 3 times in the NEPL in 2016, once in 2018 and twice in 2019.

During the 2022 season he played 11 matches in the NEPL for South North, batting 8 times with 4 not outs, he scored 76 runs at an average of 19.00. His highest score was 29, made on 23rd April at Newcastle. He took 7 catches and made 3 stumpings in 2022. He played his last NEPL game on 3rd September 2022 for South North at Sunderland.

In total Mannikar played 17 matches in the NEPL, batting 11 times with 5 not outs, he scored 98 runs at an average of 16.33. His highest score was 29, mentioned earlier. He took 15 catches and had 4 stumpings in the NEPL.

Angus Southern is a right-handed batsman who made his NEPL debut in this game on 16th April 2022 at Burnopfield. He was batted at number 8 and was dismissed first ball. He had progressed through the Northumberland Junior set up since making his debut on 20th August 2020 at Under 15 level. He played one further game for the firsts in 2022 and one further match in 2023 and he also played for the county Under 18 side in 2023.

Jonny Wightman batted at number nine; he was also dismissed first ball. He opened the bowling taking 2 for 39. Wightman entered the 2022 season having played 224 matches in the NEPL, he had batted 110 times with 41 not outs, he had scored 702 runs at an average of 10.17. His highest score was 37 scored for South North in May 2011 and mentioned earlier.

He had bowled 13326 balls with 331 maidens, conceding 8083 runs and taking 438 wickets at an average of 18.45. His best bowling figures were 8 for 31, taken on 4th June 2016 for South North at home to Gateshead Fell. He had taken 28 catches.

During the 2022 season Wightman played 21 matches, batting 9 times with 2 not outs, he scored 21 runs at an average of 3.00. His highest score was 6. He bowled 1247 balls with 21 maidens, conceding 861 runs and took 41 wickets at an average of 21.00. His best bowling figures of 2022 were 4 for 37, taken on 6th August at home to Burnmoor. He took 5 catches in the NEPL in 2022.

Calum Fletcher was listed to bat at number ten in the season opener, he didn't bat as his side ran out of overs. He did bowl, taking 0 for 42. Fletcher entered the 2022 season having played 20 matches in the NEPL, all for South North, he had batted 5 times with 2 not outs, he had scored 11 runs at an average of 3.66. His highest score was 5 not out.

He had bowled 670 balls with 18 maidens, conceding 376 runs and taking 17 wickets at an average of 22.11. His best bowling figures were 2 for 21, taken on 31st July 2021 at home to Hetton Lyons. He had taken 2 catches.

During the 2022 season Fletcher played 15 matches, batting 5 times with 3 not outs, he scored 17 runs at an average of 8.50. His highest score was 13.

He bowled 529 balls in the NEPL in 2022, with 14 maidens, conceding 295 runs and took 11 wickets at an average of 26.81. His best bowling figures of 2022 were 3 for 16, taken on 30th July at Tynemouth. He took 1 catch in the NEPL in 2022.

Lee Crozier was listed to bat at number eleven but didn't get to bat. He took 1 for 75 when he bowled. He entered the 2022 season having played 394 matches in the NEPL, batting 166 times with 81 not outs, he had scored 1371 runs at an average of 16.12. He had scored 1 half century, 89 for Benwell Hill in 2002.

He had bowled 26826 balls, with 1179 maidens, conceding 11883 runs and taking 784 wickets at an average of 15.15. His best bowling was 7 for 21 taken for South North in 2007. He had taken 55 NEPL catches.

Lee Crozier played 21 matches in the NEPL in 2022, batting 5 times with 4 not outs, he scored 12 runs at an average of 12.00. His highest score of the 2022 NEPL season was 12.

He bowled 1253 balls in the NEPL in 2022, with 24 maidens, conceding 801 runs and taking 23 wickets at an average of 34.82. His best bowling figures of the season were 3 for 51, taken on 4th June at home to Eppleton. He took 2 catches in the NEPL in 2022.

Adam Cragg missed the opening two games of 2022 but returned on 30th April at home to Felling, he started his season with 58 in a 7-wicket loss. Cragg entered the 2022 season having played 260 matches in the NEPL, he had batted 215 times with 44 not outs, he had scored 5246 runs at an average of 30.67. He had scored 29 half centuries and 2 centuries. His highest score was 102, made in May 2010 at home to Blaydon. He had not bowled since 2017 so still had 1 wicket to his name, but he had taken 191 catches and had 24 stumpings in his NEPL career so far.

Cragg played 19 matches in the NEPL in 2022, batting 15 times with 4 not outs, he scored 432 runs at an average of 39.27. He scored 4 half centuries. His highest score was 70, made on 4th June at home to Eppleton. He took 14 catches in the NEPL in the season.

Tshepang Dithole was a left-handed batsman and right arm off break bowler, he was the overseas pro for 2022, hailing from South Africa. He arrived having played first -class cricket in South Africa for Border, KwaZulu-Natal Inland, Gauteng and Central Gauteng, he had also played List A cricket for KwaZulu-Natal Inland, Dolphins, Gauteng and Central Gauteng and Twnety20 cricket for KwaZulu-Natal Inland and KwaZulu-Natal Coastal. He had also played for a South African Emerging Players XI.

He made his NEPL debut for South North on 25th June 2022 at Hetton Lyons, he scored 51 in a winning effort, his last game in the NEPL was for South North on 27th August 2022 at Benwell Hill.

Dithole played 10 matches in the NEPL in 2022, batting 9 times with 1 not out, he scored 176 runs at an average of 22.00. He scored 1 half century, the 51 on debut mentioned earlier. He did not bowl but took 6 catches in the NEPL in 2022. He returned to South African cricket after 2022, playing for Kwa Zulu-Natal Coastal.

Looking back at the 2022 season and the final few games it seems South North had built a healthy lead over both Burnmoor and Hetton Lyons as the format of the league went towards the last five games and the 50 over format. The negative thing with this format is that you don't get as many points for a win as you do in the more traditional format, effectively it's only 10 points as against 20 points and this makes overhauling a lead difficult to say the least.

With 6 games to go, after the games of 30th July 2022 the top of the table would have looked something like this.

South North 316 Points
Burnmoor 276 Points
Hetton Lyons 269 Points

South North had lost just 3 games up to this point and hosted Burnmoor on the next weekend, 6th August 2022. South North won the toss and elected to field, Burnmoor then made 195 for 9 and declared after 49.5 overs. Half centuries from Alex Simpson, 58, and Ryan Pringle, 53, supported by 22 from Ross Greenwell and 19 from Craig Stephenson setting them up with a respectable score. For South North Jonny Wightman had taken 4 for 37, Sean Tindale 2 for 38, Lee Crozier 2 for 46 and Calum Fletcher 1 for 25.

When South North batted, they never really got going, regular wickets from Burnmoor kept them in check and they never threatened to get the required runs. Despite 47 from Rob Peyton, South North were bowled out for 123 from 38.2 overs. Waqas Maqsood took 4 for 44, Ryan Greenwell had 2 for 1, Josh Coughlin took 2 for 36, Craig Stephenson 1 for 1 and Graeme Bridge 1 for 17. Burnmoor had won by 72 runs and picked up 29 points for their efforts, South North got 4.

Hetton Lyons had comfortably beaten Tynemouth after Ben McKinney had made 113 and Gary Scott 58 and then Chris Ralston had taken 3 for 41 to pick up 30 points.

The league table, although not altered position wise, had closed up a little.

South North 320 Points
Burnmoor 305 Points
Hetton Lyons 299 Points

The weekend of 13th August saw the pendulum swing back towards South North, they beat Chester le Street by 4 wickets, this was despite 81 from Chester opener Jacob McCann and 57 from Matthew Cranston as Chester posted a good score of 231 from their 50 overs. Jonny Wightman had taken 3 for 42. Chris Hewison, 50, and Sol Bell 47, had led the South North response as they picked up 20 points, winning with the first ball of the 47th over.

Both Burnmoor and Hetton lost, Burnmoor had batted first at home to Tynemouth, Matthew Brown top scored with 49 but 61 not out from Stuart Poynter had seen Tynemouth win by 4 wickets. Burnmoor got 5 points from the game. Hetton had been undone at Whitburn, Kevin Almeida, Whitburn's overseas pro had scored 100 from just

67 balls, with 11 fours and 4 sixes as Whitburn posted 330 for 6 from 50 overs. Chris Ralston top scored with 48 as Hetton gave it a go but they were dismissed for 246 from 39.2 overs. They picked up 7 points from the game.

The league table would now look like this.

South North 340 Points
Burnmoor 310 Points
Hetton Lyons 306 Points

The weekend of 20th August was washed out for South North and Burnmoor, so they picked up 5 points each. Hetton lost at home to Newcastle, once again they gave up a big score to an overseas pro, Jesse Tashkoff making 126 from 117 balls with 17 fours and 1 six as Newcastle made 290 for 8 from their 50 overs. Chris Ralston had 3 for 35.
 Ralston led the charge with the bat, making 63 and Jarvis Clay hit 59 but Tashkoff 5 for 36 and George Darwood 4 for 38, saw Newcastle win by 82 runs. Hetton got 7 points for their efforts.

Going into the weekend of 27th August 2022 the league table would now look like this.

South North 345 Points
Burnmoor 315 Points
Hetton Lyons 313 Points

South North then visited Benwell Hill, Hill batted first and 79 from Fin McCreath and 69 from Mohsin Mukhtar meant they posted a challenging 244 for 8 from their 50 overs. Oli McGee had 3 for 45 for South North. When South North batted despite 47 from Rob Peyton and the fact that the top seven all made double figures, they were bowled out for 215 from 47.2 overs. Two wickets each for Max Williamson, Callum Harding and Joe Torre. South North got 7 points from the game.
 Burnmoor had been in a bit of trouble at home to Eppleton at 134 for 7 but a stand of 108 for the eighth wicket between Josh Coughlin, 55, and Craig Stephenson, 45 not out, had seen them recover to score 245 for 8 from their 50 overs. When Eppleton batted Graeme Bridge 3 for 39 and Craig Stephenson 3 for 44 saw the win by 23 runs and also pick up 20 points.
 Hetton Lyons got back on track with a solid team win at Felling, Tyler Easton had hit 102 and Alan Mustard 57, when Felling batted as they scored 229 for 5 from their 50 overs. Robbie Talbot with 66 not out and 45 from Chris Ralston saw them home by 3 wickets with 10.2 overs to spare and pick up 20 points.

The league table heading to the weekend of 3rd September was as follows.

South North 352 Points
Burnmoor 335 Points
Hetton Lyons 333 Points

And so, to the penultimate weekend of the 2022 season, all three teams won, and all three teams picked up 20 points.
 South North dismissed Sunderland for 172, Simon Birtwisle 3 for 7. Rob Peyton making 41 as they got home for the loss of 5 wickets.
 Burnmoor, thanks to 67 not out from Ross Greenwell and 51 not out from Alex Simpson had chased down 191 at Benwell Hill to win by 5 wickets.
 Hetton Lyons had bowled Burnopfield out for 155, Cameron Grimwood taking 3 for 32. An unbeaten 54 from Gary Scott had seen them win by 6 wickets.

So, the league table, and more importantly the points difference remained unaltered.

South North 372 Points
Burnmoor 355 Points
Hetton Lyons 353 Points

Hetton Lyons were to play at South North in the last game of the season so that effectively ruled out a Burnmoor title win. A single point meant South North shared the title, two points and it was theirs outright. The weather forecast for 10th September 2022 wasn't great, South North won the toss and decided to bat, 125 required to get 1 bonus point, 150 to get two. They were 60 when the first wicket fell, Simon Birtwisle leg before to Grimwood for 18, and 67 when number three Rob Peyton was leg before to Rahatul Ferdous for 7.

122 for 3 when opener Sol Bell was caught by Gary Scott off Talbot for 51 and 171 for 4 when Chris Hewison was out for 46. 58 from Adam Cragg saw them post 230 for 7 when their innings was closed after 50 overs. I was at this game with the camera, and it poured down during the tea interval, match abandoned, South North 9 points, Hetton Lyons 8 points, South North 2022 NEPL Champions.

The Banks Salver was won by Benwell Hill, South North won the Twenty20 and Seb Allison of Felling was named as NEPL Player of the Year.

I could find very little on Seb Allison prior to his NEPL debut, he was playing for Bishops Diocesan College whilst at Durham University in 2018. He next appeared playing a couple of games for the Durham University Centre of Cricketing Excellence against Durham and Sussex in March 2022 and a further game for them against Worcestershire in April 2022.

This was Allison's first season in the NEPL, making his NEPL debut on 16th April 2022 at home to Burnmoor, he took 1 for 23, his first NEPL wicket was Ryan Greenwell, bowled for 4.

Seb Allison played 21 matches in the NEPL in 2022, batting 15 times with 2 not outs, he scored 495 runs at an average of 38.07. He scored 4 half centuries with a highest score of 87 not out, made on 3rd September 2022 at Whitburn.

He also bowled 1360 balls in the NEPL in 2022, with 38 maidens, he conceded 743 runs and took 50 wickets at an average of 14.86. His best bowling figures were 5 for 27 taken on 4th June 2022 at home to Sunderland. He took 6 catches in the NEPL in 2022.

To the end of the 2023 season Allison had played 39 matches in the NEPL, batting 31 times with 3 not outs, he had scored 778 runs at an average of 27.78. He had scored 5 half centuries with a highest score of 87 not out and mentioned earlier.

He had also bowled 2401 balls in the NEPL, with 73 maidens, conceding 1338 runs and taking 89 wickets at an average of 15.03. His best bowling figures were 5 for 27 mentioned earlier. He had now taken 8 NEPL catches.

TABLE 68   NEPL 2022.

	Played	Won	Draw/Aban	Lost	Penalty Points	Bonus Points	Points
South North	22	14	3	5	0	100	381
Burnmoor	22	12	3	7	0	115	361
Hetton Lyons	22	13	3	6	0	94	361
Felling	22	13	4	5	0	73	341
Newcastle	22	11	4	7	0	103	335
Chester le Street	22	7	8	7	0	92	269
Benwell Hill	22	7	6	9	0	97	265
Whitburn	22	9	3	10	0	59	250
Tynemouth	22	6	5	11	0	111	246
Burnopfield	22	3	7	12	0	91	215
Sunderland	22	2	6	14	0	88	208
Eppleton	22	1	6	15	5	86	186

TABLE 69   NEPL Batting Averages 2022.
Qualification 450 Runs.

Player	Club	Inns	N. O	H. S	Runs	Average
(1) J.T.A Burnham	Whitburn	16	1	147	830	55.33
(2) J. du Toit	Newcastle	21	4	101 no	898	52.82
(3 T.M Norris	Felling	19	2	135 no	775	45.59
(4) R.A Green	Newcastle	15	2	108	590	45.38
(5) K.J Coetzer	Benwell Hill	11	1	108	452	45.20
(6) C.J Hewison	South North	18	3	107 no	677	45.13
(7) P.G Bell	Benwell Hill	18	7	74 no	493	44.82
(8) J. McCann	Chester le Street	20	2	81	787	43.72
(9) B.S McKinney	Hetton Lyons	15	1	113	598	42.71
(10) S.J.D Bell	South North	22	3	106 no	799	42.05
(11) E. Rahman	Tynemouth	20	4	112	639	39.94
(12) J.R Oswell	Burnopfield	20	0	194	789	39.45
(25) R. Peyton	South North	20	3	50 no	554	32.59

TABLE 70   NEPL Bowling Averages 2022.
Qualification 20 Wickets.

Player	Club	Overs	Mdns	Runs	Wkts	Average
(1) Waqas Maqsood	Burnmoor	190.1	26	689	47	14.66
(2) S.J Allison	Felling	226.4	38	743	50	14.86
(3) Taj Wali	Eppleton	156.3	36	454	29	15.66
(4) P. Leonard	Felling	220.2	41	755	48	15.73
(5) Q.J Hughes	Chester le Street	164.0	35	444	28	15.86
(6) A. Ebdale	Eppleton	159.4	17	578	36	16.06
(7) O.F McGee	South North	190.2	13	717	44	16.30
(8) G.D Bridge	Burnmoor	160.1	16	586	35	16.74
(9) K. Waterson	Sunderland	220.5	42	769	44	17.48
(10) A. Feroz	Hetton Lyons	207.2	31	681	36	18.92
(11) C. Stephenson	Burnmoor	159.5	27	540	28	19.29
(12) C.T Harding	Benwell Hill	138.2	19	477	24	19.88
(18) J.R Wightman	South North	207.5	21	861	41	21.00
(21) S.J Tindale	South North	190.3	26	720	33	21.82

South North CC 2022.

Left to Right- Back Row- John Tindale (Coach), Calum Fletcher, Sol Bell, Chris Hewison, Nathan Gough, Rob Peyton, John Ruddick (Scorer).

Front Row -Lee Crozier, Jonny Wightman, Sean Tindale, Adam Cragg, Simon Birtwisle, Oli McGee.

Oli McGee seen here bowling at Ashington on 10th June 2023.

Seb Allison seen here bowling for Felling on 31st August 2024 at Benwell Hill.

2023

South North opened their title defence in 2023 with a home game against Newcastle on 29th April, the visitors won the toss and decided to field and South North were 184 all out in 49.1 overs. 40 from opener Rob Peyton and 38 from Oli McGee, batting at number eight, the main reasons for the score. Newcastle opening bowler George Darwood and veteran Jaques du Toit both took 3 for 24.

When Newcastle batted, they were 79 for 3 but when the wicket of George Darwood fell to go 79 for 4, they fell away to be dismissed for 104. Oli McGee took 4 for 24, Lee Crozier 3 for 18, Sean Tindale 2 for 19 and Calum Fletcher 1 for 4. South North won by 80 runs.

The South North team to start the season was as follows-

Simon Birtwisle opened the batting today and made 5. Birtwisle had played 384 matches in the NEPL going into the 2023 season, he has batted 376 times with 32 not outs, he has scored 12004 runs at an average of 34.89. He has scored 66 half centuries and 17 centuries. His highest score is 151 not out, made for Chester le Street in July 2010 and mentioned earlier.

He has bowled 6304 balls in the NEPL with 193 maidens, conceding 3612 runs and taking 182 wickets at an average of 19.84. His best bowling figures are 6 for 18 taken for South North on 7th September 2019 at home to Sacriston. He has taken 133 catches in the NEPL.

During the 2023 season Simon Birtwisle played 15 NEPL matches, batting 14 times with 0 not outs, he scored 192 runs at an average of 13.71. His highest score was 45, made on 1st July 2023 at home to Chester le Street.

He bowled 129 balls in the NEPL in 2023 with 1 maiden, conceding 66 runs and taking 5 wickets at an average of 13.20. His best bowling figures were 3 for 17, taken on 12th August at home to Tynemouth. He made 5 catches in the NEPL in 2023.

At the end of 2023 Simon Birtwisle had played 399 matches in the NEPL, he has batted 390 times with 32 not outs, he has scored 12196 runs at an average of 34.06. He has scored 66 half centuries and 17 centuries. His highest score is 151 not out, made for Chester le Street in July 2010 and mentioned earlier.

He has bowled 6433 balls in the NEPL with 194 maidens, conceding 3678 runs and taking 187 wickets at an average of 19.66. His best bowling figures are 6 for 18 taken for South North on 7th September 2019 at home to Sacriston. He has taken 138 catches in the NEPL.

At the end of the 2023 season Birtwisle, together with South North teammates Chris Hewison and Jonny Wightman were informed that they had been selected for the England Seniors Over 40 for the World Cup in South Africa in February 2024. Birtwisle travelled and played and was part of the team that finished fourth. Birtwisle had made his debut for The England Over 40's on 19th February 2024 against Zimbabwe. He scored 9.

Rob Peyton opened the batting with Birtwisle and scored 40, he also kept wicket, taking 2 catches and a stumping. Coming into the 2023 season he had played 135 matches in the NEPL, batting 104 times with 16 not outs, he had scored 1760 runs at an average of 17.60. He had scored 5 half centuries with a highest score of 80 made on 2nd September 2017 at The Riverside against Durham Academy. He had made 126 catches and had 20 stumpings so far in the NEPL.

He played 15 matches in the NEPL in 2023, batting 14 times with 0 not outs, he scored 203 runs at an average of 14.50. He scored 1 half century, 67 on 20th May 2023 at home to Whitburn. He took 15 catches and made 8 stumpings in the season.

At the end of the 2023 season Rob Peyton had now played 150 matches in the NEPL, batting 118 times with 16 not outs, he had scored 1963 runs at an average of 19.24. He had scored 6 half centuries with a highest score of 80 made on 2nd September 2017 at The Riverside against Durham Academy. He had made 141 catches and had 28 stumpings so far in the NEPL.

Nikhil Gorantla is a right-handed batsman and right arm medium pace bowler, he was making his NEPL debut for South North today, he batted at number three to open the 2023 season, he made 27. Lee Crozier almost waxed lyrically when I spoke to him about Gorantla "what a player he is! I'm really looking forward to seeing him bat with Sol Bell, I don't understand how these two are not playing first-class cricket, his performance against Durham when he made 100+ against their first and second team plus the two 40 odd scores he made in a warm up match and then his time with Worcestershire and Warwickshire to me add up to someone who deserves a chance. I really hope it's simply a case of waiting for the right place at the right time for him, it hasn't happened yet but I'm sure it will. He is a very level headed batsman, he reads conditions and situations and can base his style of innings depending on what the team needs."

Gorantla first came to note on 31st July 2016 when he played for Cambridgeshire Under 14's against Middlesex Under 14's at Impington, he didn't get to bat.

The following year he was selected to play for Cambridgeshire Under 15's against Huntingdonshire Under 15's on 21st May 2015 at Burwell, he took 1 for 17 when his side bowled and he opened the batting, making 68 not out as his side won by 9 wickets. He continued to play for the Under 14's throughout 2017 although he was selected for the Under 17's in a 2-day match starting on 25th July 2017 at Copdock against Suffolk Under 17's.

The remainder of 2017 and first part of 2018 was spent playing youth cricket across the age groups for Cambridgeshire. On 16th June 2018 Gorantla made his debut in the Cambridgeshire and Huntingdonshire Premier League for Ramsey at home to Sawston and Babraham, he made 29 batting at three.

He started the 2019 season by playing for Essex Second XI in a 50 over match on 13th April at Broxbourne against Norfolk, he didn't get to bat. On 20th April 2019 he made his debut in the East Anglian Premier League for Saffron Walden at home to Mildenhall, he scored 17 batting at number five. The 12th of May 2019 saw Gorantla make his debut for Essex Under 17's at Canterbury against Kent Under 17's, he scored 52 opening the batting. Gorantla scored his first century, 114, for Essex Under 17's in 3 -day match which started on 30th July 2019, he also scored 53 in the second innings.

On 23rd August 2019 Gorantla played for a Cambridgeshire Under 25's side against an Essex Cricket Board Development XI, he scored 44 and took 2 for 61.

During the 2020 pandemic he played for Essex Under 18's and Essex Academy, as well as continuing to play for Saffron Walden.

On 30th May 2021 Gorantla made his debut in Minor Counties Trophy matches, for Cambridgeshire at Hertfordshire. He scored 48 and took 1 for 20.

On 26th July 2021 he was selected to play in an ECB Elite Development Under 18 game between London and East and North, he made 16 opening the batting for the London side.

I found a remarkable run of form in June 2022, starting on 25th June when Gorantla scored 114 for Saffron Walden at Witham, in his next innings, in a 4-day match which started on 27th June for Essex Seconds he scored 101 in the first innings against Hampshire Seconds, he made 26 not out in the second innings.

He then played for Essex Second XI at Leeds against Yorkshire Second XI in a 4-day match which started on 4th July 2022. Essex batted first and Gorantla, batting at number seven, scored 200 not out in the first innings, he faced 215 balls, batted for 251 minutes and struck 29 fours and 4 sixes. In four innings he had scored 441 runs at an average of 220.50!

In a 3-day match which started on 27th March 2023 Gorantla was selected to play for a Durham University Centre of Cricketing Excellence side against Durham at the Riverside, he made 27 and 40 in a drawn game.

So far, Gorantla has only played one season, 2023, in The NEPL, at the end of it he was named The NEPL Player of the Year. He played 13 NEPL matches, he has batted 13 times, with 4 not out's, scoring 678 runs at an average of 75.33. He has scored 3 half centuries and 3 centuries. His highest score was his second century, 134 not out, scored on 10th June 2023 at Ashington, this innings came from 110 balls and contained 17 fours and 4 sixes.

His first century,103, for South North in the NEPL, had been at Tynemouth on 27th May 2023, it had come from 151 balls and contained 8 fours.

The third South North century,134 not out, came at home to Castle Eden on 17th June 2023, it came from 101 balls with 20 fours and 1 six.

He has bowled 30 balls in The NEPL, with 0 maidens, conceding 24 runs and failing to take a wicket. He has taken 7 NEPL catches.

Gorantla also scored a fourth century that season, 118, for Northumberland at Jesmond against Durham, that innings came from 121 balls and contained 18 fours and helped Northumberland to an upset win over a strong Durham side.

I was fortunate to be at all four of the centuries he scored, the first at Tynemouth was very impressive, Tynemouth had South North 2 for 3 and the ball was seaming all over the place, Andrew Smith had removed Simon Birtwisle and Angus Southern, Richard Stanyon had dismissed Chris Hewison. Adam Cragg then came in at five and he scored 69 as he and Gorantla added 174 for the fourth wicket as South North went on to win by 111 runs.

The second century,134 not out, at Ashington, was a classic example of pacing an innings to suit the situation. It was a beautiful sunny day at Ashington and a good batting track. Ashington had batted first and batted well, seven players got into double figures, there were half centuries from Mitchell Killeen, 52, and West Indian pro Jeremiah Louis, 51, Jack Jessop had 46 as Ashington scored 254 for 8 when their innings was closed after 58 overs.

South North had 52 overs because of the loss of overs earlier. The Ashington opening bowlers Killeen and Matthew Collins bowled well, not giving much away and Collins picking up the wickets of Rob Peyton and Sam Ewart as South North reached 38 for 2. Chris Hewison had come in at four and he hit a steady 32 from 58 balls before Killeen bowled him, although he and Gorantla had however given South North a platform at 143 for 3. Former Ashington player and now South North captain, Adam Cragg came in at five and he and Gorantla then started playing their shots. They added an unbroken 112 for the fourth wicket, Gorantla was 134 not out from 110 balls and Cragg 58 not out from 41 balls, he had hit 8 fours in his innings.

Gorantla's third NEPL hundred, 104 not out, at home to Castle Eden, was simply good batting. Castle Eden had batted first and posted a respectable 168 all out in 47.1 overs. Philip Wimpenny top scored with 49 as he and Oliver Sampson Barnes, 34, had added 59 for the ninth wicket after they had been facing a low score at 109 for 8. Oli McGee had taken 4 for 28 as the pick of the South North bowlers. South North lost Simon Birtwisle for 4 and Shayne Moseley for 3 early on but Gorantla and Chris Hewison put the innings on an even keel, they put on 50 in just 72 balls, with Hewison hitting 33 of them from 37 balls. When Hewison was dismissed, for 40 from 47 balls with 6 fours and a six, South North were 122 for 3 and although they lost Rob Peyton and Sean Tindale cheaply, Gorantla opened up and finished the innings off. South North won by 5 wickets.

The fourth century I saw Gorantla score in 2023 was for Northumberland at Jesmond against Durham. Northumberland had lost opener Alasdair Appleby in the first over but Gorantla and Ashington opener Jack Jessop, who made 38, added 98 for the second wicket at a good pace, their fifty-partnership coming from just 54 balls, once Jessop had gone Ben Robinson, 27, had added 50 in 39 balls and this allowed the rest of the Northumberland batsmen to come in and be even more aggressive. Gorantla had made 118 came from 121 balls and struck 18 fours when Liam Robinson had him caught on the boundary by Paul Coughlin to end the innings, the score was then 240 for 6 from 42.5 overs. Matthew Oswell, batting at number eight, had made 22 from 21 balls to keep the impetus going and Northumberland finished on an impressive 290 for 8 when their innings was closed after 50 overs. Luke Robinson had 3 for 33 as the most successful Durham bowler.

George Darwood got Northumberland off to a good start when he removed England test Player Alex Lees for 5, caught by Calum Fletcher when Durham were 18. The rest of the Durham top and middle order all made double figures, opener Graham Clark had 40, Michael Jones 14 and Ben McKinney 35. They were 108 for 4 when McKinney was run out. It was the fifth wicket stand, between Jonny Bushnell and Liam Trevaskis which looked like it might turn out to be the match winner, as they added 50 in 57 balls and 100 in 90 balls. They both fell in the space of 7 balls, with the score on 208 Oli McGee had Trevaskis leg before wicket with the fourth ball of the 34th over for 63. His innings had come from 45 balls and contained 6 fours and 3 sixes. With the third ball of the 35th over Max Williamson had Bushnell caught behind by wicketkeeper and captain Stuart Poynter for 47, his innings had come from 64 balls and contained 6 fours. Durham were now 214 for 6 from 35.3 overs and required 77 runs to win from 14.3 overs, still less than a run a ball but not many wickets left. Williamson removed George Drissell stumped for 4, Oli McGee had Paul Coughlin caught by George Darwood for 26, Matthew Oswell had Oliver

Gibson caught by Calum Fletcher for 5 and with the score at 261, with the fifth ball of the 45th over, George Darwood had Luke Robinson caught behind by Poynter for a single, Durhan 261 all out, Northumberland won by 29 runs.

An excellent day's cricket, a tremendous advert in fact for North East cricket in front of a decent crowd and the win, although a tremendous all-round team effort was set up by a lovely hundred from Gorantla.

Chris Hewison batted at number four to start the 2023 season, he made 32. He entered the 2023 season having played 265 matches in the NEPL, he had batted 251 times with 39 not outs, he had scored 8759 runs at an average of 41.31. He had scored 46 half centuries and 20 centuries. His highest score was 165 not out, made in June 2002 at Philadelphia. He had not bowled in the NEPL since 2010, so he still has 32 wickets at an average of 34.59 and he had taken 141 catches in his NEPL career so far.

Hewison played 16 matches in the NEPL in 2023, batting 15 times with 0 not outs, he scored 371 runs at an average of 24.73. He scored 2 half centuries, his highest score was 51, made on 1st July 2023 at home to Chester le Street. He took 3 catches in the NEPL in the season.

By the close of the 2023 season Chris Hewison had now played 281 matches in the NEPL, he had batted 266 times with 39 not outs, he had scored 9130 runs at an average of 40.22. He had scored 48 half centuries and 20 centuries. His highest score was 165 not out, made in June 2002 at Philadelphia. He had not bowled since 2010, so he still has 32 wickets at an average of 34.59 and he had taken 144 catches in his NEPL career so far.

At the end of the 2023 season Hewison, together with South North teammates Simon Birtwisle and Jonny Wightman were informed that they had been selected for the England Seniors Over 40 for the World Cup in South Africa in February 2024. Hewison travelled and played and was part of the team that finished fourth, he made his debut for The England Over 40's on 19th February 2024 against Zimbabwe, scoring 47.

Bas de Leede batted at number five to open the season, he scored 6. He also bowled five overs, taking 0 for 24 when his side were in the field. He was signed as a short-term option only as he was heading to the World Cup Qualifiers with the Netherlands. He had arrived at South North having first played for The Netherlands in 2018, and he had scored 123 in their final World Cup qualifying match against Scotland as recently as 6th July 2023. He played only twice in the NEPL in 2023, scoring just 6 runs, he took 0 for 24 when he bowled. At the 2023 World Cup he picked up 16 wickets, including four against Pakistan and three against England. He also scored 139 runs in the tournament, including 67 against Pakistan.

On 24th January 2024 de Leede was selected as The ICC Men's Associate Cricketer of the Year for 2023.

He made 7 first class appearances for Durham, scoring 494 runs and taking 17 wickets.

At the time of writing, 1st April 2024, he was playing for The Desert Vipers in Dubai in the International League T20. Update- de Leede was a regular for Durham in first class cricket throughout 2024.

Adam Cragg was captain again this season and batted at six to open the season, he was run out for a single. Cragg entered the 2023 season having played 279 matches in the NEPL, he had batted 230 times with 48 not outs, he had scored 5678 runs at an average of 31.19. He had scored 33 half centuries and 2 centuries. His highest score was 102, made in May 2010 at home to Blaydon. He had not bowled since 2017 so still had 1 wicket to his name and he had taken 205 catches and had 24 stumpings in his NEPL career so far.

He played 16 matches in the NEPL in 2023, batting 16 times, he scored 401 runs at an average of 36.45. He scored 2 half centuries, his highest score of the season was 69, scored on 27th May at Tynemouth. He also took 13 catches.

At the end of the 2023 season Cragg had now played 295 matches in the NEPL, he had batted 246 times with 53 not outs, he had scored 6079 runs at an average of 31.49. He had scored 35 half centuries and 2 centuries. His highest score was 102, made in May 2010 at home to Blaydon. He had not bowled since 2017 so still had 1 wicket to his name, he had taken 218 catches and had 24 stumpings in his NEPL career so far.

Since Cragg was first appointed as South North captain in 2017, he has seen the side win NEPL titles in 2017, 2018, 2021, 2022 and 2023 under his leadership.

Sean Tindale batted at number seven, scoring 16. He also opened the bowling taking 2 for 19 from seven overs. Tindale played 17 matches in the NEPL in the 2023 season, batting 15 times, he scored 210 runs at an average of 14.00. His highest score was 40, scored on 20th May at home to Whitburn.

He bowled 900 balls, with 16 maidens, conceding 523 runs and taking 27 wickets at an average of 19.37. His best bowling figures were 4 for 35, taken on 3rd June at home to Felling.

To the end of the 2023 season Tindale has played 193 NEPL matches, batting 160 times with 28 not outs, he has scored 2840 runs at an average of 21.51. He has scored 9 half centuries and 2 centuries, his highest score remains 108 not out scored inn April 2017 for Newcastle and mentioned earlier.

He has also bowled 9199 balls with 258 maidens, conceding 5252 runs and taking 256 wickets at an average of 20.51. His best bowling figures are 6 for 18, taken on 15th May 2021 at Whitburn and mentioned earlier. He has taken 48 NEPL catches.

Sean Tindale has now played 53 matches for Northumberland, the most recent on 6th August 2023, he has batted 70 times with 9 not outs, he has scored 1355 runs at an average of 22.21. He has scored 6 half centuries with a highest score of 95, made in a 3-day match which started on 19th June 2016 against Suffolk.

He has bowled 4050 balls for Northumberland, with 95 maidens, conceding 2920 runs and taking 74 wickets at an average of 39.45. His best bowling is 5 for 40, taken in a 3-day match which started on 31st July 2016 at Norfolk. He has taken 20 catches for Northumberland.

Oli McGee batted at number eight and scored a key 38 when South North batted, he also took 4 for 24 from seven overs when he bowled. McGee entered the 2023 season having played 190 times in the NEPL, he has batted 114 times with 44 not outs, he has scored 1196 runs at an average of 17.08. He has scored 4 half centuries. His highest score is 99, made 9th June 2018 for Newcastle against The Durham Academy at The Riverside.

He had bowled 10583 balls in the NEPL up to the end of 2022, with 297 maidens, conceding 5859 runs and taking 325 wickets at an average of 18.02. His best bowling figures were 7 for 54, taken for Newcastle on 27th August 2016. He had taken 51 NEPL catches up to this point.

McGee played 17 times in the NEPL in the 2023 season, he batted 13 times, with 4 not outs, he scored 163 runs at an average of 18.11. His highest score was 43, scored on 1st July at home to Chester le Street.

He bowled 898 balls with 21 maidens, conceding 456 runs and taking 40 wickets at an average of 11.40. His best bowling figures were 4 for 23 taken on 26th August at home to Ashington.

He has now played 207 NEPL matches, he has batted 127 times, with 48 not out's, scoring 1359 runs at an average of 17.20. He has scored 4 half centuries; his highest score is 99 made on 9th June 2018 at The Riverside against The Durham Academy.

He has bowled 11481 balls in The NEPL, with 318 maidens, conceding 6315 runs and taking 365 wickets at an average of 17.30. His best bowling figures are 7 for 54 on 27th August 2016 for Newcastle at home to South Shields. He has taken 54 NEPL catches.

Lee Crozier also says about Oli McGee that "when he first came, he was happy just to contribute, now he is only happy if his contribution is central to a team win, and that's a huge development in mindset."

Since making his debut for Northumberland Oli McGee has been a regular in the side, prior to 2024 starting, he has now played 84 matches for the County, batting 91 times with 28 not outs, he has scored 989 runs at an average of 15.69. His highest score is 49 not out, made on 13th August 2023 at Cumbria.

He has bowled 8761 balls, with 177 maidens, conceding 5707 runs and taking 213 wickets at an average of 26.79. His best bowling figures are 7 for 81, taken in a 3-day match which started on 2nd August 2015 at Jesmond against Staffordshire. He has taken 25 catches for Northumberland so far in his career with them. He has deservedly been named Northumberland captain for 2024.

Jonny Wightman batted at number nine, he was run out for nought, he also opened the bowling taking 0 for 15 from six overs. Wightman played 15 times in the NEPL for South North as they won the 2023 title, he bowled 752 balls, with 10 maidens, conceding 530 runs and taking 31 wickets at an average of 17.09. His best bowling figures were 7 for 32, taken 13th May at Burnopfield.

He has now played 260 NEPL matches, batting 128 times, with 48 not outs, he has scored 814 runs at an average of 10.17. His highest score is 37 made on 14th May 2011 at Roseworth Terrace against Blaydon.

He has bowled 15325 balls in The NEPL, with 362 maidens, conceding 9474 runs and taking 510 wickets at an average of 18.57. His best bowling figures are 8 for 31 on 4th June 2016 for South North at home to Gateshead Fell. He has taken 37 NEPL catches.

At the end of the 2023 season Wightman, together with South North teammates Simon Birtwisle and Chris Hewison were informed that they had been selected for the England Seniors Over 40 for the World Cup in South Africa in February 2024. Wightman travelled and played and was part of the team that finished fourth. Wightman made his debut for The England Over 40's on 19th February 2024 against Zimbabwe. He took 1 for 22 from five overs.

Calum Fletcher batted at number ten in the season opener, he made a single, he also bowled six overs, taking 1 for 4. Lee Crozier says of Fletcher "he's a quiet lad, a nice lad, but he found his feet very quickly both in the dressing room and on the cricket field. Calum bowls a very tight line and applies scoreboard pressure to the batsman, picking up wickets as a result. He is moving on for 2024 and he will be missed, as an important team player and nice lad around the dressing room."

His contribution with the ball to the 2023 title was that he played 16 matches and bowled 646 balls, with 21 maidens, conceding 329 runs and taking 15 wickets at an average of 21.93. His best bowling figures were 3 for 11, taken on 24th June at Hetton Lyons.

Fletcher would move on at the end of the 2023 season, having played 51 NEPL matches, all for South North, batting 16 times, with 8 not outs, scoring 56 runs at an average of 7.00. His highest score is 13 not out. He has also bowled 1845 balls in the NEPL, with 53 maidens, conceding 1000 runs and taking 43 wickets at an average of 23.25. His best bowling figures were 3 for 11 on 24th June 2023 at Hetton Lyons. He has taken 9 NEPL catches.

Lee Crozier batted at number eleven to start the season off, he was 1 not out. He took 3 for 18 from nine overs. He entered the 2023 season having played 415 matches in the NEPL, batting 171 times with 85 not outs, he had scored 1383 runs at an average of 16.08. He had scored 1 half century, 89 for Benwell Hill in 2002.

He had bowled 28079 balls, with 1203 maidens, conceding 12684 runs and taking 807 wickets at an average of 15.71. His best bowling was 7 for 21 taken for South North in 2007. He had taken 61 NEPL catches.

Looking purely at the bowling contribution to the 2023 title, Crozier played 16 matches, he bowled 734 balls with 21 maidens, conceding 436 runs and taking 33 wickets at an average of 13.21. His best bowling figures of the season were 4 for 9, taken on 29th July at home to Burnopfield.

Crozier ended the 2023 season having played 431 NEPL matches, batting 176 times with 90 not outs, he had scored 1403 runs at an average of 16.31. He had scored 1 half century, 89, for Benwell Hill, mentioned earlier.

He has bowled 28813 balls, that's 4802.1 overs, with 1224 maidens, conceding 13120 runs and taking 840 wickets at an average of 15.61. His best bowling figures were 7 for 21, mentioned earlier from 2007. He has taken 65 NEPL catches in his career.

Shayne Moseley came to South North as a West Indian test player, he arrived with the 2023 season well under way, replacing Bas de Leede, consequently he played only 10 NEPL matches, batting 10 times, with 1 not out, he scored 345 runs at an average of 38.33. He made 2 half centuries and had 1 century, 100, scored on 24th June at Hetton Lyons, the innings came from 136 balls and contained 9 fours and 3 sixes. He didn't bowl in The NEPL but took 2 catches.

Moseley had made his test debut on 3rd February 2021 for the West Indies in Bangladesh, he scored 2 and 12 and didn't bowl. He played his second, and to date, last test match starting on 11th February 2021 also against Bangladesh, he scored 7 in both innings and didn't bowl. He took 3 catches across the two matches.

He made his debut in first-class cricket for Barbados on 26th October 2017 at home against Trinidad and Tobago. To date, his last first-class game for Barbados started on 21st February 2024 at Jamaica.

He has now played 41 first class matches for Barbados, batting 77 times with 5 not outs, he has scored 2157 runs at an average of 29.95. He has scored 12 half centuries and 4 centuries. His highest score, 155 not out, was made in a 4-day match which started on 13th February 2020 against Trinidad and Tobago.

He has also played 8 List A matches for Barbados.

Sam Ewart is a right-handed batsman and wicketkeeper. He first came to attention on 18th May 2021 for Northumberland Under 15's at Cockermouth against Cumbria Under 15's. He played for Northumberland Under 15's throughout 2021.

On 7th July 2022 Ewart played for Northumberland Under 16's at Hexham against Cumbria Under 16's and on 10th August 2022 he played a 20 over match for Northumberland Under 18's at Penrith, again against Cumbria Under 18's. He continued throughout the 2022 season to play for Northumberland at both age groups.

He also played for South North First XI on 20th July 2022 when they hosted an M.C.C XI at Roseworth Terrace. Ewart opened the batting and made 31 and kept wicket, taking 3 catches.

He continued to play youth cricket for Northumberland throughout 2023 and also made his NEPL debut on 23rd May 2023 at Benwell Hill.

He has now played 12 NEPL matches, batting 11 times with 3 not outs, he has scored 127 runs at an average of 15.87. His highest score is 34 not out 20th May 2023 at home to Whitburn. He has also taken 3 catches. He suffered a bad leg break early in 2024 playing cricket, hopefully he will return in 2025.

South North won the league comfortably by 67 points, despite losing their last game of the season to relegated Hetton Lyons.

Much earlier in the book the then South North skipper John Graham referred to "pivotal moments," I think that Gorantla scoring his hundred at Tynemouth after they were 2 for 3 and they went on to win and the partnership between Gorantla and Adam Cragg at Ashington were both such moments in 2023.

There was also the moment when the title was won, and that came not from an unlikely pair, but from an unlikely pair in the role in which they won the game! I shall explain, South North hosted Ashington on 26th August 2023, the third last game of the season.

If South North win, they won the league with two games to spare, South North won the toss and asked Ashington to bat. When Ashington batted Jack Jessop and Ben O'Brien put on 66 for the first wicket before Jessop was leg before to Lee Crozier. O'Brien scored 50 from 97 balls, with 3 fours and 1 six and the score was 85 for 3 when he was dismissed. They fell away completely, after the two openers no other batsman made double figures and they were bowled out for 105 from 43.4 overs. Oli McGee took 4 for 23, Lee Crozier had 3 for 16, Sean Tindale 2 for 26 and Calum Fletcher 1 for 9.

When South North batted, they struggled to build partnerships and lost wickets regularly, Adam Cragg and Sean Tindale had added 16 for the fifth wicket but South North were in trouble at 58 for 5 when Cragg was bowled by Alex Storey for 12. Tindale top scored the innings with 23 but when he was caught by wicketkeeper Jack McCarthy off Jeremiah Louis, they were 82 for 8. This quickly became 82 for 9 when Louis bowled George Gray second ball.

This brought Lee Crozier in at number eleven to join Calum Fletcher who was batting at nine, 24 runs were still required to win the game and seal the 2023 NEPL title. In his 50 NEPL matches across the 15 innings he has batted to this point; Fletcher's highest score was 13. Lee Crozier is known as a bowler not a batsman, he does however have 1 half century, back in his Benwell Hill days, in 2002, he had a score of 89. Despite some intelligent captaincy, some hostile bowling and some loud appeals, Fletcher, 13 not out, and Crozier 9 not out, got South North home with the last ball of the 43rd over. Cameron Nicholls had 3 for 27, Jeremiah Louis 2 for 23, Alex Storey 3 for 29 and Ben Harmison 1 for 14. A great day's cricket and I'm sure South North were relieved to get this one done and celebrated long into the night!

The 2023 Banks Salver was won by Burnmoor, and they also won The Twenty20 and Nikhil Gorantla of South North was named NEPL Player of the Year.

TABLE 71   NEPL 2023.

	Played	Won	Draw/Aban	Lost	Tied	Penalty Points	Bonus Points	Points
South North	22	13	6	3	0	0	73	378
Burnmoor	22	10	4	7	1	0	67	311
Chester le Street	22	8	8	5	1	0	61	288
Burnopfield	22	9	7	6	0	0	60	281
Castle Eden	22	8	6	8	0	0	65	274
Newcastle	22	8	6	8	0	0	70	266
Ashington	22	8	5	9	0	0	71	258
Benwell Hill	22	8	6	8	0	0	39	255
Felling	22	7	7	8	0	0	62	252
Tynemouth	22	6	7	9	0	0	48	209
Hetton Lyons	22	5	6	11	0	0	65	203
Whitburn	22	4	6	12	0	0	62	170

TABLE 72   NEPL Batting Averages 2023.
Qualification 300 Runs.

Player	Club	Inns	N. O	H. S	Runs	Average
(1) N.V Gorantla	South North	13	4	134 no	678	75.33
(2) K.J Coetzer	Benwell Hill	10	2	122 no	468	58.50
(3) J.R Oswell	Burnopfield	15	2	122 no	626	48.15
(4) C.J Pearce	Burnopfield	11	4	66 no	317	45.29
(5) G.M Scott	Hetton Lyons	12	1	93	484	44.00
(6) J. McCann	Chester le Street	16	2	86	566	40.43
(7) J.W Coxon	Chester le Street	15	2	99	503	38.69
(8) S.A.R Moseley	South North	10	1	100	345	38.33
(9) M. Brown	Tynemouth	14	3	85 no	421	38.27
(10) T.M Norris	Felling	15	0	102	561	37.40
(11) K. Turner	Burnopfield	18	4	100 no	515	36.79
(12) A. Cragg	South North	16	5	69	401	36.45
(24) C. J Hewison	South North	15	0	51	371	24.73

TABLE 73   NEPL Bowling Averages 2023.
Qualification 20 Wickets.

Player	Club	Overs	Mdns	Runs	Wkts	Average
(1) Bilawal Iqbal	Castle Eden	173.4	43	518	49	10.57
(2) Waqas Maqsood	Burnmoor	162.5	33	471	44	10.70
(3) O.F McGee	South North	149.4	21	456	40	11.40
(4) F.R McGurk	Burnopfield	143.3	23	416	36	11.56
(5) L.J Crozier	South North	122.2	21	436	33	13.21
(6) A.W.G Jones	Tynemouth	98.5	13	308	22	14.00
(7) G.D Bridge	Burnmoor	131.0	15	357	25	14.28
(8) S.J Allison	Felling	173.3	35	595	39	15.26
(9) E.R MacMillan	Benwell Hill	150.0	25	531	32	16.59
(10) J. Coughlin	Burnmoor	105.1	11	419	25	16.76
(11) T.I Ntuli	Tynemouth	109.1	18	391	23	17.00
(12) J.R Wightman	South North	125.2	10	530	31	17.10
(16) S.J Tindale	South North	150.0	16	523	27	19.37

South North NEPL Champions 2023.

Left to Right- Back Row- Will Alexander, Calum Fletcher, Shayne Moseley, Chris Hewison, Jonny Wightman, Sam Ewart.

Front Row-Rob Peyton, Lee Crozier, Sean Tindale, Adam Cragg, Oliver McGee, Simon Birtwisle.

Nikhil Gorantla seen here batting for South North at Ashington 10th June 2023.

Chapter Fourteen

The Chairman's View

Having started the introduction to the book with the thoughts of the Chairmen of 25 years ago I thought it might be interesting to hear the views of the current incumbents in the role and also get a preseason update on the squads and player's the teams were relying upon this season. One or two let club representatives speak on their behalf but nonetheless it's a view of the club at a moment in time.

Ashington Media Officer Brian Bennett offers his thoughts on the upcoming 2024 season, "Ashington Cricket Club were delighted after their first season in the NEPL premier division last year. Playing in the topflight was always going to be a tough challenge but the players stepped up to the plate.

Led by Sean McCafferty, the Mighty Acorns missed the opportunity to climb up to second in the division in the closing weeks and finished the campaign in mid table. We did finish the season on a high, winning a very close Northumberland County Cup final at Benwell Hill.

The lead up to the 2024 season has been affected by the horrendous wet weather. Long serving officials claim the amount of rain which fell on the Langwell Crescent ground to be the worst ever with a 'lake' stretching for several hundred yards from the Ashbourne Crescent end past the score box.

Preparations on the field suffered a double blow with Ben O'Brien and Mitchell Killeen - the latter who was the club's Durham player - moving on. However, on the plus side, Jeremiah 'Chilly' Louis has agreed to return as the club's professional after the all-rounder had an outstanding season in 2023. The club have not brought replacements in to fill the void left by O'Brien and Killeen. They are hoping other players will rise to the challenge and take on more responsibility as well as looking for the youngsters to flourish."

Jeremiah "Chilly" Louis is a right-handed batsman and right arm fast bowler, originally from the Leeward Islands in the West Indies and after first appearing for the Islands Under 15's on 5th July 2011 he has progressed through their junior and youth setup, playing at both Under 17 and Under 19 level.

He made his debut for St Kitts in a 3-day match starting on 1st June 2012 against Antigua and Barbuda at Basseterre. He would go on to play a 3-day representative game for St Kitts and Nevis starting on 30th August 2014 against The Bangladeshis again at Basseterre.

He made his debut in first-class cricket for The Leeward Islands in a 4-day match starting on 21st November 2014 at home to Trinidad and Tobago, he made 34 not out and took 2 for 30 in the first innings. To date, he played his last first-class match for Leeward Islands in a 4-day match starting on 17th April 2024 against The Windward Islands. He has now played 54 first-class matches for The Leeward Islands, batting 89 times with 23 not outs, he has scored 1560 runs at an average of 23.63. He has scored 4 half centuries with a highest score of 78 not out, made in a 4-day match which started on 1st February 2023 at home to Jamaica.

He has also bowled 7301 balls in first-class cricket for The Leeward Islands, with 264 maidens, conceding 3743 runs and taking 149 wickets at an average of 25.12. His best bowling figures were 6 for 69, taken in a 4-day match against Barbados which started on 1st November 2017. He has taken 31 catches for Leeward Islands in first-class cricket.

He made his debut for West Indies A side on 11th February 2018 against England Lions in Jamaica. Keaton Jennings and Paul Coughlin who both played in the NEPL were in the England side, alongside Ben Foakes and Liam Livingstone. Foakes was Louis first wicket at this level, caught by Shane Dowrich for 16.

Louis played twice more for West Indies A side but was given only very limited opportunities, batting just once more and bowling just 28 more overs, leaving him with only 21 runs and 2 wickets in total. To date, he has now played 29 List A matches for The Islands, batting 21 times with 7 not outs, he has scored 248 runs at an average of 17.71. His highest score is 41 not out, made on 16th February 2017 at home to Barbados.

He has bowled 851 balls at this level, with 6 maidens, conceding 825 runs and taking 25 wickets at an average of 33.00. His best bowling figures are 5 for 33, taken on 4th October 2018 at Barbados, his first wicket that day was Sheyne Moseley, he would play for South North in the NEPL in 2023. He has taken 10 catches at this level. Louis has also played 6 Twenty20 matches for the St Kitts and Nevis Patriots, he didn't complete an innings and barely bowled, taking three wickets for 116 runs.

The 2024 season will be his second successive season as Ashington's overseas pro, he made his NEPL debut for them on 6th May 2023 at Chester le Street, his first NEPL wicket was Chester opener Jacob McCann, caught by Sean McCafferty for 85.

He played 17 matches in the NEPL for Ashington in 2023, batting 15 times with 4 not outs, he scored 351 runs at an average of 31.90. He scored 1 half century and 1 century, 126 not out, made on 29th July 2023 at Jesmond against Newcastle, it came from 113 balls and contained 13 fours and 5 sixes. For good measure he took 5 for 40 in the same game!

Louis bowled 671 balls in the NEPL in 2023, with 11 maidens, conceding 458 runs and taking 25 wickets at an average of 18.32. His best bowling figures were 5 for 5, taken on 15th July 2023 at Castle Eden. He also took 1 catch in the NEPL in 2023. Louis was handicapped by an injury during 2023, I saw him play a number of times and I saw flashes which suggest that when he is fully fit, he could be capable of some real pace.

Sean McCafferty played junior cricket for Northumberland at Under 13, Under 15 and Under 16 level. He also appeared for a Northumberland Development XI against Durham Academy at Winlaton on 9th May 2012. He first appeared on my radar in senior cricket when he played for Ashington at Boldon in a NEPL Division 1 fixture on 27th April 2019. He has now played 54 matches in NEPL Division 1, batting 46 times with 6 not outs, he has scored 1087 runs at an average of 27.17. He has scored 7 half centuries and 1 century at this level, 104, scored on 14th August 2021 at home to Gateshead Fell, the innings came from 84 balls and contained 12 fours and 3 sixes.

He also played for Ashington during the covid season of 2020 and made his NEPL debut for Ashington on 29th April 2023 at home to Castle Eden.

During the 2023 season he played 18 matches in the NEPL, batting 13 times with 1 not out, he scored 142 runs at an average of 11.83, with a highest score of 28. He took 11 catches in the NEPL in 2023.

Ashington CC 25/5/24.

Left to Right- Back Row Callum Storey, Ben Harmison, James Harmison, Jeremiah Louis, Alex Storey, Matty Collins.

Front Row- Adam Nichol, Scott Pearcey, Sean McCafferty, Cameron Nichols, Jack Jessop.

Benwell Hill Chairman Simon Lunn shares his thoughts on the upcoming 2024 campaign.

"After a difficult season in 2023 that was marred by injuries and unavailability a number of changes have been made to the First Team line up that will hopefully lead to a more relaxed summer for the Benwell Hill followers. Wicketkeeper batsman Pete Halliday will again lead the side supported by a youthful Off Spinning Vice Captain in Max Williamson. The experience in the batting will be provided by Phillip Bell and the evergreen Adam Heather whilst the pace attack will once again be led by Callum Harding supported by Daniel Gardner.

The reconstruction of the team will see three former Benwell Hill Juniors back at Denton Bank in brothers Luke and Ben Mussett and Joe Anderson. All-rounder Rory Hanley will also be available following a year spent abroad in South America. Other graduates of the BHCC Junior Ranks in Haydon Mustard and William Archbold will look to build on their solid progress in 2023 and they will be supported by a number of other promising young players coming up on the rails. The Club sees producing as many players of our own as we can as the way to build the team in what is sure to be a highly competitive league.

To support this effort Indian First-Class Cricketer Yash Kothari has been recruited as Overseas Coach/Match Professional. Yash is an opening batsman who also bowls slow left arm and whilst this is his first time in the UK he arrives with a strong reputation. Yash arrives as a replacement for Kyle Coetzer who decided at the end of last season to leave the Club after seven years largely to pursue a Full Time Career in Professional Coaching. Kyle has been a marvellous player and influence at Benwell Hill, and we wish him well.

Other players to leave the Club at the end of last season were Angus Guy and Luke Doneathy both of whom enjoyed some golden moments in the Hill colours. Again, we wish them all the best in their cricketing careers.

To conclude, it will be a rather different Benwell Hill team that takes to the field in 2024, and it is sure to be a tough challenge. It will be interesting to see whether the format reduction to 45 overs per side makes any real difference but the one thing everyone will agree with is that some decent sunshine is a must to give the season some real momentum. One final reflection from a now fully fledged Muppet is to wish for the Spirit of Cricket to prevail at all times."

Adam Heather and Callum Harding are covered elsewhere in the book, so I am going to have a look at the remainder of the Benwell Hill squad for 2024.

Pete Halliday is a right-handed batsman, wicketkeeper and captain, he made his NEPL debut for Benwell Hill on 18th April 2015 at the Durham Academy.

To the end of the 2023 season, he has played 142 matches in the NEPL, batting 113 times with 23 not outs, he has scored 1752 runs at an average of 19.46. He has scored 4 half centuries and 3 centuries. His highest score is 113 not out, made on 3rd June 2023 at Chester le Street. The innings came from 138 balls and contained 10 fours and 3 sixes. Halliday and Kyle Coetzer, 122 not out, added an unbroken 252 for the fifth wicket to chase down 284 in the game after Quentin Hughes had made 100 not out.

He has taken 148 catches and has 27 stumpings in the NEPL so far in his career.

Halliday can be found as far back as 2005 playing for Horwich RMI in the Lancashire Leagues, the last appearance I can find for Halliday at Horwich on 14th September 2014 at home to Walkden.

He made his debut for Cumberland on 8th July 2012 at Cambridgeshire and last played for Cumberland on 7th July 2019 at home to Cambridgeshire.

He played 6 matches for Cumberland, although he only had the opportunity to bat twice, scoring 25 runs. He did take 10 catches and have 1 stumping for the county.

Max Williamson is a right-handed batsman and right arm off break bowler. Williamson made his NEPL debut for Benwell Hill on 1st August 2015 at Hetton Lyons although he had to wait until 28th May at home to Durham Academy to take his first NEPL wicket, Ross Greenwell caught by Sameet Brar for 24. Williamson played the last game of this spell for Benwell Hill on 9th September 2017 at The Riverside against Durham Academy.

He made his NEPL debut for Durham Academy on 21st April 2018 at Chester le Street, his last NEPL game for them was on 28th July 2018 at Hetton Lyons. He then returned to Benwell Hill the following week, making his "second" debut for them on 4th August 2018 at home to Stockton and he has played for Benwell Hill in the NEPL ever since.

To the end of the 2023 season, Williamson has played 129 matches in the NEPL, he has batted 82 times with 28 not outs, he has scored 711 runs at an average of 13.16. His highest score is 39 not out, made on 22nd June 2019 at home to Burnmoor.

He has bowled 6561 balls in the NEPL, with 151 maidens, conceding 4209 runs and taking 169 wickets at an average of 24.90. His best bowling figure are 6 for 27, taken on 22nd April 2017 at Stockton. He has taken 36 catches in the NEPL.

He had first come to attention playing for Northumberland Under 15's, making his debut on 31st July 2013 at Lincolnshire.

He appeared for Benwell Hill First XI at Scarborough on 26th April 2015 in an ECB National Championship game. He also progressed through to the Northumberland Under 17's in 2015, playing his first game for them at Cumbria Under 17's.

On 2nd June 2016 Williamson was selected to play for a Northumberland Development XI side against The British Fire Service. Before he played for Durham Academy in the NEPL he played two other games for them, on 16th and 17th May 2017 he played games at Rothwell Castle against a Scottish Development XI. This in turn led to him playing for Durham Under 17's on 21st May 2017 at Feethams against Derbyshire Under 17's and throughout 2017 Williamson was playing for Northumberland Under 17's.

He made his debut in Minor Counties matches for Northumberland on 8th July 2018 in a 3-day match at home to Buckinghamshire.

Selection for Durham Under 19's also followed in 2018, making his debut in a 2-day match starting on 21st August 2018.

To the end of the 2023 season, Williamson has played 41 times for Northumberland, batting 37 times with 11 not outs, he has scored 309 runs at an average of 11.88, with a highest score of 33.

He has bowled 2516 balls for Northumberland, with 47 maidens, conceding 1819 runs and taking 61 wickets at an average of 29.81. His bet bowling figures are 4 for 59, taken in a 3-day match which started on 3rd July 2022. He has taken 13 catches for Northumberland.

Phil Bell is a right-handed batsman and now only an occasional right arm medium pace bowler. Bell first came to my notice on 10th July 2000 when he appeared for Durham Under 17's against Scotland in Edinburgh.

He next appeared making his NEPL debut for Gateshead Fell at home to Blaydon, he took his first NEPL wicket in this match when he had Ray Marshall caught by Chris Nicholls for 9, he finished with 1 for 38, but the game was notable for 141 not out from Blaydon's Nehemiah Perry.

On 2nd July 2001 Bell played for Durham Under 19's at Longhirst against Scotland Under 19's.

He played his last game for Fell in the NEPL on 27th July 2002 at home to Sunderland. He had played 20 matches in the NEPL for Gateshead Fell, batting 17 times with 2 not outs, he scored 370 runs at an average of 24.66. He scored 1 half century, 53 not out on 18th August 2001 at The Racecourse against Durham Academy. This was a unique game as three batsmen scored centuries, Philip Walker, 112, and David Barnes, 111 not out, for Durham and Stewart Hutton, 100 not out for Fell.

Bell also bowled 801 balls in the NEPL for Fell, with 20 maidens, conceding 507 runs and taking 13 wickets at an average of 39.00. His best bowling figures were 4 for 41, taken on 9th June 2001 at Norton and he also took 5 NEPL catches for Fell.

Bell next appeared in the NEPL for South Shields on 5th May 2007 at home to Chester le Street, he made his last NEPL appearance for South Shields on 29th August 2011 at home to Newcastle.

He played 41 matches in the NEPL for Shields, batting 36 times with 4 not outs, he scored 832 runs at an average of 26.00. He scored 4 half centuries and 1 century, 122 not out, was made on 3rd July 2010 at home to Newcastle and the innings came from 95 balls and contained 19 fours and 1 six.

He bowled 804 balls in the NEPL for Shields, with 26 maidens, conceding 519 runs and taking14 wickets at an average of 37.07. His best bowling figures were 4 for 78, taken on26th May 2007 at The Racecourse against Durham Academy. He also took 17 NEPL catches for Shields.

Bell made his NEPL debut for South North on 2nd June 2012 at Sunderland and his last NEPL appearance for them on 11th May 2013 at Stockton.

He played 6 matches in the NEPL for South North, batting 4 times with 2 not outs, he scored 18 runs at an average of 9.00. His highest score was 12. He didn't bowl in the NEPL for South North, but he did take 2 catches.

He spent the 2015 and 2016 seasons playing for Eastcote in the Middlesex County League and then made his NEPL debut for Whitburn on 21st April 2018 at Tynemouth.

He made his debut for Northumberland on 20th May 2018 at Lincolnshire, he played twice more for Northumberland in 2018, batting 3 times in total with 1 not out, he scored 59 runs at an average of 29.50. He didn't bowl for the county and took 1 catch.

He played his last NEPL game for Whitburn on 7th September 2019 at Newcastle. Bell played 34 NEPL matches for Whitburn, batting 30 times with 3 not outs, he scored 406 runs at an average of 15.03. He scored 2 half centuries and 1 century, 104, was made on 28th April 2018 at home to Chester le Street and came from 84 balls and contained 11 fours and 6 sixes. He didn't bowl in the NEPL for Whitburn, but he did take 10 catches.

Bell then made his NEPL debut for Benwell Hill on 17th April 2021 at home to Burnopfield. Up to the end of 2023 Bell played his last NEPL game for Hill on 9th September 2023 at Ashington, although he did play regularly in 2024.

To that date he has played 47 matches in the NEPL for Benwell Hill, batting 39 times with 10 not outs, he has scored 863 runs at an average of 29.75. He has scored 5 half centuries with a highest score of 74 not out, scored on 28th May 2022 at home to Felling. He has bowled 30 balls in the NEPL for Hill, taking 0 for 40 and has taken 14 catches in the league for Hill.

In his NEPL career to the end of 2023, Phil Bell has played 148 matches in the NEPL, batting 126 times with 21 not outs, he has scored 2489 runs at an average of 23.70. He has scored 12 half centuries and 2 centuries. His highest score is 122 not out for South Shields mentioned earlier.

He has bowled 1635 balls, with 46 maidens, conceding 1066 runs and taking 27 wickets at an average of 39.48. His best bowling figures are 4 for 41 taken for Gateshead Fell and mentioned earlier. He has taken 48 catches in the NEPL.

Daniel Gardner is a left-handed batsman and right arm seam bowler, he joined Hill a season and a half ago from Bomarsund, he is the grandson of Bomarsund legend John Haig.

Luke Mussett is a right-handed batsman and right arm medium fast bowler. Luke, and his brother Ben have both signed for Benwell Hill for the 2024 season.

Luke came through the Northumberland Youth set up, first coming to notice on 21st May 2012 when he played for Northumberland Under 13's at Benwell Hill against Cumbria Under 13's. He took 5 for 6 on debut! The following year he was selected for Northumberland Under 15's, playing his first match at that age group on 21st May 2014 at Lincolnshire Under 15's, he took 3 for 48.

In 2015 he was selected for Northumberland Under 17's for the first time, making his debut in a 2-day match starting on 28th July 2015 at Hipsburn against Scotland Under 17's. He continued the happy knack of taking wickets on his debuts with 4 for 31!

He made his NEPL debut for Benwell Hill on 1st August 2015 at Hetton Lyons although he had to wait until 13th August 2015 at The Riverside against Durham Academy to take his first NEPL wicket, it was a good one, Sol Bell, caught by Ata-Ur-Rahaman for 33.

He played his last NEPL game of this spell with Benwell Hill on 26th August 2017 at South North.

He then made his NEPL debut for Durham Academy on 28th April 2018 at The Riverside against Felling, he took a wicket with his second ball in the NEPL for The Academy, bowling Chris Goudie for a duck.

He played his last NEPL game for Durham Academy on 16th June 2018 at The Riverside against Whitburn.

He then returned to Benwell Hill and the NEPL on 14th July 2018 at South North and he marked the occasion with 5 for 45.

He made his debut, and so far, only, appearance for Northumberland when he made his Minor Counties Championship debut on 22nd July 2018 at Bedfordshire. He took 0 for 30 and 1 for 19 when he bowled, and he didn't bat in the game.

His last game of this spell at Benwell Hill came on 14th September 2019 at home to Newcastle.

He played for Newcastle in NEPL Division 1 in 2021 before then making his NEPL debut for Newcastle on 23rd July 2022 at Chester le Street. He only played 3 games in the NEPL for Newcastle, the last coming on 6th August 2022 at Benwell Hill.

Luke Mussett played for Tynedale in NEPL Division 1 in the 2023 season.

To the end of 2023 he has played 39 matches in the NEPL, batting 21 times with 12 not outs, he has scored 90 runs at an average of 10.00. His highest score is 19 not out.

He bowled 1740 balls in the NEPL, with 40 maidens, conceding 1112 runs and taking 48 wickets at an average of 23.16. His best bowling figures are 6 for 19, taken on 29th June 2019, for Benwell Hill at Newcastle. He has taken 3 NEPL catches.

Ben Mussett is a right-handed batsman, he came through the Northumberland Youth set up, first appearing at Under 15 level on 2nd June 2010 at Shropshire.

He spent 2010 and 2011 playing for both the Under 14 and Under 15 county sides, as well as playing for a Northumberland Development XI at Durham Academy on 9th May 2012.

He also made his debut for Northumberland Under 17's in 2012, on 17th July at Gosforth against Norfolk Under 17's, he scored 34 and 70 in the game. He represented Northumberland 4 times at this level, adding a 96 not out to the earlier half century.

Ben Mussett made his NEPL debut for Benwell Hill on 27th August 2012 at home to Durham Academy.

He also played 2 games for South North, debuting on 25th July 2015 at home to South Shields and then on 15th August 2015 at Blaydon.

He also spent time in and out of Benwell Hill Second XI in 2016, as well as the occasional game in the firsts.

He moved to Washington for the start of the 2017 season playing in NEPL Division 1, returning to Benwell Hill in 2018, although he spent 2021 at Newcastle and 2023 at Tynedale, both in NEPL Division 1. His last NEPL appearance, to the end of 2023, was on 20th April 2019 at home to Whitburn.

In total he has played 29 matches in the NEPL, batting 26 times with 2 not outs, he has scored 313 runs at an average of 13.04. He has scored 1 half century, 58, made for Benwell Hill on 31st August 2013 at Chester le Street. He hasn't bowled in the NEPL, but he has taken 10 catches.

Joe Anderson is a right-handed batsman. The first note I can find of Anderson was that he played for Benwell Hill Seconds on 23rd April 2016 at home to Chester le Street. On 20th May 2016 he made his debut for Northumberland Under 15's at Durham Under 15's.

He made his NEPL debut on 30th July 2016 for Benwell Hill at Whitburn and then made his debut for Northumberland Under 17's in a 2-day match at Lincolnshire starting on 11th July 2017.

He played 15 matches for Northumberland Under 17's, batting 15 times with 2 not outs, he scored 439 runs at an average of 33.76. He scored 3 half centuries and 1 century, 103, was scored on 17th July 2018 at Gosforth against Cumbria Under 17's, the innings came from 128 balls and contained 13 fours and 1 six. He added exactly 200 for the third wicket with Rory Hanley, Hanley scored 144 from 196 balls with 16 fours and 2 sixes. Joe Anderson played his last game of this spell at Benwell Hill on 7th August 2021 at home to Burnmoor.

He made his NEPL debut for Newcastle at Jesmond on 16th April 2022 and his last NEPL game for Newcastle was on 9th September 2023 at home to Felling.

To the end of the 2023 season, Anderson has played 43 matches in the NEPL, batting 40 times with 6 not outs, scoring 635 runs at an average of 18.67. He has scored 3 half centuries, with a highest score of 65, made on 25th June 2022 for Newcastle at Felling. He has bowled 1 ball in the NEPL, going for 1 run and he has taken 6 catches in the NEPL.

Rory Hanley is a right-handed batsman and right arm fast medium bowler; he first came to light on 31st July 2015 playing for Northumberland Under 15's against Derbyshire Under 15's. He made his NEPL for Benwell Hill on 20th August 2016 at home to Newcastle, rain ruined the game so barely any cricket was played. As well as playing for

Benwell Hill Seconds he made his way through the Northumberland Youth system, making his debut for Northumberland Under 17's in a 2-day match starting on 11th July 2017 at Lincolnshire, he took 1 for 46 and scored 40. He took his first NEPL wicket on 6th May 2017 at Whitburn, James Thompson, leg before for 20.

He made his debut for Durham Under 17's on 13th May 2018 at Derbyshire and then his debut for Northumberland on 3rd June 2018 at Cheshire in a 20 over match. Although he has now played 8 matches for Northumberland, across different formats, it's fair to say he didn't really make his mark.

He did also make his debut for Scotland Performance Academy on 18th June 2019 in a game against New South Wales at Alloway. Hanley has also represented Scotland at Under 19 level, his debut for them coming on 26th July 2019 in Rotterdam against Netherlands in the Under 19 World Cup. When representing Scotland, he has a highest score of 23 not out and his best bowling figures are 2 for 27.

Benwell Hill are his only club in the NEPL, to date, April 2024, his last game for them was on 9th September 2023 at Ashington. To that date, Hanley has played 67 matches in the NEPL, batting 51 times with 11 not outs, he has scored 631 runs at an average of 15.77. His highest score is 49, made on 18th June 2022 at Burnmoor.

He has bowled 2734 balls in the NEPL, with 43 maidens, conceding 1795 runs and taking 58 wickets at an average of 30.94. His best bowling figures are 6 for 25, taken on 7th May 2022 at Eppleton. He has taken 24 catches.

William Archbold is a right-handed batsman and right arm off break bowler, he first came to attention when he played for Benwell Hill Second XI on 23rd April 2016 at home to Chester le Street. He made his debut for Northumberland Under 15's the same year, debuting on 7th July at Derbyshire Under 15's.

He made his NEPL for Benwell Hill on 30th June 2018 at Chester le Street, he scored 35 and took 1 for 18, his first NEPL wicket was Chester opener Jacob McCann, bowled for 87.

He made his debut for Northumberland Under 17's in a 2-day match at South North starting on 17th July 2018 against Cumbria Under 17's. He went on to play 5 matches at this age group for Northumberland.

Up to the end of the 2023 season, Archbold has played 30 matches in the NEPL, batting 26 times with 4 not outs, he has scored 411 runs at an average of 18.68. He has scored 2 half centuries, with a highest score of 70 not out, made on 24th June 2023 at home to Ashington. He has bowled 327 balls, with 1 maiden, conceding 281 runs and taken 4 wickets, he has also taken 6 NEPL catches.

Yash Kothari is a right-handed batsman and slow left arm orthodox bowler; in India he has played first-class cricket for both Rajasthan and Chilaw Marians Cricket Club. He has played a total of 23 first class matches in India, batting 38 times, with 3 not outs, he has scored 1048 runs at an average of 29.94. He has scored 9 half centuries, with a highest score of 96. He has also bowled 198 balls in first class cricket, with 1 maiden, conceding 124 runs and taking 1 wicket.

He has played 20 List A matches, batting 20 times with 1 not out, he has scored 508 runs at an average of 26.73. He has scored 1 half century and 2 centuries, with a highest score of 139. He has bowled 105 balls in List A cricket, with 1 maiden, conceding 76 runs and taking 5 wickets at an average of 15.20.

He has also played 7 matches in Twenty20, all for Rajasthan, scoring 142 runs at an average of 23.66 with 1 half century, 53 not out.

Benwell Hill CC 11/5/24.

Left to Right- Back Row- Haydon Mustard, Luke Mussett, Rory Hanley, Phil Bell, Dan Gardiner, Joe Anderson, Callum Harding, Will Archbold.

Front Row-Adam Heather, Pete Halliday, Max Williamson, Yash Kothari.

Photo Courtesy of Martin Avery.

Burnmoor Chairman Alec Linsley offers his thoughts on the upcoming 2024 season.

"We are looking forward to the 2024 season and have made a couple of additions to our squad. We are delighted to have recruited Stuart Poynter, a RHB/WK and occasional off break bowler, who has represented his country Ireland on a number of occasions as well as playing for Durham CCC.

Mitch Killeen is on a Durham CCC rookie contract, and we hope we can help him progress through the ranks and the evergreen Allan Worthy and Graeme Bridge are back for another season and who, in addition to myself, help keep the average age up!!

We are captained by Ryan Pringle who played 49 games for Durham CCC. He needs no introduction and is held as one of the best players in the NEPL. He is a hard-hitting RH Batter and off break bowler. He's also an exceptional fielder.

The squad is made up of plenty of talented young cricketers. Josh Coughlin and Ross Greenwell have both played 1st Class cricket. Marcus Brown is the youngest member of the team and has plenty potential, he is a very good opening batsman. Craig Stephenson is our right arm slow off break bowler and handy lower order batsman.

We have engaged our resident overseas Waqas Maqsood for the 3rd consecutive season. Waqas, a former Pakistan international, is an outstanding left arm fast-medium bowler with some serious skills. His slower ball variations make him difficult to play. He is also a left-handed middle order batsman, who weighs in with some important contributions.

We have only been in the NEPL for 5 seasons and in that time have won it once and finished 2nd every other year. We have the team to win it and that will be our aim. It will be tough though as there are a lot of great sides in the division. However, we believe we have the ability within our ranks to go all the way in the League and build on our 3 T20 & Banks Salver trophies we won in 2023."

Of those named by Linsley as part of the expected first XI for 2024, five of them were part of the successful side which won the NEPL title in 2019, Allan Worthy, Ryan Pringle, Linsley himself, Craig Stephenson and Graeme Bridge, their stats up to the end of 2023 are covered as part of the chapter on that title winning side.

Here's a more detailed look at the remainder of the Burnmoor squad for 2024.

Stuart Poynter made his NEPL debut for Tynemouth at home to South North on 23rd April 2016, he marked the occasion with a hundred, 112 to be precise in a losing cause. He played his last game in the NEPL for Tynemouth on 9th September 2023 at home to Burnmoor.

To the end of the 2023 season Poynter has played 59 matches in the NEPL, all for Tynemouth, batting 57 times with 5 not outs, he has scored 1739 runs at an average of 33.44. He has scored 13 half centuries and 3 centuries. His highest score is 149, scored on 1st September 2018 at home to Stockton. He has taken 53 catches and made 6 stumpings in the NEPL.

Poynter started out at Middlesex as an Under 13, he progressed through the Under 15's and into the second XI, from where he was picked up by Ireland and he played his first game for them on 11th February 2008 in Kuala Lumpur against Papua New Guinea.

At this time, he was playing club cricket for Sunbury in the Surrey Premier Division. He also played for Middlesex Under 17's and Under 19's whilst representing Ireland under 19's and has also represented Clontarf in the Leinster league.

Poynter made his debut for the full Ireland side on 6th September 2011 at Belfast against Namibia. He went on to play 71 matches for Ireland, batting 66 times with 14 not outs, he scored 1013 runs at an average of 19.48. He scored 1 half century and 2 centuries. His highest score was 125, scored in a 4-day match which started on 17th October 2015 against Zimbabwe A side. He took 65 catches and had 8 stumpings for Ireland. His last game for Ireland was on 15th March 2019 in India against Afghanistan, this was actually a test match and the only test match he played.

Poynter also played 21 One Day Internationals for Ireland, batting 19 times with 5 not outs, he scored 185 runs at an average of 13.21. His highest score was 36. He took 22 catches and 1 stumping.

He also played 25 Twenty20 matches for Ireland, batting 21 times with 6 not outs, he scored 240 runs at an average of 16.00. His highest score was 39. He took 13 catches and had 2 stumpings at this level.

He played a total of 47 first class matches, for Ireland and Durham, batting 73 times with 4 not outs, he scored 1522 runs at an average of 22.05. He scored 6 half centuries and 2 centuries. His highest score was 170, made for

Durham against Derbyshire in Division 2 of the County Championship in May 2018. He took 139 catches and had 4 stumpings at first class level.

Poynter also played 47 List A matches, batting 40 times with 9 not outs, he scored 581 runs at an average of 18.74. He scored 1 century, 109, on 23rd July 2014 for Ireland against Sri Lanka A. He took 43 catches and had 3 stumpings at this level.

Poynter also played 40 Twenty20 matches for Durham, batting 29 times with 14 not outs, he scored 447 runs at an average of 29.80. He scored 1 half century, 61 not out on 15th August 2017 at Derbyshire. He took 21 catches and made 8 stumpings at this level.

Poynter undertook a career with Northumberland in recent years, making his debut on 17th April 2022 in a 20 over match at Staffordshire, he started with 62. He has now played 27 matches for Northumberland across all formats, batting 33 times with 4 not outs, he has scored 1235 runs at an average of 42.58. He has scored 7 half centuries and 2 centuries. His highest score of 171 was made on 4th June 2023 at Jesmond in a 50 over match against Herefordshire, the innings came from 120 balls and contained 18 fours and 9 sixes. He has taken 33 catches and 8 stumpings for Northumberland up to the end of the 2023 season.

Mitch Killeen is a right-handed batsman and right arm medium fast bowler, he is the son of Durham stalwart, Neil Killeen. He is a product of the Durham youth set up, starting as an Under 13 and progressing through Under 14, Under 15, Under 18 and playing for the Durham Academy during the 2020 covid season. He has also played for Durham Second XI and made his debut for England Under 19's on 8th September 2022 at Worcester against Sri Lanka Under 19's. At the time of writing, April 2024, his last game for England Under 19's was as recently as 22 November 2023 in India.

Mitch Killeen made his NEPL debut for Burnopfield at South North on 27th April 2019 and took his first NEPL wicket at Jesmond against Newcastle on 17th August 2019, Ross Greenwell, caught by John Oswell for 13.

He played his last NEPL game for Burnopfield at home to Sunderland on 27th August 2022 and then made his NEPL debut for Ashington on 29th April 2023 at home to Castle Eden and his last game in the NEPL for Ashington was on 12th August 2023 at home to Hetton Lyons.

To the end of the 2023 season, Mitch Killeen has played 47 NEPL matches, batting 46 times, with 3 not outs, he has scored 884 runs at an average of 20.55. He has scored 3 half centuries, and his highest score is 92 not out, scored on 28th August 2021 for Burnopfield at home to Washington.

He has bowled 1957 balls in the NEPL, with 52 maidens, conceding 1207 runs and taking 56 wickets at an average of 21.55. His best bowling figures are 4 for 21, taken for Burnopfield at Sacriston on 7th August 2021. He has taken 12 catches in the NEPL.

Josh Coughlin is a left-handed batsman and right arm medium pace bowler, he is the brother of Paul Coughlin, Josh came through the junior ranks at Durham, he started playing Under 13 level for them and went on to play at Under 14, Under 15, Under 17 and Under 19 level before progressing to the Durham Academy and also Durham Second XI.

He has also played 4 first class matches for Durham and 1 Under 19 test match for England. Coughlin made his debut for Durham on 26th June 2016 against Sri Lanka A at The Riverside, taking 1 for 35 and 1 for 10 when he bowled. He played twice more for Durham in 2018 and once more in 2019.

He played a 2-day warm up game for England Under 19's starting on 21st July 2016 against The Unicorns at Loughborough. Batting at number 9, he top scored the first England Innings with 64 and then took 0 for 19 and 1 for 46 as the match was drawn. He then played his one and only test match for England Under 19's, starting on 26th July 2016 against Sri Lanka at Fenner's, he scored 14 and took 2 for 45 as the match was drawn.

He has played 4 times for Northumberland after making his debut on 4th June 2017 at Staffordshire.

Josh Coughlin made his debut in the NEPL for Hetton Lyons at Stockton on 21st July 2012. He had to wait until 18th April 2015 before he took his first NEPL wicket, South Shields opener Andrew Elliott, caught by Jarvis Clay for 8. He played his last NEPL game for Hetton on 5th September 2015 at Whitburn.

He had played 33 matches in the NEPL for Hetton Lyons, batting 28 times with 2 not outs, he scored 354 runs at an average of 13.61. He scored 2 half centuries with a highest score of 73, made on 20th June 2015 at Gateshead Fell.

He bowled 778 balls in the NEPL for Hetton Lyons, with 16 maidens, conceding 523 runs and taking 26 wickets at an average of 20.11. His best bowling figures were 5 for 20, taken on 18th July 2015 at home to Blaydon. He took 9 NEPL catches for the club.

He then made his NEPL debut for the Durham Academy on 23rd April 2016 at Whitburn, his last NEPL appearance for Durham Academy was on 10th September 2016 and he returned to Hetton Lyons for the 2017 season.

He had played 17 matches in the NEPL for Durham Academy, batting 14 times with 1 not out, he scored 324 runs at an average of 24.92. He scored 2 half centuries with a highest score of 67 not out, made on 27th August 2016 at The Riverside against Gateshead Fell.

He bowled 784 balls in the NEPL for Durham Academy, with 31 maidens, conceding 407 runs and taking 16 wickets at an average of 25.43. His best bowling figures were 5 for 37, taken on 30th April 2016 at The Riverside against South North. He took 8 NEPL catches for Durham Academy.

He re-appeared for Hetton Lyons next in the NEPL on 15th April 2017 at home to South Shields and his last NEPL appearance for Hetton was on 9th September 2017 at home to Stockton.

He played 18 matches in the NEPL for Hetton Lyons during this spell, batting 16 times with 2 not outs, he scored 320 runs at an average of 22.85. He scored 1 half century, 83, made on 26th August 2017 at home to Durham Academy.

He bowled 819 balls in the NEPL in 2017, with 18 maidens, conceding 530 runs and taking 26 wickets at an average of 20.38. His best bowling figures were 4 for 50, taken on 19th August 2017 at Benwell Hill. He took 4 NEPL catches in 2017.

He joined Eppleton for the 2018 season, making his NEPL debut for them on 21st April 2018 at Hetton Lyons, his last NEPL appearance for Eppleton was on 14th September 2019 at home to Tynemouth.

Coughlin played 28 matches in the NEPL for Eppleton, batting 23 times with 1 not out, he scored 382 runs at an average of 17.36. He scored 1 half century, 78 not out, made on 19th May 2018 at home to Durham Academy.

He bowled 822 balls in the NEPL for Eppleton, with 43 maidens, conceding 316 runs and taking 23 wickets at an average of 13.73. His best bowling figures were 3 for 13, taken on 4th August 2018 at The Riverside against Durham Academy. He took 6 NEPL catches for Eppleton.

He played for Eppleton and Durham Second XI during the 2020 covid season and he then made his NEPL debut for Burnmoor on 17th April 2021 at Tynemouth.

By the end of the 2023 season Josh Coughlin had played 55 matches in the NEPL for Burnmoor, batting 39 times with 4 not outs, he has scored 664 runs at an average of 18.97. he has scored 2 half centuries, with a highest score of 55, made on 27th August 2022 at home to Eppleton.

He has bowled 2469 balls in the NEPL for Burnmoor, with 64 maidens, conceding 1436 runs and taking 82 wickets at an average of 17.51. His best bowling figures are 6 for 17, taken on 19th August 2023 at home to Newcastle. He has taken 14 NEPL catches for Burnmoor.

To date, by the end of the 2023 season, Josh Coughlin has played 151 matches in the NEPL, batting 120 times with 10 not outs, he has scored 2044 runs at an average of 18.58. He has scored 8 half centuries, his highest score is 83, scored on 26th August 2017 for Hetton Lyons against Durham Academy, he took 3 for 36 that day as well!

Coughlin has bowled 5672 balls in the NEPL, with 172 maidens, conceding 3212 runs and taking 173 wickets at an average of 18.56. His best bowling figures are 6 for 17, mentioned earlier for Burnmoor at home to Newcastle. He has taken 41 NEPL catches.

Ross Greenwell came through the Durham Junior set up, playing at Under 13, Under 14 and Under 15 level before making his NEPL debut. He then progressed further with Durham, playing Under 17 and Second XI cricket for Durham.

Greenwell made his NEPL debut for Blaydon on 6th July 2013 at home to Gateshead Fell. He took his first NEPL wicket on 23rd August 2014 at Tynemouth when Ryan Buckley caught opener Ben Debnam for 33. He played his last NEPL game for Blaydon on 5th September 2015 at Gateshead Fell.

He had played 18 matches in the NEPL for Blaydon, batting 15 times with 1 not out, he scored 105 runs at an average of 7.50. His highest score was 31 not out. He bowled 349 balls in the NEPL for Blaydon, with 9 maidens, conceding 243 runs and taking 9 wickets at an average of 27.00. His best bowling figures were 3 for 33, taken on 4th July 2015 at South Shields. He took 3 NEPL catches for Blaydon.

Greenwell then made his NEPL debut for the Durham Academy on 14th May 2016 at Jesmond against Newcastle, he opened the innings, making 92. He played his last game for The Academy on 8th September 2018 at Sacriston. He played 59 matches in the NEPL for Durham Academy, batting 57 times with 6 not outs, he scored 1871 runs at an average of 36.68. He scored 13 half centuries and 3 centuries.

His first century, 105, was made on 10th September 2016 at The Riverside against Stockton and the innings came from 186 balls and contained 12 fours.

His second century, 118 not out, was scored on 13th May 2017 at Whitburn, it came from 166 balls and contained 12 fours and 2 sixes.

His third century, 131 not out, was scored 16th June 2018 at The Riverside against Whitburn and came from 149 balls and contained 13 fours and 4 sixes.

He also bowled 320 balls in the NEPL for Durham Academy, with 14 maidens, conceding 165 runs and taking 7 wickets at an average of 23.57. His best bowling was 2 for 6 and he also took 15 NEPL catches for Durham Academy.

Ross Greenwell then made his NEPL debut for Newcastle on 20th April 2019 at Chester le Street and his Minor Counties Championship debut for Northumberland on 23rd June 2019.

Although, to date, he has only played three games for Northumberland, the last on 24th April 2022 at Gosforth against Cumbria, his highest score is 22.

His last game for Newcastle was on 14th September 2019 at Benwell Hill. He played 17 matches in the NEPL for Newcastle, batting 16 times with 0 not outs, he scored 353 runs at an average of 22.06. He scored 2 half centuries and 1 century, 136, scored on 6th July 2019 at home to Chester le Street, the innings came from 170 balls and contained 9 fours and 5 sixes.

He bowled 877 balls in the 2019 NEPL season, with 22 maidens, conceding 583 runs and taking 21 wickets at an average of 27.76. His best bowling figures were 4 for 51, taken on 22nd June 2019 at Whitburn. He took 3 NEPL catches in 2019.

He played for Burnmoor in the 2020 covid season. And went on to make his NEPL debut for Burnmoor on 17th April 2021 at Tynemouth.

By the close of the 2023 season Ross Greenwell had played 53 matches in the NEPL for Burnmoor, batting 53 times with 10 not outs, he has scored 1503 runs at an average of 34.95. He has scored 8 half centuries and 1 century, 125 not out, scored on 12th June 2021 at Eppleton, it came from 144 balls and contained 21 fours and 1 six. He has bowled 801 balls in NEPL for Burnmoor, with 24 maidens, conceding 460 runs and taking 18 wickets at an average of 25.55. His best bowling figures are 3 for 22, taken on 19th June 2021 at home to Felling. He has taken 6 NEPL catches for Burnmoor.

To the end of the 2023 season, he has played 147 matches in the NEPL, batting 141 times, with 17 not outs, scoring 3832 runs at an average of 30.90. He has scored 23 half centuries and 5 centuries, his highest score is 136, scored for Newcastle on 6th July 2019 at home to Chester le Street, the innings came from 170 balls and contained 9 fours and 5 sixes. He has bowled 2347 balls, with 69 maidens, conceding 1451 runs and taking 55 wickets at an average of 26.38. His best bowling figures are 4 for 51, taken on 22nd June 2019 for Newcastle at Whitburn. He has taken 27 catches in the NEPL.

Marcus Brown started off in the Durham Junior system, playing at Under 14, Under 15 and Under 17 level, he also played for Easington Colliery Welfare in the Durham Cricket League. He made his NEPL debut for Eppleton on 30th April 2016 at Hetton Lyons.

Brown played 8 times for Northumberland between 8th July 2018 and 11th August 2019, scoring 138 runs at an average of 13.50. He played his last NEPL game for Eppleton on 14th September 2019 at home to Tynemouth.

He had played 80 NEPL matches for Eppleton, batting 77 times with 2 not outs, he has scored 1431 runs at an average of 19.07. He scored 7 half centuries with a highest score of 80, made on 20th April 2019 at home to

Burnmoor. He hasn't bowled a lot, having taken 3 wickets for 38, his first NEPL wicket was South North batsman Jonny Craigs, bowled for 3 on 29th July 2017. He took 45 catches and made 1 stumping in the NEPL in his time with Eppleton. He also played for Eppleton during the 2020 covid season and then made his NEPL debut for Burnmoor on 17th April 2021 at Tynemouth.

By the end of 2023 Brown had played 57 NEPL matches for Burnmoor, batting 53 times with 5 not outs, he has scored 1101 runs at an average of 22.93. He has scored 5 half centuries and 1 century, 103 not out, scored on 14th August 2021 at Felling, it came from 86 balls and contained 14 fours and 1 six. He hasn't bowled for Burnmoor in the NEPL, but he has taken 32 catches.

Marcus Brown, to the end of 2023, has now played 137 NEPL matches, batting 130 times with 7 not outs, he has scored 2532 runs at an average of 20.58. He has scored 12 half centuries and 1 century, the century mentioned earlier. He has bowled 108 balls in the NEPL, with 1 maiden, conceding 58 runs and taking 3 wickets at an average of 19.33. His best bowling figures are 3 for 20 taken on 29th July 2017 for Eppleton against South North. He has taken 77 catches and has 1 stumping.

Waqas Maqsood is the overseas pro, he made his NEPL debut for Burnmoor on 16th April 2022 at Felling, his first NEPL wicket was Felling opener, Tyler Easton, leg before for a single. To the end of the 2023 season, Maqsood had played 35 NEPL matches, batting 29 times with 6 not outs, he has scored 267 runs at an average of 11.60. his highest score is 38, made on 30th April 2022 at home to Newcastle.

He has bowled 2118 balls, with 59 maidens, conceding 1160 runs and taking 91 wickets at an average of 12.74. His best bowling figures are 6 for 27, taken on 30th July 2022 at Burnopfield. He has taken 7 NEPL catches.

He has played 81 first class matches in Pakistan, batting 121 times with 29 not outs, he has scored 1178 runs at an average of 12.80. He has 1 half century, 62, scored for The Water and Power Development Authority against The Bank of Pakistan in a 4-day match which started on 18th November 2014.

He has bowled 14158 balls in first class cricket in Pakistan, with 504 maidens, conceding 7372 runs and taking 294 wickets at an average of 25.07. His best bowling figures are 9 for 32, taken for The Water and Power Development Authority against Khan Research Laboratories in a 4-day match which started on 3rd December 2017. He has taken 34 catches at this level in Pakistan.

Maqsood has played 56 List A matches in Pakistan, batting 25 times, with 14 not outs, he has scored 189 runs at an average of 17.18. His highest score is 33 not out. He has bowled 2620 balls with 26 maidens, conceding 2322 runs and taking 87 wickets at an average of 26.68. His best bowling figures are 6 for 63, taken on 3rd May 2018 for Federal Areas against Baluchistan. He has taken 14 catches at this level.

Maqsood has played 68 Twenty20 matches in Pakistan, batting 25 times, with 11 not outs, he has scored 83 runs at an average of 5.92. His highest score is 18.

He has bowled 1479 balls with 1 maiden, conceding 1901 runs and taking 77 wickets at an average of 24.68. His best bowling figures are 4 for 35, taken on 5th February 2022 for Islamabad United against Lahore Qalanders. He has taken 15 catches at this level.

Maqsood has played 1 Twenty20 match for Pakistan on 4th November 2018 in Dubai against New Zealand, he took 2 for 21.

Burnmoor CC 22/6/24.

Left to Right- Back Row Josh Coughlin, Mitchell Killeen, Ross Greenwell, Paul Craig, Alec Linsley, Allan Worthy.

Front Row-Craig Stephenson, Waqas Maqsood, Ryan Pringle, Marcus Brown, Graeme Bridge.

Burnopfield first team captain John Oswell shares a few thoughts on the upcoming season.

"The 2024 season sees the club coming into it with a strong young squad with an ambitious attitude towards their cricket. We aspire to be one of the best teams in the league and believe that we have the squad to fulfil those aspirations. The team has improved over the last couple of seasons, and we look to build on the fourth-place finish from 2023. Equally we have some very talented juniors who will be playing in the 2nd and 3rd teams this year.

Our squad has evolved over the past few seasons as we have adapted into the NEPL. This season we have recruited players such as Ben McKinney who has come in as our Durham CCC player as well as Ross Whitfield, Amaan Ul Haq and Harry Lumsden all of whom have County Second XI cricket experience.

These signings bring a lot of talent to our squad and will allow the club to build on a strong fourth place finish in 2023. We once again have Australian Finn McGurk as the overseas player who was a fantastic asset to us in 2023 and we hope that he will continue to be in 2024. "

Ben McKinney is a left-handed batsman and off break bowler; he goes into the 2024 season having made his NEPL debut for Hetton Lyons 25th May 2019 at Benwell Hill, he didn't get to bat as the game was abandoned after 47 overs. He remained with Hetton Lyons until the end of the 2023 season, his last match coming on 15th July at Whitburn. He had to wait to take his first NEPL wicket, 24th April 2021 when he had Whitburn opener Lee Henderson caught by Gary Scott for 26.

He has now played 57 NEPL matches, batting 55 times with 2 not outs, he has scored 1440 runs at an average of 27.16. He has made 11 half centuries and 1 century, 113, scored on 6th August 2022 at home to Tynemouth, the innings came from just 167 balls and contained 12 fours and 1 six.

McKinney has also bowled 617 balls in the NEPL, with 15 maidens, conceding 393 runs and taking 23 wickets at an average of 17.08. His best bowling figures are 6 for 34, taken on 3rd July 2021 at home to Felling. He has taken 23 NEPL catches.

He is a product of the Durham Youth system, having first played Under 12's for the county in August 2016. He progressed through the age groups for Durham before reaching Second Team level, making his debut at this level on 29th June 2021 in a 2-day match at Eastwood Gardens against Scotland A. In 2021 he also played a number of games for the ECB Elite Player Development North Under 18's.

On 21st August 2023 McKinney made his debut for England Under 19's in a test match at Chelmsford against Sri Lanka. He made 33 and 56, fellow NEPL player Ross Whitfield made his debut in the same match but more of him shortly!

To the end of March 2024 McKinney has now played 34 matches for England Under 19's, batting 40 times with 0 not outs, he has scored 1258 runs at an average of 31.45. He has scored 8 half centuries with a highest score of 88, made 20th January 2024 against Scotland in the Under 19 World Cup.

He has bowled 37 balls at this level, with 0 maidens, conceding 38 runs and taking 1 wicket. He has 29 catches for England Under 19's.

Although clearly in the very early stages of his professional career he has already played 3 matches for Durham in first class cricket, making his debut on 6th April 2023 in a County Championship match which started on 6th April 2023.

At the time of writing, April 2024, he had played 2 more first class matches against Zimbabwe A for Durham. He has also played 4 List A matches for Durham, making his debut on 1st August 2023 at The Riverside against Worcestershire.

McKinney made his debut for Tuskers on 3rd March 2024 in the Zimbabwe Domestic Twenty20 competition. He has now played 5 matches for them at this level.

Ross Whitfield is a right-handed batsman; he is another product of the Durham Youth system playing first of all at Under 12 level on 4th August 2017. He has also represented Durham at Under 14, Under 15, Under 18's and Second Team Level. Any look at Whitfield must mention a 3-day match against Lancashire Under 18's which started on 26th July 2022 at Southport, he batted for 225 balls and struck 34 fours and 6 sixes as he scored 270. No-one else in the side made 50 as the team posted 456 for 9 declared in 88.3 overs.

He made his NEPL debut for Sacriston on 17th April 2021 against Eppleton and he played his last NEPL match for Sacriston on 11th September 2021 at Hetton Lyons.

Whitfield then made his NEPL debut for Sunderland on 16th April 2022 at Tynemouth, he made 57. He took his first NEPL wicket on 21st May 2022 at Whitburn, Jack Burnham caught by Micky Allan for 117. He played his last NEPL match for Sunderland on 6th August 2022 at home to Whitburn.

Whitfield then made his NEPL debut for Chester le Street at home to Ashington on 6th May 2023 and he played his last NEPL game for Chester on 12th August 2023 at home to Whitburn.

To the end of the 2023 season Ross Whitfield has played 47 matches in the NEPL, batting 46 times with 4 not outs, he has scored 940 runs at an average of 22.38. He has scored 6 half centuries and 1 century, 101, scored for Chester le Street on 20th May 2023 at home to Hetton Lyons, the innings came from 78 balls and contained 12 fours and 3 sixes. His bowling career is still in the early stages, and he has taken 3 wickets and conceded 173 runs, and he has taken 20 catches in the NEPL.

On 21st August 2023 Whitfield made his debut for England Under 19's in a test match at Chelmsford against Sri Lanka, as mentioned earlier fellow NEPL player and now Burnopfield teammate Ben McKinney made his debut in the same match. Whitfield made 86 and 110, the century came from 134 balls and contained 12 fours and 1 six.

To the end of March 2024 Whitfield has now played 13 matches for England Under 19's, batting 17 times with 0 not outs, he has scored 441 runs at an average of 25.94. He has scored 3 half centuries and 1 century, the 110 on debut. He hasn't bowled at this level, but he has taken 2 catches.

Amaan Ulhaq is a right-handed batsman and leg break bowler. The first record I could find for Ul Haq was on 28th August 2018 playing for Durham Academy at Ropery Lane against an M.C.C side. He played four times for Durham Academy and then played for Chester le Street in the Covid Competition of the 2020 season.

He made his NEPL debut for Chester le Street on 17th April 2021 at Whitburn, he took 1 for 35, his first NEPL wicket was Kieran Waterson, bowled for 22.

He made his debut for Durham Seconds in a 4-day match which started on 17th May 2021 at Leicestershire. He went on to play 5 matches for Durham at this level.

Ulhaq made his debut for Northumberland in Minor Counties Trophy matches on 13th June 2021 at Jesmond against Cheshire. He has now played 9 matches for Northumberland.

He has also played second team cricket for Northamptonshire, Warwickshire and Surrey.

On 29th June 2022 he made his debut for the South Asian Cricket Academy against Surrey Second XI.

He played his last NEPL game for Chester le Street on 9th September 2023 at home to Castle Eden.

To this point he has played 54 matches in the NEPL, batting 25 times with 10 not outs, he has scored 91 runs at an average of 6.06. His highest score was 24.

He has bowled 2609 balls in the NEPL, with 24 maidens, conceding 2010 runs and taking 83 wickets at an average of 24.21. His best bowling figures are 7 for 38 taken on 12th June 2021 at Sacriston. He has taken 20 NEPL catches so far.

Harry Lumsden is a right-handed batsman and left arm medium pace bowler, he first came to note on 14th June 2018 when he played for Durham Under 14's at Nottinghamshire., he went on to play for the Under 15 side the following season.

During the covid season of 2020 he played for Gateshead Fell. He made his NEPL Division 1 debut for Gateshead Fell on 1st May 2021 at home to Castle Eden, his first wicket at this level was Lewis Williams bowled for 8.

He made his debut for Durham Under 18's on 5th July 2022 against Scotland Under 18's and his debut for Durham Seconds the same season, in a 4-day match starting on 6th September at Gosforth against Leicestershire Second XI.

To the end of the 2023 season Lumsden had played 36 matches in NEPL Division 1, batting 26 times with 5 not outs, he scored 172 runs at an average of 8.19. His highest score was 26 not out.

He bowled 1522 balls in NEPL Division 1, with 29 maidens, conceding 1252 runs and taking 47 wickets at an average of 26.63. His best bowling figures were 4 for 19, taken on 21st May 2022 against Ashington. He has taken 5 catches at this level.

Finn McGurk is a right-handed batsman and right arm off break bowler, he originally came to notice in his native Australia in 2019 playing for Australian Capital Territory.

He made his NEPL debut for Burnopfield on 6th May 2023 at Newcastle, he took 4 for 17, his first NEPL wicket was Newcastle captain Bobby Green, bowled for 4.

To the end of the 2023 season, he had played 17 matches in the NEPL, batting 10 times, with 3 not outs, he scored 84 runs at an average of 12.00. He scored 1 half century, 53, made on 24th June 2023 at home to Whitburn.

He has bowled 861 balls in the NEPL, with 23 maidens, conceding 416 runs and taking 36 wickets at an average of 11.55. His best bowling figures were 5 for 22, taken on 17th June 2023 at home to Benwell Hill. He has taken 3 catches in the league for the club.

Burnopfield CC 18/4/24.

Left to Right- Back Row-Ross Whitfield Jnr, Sam Dinning, Ben McKinney, Daniel Hogg, Matthew Oswell, Amaan Ulhaq.

Front Row-Callum Brown, Finlay McGurk, John Oswell, Harry Lumsden, Freddie Geffen.

Castle Eden Chairman John Spellman has a few thoughts on the upcoming season.

"Castle Eden Cricket Club looks forward to the 2024 season with hope, excitement, and optimism. Having been promoted to the NEPL premier league in 2023 after winning the Division 1 title in 2022, we were cautiously confident that we could survive, however I think it's fair to say that we exceeded our own expectations, finishing 5th in our first year. This gives us renewed confidence and expectation for the coming season.

We rely heavily on home-based players who have stayed with us on our journey over the years, many who have been with us since junior cricket. At least 7 of last year's first team are in that category, all of whom will play again this year.

Our Pakistan Professional, Bilawal Iqbal, returns for his 4th year and has been tremendous for us, a fast bowler and explosive batsman, his presence has complimented the group brilliantly, winning the most league wickets three years in a row.

We also welcome back JP Meade who we acquired from Billingham Synthonia last year, for his second season with us. Again, he made a significant impact with bat and bowl, explosive with the bat and complimenting that with his medium pace seamers.

We have signed another allrounder for the 2024 season, Muhaymen Majeed, a top order batsman and spin bowler, who we hope will fit into the side seamlessly and we are delighted to see the return of Alan Unsworth to the ranks, one of our veterans, who was side-lined for the majority of last year with a serious knee injury. His wily medium pace bowling will hopefully see a twenty + wicket return this year.

Led brilliantly by our captain Jonathan Malkin who captains the side again this year we're looking forward to a competitive and exciting season."

Bilawal Iqbal made his NEPL debut for Castle Eden on 29th April 2023 at Ashington, he took his first NEPL wicket in the game when he trapped Ashington opener Scott Pearcey leg before wicket for 7. He completed his first NEPL season having played 17 matches, batting 16 times with 6 not outs, he scored 186 runs at an average of 18.60. He made 1 half century, his highest score of 61 not out, scored on 29th July at home to Hetton Lyons.

Iqbal bowled 1042 balls in the NEPL in 2023, with 43 maidens, conceding 518 runs and taking 49 wickets at an average of 10.57. His best bowling figures were 7 for 18, taken on 3rd June at home to Whitburn. He has taken 3 NEPL catches.

He had made his NEPL Division 1 debut for Castle Eden on 17th April 2021 at home to Boldon and in his two seasons with the club in NEPL Division 1 Iqbal has played 36 matches, batting 34 times with 1 not out, he scored 669 runs at an average of 20.27. He scored 4 half centuries, his highest score of 88 was made on 1st May 2021 at Gateshead Fell. He bowled 2046 balls in NEPL Division 1, with 85 maidens, conceding 1004 runs and taking 105 wickets at an average of 9.56. His best bowling figures were 7 for 12, taken on 24th July 2021 at home to Ashington. He took 6 catches in NEPL Division 1.

In his home country of Pakistan, Iqbal has represented Lahore, Punjab, Central Punjab and Baluchistan, playing a total of 65 first class matches and 22 List A matches.

J. P Meade, referred to on cricket archive as Gian Piero Sergio Meade, first came to attention in South Africa, on 17th December 2014 playing for Easterns Under 19's against North West Under 19's at Pretoria. By the start of the 2016 season, on 23rd April, he was playing for Brailsford and Ednaston against Rolls Royce in Division Three of the Derbyshire County Cricket League.

On 29th October 2016 he played for Italy in a 50 over match in Denmark and he was still playing for Italy as recently as 3rd March 2024 against Vanuatu in Malaysia. This was his 64th match for Italy, he has batted 56 times, scoring 916 runs at an average of 17.96. He has scored 4 half centuries with a highest score of 62, made on 9th September 2017 in Benoni, South Africa against Qatar. He has bowled 691 balls, with 3 maidens, conceding 657 runs and taking 20 wickets at an average of 32.85. His best bowling figures are 3 for 18, taken on 19th October 2021 in Almeira against Denmark and he has taken 32 catches for Italy.

Meade first came to notice in the north east when he played for Horden in 2018. He then made his debut for Billingham Synthonia in the N.Y.S.D Premier League on 20th April 2019 at Barnard Castle and his last game for Synthonia was on 3rd September 2022 at home to Thornaby.

He made his NEPL debut for Castle Eden on 29th April 2023 at Ashington. He played 15 matches for them in 2023, batting 15 times with 2 not outs, he scored 412 runs at an average of 31.69. He scored 1 half century and 1 century, 147, scored on 1st July 2023 at home to Newcastle, it came from 148 balls and contained 15 fours and 5 sixes. He also bowled 569 balls, with 9 maidens, conceding 409 runs and taking 21 wickets at an average of 19.47. His best bowling figures were 5 for 21 on 28th August at Newcastle. He took 7 NEPL catches.

Muhaymen Majeed is a left-handed batsman who first came to notice playing for Western Warriors Under 16's at Eastern Warriors Under 16's at Edinburgh. He would go on to be selected for Scotland Under 19's in 2021, playing 10 times for them.

He made his NEPL debut for Whitburn at home to Burnmoor on 6th May 2023, scoring 29 in his first innings. He would go on to play 18 matches in the NEPL in 2023 for Whitburn, he batted 18 times with 1 not out, he scored 358 runs at an average of 21.05. He scored 1 half century, 72, made on 12th August at Chester le Street. He did not bowl in the NEPL in 2023 but did take 6 catches.

Alan Unsworth can be traced on cricket archive back to 27th April 2013, playing for Castle Eden in the Durham Cricket League, I suspect he has played for the club a bit longer than that! I did find one century, 115 not out, scored on 11th July 2015 at Philadelphia in the Durham Cricket League, he has also scored at least 9 half centuries since 2013, he has also taken at least 153 wickets at an average of 17.27 since then. Unsworth made his debut for Durham Over 50's on 2nd June 2021 at Cumbria Over 50's.

Unsworth made his debut in the NEPL on 29th April 2023 at Ashington, his first NEPL wicket was Ashington's Cameron Skinner, caught by J P Meade for a single. He played 6 NEPL matches in 2023, it was as a bowler that he made his mark, bowling 225 balls, with 4 maidens, conceding 144 runs and taking 8 wickets at an average of 18.00. His best bowling figures were 3 for 21, taken on 10th June 2023 at Benwell Hill. He took 3 NEPL catches in 2023.

Jonathan Malkin after playing for Durham Under 15 and Under 17 sides, Malkin made his NEPL debut for Blaydon on 26th April 2008 at home to Newcastle, he took 3 for 42 with the ball, his first NEPL wicket was Sean Adair, bowled for 14. He progressed through a Northumberland Development side to make his full Northumberland debut in Minor Counties Championship cricket on 21st June 2009 at Bedfordshire.

He played his last NEPL game for Blaydon on 12th September 2009, moving on to play for Hetton Lyons, debuting there on 1st May 2010 against Durham Academy.

2010 saw him selected for Durham M.C.C University and Durham Second XI a number of times.

He played his last NEPL game for Hetton Lyons on 14th September 2019 at Whitburn and joined Castle Eden for the Covid shortened season of 2020, going on to make his full NEPL debut for the club on 29th April 2023 at Ashington.

To the end of the 2023 season, Malkin has played 239 matches in the NEPL, batting 194 times, with 31 not outs, he has scored 3177 runs at an average of 19.49. He has scored 15 NEPL half centuries, his highest NEPL score is 88, made for Hetton Lyons on 16th July 2016 at Eppleton.

He has bowled 10830 balls in the NEPL, with 285 maidens, conceding 6570 runs and taking 260 wickets at an average of 25.26. His best bowling figures are 6 for 65 taken for Hetton Lyons on 6th July 2013 at Benwell Hill. He has taken 72 catches in the NEPL.

Castle Eden CC 11/5/24.

Left to Right- Back Row Philip Wimpenny, Ben Simpson, Nick Sampson-Barnes, Keith Bailey, Jon Malkin.

Front Row-Connor Crute, Ash Grant, Jonathan Brown, Alan Unsworth, Muhaymen Majeed, Bilawal Iqbal.

Chester le Street Chairman Mark Burdon shares his thoughts on the upcoming 2024 season.

"It's been a busy winter at Chester le Street with several departures and arrivals as we head in to the 2024 season full of excitement and optimism. We have lost Amaan Ulhaq, Ross Whitfield and Stanley McAlindon; we wish them all the best at their new clubs.

Our squad has been bolstered by the additions of James Thompson and Mark Watson from Washington, Cole Pearce returns from Burnopfield, and we have also signed former Scotland captain Kyle Coetzer. Our Durham player for the season is up and coming fast bowler Luke Robinson who joins from Philadelphia.

South North and Burnmoor will rightly go into the season as favourites, but we want to be up there competing. At full strength we feel we can challenge, and we are hopeful that availability is kind to us this year."

Kyle Coetzer and his career is covered earlier in the book as are James Thompson and Cole Pearce, who were both part of the title winning Chester side of 2016, let's have a look at the new additions to the Chester squad.

Mark Watson has spent his career so far with Washington, playing for them in the 2021 season, after they were promoted from NEPL Division 1. He made his NEPL debut 17th April 2021 at home to Felling, he took 1 for 56, his first NEPL wicket was opener Arun Phogat, bowled for 38. His last NEPL game for Washington was on 11th September 2021 at home to Stockton.

He had played 18 matches in the NEPL for Washington, batting 13 times with 7 not outs, he has scored 34 runs at an average of 5.66. He had also bowled 1053 balls in the NEPL for Washington, with 22 maidens, he conceded 711 runs and took 30 wickets at an average of 23.70. His best bowling figures were 5 for 41, taken on 5th June 2021 at home to Tynemouth. He took 4 catches in the NEPL for Washington.

He had previously played for Washington on NEPL Division 1, making his debut on 22nd June 2013 at Brandon. His first wicket at NEPL Division 1 level was opener and well known NEPL player, Karl Turner, caught by Ashley Thorpe for 48.

He continued to play for Washington through the covid season of 2020 and as stated earlier during their one season in the NEPL, he stayed with them following relegation from the NEPL for the 2022 season and into 2023.

To date he has played 167 matches in NEPL Division 1 for Washington, as a batsman it's fair to say he is a tailender.

He has bowled 7235 balls in NEPL Division 1, with 208 maidens, conceding 4734 runs and taking 231 wickets at an average of 20.49. His best bowling figures at this level are 5 for 22, taken on 10th June 2017 at Boldon, he has taken 29 catches at this level.

Watson has also played 2 matches for Northumberland, both in May 2019, he wasn't given any kind of opportunity and so far, that remains his career for the County.

Luke Robinson is a left-handed batsman and right arm medium pace bowler; he first came to my attention on 26th August 2016 when he played for Durham Under 12's against Cleveland Under 12's at Hetton le Hole. Ben McKinney and Mitchell Killeen were in the same side.

He played for Durham Under 13's on 15th May 2017 in a 20 over match at Cleveland.

The first record I found of him playing for Philadelphia was for their Under 15's on 23rd April 2018 at Chester le Street Under 15's.

The 2018 season also saw him continue his progress through the Durham youth system. On 14th June that year he played for the Under 14's at Nottinghamshire Under 14's.

The first trace I found of him in Philadelphia's first team was on 27th May 2019 at Dawdon Welfare in a 20 over match. He played for Philadelphia during the 2020 covid season.

On 4th July 2021 Robinson was selected to play for Durham Under 18's at Lancashire Under 18's in a 50 over match, rain ruined the day, but he would go on to represent Durham at his level throughout 2021 and 2022 as he continued his progress through the Durham system.

On 6th September 2022 he made his debut for Durham Seconds in a 4-day match at Gosforth against Leicestershire Second XI.

To the end of the 2023 season, Robinson has played 9 matches for Durham Seconds, he has a highest score of 19, but more importantly, he has taken 12 wickets with a best of 5 for 34.

Robinson made his debut for Durham in twenty over cricket on 4th June 2023 in a Vitality Blast game at The Riverside against Leicestershire, he marked his debut with 2 wickets. He played two more Twenty20 matches for Durham in 2023.

He has also made his debut in List A cricket for Durham, on 11th August 2023 at The Riverside against Derbyshire. Although he didn't bat, he opened the bowling taking his first wicket at this level, opener Harry Came, caught by George Drissell for 44, as he finished with 1 for 42 from seven overs.

He played a second List A game for Durham on 17th August 2023 against Somerset at Gosforth.

As I write this, early in 2024, Robinson has continued to prosper and has continued his journey through the Durham system.

Early in 2024 Durham played some warm up matches in Zimbabwe, on 3rd March 2024 they played a 20 over match against Mountaineers, Robinson didn't bat but took 2 for 28. Benwell Hill's Haydon Mustard made his debut at this level in the same match.

Robinson played a further 3 matches on the tour and picked up 2 more wickets.

Chester le Street CC 20/7/24.

Left to Right- Back Row- John Coxon, Seb Hughes-Pinan, Matthew Robinson, Mark Watson, Ash Thorpe, Andrew Smith.

Front Row-Liam Simpson, Cole Pearce, James Thompson, Quentin Hughes, Jake McCann.

Felling Chairman Andrew McNally shares a few thoughts on the upcoming season.

"After an underwhelming year, finishing 9^{th,} in 2023, we look to go a bit better this time around. It's been a busy winter with a few new faces. Northumberland batsman Alasdair Appleby returns to the club after 2 years away, left arm spinner and Scotland U19 international Jamie Cairns joins from Gateshead Fell, Durham U18 seamer Ishaq Khan joins from Eppleton and Jordan Watson will be the overseas player for 2024 – a talented young batter from Sydney.

Stalwart Paul Leonard continues as captain - the only man to ever record a NEPL 10-fer. All-rounder and NEPL player of the year from 2022, Sebastian Allison, is retained. Veteran Alan Mustard will once again open the batting, a regular for many years in the NEPL and still putting in match winning performances.

The league has remained very competitive, and we are in no doubt it will be again this coming season. We look forward to welcoming all teams to High Heworth Lane. Let's hope the weather gods are kinder to us all in 2024. "

Alasdair Appleby goes into the 2024 season having made his NEPL debut for Benwell Hill on 1st June 2013 at home to South Shields. He remained with Hill until the end of the 2015 season, his last match coming on 5th September at Newcastle.

He played 30 matches in the NEPL for Benwell Hill, batting 24 times with 1 not out, he scored 264 runs at an average of 11.47. His highest score was 42, made on 8th August 2015 at home to Blaydon. He bowled a little, 0 for 39, but took 6 catches in the NEPL for Benwell Hill.

He then made his NEPL debut for The Durham Academy on 23rd April 2016 at Whitburn and he took his first NEPL wicket for The Academy on 7th May 2016 when he bowled Tynemouth opener Nick Armstrong for 32. He played his last NEPL game for The Academy on 3rd September 2016 at Chester le Street.

He played 17 matches in the NEPL for Durham Academy, batting 15 times with 0 not outs, he scored 281 runs at an average of 18.73. He made 1 half century, 56, on 4th June 2016 at South Shields.

He also bowled 525 balls in the NEPL for Durham Academy, with 11 maidens, he conceded 372 runs and took 16 wickets at an average of 23.25. His best bowling figures were 4 for 38, taken on 7th May 2016 at Tynemouth. He took 1 catch in the NEPL for Durham.

He then made his NEPL debut for Newcastle on 15th April 2017 at Jesmond against Eppleton and his last game in the NEPL for them was on 14th September 2019 at Benwell Hill.

He played 39 matches in the NEPL for Newcastle, batting 38 times with 2 not outs, he scored 916 runs at an average of 25.44. He made 5 half centuries, with a highest score of 88, made on 1st July 2017 at Eppleton.

He also bowled 1941 balls in the NEPL for Newcastle, with 41 maidens, he conceded 1137 runs and took 41 wickets at an average of 27.73. His best bowling figures were 4 for 47, taken on 26th August 2017 at home to South Shields. He took 12 catches in the NEPL for Newcastle.

Appleby played for Felling in the covid season of 2020 and then made his NEPL debut for them on 17th April 2021 at Washington, his first NEPL wicket for Felling was taken in this game, Joe Thompson leg before wicket. His last game in this spell with Felling was on 11th September 2021 at home to Eppleton.

He played 20 matches in the NEPL for Felling in 2021, batting 18 times with 1 not out, he scored 334 runs at an average of 19.64. He scored 2 half centuries, with a highest score of 71, made on 21st August 2021 at Burnopfield.

He also bowled 503 balls in the NEPL for Felling in 2021, with 6 maidens, he conceded 394 runs and took 19 wickets at an average of 20.73. His best bowling figures were 6 for 11, taken on 22nd May 2021 at home to Hetton Lyons. He took 6 catches in the NEPL for Felling in 2021.

He made his NEPL debut for Burnopfield on 30th April 2022 at home to South North and his last NEPL game was for Burnopfield on 3rd September 2022 at Hetton Lyons.

He played 21 matches in the NEPL for Burnopfield, batting 20 times with 2 not outs, he scored 572 runs at an average of 31.77. He made 3 half centuries and 1 century, 123 not out, scored from 88 balls, with 11 fours and 4 sixes and was made on 18th June 2022 at Hetton Lyons.

He also bowled 939 balls in the NEPL for Burnopfield, with 10 maidens, he conceded 742 runs and took 16 wickets at an average of 46.37. His best bowling figures were 4 for 38, taken on 2nd July 2022 at Newcastle. He took 6 catches in the NEPL for Burnopfield.

He spent the 2023 season playing for Darlington Railway Athletic in The N.Y.S.D Premier League.

Up to the end of 2023, he has now played 127 NEPL matches, batting 115 times with 6 not outs, he has scored 2367 runs at an average of 21.71. He has made 11 half centuries and 1 century, 123 not out on 18th June 2022 for Burnopfield at home to Hetton Lyons, the innings came from just 88 balls and contained 11 fours and 4 sixes.

Appleby has also bowled 3950 balls in the NEPL, with 68 maidens, conceding 2684 runs and taking 92 wickets at an average of 29.17. His best bowling figures are 6 for 11, taken for Felling on 22nd May 2021 at home to Hetton Lyons. He has taken 31 NEPL catches.

Appleby made his debut for Northumberland on 19th April 2015 against Durham Second XI at The Emirates. Up to 13th August 2023 he has played 60 matches for Northumberland, batting 71 times with 3 not outs, he has scored 1614 runs at an average of 23.73. He has scored 8 half centuries and 2 centuries.

The centuries came in back-to-back games, the first, 102 not out, was scored on 8th May 2022 in a 20 over match at Gosforth against Cheshire. The innings came from 62 balls and contained 13 fours and 3 sixes.

The second century, 118, was scored on 5th June 2022 in a 50 over match at Allendale against Lincolnshire. The innings came from 111 balls and contained 16 fours and 5 sixes.

He has also bowled 1373 balls for Northumberland, with 36 maidens, conceding 1007 runs and taking 34 wickets at an average of 29.61. His best bowling figures are 4 for 33, taken in a 3-day match which started on 25th July 2021 at Carlisle against Cumbria. He has taken 19 catches for Northumberland across all formats.

Jamie Cairns has yet to appear in the NEPL although he is an established player in the Scottish youth system, having played at Under 15, Under 17 and Under 19 level as well as playing for The Scotland Performance Academy. He made his debut for Scotland A on 8th July 2022 against Namibia, taking 1 for 35.

He has also played a game for Hampshire Second XI, against Warwickshire Seconds starting on 7th September 2021 and he has played 3 games for Durham Seconds in June 2022 and twice more in September 2022.

He has played in NEPL Division 1, making his debut for Gateshead Fell on 16th April 2022 at home to Castle Eden and his last NEPL Division 1 game for Fell was on 9th September 2023 at Seaham Park.

He played 35 matches in NEPL Division 1 for Gateshead Fell, batting 28 times with 5 not outs, he scored 434 runs at an average of 18.86. He scored 2 half centuries with a highest score of 58, made on 6th August 2022 at Ashington.

He bowled 1980 balls in NEPL Division 1, with 52 maidens, conceding 1143 runs and taking 64 wickets at an average of 17.85. His best bowling figures were 5 for 35, taken on 28th May 2022 at Crook. He took 23 catches at this level.

Ishaq Khan made his NEPL Division 1 debut for Eppleton on 6th May 2023 at home to Sacriston, he took 3 for 26. He made his Durham Under 18's debut on 6th July 2023 at Darlington against Cumbria Under 18's, he played 7 times for them in 2023. His last game for Eppleton, prior to signing for Felling, was on 9th September 2023 at Tynedale.

He played 16 matches in NEPL Division 1 for Eppleton in 2023, batting 11 times with 6 not outs, he scored 37 runs at an average of 7.40.

He bowled 543 balls for Eppleton in NEPL Division 1, with 8 maidens, he conceded 447 runs and took 23 wickets at an average of 19.43. His best bowling figures were 4 for 37, taken on 12th August 2023 at Lanchester. He took 1 catch at this level.

Jordan Watson arrives at Felling from Penrith CC in New South Wales, Australia then Wollaston CC from the Northamptonshire Cricket League where he spent the 2023 season. Putting the NEPL on notice, Watson played 15 games in the league for Wollaston, batting 15 times, with 0 not outs, he scored 575 runs at an average of 38.33. He scored 5 half centuries and 1 century, 125, scored on 10th June 2023 at Desborough Town, it came from 127 balls and contained 8 fours and 6 sixes.

He also bowled 42 balls, conceding 30 runs and failing to take a wicket and he took 5 catches in the league for the club.

Paul Leonard and his 10 for 24 against Stockton on 29th July 2017 is covered elsewhere in the book, a recap of his NEPL career to the end of 2023 has seen him play 104 NEPL matches, all for Felling, scoring 1031 runs at an average of 15.16. He has scored 2 half centuries with a highest score of 80, scored on 14th August 2021 at home to Burnmoor.

He has bowled 5708 balls, with 182 maidens, conceding 3291 runs and taking 174 wickets at an average of 18.91. Unsurprisingly his best bowling figures remain the 10 for 24 mentioned earlier! He has also taken 18 NEPL catches.

Seb Allison was covered earlier in the book when he was named the NEPL Player of the Year in 2022.

Alan Mustard is covered elsewhere in the book; however, a quick recap shows that as he enters the 2024 season, he has now played 246 NEPL matches, batting 228 times, with 26 not outs, he has scored 5206 runs at an average of 25.07. He scored 27 half century and 1 century, 121 not out, scored for Chester le Street 22nd August 2009 at Norton.

He has bowled 908 balls in the NEPL, with 15 maidens, conceding 700 runs and taking 32 wickets at an average of 21.87. His best bowling figures are 6 for 69 taken on 26th August 2006 for Sunderland at Blaydon. He has taken 95 NEPL catches and 1 NEPL stumping.

Felling CC 15/6/24.

Left to Right- Back Row- Ishaq Khan, Elliot Fox, Paul Leonard, Alan Mustard, Jordan Watson, Seb Allison.

Front Row-Tyler Easton, Max Lowery, Alasdair Appleby, Ed Hurst, Marc Foster.

Newcastle Chairman Phil Hudson shares his thoughts on the upcoming 2024 season.

"Newcastle head into the 2024 season with some optimism as a young squad gets more battle hardened; and with some key additions think that the club should have a good season. The club have lost Ronan Hogarth (2023 overseas) Brodie Glendinning (Uni in Yorkshire) and Joe Anderson but have signed Rowan Shelton, a pace bowling all-rounder from Tasmania and were hugely boosted by the news that former Durham and Hampshire all-rounder Asher Hart has moved to the area and will be available for the whole season. Hart and Shelton will combine with talented youngsters George Darwood and Isaac Unsworth to form a potent seam attack which we hope will form the cornerstone of the clubs bid for honours.

The batting will once again be spearheaded by grizzled veteran Jacques du Toit, with strong support expected from captain Bobby Green and Ben Robinson as well as talented spin bowling all-rounder Mohsin Mukhtar. Kieran Trevaskis retains the gloves and provides middle order power, with Matthew Stewart offering leg spin variety and top order support.

The squad will be supported by young players in Joe Boaden, Hamza Amin, Charlie Darwood, Yuvi Chauhan and Woody Wilson who we hope will continue their development in 2024."

Rowan Shelton spent the 2022 season with Neston in the Cheshire Premier League, he played 23 matches, batting 20 times with 4 not outs, he scored 353 runs at an average of 22.06, with 1 half century, 58 not out. He also bowled 1441 balls, with 36 maidens, conceding 1145 runs and taking 53 wickets at an average of 21.60. His best bowling figures were 6 for 52.

He played at Atherton C.C in 2023 in The Northwest Cricket League around Manchester.

Asher Hart has played 2 first-class matches for Hampshire, he batted 4 times and scored 44 runs at an average of 14.66 with the highest score of 36. He bowled 263 balls in first-class cricket for Hampshire with 8 maidens, conceding 111 runs and taking 5 wickets at an average of 22.20. His best bowling figures were 3 for 17.

He also played 5 List A matches for Hampshire, batting 5 times with 0 not outs, he scored 58 runs at an average of 11.60 with a high score of 21. He bowled 144 balls in List A cricket, with 0 maidens, he conceded 144 runs and took 3 wickets at an average of 48.00. His best bowling figures was 2 for 34.

Hart made his NEPL debut for Durham Academy on 17th April 2013 at Tynemouth and his last NEPL game for the Academy was on 10th September 2016 at home to Stockton.

He had played 54 matches in the NEPL for Durham Academy, batting 49 times with 12 not outs, he had scored 829 runs at an average of 22.40. He scored 3 half centuries with a highest score of 79, made on 13th August 2013 at The Riverside against Benwell Hill.

He had also bowled 2076 balls in the NEPL for Durham Academy, with 78 maidens, he conceded 1119 runs and took 66 wickets at an average of 16.95. His best bowling figures were 4 for 6, taken on 18th June 2016 at the Riverside against Chester le Street. He took 5 catches in the NEPL for Durham Academy.

Hart has also played for Penrith in the Northern Premier League from 2018 to 2022.

Asher Hart made his NEPL debut for Newcastle on 20th May 2023 at Tynemouth, he played 4 matches in the NEPL in 2023, batting 4 times, with 1 not out, he scored 84 runs at an average of 28.00. He scored 1 half century, 53, on debut. He also bowled 252 balls, with 8 maidens, conceding 151 runs and taking 10 wickets at an average of 15.10. His best bowling figures were 6 for 46, taken on 8th July 2023 at home to Chester le Street.

Jaques du Toit is a two-time NEPL Player of the Year and his career stats up to the end of 2023 can be found in the chapter which covers the Team of the Twenty Years.

Here's a more detailed look at the remainder of the Newcastle squad for 2024.

George Darwood is a right arm fast medium bowler and right-handed batsman, he made his NEPL debut for Newcastle at home to Chester le Street on 16th April 2022. He opened the bowling, taking 2 for 15, his first NEPL wicket was opener Josh Wilson, bowled for 12 and he scored 5 not out when he batted.

To date, the end of March 2023, he played his last game in the NEPL for Newcastle on 9th September 2023 at Felling. To the end of the 2023 season Darwood has played 35 matches in the NEPL, all for Newcastle, batting

27 times with 7 not outs, he has scored 450 runs at an average of 22.50. He has scored 1 half century, 81 not out, on 7th May 2022 at Burnopfield. He has also bowled 1521 balls in the NEPL, with 33 maidens, he has conceded 958 runs and took 45 wickets at an average of 21.28. His best bowling figures are 4 for 38, taken on 20th August 2022 at Hetton Lyons. He has taken 13 catches in the NEPL.

George Darwood first came to my attention when he played for Northumberland Under 15's, 19th June 2019, he progressed through the Under 15's, playing in Northumberland Development XI side on 23rd June 2002 against Scotland Under 19's. He also started playing for the Northumberland Under 18 side on 5th July 2021 in a game at Cumbria Under 18's.

Darwood made his debut for the full Northumberland side on 24th April 2022 at Roseworth Terrace against Cumbria. Up to the end of the 2023 season, he has now played 14 matches for Northumberland, batting 6 times with 3 not outs, he has scored 51 runs at an average of 17.00. His highest score is 22.

He has bowled 425 balls, with 2 maidens, conceding 462 runs and taking 12 wickets at an average of 38.50. His best bowling figures are 3 for 22, taken on 2nd May 2022 at Shropshire. He has taken 4 catches for Northumberland.

He was part of the Northumberland side which pulled off a shock win over a strong Durham side on 30th July 2023 at Jesmond, he scored 15 and took 2 for 51, including the final wicket to secure the win.

2023 also saw him make his debut for both Durham Under 18 and Second XI sides, as well as an ECB Elite Player Development North side.

He made his first century, 101 not out for Durham Under 18's on 6th July 2023 at home to Cumbria Under 18's. Having seen Darwood a number of times I think he is one to keep an eye on as he clearly has a bright future in cricket.

Isaac Unsworth is a right-handed batsman and right arm fast medium bowler. He is a product of the Durham youth set up, starting as an Under 15 and progressing through Under 14, Under 15, Under 16 and Under 17, he has also played for The English Schools Cricket Association North at The Bunbury Festival and The Durham Emerging Players Under 16's in 2018.

He made his debut for Castle Eden in NEPL Division 1 on 16th June 2018 at home to Willington, his last appearance for them was in NEPL Division 1 on 11th September 2021 at Ashington. He played 39 matches in NEPL Division 1 for the club, batting 32 times with 3 not outs, he scored 270 runs at an average of 9.31. His highest score was 33.

He also bowled 1350 balls for Castle Eden in NEPL Division 1, with 31 maidens, conceding 1044 runs and taking 59 wickets at an average of 17.69. His best bowling figures were 6 for 67, taken on 10th July 2021 at home to Philadelphia. He took 8 catches for the club at this level.

Unsworth made his NEPL debut for Newcastle at home to Chester le Street on 16th April 2022. He opened the bowling that day and took his first NEPL wicket, a good one as it happens, Andrew Smith, bowled for 8. Up to the time of writing, early April, his last NEPL game was at Felling on 9th September 2023.

To the end of the 2023 season, Isaac Unsworth has played 37 NEPL matches, batting 17 times, with 6 not outs, he has scored 43 runs at an average of 3.90. His highest score is 12 not out.

He has bowled 1472 balls in the NEPL, with 17 maidens, conceding 1161 runs and taking 39 wickets at an average of 29.76. His best bowling figures are 5 for 39, taken on 11th June 2022 at Whitburn. He has taken 7 catches in the NEPL.

He has also played two games for Northumberland, making his debut on 19th June 2022 at Jesmond against Oxfordshire, he took 2 for 81 and scored 16, and then he played again on 3rd July 2022, at Preston Avenue against Cumbria, he scored 1 and 0 not out and took 0 for 18 and 0 for 13.

Bobby Green after playing for the Royal Grammar School Green played for Northumberland Under 15's in June 2018, he played 9 times at this age group before moving on to the County Under 18's. The pandemic disrupted his junior cricket so that accounts for the jump in age groups progressing to the Durham Academy.

Green made his debut in the NEPL for South North at home to Tynemouth on 11th August 2018, scoring 7. He played 1 more game for South North in the NEPL, on 8th September 2018 at home to Felling, he made 3 not out and took a catch.

He made his NEPL Division 1 debut for Crook on 11th May 2019 at Washington and his last appearance for Crook in NEPL Division 1 was on 14th September 2019 at Shotley Bridge. He played for Crook during the 2020 Covid season in The Banks Salver.

He made his NEPL Division 1 debut for Newcastle on 17th April 2021, at Lanchester and his last NEPL Division 1 match was on 11th September 2021 at home to Boldon.

He played 16 matches in the NEPL Division 1 for Newcastle, batting 13 times with 2 not outs, he scored 193 runs at an average of 17.54. His highest score was 34 not out, made on 7th August 2021 at Shotley Bridge. He didn't bowl in the league in 2012 but took 7 catches.

He made his NEPL debut for Newcastle on 21st May 2022 at home to Benwell Hill, scoring 37 and his last NEPL appearance to date early April 2023 for Newcastle was on 9th September 2023 at Felling.

He has now played 33 matches in the NEPL for Newcastle, batting 33 times with 2 not outs, he has scored 940 runs at an average of 30.32. He has scored 5 half centuries and 1 century, 108, scored on 6th August 2022 at Benwell Hill and was scored from 141 balls, with 13 fours and a six. Green has bowled 18 balls in the NEPL, conceding 15 runs for no wickets and he has taken 18 catches in the NEPL for Newcastle.

Ben Robinson is a right-handed batsman and right arm off break bowler, his brother, Charlie, also plays for Newcastle. He first came to my attention playing for York on 15th September 2018 against Wakefield Thornes in the Yorkshire Premier League. His last game in the Yorkshire Premier League was for York on 7th September 2019 at Scarborough, he made 72 not out.

Robinson made his NEPL debut for Burnopfield on 17th April 2021 at Benwell Hill, he scored exactly 50, opening the batting. He also took his first NEPL wicket in this match, Kyle Coetzer, caught by Jonathan Pears for 107. He played his last NEPL game for Burnopfield 11th September 2021 at Chester le Street, he scored 42.

Robinson played 19 matches in the NEPL for Burnopfield, batting 19 times with 0 not outs, he scored 240 runs at an average of 12.63. He scored 1 half century, his highest score was 50, made on debut and mentioned earlier.

He bowled 687 balls in the NEPL in 2021, with 4 maidens, he conceded 532 runs and took 22 wickets at an average of 24.18. His best bowling figures were 4 for 49, taken on 24th April at Eppleton.

Robinson then made his NEPL debut for Newcastle on 16th April 2022 at Jesmond against Chester le Street.

Robinson has now played 39 matches for Newcastle in the NEPL, batting 39 times with 0 not outs, he has scored 1209 runs at an average of 31.00. he had scored 7 half centuries and 2 centuries.

His first century, 106, was scored for Newcastle at home to Sunderland on 28th May 2022, the innings had come from 182 balls and contained 17 fours and 1 six.

His second century, 102, was scored on 16th July 2022 at home to Burnmoor, the innings came from 141 balls and contained 13 fours and 3 sixes.

He has bowled 221 balls in the NEPL for Newcastle, with 3 maidens, conceding 159 runs and taking 8 wickets at an average of 19.87. His best bowling figures were 2 for 1, taken on 9th September 2023 at Felling. He had taken 9 catches in the NEPL for Newcastle up to this point.

To date, the end of the 2023 NEPL season, Robinson has played 58 matches in the NEPL, batting 58 times with 0 not outs, he had scored 1449 runs at an average of 24.98. He had scored 8 half centuries and 2 centuries to this point.

He had bowled 908 balls in the NEPL, with 7 maidens, conceding 691 runs and taking 30 wickets at an average of 23.03. His best bowling figures were 4 for 49, taken on 24th April 2021 for Burnopfield at Eppleton. He has taken 14 catches in the NEPL.

Ben Robinson made his Minor Counties Championship debut for Northumberland in a match starting on 3rd July 2022 at Preston Grange against Cumbria, he scored 19 and 30.

To the end of the 2023 season, he has played 12 matches for Northumberland, batting 17 times, with 1 not out, scoring 372 runs at an average of 23.25. He has scored 2 half centuries with a highest score of 88, made on 4th June 2023 against Herefordshire at Jesmond. He has bowled 66 balls for Northumberland, with 1 maiden, conceding 50 runs and taking 0 wickets, he has yet to take a catch for Northumberland.

He was part of the Northumberland side which beat Durham on 30th July 2023 at Jesmond, scoring 27 from 28 balls with 3 fours and 2 sixes.

Mohsin Mukhtar is a right-handed batsman and slow left arm bowler, he played for Northumberland Under 15's on 21st May 2014 at Lincolnshire Under 15's. He was a regular throughout 2015 for the County Under 15 side and he was selected for a Northumberland Development XI on 5th May 2016, Durham Under 16's on 1st July 2016 against a North of England Under 15's side and Northumberland Under 17's in a 2-dy match starting on 19th July 2016.

He was a regular for Northumberland Under 17's in 2017 and also played for Durham Under 15's on 22nd August 2017 at Derbyshire. In 2018 Mukhtar was twice selected for Durham Under 17's,

He made his NEPL debut for Benwell Hill on 28th April 2018 at home to South North and his debut for Northumberland on 3rd June 2018 at Cheshire in a T20 match.

He has now played 16 matches for Northumberland across all formats, batting 16 times with 1 not out, he has scored 84 runs at an average of 5.60. his highest score is 33 not out. He has bowled 162 balls, with 1 maiden, conceding 149 runs and taking 2 wickets at an average of 74.50 and he has taken 7 catches for the County.

He played his last NEPL game for Benwell Hill on 3rd September 2022 at home to Burnmoor. He had played 65 matches in the NEPL for Benwell Hill, batting 60 times with 9 not outs, he scored 1112 runs at an average of 21.80. He scored 6 half centuries, with a highest score of 94.

He also bowled 1885 balls in the NEPL for Hill, with 36 maidens, conceding 1228 runs and taking 64 wickets at an average of 19.18. His best bowling figures were 5 for 41, taking on 3rd July 2021 at home to Eppleton. He took 21 NEPL catches for Hill.

He made his NEPL debut for Newcastle on 29th April 2023 at South North.

To the end of 2023, he had played 83 matches in the NEPL, batting 78 times with 11 not outs, he has scored 1414 runs at an average of 21.10. He has scored 7 half centuries with a highest score of 94, made on 4th September 2021 for Benwell Hill at home to Sacriston.

He has bowled 2791 balls in the NEPL, with 51 maidens, conceding 1813 runs and taking 87 wickets at an average of 20.83. His best bowling figures are 5 for 24, taken on 2nd September 2023 at home to Whitburn. He has taken 23 catches in the NEPL.

Kieran Trevaskis is a left-handed batsman and wicketkeeper; he is the brother of Liam Trevaskis who also features in the book. He first came to my attention on 4th June 2012 when he played for Cumbria Under 15's against Derbyshire Under 15's at Great Salkeld.

On 19th April 2014 he played for Penrith against Kendal in a Northern Premier League match, and he would play for Penrith Second XI and First XI from 2014 until the end of 2017.

Kieran Trevaskis made his NEPL debut for Durham Academy 26th August 2017. He played just 3 matches in the NEPL for them, his last game was on 9th September 2017. His highest score for the Academy was 18.

He made his NEPL debut for Newcastle on 28th April 2018 at home to Tynemouth.

On 30th May 2018 he was selected for a Cumberland Development XI against Myerscough College, he made 78 when they played the same opposition the following day.

He played for Newcastle during the pandemic season of 2020 and during the 2021 season when they were in NEPL Division 1. He played 14 matches in NEPL Division 1 in 2021, his highest score was 42 not out, made on 4th September 2021 at Crook. He took 10 catches and had 2 stumpings in NEPL Division1 in 2021. His last NEPL game to date, early April 2024, was on 9th September 2023 at Felling.

To the end of the 2023 season, Kieran Trevaskis had played 66 NEPL matches, he has scored 2 half centuries, his highest score is 64, made on 8th September 2018 at home to Stockton. He has never bowled in the NEPL, but he has taken 56 NEPL catches and made 9 stumpings.

Matthew Stewart is a leg break bowler; he first came to note on 5th June 2018 playing for Northumberland Under 15's against Durham Under 15's at Gateshead. He played for Northumberland Under 15's throughout 2018 and 2019 and played 1 game for the Under 18's in the covid season of 2020 and 1 in 2021, he also played 1 game for a Northumberland Development XI in June 2021.

He played 7 matches in NEPL Division 1 for Newcastle in the 2021 season, batting 6 times with 3 not outs, he scored 135 runs at an average of 45.00. He scored 1 half century, 68 not out, made on 14th August 2021 at home to Sunderland. His best bowling figures were 1 for 15 and he took 1 catch at this level.

He made his NEPL debut on 16th April 2022 at Jesmond for Newcastle against Chester le Street and his first NEPL wicket was taken on 9th July 2022 at South North, Sean Tindale, caught by Bobby Green for 8.

Up to the end of the 2023 season, he had played 24 matches for Newcastle in the NEPL. His highest score is 41, made on 2nd September 2023 at home to Whitburn. His best bowling figures are 3 for 45, taken on 13th May 2023 at Ashington and he has taken 2 NEPL catches up to this point.

Newcastle CC 11/5/24.

Left to Right- Back Row-George Darwood, Mohsin Mukhtar, Rowan Shelton, Isaac Unsworth, Asher Hart, Ben Robinson, Kieran Trevaskis, Charlie Darwood.

Front Row-Matthew Stewart, Bobby Green, Jaques du Toit.

Photo Courtesy of Martin Avery.

South North Chairman Howard Sidney- Wilmot shares a few thoughts on the upcoming season and one or two squad changes.

"As ever the competition in the NEPL will be fierce. Being champions for three consecutive years raises expectation levels and encourages other teams to challenge strongly. The hard work and practice to maintain the level and to aim for continuous improvement is always recognized. In 2024 we say goodbye and thank you to coach Shayne Moseley and Calum Fletcher (Undercliffe CC) and welcome back Sol Bell, The NEPL Player of the Year in 2021, from Sacriston.

Nik Gorantla, The NEPL Player of the Year in 2023, will play when County and University commitments allow. He had an outstanding first season, (Inns 13, no 4, runs 768, avg 75.33, 50 x 3, 100 x 3, highest score 134*, 7 catches). His 118 for Northumberland in their showcase win over Durham CCC was special.

Evergreen Lee Crozier, leading NEPL wicket taker with 840, will continue, as will our three England Over 40 representatives Simon Birtwisle, leading NEPL run score with 12206, Chris Hewison, now 9122 runs and Jonny Wightman 510 wickets.

Outstanding all-rounder Sean Tindale, 2840 runs and 256 wickets, whose bowling partnership with Wightman and impressive middle order batting have been a key part of our success, continues.

Effervescent wicketkeeper/batsman Rob Peyton, 1963 runs, 141 catches and 28 stumpings, adds fast hands & batting depth and we congratulate Oli McGee on becoming Northumberland CCC captain & hope he can build on his enviable record of 365 wickets & 1359 runs.

Sam Ewart's serious leg injury is a blow from which we are assured he will make a full recovery. We are keen to watch the progress of talented juniors, such as Will Alexander & George Gray, both of whom made first XI debuts in 2023 & had success on a Durham Academy tour to the UAE, as well as Angus Southern, Alex Charnley, Ben Hobbs and Will Carr.

Adam Cragg (6079 runs, 218 catches) begins his 8th season as Captain, hoping for a sixth title since 2017. His outstanding fielding sets the example. An overseas coach appointment is imminent.

Expectations are high both for NEPL league & cups & in the 2 national competitions. We must continue to be competitive but play with a smile & enjoy the game, hoping all teams feel welcome on their visits to Roseworth Terrace.

Australian Tom Rogers has now been recruited as an overseas coach. A left-handed batsman and right arm quick bowler, Tom has played for Australia A, Tasmania, Hobart Hurricanes and Melbourne Renegades. We are looking forward to benefitting from his expertise.

We also look forward to seeing the progress of promising Northumberland County Juniors, Will Alexander, George Gray, Angus Southern, Alex Charnley, Ben Hobbs and Will Carr. Will and George made their 1st XI debuts in 2023, and both represented Durham Academy in the U17 section of the Gulf Cup in The UAE in January 2024."

South North CC 11/5/24.

Left to Right- Back Row- Chris Hewison, Tom Rogers, Lee Crozier, Jonny Wightman, Sean Tindale, Rob Peyton.

Front Row- David Edwards, Sol Bell, Adam Cragg, Oli McGee, Simon Birtwisle.

Sunderland Chairman John Gillon shares a few thoughts on the upcoming 2024 campaign and the Sunderland squad assembled to fight it!

"Following a fantastic season last year, Sunderland CC are aiming to shrug off the 'yo-yo' club brush they have been tarnished with over the past few years following promotion and then immediate relegation in 2022. Having won the first division by 65 points last year, the atmosphere around the club is very positive. Experienced wicket-keeper batsman Chris Youldon has taken over as club captain following a successful ten years in charge from Greg Applegarth. Recruitment has been very promising with many young, promising cricketers from across the region coming to ply their trade at Ashbrooke. In addition to this, experienced cricketers such as Michael Nunn and Graeme Race have arrived to bridge the gap between first team and second team cricket."

The Sunderland Squad for 2024-

Chris Youldon- Captain/Wicketkeeper-Batsman- Nearly 20 years NEPL experience. Fine season last year, 573 league runs @44.08, and 44 dismissals, breaking the Division 1 league record, he was part of the Northumberland CCC team who were runners up in MCCA Trophy 2015 and he has returned to play for the minor county this season.

Youldon had first appeared on my radar on 16th June 2004 when he appeared for Durham Under 13's at Oldham against Lancashire Under 13's. He went on to represent Durham at Under 15 and Under 17 level as well as representing English Schools Cricket Association North Under 15's. Fellow teammates in the North School side included Joe Root and Ben Stokes.

He made his NEPL debut for Sunderland on 9th September 2006 at home to Durham Academy, he took his first NEPL catch, Karl Turner, off the bowling of Greg Davison for 14, and his first NEPL stumping, Richard Hopwood off the bowling of Imran Shah for 16 in the game. He scored 16 when he batted.

Youldon was selected to play in a 2-day match for Durham Academy starting on 30th June 2009 at Cheshire.

On 29th May 2012 he played for Durham Second XI at Derbyshire Seconds, this was the first of four appearances he made in May 2012 for Durham Seconds.

He played his last NEPL game for Sunderland on 8th September 2012 at Hetton Lyons.

He played 102 matches in the NEPL for Sunderland in this period, batting 72 times with 19 not outs, he scored 813 runs at an average of 15.33. He scored 3 half centuries with a highest score of 75 not out, made on 16th May 2009 at home to South Shields. He took 96 catches and made 20 stumpings in this period.

He made his NEPL debut for Chester le Street on 27th April 2013 at Hetton Lyons and he played his last NEPL game for Chester on 16th August 2014 at home to Newcastle.

He played 36 matches in the NEPL for Chester le Street, batting 28 times with 6 not outs, he scored 408 runs at an average of 18.54. He scored 1 half century, his highest score of 69 not out, made on 16th August 2014 at home to Newcastle. He took 30 catches and made 6 stumpings in this period.

He then made his NEPL debut for Newcastle on 23rd April 2016 at Eppleton and played his last NEPL appearance for Newcastle on 10th September 2016 at home to Chester le Street.

He played 20 matches in the NEPL for Newcastle, batting 15 times with 5 not outs, he scored 181 runs at an average of 18.10. His highest score was 47 not out, made on 13th August 2016 at home to South Shields. He took 15 catches and made 5 stumpings in this period.

He next appeared in the NEPL on 16th April 2022 for Sunderland at Tynemouth and his last NEPL game, up to the end of the 2023 season was for Sunderland at Burnmoor on 10th September 2022.

He played 21 matches in the NEPL for Sunderland in 2022, batting 19 times with 1 not out, he scored 322 runs at an average of 17.88. His highest score was 48, made on 13th August 2022 at home to Newcastle. He took 21 catches and made 2 stumpings in the NEPL in 2022.

Up to the end of the 2023 season, Youldon has played 179 matches in the NEPL, batting 134 times with 31 not outs, he has scored 1724 runs at an average of 16.73. He has scored 4 half centuries with a highest score of 75 not out, made on 16th May 2009 at home to South Shields. He has taken 162 catches and made 33 stumpings in the NEPL.

Youldon feels that in the early stages of his career he focused solely on wicketkeeping and that his batting has dramatically improved since 2018 as he worked on becoming a more complete cricketer.

Youldon has also played 17 matches for Northumberland, batting 17 times with 4 not outs, he has scored 423 runs at an average of 32.53. He has scored 1 half century for the county, 53 not out, made on 15th May 2016 at Cumberland. He has also taken 24 catches and 2 stumpings for Northumberland.

Daniel Shurben- Vice-captain- Batsman- One of the most decorated batters in NEPL history. 591 league runs last season. Played many years for Northumberland CCC, part of MCCA trophy winners in 2006. Current Northumberland first team coach.

Shurben won an NEPL title in 2001 with Chester le Street and was named as part of the Team of the Decade in 2009.

His career is covered as part of that chapter, but a quick recap shows that up to the end of 2023 he has now played 347 matches in the NEPL, batting 336 times with 30 not outs, he has now scored 10069 runs at an average of 32.90. He has scored 51 half centuries and 15 centuries, his highest score is 180 not out, made on 30th May 2015 for Whitburn at Gateshead Fell, the innings came from 175 balls and contained 25 fours and 5 sixes.

Greg Applegarth- Batsman- The former captain will take an active role in the team this year despite resignation from leadership, he is a hard-hitting left-handed batter with over 6000 league runs for the first team, with a highest score of 158. Greg Applegarth made his NEPL debut for Sunderland on 2nd August 2003 at home to Stockton.

He played for Northumberland Under 17's in a 2-day match at Jesmond starting on 26th July 2004 against Huntingdonshire Under 17's.

He played for the NEPL representative side on 23rd July 2006 in a President's Trophy Quarter Final match at the Derbyshire Premier League.

Greg Applegarth was also selected to play for Durham Pilgrims in a 2-day match starting on 13th August 2013 at Castle Eden against East Lancashire Cryptics. His father Adam was also in the Pilgrims side.

He has played his entire career for Sunderland, including their spells in NEPL Division 1.

Up to the end of 2023 Greg Applegarth has played 147 matches in the NEPL, batting 129 times with 10 not outs, he has scored 2174 runs at an average of 18.26. He has scored 6 half centuries and 1 century, 123, scored for Sunderland at Tynemouth on 4th May 2013, the innings came from 107 balls.

He has bowled 751 balls in the NEPL, with 21 maidens, conceding 480 runs and taking 13 wickets at an average of 36.92. His best bowling figures are 3 for 85, taken on 20th July 2013 at home to Tynemouth.

He has taken 33 NEPL catches.

George Drissell is an all-rounder and Durham CCC contracted player he also has county experience with Somerset and Gloucestershire. This is his third year with the club. He had a promising pre-season taking five wickets for Durham CCC v Durham UCCE.

Drissell has played 7 matches in first class cricket for Gloucestershire and 4 first-class matches for Durham. He has scored 135 runs and taken 9 wickets in first-class cricket.

He has also represented Gloucestershire, Somerset and Durham in List A cricket, playing a total of 17 matches, scoring 189 runs and taking 13 wickets.

He has also played 5 Twenty20 matches, all for Durham although he was given almost no opportunity to make any kind of mark.

Drissell made his NEPL debut for Sunderland on 16th April 2022 at Tynemouth, he took 1 for 55 and scored 56. His first NEPL wicket was Joe Snowdon, caught by Adam Shaw for 20.

Up to the end of 2023, he has now played 9 matches in the NEPL, batting 7 times with 0 not outs, he has scored 166 runs at an average of 23.71. He has scored 2 half centuries with a highest score of 74, made on 28th May 2022 at Newcastle.

He has bowled 456 balls in the NEPL, with 8 maidens, conceding 347 runs and taking 11 wickets at an average of 31.54. His best bowling figures are 3 for 85, taken on 28th May 2022 at Newcastle. He has taken 6 catches in the NEPL to the end of 2023.

Drissell made his debut for Northumberland on 23rd April 2023, playing in two Twenty20 matches against Staffordshire, again he had very little opportunity but having seen him play a number of times I'm sure a bright cricket future is ahead of him.

Kieran Waterson- Seamer- One of most successful seamers in NEPL history. Over 500 NEPL wickets across all divisions with spells at Hetton Lyons, Whitburn and Sunderland. Hoping to add to this tally this year.

Waterson was named the NEPL Player of the Year in 2018 for his efforts with Whitburn, he was also named as part of the NEPL Team of 20 Years and his career is covered there.

As a quick recap, he has now played 197 matches in the NEPL and has taken 422 wickets at an average of 17.95.

Joe Stuart- Spinner- Breakout season for the 23-year-old, leading the league wicket taking tallies with 44 wickets @11 in 2023. Nominated for league player of the year. Trained with the Minor County over the winter and hoping to be involved in the summer.

Stuart made his NEPL debut for Sunderland on 23rd April 2022 at home to Eppleton, he took 1 for 14, his first NEPL wicket was Colin Mann, caught by Ross Whitfield for a duck.

The breakout season referred to in 2023 saw Stuart play 16 matches in NEP Division 1, he bowled 840 balls, with 14 maidens, conceding 505 runs and taking 44 wickets at an average of 11.47. His best bowling figures were 6 for 25, taken on 26th August 2023 at home to Eppleton.

To the end of the 2023 season he has played 20 NEPL matches, batting 16 times with 3 not outs, he has scored 101 runs at an average of 7.76. His highest score is 24, made on 27th August 2022 at Burnopfield.

He has bowled 877 balls in the NEPL, with 9 maidens, conceding 622 runs and taking 17 wickets at an average of 36.58. His best bowling figures are 3 for 25, taken on 4th June 2022 at Felling. He has taken 4 NEPL catches so far in his career.

Brett Hutchinson- Seamer- The 17-year-old left arm swing bowler is currently dual registered with Durham Academy and is highly rated by management at the county. Striving to play a leading role in the Sunderland CC bowling attack.

Hutchinson started as a junior for Sunderland, progressing to play for Durham Under 14's in May 2021, he went on to play numerous games at Under 16 and Under 18 level for Durham.

Hutchinson made his NEPL debut for Sunderland on 23rd July 2022 at home to Tynemouth, he took 1 for 15, his first NEPL wicket was Esam Rahman, leg before wicket for 16.

He played 6 matches in the NEPL in 2022, with the highest score of 22 not out and he took 5 wickets for 191 runs as he started out on his career in senior cricket.

Robbie Potts- Batsman- Having come through the junior system, the hard-hitting middle order batsman is looking to cement his place in the club's first team. Played a major role in some important partnerships last year in promotion winning season. Highest first team score of 45.

Jack Johnson- All-rounder- He returns to the club from Seaham Park, having come through the junior system at Sunderland CC. Vital experience opening the batting at Seaham Park, including 95 runs in a league record partnership v Washington. Has worked incredibly hard over the winter and ready to take a big role in the Sunderland CC side.

The first trace I could find of Johnson was on 16th April 2022 when he played for Seaham Park at home to Ashington in NEPL Division 1. He last played for Seaham Park in NEPL Division 1 on 9th September 2023 at home to Gateshead Fell.

During those two years in NEPL Division 1, Johnson played 34 matches at his level, batting 32 times with 6 not outs, he scored 674 runs at an average of 25.92. He scored 4 half centuries with a highest score of 95 not out, made on 10th June 2023 at home to Washington.

He bowled only 118 balls, taking 2 wickets for 135 runs, he took 10 catches in this period.

Micky Allan- All-rounder- Fantastic season last year, nominated for NEPL player of the year alongside Joe Stuart. 643 league runs @40.19 and 24 wickets @20.04. Part of the leadership team within the squad. Part of the Northumberland CCC team who were runners up in MCCA Trophy 2015.

Allan had started out playing for Durham Under 13's, then playing at Under 15 and Under 17 level before moving on to play for Durham Academy.

He made his NEPL debut for Durham Academy on 26th April 2008 against South Shields at The Racecourse. He didn't bat but he did take his first NEPL wicket, Shields opener Dan Shurben, caught by Andrew Smith for 20.

He made his debut for Durham Second XI on 6th June 2008 at Surrey and he was also selected a number of times for an ECB North Under 17 side in 2008.

He played his last NEPL game for Durham Academy on 12th September 2009 at Norton.

On 7th July 2013 Allan played for a Northumberland and Tyneside Senior League representative side against the Nottinghamshire Premier League in a President's Trophy match.

He next re-appeared in the NEPL for Newcastle on 18th April 2015 at Jesmond against South North and he played his last NEPL match for Newcastle on 10th September 2016 at Jesmond against Chester le Street. There was another gap before he appeared in the NEPL again, for Sunderland on 16th April 2022 at Tynemouth.

Up to the end of the 2023 season Allan had played 74 matches in the NEPL, batting 62 times with 5 not outs, he has scored 1165 runs at an average of 20.43.

He has scored 6 half centuries and 1 century, the century, 106 not out, was made for Newcastle at Gateshead Fell on 18th July 2015, the innings came from 112 balls and contained 14 fours and 2 sixes.

He has bowled 3441 balls in the NEPL, with 87 maidens, conceding 2114 runs and taking 93 wickets at an average of 22.73. His best bowling figures are 4 for 6, taken on 25th June 2022 for Sunderland at home to Burnmoor. He has taken 33 catches in the NEPL.

Allan had made his Northumberland debut in Minor Counties Championship matches in a 3-day match starting on 22nd June 2014 at Gosforth against Lincolnshire.

Allan has now played 38 matches for Northumberland, batting 44 times with 6 not outs, he has scored 926 runs at an average of 24.36. He has scored 3 half centuries and 1 century, 107, made in a 3-day match at Jesmond against Suffolk which started on 20th July 2014.

Allan has also bowled 1928 balls for Northumberland, with 41 maidens, he has conceded 1374 runs and taken 54 wickets at an average of 25.44. His best bowling figures were 4 for 21, taken on 15th July 2018 at Cumberland. He took 17 catches for Northumberland.

He played his last match for Northumberland on 20th July 2021 at Yorkshire.

Charlie Coulthard-Batsman- New signing from Willington CC. Former experience with Durham Cricket Academy. Wants to challenge himself at a high level and to score consistent runs at the highest level on Northeast cricket. Current student at Barnard Castle.

Coulthard first came to my attention when he played for Willington during the covid season of 2020, he subsequently went on to play for Durham Under 15's, Under 16's and Under 18's, as well as play for Willington in NEPL Division 1.

To the end of 2023 he had played 27 matches in NEPL Division 1, batting 22 times with 2 not outs, he has scored 235 runs at an average of 12.10. His highest score is 35, made on 7th May 2022 at Washington. He has hardly bowled but has taken 6 catches in NEPL Division 1.

Jack Brassell- Bowler- Signed from Washington. Played for Namibia in the U19 World Cup, taking three wickets against Australia and made his full international debut following this. Anticipated to be part of the full world cup squad for the 2020s in June. Part of the Durham Cricket Academy.

Brassell is clearly starting out on his cricketing path, first coming to note in 3-day match starting on 9th August 2022 for Durham Under 18's at Nottingham.

He made his NEPL Division 1 debut for Washington on 29th April 2023 at Shotley Bridge and marked the occasion with 5 for 45, he also scored 31 not out.

He played 10 matches for Washington in NEPL Division 1 in 2023, bowling 518 balls, with 9 maidens, conceding 352 runs and taking 12 wickets at an average of 29.33. His best bowling figures were 5 for 45, taken on debut and mentioned earlier.

He made his debut for Namibia Under 19's on 13th January 2024 in a match in Pretoria against the United States as part of a world cup warm up. He went on to play 4 matches in the 2024 Under 19 World Cup for them.

He made his full debut for Namibia in a 50 over match on 15th February 2024 in Kirtipur against Nepal, he took 2 for 11.

At the time of writing, April 2024, Brassell had last played for Namibia on 7th April 2024 against Oman.

Joe Coyne- All-rounder- Second spell at Sunderland CC following stints at Boldon CC, South Northumberland CC and Whitburn CC. He can't always play due to work commitments but is a vital part of the squad. He scored a double hundred for Durham Second XI in time as Durham Cricket Academy player.

Coyne was part of the South North side which won the NEPL in 2012, up to the end of the 2023 season he has now played 136 matches in the NEPL, batting 132 times with 18 not outs, he has scored 2846 runs at an average of 24.96. He has scored 16 half centuries and 2 centuries, with a highest score of 126 not out, made for Whitburn at home to South Shields on 21st May 2016, the innings came from 162 balls and contained 13 fours and 2 sixes.

He has also bowled 4274 balls in the NEPL, with 149 maidens, conceding 2343 runs and taking 123 wickets at an average of 19.04. His best bowling figures are 5 for 30, taken for South North at Sunderland on 25th May 2013. He has taken 64 NEPL catches in his NEPL career.

George Fishwick- Batsman- Current Durham School scholar, exciting opening batsman who has a fantastic temperament and work ethic. Signed this year from Durham City, with aspirations to become a Durham Cricket Academy player. Reserve wicketkeeper.

All records I could find pertaining to Fishwick are in relation to Durham Under 14's and Under 16's.

To date the end of April 2024, he has 2 half centuries and 1 century to his name in Durham colours, the century, 107 not out, made for the Under 16's at Cumbria on 25th July 2023 and the innings came from 92 balls and contained 17 fours and 3 sixes.

Michael Nunn- Batsman- Returns from Washington CC as second team coach to the club where he has spent the majority of his career. Gritty batsman who makes it very difficult for the opposition.

Nunn made his debut in the NEPL with Sunderland on 6th May 2000 and played 4 matches in that title winning season.

To date the end of the 2023 season, he has played 165 matches in the NEPL, batting 131 times with 34 not outs, he has scored 1390 runs at an average of 14.32. He has scored 3 half centuries in the NEPL, with a highest score of 74 not out, made on 5th September 2009 for Sunderland at home to Norton.

He has bowled 32 balls in the NEPL, with 0 maidens and figures of 0 for 42 and he has taken 40 catches in his NEPL career.

Graeme Race- Seamer- Comes to Sunderland from Washington. Vast NEPL experience with Washington, Benwell Hill and Chester le Street. Has combatted injury over the past few seasons but looking to find his best cricket again at Ashbrooke.

Race made his NEPL debut for Chester le Street on 19th May 2001 at Sunderland.

His career, up to the end of 2015, is covered as part of the chapter which covers Chester le Street winning the league title in 2001.

On 30th April 2016 Race made his debut for Washington in NEPL Division 1 at Blaydon, and he played his last match for Washington in NEPL Division 1 on 9th September 2023 at Lanchester.

During that period Race has played 127 matches in NEPL Division 1, batting 91 times with 25 not outs, he has scored 1028 runs at an average of 15.57. He has scored 1 half century, 53, made on 13th August 2016 at Sacriston.

He has bowled 4596 balls in NEPL Division 1, with 129 maidens, conceding 2962 runs and taking 134 wickets at an average of 22.10. His best bowling figures are 6 for 16, taken on 2nd September 2017 at Mainsforth. He has taken 19 catches at this level.

To the end of the 2023 season, Race has played 262 matches in the NEPL, batting 169 times with 26 not outs, he has scored 2080 runs at an average of 14.54. He has scored 6 half centuries, with a highest score of 78, made for Benwell Hill at home to Chester le Street on 1st September 2007.

He has bowled 8979 balls in the NEPL, with 234 maidens, conceding 2080 runs and taking 188 wickets at an average of 29.97. His best bowling figure are 5 for 34, taken for Benwell Hill on 2nd June 2012 at home to Gateshead Fell. He has taken 61 catches in the NEPL.

Sunderland CC 25/4/24.

Left to Right- Back Row-Dan Shurben, George Drissell, Greg Applegarth, Jack Johnson, Charlie Coulthard, Micky Allan.

Front Row-Brett Hutchinson, Joe Stuart, Kieran Waterson, Chris Youldon, George Fishwick, C. Grimes (Scorer).

Tynedale Fixtures Secretary Graeme Robbie shares his thoughts on the upcoming 2024 season.

"After a number of years competing at the top of the Northumberland and Tyneside Cricket League Division One, 2022 marked a milestone for the club as we finished top of Division 1, securing promotion to the NEPL. While promotion was fully celebrated at the end of that season, it's fair to say that it also generated a fair bit of discussion over the winter.

Although the club welcomed the challenge posed by promotion to the NEPL, there were some misgivings from players faced with different playing conditions, different start times, travel challenges, and of course the higher standard of cricket offered within the NEPL. As it turned out the first season in the NEPL exceeded expectations. It was a challenge, both on and off the field, at times, but overall, the year couldn't have been better for the club, and fair better than we could have hoped for over the winter of 2022/23.

In NEPL Division 1, the 1st XI enjoyed a good degree of consistency with availability and strong performances throughout the season. Three batters in the league top 20 averages was a promising return for a first season in in the NEPL. 500+ run seasons for long-standing club members James Rainford, Tom Cant and Euan Stephenson, supported by Saturday skipper Dan Parker and new-signing Ben Mussett provided solidity in the batting line up whilst the bowling unit, led by u18 Archie Fletcher with 38 wickets and Aaron Rourke (signed from Stocksfield) with 31, but supported by Luke Mussett with 28 wickets proved a strong attack.

The result in 2023; promotion to the Premier Division at the first time of asking, finishing runners up and securing back-to-back promotions. For 2024, the club's aim of being a focal point for cricket in the west of Northumberland continues as we welcome back a number of former players. Whilst the Mussett's have moved on, former club juniors Matty Scott and Ed Foreman return, bringing Premier Division experience with them, whilst Joe Barber, another former club junior also returns for a full season from stints at a number of clubs. Tom Cant will continue to juggle Northern Diamonds commitments with Saturday cricket to provide experience with bat and ball, whilst a number of juniors (and recent juniors) look to establish themselves in the first team.

The likes of Will Marrow, Seth Robbie, Ted Fletcher, Josh Wallace and Dan Nevin will all look to build on their first NEPL season performances, push towards the 1st XI and support other juniors into Saturday senior cricket."

Here's a more detailed look at the Tynedale squad for 2024.

James Rainford is a right-handed batsman. He first came to attention playing for Northumberland Under 15's on 27th May 2005 at Preston Avenue against Cumbria Under 15's. Ben Stokes made 41 for Cumbria that day and Mark Wood had 41 for Northumberland. Rainford had scored 14 opening the batting, future fellow Tynedale player Tom Cant was also in the Northumberland side that day, taking 4 for 55 and scoring 17 not out. He played 4 times for Northumberland Under 15's.

Although I'm sure it wouldn't have been his first or indeed only appearance at this time for Tynedale First XI, he did play a game at home to Benwell Hill on 28th May 2009.

On 2nd June 2011 Rainford was selected for a Northumberland Development XI against the British Fire Service.

On 15th April 2012 Rainford was selected to play for an International Students XI at Perth against The Scottish Students, he made 43, top scoring the innings. He would go onto play for the Scottish Students on 3 different occasions.

During the 2023 season Rainford played 17 matches in NEPL Division 1 for Tynedale, batting 17 times with 3 not outs, he scored 516 runs at an average of 36.85. He scored 3 half centuries with a highest score of 77, made on 17th June 2023 at home to Willington. He didn't bowl in NEPL Division 1 in 2023 but did take 10 catches.

Tom Cant is a right-handed batsman and right arm off spin bowler. He is a product of the Northumberland youth set up, starting as an Under 15 and progressing through Under 16, and Under 17 sides, making his debut for the full Northumberland side in a Minor Counties Championship match at Hertfordshire which started on 23rd July 2006.

His last game for Northumberland was on 15th August 2021 at Jesmond against Bedfordshire, he scored 53 and 4 and took 0 for 19. He has played 70 matches for Northumberland, batting 82 times with 16 not outs, he has scored 1749 runs at an average of 26.50. He scored 10 half centuries with a highest score of 90, made in a 3-day match which started on 7th July 2013. He also bowled 3963 balls for Northumberland with 68 maidens, conceding 2855 runs and taking 77 wickets at an average of 37.07. His best bowling figures were 5 for 40, taken on 22nd July 2018 at Bedfordshire. He took 29 catches for the county.

He can also be found on 24th August 2006 playing in a JustSport Trophy match for Tynedale at Benwell Hill.

Cant made his NEPL debut for Benwell Hill on 28th April 2007 at Sunderland and he took his first NEPL wicket the following week, 5th May 2007 at Denton Bank against Durham Academy when he had Richard Coughtrie leg before wicket for 31. He played his last NEPL game for Benwell Hill on 28th August 2010 at home to Blaydon.

To the end of the 2023 season, Cant had played 76 NEPL matches, batting 45 times, with 19 not outs, he has scored 302 runs at an average of 11.61. His highest score is 45, made on 25th April 2009 at home to Newcastle. He has bowled 3809 balls in the NEPL, with 92 maidens, conceding 2345 runs and taking 75 wickets at an average of 31.26. His best bowling figures are 7 for 57, taken at home to Blaydon on 25th August 2008. He has taken 18 catches in the NEPL.

On 22nd July 2012 Cant played for The Northumberland and Tyneside Senior League side in the quarter final of The Presidents Trophy.

During the 2023 season, Cant played 13 matches in NEPL Division 1, batting 13 times with 1 not out, he scored 512 runs at an average of 42.66. He scored 3 half centuries and 1 century, 131, scored on 2nd September 2023 at Willington, it came from 125 balls and contained 9 fours and 5 sixes.

He also bowled 437 balls in NEPL Division 1, with 4 maidens, conceding 284 runs and taking 11 wickets at ana average of 25.81. His best bowling figures were 3 for 20, taken on 12th August 2023 at home to Crook. He took 9 catches in NEPL Division 1 in 2023.

Euan Stephenson is a left-handed batsman, he came through the junior ranks at Northumberland, he started playing Under 15 level for them, making his debut on 10th July 2014 at Gosforth against Durham. He went on to make his debut at Under 17 level for Northumberland on 5th July 2016 at Hipsburn against Scotland Under 17's.

Stephenson played 17 matches for Tynedale in NEPL Division 1 during the 2023 season, batting 17 times with 3 not outs, he scored 506 runs at an average of 36.14. He scored 4 half centuries with a highest score of 74 not out, scored on 19th August 2023 at Shotley Bridge.

He has also bowled 2 balls in NEPL Division 1, taking 1 wicket for 0 runs and he took 9 NEPL Division 1 catches in 2023.

Dan Parker is a left-handed batsman, the first trace I can find of Parker was playing for Tynedale in July 2011 in The Northumberland Cup Final at Benwell Hill. He next appeared on my radar on 31st July 2016 playing for the West Tyne Cricket League Under 21's in a game against the NEPL Under 21's at Stocksfield.

During the 2023 season Parker played 18 matches in NEPL Division 1 for Tynedale, batting 17 times with 1 not outs, he scored 310 runs at an average of 19.37. He scored 3 half centuries with a highest score of 72, made on 2nd September 2023 at Willington. He also took 9 catches in the League in 2023.

Aaron Rourke is a right-handed batsman and right arm off spin bowler, he first came to my attention playing in the village cup in 2017 for Stocksfield. It appears that he was still at Stocksfield as late as 5th June 2022 when he appeared in The Group 2 Final of The Village Cup for Stocksfield against Wolviston.

He played 17 matches in NEPL Division 1 for Tynedale, batting 14 times with 5 not outs, he scored 184 runs at an average of 20.44. His highest score was 32 not out.

He bowled 892 balls in NEPL Division 1 in 2023, with 22 maidens, conceding 527 runs and taking 31 wickets at an average of 17.00. His best bowling figures were 4 for 21, taken on 13th May 2023 at home to Lanchester. He took 8 catches at this level in 2023.

Tim Raglan is a right-handed batsman, he came through the County Youth setup after first appearing for Durham Under 12's 11th June 2006 in Edinburgh against Scotland Under 12's. Approximately a month later, on 12th July 2006 he appeared again at Edinburgh, this time for Northumberland Under 12's against Scotland Under 12's.

He progressed through the Northumberland Junior setup, playing for the Under 13's in 2007, the Under 14's in 2008 and the Under 15's in 2009 and then made his debut for Durham Under 17's on 18th July 2010 at Derbyshire.

On 2nd June 2011 Raglan was selected to play for Durham Second XI at Brandon against a Unicorns A side. He was in good company in the Durham side, Keaton Jennings, Kyle Coetzer and Mark Stoneman also in the team. He would also play a couple of games for Durham Academy in 2011.

Raglan made his NEPL debut for Gateshead Fell on 21st April 2012 at South North, rain ruined the game after just 26 overs. He played twice more for Fell that season, the last on 11th August, he did take two wickets, his first NEPL wicket was taken on 4th August 2012 at home to Blaydon, Geoff Stewart was leg before wicket for a duck.

On 3rd April 2013 Raglan played the first of 5 matches for Cambridge Marylebone Cricket Club University, Essex Second XI were the opposition for the debut.

On 7th December 2013 Raglan was to be found playing in a 2-day match for Waikato Valley against Poverty Bay in New Zealand.

On 31st July 2016 Raglan was selected by the West Tyne Cricket League Under 21's in a match against the North East Premier League Under 21's at Stocksfield, he took 1 for 52 and scored 47.

In the period between 2013 and his return to Tynedale in 2022 Raglan played for Allendale in The West Tyne League and the Northumberland and Tyneside Senior League.

In 2018 he scored 1592 runs at an average of over 100, with 10 centuries, his highest score was 162 not out and in 2019 he scored 1499 runs, again at an average of over 100, and with 6 centuries, his highest score was 266 not out.

During the 2023 season Raglan played 5 matches in NEPL Division 1, batting 5 times with 0 not outs, he scored 122 runs at an average of 24.40. His highest score was 46, made on 6th May 2023 at Philadelphia. He also took 2 wickets for 21 runs and took 1 catch.

James Crichton is a right-handed batsman and wicket keeper, the first record I found for him was making his Minor Counties debut for Northumberland in a match starting on 29th June 2003 at Jesmond against Buckinghamshire. He played 5 matches in total for Northumberland that season, and also made his debut for the county at Under 17 level that season.

He next appeared in the records playing for Tynedale in 2006 and I can find nothing in between to suggest that he has ever played anywhere else.

He played 17 matches in NEPL Division 1 in 2023, with a highest score of 37 not out, made on 28th August 2023 at home to Seaham Park. He took 11 catches and had 1 stumping in the league in 2023.

Matty Scott is a right-handed batsman and fast bowler, he came through the Northumberland Youth setup, playing for the Under 15's first of all on 5th June 2018 at Durham Under 15's, he took 1 for 40 and scored 39.

He went on to represent Northumberland at Under 17 and Under 18 level, making his debut for the full Northumberland side on 23rd June 2019 at home to Bedfordshire. He last played for Northumberland on 21st August 2022, to that date he has played 16 matches for Northumberland, with a highest score of 41 not out, he has also bowled 1038 balls, with 22 maidens, conceding 791 runs and taking 26 wickets at an average of 30.42. His best bowling figures are 6 for 54, taken on 22nd August 2021 at Buckinghamshire. He has taken 2 catches for Northumberland.

Scott made his NEPL debut for Burnopfield on 21st May 2022 at home to Chester le Street, he took his first NEPL wicket in the game, and it was a good one, Quentin Hughes bowled for 4. He played his last NEPL match for Burnopfield on 9th September 2023 at Whitburn.

To that date he has played 31 matches in the NEPL, batting 17 times with 7 not outs, he has scored 125 runs at an average of 12.50. His highest score is 16 not out.

He has bowled 1205 balls in the NEPL, with 12 maidens, conceding 945 runs and taking 33 wickets at an average of 28.63. His best bowling figures are 5 for 35, taken on 28th May 2022 at home to Eppleton. He has taken 5 catches in the NEPL.

Scott played 1 match for Nottinghamshire Second XI starting on 20th June 2022 against Lancashire Second XI, he took 1 for 16 from 9.1 overs in the second innings.

Ed Foreman is a right-handed batsman and right arm off spinner, who first came to my attention on 5th June 2018 when he played for Northumberland Under 15's at Durham Under 15's. He took 1 for 31 and scored 13. On 8th July 2019 he made 75 for Northumberland Under 15's against Scotland Under 15's in Alloway and on 1st August 2019 he made his debut for Northumberland Under 17's against Cumbria Under 17's.

He played for Sacriston during the covid 2020 season and made his NEPL debut on 22nd May 2021 for Sacriston at South North. On 23rd June 2021 he was selected for a Northumberland Development XI against Scotland Under 19's at Hipsburn. He played his last NEPL match for Sacriston on 28th August 2021 at home to Tynemouth.

On 29th April 2023 Foreman made his NEPL debut for Tynemouth at home to Felling, he played his last NEPL match for Tynemouth on 9th September 2023 at home to Burnmoor. To the end of the 2023 season Foreman has a highest score of 33 in the NEPL and has taken 1 wicket for 28 runs. He has taken 4 NEPL catches.

Archie Fletcher is a right-handed batsman and right arm fast medium bowler. Fletcher made his debut for Northumberland Under 15's during the covid season of 2020, on 20th Augusts he played at Sunderland against Durham Under 15's, he took 2 for 18 and scored 9. He made his debut for Northumberland Under 16's on 27th July 2022 at Yorkshire, when Northumberland batted, he top scored the innings with 26.

He played 18 matches in NEPL Division 1 for Tynedale in 2023 and while he didn't make his mark with the bat he did bowl 1036 balls, with 38 maidens, conceding 616 runs and taking 40 wickets at an average of 15.40. His best bowling figures were 4 for 14, taken on 8th July 2023 at home to Washington. He took 1 catch at this level in 2023.

Nathan Byerley is a right-handed batsman and right arm fast medium bowler, he is clearly just starting out on his cricket career, so there is very little record of him. He did play 13 matches in NEPL Division 1 for Tynedale in 2023, with a highest score of 35 and he bowled 436 balls, with 4 maidens, conceding 374 runs and taking 18 wickets at an average of 20.77. His best bowling figures were 6 for 48, taken on 19th August 2023 at Shotley Bridge. He has taken 2 catches at this level.

Oliver Fletcher is a right-handed batsman and a product of the Northumberland Youth setup, playing for the county under 15's first of all on 24th May 2017 at Lincolnshire. He was selected for a Durham Under 16's Emerging Players XI which played Lancashire Under 16's on 16th August 2018. He then progressed to Northumberland Under 17's, playing his first game for them starting on 9th July 2019 against Leicestershire and Rutland Under 17's, he made 26, opening the batting.

On 1st September 2020 he continued his progress with Northumberland, debuting for the Under 18's at Gosforth against Cumbria Under 18's, he made 55, again, opening the batting.

He played 7 matches in NEPL Division 1 in 2023, with a highest score of 35 and he took 6 catches.

Sam Peter is a right-handed batsman and right arm fast bowler, he made his debut for Northumberland Under 15's on 24th May 2017 at Lincolnshire Under 15's, taking 2 for 27 when he bowled. On 17th July 2018 he made his debut for Northumberland Under 17's in a 2-day match at Gosforth against Cumbria Under 17's. Just five days later on 22nd July 2018 he started in a 3-day match for Northumberland Senior side at Bedfordshire.

On 14th April 2019 Peter made his debut for Durham Academy in a 50 over match against Chester le Street. During the covid season of 2020, Peter made his debut for Northumberland Under 18's on 1st September at Gosforth against Cumbria Under 18's. On 19th July 2021 he was selected for a Northumberland Development XI to play against their Cumbria counterparts at Cockermouth.

He played 16 matches for Tynedale in NEPL Division 1 in the 2023 season, batting 12 times with 4 not outs, he scored 158 runs at an average of 19.75. His highest score was 47, made on 10th June 2023 at home to Sacriston. He also bowled 612 balls in NEPL Division 1 in 2023, with 5 maidens, conceding 531 runs and taking 14 wickets at an average of 37.92. His best bowling figures were 3 for 21, taken on 13th May 2023 at home to Lanchester. He took 5 catches at this level in 2023.

Joe Barber is a right-handed batsman and right arm medium pace bowler; he first came to my attention on 8th July 2002 when he was selected for Northumberland Under 13's against Scotland Under 13's. The following season, on 1st June 2003 he was selected for Northumberland Under 15s at Lincolnshire.

By 2004 he had progressed to Northumberland Under 17's, making his debut on 10th August 2004 at Herefordshire. On 3rd May 2006 Barber played for Durham Second XI in Edinburgh against Scotland A side, he also played 2 games for Durham Academy in 2006, although he wasn't given much opportunity.

On 24th August 2006 he appeared for Tynedale in a JustSport match at Benwell Hill and in July 2008 he was selected for a Northumberland Development XI at Cheshire A.

Tynedale CC 27/4/24.

Left to Right- Back Row-Seth Robbie, Ed Foreman, Joe Barber, Dan Parker, Tim Raglan, Euan Stephenson.

Front Row-Aaron Rourke, Jamie Crichton, Matty Scott, Nathan Byerley, Archie Fletcher.

Tynemouth Chairman Graeme Hallam shares his thoughts on the upcoming season.

"Tynemouth CC enter the 2024 season as one of only four Clubs to have played in all 25 years of the North East Premier League. Our long-term plans of building sides largely around the development of our own young players and then adding a touch of stardust to make us truly competitive works for us and will be at the heart of plans again this year.

The last two years we have only just avoided relegation so this year we want to look to move back to the middle of the table, maybe win a trophy and see further improvements from our young players across all teams.

The core of the team will remain the same as last year with one Club players like Ben Debnam, Matty Brown and Andrew Smith looking to add to their reputation. The experienced Martin Pollard will captain the side that otherwise should have a youthful look.

New players brought in include Josh Moors, a spin bowling all-rounder from the famous St George CC in Sydney, leg spinner Fred Harrison from Durham University and fast bowler Stan McAlindon who will play when available from Durham CCC commitment. Look out too though for our young guns coming through where we hope to see the likes of Joe Snowdon, Dan Thorburn, Patrick Hallam, Joel Hull Denholm and Robbie Bowman making good contributions through the season."

Let's have a closer look at the player's Hallam has mentioned.

Ben Debnam goes into the 2024 season having made his debut for Tynemouth in The NEPL on 21st June 2003. He has now played 322 NEPL matches, batting 303 times with 14 not out's, he has scored 5692 runs at an average of 19.69. He has made 24 half centuries and 3 centuries, his highest score is 132 not out on 23rd June 2018 at home to Eppleton. He has taken 61 NEPL catches.

Matthew Brown is a right-handed batsman, right arm medium pace bowler and wicketkeeper, he first came to notice on 6th June 2004 when he played for Northumberland Under 13's at Cumbria, he made 54 not out. He progressed through to the Under 15's, making his debut at this level on 5th June 2006 at Durham and continued into the Northumberland Under 17's when he played in a 2-day match at Cambridgeshire, starting on 9th July 2007. He made his NEPL debut for Tynemouth on 31st May 2008.

On 5th May 2009 Brown was selected to play for a Northumberland Development XI against Durham Academy at Winlaton and on 29th July 2009 he played for Northumberland Second XI in a 2-day match against Huntingdonshire at Preston Avenue. He was also selected for a number of different university sides over the 2009 and 2010 seasons.

He made his debut for the Northumberland Senior side on 23rd April 2017 at Cambridgeshire. To date, his last appearance for Northumberland was on 31st July 2022 at Gosforth against Yorkshire in a Royal London Cup warm up match.

He has played 31 matches for Northumberland, batting 32 times with 7 not outs, he has scored 593 runs at an average of 23.72. He has scored 2 half centuries with a highest score of 77 not out, made on 6th May 2018 at Jesmond against Lincolnshire. He hasn't bowled at this level for Northumberland, but he has taken 24 catches and had 5 stumpings.

Up to the end of 2023, Matthew Brown has now played 245 NEPL matches, batting 223 times with 21 not outs, he has scored 5164 runs at an average of 25.56. He has made 29 half centuries and 2 centuries, his highest score is 123 made on 15th April 2017 at Benwell Hill.

Brown has also bowled 475 balls, with 6 maidens, conceding 304 runs and taking 16 wickets at an average of 19.00. His best bowling figures are 3 for 16 taken on 4th September 2021 at home to Eppleton. He has also taken 196 catches and has 33 stumpings to his name.

Andrew Smith is a right-handed batsman and right arm medium pace bowler, he is a product of the Northumberland Youth setup, coming first to my attention on 8th July 2002 in a match against Scotland Under 13's. The following season, on 1st June 2003 he was selected for Northumberland Under 15's at Lincolnshire Under 15's.

He made his NEPL debut for Tynemouth on 30th April 2005 at Sunderland.

He played in a 2-day match for Northumberland Under 17's at Derbyshire starting on 19th July 2005, he made 58 and 19 not out when he batted and took 1 for 19 in Derbyshire's only innings.

On 9th July 2008 he was part of a Northumberland Developmental Side which took on Huntingdonshire at Preston Avenue in a 2-day match. He made his debut for the Northumberland Senior side on 31st May 2009 at Suffolk, making 37 when he batted, and he last played for Northumberland in a 3-day match starting on 19th July 2015 at Jesmond.

He has played 8 matches for Northumberland, batting 12 times with 4 not outs, he has scored 128 runs at an average of 16.00. His highest score is 37. He has also taken 5 wickets for Northumberland at a cost of 272 runs and taken 3 catches.

Andrew Smith has now played 285 NEPL matches, batting 239 times with 44 not outs, he has scored 3263 runs at an average of 16.73. He has made 8 half centuries and 1 century, 101 not out, made on 28th June 2014 at Sunderland.

Smith has also bowled 11516 balls, with 273 maidens, conceding 7447 runs and taking 287 wickets at an average of 25.94. His best bowling figures are 6 for 37 taken on 26th August 2016 at home to Eppleton. He has also taken 50 NEPL catches.

Martin Pollard is vastly experienced in the NEPL, making his debut on 28th April 2001 for Benwell Hill. He won the NEPL title in 2002 with Benwell Hill, he has also played for Blaydon and Hetton Lyons before joining Tynemouth in 2016.

Up to the end of 2023 he has played 381 NEPL matches, batting 159 times with 87 not outs, he has scored 547 runs at an average of 7.59. His highest score is 39 not out, made for Hetton Lyons on 16th May 2015 at home to Chester Le Street.

Pollard has also bowled 21000 balls, with 737 maidens, conceding 10845 runs and taking 511 wickets at an average of 21.22. His best bowling figures are 7 for 27 taken on 4th August 2018 at home to Felling. He has also taken 110 NEPL catches.

Stan McAlindon is a right-handed batsman and right arm fast medium bowler, he first came to my attention on 4th June 2018 when he was selected for Cumbria Under 14's against Cheshire Under 14's at Carlisle, he took 4 for 50 when he bowled.

The following season he was selected by Durham Academy on 14th April 2019 in a match against Chester le Street and he was also selected a number of times in 2019 by Cumbria Under 15's, as well as playing for Carlisle.

On 4th August 2019 he was selected for the first of six appearances by an ECB North Under 15 side to play in the Bunbury Festival.

He made his NEPL debut for Sacriston on 17th April 2021 at home to Eppleton.

On 14th June 2021 McAlindon was selected to play for Durham Second XI at Ropery Lane against Lancashire Second XI and on 27th June 2021 he played for Durham Under 18's at Cheshire Under 18's.

He moved to Chester le Street in 2022, making his debut for them on 16th April at Newcastle and he played there until the end of the 2023 season.

He made his debut in First-Class matches for Durham on 11th July 2022 at The Riverside against Derbyshire in a Division 2 County Championship match. He took 2 for 63 and 0 for 50 and scored 26 not out and 18 not out when he batted.

Stan McAlindon has now played 29 NEPL matches, batting 24 times with 3 not outs, he has scored 227 runs at an average of 10.80. His highest score is 38 made in his last appearance for Chester Le Street on 9th September 2023 at home to Castle Eden.

McAlindon has also bowled 1298 balls, with 22 maidens, conceding 942 runs and taking 47 wickets at an average of 20.04. His best bowling figures are 5 for 21 taken for Chester le Street on 4th June 2021 at Burnmoor. He has also taken 9 NEPL catches.

As recently as 22nd February 2024 he played for Durham against Zimbabwe A in Harare, he took 3 for 34 when he bowled. Up to that date he has played 14 matches for Durham, batting 12 times with 5 not outs, he has scored 173 runs at an average of 24.71. He has scored 1 half century, exactly 50 on 23rd August 2023 at Leicestershire in the Royal London Cup.

He has bowled 751 balls for Durham, with 8 maidens, conceding 738 runs and taking 15 wickets, his best bowling figures are 4 for 29, taken in the same match he scored his 50. He has taken 2 catches so far for Durham.

Joe Snowdon made his NEPL debut on 7th September 2019 for Tynemouth at home to Chester Le Street. He originally came to my notice on 12th June 2018 when he played for Northumberland Under 15's at Lincolnshire. He played his last game at this level on 18th July 2019 at Hipsburn against Scotland Under 15's. He represented Northumberland eight times at this level and had a highest score of 69.

He made his debut for Northumberland Under 18's on 5th July 2021 at Keswick against Cumbria Under 18's, he made 56 opening the batting. He played his last game for Northumberland Under 18's on 11th August 2022 in a T20 match at Northwich against Cheshire, he represented Northumberland seven times at Under 18 level and had a highest score of 56.

On 2nd May 2023 Snowdon was part of a Northumberland Development XI which travelled to Kendal to take on a Cumbria Development XI.

Joe Snowdon, to the end of 2023 has now played 44 NEPL matches, batting 38 times, with 2 not out's, he has scored 589 runs at an average of 16.36. He scored 2 half centuries; his highest score is 59 not out which came on 14th May 2022 at South North. He has never bowled in the NEPL, although he has taken 18 NEPL catches.

Dan Thorburn made his NEPL debut on 10th July 2021 for Tynemouth at Eppleton, he first came to my attention on 19th June 2019 for Northumberland Under 15's at Keswick against Cumbria Under 15's.

He played six times at Under 15 level for Northumberland before moving on to the Under 18 age group on 5th July 2021 and Under 16 level on 21st July 2022.

His highest score is 71, made for the Under 18's at Longhirst against Cumbria Under 18's on 31st May 2023, his innings came from 57 balls and contained 7 fours.

He has played 15 NEPL matches, batting 14 times, with 1 not out, he has scored 144 runs at an average of 11.07. He scored 1 half century, 53, made on 9th July 2022 at Benwell Hill. He bowled 6 balls and taken 0 for 7 and has taken 1 NEPL catch.

Patrick Hallam has played just 1 NEPL match so far, on 7th August 2021 at home to Chester Le Street, he scored 1 when he batted.

Joel Hull Denholm has also played just 1 NEPL match so far, on 27th August 2022 at home to Chester Le Street, he scored 10 and took 2 catches. Denholm is clearly still in the very early stages of his cricket career; he was selected to play for Northumberland Under 15's on 18th May 2021 at Cumbria Under 18's and he has represented Northumberland six times at Under 15 level.

On 7th July 2022 he was selected for Northumberland Under 16's at Hexham against Cumbria Under 16's. He opened the batting and made 75, the innings came from 63 balls and contained 8 fours and 3 sixes.

Up to the end of 2023 he has played ten matches at Under 16 level for Northumberland, on his last appearance, on 16th August 2023 he scored 70 at Derbyshire Under 16's.

Robbie Bowman made his NEPL debut on 3rd June 2023 for Tynemouth at Ashington, his junior career to this point has been a yoyo of representative age groups, culminating with him joining Durham CCC as an Academy player.

He first came to my attention on 7th July 2022 when he made his debut for Northumberland Under 18's at Alnmouth against Scotland Under 18's, he scored 51 from 53 balls with 7 fours and 1 six. Just one week later he was playing for Northumberland Under 16's at Alnwick against Scotland Under 16s, he scored 24 opening the batting.

He played three more matches at Under 16 for Northumberland before, on 11th August 2022 he was selected to play for Durham Under 16's at Derbyshire. When he batted, he was run out for 49.

He next appeared on my radar on 21st May 2023 for Durham Under 18's at Yorkshire Under 18's. He played four more matches early in the 2023 season at this age group for Durham before then next appearing on 3rd July 2023 for Northumberland Under 16's at Lancashire Under 16's. He opened the batting and scored 73 from 50 balls with 4 fours and 6 sixes. He played one more match at this level and then four matches for four different teams, Durham Under 18's, Durham Under 16's, Tynemouth and an ECB North Elite Under 15 side.

He saw out the 2023 season at youth level playing for Durham at both Under 16 and Under 18 level as well as Tynemouth in the NEPL.

Robbie Bowman played 10 NEPL matches in the 2023 season, batting 9 times, with 1 not out, he scored 211 runs at an average of 26.37. He scored 1 half century, 54 not out which came on 19th August 2023 at home to Ashington. He has never bowled in the NEPL but has taken 2 catches.

Tynemouth CC 29/6/24.

Left to Right- Back Row- Josh Koen, Matthew Brown, Martin Pollard, Matthew Kimmitt, Ben Debnam, Joel Hull- Denholm.

Front Row-Robbie Bowman, Josh Moors, Fred Harrison, Barry Stewart, Stanley McAlindon.

CHAPTER FIFTEEN

The Opening Session 2024

After the 2019 season the NEPL planned to change the format and split the season, because of the covid pandemic and in effect no traditional NEPL cricket in 2020, it was put back to the start of the 2021 season. The first five matches and last six would be 11.30am starts, 50 overs a side win or lose, no draws, coloured clothing using an orange ball. This was changed again going into the 2024 season, the first six matches would now be 45 overs a side and start at noon. The middle eleven matches of the season would be traditional NEPL cricket, starting at 11.30am, with white clothing and a red ball, the first innings can be up to 65 overs, total overs in the match is no more than 110.

It therefore makes sense to me to break the 2024 season into three chapters and look at each segment in that way.

There were a couple of more format changes prior to the 2024 season, the Saturday win/lose matches reduced to 90 Overs from 100 overs and both The Banks Bowl and Banks Bowl Salver will be played as a Hundred Competition. Following a wet winter and probably even wetter spring, the NEPL match-play committee unanimously decided to postpone game week one of the 2024 season and reschedule the games for Sunday 1st September. Therefore, the season got underway a week later than planned on 27th April, unless of course you were Ashington or Tynemouth whose fixture at Langwell Crescent was still cancelled! Unfortunately, that still wasn't the end of the British weather as the following week's program was once again completely washed out.

Saturday 27th April 2024

Ashington v Tynemouth still fell victim to the weather, 5 points each side.

Benwell Hill won the toss and elected to field at home to Castle Eden. Daniel Gardner with 2 wickets and Callum Harding with 1 had Castle in a bit of trouble at 27 for 3, J P Meade,18, and Keith Bailey, 26, steadied things with a partnership of 40 but another flurry of three quick wickets saw them fall to 88 for 6. Bilawal Iqbal, 21, and Philip Wimpenny,26, then added 57 for the seventh wicket to take them to 145 for 7 but they were dismissed for 159 from 41.3 overs. Callum Harding had 2 for 32, Daniel Gardner 2 for 39, Max Williamson 2 for 30, Rory Hanley 2 for 15 and William Archbold 1 for 26.

Benwell Hill started disastrously when opener Adam Heather was run out without facing a ball and quickly fell to 9 for 2 when Arun Phogat was leg before to Bilawal Iqbal for 3. This was Iqbal's 50th wicket in the NEPL. Only three Benwell batsmen made double figures, Haydon Mustard 18, Peter Halliday 11, and Phil Bell, 13, as they were bowled out for 88 in 34.2 overs. Iqbal had 1 for 18, Alan Unsworth 3 for 14, Jonathan Malkin 1 for 9, Ash Grant 1 for 20 and Connor Crute 3 for 4. Castle Eden won by 71 runs and picked up 24 points, Benwell got 4 points.

Burnopfield were at home to South North, this game marked the 400th NEPL appearance of Simon Birtwisle, only teammate Lee Crozier has more! For Burnopfield Matthew Oswell made his 100th NEPL appearance. The visitors won the toss and elected to field. Openers Ben McKinney, 34, and John Oswell, 40, had added 55 for the first wicket when Sean Tindale had Oswell leg before wicket with the fourth ball of the eleventh over. Next ball he caught and bowled Ross Whitfield Jnr, 55 for 2, which quickly became 55 for 3 when he completed his hat trick with the last ball of the over by bowling Sam Dinning first ball. Burnopfield 55 for 3. Oli McGee then nipped in to take 2 wickets and Lee Crozier 3 more, when Tindale caught Finlay McGurk off the bowling of Lee Crozier that was his 50th NEPL catch. Matthew Oswell 24 not out and 20 from Harry Lumsden down the order got Burnopfield to a score of 128 for 9 from their 45 overs. New coach Tom Rogers had taken his first NEPL wicket when he removed Ben McKinney leg before for 34 and finished with 1 for 22, Tindale had 3 for 27, McGee 2 for 8 and Crozier 3 for 13.

When South North batted Matthew Oswell quickly picked up Sol Bell and Chris Hewison and South North were 21 for 2. Opener Simon Birtwisle, 29, and Sean Tindale, 18, took the score to 60 before Finlay McGurk had Tindale leg before. When Birtwisle and then Adam Cragg fell within seven runs of each other South North were 82 for 5 and still required 47 to win. Rob Peyton and Tom Rogers got South North closer, when the score was 106 Peyton was caught by Sam Dinning off the bowling of Amaan Ulhaq for 12. Rogers finished 22 not out and Will Alexander 6 not out as South North won by 4 wickets. McGurk had 2 for 28, Matthew Oswell 2 for 33, and Ulhaq 2 for 41. South North collected 24 points, Burnopfield 3 points.

Felling hosted Chester le Street at High Heworth Lane and were asked to bat when Chester won the toss. Opener Travis Norris carried his bat as he made 127 not out from 135 balls, the innings contained 11 fours and 4 sixes, this was his fifth NEPL century. He was well supported by veteran Alan Mustard, 23, Alasdair Appleby 22, and Seb Allison 23. For Chester Quentin Hughes took 2 for 17, John Harrison 2 for 49 and Josh Wilson 2 for 41 as Felling made 229 for 6 wickets from their 45 overs.

Felling opening bowlers Seb Allison and Ishaq Khan made good use of the new ball, Allison taking 3 wickets and Khan 1 as they reduced Chester to 9 for 4. Opener Jacob McCann, 18, helped the evergreen Quentin Hughes to restore respectability to Chester, adding 29 before McCann was bowled by Travis Norris. Hughes, for the 83rd time in his NEPL career, was not out, making a solid 40 from just 53 balls but the Chester tail failed to wag, and they were bowled out for 103 from 28.5 overs. Seb Allison took 3 for 6, Ishaq Khan 1 for 20, Paul Leonard 1 for 17, Norris had 1 for 18, Alasdair Appleby 1 for 17 and Jamie Cairns, who had taken the last three wickets, had 3 for 6. Felling had won by 126 runs and pick up 24 points for their troubles, Chester a consolation 2 points.

Last season's NEPL Division 1 champions, Sunderland, were the hosts for Newcastle in cricket's Wear Tyne derby. Sunderland won the toss and elected to field. Despite losing Ben Robinson, caught by Chris Youldon off the bowling of Jack Brassell for 10, Bobby Green and Mohsin Mukhtar made good progress and had taken the score to 66 when Mukhtar was leg before to Micky Allan for 18. The score was unchanged at 66 when Green was leg before to George Drissell for 22. This became 68 for 4 when Allan picked up another leg before and then two more quick wickets, Newcastle fell to 73 for 6, and despite 33 from Jaques du Toit at almost a run a ball, Newcastle were bowled out for 134 in 43.3 overs. Brassell had 1 for 21, Brett Hutchinson 2 for 16, George Drissell 1 for 28, Allan finished with 4 for 28, and Joseph Stuart, 1 for 28.

When Sunderland batted openers George Drissell and Dan Shurben put on 48 for the first wicket before Bobby Green caught Drissell off the bowling of Asher Hart for 28. Charlie Coulthard, batting at three, and Shurben had taken the score to 123 when Shurben was caught by du Toit off Matthew Stewart for 47. Coulthard finished unbeaten on 48 and Micky Allan 0 not out when Sunderland hit the winning runs, 136 for 2, to get home by 8 wickets. Hart took 1 for 19 and Matthew Stewart 1 for 18 for Newcastle. Sunderland get 24 points for the win; Newcastle cap a disappointing day with 0 points.

I went with the camera to photograph newly promoted Tynedale host the strongly fancied Burnmoor. Tynedale won the toss and elected to bowl and on a slow wicket had Burnmoor in a little trouble at 34 for 3, Matthew Scott had taken all 3 wickets, assisted in the dismissal of Ryan Pringle by a brilliant diving catch in the outfield by Ed Foreman. This brought Stuart Poynter to the crease to join opener Marcus Brown. This was Poynter's NEPL debut for Burnmoor after he joined them from Tynemouth in the close season. He and Brown added a new NEPL highest partnership score of 369 before Poynter was dismissed for 247! This is only the third double century in NEPL history and the highest score by any individual, his 100 came from 74 balls and contained 15 fours and 2 sixes. Poynter's double hundred came from 107 balls, with 23 fours and 10 sixes. When he was dismissed, he had scored 247 runs from 124 balls, he had struck 29 fours and 13 sixes. For the record he was caught by Aaron Rourke off the bowling of Nathan Byerley. Watching the innings Poynter was absolutely clinical in dealing with length, he was all over the short ball, on both sides of the wicket, and he punished everything over pitched, it's probably an overused phrase to say you couldn't bowl to someone but on this occasion it was true. He has previously scored 3 NEPL centuries, all for Tynemouth, with the highest score of 149.

Marcus Brown's century will no doubt be overshadowed by the quality and magnitude of Poynter's effort but his hundred was absolute quality as well, he looked comfortable throughout, including the early difficult spell with the new ball and he paced his innings very well, rotating the strike and putting the bad ball away. When he was caught by Seth Robbie off the bowling of Archie Fletcher, he had scored 101 from 110 balls, scoring 12 fours. This was his second NEPL century, his other, 103 not out, was scored for Burnmoor at Felling on 14th August 2021. When the Burnmoor innings was closed they had 435 for 5 from their 45 overs. This is the highest innings NEPL score in the history of the league. Josh Coughlin was 21 not out and Allan Worthy 4 not out. Matthew Scott finished with 3 for 46, Archie Fletcher 1 for 53 and Nathan Byerley 1 for 52.

When Tynedale batted, they, unsurprisingly never threatened the massive Burnmoor score, Tim Raglan, 33, and skipper Daniel Parker, 27, both showed enough quality to suggest that they belong at this level, and tailender's Aaron Rourke with 26 and Seth Robbie, 15 not out, showed enough fight to get Tynedale to 144 all out from 36 overs. All six of the Burnmoor bowlers used picked up at least one wicket and got a run out, Josh Coughlin 1 for 17, Daniel Reed 1 for 29, Graeme Bridge 1 for 11, Craig Stephenson 4 for 25, Ryan Pringle 2 for 29 and Ross Greenwell 1 for 27. A strong batting line-up and an excellent spin bowling attack, with their overseas pro still to join them, Burnmoor showed why they are strongly fancied for the title. Burnmoor collect 24 points and Tynedale 3 points.

Congratulations to Marcus Brown and Stuart Poynter on their performances, a day to say, "I was there!"

There were 3 centuries on the opening day of the season and no bowler took 5 wickets, although there was a hat trick!

Saturday 4th May 2024

Heavy overnight rain washed out the entire program this weekend without a ball being bowled, each team picking up 5 points. The game at Chester le Street did tease those of us in attendance by waiting until a pitch inspection at twelve o'clock before being called off but called off it certainly was!

Burnmoor v Sunderland
Castle Eden v Burnopfield
Chester le Street v Benwell Hill
Newcastle v Felling
South North v Ashington.
Tynemouth v Tynedale

11th May 2024

Ashington looked to get their 2024 campaign underway hosting newly promoted Tynedale after two wash outs. Tynedale were looking to recover from their mauling at the hands of Burnmoor when they had debuted in the NEPL two weeks ago. The visitors won the toss and elected to bat. Of their first eight batsman only one, Ed Foreman, with 26, made double figures as they slumped to 80 for 9 as Ashington's bowlers all weighed in with wickets. It took a tenth wicket stand of 68 between number 10, Aaron Rourke, who made 61 from 57 balls, with 3 fours and 3 sixes, and Archie Fletcher, 10 not out to get Tynedale a target to defend. They got to 148 all out from 40.4 overs. Jeremiah Louis took 2 for 27, Matthew Collins 3 for 26, Ian Sharkey 2 for 23, Cam Nicholls 1 for 39 and James Harmison, 1 for 8.

When Ashington batted they lost opener Adam Nichol for 6, bowled by Archie Fletcher with the score on 8. Northumberland opener Jack Jessop then took command of the innings, going on to make 71 not out, with wicketkeeper Jack McCarthy batting three and scoring 44 before Ted Fletcher caught and bowled him, these two had taken the score to 94. This was Jessop's second half century in the NEPL, his innings came from 95 balls and contained 6 fours and a six. Sean McCafferty came in at number 4 and in true captain's style made 15 not out to see his side home by eight wickets with almost 13 overs to spare. Ashington collected 24 points for the win, Tynedale a single point.

Benwell Hill were home to visitors Newcastle with both teams looking to put disappointing starts behind them and get that first win. Phil Bell had been named in the Benwell Hill lineup and this was his 150th NEPL appearance as Hill won the toss and elected to field. Newcastle were quickly in trouble at 13 for 2 as Callum Harding picked up Ben

Robinson and Mohsin Mukhtar for 2 each. Opener and captain Bobby Green had made 46 and the score was 72 when he was caught by Haydon Mustard to give Yash Kothari his first NEPL wicket. When Green scored his 28th run that was his 1000 run in the NEPL.

His dismissal brought Jaques du Toit to the crease, less than 24 hours earlier, on the Friday night, du Toit had scored 142 not out from 38 balls in a T20 game at Tynedale. His innings had contained 9 fours and 13 sixes! When Matthew Stewart was caught by Dan Gardiner off Max Williamson for 20, Newcastle were 97 for 4. Williamson also dismissed du Toit, leg before for 27, a quickfire 55 from Asher Hart, his 5th NEPL half century, from just 34 balls with 3 fours and 5 sixes and 24 from Rowan Shelton, got Newcastle to a decent score of 210 all out form their 45 overs, Callum Harding picking up his sixth wicket when he bowled last man Charlie Darwood with the last ball of the innings to finish with 6 for 48. Kothari had 2 for 26 and Williamson 2 for 31 the other Hill wicket takers.

When Benwell Hill batted they lost early wickets regularly, 27 for 1, 34 for 2, 49 for 3 and 63 for 4 when Bell was leg before to Mukhtar for 5. They did however have new professional Yash Kothari at the crease, he had come in at number three. He was the difference maker, scoring 50 from 63 balls with 4 fours and 100 from 100 balls with 10 fours. He was eventually caught by Bobby Green off the last ball of the 44th over of the innings, bowled by George Darwood for 110 with the score on 205 for 8. His innings had come from 119 balls and contained 10 fours. Benwell Hill veteran, and now league statistician David McKay, remarked that the style and concentration of Kothari's batting reminded him of former Ryton pro Surendra Bhave, and he has previously described him as the best batsman he has seen!

Benwell Hill now required two runs to win from six balls with two wickets left. Rowan Shelton bowled a dot ball with the first ball of the last over to Dan Gardiner, Gardiner took a single off the second ball, scores tied, 4 balls left, Luke Mussett then hit a boundary from the third ball and Hill had won by 2 wickets. Shelton finished with 3 for 28, George Darwood 3 for 45, Mukhtar 1 for 32 and du Toit 1 for 51. Benwell Hill got 24 points, Newcastle 7 points.

Burnopfield at home to Chester le Street was another fixture between two clubs looking to kick start their season after disappointing losses in their first games. Burnopfield won the toss and elected to field and both sides made steady starts to the game, Chester reaching 86 for 3 when John Coxon was caught by Callum Brown off Finlay McGurk for 28. Kyle Coetzer had come in at four and he dominated the Chester innings from this point, he reached his 50 from 45 balls with 8 fours, and he went on to reach his 100 from 104 balls with 13 fours and 2 sixes. He reached his hundred with a boundary off the eighth ball of the last over after a wide and a no-ball extended the over. This was his 17th NEPL hundred. Quentin Hughes had chipped in with 13, Liam Simpson 21 and Ash Thorpe 11 not out as the Chester batsman had both pursued quick runs and supported Coetzer as Chester made 246 for 8 from their 45 overs. Matthew Oswell took 2 for 50, Harry Lumsden 2 for 71, Finlay McGurk 1 for 38and Amaan Ulhaq 3 for 46 for Burnopfield.

I'm not sure where to start with the Burnopfield reply, the first pair had added 245 for the first wicket when John Oswell was run out for 171! He had reached 50 from 53 balls with 6 fours and 3 sixes, his 100 had come from 83 balls with 8 fours and 7 sixes, the 150, from 105 balls with 12 fours and 12 sixes! When he was dismissed, Oswell had faced 115 balls, he had struck 12 fours and 14 sixes. This was his 7th NEPL century, but not his highest NEPL score, this remained the 194 he scored on 7th May 2022 against Newcastle. Ben McKinney was 67 not out, his 50 had come from 84 balls with 4 fours and 2 sixes. This was his 12th NEPL half century. When McKinney reached 26 that was his 1500 runs in the NEPL. On a day when there was almost 500 runs scored and two centuries, Burnopfield got 24 points and Chester le Street 4 points.

Felling at home to Burnmoor was likely to be a tightly contested affair, both sides with strong wins to start the season and undoubtedly high hopes at the top end of the league table. Burnmoor won the toss and elected to bat. Similar to their opening win Burnmoor had a mixed start, falling to 40 for 3 as Ishaq Khan, Elliot Fox and Paul Leonard all picked up a wicket each in the first dozen overs. Mitch Killeen and Stuart Poynter then got Burnmoor back on track, adding 71 for the fourth wicket when Killeen was caught by Ed Hurst off the bowling of Seb Allison for 37. Poynter and veteran Allan Worthy had taken the score to 146 when Poynter was stumped by Hurst off the bowling of Alasdair Appleby for 52. Poynter's innings had come from 61 balls and contained 7 fours and 1 six. This dismissal meant Poynter had scored 299 runs in his two innings so far this season, his average however had plummeted from 247.0 to 149.50! When he had scored 14, Poynter reached 3,000 NEPL runs. Worthy, 16, Josh

Coughlin 22, and Waqas Maqsood 20 saw Burnmoor reach 200 all out from 40.1 overs. Seb Allison had 1 for 26, Ishaq Khan 2 for 26, Leonard 2 for 55, Fox 3 for 39 and Appleby 2 for 48.

At this point Burnmoor were probably happy to have posted 200 but probably a little disappointed not to have batted the overs, Felling, chasing a fraction over 4 runs an over were probably happy with their efforts. No Travis Norris for Felling today so Tyler Easton and Alan Mustard opened the batting, putting on 42 for the first wicket when Easton was caught behind by Alec Linsley off Mitch Killeen for 14 with the fifth ball of the tenth over. With the last ball of the next over Josh Coughlin had Ed Hurst caught behind for a duck and in his next over Coughlin had Alan Mustard caught by Marcus Brown for 36, Felling were now 60 for 3. This became 60 for 4 when Alasdair Appleby was caught by Worthy for 5 off Killeen, Felling now in a little trouble. Jordan Watson batting at five and Seb Allison, batting at six then got Felling back into the game, adding 59 for the fifth wicket when Watson was caught by Maqsood off Ross Greenwell for 21. Felling were 119 for 5 and just two balls later Elliot Fox was caught and bowled by Greenwell for a duck. 119 for 6.

Leonard and Allison got the score to 156 when Allison was leg before to Graeme Bridge for 52, this was his 6th NEPL half century, the innings coming from 96 balls with 3 fours and a six. Burnmoor then ruthlessly mopped up the Felling tail, 156 for 7 became 162 for 8, then 163 for 9 and then 166 all out from 42.1 overs. Maqsood had 1 for 20, Coughlin 3 for 53, Killeen 2 for 11, Bridge 1 for 21 and Greenwell 2 for 27. Burnmoor 24 points and Felling 6 points.

South North opening their home fixture list against Castle Eden is an intriguing fixture, South North are always there or there abouts, but I think Castle Eden are one of the chasing pack. I went to this game with my camera and wasn't disappointed! Castle Eden were missing three regular first teamers through injury and unavailability. South North won the toss and elected to bat. Castle Eden opening bowler's Bilawal Iqbal and Keith Bailey soon made them regret the decision as they attempted to defy the laws of physics and had the ball "hooping around corners!"

Simon Birtwisle struck a boundary through the offside off the first ball of the opening over, but Iqbal got him leg before with the second! After a Chris Hewison single, Sol Bell was then bowled with the last ball of the over and South North were 5 for 2 after six balls! When left armer Keith Bailey bowled Chris Hewison with the first ball of his opening over with an absolute beauty, South North were 5 for 3! Captain Adam Cragg came in at number five and he struck 17 from 16 balls with 2 fours and a six as he counterattacked the bowlers, he was undone when he left one alone outside off stump form Iqbal and it swung back a mile and bowled him. South North now 26 for 4. This quickly became 26 for 5 when number six, coach Tom Rogers was also bowled by Iqbal! Rob Peyton came to the crease to join Sean Tindale who had come in at four and seen two wickets fall in ten balls. Tindale has two NEPL centuries to his credit and Peyton has done well in previous seasons opening the batting. When Iqbal was rested, he had taken 4 for 21 from six overs.

Peyton and Tindale then set about trying to limit the damage, initially taking few risks but Peyton then going a bit more aerial as Tindale settled into being the rock around which the innings could be built. When Peyton reached 25 that was his 2000th NEPL run, he completed his 50 from 73 balls with 9 fours. Tindale completed his 50 from 96 balls with 4 fours and 1 six. When Peyton was bowled Nicholas Sampson-Barnes he had made his highest NEPL score, 82 from 111 balls with 12 fours. He beat his previous highest score of 80, made on 2nd September 2017 at The Emirates against the Durham Academy. South North were now 191 for 6 after the pair had added 165 for the sixth wicket and dug them team out of a rather deep hole! Iqbal bowled David Edwards for a single to complete a well-deserved 5 for 41, but Oli McGee, 9 not out, and Tindale 86 not out got South North to 213 for 7 from their 45 overs. Tindale's innings came from 123 balls and contained 6 fours and a six. It was his tenth NEPL half century. The other wicket takers were Bailey 1 for 20 and Sampson-Barnes 1 for 32.

When Castle Eden batted, they also found the going difficult against the new ball, after Tom Rogers had opened with a maiden, Jonny Wightman trapped Oliver Sampson-Barnes leg before for a duck with the second ball of his first over. The score was 19 when Wightman then had Ben Simpson caught behind by Rob Peyton for 13. Rogers then bowled Keith Bailey with the score on 20 and Lee Crozier had Majeed leg before for 11 when the score was 26. This quickly became 29 for 5 when Philip Wimpenny was caught by Chris Hewison off Sean Tindale for a single. Bilawal Iqbal struck 44 at a run a ball as he also adopted a counter attacking strategy and he was well supported by Nicholas Sampson-Barnes as the pair got the score to 72 when Sampson-Barnes was bowled by Tom Rogers for 14. A partnership of 20 for the seventh wicket between Iqbal and Jonathon Brown, got the score to 92 when Brown was bowled by Wightman for 6. When Iqbal was caught by a brilliant Sean Tindale catch at long off from the bowling of McGee on the same score, the game was done, McGee took the last two wickets in consecutive balls and Castle Eden were 95 all out from 30.5 overs. Rogers had 2 for 12, Wightman 3 for 27, Tindale 1 for 7, Crozier 1 for 23 and McGee 3 for 26. South North had won by 118 runs and got 24 points for the win, Castle Eden picking up 3 points for their efforts. This book has been written about pivotal moments, and its very early days in the season, but I wonder if today turns out to be one.

Sunderland at home to Tynemouth saw an experienced Sunderland side look to build upon a very solid win in their first game, Tynemouth, still to play a single delivery were looking for a winning start. Sunderland won the toss and elected to bat. An early wicket each for opening bowlers Josh Koen and Barry Stewart had Sunderland 45 for 2 and when George Drissell was caught by Koen off the bowling of Josh Moors, 62 for 3 was a scorecard which could go in favour of either team. Micky Allan batting at four and Chris Youldon at five then ensured Sunderland posted a total as they added 80 for the fourth wicket. Although they were both dismissed in the space of 2 runs, 142 for 4 and 144 for 5, Allan had made 54, from 59 balls with 6 fours and a six, Youldon 27, from 47 balls with 3 fours. When Greg Applegarth was caught by Moors off Martin Pollard Sunderland were 161 for 6 and once again things were in the balance. An unbroken stand of 51 between Jack Johnson, 36 not out, and Robert Potts, 22 not out, saw Sunderland reach a good score of 212 for 6 from their 45 overs. Josh Koen took 1 for 41, Barry Stewart 1 for 33, Josh Moors 1 for 33, Freddie Harrison, who had   caught and bowled Youldon, 1 for 41 and Martin Pollard, whose first wicket was Allan, had 2 for 33.

When Tynemouth batted, they got a steady start, Matthew Kimmitt and Ben Debnam adding 21 before Kimmett was caught by Micky Allan off the bowling of Kieran Waterson for 14. This quickly became 29 for 2 and then 30 for 3 as first of all Robbie Bowman was caught by Greg Applegarth off the bowling off Brett Hutchinson for 4 and then Debnam was leg before to Allan for 5. Joe Snowdon and Josh Moors then took the score to 96 when Snowdon was caught by Hutchinson off the bowling of George Drissell for 15. Moors then dominated proceedings, he made 50 from 39 balls with 6 fours and 2 sixes and he completed his century from 66 balls, it contained 11 fours and 4 sixes. He was well supported by Dan Thorburn, he had scored 28 when he was stumped by Youldon off the bowling of Drissell for 28. The pair had added 110 for the fifth wicket and at 206 for 5 had put Tynemouth well on the way to victory. With the score on 208, and just five runs required to win the game, Moors was caught by Hutchinson off the bowling of Joseph Stuart for 119. His innings had come from 76 balls and contained 13 fours and 5 sixes. Freddie Harrison 7 not out and Barry Stewart 2 not out, saw Tynemouth home by 4 wickets. Harrison struck a six to win the match as Tynemouth, 216 for 6 from 36.1 overs collected 24 points and Sunderland 6 points. The wicket takers for Sunderland were Waterson 1 for 46, Hutchinson 1 for 29, Allan 1 for 28, Drissell 2 for 59 and Stuart 1 for 45.

This weekend had seen four centuries scored and two bowlers took 5 wickets in an innings.

Saturday 18th May 2024

As the league starts to settle into its rhythm there is a familiar feel at the top of the table, Burnmoor and South North winning both their games and top of the table on 53 points. Ashington and Tynemouth are also unbeaten but have effectively only played one game, a game which they both won, but the game between the two of them was washed out earlier. Tynedale are enduring a tough start after two heavy defeats.

Burnmoor hosting Benwell Hill looked like an interesting game following the arrival of Hill pro Yash Kothari a week earlier. He announced himself to Hill with 110 on Saturday in the NEPL and 123 on Sunday in The National Knock Out Cup that weekend. For Burnmoor Ross Greenwell made his 150th NEPL appearance and Mitch Killeen his 50th NEPL appearance. Benwell Hill won the toss and elected to bat, but not a lot went right for their batsmen as the Burnmoor bowlers showed why many observers make them a strong bet for a run at the title. Waqas Maqsood had opener Haydon Mustard caught by Marcus Brown for a single, Kothari was caught behind by Alec Linsley for 4, again off Maqsood and when Maqsood had Joe Anderson caught by Allan Worthy for a duck, Hill were 25 for 3. Opening batsman Phil Bell had provided some resistance, making 18 when he was leg before to Graeme Bridge, Hill now 36 for 4. Without any addition to the team score, Mitch Killen had Peter Halliday caught by Marcus Brown for 5 and just eight runs later this became 44 for 6 when Worthy got his second catch of the day and Bridge his second wicket with the dismissal of William Archbold for 2. Daniel Gardiner, 18 not out and Luke Mussett, 12, added 15 for the ninth wicket but Hill were bowled out for 89 in 29.1 overs. Only Josh Coughlin didn't take a wicket as Maqsood 4 for 22, Bridge 2 for 18, Killeen 1 for 13 and Ryan Pringle 3 for 12 proved too much for the visitors.

Benwell Hill's bowlers did show some fight as they reduced Burnmoor to 22 for 3 but Ross Greenwell, 39 not out and Stuart Poynter, 29 not out, made sure Burnmoor got the required 90 runs in just 21.3 overs to take a seven-wicket win. Kothari had 1 for 31 and Callum Harding 1 for 12, the other Burnmoor wicket falling to a run out. Burnmoor got 24 points for the win and Benwell Hill 1 point.

Castle Eden played host to Ashington, Ashington as a club were still reeling from a break in at the club house the previous weekend and were looking to their players to give the club a much-needed lift, they won the toss and elected to field. Castle Eden welcomed opening bat Jonathan Malkin back to their ranks after he missed last week's game. They were soon in trouble as Matthew Collins went about his work and picked up three early wickets, Ben Simpson for 7, Malkin for 14 and Bilawal Iqbal for 4 as Castle Eden slumped to 31 for 3, when pro Jeremiah Louis picked up Muhaymen Majeed for 10 they were 4 down for 41. Louis nipped out another when he had Nicholas Sampson-Barnes leg before and Collins got a fourth wicket when he dismissed Philip Wimpenny leg before second ball for a duck, Castle Eden were now 49 for 6. When Jack McCarthy caught Keith Bailey for 7, again off Louis, Castle Eden were 51 for 7. Jonathon Brown 14 not out and Aalan Unsworth 11, pushed the score to 72 before Ian Sharkey had Unsworth leg before, James Harmison picked up a wicket and another one for Sharkey saw Castle Eden all out for 82 in 27.3 overs. Louis, 3 for 35, and Collins, 4 for 32, had both bowled their nine overs straight out, James Harmison took 1 for 8 and Ian Sharkey 2 for 6.

Ashington made a rough start themselves, Iqbal bowling Adam Nichol for a duck and Jack McCarthy was caught for 5, again off the bowling of Iqbal, as they were 8 for 2. Opener Jack Jessop, who had made 71 not out last week, was in good form again and with captain Sean McCafferty he steadied Ashington nerves, the pair had added 60 to take the score to 68 when Iqbal had McCafferty leg before for 26. Jessop finished on 40 not out from 49 balls with 6 fours and a six and Ben Harmison was 5 not out as Ashington reached 85 for the loss of 3 wickets from 17.4 overs to take home a seven-wicket win. Bilawal Iqbal had taken 3 for 36 as the only bright spot for the hosts. Ashington 24 points, Castle Eden 1 point.

Chester le Street played host to their old foes South North at Ropery Lane, Chester won the toss and elected to field. Familiar faces Simon Birtwisle and Sol Bell put on 49 for the first wicket with Bell being the first to fall, bowled by Mark Watson for 20. Opener Birtwisle was next to go when he was leg before to Josh Wilson for 29 with the score on 63. Chris Hewison and Adam Cragg had taken the score to 71 when Hewison was caught by Andrew Smith off the bowling of Seb Hughes-Pinan for 11.

Captain Adam Cragg was in an aggressive mood as he and all-rounder Sean Tindale had moved the score to 115 when Tindale was bowled by Mark Watson for 20. Coach Tom Rogers joined Cragg at this point and they added 54 for the fifth wicket, Rogers next man out for 33 from just 14 balls when he was caught by Andrew Smith off Josh Wilson. The only other wicket to fall was Rob Peyton, run out for 2, as Cragg finished on 83 not out from 57 balls, his innings had contained 6 fours and 5 sixes and was his 36th NEPL half century. Nathan Gough was 7 not out as South North scored 217 for 6 from their 45 overs. For Chester, only three bowlers picked up wickets, Josh Wilson 2 for 33, Mark Watson 2 for 49 and Seb Hughes-Pinan 1 for 40, given later events its worth mentioning Quentin Hughes who bowled nine overs for just fifteen runs at an economy rate of 1.67.

When Chester batted John Coxon and Jacob McCann made a steady start, making 32 before Coxon was caught behind by Rob Peyton off Tom Rogers for 12. Andrew Smith was next man in and next man out, but not before he had scored 26 and moved the score to 89, he was caught by Adam Cragg off the bowling of Oli McGee. This brought Kyle Coetzer to the crease at number four, and they had reached 106 when opener McCann was caught by Rob Peyton off Tom Rogers for 55. This was McCann's 19th NEPL half century, his innings came from 65 balls and contained 5 fours and 1 six. Coetzer was joined by captain James Thompson as the game hung in the balance. They added 99 for the fourth wicket, taking the score to 205 when Thompson was stumped by Peyton off McGee for 27. Cole Pearce struck two boundaries as he made 11 off just 4 balls and Coetzer was 77 not out as Chester got home by 6 wickets with 2 overs to spare. This was Coetzer's 42nd NEPL half century and his innings came from 78 balls and contained 7 fours and 2 sixes. For South North, Tom Rogers had 2 for 37, Oli McGee 1 for 35 and Lee Crozier 1 for 52. Chester collect 24 points for their win, South North 5 points.

I chose to attend Jesmond with the camera as Newcastle hosted Burnopfield. The visitors won the toss and elected to field on a hot sunny day, and they made a good start when Daniel Hogg trapped Newcastle captain Bobby Green leg before for a single with the score on 6. Mohsin Mukhtar and opener took the score to 57 before Mukhtar was leg before to change bowler Callum Brown for 20. Robinson and new batsman Jaques du Toit then picked up the scoring, du Toit in particular looking in good nick with some lovely cricket shots and clean hitting. Ben Robinson had completed his 1500 NEPL runs when he reached 39 and when he reached 50 that was his 9th NEPL half century. He was on 58, and the score 148 for 2 when he was dismissed in a rare fashion, I'm 60 years old and I can't recall ever seeing someone given out for obstructing the field in all those years playing and watching club cricket.

I can't remember the bowler, but Robinson played a defensive shot, the ball landing at his feet, it was however spinning slowly back towards the stumps when he bent down and picked it up and threw it to a fielder! Howzat? An appeal was made, over to the umpires, a quick conference and the finger is raised. I spoke to Robinson as the innings progressed and he confirmed that the ball was still moving, albeit slowly, when he picked it up and, although his intention was to return the ball to the fielder, he totally accepted that the laws of the game meant the fielding team were entitled to appeal and that the umpire was right to give him out, he assured me he wouldn't be making that mistake again! The manner of dismissal shouldn't cloud an excellent half century, his innings coming from 71 balls with 8 fours and 2 sixes. Despite being in a strong position after Robinson's dismissal and with around 20 overs left Newcastle's batting fell away, none of the new batsmen made double figures as they lost 7 wickets for 59 runs, du Toit had been caught and bowled by Daniel Hogg for 73. His innings had come from 45 balls and contained 8 fours and 4 sixes, it was his 45th NEPL half century and came in his 200th NEPL appearance. Newcastle were 207 all out in 41.2 overs, Daniel Hogg had 3 for 15, Callum Brown 3 for 47 and Amaan Ulhaq 3 for 37, no bowler is credited with the obstruct the field dismissal.

I would think, given the strong nature of their batting lineup, Burnopfield would have been happy to chase 208, certainly the two or three people I spoke to at tea thought Newcastle were 20 or 30 light. When Burnopfield batted John Oswell started like a man with a train to catch, as he struck 3 fours and a six to quickly go to 20. Two consecutive fours, one between mid-wicket and mid-on and another through mid-on were lovely shots on the eye, both pure timing. However, with the score 23, he hit one in the air to deep midwicket off Rowan Shelton, George Darwood had to make 12-15 yards before he could leap to complete the catch, tumbling to the ground as he did so but holding on to the ball, Newcastle's relief was palpable. Ross Whitfield Jnr came in at three, making his 50th NEPL appearance, with the score on 30 and Whitfield having made 3, he was caught smartly at a wide slip by Jaques du Toit off the bowling of Shelton. Just 5 runs later George Darwood induced a nick from opener Ben McKinney and Euan Stenhouse took the catch behind the stumps. 35 for 3 became 56 for 4 when Stenhouse caught Sam Dinning off the bowling of du Toit for 10. At 67 Freddie Geffen was caught at slip by du Toit off Issac Unsworth for 19, Burnopfield now 5 down. Daniel Hogg, batting at six, hit 2 fours and 2 sixes as he went on the offensive, but with the score on 108 he was leg before to du Toit for 30. Burnopfield then lost their last four wickets for 1 run as they fell from 124 for 6 to 125 all out as Mohsin Mukhtar picked up three quick wickets and du Toit administered the last rites. Callum Brown was 22 not out as Burnopfield were bowled out for 125 from 26.3 overs. Shelton had 2 for 19, Darwood 1 for 36, du Toit 3 for 30, Unsworth 1 for 33 and Mukhtar 3 for 7. Newcastle got 24 points for their 82-run win, Burnopfield 5 points for their loss.

Tynedale were still looking for their first NEPL win when they hosted Sunderland. This game saw several Sunderland veterans reach career milestones, Dan Shurben made his 350th NEPL appearance, Kieran Waterson his 200th NEPL appearance and Greg Applegarth his 150th NEPL appearance. Tynedale won the toss and elected to bat. They were soon in trouble as both opening bowlers, Brett Hutchinson and Kieran Waterson picked up a wicket each as Tynedale slipped to 17 for 2. However, each of the next eight Tynedale batsman made double figures, Euan Stephenson top scoring with 36 and Matthew Scott 24, Jamie Crichton 20 and Seth Robbie 20, all giving valuable support as they battled their way to 190 all out from 44 overs and gave their bowlers something to bowl at. Each of the Sunderland bowlers used picked up at least one wicket, Hutchinson finished with 1 for 34, Waterson 2 for 29,

Micky Allan 2 for 51, Joseph Stuart 1 for 22, Jack Johnson 2 for 32 and Graeme Race 1 for 18. When Allan dismissed Matthew Scott, that was his 100th NEPL wicket.

When Sunderland batted, they made a steady start, despite losing Dan Shurben for 8 when the score was 20, he was caught by Tom Cant off the bowling of Matthew Scott. Opener Jack Johnson and Greg Applegarth had taken the score to 63 when the latter fell leg before to Aaron Rourke for 29.

Johnson and number four, Micky Allan had brought up the Sunderland hundred but with the score on 105, Allan, who had made 28 from just 16 balls, was leg before to Nathan Byerley. Captain and wicketkeeper Chris Youldon was next to fall, caught by Seth Robbie off Nathan Byerley for 9 as Sunderland were now 127 for 4, still requiring 64 runs to win. With the score on 148 Tynedale got the wicket they needed most when Johnson was leg before to Byerley for 61. This was his maiden NEPL half century and his innings came from 115 balls and contained 5 boundaries. Despite 21 not out from Bruce Pritchard some tight Tynedale bowling and regular wicket taking saw them restrict Sunderland to 183 for 9 from their 45 overs as Tynedale won by 7 runs. Tynedale's wicket takers were Matthew Scott 1 for 31, Aaron Rourke 1 for 26, Tom Cant 1 for 37 and Nathan Byerley 6 for 39. Tynedale pick up their first NEPL win and earn 24 points, Sunderland get 7 points for the loss.

Tynemouth welcomed Felling to Preston Avenue, Felling won the toss and elected to bat and despite losing veteran Alan Mustard for a single, caught by Robbie Bowman off fellow veteran Barry Stewart, they made a strong start. A second wicket stand of 94 between opener Travis Norris and number three Tyler Easton gave them a solid platform to post a good score. Josh Moors separated the pair when he caught and bowled Norris for 68 with the score 103. When he scored his 37th run that took Norris to 1500 NEPL runs, this was his 6th NEPL half century and his innings came from 59 balls and contained 8 fours and 2 sixes. Two relatively quick wickets, Alasdair Appleby bowled by Josh Moors for 18 and Jordan Watson caught and bowled by Pollard for a single, saw Felling stutter a little at 129 for 4 this became 150 for 5 when Tyler Easton was caught and bowled Martin Pollard for 45. When Easton reached 12 that completed his 1500 runs in the NEPL. Seb Allison had come in at 6 and he then dominated the remainder of the innings as he and Ed Hurst added 117 for the sixth wicket. When Allison was caught by Matthew Brown off the bowling of Barry Stewart with the fifth ball of the last over, he had scored 80 from 54 balls with 3 fours and 6 sixes. This was his 7th NEPL half century. Paul Leonard was stumped off the last ball of the innings by Bowman again off Barry Stewart as Felling posted a daunting 267 for 7 from their 45 overs. The wicket takers for Tynemouth were Stewart 3 for 34, Moors 2 for 53 and Pollard 2 for 31.

When Tynemouth batted openers Ben Debnam and Matthew Kimmitt made an excellent start, scoring 92 for the first wicket before Paul Leonard bowled Kimmitt for 40. Debnam had added just three more to his own score, and with the total now 103, when he was bowled by Elliott Fox. Arguably the innings and the game was now in the balance, two new batsman at the crease and still over 150 required for the win. Tynemouth need not have worried, Robbie Bowman, 81 not out and Matthew Brown 92 not out saw them home by 26 balls to win by eight wickets. This was Bowman's second NEPL half century and his highest NEPL score to date, his innings had come from 77 balls and contained 5 fours and 3 sixes. For Matthew Brown this was his 30th NEPL half century, his innings had come from just 51 balls and contained 7 fours and 5 sixes. Paul Leonard, 1 for 28 at a very creditable economy rate of 3.11, and Elliot Fox, 1 for 56 were the two wicket takers, I mention Leonard's economy rate as he went at a rate around half of that of his fellow bowlers. Tynemouth thus join Ashington and Burnmoor as the only three unbeaten clubs this season and collected 24 points for their efforts, Felling got 4 points for their toil.

Burnmoor now sit alone at the top of the league with 77 points from Ashington, South North and Tynemouth with 58 points.

Saturday 25th May 2024

Unbeaten Ashington welcomed Sunderland to Langwell Crescent on a sunny day, I attended this one with my camera. Sunderland won the toss and elected to field. Ashington's openers struggled to score against a disciplined Sunderland opening bowling attack and it was no surprise when Adam Nichol chased a wide one from Brett Hutchinson and was caught behind by Chris Youldon with the score on 19 after 7.2 overs. Second team regular Scott Pearcey batted at three and although he rarely looked comfortable, he and Jack Jessop took the score to 76 when

Pearcy hit one to mid-on, Brett Hutchinson, off spinner George Drissell to depart for 20. Jessop departed 2 runs later for 39, leg before to Micky Allan. This was Allan's 100th NEPL wicket and was a key one in the context of the innings. Ashington then slipped to 102 for 6 as George Drissell picked up three more quick wickets. James Harmison's 33 included 2 fours and 2 sixes and Alex Storey hit 20, including the last ball of the innings for six as Ashington made 167 for 9 from their 45 overs. Sunderland's wicket takers were Kieran Waterson, 1 for 35, Brett Hutchinson 2 for 30, Micky Allan 1 for 43, Drissell had 4 for 24 and Joe Stuart 1 for 32.

Sunderland showed all their experience as they chased Ashington's score down, their lowest partnership was the opening stand of 21, with Micky Allan hitting the only half-century of the game, 58 not out, as the backbone, his teammates contributed five of the other six who batted made double figures, Jack Johnson being 22 not out at the end. This was Allan's second half century of the season, and his 7th NEPL half century, his innings came from 89 balls and contained 3 fours and 2 sixes. Only three wicket takers for Ashington, Jeremiah Louis had 1 for 55, Matt Collins 2 for 30 and Cam Nichols 2 for 28 as Sunderland won by 5 wickets. Sunderland 24 points, Ashington 4 points.

Benwell Hill were hosts to unbeaten Tynemouth at Denton Bank, Benwell Hill won the toss and elected to field. Tynemouth started well with veteran Ben Debnam and Matthew Kimmitt with an opening stand of 45 before Debnam was caught by Peter Halliday off the bowling of Luke Mussett for 15. They had reached 73 when Kimmitt was caught by Mussett off Dan Gardiner for 42. Matthew Brown with 69 made sure Tynemouth got a decent score, he was well supported by Josh Moors, 33 and Barry Stewart, batting at nine, made 28. This was Brown's second successive half century and his 31st in the NEPL, his inning shad come from 74 balls and contained 1 four and 5 sixes. Tynemouth made 240 all out from their 45 overs, Callum Harding took 1 for 36, Luke Mussett 2 for 33, Rory Hanley 1 for 34, Max Williamson 2 for 53, Dan Gardiner 1 for 40 and Yash Kothari 2 for 38 as all bowlers used took at least one wicket.

When Benwell Hill batted they lost wickets at regular intervals to fall to 67 for 5. One of the five men out was overseas pro and undoubted danger man, Yash Kothari, who fell leg before to a footballer, Newcastle United's Sean Longstaff dismissing him for 9. Will Archbold,15, and Rory Hanley, 20, had taken the score to 107 when Archbold was caught by Longstaff off Josh Moors and just three balls later Moors had new batsman Dan Gardiner caught by Robbie Bowman and Hill were now 107 for 7. Luke Mussett hit a couple of fours and a six in his 19 but when he was bowled by Freddie Harrison for 19, Benwell Hill were 145 all out from 39. 1 overs to give Tynemouth a 95-run victory.

Following Ashington's defeat and Burnmoor's lack of a game, Tynemouth remain as one of only two unbeaten teams in the league and they collect 24 points for their win, Benwell Hill picked up 5 points for their loss.

Burnopfield were due to be at home to the last of the three unbeaten teams this season, league leaders, Burnmoor, unfortunately this one fell victim to the previous heavy rain and was abandoned without a ball being bowled. I can only imagine Burnmoor's frustration at this, having opened up a lead at the top of the table, the 5 points each side is awarded for an abandonment must feel like a loss as all the other games were played.

Castle Eden were at home to Chester le Street, the visitors won the toss and elected to field. The home openers had made 24 for the first wicket when Mark Watson had Ben Simpson caught by Andrew Smith for 5, fellow opener Jon Malkin was dismissed for 20 just 5 runs later, Watson again the bowler, as he was caught by James Thompson. From there it was pretty much a steady procession of wickets as no Chester bowler had an economy rate over 2.57 and they bowled the hosts out for 82 in 36.5 overs. Watson finished with 3 for 15, Josh Wilson had 3 for 22 and Seb Hughes-Pinan 3 for 19, Quentin Hughes completed the wicket takers, 1 for 14.

When Chester le Street batted, they also struggled with conditions but 33 from Jacob McCann and 17 not out from Josh Wilson saw them home by 4 wickets in 20.4 overs. Keith Bailey had been the main cause of the Chester discomfort, taking 5 for 20, Alan Unsworth taking 1 for 14. Chester le Street got 24 points for the win; Castle Eden collect 2.

Felling won the toss at home to Tynedale and as with everyone else, elected to field, for Felling, Alan Mustard made his 250th NEPL appearance. Seb Allison quickly made inroads into the Tynedale batting, removing overseas pro Nkosana Mpofu for two with the third ball of the first over and then Oliver Fletcher with the second ball of his second over. Opener Ed Foreman and captain Dan Parker then added 77 for the third wicket as Tynedale looked to post a score, both batsmen were dismissed with the score on 85, Foreman run out for 46 and Parker stumped by Ed Hurst off the bowling of Alasdair Appleby for 28. The experienced Joe Barber, 39, and Euan Stephenson 43, had added 66 for the fifth wicket when Elliot Fox dismissed Stephenson, this was the first of four wickets for Fox as Tynedale lost their last five wickets for 39 runs and were bowled out for 190 from 44.1 overs. Fox finished with 4 for 24, Seb Allison 3 for 47 and Appleby 1 for 17.

When Felling batted, they were in trouble at 39 for 3 after Archie Fletcher dismissed Alan Mustard and Mpofu accounted for Tyler Easton and Alasdair Appleby. A partnership then developed between Jordan Watson and Seb Allison, giving Felling a platform to kick on but Watson then fell for 54, caught by Joe Barber off Mpofu after the pair had added 55. When Allison was dismissed for 17 with the score on 115 and then Jamie Cairns got out on the same score, Felling were suddenly 115 for 7. Despite 31 not out from number nine Paul Leonard, Felling couldn't maintain any momentum and were bowled out for 169 from 41.5 overs. Matthew Scott took 1 for 26, Archie Fletcher 1 for 36, Nkosana Mpofu 3 for 22, Aaron Rourke 1 for 47 and Nathan Byerley 3 for 32 as Tynedale collected their second successive NEPL win and 24 points, Felling pick up 6 points in defeat.

South North played host to Newcastle in the Tyneside derby. Newcastle won the toss and elected to field to complete all 5 sides winning the toss not fancying a bat in damp conditions! There was an issue with play-cricket this weekend and it's difficult to paint an accurate picture of this game. South North made a steady start, putting on 31 for the first wicket before Simon Birtwisle was caught by Rowan Shelton off the spin bowling of Mohsin Mukhtar for 17. When Nikhil Gorantla, on his first NEPL appearance of the season, was caught by George Darwood off Woody Wilson for 13, South North were 66 for 2. A third wicket stand of 63 between Sol Bell and Chris Hewison had South North on 129 for 3 but Newcastle and Jaques du Toit in particular kept chipping away at them with wickets falling regularly. Bell was dismissed for 66, his innings coming from 86 balls and containing 10 fours. This was his 16th NEPL half century. Sean Tindale, batting at five, scored his second unbeaten half century of the season, 52 not out to guide South North to 220 for 8 from their 45 overs. Tindale reached 3,000 career NEPL runs when he scored his 36th run of the innings and this was his 11th NEPL half century. His innings had come from 58 balls and contained 4 boundaries. Jaques du Toit picked up 3 for 31, with the other Newcastle wicket takers being Rowan Shelton, 1 for 52, Mohsin Mukhtar 1 for 27 and Woody Wilson 1 for 18.

When Newcastle batted, they got off to a disastrous start, Tom Rogers trapping Newcastle captain Bobby Green leg before second ball. They too lost their second wicket on 66, Ben Robinson caught by Simon Birtwisle off Jonny Wightman for 17. A partnership of 52 between Asher Hart and Jaques du Toit was ended when du Toit was caught by Will Alexander off Oli McGee for 25, crucially his runs had come at a run a ball and contained a four and two sixes. A stand of 75 between Hart and Mohsin Mukhtar then took Newcastle to 160 when the latter was bowled by Oli McGee for 33. Just 13 runs later Hart was caught by Sean Tindale off Wightman for 82, and the game was once more in the balance, Newcastle 173 for 5. Hart had faced 119 balls and had struck 5 fours and 3 sixes in his innings; this was his second successive NEPL half century, his highest NEPL score to date and his 6th NEPL half century. When he reached 30, he scored his 1,000[th] NEPL run. Matthew Stewart and Rowan Shelton got Newcastle to 200 when Shelton was bowled by Tom Rogers for 14. Rogers then then bowled George Darwood first ball, Newcastle 200 for 7. This became 215 for 8 when Levi Olver was caught and bowled by Jonny Wightman for 9. It all came down to the last ball two required to win, Euan Stenhouse was run out by Sean Tindale for 4 as he tried to scramble the winning run, match tied, Newcastle 220 for 9 wickets! Matthew Stewart was 21 not out for Newcastle, Tom Rogers, 3 for 26 and Jonny Wightman 3 for 48 were the main wicket takers, Oli McGee also picked up 2 for 33. South North got 16 points and Newcastle 15 points for their efforts.

The league table now has a real air of familiarity about it, Burnmoor and South North first and third but Tynemouth a surprise package to many, still unbeaten and no doubt wishing they hadn't lost their first match of the season to the weather. After a tough introduction to the NEPL Tynedale have put together back-to-back wins and every team has now won at least one game. Next week sees the return to red ball cricket and the more traditional format.

I would like to make a couple of observations at this point, the first one relates to the balance of the league. It appears to me that, despite the damp wickets, new balls and quality of bowlers, it is easier to score a hundred than take five wickets, so far there have been seven centuries and only two five wicket hauls in the league, I think that reflects the fact that limited over cricket was set up to entertain rather than the grind which timed cricket can be, it will be interesting to see if the red ball changes things in the coming weeks.

The second matter relates to American Football, I am a huge fan of the sport, there's a saying in the NFL "on any given Sunday" it's widely interpreted as "anything can happen on any particular day," Sunday being the day most NFL games are played! In respect of the NEPL I would look at the fact that after each team has played five games, in reality only four, and in the case of four teams only three, there are only two unbeaten teams, Burnmoor and Tynemouth, and without taking anything away from them, they are amongst the teams that have played three games. Every team has won at least one game, proving that on any given day any team can beat any other! This is why we play the games, because on paper Team A should beat Team B, whilst the NFL strives for parity, hence the draft system to try and level up every season, I don't think the NEPL does, but I would say there is an early case for this being at the very least an interesting season, and possibly the most open for a few years.

TABLE 74   NEPL Table Sunday 26th May 2024.

	Played	Won	Draw/Aban	Lost	Tied	Penalty Points	Bonus Points	Points
Burnmoor	5	3	2	0	0	0	0	82
Tynemouth	5	3	2	0	0	0	0	82
South North	5	2	1	1	1	0	13	74
Sunderland	5	2	1	2	0	0	13	66
Ashington	5	2	2	1	0	0	4	62
Chester le Street	5	2	1	2	0	0	6	59
Tynedale	5	2	1	2	0	0	4	57
Newcastle	5	1	1	2	1	0	15	52
Felling	5	1	1	3	0	0	16	45
Burnopfield	5	1	2	2	0	0	8	42
Benwell Hill	5	1	1	3	0	0	10	39
Castle Eden	5	1	1	3	0	0	6	35

Chapter Sixteen

The Middle Session 2024

Saturday 1st June 2024

With the first part of the season now a matter of record, the middle part of the season, the next 11 games revert to a red ball, traditional white clothing and 110 overs in a day, the team batting first with the option of batting up to 58 overs and a draw now back on the table.

The return of the red ball and some heavy midweek rain meant, for the second week in a row, every team who won the toss elected to field, with only two teams reaching 200, and one falling just short, the game between arguably the leagues two strongest batting sides produced just 228 runs in total, and with a result in every game, I suspect the captain's instincts were correct to bowl.

Unbeaten joint league leaders Burnmoor hosted reigning champions South North today, I'm sure it's far too early to attach any significance to this match in respect of the title, but this fixture always represents a challenge for both teams and can result in some hard-edged cricket.

South North captain Adam Cragg made his 300th NEPL appearance when he called the toss and invited Burnmoor to bat. Burnmoor made a steady start, they were 15 when the first wicket fell and 43 when the second went down, both batters falling to Oli McGee. Tom Rogers then fired out Mitch Killeen, Stuart Poynter and Allan Worthy for the addition of just five runs as Burnmoor slipped to 48 for 5. Opener Marcus Brown was still there and holding one end up, but Burnmoor struggled to reach 94 for 9 when Brown was bowled by Jonny Wightman for 38, he had faced 106 balls and hit three boundaries in his innings. Number ten Craig Stephenson then played what turned out to be a pivotal innings, with wicketkeeper Alec Linsley scoring 7 not out from 26 balls, Stephenson hit two fours and a six as he made 25 from 33 balls before Sean Tindale caught him off the bowling of Oli McGee. Burnmoor 125 all out in 45.4 overs, Oli McGee finished with 4 for 34, Tom Rogers 4 for 35 and Jonny Wightman 2 for 23.

When South North batted Josh Coughlin dismissed Simon Birtwisle for 7 and Nikhil Gorantla for 5 as Burnmoor looked to get among the visiting batsman. Sol Bell and Chris Hewison had brought the South North 50 up when Bell was caught by Ryan Pringle off the spin of Graeme Bridge for 22. Bell's score would prove to be the highest of the innings, when Maqsood had Hewison caught by Stu Poynter for 21, South North were in a bit of trouble, 58 for 4, when Maqsood removed Cragg with the score on 68 and Bridge then picked up three quick wickets they had stumbled to 98 for 9. Mitch Killeen then bowled Wightman and Lee Crozier with successive balls and McGee was stranded on 12 not out. Burnmoor's bowlers had the following stats, Maqsood 2 for 16, Josh Coughlin 2 for 23, Mitch Killeen 2 for 11, and Graeme Bridge 4 for 36. South North were 103 all out in 40.3 overs, Burnmoor had won by 22 runs and collected 23 points, South North got 4 points

Chester le Street entertained Ashington at Ropery Lane, the visitors looking to bounce back after their first loss of the season last week. Ashington won the toss and elected to field, they quickly saw a result from that decision when Matt Collins had Jacob McCann caught by Sean McCafferty for a duck with the score on 4.

When Collins removed the dangerous Andrew Smith with the last ball of his next over and just four balls later Jeremiah Louis had James Thompson caught by Jack McCarthy, Chester were now 13 for 3. Opener John Coxon and Charlie Purdon had added 40 for the fourth wicket when Coxon was bowled by Collins for 23. Purdon continued to bat well, as he and Cole Pearce continued the fightback. They were 83 when the fifth wicket fell, Purdon caught by McCarthy off Alex Nice for 39. Chester then fell from 100 for 5 to 112 all out as Ashington's bowlers kept at them.

Pearce was out for 21, with Ashington's wicket takers being Jeremiah Louis 2 for 26, Matt Collins, continuing his impressive early season form, 3 for 28, Cam Nichols 3 for 34 and Alex Nice, on debut 2 for 8.

Ashington also struggled at the start of their innings, losing the in-form Jack Jessop for 7 and Jack McCarthy for 5 as they reached 24 for 2. Liam Simpson and Quentin Hughes had been the successful bowlers. Opener Cam Nicholls and captain Sean McCafferty then added 51 for the third wicket as Ashington looked to be heading for a comfortable win, even when McCafferty was caught by Charlie Purdon off the bowling of Mark Watson for 17, 75 for 3, Ashington must have still felt in control. Any complacency was soon removed as they lost two more quick wickets whilst adding just one more run, Nichols going for 43, being one of those wickets, 76 for 5. Ben Harmison and Jeremiah Louis then settled Ashington nerves as they took the score to 91 when Harmison was caught by McCann for 7, Mark Watson was again the bowler. Ashington then again lost quick wickets, as they slipped once more, Seb Hughes- Pinan dismissing Greg Williams and Ian Sharkey in the space of three balls, 92 for 8, still 21 required. A ninth wicket stand of 23 between Louis and Alex Nice saw The Mighty Acorns home,115 for 8 from 42.2 overs, to win by 2 wickets, Louis finished 24 not out and Nice 8 not out. Chester le Street's wicket takers had been Quentin Hughes 1 for 22, Liam Simpson 1 for 28, Mark Watson 3 for 26 and Seb Hughes-Pinan 3 for 35. Ashington collected 22 points and Chester le Street 3 points.

At Jesmond, Newcastle, after tying last week, were hoping to get across the line against a struggling Castle Eden batting line up, the hosts won the toss and elected to field. Castle Eden cast aside any doubts I may have had about their batting to post the highest team score of any team batting first today, they were also the only team to get over 200 as six batsmen made double figures. Bilawal Iqbal top scored with 56 not out, his innings coming from 86 balls with 7 fours and 2 sixes, this was his second NEPL half century. Ben Simpson had 40, Jon Malkin and Muhaymen Majeed 27 each and 25 from Chris Tudball all made valuable contributions. Castle Eden scored 216 all out from 54.2 overs, for Newcastle George Darwood had 1 for 41, Rowan Shelton 2 for 48, Issac Unsworth 1 for 67, Mohsin Mukhtar 3 for 45 and Matt Stewart 2 for 9. When Darwood had Nicholas Sampson-Barnes caught by Euan Stenhouse that was his 50th NEPL wicket.

When Newcastle batted, they lost Ben Robinson in the second over, caught by JP Meade off the bowling of Richard Ede for a duck. Captain Bobby Green then made his way towards his 6th NEPL half century, going on to make 67 in total, from 98 balls with 10 fours, as he and Asher Hart had put on 70 for the second wicket when Hart was caught by Iqbal off the bowling of Malkin for 43. Nicholas Sampson-Barnes then picked up two quick wickets as Newcastle wobbled a little at 87 for 4, but with Green still there and Rowan Shelton now giving good support, they were inching closer to the win. When Green was caught with the score on 133, now with 5 wickets down, the game hung in the balance. Matt Stewart went some way to calming Newcastle nerves but when he was leg before to Iqbal for 19, Newcastle were now 179 for 6. George Darwood came and went for 6, bowled by Richard Ede, Newcastle now 204 for 7 and the overs now ticking by, just 9 balls left and still 13 to win. Shelton hit a six off the last ball of the 54th over which meant they now needed six to win from the last of their 55 overs. Newcastle couldn't tie two weeks in a row, could they? Jon Malkin bowled the last over, leg bye first ball, dot to Shelton second ball, a single from the third ball and new batsmen Issac Unsworth taking two and then a single, scores level, one ball left, Shelton facing, now on 51. He hit a four to take Newcastle to 220 for 7 from 55 overs and a 3-wicket win. This was Shelton's first NEPL half century, he finished on 55 not out from 97 balls with 6 fours and 1 six, Unsworth was 4 not out. For Castle Eden, Iqbal had 1 for 46, Ede 2 for 30, Malkin 1 for 66, Nicholas Sampson-Barnes 2 for 40 and Alan Unsworth 1 for 18. Newcastle 25 points, Castle Eden 6 points.

Sunderland, after a good away win last week, were another team looking for consistency as they played host to Felling, the visitors won the toss and, as with everyone else, opted to field. Sunderland's top four all made double figures, George Fishwick 32, Dan Shurben 19, George Drissell 27 and Micky Allan 40, as they batted sensibly to try and get their team to a defendable total. Elliot Fox had accounted for three of the top four to go and he would go on to take a five for, but 22 from Jack Johnson and 36 not out from Greg Applegarth got Sunderland the sort of score they would want, 198 all out from 52.4 overs. Fox took 6 for 22, Seb Allison had 2 for 46, Ishaq Khan 1 for 37 and Alasdair Appleby 1 for 17 for Felling.

When Felling batted, they were hindered almost immediately when opener Alan Mustard had to retire hurt after just three overs with the score on 6 for no wicket. Disaster followed just nine balls later, Mustard's replacement,

Jordan Watson was caught and bowled by Brett Hutchinson second ball with no runs added. When Alasdair Appleby was bowled by Hutchinson with the score 22, Felling were in a little trouble. Opener Tyler Easton and number four Seb Allison then got Felling back on track, taking the score to 45 when Easton was caught by Applegarth off the bowling of Joe Stuart for 21. Felling then fell away badly as they slumped to 58 for 7 as Joe Stuart found his line and length and removed Ed Hurst and Seb Allison, the run out of Paul Leonard compounded matters for Felling and it was no surprise when they were eventually all out for 92, in fairness to them they had batted as a team for 53.4 overs and the Sunderland bowlers all had exceptional economy rates, the highest being 2.22! Joe Stuart finished with 6 for 19, Brett Hutchinson 2 for 21 and George Drissell 1 for 10, Kieran Waterson and Micky Allan had shared 18 overs equally between them for a total of just 32 runs. Sunderland's win by 106 runs earned them 25 points and Felling pick up 4 points.

Tynedale played host to Benwell Hill, Tynedale looking for three wins in a row, Benwell Hill looking to find some form. Tynedale won the toss and elected to field and after just sixteen balls I'm pretty sure they felt they had made the right decision, Benwell Hill making a disastrous start at 3 for 4, opening bowlers Matt Scott and Archie Fletcher taking two wickets each. Indian pro Yash Kothari had come in at three and he had to be the rock around which Benwell Hill batted and so it proved.

Although the score was only 26 when Scott bowled William Archbold for 14, Kothari lived up to his growing reputation and batted on. The score was 51 when number seven Joe Anderson was dismissed for 2. Kothari then made his first NEPL half century, to go with his earlier century, and with good support down the order form Dan Gardiner, 14, and Max Williamson 19, he would go on to be last man out for 89, his innings coming from 124 balls, with 10 fours and 1 six. Credit to the Hill batsman who dug in and got them to 158 all out from 44.1 overs after such a disastrous start. For Tynedale, Matt Scott finished with 5 for 33, Archie Fletcher 3 for 44 and Aaron Rourke 2 for 29.

Tynedale's batters fared than Benwell Hill's but not by too much, falling to 30 for 3, then 57 for 5 and 84 for 7 as Benwell's bowlers, led by Callum Harding and Luke Mussett fought back. The eighth wicket stand between Aaron Rourke and Matt Scott would prove to be the decisive partnership of the match, adding 58 to take the score to 145 before Rourke was caught by Haydon Mustard off Mussett for 33. However, Matt Scott finished on 30 not out and Nathan Byerley 6 not out as Tynedale got home by 2 wickets in the 51st over. Four Hill bowlers took wickets, Harding had 2 for 29, Mussett 3 for 34, Kothari 1 for 42 and Dan Gardiner 2 for 33. Tynedale 24 points, Benwell Hill 5 points.

Tynemouth, still unbeaten, welcomed Burnopfield to Preston Avenue, I chose this one to attend with my camera. Burnopfield won the toss and elected to field. I had been told that both ends of the wicket were under water on Thursday, so it was no surprise when the new red ball moved around off the wicket and Daniel Hogg and Matthew Oswell had both openers back in the pavilion with just 12 on the board. Number three Robbie Bowman and number four Matthew Brown then rode the storm, adding 61 for the third wicket, they were separated with the first ball of the 18th over by a catch from Ross Whitfield Jnr off the bowling of Harry Lumsden, Bowman the batsman to go for 35. When Lumsden bowled Josh Moors for four in the same over, Tynemouth were now 78 for 4. Joe Snowdon then joined Brown and Tynemouth consolidated once again, Snowdon had scored 19 when he drove a low catch back to spinner Finlay McGurk. 119 for 5 then became 119 for 6 when Brown was dismissed for 42. The Tynemouth tail couldn't wag, and they slid to 145 all out from 40.4 overs. Dan Hogg took 2 for 25, Matt Oswell 1 for 28, Harry Lumsden 2 for 21, Callum Brown 2 for 44 and Finlay McGurk 3 for 21.

Burnopfield soon found themselves in difficulty, a wicket each for the veteran Barry Stewart and Newcastle United midfielder Sean Longstaff had them 8 for 2. Stewart was forced off with an arm/shoulder injury after bowling the third ball of his second over in a blow to Tynemouth. Longstaff would go on to bowl 15 consecutive overs at one end, at times showing genuine pace, as he collected four wickets, the highlight of which was a smart caught and bowled but despite reducing Burnopfield to 89 for 5, they couldn't separate opener Ben McKinney and Dan Hogg as Burnopfield went on to win by 5 wickets. McKinney finished on 92 not out from 91 balls, with 8 fours and 5 sixes, this was his 13th NEPL half century, Hogg was 27 not out at the other end. Longstaff finished with 4 for 39 and Stewart 1 for 4. Burnopfield 23 points, Tynemouth 3 points.

The balance between bat and ball had now swung in favour of the bowlers; the red ball and damp wickets saw three bowlers take five wickets or more this week and no centuries. The league table now sees Burnmoor with a 14-point lead over Sunderland, Tynemouth in third place.

Saturday 8th June 2024

Benwell Hill at home to Sunderland sees Hill struggling with the bat as the visitors look like a side very much on the up. Sunderland won the toss and elected to field. At first glance the Benwell Hill scorecard looks like they had put their recent batting troubles behind them as they scored a healthy 227 for 8 from 58 overs, a close inspection however shows that veteran Adam Heather, back opening the batting again, scored 68, his 50th NEPL half century, Yash Kothari scored the second century of his very short NEPL career, 130 not out. He had also made 102 not out in a cup game during the week! Heather's innings came from 154 balls and contained 8 fours, Kothari faced 145 balls and struck 12 fours and 2 sixes. No other Benwell Hill batsman made double figures. Sunderland's wicket takers were Kieran Waterson 1 for 30, George Drissell 3 for 45 and Joe Stuart 4 for 68.

When Sunderland batted, they lost both openers with just 4 on the board, and another at 24, but 104 not out from George Drissell and 57 from Chris Youldon and 50 not out from Greg Applegarth was enough to get Sunderland home comfortably with just over 10 overs to spare. This was Drissell's first NEPL century and the innings came from 116 balls and contained 13 fours and 1 six. Chris Youldon faced 64 balls for his 57 runs, and he struck 10 fours in his innings, this was his 5th NEPL half century. Greg Applegarth made his 7th NEPL half century, his innings came from 52 balls with 8 fours and 1 six, the six being struck to win the match and bring up his half century in style. One wicket for Callum Harding, 1 for 48, and 2 for Luke Mussett, 2 for 65 for Hill. For their 7-wicket win, Sunderland got 25 points, Benwell Hill 3 points in the loss.

Burnopfield at home to Tynedale is an intriguing game, there is no doubting the quality Burnopfield have, and Tynedale have put their rocky start behind them to get three wins in a row. Burnopfield won the toss and elected to field. The fragility in Tynedale's batting returned again this week as they quickly tumbled to 17 for 4, Matthew Oswell picking up 3 early wickets and Harry Lumsden 1, but as in recent weeks, Tynedale will fight together and dig in for each other and the middle order, led by 32 from Jamie Crichton, all made double figures as they at least got something to bowl at, 129 all out. Oswell finished with 4 for 31, Lumsden 1 for 30, Finlay McGurk 2 for 26 and Amaan Ulhaq 3 for 14 the wicket takers for Burnopfield.

An opening stand of 47 between Callum Brown and Ben McKinney more or less assured the home side the win, an unbeaten 50 from Ross Whitfield Jnr definitely did. This was Whitfield's 7th NEPL half century, his innings, exactly 50, came from 33 balls and contained 6 fours and 2 sixes.

Struggling Castle Eden at home to Burnmoor was always going to be a tough one for the home side, Burnmoor now the NEPL'S only unbeaten side. This game was not digitally scored and therefore is based on scorecard info only, the visitors winning the toss and electing to field. Their opening bowlers were soon among the home batsmen as Waqas Maqsood and Josh Coughlin both picked up an opening batsmen each early on and things didn't really improve much for the home side as only Muhaymen Majeed, with 36, and Chris Tudball with 28, made double figures as they were bowled out for 126 in 46 overs. Each of the Burnmoor bowlers got at least one wicket, Maqsood 1 for 26, Josh Coughlin 1 for 19, Graeme Bridge 3 for 28, Mitch Killeen 2 for 7, Craig Stephenson 2 for 10 and Ryan Pringle 1 for 15.

Despite losing Ross Greenwell for 26, Marcus Brown for 11 and Mitch Killeen run out without facing a ball, Ryan Pringle made 57 not out and Stu Poynter continued his good early season form with 32 not out to see Burnmoor home by 7 wickets. This was Pringle's 25th NEPL half century as Burnmoor collected 23 point and Castle Eden 2 points.

Chester le Street hosted Newcastle at Ropery Lane, both sides capable of winning this one as they strive for consistency. Chester le Street won the toss and elected to field. Newcastle's scorecard shows a lot of double figure partnerships without one going on to make a game changing difference, Jaques du Toit top scored with 55, his 46th NEPL half century, his innings had come from 50 balls with 6 fours and 3 sixes. Newcastle made 191 for 9 from 58 overs. For Chester there were wickets for Quentin Hughes, 1 for 33, Ash Thorpe 3 for 45, Mark Watson 3 for 58 and Seb Hughes-Pinan 2 for 47.

When Chester le Street batted opener John Coxon reached 7,000 NEPL runs when he had scored 27, as he and Jacob McCann had put on 82 for the first wicket. The fall of McCann to du Toit, a rare failure for Andrew Smith and the demise of Coxon, both to Levi Olver, all in the space of 4 runs saw a stutter from the home side. When Olver picked up Charlie Purdon with the score on 91, the stutter had become more pronounceable! Captain James Thompson had come in at four and he played the key innings of the game, going on to make 61 not out as he guided his side to victory. His innings had come from 113 balls and contained 6 fours; this was his 19th NEPL half century. He was well supported by 31 from Cole Pearce and the obligatory not out, for 9 in this case, from Quentin Hughes, as Chester won by 4 wickets with 7 balls to spare. Newcastle's wicket takers were George Darwood 2 for 61, Jaques du Toit 1 for 32 and Levi Olver 3 for 29. Chester received 25 points for a hard-fought win, Newcastle 5 points for their efforts.

A Felling side that is looking for some improved batting, hosted an Ashington side that is going well, bouncing back in a tight game last week following their first loss the week before. Felling won the toss and, showing faith in their batting line up, bucked the trend of every toss winning side in the last three weeks, elected to bat! Ashington's pro Jeremiah Louis put the bat first theory to the test as he removed both openers with the score on 15, but a stand of 106 between Felling's pro Jordan Watson and Alasdair Appleby restored the faith in the home wicket. Appleby was caught by Adam Nichol off Ben Harmison for 48. Any hopes Ashington had of making inroads into the Felling batsmen were soon dispelled as Watson continued on to his first NEPL century, finishing 151 not out, and Seb Allison hit 81 not out at better than a run a ball. Watson's innings came from 145 balls and contained 21 fours and 3 sixes and Allison's innings from 71 balls with 2 fours and 6 sixes. The pair added an unbroken 179 for the fourth wicket as Felling posted 300 for 3 from just 50 overs. Louis finished with 2 for 39 and Ben Harmison 1 for 45 as Ashington's only wicket takers.

When Ashington batted Jeremiah Louis top scored with 54 from 35 balls as he took the attack to Felling, despite 42 from Scott Pearcey and 23 from Ben Harmison, I'm not sure Ashington were ever on pace to chase down 300. Louis's 54 came from 35 balls and contained 7 fours and 2 sixes, it was his 2nd NEPL half century and when Ben Harmison reached 16 this was his 2000th NEPL run. With at least one wicket for each of their six bowlers Felling won by 104 runs, Ashington being dismissed for a creditable 196 from 47.3 overs.

The bowling figures show Seb Allison 3 for 30, Paul Leonard 2 for 33, Elliot Fox 1 for 24, Ishaq Khan 2 for 37, Alasdair Appleby 1 for 51 and Jamie Cairns 1 for 15. Felling 30 points, Ashington 4 points.

Roseworth Terrace is the NEPL ground closest to my home and it's often the choice with the camera for that reason, however, I saw South North hosting Tynemouth as an interesting fixture for a number of reasons. After an uncharacteristic start to the season, with two losses and a tie in their last three NEPL games, I saw South North seemingly get back on track last Sunday as they beat Norton by 122 runs in the ECB cup. That said, they were 25 for 3 and it took a stand of 161, Chris Hewison 154, and Sean Tindale, 54, to get them to a strong position. I saw Tynemouth lose their unbeaten record to Burnopfield last week and I think this game is a good one to see exactly where Tynemouth fit into this season, title challengers or middle of the pack?

Hosts South North won the toss and elected to field, their opening bowlers, Tom Rogers and Sean Tindale, provided a thorough examination of the visitor's top order, using the short ball to good effect, Tindale having Ben Debnam caught behind by Rob Peyton for 6 with the score on 13. When Rogers struck youngster Robbie Bowman on the helmet, leading to him retiring hurt, Tynemouth were 16 for 1 after 4.5 overs. However, whilst the bowlers were proving unwelcoming to their guests, the South North fielders were proving a bit more friendly, as one South North spectator pointed out to me, "they put five bl**** catches down in five overs," that's harsh in many respects as the difficulty of the potential catches put at least two of them in the very difficult category but given how well Stan McAlindon and Matthew Brown batted once they got past that period, I understood his frustration! The pair added 102 before they were separated when Brown got an inside onto his leg stump to a one from Tom Rogers that nipped back at him, he had made 53 from 65 balls with 6 fours. This was Brown's 31st NEPL half century. Tom Rogers then continued to hit back for South North as he removed Matt Kimmitt, Josh Moors and Joe Snowdon as Tynemouth slipped from 118 for 1 to 132 for 5 in the space of 40 balls. Robbie Bowman then "unretired hurt" and, it has to be said, showed great courage as he batted beautifully as he and McAlindon took the score to 199 before Will Alexander bowled the opener with the first ball of the 49th over. McAlindon had made 81 from 133 balls with

8 fours and 1 six, this was his first NEPL half century. Bowman went onto make his third NEPL half century, being dismissed for 69 from 67 balls, his innings contained 7 fours and 4 sixes. Some clever batting and hard running from Freddie Harrison, who made 25, and Sean Longstaff, who was 22 not out, got Tynemouth to 273 for 8 from 58 overs. South North's wicket takers were Tom Rogers 4 for 66, Sean Tindale 1 for 46, Oli McGee 1 for 39 and Will Alexander 2 for 44.

Tynemouth's opening bowlers proved just as unhospitable as their South North counterparts, Owen Gourley and Sean Longstaff removing a batsman each as South North found themselves 9 for 2 inside 16 balls. When Chris Hewison fell to a smart low catch in the covers by Freddie Harrison off the bowling of Longstaff, South North were 32 for 3. Nikhil Gorantla and Sean Tindale then set the game up nicely as they added 78 for the fourth wicket, Gorantla had scored his fourth NEPL half century, 54, when he got underneath a delivery from Matthew Brown and put one straight up in the air into the leg side for Ben Debnam to take a straightforward catch. His innings had come from 72 balls and contained 8 fours. South North were now 110 for 3 from 27 overs, however Tindale was dismissed just six runs later for 31 and Adam Cragg just two runs after that, they had now slipped to 118 for 6.

Despite losing 2 more wickets and facing some testing bowling and attacking fields, Tom Rogers with 32 not, saw South North hang on for the draw, finishing on 173 for 8 wickets from their 52 overs. Sean Longstaff had 3 for 53, Owen Gourley 1 for 4, Mtthew Brown 2 for 32 and Freddie Harrison 2 for 46. Tynemouth got 17 points and South North 9 points.

A couple of things in summary from this game, that's two weeks in a row I have seen Tynemouth, they came through today with flying colours, but a word of caution, Sean Longstaff has bowled more than a third of their overs in that time and accounted for 7 of the 13 wickets they have taken, when he resumes "work "he is going to leave a big hole to fill, a challenge to their other bowlers.

For South North, uncharacteristically dropping catches in the field, a mis-firing top order is probably a bigger headache right now, the two other games I saw them win this season, they were 25 for 3 and 25 for 4 if memory serves me right, but form is temporary, class is permanent, there are plenty of bowlers who will testify to the quality of their top order, the question is will they come good in time to defend their current NEPL title?

A bit of sunshine and drying winds during the week didn't do too much to deter captain's inviting the opposition to bat, fair play to Felling's Alan Mustard for using all of his experience to back his batsmen in the battle between bat and ball, three more centuries this week in improved batting conditions and no five wicket hauls means that there are now ten centuries to five bowlers taking five wicket hauls, an even contest between bat and ball?

Burnmoor now sit 12 points clear of Sunderland at the top of the table, with Tynemouth a further 14 points behind them. Benwell Hill in eleventh and Castle Eden in twelfth need to change their fortunes quickly before they find themselves cut off at the wrong end of the table.

Saturday 15th June 2024

Ashington hosting Newcastle was an interesting one prior to play, just six points separated these two teams, in fact six points separate six teams and nine points separate seven teams in mid to lower table! Newcastle won the toss and elected to field. An opening stand of 49 between Jack Jessop and Cam Nichols set the tone for Ashington as three of the top four made scores in the thirties and the fourth scored 23, Scott Pearcey top scoring with 37. This got them to a score of 201 all out from 54 overs, the Newcastle wicket takers were George Darwood 1 for 31, Issac Unsworth 1 for 17, Asher Hart 1 for 28, Mohsin Mukhtar 4 for 37 and Jaques du Toit, 2 for 32.

When Newcastle batted their top order couldn't find the consistency of their hosts and the quickly slipped to 17 for 3 and 47 for 4. Jaques du Toit, with his 47th NEPL half century, top scored with 53 from 43 balls with 5 fours and 3 sixes but when Ian Sharkey had him caught, Newcastle had fallen to 82 for 5 and they never quite recovered, being bowled out for 127 with the third ball of the 43rd over. Ashington had won by 74 runs and collected 28 points, Newcastle 5 points.

Unbeaten Burnmoor lead the league and visiting Chester le Street always provide difficult opposition, whoever they play, another interesting fixture. Chester le Street won the toss and elected to field.

Watson dismissed Marcus Brown with his second delivery, the second ball of the second over and when Quentin Hughes bowled Mitch Killeen with the last ball of the fifth over, Burnmoor looked to be in trouble. Opener Ross Greenwell then scored his 24th NEPL half century, making exactly 50 from 72 balls with 6 fours and 2 sixes and captain Ryan Pringle with 46 got Burnmoor back on track. Stuart Poynter, batting at five, then continued his remarkable season with his second century, he was 100 not out when Burnmoor declared on 238 for 4 wickets from 51 overs. This was Poynter's fifth NEPL century, his innings came from 75 balls with 10 fours and 5 sixes. By my reckoning Poynter has already now scored 464 runs this season at an average of 154.6! Allan Worthy was 27 not out and there were wickets for Quentin Hughes 1 for 23, Mark Watson 2 for 53 and Seb Hughes-Pinan 1 for 89.

When Chester batted, John Coxon, making his 350th NEPL appearance, was dismissed for 6 and Andrew Smith for a duck, both by Waqas Maqsood in consecutive balls, but with the score 34 for 2 the match was abandoned after just 13 overs of the innings. Maqsood had 2 for 11. Burnmoor remain unbeaten and picked up 9 points, Chester le Street got 6 points.

I decided to turn back the clock and make my first NEPL visit to Felling today. The last time I was here I was playing for Seaton Burn in the Tyneside Senior League and Madan Lal and Chris Pleasants opened the bowling for the home side! I saw the visit of Benwell Hill as a big game for both teams. Going into the game, Felling were tenth, Hill eleventh, with 32 points separating them and both professionals coming off centuries last week. Felling for the second week in a row won the toss, went against everyone else and elected to bat. An opening stand of 145 by Tyler Easton and captain Alan Mustard once again supported Mustard's decision to bat first. Mustard was caught at long off by Jake Robson off the bowling of Max Williamson for 75, this was his 28th NEPL half century and came from 94 balls with 14 fours and 2 sixes. Easton was the third wicket to fall but Felling had reached 229 by that point and a big score was looming. Easton had scored 75 from 123 balls with 9 fours, this was his 8th NEPL half century. Arguably with one eye on the weather Felling's batsmen, led by Alasdair Appleby with 43 from 41 balls, then played a succession of big shots and they were subsequently declared on 273 for 9 wickets from 51 overs. For Benwell Hill, Dan Gardiner finished with 4 for 71, Yash Kothari 4 for 60 and Max Williamson 1 for 78. Going forward, Callum Harding only bowled 3 overs for Hill due to injury and that must be a concern for the visitors.

When Benwell Hill batted Felling's Seb Allison got an early breakthrough, and they were in trouble at 57 for 5 when rain stopped play and forced the eventual abandonment. Yash Kothari had top scored with 15 but Allison 3 for 25 and Paul Leonard 2 for 20 had given Felling every chance of going on to take the win. Felling 11 points, Benwell Hill 9 points.

Going into this week and next, Sunderland, who currently sit second in the table, had one or two availability issues, today's visitors, Burnopfield with their powerful batting line up, always have the potential to be problematic. Sunderland won the toss and elected to field. Burnopfield openers Callum Brown and Matthew Oswell put on 56 for the first wicket, Brown dismissed for 27, Oswell went on to top score the innings with 46, further support from John Oswell 40, Ross Whitfield Jnr 29, Max Moen 27 and 18 each from George Weston and Harry Lumsden got Burnopfield to 222 for 9 declared from 51.1 overs. Kieran Waterson continues to take wickets for Sunderland, finishing with 4 for 71, the other wicket takers, Phillip Smith, 3 for 23, Micky Allan 1 for 49 and Joe Stuart 1 for 67.

When Sunderland batted the threatened poor weather duly arrived with Sunderland sitting at 57 for 1 from 12.5 overs, Dan Shurben was 19 not out and George Fishwick 10 not out, Callum Brown had the one wicket to fall, 1 for 17. Both teams got 9 points from a finely balanced match which could have had a good finish!

Just five points separated Tynedale and their visitors today, South North, a big weekend all round for South North with an ECB cup match on Sunday as well as this one. South North followed the expected pattern and invited Tynedale to bat. Coach Tom Rogers quickly had three wickets and Jonny Wightman, refreshed from his holidays, picked up another as Tynedale found themselves 14 for 4. A series of small partnerships and a stand of 40 between Aaron Rourke and Matt Scott got them to 93 for 8 and then Rourke and Nathan Byerley added a further 37 as Tynedale fought hard for any kind of total. Rourke was eventually out for 40, Byerley made 30 and Scott had 11 as Tynedale were bowled out for 144 from 33.5 overs. For South North Sean Tindale finished with 4 for 44, Tom Rogers 3 for 21, Wightman 1 for 44 and Oli McGee 1 for 21.

When South North batted, with one eye on the weather and a re-jigged batting order, they also found it hard against the new ball. Matt Scott, after going for 17 in his first over, then made life awkward for the visitors, taking 2 wickets in his second over as he picked up 3 wickets and South North found themselves 42 for 3. Opener Sol Bell ended up 49 not out, scored from 39 balls with 9 fours and 1 six and England Over 40's batsman Simon Birtwisle hit 75 from just 38 balls with 16 fours and 1 six as South North went on to win by 6 wickets, scoring the required runs to finish on 148 for 4 from 16 overs. This was Birtwisle's 67th NEPL half century. Scott finished with 3 for 50 and Nkosana Mpofu took the other wicket, 1 for 12. South North picked up 23 points for beating the weather, Tynedale 2 points.

The weather ruined their ECB game on the Sunday, 38.5 overs only were possible with Woodlands CC 199 for 9, 5 wickets for Jonny Wightman but the Yorkshire side having to come back next week following the abandonment due to rain.

Third placed Tynemouth were looking to maintain their strong start to the season as Castle Eden looked to get their season back on track. As it turned out, this game was an epic in itself and I'm pretty sure I can't do it justice here! The game saw Tynemouth's Joe Snowdon make his 50th NEPL appearance.

Tynemouth won the toss and elected to field, and despite a wicket in the second over Castle Eden put together a series of partnerships, six of their batsmen making double figures and led by 64 from Nicholas Sampson-Barnes, made a good score of 206 all out in 55.2 overs. This was Sampson-Barnes second NEPL half century, and his highest NEPL score to date, his innings came from 74 balls and contained 7 fours and 2 sixes. For Tynemouth, Matthew Brown, making his 250th NEPL appearance, finished with 3 for 34, Martin Pollard had 1 for 25, Josh Moors 2 for 50 and Freddie Harrison 4 for 49.

When Brown caught Muhaymen Majeed off the bowling of Martin Pollard for 27, that was his 200th NEPL catch.

Tynemouth made a steady start in their reply, despite losing a wicket with the score on 23, they were 43 when the next wicket fell, they lost two more by the time they were 45 as they stumbled to 45 for 4, Keith Bailey with 1 wicket and Nicholas Sampson-Barnes continuing his good day with 2 wicket more. A partnership of 47 between Matthew Brown and Josh Moors took the score to 81 for 4 at tea off 25 overs but the expected rain delayed matters for an hour, a revised score of 207 from 38 overs was then the Tynemouth target, Tynemouth 92 for 5 for 5 when Brown was dismissed for 27. Tynemouth were still attacking the bowling, looking for the extra points from a winning draw but at 122 Moors was out for 38 to Alan Unsworth with the last ball of the 31st over, Unsworth then picked up two more wickets in successive balls in the 33rd over, Tynemouth were in real danger of a heavy loss at 126 for 8. This was made worse when Bilawal Iqbal removed Joe Snowdon with the first ball of the 34th over to leave Tynemouth 126 for 9. The last pair of Andrew Smith, 4 not out, and Martin Pollard, 1 not out, faced 30 balls between them until the rain came, Tynemouth finished on 131 for 9 from 38 overs to frustrate Castle Eden and cost them a much-needed win. Tynemouth got 9 points and Castle Eden 17 points for the abandonment.

Only one captain fancied batting again this week when winning the toss, Felling's Alan Mustard, as the damp conditions and further threat of rain once again influenced the outcomes of the games, five wicket hauls still proving a rarity as one more century was added to the batting honours! Burnmoor continue unbeaten, although the weather seems to be having a good go at making sure they don't run away with anything just yet! Sunderland just 12 points behind in second place, ahead of two unexpectedly placed Northumberland teams, Ashington third and Tynemouth now fourth, South North back on track with a win this week, now fifth, 27 points behind Burnmoor. At the wrong end of the table, Castle Eden's strong effort at Tynemouth sees them climb above Benwell Hill by 4 points.

Saturday 22nd June 2024

Ashington played hosts to Benwell Hill today, the home side looking to maintain a strong season so far with the visitors looking up the table at everyone else. Ashington won the toss and elected to field and picked up to a steady stream of wickets to reduce the visitors to 110 for 8, Joe Anderson, with 32 on his 50th NEPL appearance the only highlight for Hill, however Dan Gardiner, batting at nine hit 20 from 38 balls and Max Williamson, batting at ten, scored 63 not out from just 43 balls with 4 fours and 3 sixes as he counterattacked his way side to a decent score of 201 for 9 from 58 overs. This was Williamson's first NEPL half century and eclipsed his previous best of 39 not out. For Ashington, the wicket takers were Jeremiah Louis, 2 for 31, Alex Nice, 3 for 22 and James Harmison 4 for 40.

When Ashington batted they quickly lost Cam Nichols for 6 with the score on 11, but a partnership of 146 for the second wicket between opener Jack Jessop and Matthew Potts put the hosts firmly in the driving seat. Potts was out for 75, his innings coming from 101 balls with 9 fours, this was just his fifth NEPL game and his first half century. Jessop was dismissed for 64, his 3rd NEPL half century, his innings came from 95 balls with 4 fours and a six. For Benwell Hill, there were wickets for Kothari 2 for 57, Dan Gardiner 2 for 24, Max Williamson 1 for 47 and Jake Robson 1 for 34. When Peter Halliday caught Sean McCafferty off the bowling of Robson, that was his 150th NEPL catch.

Ashington, who scored their 202 for 6 from 43.2 overs, won by 4 wickets and collect 26 points for their win, Benwell Hill, 3 points in the loss.

Just seven points separated hosts Burnopfield from their guests from Felling prior to this one, a tight game was expected. Burnopfield won the toss and elected to field and almost immediately must have been happy with the decision as two wickets for Harry Lumsden and one for Matt Oswell reduced Felling to 21 for 3. The Felling middle order of Alasdair Appleby, 47, Seb Allison, 29, and Ed Hurst with 24, plus 18 in just 17 balls from Paul Leonard batting at eight, got them to 157 all out from 32.2 overs. Amaan Ulhaq with 6 for 31 was the main problem for the Felling batsmen, with wickets for Matt Oswell, 1 for 23, Harry Lumsden 2 for 17 and Finlay McGurk 1 for 47.

When Burnopfield batted their batsmen also found life difficult, only Ross Whitfield Jnr with 70 made double figures as they were bowled out for 125 in 43 overs. This was Whitfield's 4th NEPL half century and his innings came from 97 balls with 8 fours and 1 six. There were wickets for Seb Allison, 1 for 23, Alasdair Appleby 3 for 46, Paul Leonard 4 for 21 and Elliot Fox 2 for 12. When Appleby had Matt Oswell caught by Jordan Watson, that was his 100th NEPL wicket. Felling picked up 24 points for the win and Burnopfield 5 points.

After a good all round team performance last week Castle Eden were looking to get the better of a Tynedale side which arrived 24 points and one place above them in the table. Castle Eden won the toss and elected to field and were soon in the game, opening bowlers Bilawal Iqbal with two wickets and Keith Bailey with one, reducing the visitors to 26 for 3. Jonathan Malkin had been brought on as early as the eighth over and remarkably he went on to take the next seven Tynedale wickets, finishing with the figures of 9 overs, 4 maidens, he conceded 14 runs for his 7 wickets. Iqbal finished with 2 for 25 and Bailey 1 for 6 as Tynedale were dismissed for 61 from 24 overs.

When Castle Eden batted Malkin's good day continued as he made 34 not out opening the batting, his fellow opener, with Ben Simpson 28 not out the hosts won by ten wickets in 8.3 overs. Castle Eden got 22 points for the win, Tynedale got nothing and the gap between the two sides was now closed to just two points at tenth and eleventh in the table.

Chester le Street's visit by Tynemouth saw two teams square off whose games, albeit in very different circumstances, were both affected by the rain last week. Chester le Street won the toss and elected to field and quickly picked up danger man Stan McAlindon for 3, bowled by Liam Simpson. Robbie Bowman, with his 4th NEPL half century, top scored the innings with 67 from 123 balls with 5 fours and a six, and he found good support from Matt Brown 36, Marcus Turner 26 and Josh Moors 24, as Tynemouth reached 206 all out from 55.3 overs. Liam Simpson finished with 1 for 28, Mark Watson 1 for 32 and Seb Hughes-Pinan 2 for 62, but it was the veteran Ash Thorpe who had stolen the limelight with the ball, with 6 for 46, this takes him to 188 NEPL wickets in his career.

When Chester le Street batted John Coxon 102 not out from 138 balls with 16 fours, his eight NEPL century and Jacob McCann 100 not out from 121 balls, with 14 fours, his fourth NEPL century, saw them home by ten wickets, Coxon hitting a boundary off the last ball of the 43rd over to secure the win and his century. Chester get 26 points for the win and Tynemouth 3 for the loss.

Newcastle hosting unbeaten Burnmoor was my choice with the camera this week and I saw a good game of cricket, over 400 runs scored and some big shots from both sides. Burnmoor won the toss and elected to field, Newcastle had opened with a steady partnership of 47 when Ben Robinson hit one straight up into the air from Maqsood and was caught for 9. A third wicket stand of 57 between Bobby Green and Mohsin Mukhtar took Newcastle to 115 when Green was leg before to the spin of Craig Stephenson for 68, this was his 7th NEPL half century, the innings coming from 107 balls with 9 fours. Newcastle then stumbled to 126 for 5 and then 166 for 7 when Mukhtar was out for 41, but a boundary and 4 sixes in one over from Hamzah Amin, who made 34, got Newcastle to 220 for 8 wickets from 58 overs. Maqsood took 3 for 46, Josh Coughlin 1 for 40, Mitch Killeen 2 for 29 and Craig Stephenson 2 for 58 were Burnmoor's wicket takers.

When Burnmoor batted their top order, despite an early loss of Ross Greenwell for 7, had set about their business in a professional manner. Mitch Killeen at three, had made 53 from 74 balls with 8 fours, his 4th NEPL half century as he continues to mature with bat and ball, when he was dismissed with the score on 97. When opener Marcus Brown was bowled by George Darwood for 37, they were still in a strong position at 135 for 3. Veteran Allan Worthy was hampered by a hand injury picked up when he was fielding and he was out for 4 and with Paul Craig making just a single they could have been in a little trouble, but Ryan Pringle was in a very destructive mood, some clean hitting and very big shots as he made 67 from just 32 balls with 8 fours and 4 sixes. When Pringle was also bowled by Darwood, Burnmoor still required 35 to win but 21 not out from Josh Coughlin and 16 not out from Waqas Maqsood saw them home by 4 wickets in 45.2 overs to collect the win and 25 points. Newcastle got 4 points. George Darwood had 4 for 74, Asher Hart 1 for 20 and Jaques du Toit 1 for 37.

Fifth placed South North at home to second placed Sunderland was a tempting fixture for the neutral, a strong showing by the reigning champions last week up against a well-balanced Sunderland side this week. South North won the toss and completed the set of those winning the toss electing to field. Tom Rogers bowled George Fishwick early on for 5 but Sunderland were going steady at 29 for 1 when Dan Shurben was adjudged caught behind off the bowling of Rogers for 11, this sparked off a collapse as Rogers and Sean Tindale, apparently both bowling at a good pace, picked up 9 wickets between them and Sunderland were dismissed for 74 from 29 overs. Only Jack Brassell with 19 and joined Shurben in double figures, Rogers finished with 4 for 25, Tindale 5 for 21 and Oli McGee nipped in for 1 for 7.

When South North batted two wickets in successive balls for Jack Brassell with the score on 38 offered him, and Sunderland, a little comfort, but 41 not out from Sol Bell was enough to see South North win by 8 wickets and collect 22 points, Sunderland getting nothing for their day.

In summary, another week where Burnmoor maintain their unbeaten start and Castle Eden stir the pot at the other end of the table, the winning captains all elected to field, again, and two centuries, both in the same match and three 5 wicket hauls. This weekend also saw the start of the NEPL 100 competition, replacing the Banks Salver, personally I have never seen a "100" game at any level but I will update the final at a later date!

South North lost their ECB cup game on the Sunday, 124 all out was never going to be enough against a strong Woodlands batting line up and so the region's national ambitions are over following Benwell Hill's demise in the earlier round.

Saturday 29th June 2024

Benwell Hill welcomed Burnopfield to Denton Bank looking for an upturn in their fortunes, Burnopfield won the toss and elected to field. Hill made a steady start, making 39 for the first wicket between Arun Phogat and Adam Heather, when Phogat was bowled for 15 by Finlay McGurk. Yash Kothari came to the crease and he and Heather put on 147 for the second wicket, Heather with his 51st NEPL half century, having scored 50 from 104 balls with 5 boundaries when he retired hurt. Kothari went on to his 2nd NEPL half century, making 87 from 99 balls with 11 fours, Joe Anderson then scored 51 from 66 balls with 4 fours and a six, his 4th NEPL half century, Max Williamson 30 and Rory Mustard 13 not out then got Hill to a challenging 271 for 4 from 58 overs. Matt Oswell had 1 for 38, Harry Lumsden 1 for 62, Finlay McGurk 1 for 63 and Amaan Ulhaq 1 for 83.

When Burnopfield batted they made surprisingly short work of such a good score, an opening stand of 110 between Matt Oswell and Ben McKinney got them underway. When McKinney was out for 57, his 14th NEPL half century, the innings coming from 61 balls with 7 fours and a six, Ross Whitfield Jnr then came to the crease and he and Oswell added a further 83 for the second wicket. Oswell had struck 9 fours in his 87, the innings coming from 120 balls, this was his 5th NEPL half century. Whitfield had completed his 9th NEPL half century when he was dismissed for 54, his innings coming from 51 balls and containing 7 fours and a six, the score was now 223 for 3. A typically belligerent 34 not out from 28 balls with 3 fours and a six from John Oswell and 35 not out from just 23 balls, with 7 fours, from Tom Hazell-Evans saw Burnopfield, 273 for 3, win by 7 wickets, getting the runs in just 47.1 overs. Kothari, with both openers, had 2 for 69 and Luke Mussett, 1 for 70, were the wicket takers as Burnopfield collected 23 points and Benwell Hill 5 points.

A top of the table clash at unbeaten Burnmoor today as they hosted second place Ashington. Mixed news in the buildup for the visitors as pro Jeremiah Louis has been called into the West Indian touring side to face England this summer and he will miss this game and all of July because of this. On the positive side Ashington, and by default, the NEPL, could have two players in the series going head-to-head as Mark Wood is expected to play for England and he is also registered to the club!

Burnmoor won the toss and elected to field and very quickly got their rewards as Waqas Masood took three early wickets to have Ashington on 9 for 3. Opener Jack Jessop and Scott Pearcey led the visitors fightback, Jessop going for 25 and Pearcey making his first NEPL half century, 51 from 75 balls with 7 fours. It was Ben Harmison, with his 14th NEPL half century, who went on to score 76 from 84 balls with 8 fours and a six, who made sure Ashington got to a decent total, eventually being all out for 202 in 57.4 overs. Maqsood finished with 4 for 31, the other Burnmoor wicket takers being Josh Coughlin, 2 for 64, Graeme Bridge 1 for 17 and Craig Stephenson 1 for 14.

Burnmoor once again showed why they are still unbeaten when they batted, opener Ross Greenwell finished on 75 not out from 121 balls with 8 fours, his 25th NEPL half century, when he had scored 31, this was his 4,000th NEPL run, Marcus Brown had 26, Ryan Pringle 41 and Mitch Killeen had made 57, his 5th NEPL half century, his innings had come from 65 balls with 7 fours and when he scored his 11th run that took him to 1,000 NEPL runs, Stu Poynter was 5 not out as they reached 206 for 3 from just 45.5 overs for a seven wicket win. For the visitors a wicket each for Alex Nice, 1 for 52, Cam Nichols, 1 for 52 and James Harmison 1 for 60, as Burnmoor picked up 26 points and Ashington 3 points.

Felling at home to South North at High Heworth was an interesting one going into it, South North winning the toss and electing to field. A series of 20+ partnerships and then a couple of quick wickets saw Felling at 72 for 4 and a scorecard which could go either way, fortunately for Felling Alasdair Appleby, 58, and Joe Carroll 31 got them to a defendable score of 175 all out from 47.5 overs. This was Appleby's 12th NEPL half century, his innings coming from 65 balls with 5 fours and 4 sixes. For South North, Oli McGee had 5 for 38, Sean Tindale 2 for 41, Will Alexander 1 for 12, Lee Crozier 1 for 38 and Tom Rogers 1 for 31.

When South North batted the veteran Paul Leonard removed both openers as they battled to 32 for 2, slipping to 53 for 4, as Leonard bagged another wicket and Ishaq Khan trapped Nik Gorantla for 25. This would prove to be the top score of the innings as Alasdair Appleby's good day continued with three wickets and South North were bowled out for 113 in 37.4 overs. All five Felling bowlers took at least one wicket, Leonard and Appleby both finishing with 3 for 18, Elliot Fox 2 for 28, Seb Allison 1 for 23 and Ishaq Khan 1 for 16. Felling won by 62 runs and collected 25 points, South North 4 points.

Sunderland were looking to move on after last week's loss and were at home to a Castle Eden side seemingly on the up, Sunderland won the toss and elected to field. Despite the top four all making a good start, Jon Malkin 32, Ben Simpson 24, Muhaymen Majeed 26 and J. P Meade 34, only one other player made double figures and Castle Eden were bowled out for 159 in 51.5 overs. For Sunderland Jack Brassell had 2 for 22, Kieran Waterson 1 for 10, Micky Allan 1 for 39, Joe Stuart 3 for 40 and George Drissell 2 for 27.

The Sunderland batsmen quickly set about their work, Dan Shurben leading the charge with 80 from 81 balls, this was his 52nd NEPL half century and contained 12 fours and 2 sixes, George Fishwick, 53 not out from 82 balls with 5 fours and a six, made his maiden NEPL half century. With George Drissell 21 not out, Sunderland, 162 for 1 from 28 overs, had won by 9 wickets and collected 24 points, Castle Eden, got 2 points.

Tynedale hosting Chester le Street was potentially a nervous one for the home side after both Chester openers posted unbeaten centuries last week, but they still took the challenge on, winning the toss and asking Chester to bat first. John Coxon and Jacob McCann looked like their good form was continuing with an opening partnership of 62 at just over five an over, Coxon the first to go, caught by Jamie Crichton off the bowling of Mathew Scott for 21. McCann went on to top score the innings with his 20th NEPL half century, finishing with 59 from 51 balls with 9 fours and 2 sixes. With good support from James Thompson, 38, and Ash Thorpe 23 not out, Chester reached 212 all out from 51.4 overs. When Ash Thorpe reached 7, that was his 5,000th NEPL run. Only one of Tynedale's bowlers failed to collect a wicket, Tom Cant 4 for 24 the best of them, with wickets for Aaron Rourke, 3 for 54, Nkosana Mpofu 1 for 7, Seth Robbie 1 for 27 and Matthew Scott 1 for 67.

Tynedale made a disastrous start, losing a wicket to the second ball of the innings, to the wily veteran, Quentin Hughes, they stuttered to 21 for 3, before a partnership of 40 got them back into the game, Joe Barber, 39, and Euan Stephenson 45, were the main scorers for Tynedale but they never really challenged Chester's score, a last wicket partnership of 37 taking them to 143 all out in 47.5 overs. Quentin Hughes caused more problems as he finished with 4 for 22, there was 3 wickets for Mark Watson at a cost of 32, Seb Hughes-Pinan took 2 for 42 and Liam Simpson, 1 for 8. Chester le Street 26 points, Tynedale 5 points.

Tynemouth at home to Newcastle saw both teams looking to bounce back after a loss last week. The home side celebrated the official naming of their new pavilion terrace today, The Duncan Nisbet Terrace was duly opened at lunch, and I attended this one with the camera after an early season promise to Tynemouth's Vince Howe. Newcastle, in keeping with every other side which won the toss this week, elected to field, since we moved to red ball cricket every captain who wins the toss, except Felling at home, twice, has elected to field. A nice opening partnership of 56 between Ben Debnam and Stan McAlindon gave Tynemouth a steady start, Debnam the first to go, leg before to Rowan Shelton for 17. McAlindon and Robbie Bowman had added a further 54 when Bowman was out for 32, 110 for 2 and another 50 plus partnership between McAlindon and Matthew Brown took them to 166, when Brown flat batted a lovely pull shot straight to the only man on a huge leg side boundary for 31. A rare failure today and then McAlindon dismissed for 84 from 118 balls with 10 fours, his second NEPL half century. The innings was arguably now in the balance at 190 for 5, step forward young Australian Josh Moors, he hit 100 from 53 balls, with 12 fours and 4 sixes, a couple of the sixes going over my head, bouncing on the road and into the rugby field! This was his 2nd NEPL century and in just his 7th game in the league. Tynemouth declared on 304 for 7 after 53 overs, Rowan Shelton had 3 for 53, Jaques du Toit 2 for 40, Mohsin Mukhtar 1 for 45 and Matt Stewart 1 for 58.

Newcastle made a good start in reply, Bobby Green and Ben Robinson with an opening stand of 58, Robinson adjudged leg before to Matt Brown for 27. Green then fell leg before to Martin Pollard for 30 with the score on 80, and the key partnership of Asher Hart and Jaques du Toit were together for Newcastle. The pair added 55 when du Toit, for 27, became the third visiting batsmen to go leg before, Freddie Harrison the successful bowler this time. Hart went on to make 79 from 96 balls with 11 fours, his 7th NEPL half century but with two more leg before's the accurate home bowling saw Newcastle bowled out for 202 in 45.1 overs, Harrison finished with 4 for 43, Josh Moors added to a good day with 3 for 31, Martin Pollard 2 for 42and Matt Brown 1 for 41. Tynemouth a healthy 30 points for the win and Newcastle 7 points in defeat.

Burnmoor now sit on 188 points, 39 clear of Sunderland in second, there are six teams separated by just 13 points behind them, down to South North in seventh with 136, Benwell Hill 20 points adrift of Castle Eden's 84 points at the wrong end of the table, Tynedale hovering a further two points ahead of them.

Saturday 6th July 2024

Third placed Ashington were at home to the potentially dangerous Burnopfield batting line up this week, Ashington won the toss and elected to field. I had planned all week to go to this one with my camera, but a dodgy weather forecast led to me trying to second guess the weathermen and going elsewhere at the last minute. It was a mistake; this was the only fixture of the day to get a completed game of cricket.

Burnopfield were in trouble almost immediately at 6 for 3 and then 15 for 4, Alex Nice with three wickets and Cam Nichols with one, it took 25 not out from Harry Lumsden, batting at ten, to get Burnopfield to 85 all out from 27. 2 overs. Nice went on to claim 5 for 33, Nichols, 1 for 32, Ian Sharkey took 1 for 11, Ben Harmison had 1 for 6 and James Harmison had 2 for 3.

When Ashington batted, an opening stand of 35 and then a second wicket stand of 31, both anchored by Jack Jessop, meant that the win was assured if they could beat the weather, they duly did, 89 for 4 from 21.4 overs, Jessop was 38 not out. There were wickets for Matt Oswell, 1 for 32, Finlay McGurk 1 for 21 and Amaan Ulhaq, 2 for 13 as Ashington won by 6 wickets and collected 22 points, Burnopfield got a solitary point.

Benwell Hill would be looking to pro Yash Kothari again this week as they continue their improvement with the bat against an out of sorts South North batting line up, more news from South North when it was announced on

Thursday that coach Tom Rogers was joining Kent Spitfires for the remainder of the T20 Blast, and it remains to be seen how that will impact them. South North won the toss, and in a rarity amongst all winning captains, decided to bat first, almost all of their batsmen got some kind of a start with Sean Tindale, 44, leading the way as they were 162 for 7 from 37.4 overs when the game was abandoned. For Hill, Callum Harding took 4 for 44, Luke Mussett 1 for 31, Dan Gardiner had 1 for 34 and Prahalad Nadella 1 for 26. When Harding had Simon Birtwisle caught by Haydon Mustard, that was his 350th wicket in the NEPL, this game also marked the 150th NEPL appearance by Pete Halliday.

Felling, always strong, especially with the bat at High Heworth, hosted Castle Eden, won the toss and possibly with one eye on the weather and unusually for them at home, elected to field. Opener Jonathan Malkin, 43, and number three Muhaymen Majeed, 31 not out and J.P Meade, 35 not out, had Castle Eden well placed on 123 for 2 from 33 overs when this one was abandoned. Paul Leonard, 1 for 39, and Elliot Fox, 1 for 35, were Felling's wicket takers. Both sides collected five points for their efforts.

Ninth placed Newcastle hosting tenth placed Tynedale at Jesmond was a big game for both teams this week, Tynedale won the toss and elected. After a disastrous start at 7 for 3, Newcastle went on to make 215 all out from 46.1 overs, Asher Hart scored his 8th NEPL half century, 55 at a run a ball with 6 fours and 3 sixes and Rowan Shelton made 69, his 2nd NEPL half century and highest NEPL score to date, his innings coming from 92 balls and containing 7 fours. For Tynedale there were wickets for Matthew Scott, 2 for 60, Archie Fletcher 5 for 52 and Thomas Cant 3 for 39. Fellow photographer Ken Waller was at this one and he assures me that the field was under water in places in no time at all when the heavens did open on this one, game abandoned before Tynedale faced a ball, both sides getting 9 points.

Sunderland, sitting second in the table entertained fourth placed Chester le Street at Ashbrooke, the hosts winning the toss and electing to field, for the second time in just a few weeks Sunderland's strong batting lineup was underachieving when the game was abandoned with them on 74 for 8 from 42 overs, Liam Simpson had 5 for 30, Seb Hughes-Pinan 2 for 4 and Quentin Hughes 1 for 29. Chester got 8 points and Sunderland 5 points.

I decided to attend Tynemouth hosting Burnmoor with my camera after a long look at the weather forecast, I thought I would have another look at potential champions Burnmoor as they defended their unbeaten record at Preston Avenue. The visitors won the toss and elected to field and a smart low catch to his right from Alec Linsley off the bowling of Waqas Maqsood, gave them a good start. This was followed by Allan Worthy rolling back the years to take a slightly less graceful catch at fly slip/short third man and Tynemouth were suddenly 15 for 2, this became 20 for 3 and 28 for 4 as Maqsood and Josh Coughlin picked up two wickets each. A further wicket for Maqsood and then two in two balls from Graeme Bridge had the visitors smelling blood, but Matthew Kimmitt with 37 not out and Barry Stewart with 27 not out, added an unbroken stand of 53 when the weather finally won the day after 35 overs. Maqsood finished with 3 for 35, Coughlin 2 for 23 and Bridge 2 for 23, no wicket for Craig Stephenson on his 100th NEPL appearance as Burnmoor collected 8 points and Tynemouth 5 points.

The wet conditions seemed to help the bowlers out this week, three of them taking 5 wickets in the innings and no batsman anywhere near a hundred this week, 12 centuries and 10 five wicket hauls so far in the season. At the top of the table, Burnmoor remain unbeaten at the halfway point, Ashington reap the benefits of getting an early win this weekend, now second, 28 points behind. Eleven points cover Sunderland in third down to South North in seventh, no change at the bottom for Benwell Hill.

Saturday 13th July 2024

The entire fixture list was washed out this week, not surprising given the amount of rain that fell! The fixtures should have been-

Burnmoor v Tynedale
Castle Eden v Benwell Hill
Chester le Street v Felling
Newcastle v Sunderland
South North v Burnopfield
Tynemouth v Ashington

Saturday 20th July 2024

Ashington ran South North very close in both games last season, and would no doubt see today's game at Langwell Crescent as a good test of where they are as a team. South North won the toss and elected to bat. They were soon in familiar territory for this season, 7 for 2, although opener Simon Birtwisle, 21, and Chris Hewison, 23, got them back on track, they both departed within 3 runs of each other and 54 for 4 meant that the innings was once gain in trouble and they fell away to 88 for 8. 12 Sean Tindale, who was batting at five, hit is third NEPL half century of the season, and the 12th NEPL half century of his career as he made 80, the innings coming from 107 balls with 2 fours and 4 sixes. He was supported by Jonny Wightman who made 21 as South North were eventually bowled out for 181 in 54.1 overs. For Ashington there was wickets for Matt Collins, 1 for 33, Alex Nice, 2 for 47, Ben Harmison 3 for 14, James Harmison 1 for 43 and Ian Sharkey 1 for 18.

When Ashington batted only opener Adam Nichol didn't make double figures, Jack Jessop had 24, Cam Nichols made 50, his maiden NEPL half century, from 57 balls with 10 fours, Jack McCarthy in his 50th NEPL game made his maiden NEPL half century, 63 not out from 117 balls with 7 fours, and Ben Harmison was 38 not out. Ashington 184 for 3 from 40 overs had won by 7 wickets and picked up 25 points, South North got 3 points.

I chose this one with the camera today as Benwell Hill hosted Chester le Street, I haven't seen the visitor's this season and I needed a team photo of them! Benwell Hill won the toss and elected to field. A steady opening partnership of 33 and the second wicket, John Coxon holing out for 34 when the score was 99, meant this one was in the balance. Andrew Smith, who was bowled off a no-ball at the very start of his innings, and James Thompson made sure Chester got a big score and took the game away from their hosts. Smith scored his 23rd NEPL century, when he reached 72, which he did with a six, he scored his 11,000th NEPL run, he went on to make 162 from 114 balls with 17 fours and 6 sixes, Thompson made 51, his 20th NEPL half century in his 150th NEPL innings, his runs came from 62 balls with 5 fours and a six. Chester declared on 319 for 7 from 50 overs, there were wickets for Callum Harding, 1 for 64, Yash Kothari 3 for 78, Luke Mussett 2 for 72 and Max Williamson 1 for 34.

Rory Hanley and Adam Heather started the innings with an opening stand of 65, Hanley the unlucky bowler with the no-ball earlier, had a spot of luck of his own when batting, the ball struck the bails, which lifted and then dropped back into place, a good not out decision from visiting umpire Matt French, despite the appeals for caught behind. French is actually guesting for the second season in a row from the Sussex Premier League as he holidays in the area and does a bit of umpiring whilst here! Hanley was eventually the first wicket to fall for 25. Heather went on to make his 52nd NEPL half century, 53, from 111 balls with 8 fours. Haydon Mustard with 49 led the remaining Hill batsmen, as they comfortably hung on for the draw. Max Williamson was 29 not out as they made 210 for 6 from 60 overs. Three Chester bowlers had two wickets each, Mark Watson 2 for 34, Matt Robinson 2 for 43 and Seb Hughes-Pinan 2 for 55. Chester 16 points, Benwell Hill 9 points.

Burnopfield welcomed Castle Eden today, the hosts winning the toss and electing to bat, although they were 17 for 3 inside 7 overs, Tom Hazell-Evans with 42, Callum Brown with 31 and John Oswell, 59 ensured they got a defendable total. This was Oswell's 14th NEPL half century, his innings coming from 56 balls with 7 fours and a six. Castle Eden's bowlers shared the wickets around, Bilawal Iqbal had 3 for 49, Richard Ede 2 for 15, Charlie Scorer 2 for 63 and J.P Meade 2 for 27 as Burnopfield scored 179 all out from 43.2 overs.

When Castle Eden batted their top order found the new ball as difficult to deal with as Burnopfield, 22 for 4, Philip Wimpenny top scored with 27 and Iqbal had 23 not out but Matt Oswell 2 for 18, Harry Lumsden 1 for 19, Amaan Ulhaq had 5 for 58 and Finlay McGurk 1 for 25 saw Castle Eden bowled out for 133 from 30 overs, Burnopfield winners by 46 runs collected 25 points, Castle Eden 5 points.

Felling hosting Newcastle saw, in my opinion, two of the leagues unpredictable sides going head- to -head, both sides capable of beating anyone but seem to struggle a little with consistency. Newcastle won the toss and elected to field. Opener Tyler Easton with 30, set the tone for Felling but it was 83 from Seb Allison and 53 from veteran Paul Leonard which got Felling to 218 for 9 declared from 49.2 overs. This was Allison's 50th NEPL match and his 9 NEPL half century, the innings came from 88 balls with 11 fours and 2 sixes, Paul Leonard made his 3rd NEPL half century, his innings came from 100 balls and contained 6 fours and a six. Woody Wilson, 4 for 32, was the most successful bowler, with wickets for Mohsin Mukhtar, 1 for20, Asher Hart 1 for 21, Jaques du Toit 1 for 33 and Rowan Shelton 2 for 40.

All six Newcastle batsmen used made double figures, but it was an unbeaten 80 from Asher Hart which led Newcastle to the win, this was Hart's 4th half century of the season and the 9th of his NEPL career, he scored his runs from 98 balls with 12 fours and a six. He was supported by Mukhtar with 46 and du Toit with 39. Seb Allison completed a useful day with 3 for 33 and Ishaq Khan had 1 for 51 but Newcastle, 223 for 4 from 45 overs won by six wickets and picked up a much needed 26 points, Felling got 5 points.

Going into today's game Sunderland would be hoping to give unbeaten Burnmoor a tough test at Ashbrooke, and they did! Burnmoor won the toss and elected to field. Charlie Coulthard scored his maiden NEPL half century, in just his fifth NEPL match, as he led the way for Sunderland with 53 from 91 balls, the innings included 6 fours and a six, he was aided by Chris Youldon with 28 as Sunderland were dismissed for 146 from 57 overs. Graeme Bridge 6 for 30 was the key figure in Burnmoor's bowling effort, he was well supported by Waqas Maqsood, 2 for 37, Ryan Pringle 1 for 13 and Craig Stephenson 1 for 27.

Burnmoor found themselves on 33 for 3 as Kieran Waterson and Brett Hutchinson made life difficult for them but a partnership of 68 for the fourth wicket between Marcus Brown and Stuart Poynter had seemingly put Burnmoor on the path to victory. They were 101 for 4 when Poynter was leg before to Micky Allan for 35. Poynter passed 500 runs for the season when he scored his 31st run. There was a small scare when they lost two wickets in two balls to Micky Allan with the score on 136, but Brown was still there with 49 not out and Craig Stephenson 7 not out as Burnmoor, 147 for 7 from 28.3 overs, won by 3 wickets and pick up 23 points, Sunderland got 4 points. For Sunderland Micky Allan 3 for 34, Kieran Waterson 3 for 35 and Brett Hutchinson 1 for 35 put in a great effort but not enough runs on the board to get home.

Tynedale hosted Tynemouth in the battle of the river Tyne! The visitors won the toss and elected to field. Tom Cant top scored the innings with 36 and Oliver Fletcher had 25 but three ducks in the middle order saw Tynedale dismissed for 125 from 41.4 overs. Josh Moors continued his fine season with bat and ball as he took 6 for 34, Joe Hull-Denholm had 2 for 24 and Matt Brown had 1 for 36.

Opener Matthew Kimmitt with his third NEPL half century, and highest score to date, 82 not out from 68 balls with 11 fours and 3 sixes, saw Tynemouth win by 8 wickets. For Tynedale Archie Fletcher had 1 for 29 and Nathan Byerley 1 for 25. Tynemouth 23 points, Tynedale 1 point.

Another week in the books and another win for Burnmoor who remain unbeaten, unfamiliar faces in second and third in Ashington and Tynemouth, both clubs no doubt ruing the fact that the brilliant English summer meant that both games between the two sides were washed out without a ball bowled. Benwell Hill remain bottom, but a hard-earned draw saw them make up ground on both Castle Eden and Tynedale above them. Three bowlers taking five wickets or better and one century this week means the battle between bat and ball now sits at fifteen each!

Saturday 27th July 2024

A damp or delayed start for many teams this weekend with overs being reduced as a result. Unbeaten Burnmoor hosted Felling today, the visitors won the toss and elected to field. An opening stand of 70 and a third wicket stand of 62 saw Burnmoor declare on 183 for 3 after 43 overs, Marcus Brown, following an unbeaten 49 last week, carried his bat this week for 82 not out, the innings coming from 132 balls with 6 fours, this was his 13th NEPL half century, Ross Greenwell had contributed 36 and Paul Craig 30. For Felling there were wickets for Ishaq Khan, 1 for 32, Elliot Fox, 1 for 42, and Paul Leonard 1 for 50.

Dan Brown made an early breakthrough when Felling batted, bowling Alan Mustard for 3, but Tyler Easton, 60 and Jordan Watson 38, made a result unlikely. This was Easton's 9th NEPL half century, the innings came from 102 balls and contained 5 fours. Felling did stumble from 114 for 2 to 148 for 7 as Waqas Maqsood removed their middle order but their innings was closed after 38 overs with their score on 152 for 7 wickets and the match was drawn, Maqsood finished with 3 for 17, Graeme Bridge 2 for 46, and Ross Greenwell 1 for 40 and Dan Brown 1 for 10 picked up a wicket each, Burnmoor collected 16 points, Felling 7 points.

Castle Eden lost the toss at home to South North and were invited to bat, they were 49 for 4 when J P Meade was dismissed for 6, two wickets each for Sean Tindale and Lee Crozier, but a fifth wicket partnership of 103 between Nicholas Sampson-Barnes, 65 and Bilawal Iqbal, 83 repaired the early damage. This was

Sampson-Barnes 3rd NEPL half century, the innings came from 94 balls and contained 8 fours and 2 sixes, it was Iqbal's 3rd NEPL half century, and his highest NEPLL score to date, his innings had come from 108 balls and contained 11 fours and 3 sixes. A further 36 from Philip Wimpenny meant that Castle Eden reached 251 for 9 wickets when their innings was closed after 58 overs. Tindale finished with 5 for 58, Crozier 2 for 53, and Oli McGee and Chris Hewison both had 1 for 45. When Hewison trapped Sampson-Barnes leg before this was his first NEPL wicket since 9th September 2006!

When South North batted, they were 170 for 3 from 33 overs when the game finished as a draw. Opener Simon Birtwisle made 51 from 54 balls with 9 fours, his 68th NEPL half century, and Nik Gorantla had made 54 from 51 balls with 7 fours and a six, this was his 5th NEPL half century. Chris Hewison was 39 not out. Charlie Scorer took 1 for 20, Jon Malkin 1 for 34 and Richard Ede, 1 for 41, Castle Eden picked up 8 points and South North 16 points for their efforts.

Chester le Street entertained Burnopfield today with the visitors winning the toss and electing to field. Not for the first time this season John Coxon, 43, and Jacob McCann 17, gave the hosts a steady start with an opening stand of 39. This brought Andrew Smith to the crease, you may remember last week he was bowled for nought and went on to make 162, I'm not aware of any drama this week but I do know he scored his second successive century, the 24th of his NEPL career, as he was dismissed for 138 from 107 balls with 16 fours and 8 sixes! Chester declared on 271 for 6 from 46 overs, the wicket takers for Burnopfield were Matt Oswell 2 for 57, Harry Lumsden 1 for 62, Amaan Ulhaq 1 for 67 and Finlay McGurk 2 for 59. When McGurk took his second wicket, Smith caught by Matt Oswell, that was the 50th NEPL wicket of his career.

When Burnopfield batted it was a story of two Oswell's, opener Matt made 50 not out from 114 balls with 5 fours, his 6th NEPL half century, brother John was 55 not out from 26 balls with 4 fours and 5 sixes, his 15th NEPL half century. John Oswell, when he reached 22, scored his 3,000th NEPL career run. For Chester, Quentin Hughes bowled 10 overs 1 for 8, Matt Robinson had 1 for 44 and Seb Hughes-Pinan 1 for 28, as Burnopfield, 161 for 3 from 41 overs got a draw, it sounds as if this match was set up for a great finish either way, Chester 15 points, Burnopfield 8 points.

Newcastle were at home to Benwell Hill today, both sides at the wrong end of the table. Newcastle won the toss and elected to field. Hill lost two wickets with just 17 on the board, including the dangerous Yash Kothari but 100 not out from Joseph Fletcher and 69 not out from Joe Anderson saw them add 133 for the fourth wicket. This was Fletcher's fourth NEPL game, his innings came from 108 balls with 8 fours and 3 sixes. Joe Anderson's 68 came from 57 balls with 7 fours and a six, this was his highest NEPL score to date and his 5th NEPL half century. Hill declared on 207 for 3 from 38 overs, the rain meant that Newcastle had 30 overs to score the 208 runs required to win.

Only three Newcastle batsmen made double figures, Ben Robinson had 12 and Mohsin Mukhtar with 10, it was Jaques du Toit with 60 from 73 balls and 8 fours and a six who saved Newcastle from defeat. This was his 48th NEPL half century. Newcastle finished on 106 for 9 from 39 overs, Levi Olver 0 not out from 14 balls and youngster Charlie Darwood 0 not out from 3 balls the not out batsmen. When Phil Bell caught Robinson off the bowling off Callum Harding that was his 50th NEPL catch. Harding finished with 1 for 20, Luke Mussett 2 for 19, Rory Hanley 2 for 39 and Yash Kothari had the remarkable figures of 5 overs, 4 maidens, he conceded 1 run and took 4 wickets. Newcastle got 5 points and Hill 18 points but crucially for Hill, not the win and the extra points that go with it.

I attended Prior's Flat today for Tynedale against Ashington and I was rewarded with an excellent game of cricket that ebbed and flowed like the nearby River Tyne! Ashington won the toss and elected to field on a very green looking wicket and a start delayed to 12.45. The game was reduced to 53 overs maximum for the first innings and 45 for the second. Ed Foreman, 25 and Nkosana Mpofu, 31, got Tynedale off to a good start, 40 for the first wicket, as the wicket played much better than many of us thought it might! Tynedale then slipped to 62 for 5 before a stand of 44 between Daniel Parker, 18, and Jamie Crichton, 38, put them on target for a defendable score. They had looked pretty comfortable until Ben Harmison and Jack McCarthy pulled off a smart run out of Parker. Tynedale ended up 145 all out from 50.5 overs. This was my first look at Ashington bowler Alex Nice, I know Brian Bennett and those around Ashington are impressed with him since he joined the club early in the season, he looks to have a nice action and I look forward to seeing him on a faster track, he took 3 for 30, Cam Nichols had 2 for 36, Alex Storey 1 for 18 and James Harmison 3 for 22.

Ashington, perhaps with one eye on the weather, set off like a train, Jack Jessop hitting the second ball for 6 and taking ten off the first over. They were 24 when Jessop skied the fifth ball of the third over to mid-wicket where Aaron Rourke took a good catch. They were 36 from 4 overs when the next wicket fell and slipped to 71 for 6 as Matt Scott took the first 4 wickets and was well supported by Tom Cant. Captain Sean McCafferty then played a key innings of 39 as he and Matt Potts added 68 for the seventh wicket, when McCafferty departed after holing out and Alex Storey fell first ball, Ashington were still 7 runs short with two wickets left. Potts saw them home with 46 not out, number 10 Alex Nice made two not out, including the winning run, from 27 balls as Ashington got home by two wickets. Scott finished with 4 for 62, Cant 2 for 21 and Mpofu had those 2 late wickets for 3 runs. Ashington 23 points, Tynedale 4 points.

A few weeks ago, I tried to beat the weathermen and went to Tynemouth and the game was abandoned, I nearly tried again today for the visit of Sunderland but stuck with my original plan. It turns out I finally made a good call, Sunderland won the toss and elected to field and had Tynemouth 91 for 3 from 23.2 overs when the players came off and the game was subsequently abandoned. Matt Brown continued with his consistent season and was 32 not at the time and Kieran Waterson had 2 for 28 and Brett Hutchinson 1 for 15, Tynemouth collected 5 points, Sunderland 6 points.

With just 2 weeks of red ball cricket left before we switch format to orange ball and only win or lose, this could have been a pivotal weekend at both ends of the table. At the top Burnmoor drawing and Ashington taking an unlikely win sees the gap down to just 14 points, these two teams meet in the last game of the season and, whilst I know there is a lot of cricket still to be played, as a neutral, I hope both teams take things that far. Chester le Street lead the pack in third place, 37 points behind Ashington, but just 28 points cover the teams down to Felling in eighth. Newcastle appear to be in no-man's land in ninth with 142 points and it's very tight amongst the bottom three, Tynedale 108 points, no doubt disappointed they couldn't get over the line at home to Ashington, Castle Eden have 107 points and an improving Benwell Hill 104 points. Tynedale still have the other two bottom teams to play, Castle Eden and Benwell Hill both just play Tynedale. I have some interesting choices where I go with the camera in the forthcoming weeks!

Saturday 3rd August 2024

An under strength Ashington hosted Castle Eden in a key match at both ends of the table, the hosts won the toss and elected to field. I was at this one with my camera. An opening stand of 34 before two wickets for one run saw Castle Eden at 35 for 2, this became 55 for 3 when Jonathan Malkin was dismissed by David Rutherford for 30. J P Meade and Nicholas Sampson-Barnes then took the game away from Ashington with a stand of 161, Meade was eventually out for 107, his second NEPL century, the innings came from 116 balls and contained 5 fours and 6 sixes, several of which went over my head at long off or long on! Sampson Barnes made 74 from 91 balls with 7 fours and 2 sixes, this was his 4th NEPL half century and his highest NEPL score to date. To further add to Ashington's problems Bilawal Iqbal then followed up his NEPL career best last week with a 52 not out this week! His innings came from 36 balls and contained 3 fours and 3 sixes; this was his 4th NEPL half century. With Ben Simpson adding 22 not out, Castle Eden reached 297 for 5 wickets in 58 overs. For Ashington Ben Harmison took 3 for 49 and David Rutherford had 2 for 62.

Ashington made a brisk start in the opening overs, but they also lost two wickets in the thirties and were 38 for 2. Number four batsman Matt Storey was seriously hampered by a hamstring injury he had suffered whilst fielding but he went on to make a determined 37 and captain Sean McCafferty made 40 but the steady fall of wickets saw Ashington holding on desperately for the draw, Bilawal Iqbal tested the technique of the batsmen with a combination of short pitched bowling and excellent fast yorkers but he couldn't find a way past James Harmison who had 15 not out from 58 balls, with Ian Sharkey 3 not out Ashington hung on for the draw, 164 for 9 from 52 overs. Iqbal finished with 3 for 30, Ryan Ball, in his first appearance of the season, had 3 for 24, Phil Wimpenny 1 for 27 and Jonathan Malkin 2 for 28. As a footnote Charlie Harmison made his NEPL debut, wearing the shirt number, 10, of his father, Stephen, one to watch for the future? Ashington collected 12 points, Castle Eden 18 points.

Benwell Hill at home to Burnmoor saw the bottom team in the table host the top team, Burnmoor won the toss and elected to field. They got their reward immediately when Waqas Maqsood bowled Hill's overseas pro and main batting danger, Yash Kothari first ball of the innings. When Maqsood had Max Williamson leg before with the last ball of the opening over Hill were 0 for 2. This became 13 for 3 when Phil Bell was caught behind by Alec Linsley off the bowling of Josh Coughlin. Opener Rory Hanley top scored the innings with 42 and captain Peter Halliday had 32 not out but Hill only got to 109 all out from 40.5 overs. Maqsood finished with 3 for 33, Josh Coughlin 1 for 9, Graeme Bridge 1 for 13, Mitch Killeen 1 for 24, and Ryan Pringle 4 for 20.

Ross Greenwell, 43 not out and Marcus Brown 61, put on 103 for the first wicket as Burnmoor made 111 for 1 from 23.1 overs, Greenwell hitting a six to finish the game off. This was Brown's 14th NEPL half century, his innings came from 72 balls with 8 fours. Max Williamson was the only wicket taker, 1 for 19, as Burnmoor picked up 22 points and Hill got nothing for their efforts.

Burnopfield played host to Newcastle, the visitors won the toss and elected to bat and things took a bad turn from the start, Dan Hogg, who had made his List A debut for Durham on Wednesday, bowled Bobby Green with the first ball of the innings. Seven Newcastle players made double figures, Mohsin Mukhtar with 25 top scoring but they were all out for 141 in 46.1 overs. Hogg finished with 5 for 36, Harry Lumsden 3 for 11, Callum Brown 1 for 30 and Finlay McGurk 1 for 30.

When Burnopfield batted the first wicket put on 56, Matthew Oswell out for 24, the second wicket added 65, Ben McKinney out for 61. This was his 15th NEPL half century, the innings came from 50 balls and contained 7 fours and 3 sixes, he had also scored 80, his maiden List A half century for Durham on 28th July against Worcestershire. With Ross Whitfield Jnr making 45 not out Burnopfield made the required 142 runs in 27.1 overs, Mukhtar took 2 for 22 and Jaques du Toit had 1 for 19, Burnopfield collected the maximum 30 points, Newcastle 2 points.

Felling at home to Tynemouth was always going to be a pretty even contest, Felling won the toss and elected to bat. Their innings went on to contain three half centuries, both openers amongst them, Tyler Easton made 64 from 126 balls with 6 fours, Alan Mustard made 50 from 71 balls with 9 fours and Seb Allison made 57 from 31 balls with 1 fours and 6 sixes. This was Easton's 10th NEPL half century, it was Mustard's 29th NEPL half century and Allison's 10th. With Jordan Watson weighing in with 37 and Alasdair Appleby 34, Felling posted 314 for 6 from 58 overs. Josh Moors 3 for 102, Dan McGee 2 for 43 and Martin Pollard 1 for 50.

Despite losing Matthew Kimmitt early in the innings to Paul Leonard, the Felling wicket remained true, Joe Snowdon top scored with 71 not out from 99 balls with 9 fours and a six and Matthew Brown made 67 from 92 balls also with 9 fours and a six. This was Snowdon's third NEPL half century and his highest score in the league to date, for Brown, this was his 33rd NEPL half century. With Robbie Bowman, who had played for Durham Under 16's during the week, making 48 and Stan McAlindon and Dan McGee both making 18, McGee unbeaten, Tynemouth 229 for 5 from 52 overs appear to have comfortably got a draw. Felling, 16 points, Tynemouth 10 points.

South North at home to Chester le Street is always a tough contest for both sides, a lot of good battles over the years with these two, South North won the toss and elected to bat against a Chester side missing one or two faces. Simon Birtwisle opening the innings with 48 and Chris Hewison with his 49th NEPL half century, 65 from 90 balls with 9 fours, saw the hosts reach 223 for 8 from 58 overs, as a footnote Will Alexander, who made 17 today, had made 45 not out for Durham Under 16's against Scotland earlier in the week. For Chester Hedley Windows took 3 for 54, John Harrison had 3 for 48 and Ash Thorpe 1 for 41.

In Chester's reply Josh Wilson made his 3rd NEPL half century, 58 from 51 balls with 6 fours and a six, and John Coxon had 42, but Chester fell short of their target, they came within four balls of getting a draw, but Sean Tindale bowled last man John Harrison for 10 with the second ball of the last over. Tindale finished with 3 for 39, Oli McGee 2 for 29, Jonny Wightman, who had five wickets for England Over 40's during the week, had 1 for 32 and Lee Crozier took 2 for 24. When Crozier took his second wicket, John Coxon, who was caught behind by Rob Peyton, this was his 850th NEPL wicket, I will retype that, in case anyone thinks it's a typo, his 850th NEPL wicket! Congratulations Lee, an unbelievable achievement. South North had won by 44 runs and collected 25 points; Chester got 6 points.

Congratulations also to Chester's Seb Hughes-Pinan for 5 wickets for 12 runs for in an International T20 match for Spain against Croatia.

Sunderland, who the lead the pack chasing the top four welcomed Tynedale to Ashbrooke today, Sunderland won the toss and elected to field. Tynedale lost an early wicket, but the real damage was done to them with the score on 28, when they lost three wickets to fall from 28 for 1 to 28 for 4. Nathan Byerley top scored the innings with 32 but it was the Sunderland bowlers who came out on top, Joe Stuart had 4 for 32, Brett Hutchinson 3 for 29, Kieran Waterson 2 for 23 and Micky Allan 1 for 35. Tynedale were all out for 119 in 42.5 overs.

For Sunderland opener Dan Shurben hit 53 not out from 83 balls with 5 fours and 2 sixes, this was his 53rd NEPL half century, as Sunderland, 120 for 4 from 33.4 overs, won by 6 wickets, they collect 22 points, Tynedale a single point. For completeness, Tynedale's successful bowlers were Archie Fletcher 1 for 27, Nathan Byerley 1 for 10 and Aaron Rourke 2 for 16.

With Burnmoor winning and Ashington hanging on for a draw the points gap at the top has now opened to 28, Chester le Street remain third 43 points behind Ashington, with just 5 points covering the next five teams. At the bottom Castle Eden looked strong in their draw at Ashington, they now have 125 points, Tynedale 109 points and Benwell Hill 104 points.

Saturday 10th August 2024

The last week of red ball and traditional white clothing saw some interesting fixtures, no easy games at this stage of the season and teams trying to set themselves up for the remaining half dozen win/lose games. It's difficult to know how to describe this weekend's results, I think a couple were predictable, the other four, not so much! I will do it alphabetically as normal, but if this weekend proves anything it's why we play the games, nothing is won on paper!

Burnmoor defended their unbeaten record at home to Burnopfield, the home side won the toss and elected to field. With Ben McKinney on duty with Durham, he scored his maiden hundred, 115, for the county the next day at Canterbury against Kent, Matthew Oswell and Harry Lumsden opened the innings. There was an opening stand of 18 before Lumsden fell LBW to Josh Coughlin for 9. Oswell and Ross Whitfield Jnr then added 69 for the second wicket, before Whitfield was leg before to Maqsood. The next two batsmen both made ducks as Burnopfield stumbled from 87 for 1 to 89 for 4. Oswell stood firm though, making 53 from 87 balls with 7 fours, his third NEPL half century as the visitors battled their way to 150 all out in 45.3 overs. Maqsood finished with 3 for 36 and for the second week in a row there was 4 wickets for Ryan Pringle, 4 for 22 to be precise! Josh Coughlin 1 for 16, Graeme Bridge 1 for 32 and Craig Stephenson 1 for 40 rounded up the bowling figures.

Burnmoor got off to a bad start when Matthew Oswell had Marcus Brown, on his 150th NEPL appearance, caught behind by brother John from just the fourth ball of the innings. Opener Ross Greenwell, who would top score the innings with 35, and Craig Stephenson added 54 for the second wicket but with 20 each for Stuart Poynter and Waqas Maqsood Burnmoor were dismissed for 109 from 34 overs. Amaan Ulhaq with 6 for 38, his second six for of the season and his third five for, was the chief destroyer, with Finlay McGurk taking 3 for 30 and Matt Oswell 1 for 22. Burnopfield won by 41 runs and collected 24 points and Burnmoor 4 points in defeat. Given the standard of the league, it's still an achievement to only lose your first game in week 16 as Burnmoor have just done, so well done to them for that.

Chester le Street welcomed Castle Eden to Ropery Lane today, the visitors won the toss and elected to bat. An opening stand of 85 between Jonathan Malkin and Muhaymen Majeed had seemingly set them up for a big score when Malkin was bowled by Seb Hughes-Pinan for 47. Father Quentin Hughes then removed the dangerous JP Meade and Seb dismissed Nicholas Sampson-Barnes and suddenly Castle Eden were 89 for 3 and the innings faltering. Majeed went on to score 63 from 113 balls with 4 fours, his second NEPL half century, and with solid contributions down the order from Bilawal Iqbal, 23, Ben Simpson, 28 not out and Chris Tudball 23, Castle Eden got themselves to a decent total of 210 for 7 wickets from 58 overs. Seb Hughes -Pinan finished with 2 for 44, John Harrison 1 for 21, Quentin Hughes 1 for 31 and Matt Robinson 1 for 52, there had also been two run outs.

Despite Chester having a third wicket stand of 109 between John Coxon and James Thompson, both batsmen making half centuries, they never really threatened the target, their lower middle order and tail falling away badly from 159 for 4 to 188 all out in 49.2 overs. Coxon made 53 from 76 balls with 7 fours and a six, his 37th NEPL half century, and Thompson 59 from 79 balls with 8 fours and a six, his 21st NEPL half century. Bilawal Iqbal continued his good form with the ball taking 4 for 42, Jonathan Malkin also had 4 wickets, 4 for 32 and Charlie Scorer, 2 for 55, completed the wicket takers. Castle Eden, who won by 22 runs, got 24 points for the win; Chester picked up 6 points in defeat.

Newcastle were at home to South North in the Tyneside derby, the visitors won the toss and elected to field. They got an early breakthrough, but a second wicket stand of 74 between Ben Robinson, 32, and Asher Hart, 36, had Newcastle nicely set up at 78 for 1. The fall of Hart sparked a collapse as they slumped to 136 for 9. A last wicket stand of 36 between George Gibson, 3, and Woody Wilson 24 not out, gave Newcastle a total to defend, 172 all out in 48.1 overs. Oli McGee had 4 for 61, Tom Rogers, back from his spell with Kent, 3 for 23, Sean Tindale 1 for 17 and Jonny Wightman 1 for 29.

There were one or two unfamiliar names in the South North side, Alexander Charnley making his NEPL debut as a new opening partner for Sol Bell. Charnley made 12 before he was bowled by Mohsin Mukhtar with the score on 39. The familiar Rob Peyton batted at three and he and Bell added 113 for the second wicket to pave the way for the win. Peyton was dismissed for 46 and Bell fell for 92 with the score on 156. The innings came from 107 balls and contained 11 fours; this was his 17th NEPL half century. Mukhtar finished with 2 for 50 and Jaques du Toit had 1 for 19 but South North, who picked up 24 points for the victory, won by 7 wickets. Newcastle got 3 points in defeat.

When Sunderland had met Ashington earlier in the season they inflicted the first defeat of their season on today's visitors. Sunderland were without George Drissell who is now starting to establish himself in the Durham set up, he took 4 for 38 the day after this match at Kent. Ashington won the toss and elected to field. Although they lost Dan Shurben for 10 with the score on 30, they went on to post a good score, a second wicket partnership of 78 between opener George Fishwick and number three Micky Allan put the hosts in a good place, Fishwick out for 44 and Allan making 54 from 70 balls with 10 fours, his 8th NEPL half century. Sunderland captain Chris Youldon took full advantage of the platform his top order had provided as he struck 85 from 79 balls with 9 fours and 2 sixes, this was his 6th NEPL half century and his highest score in the NEPL to date. Youldon added 122 for the fifth wicket with Jack Johnson who finished on 42 not out from 47 balls. The Sunderland closed on 253 for 5 wickets from 58 overs. Ben Harmison had 3 for 14, David Rutherford 1 for 17 and Alex Nice 1 for 74.

Ashington, missing usual opener Jack Jessop, made a steady start, Cam Nichols making 40, but soon fell to 57 for 3, then 62 for 5, as in recent weeks the lower middle order rallied around captain Sean McCafferty but despite 24 from him and also Matt Potts, they were dismissed for 142 from 48.1 overs. Micky Allan continued his good day with 4 for 42, Jack Brassell had 2 for 25, Milo Coates 2 for 28 and Joe Stuart 1 for 16, there was also a run out. Sunderland had won by 111 runs, they collected 24 points, Ashington 3 points.

Tynedale welcomed Felling today, the visitors won the toss and elected to bat. A steady opening partnership of 36 and a further 36 for the second wicket saw them reach 72 for 2, a rare batting collapse from the strong Felling batting line up saw them 104 for 7 and suddenly in a lot of trouble. Wicket keeper Ed Hurst and veteran bowler Paul Leonard then added 72 for the eighth wicket, Hurst out for 51 from 69 balls with 8 fours, this was his 11th NEPL half century, Leonard also reached his half century, he was out for exactly 50 from 58 balls with 2 fours and 3 sixes, this was his 4th NEPL half century. Tom Cant had been the main problem for the visiting batsmen as he took 5 for 37, Matt Scott took 2 for 41, Nkosana Mpofu had 1 for 34, Aaron Rourke 1 for 39, and Archie Fletcher 1 for 44 as Felling reached 202 all out from 51.1 overs.

Tynedale soon found themselves up against it as Seb Allison picked up two quick wickets before they had reached 30, 27 for 1 and 29 for 2, when Paul Leonard had Mpofu caught behind for 22 they were now 45 for 3. Joe Barber, the Tynedale number five, turned the game in favour of the home side, he made 82 from 88 balls with 9 fours and 3 sixes, this was his maiden NEPL half century. He was well supported throughout the innings with Nathan Byerley, 16, Tom Cant 23 and Aaron Rourke, 13 not out, all making double figure scores, Rourke ended the game with a six as Tynedale made 206 for 7 wickets from 44.5 overs to win by 3 wickets. The Felling wicket takers were led by Seb Allison, 3 for 54, Elliot Fox had 2 for 38, Paul Leonard 1 for 33 and Alasdair Appleby 1 for 52. Tynedale collected a much needed 30 points, Felling 6 points.

Tynemouth at home to Benwell Hill was my choice with the camera this week and it was another game to say, "I was there!" Benwell Hill were missing Haydon Mustard for this one as he was also away with Messrs. McKinney and Drissell at Kent with Durham, he didn't have a bad Sunday either as he made 35 and took 2 catches to complete a successful day out for the NEPL youngsters! Back at Preston Avenue Tynemouth won the toss and elected to bat. They looked vindicated in the decision almost every step of the way, partnerships of 69 between Stan McAlindon, 35, and Ben Debnam, 65 between Debnam and Robbie Bowman, 88 between Bowman and Matthew Brown meant they were 253 for 4 when Brown was dismissed for 24, Debnam was out for 53 from 96 balls with 8 fours, this was his 29th NEPL half century. Robbie Bowman was the undoubted star of the show though, still only 16 he produced a remarkable innings, 134 from 102 balls with 10 fours and 10 sixes, this was his maiden NEPL century. Having seen him produce a brilliant innings under entirely different circumstances earlier in the season at South North, I suspect I'm one in a long line of people predicting a bright cricketing future for the lad! Tynemouth declared on 302 for 7 from 53 overs. Luke Mussett took 2 for 50, Callum Harding 2 for 69, Prahalad Nadella had 1 for 38, Dan Gardiner 1 for 28 and Yash Kothari 1 for 32, Kothari's figures coming from 15 overs.

I can't close this round up without mentioning an incredible catch from Dan Gardiner. Joe Snowdon, who had made 15, top edged a pull shot from Luke Mussett to deep fine leg, Gardiner came racing in to get underneath it and as he got where he needed to be, both his feet shot out from under him, leaving him falling backwards and his arms flailing about, he somehow had the presence of mind to reach up with his right hand and unbelievably he found the ball, it somehow stuck in his hand and he kept it there as he fell flat on his back! The photos are good, but they honestly don't do the catch justice!

The Tynemouth wicket looked good and was a great batting strip, a credit to grounds man Paul Jackson, I assumed that given the quality of the wicket and concern about Benwell Hill's Yash Kothari had led to Tynemouth batting on too long. I couldn't have been more wrong; they should have batted longer! That said, Kothari was dropped in the first over off Joel Hull-Denholm, when he had scored two. He went on to make 171 not out from 153 balls with 19 fours and 2 sixes, this was his third NEPL century of his first NEPL season. Kothari was well supported by Max Williamson, a half century just evading him as he was out for 49 from 57 balls with 5 fours and 2 sixes, and Peter Halliday 21 not out. Benwell Hill reached their target with the first ball of the 55th over when Kothari hit a four off Matthew Brown when the scores had been level, Benwell Hill 306 for 6 from 54.1 overs had won by 4 wickets and collected 27 points, Tynemouth 6 points. For completion, the home wicket takers were Dan McGee, 1 for 27, Joe Hull-Denholm 1 for 37, Matthew Brown 1 for 37 and Phil Morse 3 for 78. Over 600 runs scored in the day and a couple of stellar innings, congratulations to all involved in a great day's cricket.

At the top of the table Burnmoor still lead the way, 29 points ahead of Ashington, Burnopfield are now in third a further 19 points behind them. Just 20 points cover third down to Tynemouth in seventh with 198, with Felling now a further 16 points in eighth. In the last three weeks I have seen the then bottom three clubs in action, all three gave excellent performances and got either a win or a winning draw in those games and after three games without a win, Newcastle now find themselves overtaken by Castle Eden, making it a bottom four now fighting relegation! Just 18 points between Castle Eden fourth bottom and Benwell Hill bottom, with Newcastle now third bottom and Tynedale second bottom.

I touched upon it briefly during the round up, Ben McKinney, George Drissell and Haydon Mustard all playing, and playing well, for Durham at Kent the day after these NEPL fixtures, it's worth taking a moment to reflect on one of the main objectives of the league when it was established, to provide a bridge between club and first-class cricket for promising young cricketers, with at least three others in the same Durham side who have played in the league, I will leave it to you to decide if you think the NEPL is successful in respect of one of its long held main aims.

At the end of the red ball cricket, the bowlers have one more five wicket performance than the batsmen have centuries, still a very even contest.

Robbie Bowman seen here on 10th August 2024 on his way to his maiden NEPL century v Benwell Hill.

TABLE 75   NEPL Table Sunday 11th August 2024.

	Played	Won	Draw/Aban	Lost	Tied	Penalty Points	Bonus Points	Points
Burnmoor	16	9	6	1	0	0	51	266
Ashington	16	8	4	4	0	0	62	237
Burnopfield	16	7	4	5	0	0	62	218
South North	16	6	4	5	1	0	59	216
Sunderland	16	7	4	5	0	0	52	215
Chester le Street	16	5	5	6	0	0	59	201
Tynemouth	16	5	9	2	0	0	47	198
Felling	16	4	6	6	0	0	71	183
Castle Eden	16	3	6	7	0	0	50	149
Newcastle	16	3	4	8	1	0	60	147
Tynedale	16	4	3	9	0	0	36	135
Benwell Hill	16	2	6	8	0	0	55	131

CHAPTER SEVENTEEN

The Final Session 2024

Saturday 17th August 2024

And so, we revert to the coloured clothing, orange balls, 45 overs and a noon start. Every game this week has an impact somewhere in the league table, personally, I circled South North at home to Burnmoor when the fixtures came out way back when!

Ashington hosting Chester le Street was an appealing fixture for the neutral, could Ashington, who have faltered recently, keep any kind of pressure on leaders Burnmoor, against a capable Chester side pursuing a top four finish as well. The visitors won the toss and elected to field. An opening stand of 47 between Jack Jessop and Cam Nichols might have had them questioning the decision but the veteran Quentin Hughes picked up the wickets of Nichols for 32 and two balls later, the in-form Sean McCafferty, Ashington then found themselves 47 for 2. Jessop and Ben Harmison then added 66 for the third wicket when Jessop was leg before to Ash Thorpe for 39. Harmison went on to make his 15th NEPL half century, 80 from 90 balls with 7 fours and a six as he guided Ashington to 201 all out from 45 overs. For Chester five bowlers took wickets, Cole Pearce had 3 for 29, Quentin Hughes 2 for 16, from 9 overs, Matt Robinson 2 for 64, Seb Hughes-Pinan 1 for 27 and Ash Thorpe 1 for 38.

No John Coxon this week so Matthew Cranston opened with Jacob McCann, the pair putting on 36 for the first wicket when McCann was out for 16. Andrew Smith then made 31 and James Thompson 42, but it was 87 not out from Cranston which saw Chester win by 7 wickets. This was his 3rd NEPL half century and highest score in the NEPL to date, the innings came from 91 balls with 11 fours and 2 sixes. For Ashington Cam Nichols had 1 for 25, Ian Sharkey 1 for 38 and Matt Collins 1 for 47. Chester le Street 24 points, Ashington 4 points.

Benwell Hill went into a huge match against Tynedale without their overseas pro, Yash Kothari who has returned home for a short period, he is expected back before the end of the month. Visiting Tynedale won the toss and elected to field. Dan Gardiner, whose previous highest score in the NEPL was just 20, batted at three for Hill and he made his maiden NEPL half century, 58 from 91 balls with 7 fours, he was well supported by 46 from captain Pete Halliday as the home side reached 194 all out from 44.2 overs. There was 5 wickets for Archie Fletcher, 5 for 47, Nkosana Mpofu had 2 for 24, and three bowlers with a wicket each, Nathan Byerley had 1 for 18, Tom Cant 1 for 25 and Aaron Rourke 1 for 29.

I would think that both sides would have been happy at the break, but an opening stand of 50 between Mpofu, dismissed for 28, and Ed Foreman, followed by 77 between Foreman and Oliver Fletcher, Fletcher making 36, and then 30 more between Foreman and Joe Barber, 21, saw Tynedale well placed at 157 for 3. When Foreman was bowled by Rory Hanley for 67, his maiden NEPL half century, and the innings coming from 114 balls with 9 fours, the score was 174 and victory in sight. They won without losing anyone else to claim victory by 6 wickets, 195 for 4 from 42.1 overs. Luke Mussett had taken 1 for 26, Dan Gardiner 1 for 29, Max Williamson 1 for 31 and Rory Hanley 1 for 41. Tynedale got a crucial 24 points for a huge win, Benwell Hill 4 points.

Burnopfield hosted Tynemouth fresh from taking the last unbeaten record in the league from Burnmoor last week, Tynemouth having not won since 20th July and scoring and giving up 300 last week looking to get back on track. Burnopfield won the toss and elected to field. Tynemouth were seemingly going along nicely at 74 for 1 when opener Ben Debnam was leg before to Finlay McGurk for 32, despite three players making 20 plus, they fell away badly to be all out for 140 from 35.5 overs. McGurk finished with 4 for 27, Amaan Ulhaq continued his stellar season with 3 for 18, Ross Whitfield Jnr had 2 for 25 and Matt Oswell had 1 for 10.

The loss of both John, 3, and Matthew Oswell,33, saw Burnopfield at 39 for 2 but an unbeaten 55 from Ross Whitfield Jnr, his 10th NEPL half century, and the innings coming from 52 balls with 9 fours, saw the home side, 144 for 4 from 23 overs, win comfortably and pick up 24 points, Tynemouth got 2 points, for completeness there were 3 wickets for Martin Pollard, 3 for 30 and 1 for 38 for Dan McGee.

Castle Eden, who seem to have at last found some consistency, were at home to a struggling Newcastle today, another big game for both sides. The home side won the toss and elected to bat, they were 43 for 2 when Jonathan Malkin was joined at the crease by J P Meade, they had added 67 and were 110 when Malkin was caught by Bobby Green off Jaques du Toit for 24, and without addition to the score, Meade was out for 47, caught by George Gibson off the bowling of Mohsin Mukhtar. That was as good as it got for Newcastle in the field, Nicholas Sampson- Barnes, batting at five, hit 100 not out from 72 balls, with 13 fours and 4 sixes, this was his maiden NEPL century, number six batsman Bilawal Iqbal also scored his maiden NEPL century, 112 not out from 69 balls with 9 fours and 10 sixes, the pair added an unbeaten 219 for the fourth wicket as Castle Eden made 329 for 4 from their 45 overs. For Newcastle, Rowan Shelton took 2 for 83, du Toit had 1 for 29 and Mukhtar had 1 for 55.

Newcastle made a disastrous start to their innings and were quickly 5 for 2 and then 27 for 3, when this became 48 for 4 it looked like game over. A half century each from opener Ben Robinson and number six Rowan Shelton at least meant Newcastle picked up some bonus points. When Robinson was out for 58 from 68 balls with 9 fours and 2 sixes, his 10th NEPL half century, the score was now 149 for 5. Shelton fell with the score on 180, out for 55 from 73 balls with 9 fours, his 3rd NEPL half century, George Darwood with 27 Hamzah Amin with 24 helped get Newcastle to 252 all out in 42.4 overs. Jonathan Malkin led the home bowlers with 4 for 44, Iqbal had 3 for 35, Richard Ede 2 for 31 and Keith Bailey 1 for 31. Castle Eden had won by 77 runs and collected 24 points; Newcastle got 5 points.

Felling at home to Sunderland was another fixture that would be hard for the neutral to predict. The home side won the toss, and as they especially like to do at home, chose to bat. Opener Alasdair Appleby hit his 2nd NEPL century, 111 to be precise, from 66 balls with 14 fours and 7 sixes, and Jordan Watson hit his 2nd NEPL century of the season and his career as he made 102 from 105 balls with 14 fours, Felling posted 311 for 6 from their 45 overs. For Sunderland Jack Johnson had 2 for 27, George Drissell 2 for 44 and Milo Coates 1 for 24, there was also a run out.

Sunderland lost two wickets with the score on 13, and were up against it from there, although they were 54 when the third wicket fell, two more wickets going down on 61 and it was really game over, a last wicket stand of 35 got them to 141 all out in 27.3 overs, opener George Drissell had made 48 and 22 each from number eight Bruce Pritchard and number ten Joe Stuart, who was not out, had been the main resistance. Appleby had continued his good day when he bowled picking up 4 for 39, Paul Leonard had 3 for 22, Seb Allison 2 for 21 and Elliot Fox 1 for 13. Felling won by 170 runs and got 24 points, Sunderland 3 points.

I attended this one with the camera as South North hosted Burnmoor, the home side won the toss and batted. When South North opener Sol Bell made his second run that brought up his 3,000 runs in the NEPL, he and Simon Birtwisle had added 33 when Bell was bowled by Dan Brown for 15. This set the tone for the innings, the top order all made double figures but on a slow difficult wicket, no-one kicked on, Chris Hewison top scored with 39 and Oli McGee, batting at nine, made 33 not out from 35 balls, South North were 174 for 9 from 45 overs when the innings closed. Although pace opening bowler Dan Brown had picked up two early wickets, both bowled and both sending a stump flying out of the ground, (and both missed by me with the camera), he finished with 2 for 27, and Waqas Maqsood took 1 for 36, it was the spinners who had controlled the innings, Graeme Bridge took 4 for 16, Craig Stephenson 1 for 9, and Ryan Pringle 1 for 34.

Burnmoor made a difficult start and were soon 23 for 2 with opener Ross Greenwell standing firm, he was then joined by Ryan Pringle. Pringle, as he often does, went on the counter attack, hitting 40 from 25 balls with 5 fours and 2 sixes, he had contributed 40 of the 65-run partnership when he was caught at slip by Simon Birtwisle, Burnmoor were now 88 for 3. This became 96 for 4 when Sean Tindale bowled Greenwell for 38 and 107 for 5 when Stuart Poynter was the second excellent leg side catch taken by wicket keeper Rob Peyton. Waqas Maqsood then added 32 with Josh Coughlin, he was on 14 when Lee Crozier trapped him leg before. At 139 for 6 the game, and arguably the chance to put away the league title was now hanging in the balance, Coughlin who had initially counter attacked when he first came to the crease, seemed to settle in and was now looking to put the bad ball away and keep the good ball out, new batsman Dan Brown hit some nice drives through the off side and Burnmoor were done, 175 for 6 from 35.2 overs. Coughlin finished on 40 not out from 51 balls with 4 fours and a six, and Brown was 14 not out. For South North Sean Tindale had 2 for 51, Oli McGee 1 for 22, Lee Crozier 1 for 23, Jonny Wightman 1 for 27 and Tom Rogers 1 for 41. As always with games between these two teams the game bordered on the "tetchy" side, both teams unhappy with decisions which were or weren't given, I don't know which ones were or weren't right but as they used to say in my day "read the paper tomorrow!" Burnmoor for their four-wicket win collected 24 point, South North 4 points.

In the wider picture of things, Burnmoor have two tough games coming up in a resurgent Castle Eden and a good Chester le Street side, I think with the run in they have, and the last three fixtures they have, today was a big win, and, in the language of this book, a pivotal moment. They now have 290 points and lead joint second place Ashington and Burnopfield, 242 points, by 48 points, Ashington have slipped a little in recent weeks, the loss of overseas pro Jeremiah Louis with injury following his spell with West Indies test squad no doubt a contributing factor. Chester le Street are now fourth on 225 and lead the clubs chasing a top four finish, South North sit fifth on 220 and Sunderland sixth on 218. Felling are now seventh on 207 points and Tynemouth, who are having a lean spell, are now eighth on 200 points. Castle Eden have put their earlier woes behind them and are now one of the form sides in the league, they have risen to ninth with 173 points, Tynedale are tenth, 163 points, Newcastle, seemingly safe from the prospect of relegation a few weeks ago, have now slumped to eleventh with 152 points and Benwell Hill have now seen a gap open up between them and safety as they sit bottom on 135 points.

Four batsmen made centuries this week against one 5 wicket haul, as the battle between bat and ball now once again goes in the batsman's favour, 23 centuries over 21 five fer's.

Saturday 24th August 2024

In the build up to this week's fixtures Mitch Killeen of Burnmoor, made his maiden century for Durham Second XI, congratulations to him and further congratulations to Burnopfield's Daniel Hogg who took four wickets on his first-class debut for Durham whilst today's NEPL fixtures took place.

Ashington were looking to rediscover their early season form when they welcomed Felling to Langwell Crescent today. Ashington won the toss and elected to field, the first over went for 12 and the second for 10 as Alasdair Appleby and Tyler Easton made an aggressive start. Easton was caught by Sean McCafferty for 19 off the bowling of Alex Nice with the score on 61 from just 7.3 overs. The fall of the wicket invariably slowed things down and the dismissal of Appleby for 56 helped further. Appleby's innings came from 34 balls with 7 fours and 3 sixes, this was his 13th NEPL half century. Paul Leonard with 33 and Jordan Watson 32, got Felling to a healthy 226 for 9 from their 45 overs. James Harmison finished with 3 for 29, Alex Nice 3 for 49, Ian Sharkey 1 for 29, Cam Nichols 1 for 36 and Matty Collins 1 for 58.

Seb Allison made an early breakthrough to reduce Ashington to 4 for 1, but Jack Jessop and Jack McCarthy put on 37 for the second wicket before Jessop went for 20. McCarthy was next out for 24 as Ashington fell to 68 for 3. Despite 28 from James Harmison and 25 from Ben Harmison I'm not sure Ashington ever truly threatened the Felling score, and they were eventually bowled out for 145 from 36.4 overs. The wickets were shared around, no-one with more than two but a solid team effort from Felling, Appleby had 2 for 20, Calum Wright 2 for 24, Seb Allison had 2 for 35, Paul Leonard 2 for 39, Hashmatullah Hemat 1 for 6 and Ishaq Khan 1 for 20. Felling got 24 points for the 81-run win, Ashington 5 points in defeat.

Burnmoor hosting Castle Eden was an interesting fixture given the visitors recent good batting form. Burnmoor won the toss and elected to field. When Waqas Maqsood caught and bowled Jonathan Malkin for 3, they would have been happy with the decision. Opener Muhaymen Majeed would prove to be the foundation upon which the visitor's then built their innings, making 59 from 109 balls with 4 boundaries. This was his 2nd NEPL half century. Bilawal Iqbal continued his recent good form with the bat as he made 34 not at almost a run a ball as Castle Eden finished their 45 overs on 170 for 9. Graeme Bridge was the most successful bowler with 3 for 37, Josh Coughlin 2 for 39, Ryan Pringle 2 for 41, Maqsood 1 for 13 and Daniel Brown 1 for 18.

No Ross Greenwell for Burnmoor this week so the veteran Allan Worthy stepped up to the plate to open with Marcus Brown. They put on 35 for the first wicket when Worthy was bowled by Iqbal for 20. Two more wickets relatively quickly saw Burnmoor stumble a little to 49 for 3. The second of those wickets brought Stuart Poynter to the crease to join Ryan Pringle, funnily enough I had checked Poynter's average for the season before I left the house today and saw that it had slipped to 88.00. These two took the score to 123 when Pringle was dismissed for 33. Despite losing Josh Coughlin cheaply with the score on 149, Poynter with 75 not out from 70 balls with 10 fours and a six. This was his second half century of the season to go with his two centuries, his 15th NEPL half century in his career, for the record he now has 603 runs at an average of 100.50. For the visitors Iqbal had 2 for 29, Jonathan Malkin 2 for 53 and Keith Bailey 1 for 28 in the five-wicket loss. Burnmoor 24 points, Castle Eden 4 points.

Newcastle hosting Chester le Street at Jesmond was my choice with the camera today, the home side desperately in need of a win to fight off relegation, the visitors looking to mount a challenge to get into the top three. The game marked the 400th NEPL appearance of Quentin Hughes, he went into the game with 10190 runs at an average of 38.59 with 68 half centuries and 6 centuries, for good measure he also has 388 wickets at an average of 18.93, oh and the small matter of 134 catches, his son Seb was missing today so he didn't share his father's achievement but as he was away playing in a tournament with Spain, I'm sure dad would understand!

Newcastle won the toss and elected to field, Jacob McCann and Matthew Cranston had put on 42 for the first wicket when Cranston skied one into the covers, George Darwood took an excellent running catch over his right shoulder to remove Cranston for 17. McCann and Andrew Smith both looked in good nick as they put on 68 for the second wicket, Smith out first for 47 with the score on 114. When McCann was out for 42 with the score on 131 the game was in the balance. The Newcastle bowler's stuck to their task and ultimately restricted Chester to 182 all out in 44.3 overs, James Thompson 18 and Ash Thorpe 14 helping the score along. Rowan Shelton bowled well for his 3 for 19 and George Darwood's 3 for 31 included a brilliant diving caught and bowled, unfortunately the only photographer present missed this, blaming the batsman for standing in his way as a weak excuse, Mohsin Mukhtar had 2 for 23 and Asher Hart 2 for 44 and a trip to the cemetery to try and retrieve the ball after a huge Andrew Smith six completed the wicket takers.

Newcastle made a dreadful start to their reply, captain Bobby Green, in his 50th NEPL appearance, after reverse sweeping the third ball of the innings from Quentin Hughes straight to a fielder, tried again with the fourth ball and was leg before wicket for nought. When his fellow opener Hamzah Amin danced down the wicket and failed his audition for Strictly, he found himself bowled by the same bowler for 3. With Asher Hart then dismissed for 17 and no further runs scored, Newcastle were 21 for 3 and all too familiar territory for this season. Mohsin Mukhtar with 56 from 84 balls with 5 fours and a six, his 8th NEPL half century and Ben Robinson, 53 from 88 balls with 5 fours, his 11th NEPL half century, had a fourth wicket partnership of 112 to set the game up, they both fell in successive overs, Mukhtar caught in the covers and Robinson hitting the only fielder in the deep leg side postcode with a sweetly timed pull shot, Newcastle 137 for 5. I think everyone in the ground, including both sets of players would have been aware of the next scenario, Jaques du Toit, batting at six would probably hold the key to the game, if he was there at the end, Newcastle would win, if he wasn't, they probably wouldn't. With six overs to go they required 36 to win, as they counted the runs down, losing another wicket on the way, they needed six to win with seven balls left, du Toit inevitably hit the last ball of the 44th over for six to get Newcastle a vital 3 wicket win, he finished on 25 not out. Chester's wicket taking bowlers were Josh Wilson 3 for 15, Quentin Hughes 2 for 33, Matthew Robinson 1 for 29 and Kyle Coetzer, in just his 4th NEPL appearance of the season, 1 for 37. Newcastle picked up a vital 24 points, Chester 6 points.

Sunderland looking towards the top four hosted bottom club Benwell Hill at Ashbrooke, the visitors won the toss and elected to field. Both openers were back in the pavilion with the score on 26 as Benwell Hill made a good start, when two wickets fell in successive balls to Dan Gardiner with the score on 52, they must have been happy with their decision to bowl. A stand of 72 between Micky Allan and George Fishwick got the Sunderland innings back on track, Fishwick out for 27 with the score on 124. Allan went on to make 62 from 97 balls with 7 fours, his 8th NEPL half century, a run out off the last ball of the 45th over saw them restricted them to 183 all out. Dan Gardiner took 4 for 22, Max Williamson 2 for 31, Luke Mussett 1 for 29 and Callum Harding 1 for 37.

Micky Allan's good day continued when he dismissed Hill opener Rory Hanley for 13 with the score 16, but a second wicket stand of 105 between veteran opener Adam Heather and Dan Gardiner looked to have positioned Hill nicely at 121 for 2. When Heather was out for 46, Gardiner, after making his maiden NEPL half century last week, went on to make his second this week, 82 not out from 103 balls with 6 fours and a six. His innings would prove decisive, despite losing four relatively cheap wickets Gardiner saw his side home to 184 for 6 from 41 overs and win by 4 wickets. Allan finished with 3 for 36, Joe Stuart had 2 for 44 and Jack Brassell 1 for 38. Benwell Hill collected 24 points, Sunderland 5 points.

Tynedale hovering just outside a relegation spot hosting joint second placed Burnopfield had implications at both ends of the table, the visitors won the toss and elected to field. Tynedale went on to post an impressive 245 for 7 from their 45 overs. Overseas pro and opening bat Nkosana Mpofu made his maiden NEPL half century, 59 from 69 balls with 9 fours and a six, Thomas Cant had 58 not out from 66 balls with 3 fours, this was his maiden NEPL half century, and they were well supported by Oliver Fletcher 24, Ted Fletcher 22 and Joe Barber 20. Amaan Ulhaq took 2 for 41, Matthew Oswell had 2 for 45, Ross Whitfield Jnr 1 for 35 and Harry Lumsden 1 for 57.

The Oswell's Matthew and John put on an impressive 91 in 10.4 overs for the first wicket when Burnopfield replied, Matthew falling first for 37, a couple more wickets saw them slip to 101 for 3 and then one more and they were 124 for 4. The fifth wicket fell at 147 and then the crucial one, John Oswell caught by Seth Robbie off the bowling of Thomas Cant for 73, with the score on 153. This was John Oswell's 16th NEPL half century and came from 62 balls with 9 fours and 3 sixes. Although three other batsmen made scores in their teen's, Burnopfield never recovered from the loss of Oswell and were bowled out for 202 from 35.5 overs. Mpofu took 3 for 35, Thomas Cant had 3 for 38, Matthew Scott 2 for 53, Ted Fletcher 1 for 19 and Seth Robbie 1 for 27. Tynedale winners by 43 runs collect 24 points, Burnopfield 7 points.

Tynemouth hosting South North saw unfamiliar names in both teams, as the home side won the toss and elected to field. Both South North openers got into the thirties and then got out, Simon Birtwisle made 37 and Sol Bell 32. With the score on 106 for Nikhil Gorantla was joined at the crease by Rob Peyton, the pair added 153 for the third wicket, Gorantla being next out for 107 from 75 balls with 14 make 77 from 72 balls with 7 fours and a six, his 8th NEPL half century, Sean Tindale added a quick-fire 34 from 20 balls and Adam Cragg 17 from 10 balls as South North made the best of another beautiful Tynemouth batting wicket and posted 329 for 6 from their 45 overs. For the home side Owen Gourley had 3 for 53, Freddie Harrison 1 for 49, Phil Morse 1 for 63 and Matthew Brown 1 for 67.

Sean Tindale removed both openers and then Jonny Wightman nipped in with two more wickets as Tynemouth fell to 54 for 4, it was Matthew Brown, who remains one of the most consistent run scorers in the league, and Joe Snowdon who got the home side back into the game, at least for a while, as they added 69 for the fifth wicket, Brown was the first to go, leg before to Lee Crozier for 55, his innings came from 34 balls and contained 7 fours and 2 sixes and was his 34th NEPL half century, Snowdon was dismissed for 58 from 78 balls with 6 fours, this was his 4th NEPL half century. The next highest score among the lower order was 15 as Tynemouth were bowled out for 205 from 39.5 overs. Jonny Wightman had 3 for 44, Gavin Paton 2 for 28, Oli McGee 2 for 45, Sean Tindale 2 for 50 and Lee Crozier 1 for 37. Comment must also be made of Rob Peyton, as well as his effort with the bat. He also took 2 catches and had 3 stumpings, according to someone present two of the three stumpings were off leg side wides and were remarkable efforts. South North won by 124 runs and collected 24 points, Tynemouth 6 points.

Where to start with the summary of the week? I do a football predictor, Soccer 6, as I'm sure many of you do, you try and select the correct scores from 6 football matches, if you were to apply the same rules and try to predict the results of the NEPL for the last few weeks I wonder how well anyone would have done?

Burnmoor top of the table and with another win this week, keep marching on, now 65 points clear, but the second, third and fourth teams all lost, and the three bottom teams all won this week, Burnopfield 249 points are still second, Ashington third, 247 points and South North are up to fourth on 244 points. Felling and Chester le Street are joint fifth with 231 points with Sunderland seventh on 223 and Tynemouth eighth on 206, they have a tough run in and a last game at Newcastle, Tynedale in ninth are 19 points adrift of Tynemouth and ten ahead of Castle Eden, who have 177, Newcastle are eleventh with 176 and Benwell Hill, still fighting hard have 159 points.

With one or two teams in freefall and finding winning ever more difficult, the end of the school holidays may impact positively on players availability in the forthcoming weeks and thus team performances. With the title all but mathematically belonging to Burnmoor and only 24 points for a win, Benwell Hill may need to win three out of the last four to have a chance of staying up, the picture will be a lot clearer after the upcoming "double" weekend with league games on the Saturday and Sunday.

The change to orange ball once again gives the batter the advantage over the bowler, only one century and no five wickets this week, the batsmen in the ascendency, 24 centuries over 21 five wickets for the bowlers.

Anyone fancy an NEPL Super 6?

Saturday 31st August 2024

This weekend sees a rare NEPL "double header" with league games on the Saturday and the Sunday, Sunday's games being the rearranged games from the washed-out opening weekend of the season back in April. As someone who played in The Tyneside Senior League we played four double weekends per season, one of which was a Bank Holiday Monday, I always enjoyed playing in them, as a now neutral and amateur photographer, possibly even more so, as a would-be author of a book about the NEPL I love it, it's a chance for a major change if any club can win both games and could turn a season around, bring it on!

Benwell Hill faced a tricky home fixture against the potentially destructive Felling batting line up. I chose this one to attend with the camera, with the title as good as over in my opinion I wanted to have a look at the bottom three teams this weekend. The news that Yash Kothari wouldn't be returning for the remainder of the season was no doubt a blow for Benwell Hill, as the top aggregate run scorer so far this season and a useful bowler I'm sure they could have used him in the run to the season's end. The toss was won by Felling, and they elected to field. Ishaq Khan quickly gave Felling a start, bowling Rory Hanley for 9 with the score on 16. However veteran opener Adam Heather and the upcoming Dan Gardiner then added 63 for the second wicket, Gardiner falling for 25 when he holed out to deep square leg with the score on 79. This brought Haydon Mustard to the crease and he and Heather showed what a good wicket this was by adding 96 for the third wicket, Heather was bowled by Ishaq Khan for 76, his innings came from 105 balls with 8 fours, this was his 53rd NEPL half century, for the record he also has 11 NEPL centuries and after today he now has 9812 NEPL runs, a truly remarkable NEPL career. Mustard, at the other end of the NEPL spectrum and barely just starting out, went on to make 80 from 80 balls with 8 fours and a six, the six sailing right over my head at long off! This was his 4th NEPL half century and his highest NEPL score to date. With Will Archbold making 20 and being run out from the last ball of the innings, Benwell Hill reached 255 for the loss of 7 wickets from their 45 overs. Alasdair Appleby took 3 for 53, the impressive Ishaq Khan 2 for 46 and Elliot Fox had 1 for 55.

Talking to one or two around the ground the feeling was that despite the 255, that the wicket was so good that Hill might be 20 or 30 short of a winning total. And so, it proved, an opening partnership of 182 between Alasdair Appleby and Tyler Easton in 23.4 overs saw Felling racing towards victory. Appleby was first out when he was bowled for 131 by Dan Gardiner, his innings had come from 82 balls with 19 fours and 6 sixes, this was his 3rd NEPL century and his highest NEPL score to date. Easton, on his 100th NEPL appearance, was out for 50 from 75 balls with 7 fours, his 11th NEPL half century. Both batsmen had fallen to Dan Gardiner, who would finish with 4 for 69, but 37 not out from Seb Allison saw Felling home by six wickets, 256 for 4 from 34.1 overs. Felling, 24 points, Benwell Hill 5 points.

Burnopfield, pushing for second place against a Sunderland side still aiming for a top four finish of their own was an interesting looking fixture, Burnopfield won the toss and elected to field. An opening stand of 49 between George Fishwick and Dan Shurben got Sunderland off to a promising start, but Fishwick fell for 28 with the score on 49 and Shurben went one run later for 19 and Sunderland were 50 for 2. The innings was then built around a half century from Chris Youldon, his 58 from 74 balls contained 9 fours and was his 6th NEPL half century, he was last man out with the score on 169 from 44.1 overs. Amann Ulhaq took 4 for 34, Ross Whitfield Jnr 2 for 34, Finlay McGurk 1 for 28, Harry Lumsden 1 for 29 and Matthew Oswell 1 for 38.

Burnopfield made a nightmare of a start when they replied, the ever-dangerous John Oswell run out from the last ball of the first over without facing a ball, 0 for 1. This became 15 for 2 and 20 for 3 shortly afterwards, Matthew Oswell was then out for 20 to make it 37 for 4 and from there only Harry Lumsden, with 21, presented any real resistance as Burnopfield were disappointingly bowled out for 107 in 34.5 overs. Not surprisingly there were some excellent bowling figures from the Sunderland lads, Jack Johnson had 4 for 27, Jack Brassell 3 for 13, and Joe Stuart 2 for 18. Sunderland 24 points for their 62 runs win, Burnopfield 4 points.

Castle Eden, with a little breathing space over the bottom club Benwell Hill, would see today as a chance to put further daylight between them and relegation and also give visitor's Tynemouth, next above them in the table, a sleepless night or two! Castle Eden won the toss and elected to bat. Castle Eden made steady progress without the big partnership they needed to get them a big score, Nicholas Sampson-Barnes top scored with 60 from 62 balls with 8 fours and 3 sixes, his 5th NEPL half century, but with the next highest score 18 from Chris Tudball, they managed a par score of 170 all out from 32.5 overs. For Tynemouth Martin Pollard took 3 for 19, Freddie Harrison 3 for 36, Matthew Brown 2 for 39, Phil Morse 1 for 13 and Barry Stewart 1 for 39.

An opening stand of 91 between Ben Debnam and Matthew Kimmitt saw the visitors well placed to kick on and take the win, Debnam was first out for 36. Kimmitt and Robbie Bowman then took the score to 134 when Bowman was out for 20 to give the host's a glimmer of hope but Kimmitt went on to make 67 from 82 balls with 7 fours and 3 sixes, his 4th NEPL half century, and although he was out with the score on 151, 12 each from Matthew Brown and Stan McAlindon, the latter not out, and 9 not out from 5 balls from Josh Moors saw Tynemouth reach their target for the loss of 4 wickets and take the win, Tynemouth 24 points, Castle Eden 3 point. Tynemouth no longer looking over their shoulder at the league table! To round this one up, Charlie Scorer took 2 for 20, J.P Meade 1 for 15 and Bilawal Iqbal 1 for 44.

Chester le Street hosted champions elect Burnmoor today, still with top four ambitions of their own, Burnmoor won the toss and elected to field. All of their top three batsmen made double figures, Ethan Connolly 18, Jacob McCann, 21, and Andrew Smith 36, but no-one went on to make a half century, Waqas Maqsood picked up his now obligatory three wickets, 3 for 30 and Craig Stephenson took 5 for 16 from nine overs, with Ryan Pringle also taking 1 for 21 and Graeme Bridge 1 for 22, Chester were bowled out in 42 overs for 133.

Burnmoor made a steady start in reply, 28 for the first wicket and although they were 62 for 3 at one point, Stuart Poynter, batting at five, continued his remarkable season with 42 not out to ensure his side got over the line, Mitch Killeen had earlier hit 34 and Allan Worthy with 7 not out was there at the end, Burnmoor 134 for 4 wickets, winning by six wickets. For Chester Matthew Robinson had 1 for 23, Quentin Hughes 1 for 36 and Seb Hughes-Pinan 2 for 54. Burnmoor 24 points, Chester le Street got 2 points.

After Quentin Hughes recently joined a very select group of players with 400 NEPL appearances, he was joined today by Allan Worthy, prior to today Worthy has scored 12141 runs at an average of 36.45, with 73 half centuries and 20 centuries, he has also taken 114 wickets at an average of 25.13 and best figures of 8 for 12, he is also still one of the league's best slip catchers and has 203 NEPL catches to his credit before today's game.

Newcastle would be hoping a home game against an out of form Ashington side would give them a chance to keep their relegation fight going, Newcastle won the toss and elected to field. Although Newcastle took two wickets inside eight overs, 33 for 2, Jack McCarthy and Ben Harmison put them back on track with a partnership of 70 for the third wicket, Harmison out for 20. McCarthy went on to make 95 from 110 balls with 7 fours and 4 sixes, this was his highest NEPL score to date, beating his previous high of 63 not out by some distance. With Callum Storey batting at eight, adding an NEPL career best 41, Ashington went on to make 255 for 9 wickets from 45 overs. George Darwood picked up 5 for 70, Asher Hart 3 for 44 and Mohsin Mukhtar 1 for 33.

When Newcastle batted Charlie Harmison removed Hamzah Amin for 5 and Matt Collins dismissed Asher Hart for 18, to leave Newcastle on 58 for 2. In recent weeks the three key batsmen for the home side have been Ben Robinson, Mohsin Mukhtar and Jaques du Toit, this proved to be the case once again, Robinson carried his bat for 102 not out from 129 balls with 12 fours and 2 sixes, this was his 3rd NEPL century, Mukhtar made 46 from 52 balls with 5 fours, and du Toit hit 62 not out from 38 balls with 6 fours and 4 sixes for his 49th NEPL half century. Newcastle, 257 for 3 wickets from 41.5 overs, won by 7 wickets to collect 24 points, Ashington, 5 points in defeat. For completeness, Callum Storey finished with 1 for 18, Matty Collins 1 for 34 and Charlie Harmison 1 for 56.

South North, despite an inconsistent season and missing Tom Rogers, recalled earlier in the month than expected by his state side in Australia, still find themselves with runners-up spot as a realistic proposition, with visitor's Tynedale scrapping for every point, this was another interesting game for the neutral. Tynedale won the toss and elected to bat. Oliver Fletcher was the standout batsman with 58 from 79 balls with 6 fours and 2 sixes, this was his maiden NEPL half century, Joe Barber gave good support with 35 and six other batsmen made double figures as Tynedale posted a respectable 213 for 9 from their 45 overs. All five South North bowlers used took wickets, Oli McGee had 2 for 41, Jonny Wightman 2 for 53, Will Alexander 2 for 58, Sean Tindale 1 for 26 and Lee Crozier 1 for 33.

Matthew Scott removed Sol Bell early doors for 6 when South North were 17, but unfortunately for Tynedale that was as good as it got, Simon Birtwisle hit 80 not out from 110 balls with 8 fours, this was his 69th NEPL half century, and Nikhil Gorantla made 122 not out from 80 balls with 16 fours and 4 sixes, his 6th NEPL century. When he scored his second run that was his 1,000 NEPL career runs in just his 26th appearance and innings. South North were 214 for 1 from 33.3 overs to win by 9 wickets and collect 24 points, Tynedale, 4 points in defeat. Scott, the only wicket taker finished with 1 for 21.

I did feel a little for the two sides who both posted first innings scores of 255 from their 45 overs and lost, Benwell Hill in particular must have been a difficult one to take as it makes their relegation fight now all but over, but such is the game of cricket and the strength of the league. With Tynemouth getting a crucial win at Castle Eden, it now looks a three-way fight between Newcastle on 200 points, Tynedale on 191 points and Castle Eden on 177 for the last relegation spot.

Burnmoor now find themselves 70 points clear at the top of the league table with a maximum of 72 points to play for, I suspect we will be talking a bit more about that after tomorrow's games.

Sunday 1st September 2024

With yesterday's games now a matter of record, Burnmoor look home and dry and can win the title today, South North are now making a determined charge for runners up spot as others fall away, and at the bottom of the table, a big win for Newcastle and the other bottom three sides all losing should set them up nicely for a huge game at Tynedale.

Burnopfield at home to Ashington saw two of the clubs challenging for a top four spot, with Burnopfield a single point of Ashington and placed fourth prior to the game, both teams would have relished this one. Burnopfield won the toss and elected to field. They got a big wicket early on, Jack McCarthy who had just missed out on a ton yesterday was caught by Matthew Oswell off the bowling of Harry Lumsden for 4 with the score at 21. Jack Jessop and Matthew Potts then added 46 for the second wicket but it was a partnership for the fourth wicket of 111 between Ben Harmison and Sean McCafferty which established the innings. Harmison scored 54 from 83 balls with 4 fours and 2 sixes, this was his 16th NEPL half century. McCafferty was dismissed for 47 but James Harmison then hit 34 not out from 30 balls to get Ashington to their second 200 plus score of the weekend, 242 for 6 from their 45 overs. Burnopfield's wicket takers were Finlay McGurk, 3 for 31, Matthew Oswell 1 for 45 and Harry Lumsden 1 for 66.

In reply Burnopfield lost both openers for a single apiece and found themselves at 4 for 2, they did recover, largely due to the efforts of Ross Whitfield Jnr who hit 78 from 59 balls with 10 fours and a six, this was his 11th NEPL half century, but with the next highest score just 17 not out from George Weston, they never really challenged the total and were bowled out for 148 from 31.3 overs. The wickets were shared around among the Ashington bowlers, Alex Nice 2 for 2, James Harmison 2 for 28, Cam Nichols 2 for 43, Ian Sharkey 2 for 46, Matthew Collins 1 for 27 and there was a run out. Ashington picked up 24 points, Burnopfield 3 points.

Burnmoor at home to Tynemouth saw the home side looking to win the league at their own ground, they won the toss and elected to field. Tynemouth made a good start, Ben Debnam and Matthew Kimmitt scoring 69 for the first wicket, Kimmitt the first to go for 22. Debnam went on to score his 25th NEPL half century, 81 from 96 balls with 10 fours and a six, unfortunately for Tynemouth no-one else made double figures as they were bowled out for 161 from 36 overs. Waqas Maqsood took 3 for 17, Graeme Bridge 2 or 18, Josh Coughlin 2 for 36, Craig Stephenson 2 for 33 and Ryan Pringle 1 for 33.

There was a rare double failure for Burnmoor's openers as both were dismissed early on to leave them on 16 for 2, Allan Worthy and Ryan Pringle then added 54 for the third wicket, Worthy out for 8 as they reached 70 for 3. When Ryan Pringle was out for 50 from 30 balls with 7 fours and 2 sixes, his 27th NEPL half century, they were now 87 for 4. Stuart Poynter was next out for 22 with the score on 122 but for the second time in a few weeks Josh Coughlin saw them home with a score in the forties, 42 not out to be exact, although they did lose one more wicket on the way. Burnmoor 164 for 6 from 25.2 overs. Freddie Harrison had 2 for 36, Josh Moors 2 for 45, Barry Stewart

1 for 18 and Martin Pollard 1 for 18. Burnmoor collected 24 points for their 4-wicket win, Tynemouth 4 points and therefore congratulations to Burnmoor on winning their second NEPL title, with two games to go and only one loss in the season, they are undoubtedly "Worthy" champions, a powerful batting line up and an excellent overseas fast bowling pro, well supported by an experienced and varied spin attack made them formidable competition throughout the season. The league batting and bowling averages will further enhance the reputations of many of the individuals and will no doubt reflect the strong seasons many of their players have had.

Castle Eden at home to Felling was affected by the weather as both innings were restricted to 24 overs. Felling won the toss and elected to field. Openers Jonathan Malkin with 44 from 57 balls and Muhaymen Majeed with 24 from 21 balls set the tone for the home side but it was J.P Meade who was to define it, he hit 79 from just 39 balls with 6 fours and 6 sixes, this was his 2nd NEPL half century, and he guided Castle Eden to 203 for 6 wickets in their 24 overs, the Felling wicket takers were Tony Trotter with 2 for 32, Alasdair Appleby 2 for 55 and Elliot Fox 1 for 18 with one run out.

Felling made a good start when they replied, the opening pair of Alasdair Appleby and Alan Mustard putting on 45, but this was the biggest partnership of the innings they lost wickets at regular intervals, Ed Hurst with 30 and Elliot Fox with 30 not out were the highest scorers but Felling were restricted to 168 for 9 from their 45 overs. Bilawal Iqbal took 3 for 28, Jonathan Malkin 2 for 33, Robbie McGlasham 2 for 38 and Alan Unsworth 1 for 25, they also had a run out. Castle Eden got 24 points for winning by 37 runs, Felling, 4 points in defeat.

Chester le Street hosting Sunderland was another game with both sides harbouring top four ambitions, Sunderland won the toss and elected to field. The early loss of Ethan Connolly, bowled by Micky Allan for 4, brought Andrew Smith to the crease, he and opener Jacob McCann put on a healthy 93 for the second wicket, Smith scored 61 from 47 balls with 9 fours and 2 sixes, his 65th NEPL half century. With his departure James Thompson was next in, he would score 65 from 62 balls with 6 fours, this was his 21st NEPL half century as he and McCann added a further 139 for the third wicket. McCann was eventually bowled by Milo Coates having made exactly 100 from 121 balls with 10 fours and a six, this was his 5th NEPL century. Chester would close their innings on 277 for 5 from 45 overs, only three bowlers took wickets, Micky Allan took 2 for 34, Milo Coates had 2 for 49 and Joe Stuart took 1 for 50.

Sunderland lost George Fishwick to Quentin Hughes third ball of the innings and never really recovered, Chris Youldon hit 25 and Robert Potts 20 but no-one else made double figures as they stumbled to 102 all out from 28.5 overs. Ash Thorpe took 4 for 19, Matthew Robinson 3 for 22, Quentin Hughes 2 for 36 and Hedley Windows 1 for 16. Chester won by 175 runs and collected 24 points, Sunderland 2 points.

South North and visiting Benwell Hill had implications for both sides, South North looking to finish the season strongly as runners up, Benwell Hill looking to avoid relegation. South North won the toss and elected to field. Seven Benwell Hill batsmen would make double figures, South North "old boy" Adam Heather top scoring with 32 but with no-one getting to 50, they probably would have felt that their score of 181 all out in 41 overs might not be challenging enough. Sean Tindale continued his good season with bat and ball, taking 4 for 24, he was well supported by Oli McGee 2 for 38, Lee Crozier 2 for 44, Will Alexander 1 for 32 and Jonny Wightman 1 for 37.

The poor weather which has blighted this season intervened in this game and South North found their target was cut to 129 from 28 overs. Although they lost Simon Birtwisle for 24 and Nikhil Gorantla for 6, Sol Bell with his 18th NEPL half century, 56 not out from 48 balls with 8 fours, and 26 not out from Chris Hewison saw South North win comfortably, 131 for 2 from 17.5 overs. Bell also passed 3000 NEPL career runs when he scored his 41st run. For Benwell Hill, Rory Hanley took 1 for 22 and Luke Mussett 1 for 35 as South North got 24 points and Benwell Hill 3 points.

Tynedale at home to Newcastle was a massive fixture in the context of the relegation battle, Newcastle 9 points ahead of the hosts, second bottom Castle Eden a further 14 points behind Tynedale. I attended this game with my camera, Tynedale won the toss and elected to field. A slight delay in the start meant the game was cut to 40 overs a side. It was another green looking Tynedale wicket, but, although it was on the slow side, it played well, nothing misbehaved. Seven Newcastle batsmen got into double figures, Ben Robinson after an unbeaten century yesterday battled hard for the top score of 49, Jaques du Toit with 20 was the next best performing batsmen. The highlight of the innings was an excellent caught and bowled by Seth Robbie, du Toit smacked a full toss back at him and Robbie got both hands on it to pull off a smart catch. Newcastle made 181 from their 40 overs, Nkosana Mpofu had 2 for 23, Matthew Scott 2 for 26, Aaron Rourke 2 for 32, Seth Robbie 2 for 47 and Archie Fletcher 1 for 37.

Tynedale made a steady start but with the score on 17 Mpofu tried a cut shot to a ball outside off stump from George Darwood and was well caught at first slip by Asher Hart for 8. Not much happened until the score reached 28 when Mohsin Mukhtar got two leg before decisions in two balls to reduce Tynedale to 28 for 3 from 10 overs. Before another ball was bowled it started to rain, heavily, the umpires sensibly took the players off and that's where the game sat when it was abandoned. George Darwood had 1 for 14 and Mohsin Mukhtar one over for two wickets and one run. Both sides got 9 points for the abandonment, and I suspect given their own excellent win, the real winners of today's game was Castle Eden, they visit Tynedale next week and the double weekend has certainly kept things interesting at the bottom of the table.

Saturday 7th September 2024

Going into this week there are two battles taking place, the push for runners up and a top four place and the fight to stay in the league. South North, 292 points, are well placed in second, 16 points ahead of Ashington, 276 points, who are third. Ashington are themselves 16 points ahead of fourth placed Felling, 260 points, with just a three-point gap to Chester le Street, 257 points, in fifth, and Burnopfield one point behind them in sixth. At the other end, with just 48 points to play for, Benwell Hill, 167 points are now 33 points adrift of now second bottom Tynedale, 200 points. Castle Eden with 204 points are third bottom with Newcastle on 209 points. With Newcastle at Burnmoor this week, the Tynedale v Castle Eden game takes on epic proportions, I just hope as I write this that the weather allows a full programme today.

Benwell Hill at home to Ashington is probably an appropriate place to start, the visitors winning the toss and electing to field. An opening stand of 70 between Adam Heather, who was first out for 20, and Haydon Mustard set the tone for Benwell Hill. Mustard went on to score 107 from 133 balls with 7 fours and 2 sixes, this was his maiden NEPL century and eclipsed his previous best score of 80 made last week! Ashington succeeded in picking up wickets regularly enough to make sure the home side never got away from them and Hill closed their innings on 203 for 9 from their 45 overs. James Harmison took 2 for 30, Ian Sharkey 2 for 32, Cam Nichols 2 for 45, Alex Nice 1 for 24 and Charlie Harmison 1 for 39, there was also a run out.

Ashington's Jack Jessop and Sean McCafferty bettered the opening stand of their hosts as they had an opening stand of 75, Jessop the first to go for 48. When McCafferty was out for 26 with the score on 90, Hill must have hoped this was their chance to take a few wickets and keep their season alive, sadly for them it wasn't, Jack McCarthy and Ben Harmison took the score to 202 before Harmison was dismissed for 69, the innings coming from 63 balls with 11 fours and a six, this was his 17th NEPL half century. McCarthy was 50 not out from 51 balls with 4 fours and a six as he hit his 3rd NEPL half century, Cam Nichols faced one ball from which he hit for 4 as Ashington 206 for 3 wickets from 35.4 overs to win by 7 wickets. The wicket takers for Benwell Hill were Callum Harding 1 for 45, Prahalad Nadella 1 for 45 and a run out. Ashington 24 points, Benwell Hill 5 points and thus, relegated for the first time in their NEPL history.

Burnmoor at home to Newcastle was an important game for the visitors, the hosts looking to maintain their fine record of only one loss this season weren't going to ease up, so the game was set up nicely. Newcastle won the toss and elected to field and were soon confident they had made the right decision as George Darwood took 3 quick wickets to have the home side reeling at 15 for 3, the third wicket had brought Stuart Poynter to the crease to join Noah Worthy and these two restored some order to Burnmoor, although Poynter had to retire hurt when he had scored 20. Worthy Junior was joined briefly at the crease by his dad, Allan, but Noah fell soon after for 20 with the score on 58. Allan Worthy then went on to complete his 74th NEPL half century as he made 59 from 55 balls with 6 fours and 3 sixes. Poynter returned to bat later, out for 24 and with 20 not out from Craig Stephenson and 18 from Josh Coughlin, Burnmoor reached a respectable total of 181 for 9 from their 45 overs. For Newcastle Levi Olver took 3 for 15, George Darwood 3 for 24, Asher Hart 1 for 20 and Mohsin Mukhtar, on his 100th NEPL appearance, 1 for 37.

Newcastle made an unsteady start as they had lost both openers by the time the score was 22, both to Waqas Maqsood. They fell away quickly to be 70 for 8 as Burnmoor showed why they have only lost once this season;

it took a stand of 96 for the ninth wicket between Levi Olver and George Darwood to get Newcastle close to the Burnmoor score. When Darwood was out for 52 from 57 balls with 6 fours, his 2nd NEPL half century, the score was 164 for 9. Olver would remain 41 not out and Woody Wilson 4 not out as Newcastle fell just short, 171 for 9 from their 45 overs, Graeme Bridge took 3 for 30, Maqsood 2 for 20, Craig Stephenson 2 for 30, Mitch Killeen 1 for 35, and Josh Coughlin 1 for 37. Burnmoor had won by 10 runs and collect 24 points, Newcastle get 6 useful points in their fight against relegation.

Felling played host to Burnopfield with just 4 points separating the two teams, the visitors won the toss and elected to field. Felling opener Alasdair Appleby continued his fine recent form as he made 61 from 45 balls with 11 fours and a six, this was his 14th NEPL half century and when he scored his 14th run that brought up his 3000th NEPL run, when you see that he also has 117 wickets to his credit before today's game, you would have to put him in the conversation to be among the league's current crop of best all-rounders. Despite their top five all making double figures Felling never quite posted the big score it often takes to beat Burnopfield as they were bowled out for 176 in 37.1 overs. Amaan Ulhaq continued to collect wickets at a good rate and took 4 for 38 and he was well supported by Ross Whitfield Jnr with 3 for 19 and Finlay McGirk 3 for 25.

Felling's Seb Allison made sure Burnopfield weren't going to have an easy ride to victory, taking two wickets in successive balls in the fifth over to leave them 21 for 2. When Elliot Fox removed the dangerous John Oswell for 23 and the score 41 for 3, the game was in the balance, when Burnopfield slipped to 67 for 5 the balance appeared to have tipped in Felling's direction. It took a stand of 83 for the sixth wicket between Callum Brown and Sam Dinning to tip the balance the other way, Brown was out for 52 from 67 balls with 4 fours and 2 sixes, this was his 2nd NEPL half century, Dinning was unbeaten on 39, including hitting two fours from consecutive balls to win the game as Burnopfield 179 for 6 from 35.3 overs won by 4 wickets. Burnopfield 24 points, Felling 5 points.

Sunderland welcomed South North to Ashbrooke today, the visitors winning the toss and electing to field. Sean Tindale removed both openers to have Sunderland on 27 for 2 but 57 from 76 balls with 11 fours from Charlie Coulthard, his 2nd NEPL half century and highest score in the league to date, and 42 from wicketkeeper and captain Chris Youldon, saw Sunderland give themselves a good score, 221 all out from 44.1 overs. Youldon reached 2000 NEPL career runs when he reached 39, for South North Tindale finished with 4 for 34, Oli McGee had 2 for 35, Will Alexander 2 for 48 and Lee Crozier 2 for 54. A word here on South North's Oli McGee, when he took his first wicket today, Micky Allan stumped by Rob Peyton for 13, that was his 400th NEPL career wicket, a tremendous achievement, I recall when I started this book chatting with an umpire about Lee Crozier and his wicket haul, (after today he has 857), the umpire, far more knowledgeable about the league than I, said that, in his opinion, the only person he has seen capable of beating Crozier's wicket total, was Oli McGee, I think that's high praise indeed and will be something for the next generation to keep an eye on!

South North made a good start when they replied, Simon Birtwisle and Sol Bell putting on 66 for the first wicket, Birtwisle the first to go for 11. Sunderland then dismissed Nikhil Gorantla, Chris Hewison and Sean Tindale to leave the visitors 87 for 4, this became 107 for 5 when Bell was out for 77 from 71 balls with 10 fours and a six, this was his 19th NEPL half century. Adam Cragg with 45 led the lower order as South North kept fighting to get to the total but in the end, they were bowled out for 194 from 37.4 overs, Sunderland won by 27 runs. Their bowlers were led by 3 for 26 from Brett Hutchinson, Jack Johnson had 2 for 38, Jack Brassell 2 for 45, George Drissell 1 for 21, Joe Stuart 1 for 25, and Micky Allan 1 for 33. Sunderland 24 points, South North 7 points.

Tynedale 11th in the table at home to Castle Eden was a huge game for both teams with just 4 points between them and relegation a real possibility for the side which lost. I was at this game with my camera as Tynedale won the toss and invited Castle Eden to bat. Winning the toss was probably about as good as the day got for the hosts, 19 were scored from the opening over and an opening stand of 85 between Jonathan Malkin and Muhaymen Majeed set the innings up. Malkin was out for 15 but all that did was bring J.P Meade to the crease and if anything, the tempo of the innings picked up. Majeed went on to make his maiden NEPL century, 134 from 130 balls with 14 fours and 4 sixes and Meade 61 from 59 balls with 2 fours and 5 sixes for his 3rd NEPL half century. Nicholas Sampson-Barnes added 29 not out from 27 balls as Castle Eden reached a daunting 290 for 6 form their 45 overs. Thomas Cant had bowled well for his 2 for 37 at an economy rate of 4.11, and there were wickets for Archie Fletcher 1 for 36, Nathan Byerley 1 for 50 and Matthew Scott 1 for 70.

Where to start with the reply…. Tynedale had got to 3 when Bilawal Iqbal took the first wicket, Keith Bailey took the second with the score still on 3, and then Iqbal removed another one without any addition to the score, Tynedale 3 for 3. Iqbal then took four more wickets in next to no time to leave Tynedale reeling on 11 or 7 and this rapidly became 11 for 8 when Bailey nipped in for his second wicket. Number nine Aaron Rourke then played a shot or two as he made 14, the only batsman in double figures, when he also fell to Iqbal the score was now 30 for 9 and it was no surprise when Iqbal bowled the last man with the score on 34, in keeping with Tynedale's day, the last wicket was a thick inside edge which had just enough momentum to topple the off bail. The manner of the last wicket shouldn't detract from an outstanding example of swing bowling at a fast pace, the phrase "unplayable" is often used in cricket, today I think Bilawal Iqbal was, he finished with 8.5 overs, 3 maidens, 8 for 18, Keith Bailey was the other wicket taker with 2 for 10 and he bowled a fine spell also. Castle Eden 24 points for the win, Tynedale 2 points, a huge win for the visitors who now enter the last week of the season free from the threat of relegation.

Tynemouth at home to a Chester le Street side with top four ambitions was an interesting fixture, the visitors won the toss and elected to field. Tynemouth made a steady start, but their innings and the game turned when the score was 33 for 1 and Seb Hughes-Pinan was introduced to the bowling attack. He took wickets with his second and third balls to reduce Tynemouth to 33 for 3, when his father Quentin repeated the trick the next over, father and son had reduced their hosts to 33 for 5, taking four wickets in the space of seven balls. Joe Snowdon, with 26, and Dan McGee with 33 restored respectability to the home side but a total of 133 all out in 42.3 overs was a below par score. Seb Hughes-Pinan finished with 3 for 24, Ash Thorpe 2 for 14, Quentin Hughes 2 for 22, Josh Wilson 1 for 21 and Matthew Robinson 1 for 34.

Although Jacob McCann fell with the score on 7, opening bat Ethan Connolly made 30 not out and Andrew Smith 92 not out with 13 fours and 3 sixes as Chester won by 9 wickets, 134 for 1 from 23 overs, the solitary wicket taker for Tynemouth was martin Pollard, 1 for 34. Chester took 24 points back to Ropery Lane, Tynemouth 1 point.

Weather permitting, one game to go, Burnmoor already confirmed as champions, Benwell Hill already relegated, that leaves Ashington who are second, one point ahead of South North in the race for runners up spot, although fourth place Chester le Street and fifth placed Burnopfield have a mathematical shot at it. Sunderland, Felling, Tynemouth and Castle Eden now have mid table security and that leaves Newcastle tenth on 215 points and Tynedale on 202 points to fight for the last relegation place.

Saturday 14th September 2024

In a season where the British weather caused the loss of a number of games, the last weekend…we were fortunate to get a full programme completed to finish the season off. The game of the day was arguably Ashington, occupying and looking for a win to cement second place at home to new Champions Burnmoor. Ashington had won the Northumberland County Cup the evening before, limiting Newcastle City to 97 for 8 from their 15 overs, and then Jack Jessop with an unbeaten 46 from 22 balls, and Jack McCarthy an unbeaten 49 from 22 balls, saw them reach 100 for 1 from just 7.5 overs, as they won by 9 wickets.

Burnmoor won the toss and elected to bat on what looked to be a good wicket. I attended this one with my camera as Ross Greenwell and Marcus Brown took fourteen from the first two overs and set Burnmoor on their way. They had scored 58 for the first wicket when Brown nicked one from Ian Sharkey for 35. Greenwell went on to make 26 and Ryan Pringle 18, both falling to Charlie Harmison to leave Burnmoor on 102 for 3, but three batsmen made scores in their 40's, Mitch Killen had 45, Josh Coughlin 44 and Waqas Maqsood 48 not out, and Stuart Poynter hit his 16th NEPL half century, 72 from 34 balls with 10 fours and 4 sixes, as Burnmoor posted 321 for 8 from their 45 overs. For Ashington Charlie Harmison had 2 for 37, Matthew Potts 2 for 59, Sean McCafferty 1 for 39, Alex Nice 1 for 40, Ian Sharkey 1 for 41 and Alex Storey 1 for 94. Spare a thought for Cam Nichols who only bowled one over before badly injuring his knee whilst fielding and was subsequently unable to bat.

After Maqsood struck an early blow for Burnmoor, Jack Jessop and Jack McCarthy both continued their fine form of the previous evening, McCarthy made 85 from 54 balls with 8 fours and 5 sixes, his 4th NEPL half century, and Jessop made 81 from 73 balls with 8 fours and a six, his 4th NEPL half century, as the pair added 118 for the second wicket. It was captain Ryan Pringle who had dismissed McCarthy, and he went on to cause the rest of the Ashington batting line up all sorts of problems, taking 6 for 46, with Maqsood chipping in with 3 for 46 and the unfortunate Nichols being unable to bat, Ashington were all out for 224 from 33.3 overs. A word on Burnmoor wicket keeper Alec Linsley, he took 4 catches and 2 stumpings in this match, a wicket keeping five for! Burnmoor won by 97 runs and collected 24 points, this takes them through the 400-point barrier to finish the season on 410 points, for Ashington, they collected 7 points, to finish on 307 and, given results elsewhere, finish third.

Burnopfield were looking to finish on a high at home to relegated Benwell Hill, the visitors won the toss and elected to bat. They were soon showing the very frailties which had got them demoted as they slipped to 31 for 5. Phil Bell, batting at six and captain Peter Halliday at seven restored some respectability to the score, adding 143 for the sixth wicket, Bell was out for 65 from 77 balls with 7 fours, his 13th NEPL half century, and Halliday 59 from 79 balls, also with 7 fours, his 5th NEPL half century. For Burnopfield five bowlers took wickets, Matthew Oswell had 3 for 36, Finlay McGurk 2 for 31, Harry Lumsden 2 for 33, Callum Brown 1 for 10 and Amaan Ulhaq 1 for 42, there was also a run out as Hill reached 203 all out in 39.2 overs.

Not for the first time with Burnopfield this season, I find myself not sure where to start, so I will keep this simple, Ben McKinney hit his 2nd NEPL century, 100 not out from 55 balls with 10 fours and 4 sixes, his opening partner, John Oswell, hit his 17th NEPL half century, 91 not out from 53 balls with 11 fours and 4 sixes, the pair had an unbroken opening stand of 204 from just 18 overs as Burnopfield won by 10 wickets. They collected 24 points for the win, Benwell Hill 4 points in defeat. Burnopfield finished just outside the top four, 1 point behind Chester le Street.

Castle Eden at home to Sunderland was a game with nothing but finishing the season well at stake, the home side safe from relegation, Sunderland with the top four just beyond them but a good season none the less. The home side won the toss and elected to bat, several small partnerships developed but the innings was defined by 45 from John Spellman and exactly 50 from Bilawal Iqbal. The latter, Iqbal, has had a good season with the bat, he scored his 5th NEPL half century, the innings came from 43 balls with 2 fours and 5 sixes. Castle Eden were 186 all out from 43 overs, the wickers were shared around, Joe Stuart 2 for 15, Micky Allan 2 for 34, Jack Johnson 2 for 35, Brett Hutchinson 2 for 37, there was also 1 for 58 from George Drissell and a run out.

The home bowlers found Sunderland's batsmen a bit more difficult than those of Tynedale the previous week as George Fishwick and George Drissell put on 140 for the first wicket. Drissell was the first to go for 81 from 69 balls with 6 fours and 6 sixes, this was his 3rd NEPL half century. Fishwick would remain unbeaten on 63, his innings coming from 69 balls with 7 fours and 3 sixes. Sunderland reached 187 for the loss of three wickets from 24.5 overs to win by 7 wickets. Jonathan Malkin had 2 for 20 and Connor Crute 1 for 41 for the home side. Sunderland 24 points, Castle Eden 4 points.

Chester le Street hosting Tynedale was a big game at both ends of the table, Chester looking to finish the season well and with a top four finish, Tynedale, despite winning six games in the course of the season, must win to have a chance of fending off relegation. They started the day 13 points behind Newcastle, they won the toss and elected to field. They quickly picked up a wicket to reduce the home side to 15 for 1. Andrew Smith then hit 69 from 61 balls with 11 fours, his 67th NEPL half century, he also passed 11500 NEPL runs when he had scored 5, he was well supported by James Thompson with 47 and Jacob McCann who made 43. Chester went on to score 243 for 7 from their 45 overs. Matthew Scott took 2 for 30, Nkosana Mpofu 2 for 37, Aaron Rourke 1 for 30, Thomas Cant 1 for 47 and Archie Fletcher 1 for 64.

Tynedale therefore needed 244 from 45 overs and Newcastle to lose to retain their NEPL status, after the first game of the season I'm sure they would have settled for that opportunity. When the evergreen Quentin Hughes had Ed Foreman stumped by Jacob McCann off the fourth ball of the innings, Tynedale must have feared the worst. Their innings would form around 54 from 74 balls with 3 fours from Nkosana Mpofu, their overseas pro, this was his 2nd NEPL half century. He was well supported by 33 from captain Daniel Parker and 58 from 54 balls with 4 fours and 3 sixes from Thomas Cant, this equalled his previous and only other NEPL half century. Despite some attacking lower order batting from Euan Stephenson, 24, Matthew Scott 13 not out and Archie Fletcher 12 not out, Tynedale fell just short and as they finished on 233 for from their 45 overs, they lost by just 10 runs. For Chester, Ash Thorpe and Josh Wilson both had 2 for 43, Seb Hughes-Pinan 1 for 26, Matthew Robinson 1 for 33 and Quentin Hughes

1 for 41. Chester 24 points, Tynedale 7 points, and now sitting on 209 points, still 6 points behind Newcastle and therefore relegated.

Newcastle had their destiny in their own hands at home to Tynemouth, win and you definitely stay in the NEPL, lose and you may be relegated. Newcastle won the toss and elected to field. Both openers were back in the dressing room with the total on 25 and they must have been relatively happy with the start they made. It was two promising younger players who repaired the early damage to the innings, Robbie Bowman making 42 and Stan McAlindon 52 from 74 balls with 6 fours, this was his 3rd NEPL half century. Both sides would have been happy enough at the break, Tynemouth 219 all out from 44.5 overs. Newcastle's successful bowlers were George Darwood, 3 for 33, Mohsin Mukhtar 2 for 31, Jaques du Toit 2 for 35, Rowan Shelton 2 for 52 and Asher Hart 1 for 46.

Newcastle made another poor start of their own, losing Bobby Green second ball without scoring, but Ben Robinson and Asher Hart put on 57 for the second wicket to put the game nicely in the balance. Robinson fell first, bowled by Barry Stewart for 16, this provoked a mini collapse as Newcastle fell away to 75 for 6, and although they recovered to reach 168 all out in 36.2 overs, it seems they never really pushed the Tynemouth total as they lost by 51 runs. Barry Stewart took 4 for 34, Martin Pollard 3 for 30, Josh Moors 1 for 22, Matthew Brown 1 for 33 and Stan McAlindon 1 for 43. Tynemouth 24 points, Newcastle 6 points, and because of the result at Ropery Lane, safe from relegation.

South North started the day one point and one place behind second placed Ashington and were at home to the powerful, if unpredictable Felling batting line up. South North won the toss and took the bull by the horns and elected to bat, and in doing so quickly lost both openers to be a shaky 25 for 2. Nikhil Gorantla batting at three then hit his 6th NEPL century, his third in just five NEPL innings, 103 from 104 balls with 11 fours and 2 sixes, he was supported by 41 from Adam Cragg, 26 from Chris Hewison and 25 from Rob Peyton as South North posted 235 for 9 from their 45 overs. Felling's Elliot Fox had 3 for 48, Alasdair Appleby 3 for 57, Seb Allison 2 for 49 and Ishaq Khan 1 for 40.

When Felling replied, Joe Cracknell hit 47 but his next highest scoring team mate was Tyler Easton on 23 as South North's bowlers picked up wickets at regular intervals. Felling were dismissed for 144 from 35.4 overs, Oli McGee took 4 for 24, Jonny Wightman 3 for 29 and Lee Crozier 3 for 48. South North won by 91 runs to pick up 24 points, Felling collected 5 points. With Ashington losing, South North had done enough to finish runners up, a bit of a strange season for them but still a great achievement.

The reason I wrote about this game last was purely alphabetical, but it was pointed out to me that the last wicket of the last match of the 2024 season was taken by Oli McGee when he had Joe Carroll leg before wicket. Just one wicket earlier Lee Crozier had bowled Liam Stamper for 6, this was Crozier's 860th NEPL wicket. Crozier had played in the very first NEPL weekend on 6th May 2000 and it seems has now bowled his last delivery for South North. Crozier has been there throughout the 25-year span of this book and therefore this league. He has 15 NEPL titles to his credit and his 860 wickets have taken him 4931.1 overs and cost him 13662 runs, each wicket has fallen at an average of 15.89.

The battle between bat and ball had seen 29 centuries and 25 occasions when bowlers picked up 5 wickets or better, a pretty even contest I would say. A final few words on the season overall, once again congratulations to Champions Burnmoor and runners up, South North. Commiserations to Tynedale and Benwell Hill, both relegated, the loss of Benwell Hill, one of the original founders of the NEPL and ever present throughout the 25 years, means only Chester le Street, South North and Tynemouth remain next season of the originals who will have been ever present. The two departing sides were replaced by Shotley Bridge and Hetton Lyons, congratulations to those two clubs.

Burnmoor managed to keep the core of their side the same throughout the season, the team that opened the season at Tynedale on 27th April 2024 was as follows-

Ross Greenwell, a right-handed batsman and regular opener as well as a useful right arm medium-fast bowler, opened the batting, making a single, he also took 1 for 27. He played 18 matches in the NEPL in the season, batting

17 times, with 3 not outs, he scored 427 runs at an average of 30.50, with 2 half centuries, his highest score of the season was 75 not out, made on 29th June 2024 at home to Ashington.

He also bowled 186 balls in the NEPL season, with 1 maiden, he conceded 155 runs and took 4 wickets at an average of 38.75. His best bowling figures were 2 for 27, taken at Felling on 11th May 2024, he also took 4 catches in the league this season.

Marcus Brown was the other opening bat to start the season, another right-handed batsman, he made 101 to get his season underway. He played 19 matches in the NEPL in the season, batting 18 times, with 2 not outs, he scored 517 runs at an average of 32.31, with 1 century and 2 half centuries, his highest score of the season was the 101, made on the opening day of the season at Tynedale on 27th April 2024. He didn't bowl in the NEPL in the season, but he did take 19 catches, a remarkable number for an outfielder.

Ryan Pringle captained the side and is well known around the NEPL as a destructive right-handed batsman and off spin bowler. He batted at three in the season opener, making 13 before falling to a brilliant catch in the covers, he took 2 for 29 when he bowled. He played 18 matches in the NEPL in the season, batting 16 times, with 2 not outs, he scored 431 runs at an average of 30.78, with 3 half centuries. His highest score of the season was 67, made at Newcastle on 22nd June 2024.

He also bowled 469 balls in the NEPL season, with 5 maidens, he conceded 316 runs and took 26 wickets at an average of 12.15. His best bowling figures were 6 for 46, taken at Ashington on 14th September 2024. He also took 6 catches in the league this season.

Mitch Killeen batted at four on his Burnmoor NEPL debut at Tynedale, he scored 2. A right arm fast bowler and right-handed batsman. His appearances for Burnmoor were limited by his success with Durham, starting the season in the Second XI, and including a century, and by season's end also playing one day cricket for the county. Killeen also demonstrates perfectly one of the things those of us from the older generation find both amusing and a bit odd, he played for Northumberland in a 3-day match at Jesmond starting on 7th July against Cumbria. He took 1 for 28 and 2 for 23 and scored 15 in his only innings. Just two weeks after that finished, on Sunday 21st July he turned out for Durham at Jesmond against Northumberland! He took 1 for 19 and scored 13. As the modern young cricketer strives for a professional contract they have to play where and when they can to showcase their talents.

Back to the NEPL and Killeen played 15 matches in the NEPL in the season, batting 14 times, with 1 not out, he scored 248 runs at an average of 19.07. He scored 2 half centuries, his highest score of the season was 57, made at home to Ashington on 29th June 2024.

He also bowled 411 balls in the NEPL season, with 13 maidens, he conceded 210 runs and took 11 wickets at an average of 19.09. His best bowling figures were 2 for 7, taken at Castle Eden on 8th June 2024, he also took 4 catches in the league this season.

Stuart Poynter was another making his NEPL debut for Burnmoor at Tynedale, a right-handed batsman and wicket keeper he marked the occasion with 247, only the third ever double century in the league and the highest individual score ever made in the NEPL. He played 17 matches in the NEPL in the season, batting 15 times, with 6 not outs, he scored 763 runs at an average of 84.78. He scored 2 centuries and 3 half centuries, his highest score of the season was the 247, made on the opening day at Tynedale. He didn't bowl in the NEPL in the season, but he did take 3 catches and a stumping.

Allan Worthy batted at six to start the season, he was 4 not out, his pedigree is well documented elsewhere in this book, his experience and knowledge of the league as well as his catching ability were valuable to Burnmoor throughout the season. He played 18 matches in the NEPL in the season, batting 13 times, with 3 not outs, he scored 160 runs at an average of 10.66 He scored 1 half century, his highest score of the season 59, was made at home to Newcastle on 7th September 2024. He took 10 NEPL catches in the 2024 season.

Josh Coughlin is a left-handed batsman and right arm medium pace bowler. He batted at number seven to start the season, making 21 not out and took 1 for 21. He played 18 matches in the NEPL in the season, batting 11 times, with 4 not outs, he scored 234 runs at an average of 33.42. His highest score of the season of 44, made on 14th September 2024 at Ashington.

He also bowled 814 balls in the NEPL season, with 20 maidens, he conceded 547 runs and took 19 wickets at an average of 28.78. His best bowling figures were 3 for 53, taken at Felling on 11th May 2024, he also took 3 catches in the league this season.

Graeme Bridge was listed to bat at eight but didn't get to bat when the season opened, he did take 1 for 11 with the ball with his slow left arm orthodox spin. He played 19 matches in the NEPL in the season, batting 4 times, with 0 not outs, he scored 7 runs.

He also bowled 882 balls in the NEPL season, with 16 maidens, he conceded 436 runs and took 37 wickets at an average of 11.78. His best bowling figures were 6 for 30, taken at Sunderland on 20th July 2024 he also took 4 catches in the league this season.

Alec Linsley was listed at nine on the scorecard, but he didn't bat when the season got underway. He is the first-choice wicket keeper and took 2 catches and gave up no byes at Tynedale. He played 17 matches in the NEPL in the season, batting 5 times, with 5 not outs, he scored 20, with his highest score of the season 9 not out, made on 14th September 2024 at Ashington. As a wicket keeper he took 25 catches and had 3 stumpings in the NEPL in 2024.

Daniel Reed was listed at number ten, he opened the bowling, taking 1 for 29 at Tynedale but didn't feature in the NEPL again this season as he joined Philadelphia in NEPL Division 1, his debut for them coming on 29th June 2024 at Whitburn.

Craig Stephenson was listed at number eleven to start the season; he didn't bat at Tynedale but took 4 for 25 with his off spin. He played 18 matches in the NEPL in the season, batting 6 times, with 2 not outs, he scored 70 runs at an average of 17.50, his highest score of the season was 25, made at home to South North on 1st June 2024.

He also bowled 636 balls in the NEPL season, with 13 maidens, he conceded 359 runs and took 21 wickets at an average of 17.10. His best bowling figures were 5 for 16, taken at Chester le Street on 31st August 2024, he didn't take a catch in the league this season.

Waqas Maqsood was their overseas pro, although he missed the first game at Tynedale, he went on to play 18 matches in the NEPL in the season, batting 9 times, with 2 not outs, he scored 143 runs at an average of 20.42. His highest score of the season was 48 not out made in the last game of the season at Ashington on 14th September 2024.

He also bowled 1104 balls in the NEPL season, with 48 maidens, he conceded 492 runs and took 44 wickets at an average of 11.18. His best bowling figures were 4 for 22, taken at home to Benwell Hill on 18th May 2024, he also took 8 catches in the league this season.

Hetton Lyons won the Banks T20 competition, defeating Whitburn in the final by 3 wickets and the inaugural Banks Salver Hundred competition was won by Burnmoor, a special mention should go to Ryan Pringle for his performance in the final against South North he scored 138 from 49 balls with 14 fours and 11 sixes, a remarkable knock by all accounts.

Stuart Poynter was named as The NEPL Player of the Year.

Burnmoor NEPL Champions 2024.

Left to Right- Back Row Stu Poynter, Mitch Killeen, Ross Greenwell, Waqas Maqsood, Marcus Brown, Craig Stephenson.

Front Row- Josh Coughlin, Alec Linsley, Ryan Pringle, Allan Worthy, Graeme Bridge.

Stuart Poynter, on his way to 247 at Tynedale on 27th April 2024.

This season also saw the introduction of the NEPL Hall of Fame, to celebrate the players and officials who have contributed to the NEPL. The individuals must not have played during the previous season. The inductees, who were announced at the NEPL Presentation Dinner on 15th November 2024 were as follows-

Players

Stephen Humble
John Graham
Richard Waite
Phil Nicholson

All four players have been well covered as the story of the 25 years of the league has unfolded, congratulations to them.

In addition to the players, it was decided to recognise those people who are behind the scenes of the league and deserved a place in the NEPL Hall of Fame as well, the first non-player to be inducted is Alan McKenna, here is a little about Alan and his role in shaping the NEPL.

He was the first Chairman of the NEPL and was also instrumental in its conception and inception. His cricket career started out slowly, he never played any organised cricket until he started work at the Ministry in 1960, to give it the full title, The Ministry of Pensions and National Insurance. They were having a cricket tournament, and he was asked to play, as a medium pace swing bowler he took nine wickets in a match and was subsequently asked to play for the Ministry Second XI. Success there led to him playing Sunday cricket for The Cavaliers, a team of players from across the Northumberland Division A sides of the time, run by John Bradford. This in turn led to Arthur Brown, for whom there is now a cup played for, asking him to North Durham in 1966. McKenna has a distinct memory of the 1966 World Cup Final, North Durham were playing at Wearmouth, one of the few leagues to play on that day, and Wearmouth, with one eye of the football, won the toss and batted. However, due to the extra time, Alan fondly recalls seeing the second half of extra time and England winning the World Cup!

As he was living at Westerhope whilst playing for North Durham, he decided to play for Backworth in 1967, he played there regularly until 1974, only stopping due to his wife becoming seriously ill and then unfortunately passing away in 1975. He then joined Benwell in 1976, playing until 1982 with the odd game here and there until 1984.

His administrative skills had started early in his career at the Ministry, he became secretary early in his playing days and this side of the game would lead him to become Chairman of Benwell in 1985 and Chairman of the Northumberland County League in 1988, a post he held until 1999.

He was elected to the management committee Northumberland County Cricket Club in 1987 and later, in 2001, became its Chairman until 2017. He is currently President of the County.

He recalls writing a letter to Don Robson, the Tyneside Senior League Chairman, and Ray Pallister, President of the Durham Senior League, suggesting that local league cricket was, in his opinion, "going stale", he suggested that amalgamating the various leagues across Durham and Northumberland into one league would help to freshen things up and provide more competition for the better players. However little interest was shown by the other two parties. If you think that the McLaurin Report, which ultimately brought about Premier Leagues, was published in 1997, Alan McKenna was ahead of the game by about three years!

He remained as Chairman of the Northumberland County League and, with others, began the process of writing the rules of the soon to be NEPL, this included start times, limitation of overs, etc. Bobby Smithson, for whom the Northumberland County Cup is now named, was Chairman of Northumberland County Cricket and a solicitor by trade and he went over and finalised the rules. Mckenna says suddenly the committees got larger and the meetings more frequent until the day came when the NEPL was formed and at the first meeting of its member clubs, he was voted in as its first Chairman.

He is quick to point out that he had many people who supported him over the years, naming Bobby Smithson, Don Robson and Bob Jackson in particular, and he was grateful to all who helped him throughout this difficult period. We have all no doubt seen "politics" at our own clubs, can you imagine trying to pull across two counties, especially Northumberland and Durham, and deal with a seemingly infinite amount of clubs, all with opinions on the new league, and then trying to come to some agreement on the best way forward?

Having overseen the initial introduction and then the league establish itself Alan McKenna stepped down as the NEPL Chairman in 2008. He is still seen regularly walking the boundary at North East Cricket grounds, I, without knowing it, saw him myself at Jesmond one day this season! I have touched upon the formation of the NEPL in the introduction to this book, without people like Alan McKenna to do both the heavy lifting and the fine detail, I can't help but wonder what sort of mess might have been made of it, it's fair to say that he has made a valuable contribution to the league and is one of the main reasons it is the success that it is.

The first NEPL Hall of Fame Inductees seen here on 15th November 2024, the night their induction was announced.

Left to right- Phil Nicholson, John Graham, Alan McKenna, Stephen Humble, Richard Waite.

Photo Courtesy of Martin Avery.

TABLE 76   NEPL Final Table 2024.

	Played	Won	Draw/Aban	Lost	Tied	Penalty Points	Bonus Points	Points
Burnmoor	22	15	6	1	0	0	51	410
South North	22	10	5	6	1	0	70	323
Ashington	22	10	4	8	0	0	84	307
Chester le Street	22	9	6	7	0	0	67	305
Burnopfield	22	10	5	7	0	0	76	304
Sunderland	22	10	5	7	0	0	62	297
Felling	22	7	6	9	0	0	80	269
Tynemouth	22	7	8	7	0	0	60	259
Castle Eden	22	6	6	10	0	0	61	232
Newcastle	22	5	5	11	1	0	81	221
Tynedale	22	6	4	12	0	0	57	209
Benwell Hill	22	3	6	13	0	0	76	176

TABLE 77   NEPL Batting Averages 2024.
Qualification 400 Runs.

Player	Club	Inns	N. O	Runs	H.S	Average
(1) S.W Poynter	Burnmoor	15	6	763	247	84.78
(2) B.S McKinney	Burnopfield	10	3	469	100 no	67.00
(3) Y.B Kothari	Benwell Hill	12	2	653	171 no	65.30
(4) M. Brown	Tynemouth	16	3	583	92 no	44.85
(5) J.R Oswell	Burnopfield	18	3	640	171	42.67
(6) Bilawal Iqbal	Castle Eden	18	5	548	112 no	42.15
(7) G.M Drissell	Sunderland	12	2	415	104 no	41.50
(8) A.L Smith	Chester le Street	18	1	688	162	40.47
(9) J.H Jessop	Ashington	18	3	590	81	39.33
(10) R.S.W Bowman	Tynemouth	17	1	615	134	38.44
(11) N.W Gorantla	South North	16	1	551	122 no	36.73
(12) A.W.O Appleby	Felling	19	0	686	131	36.11
(23) M. Brown	Burnmoor	18	2	517	101	32.31

TABLE 78   NEPL Bowling Averages 2024.
Qualification 20 Wickets.

Player	Club	Overs	Mdns	Runs	Wkts	Average
(1) Waqas Maqsood	Burnmoor	184.0	48	492	44	11.18
(2) G.D Bridge	Burnmoor	147.0	16	436	37	11.78
(3) R.D Pringle	Burnmoor	78.1	5	316	26	12.15
(4) T. Rogers	South North	122.0	17	371	28	13.25
(5) T.J Cant	Tynedale	97.3	7	305	22	13.86
(6) Amaan Ulhaq	Burnopfield	137.5	10	655	46	14.24
(7) Bilawal Iqbal	Castle Eden	170.2	27	602	40	15.05
(8) O.F McGee	South North	175.0	29	633	40	15.83
(9) J. Malkin	Castle Eden	110.4	14	454	28	16.21
(10) C. Stephenson	Burnmoor	111.0	13	359	21	17.10
(11) S.J Tindale	South North	168.3	23	666	38	17.53
(12) E. Fox	Felling	140.3	13	616	34	18.12

TABLE 79   NEPL Top Run Scorers.

Player	Club	Inns	N. O	Runs	Highest Score	Average	100's	50's
(1) S.J Birtwisle	South North	409	33	12694	151 no	33.76	17	69
(2) A. Worthy	Burnmoor	384	47	12222	156 no	36.27	20	74
(3) A.L Smith	Chester le Street	342	32	11564	180 no	37.30	24	67
(4) J.A Graham	Tynemouth	358	50	11070	132	35.94	12	78
(5) D.G Shurben	Sunderland	351	32	10385	180 no	32.55	15	53
(6) Q.J Hughes	Chester le Street	350	85	10213	136 no	38.54	6	68
(7) A.T Heather	Benwell Hill	363	39	9915	140 no	30.60	11	52
(8) C.J Hewison	South North	283	42	9473	165 no	39.31	20	49
(9) R.P Waite	Stockton	302	26	8867	150 no	32.13	15	48
(10) G.M Scott	Hetton Lyons	278	33	8073	143	32.95	13	43
(11) J. du Toit	Newcastle	200	29	7863	183	45.98	16	49
(12) J.W Coxon	Chester le Street	320	48	7434	125	27.33	8	37

TABLE 80 NEPL Top Wicket Takers.

Player	Club	Overs	Mdns	Runs	Wkts	Average	5 WI	Best Bowl
(1) L. J Crozier	South North	4955.3	1239	13649	860	15.87	40	7-21
(2) G.D Bridge	Burnmoor	3430.2	696	9652	638	15.13	26	6-21
(3) M.J Muchall	Whitburn	3108.2	653	11007	582	18.91	31	8-34
(4) R.P Waite	Stockton	3675.5	785	11509	575	20.02	25	8-28
(5) S. Humble	Burnopfield	2888.0	730	7945	547	14.52	30	8-55
(6) J.R Wightman	South North	2778.4	376	10042	532	18.88	22	8-31
(7) M.L Pollard	Tynemouth	3621.0	738	11276	530	21.28	16	7-27
(8) K. Waterson	Sunderland	2368.5	492	7957	439	18.13	21	8-53
(9) O.F McGee	South North	2088.3	347	6948	405	17.16	14	7-54
(10) Q.J Hughes	Chester le Street	2642.5	572	7547	397	19.01	8	6-38
(11) C.T Harding	Benwell Hill	2120.3	380	7402	356	20.79	7	8-17
(12) L. Simpson	Chester le Street	2267.3	449	7218	333	21.68	13	8-40

Chapter Eighteen

Close of Play

I'm an outsider to the NEPL, I never played in The NEPL and have no real connection to it.

As stated much earlier in the book, I did play at Seaton Burn with John Graham for a couple of seasons when he was a junior, before he went on to bigger and better things, I also knew Neil Corby who played at South North and Newcastle, as I played cricket with his father, Kevin, and he and my eldest son, David, used to hang around together as kids. I also played a lot of cricket with Eddie Collins, a well-known umpire in the NEPL for many seasons.

My only connection therefore to the NEPL, and it's a tenuous one, was that for the last two years, the 2022 and 2023 seasons, I have been taking photos of the league and putting them on Facebook to be viewed by anyone who cares enough to have a look. I had only missed a handful of weekends in that period, due to a holiday and a knee replacement, I managed to photograph 17 games in 2023, covering 11 of the 12 teams, thwarted by the weather on a couple of occasions from getting all 12. That's it. No real connection.

So, I was probably an unexpected proposition when I approached The League Management Committee with the idea of writing a book about the NEPL. I got the idea when sitting at home between Xmas and New Year, I saw on Facebook that Russell Perry was giving away some League handbooks and he was asking if anyone wanted them. I have previously written a book on cricket as I have alluded to during this one, approximately four years ago, I self-published it and sold 103 copies! So, I contacted Russell, and he kindly dropped the handbooks off at my house. From chatting to him and seeing the content of the handbooks, I realized that I could probably pull something together if I could find enough people to assist me with their stories. From the quality of people, I had met over those two years taking photos I believed from the off that it would be possible to write the book, having had my wife Carol fully support me, and the financial loss I made on the first book, I knew I had to find some funding though to get it to print! A meeting with Phil Haves and Phil Nicholson at Benwell Hill and a message to Duncan Stephen at South North and I suddenly had a pile of material to go to work on and the writing was underway.

My cunning plan was to write the introduction, and the early chapters then approach the league to see if they would fund the production costs of the book. To write those early chapters I contacted a group of people I had never met, who had never heard of me and who I was instantly going to ask for help........Greg Applegarth, Dan Shurben and Allan Worthy take a bow, you all responded quickly and positively, Dave McKay, the league statistician, and fellow photographers Martin Avery, the official NEPL Photographer, and Ken Waller also agreed to help, Tara Wilson at Wilson on the Wall Photography designed the front and rear cover for me, and then John Graham came on board, and was followed by others.

Anthony Trotter arranged for me to address the League Management meeting on 7th February 2024, armed with a mock up-front cover and a few team photos, I did a short presentation, showed them a few chapters I had already written and fortunately they agreed to fund the production costs of the project.

The composition of the book itself was initially relatively straightforward, an introduction, a chapter on each title winning team, on the year's a team won more than one title in a row, put those year's together as the bulk of the team won't change much year to year, then focus on the 2024 season, the 25th year of the league.

That 2024 season would be broken into three parts, the first six games, coloured clothing, orange balls, 45 overs, would be part one, white clothing, red balls,120 overs, the middle part, back to coloured clothing for the last part, do a weekly round up on each. A chapter at the end to round things off, book sorted.

Once I started writing it, I remembered how many different directions a story can go, I wanted to include the machinations which had led to the league forming and the history of the time plus that of the clubs who took the leap of faith and started the league off. I also wanted to make an observation regarding the clubs left behind, I was advised not to mention my own club, Seaton Burn, as they have never played in the NEPL, and they weren't part of NEPL history. I felt they were, there are links, however tenuous, across Northeast cricket to the NEPL.

I thought at the time, and having done this project, I believe it even more, most clubs have been left behind by the NEPL, they don't have the financial means of competing at the level it takes for a club to reach and stay in the league. Then again, it was never the intention of Lord McLaurin and The ECB to look after the interests of those clubs, their intention was to "raise the standard and to bridge the gap between club and first-class cricket and to provide a pathway from junior cricket."

Did they succeed?

You saw earlier I had spoken to Mark Wood, to me he is the classic example of what the NEPL was meant to do.

Wood is himself, unequivocal, "I have no doubt my time in the NEPL helped shape my career. Week in and week out you were playing against top quality local cricketers, some were ex Durham lads, others were local lads who didn't quite make it, but all very good cricketers just the same. I had to learn what my faults and shortcomings were and, with help, how to correct them.

John Windows pushed me on, but the standard of cricket also dragged me on too, if you were playing for The Academy against South North or Chester le Street, you knew it was going to be a tough game. In my case I think that without the lessons I learned in the League the step up from club to first class cricket may have been too great. Sometimes it was easier playing in midweek for Durham Seconds than playing in the NEPL at the weekend, a trip to Stockton where Richard Waite was playing or Chris Hewison at South North, Allan Worthy wherever he was playing. These guys were the best of the best in the region, competing with and against them made me a better cricketer, it really was sink or swim.

Some people couldn't hack that competitive side to it, you would sometimes see an Academy player who just couldn't get past the best of the club players, you had to grab your chance, because if you didn't the region was full of excellent young cricketer's who were trying to take your place.

You could see lads like Ben Stokes and Scott Borthwick were going to keep moving upwards, Andrew Smith did really well for us, but the Durham sides were so strong at the time his chances were limited, in a different time, he for one, could well have become a first-class cricketer.

John Windows got the Academy just right as well, it was pointless if we were the best team and winning everything and equally pointless if we were the worst team, we had to be competitive but more importantly we had to learn to win, and learn to lose, we had to grow as cricketer's, we would beat some teams, but when it came to the very top teams, we had to learn to compete, we had to develop as a team but, possibly more importantly, develop as individual cricketer's, the NEPL gave us the platform to do all of these things."

I only realised this one day when I was writing about Liam Plunkett, and I covered this earlier, the England team that won the 2019 World Cup had three NEPL players in it, Plunkett, Ben Stokes and Mark Wood.

Would they have gone on to reach the heights they did without the experience of their formative years in the NEPL and their days with The Durham Academy in the case of Plunkett and Stokes, and spells at The Academy, South North and Tynemouth in the case of Wood?

Closer inspection of The World Cup Final of 2019 reveals that two of the Kiwi side that day had also played in the NEPL. Tom Latham played at Gateshead Fell and South Shields and Henry Nicholls played at Blaydon. Did their NEPL experience help them all reach the heights they did? I asked Mark Wood for his thoughts on this, he has no doubt that the time that he, Plunkett and Stokes spent in the NEPL had contributed to who they were as cricketers and people.

"It was brilliant that the North East and North East cricket in particular was show cased in this way, it's a great measure of the standard of the league from that earlier period in time that so many players were in that final, if you look further afield at that time, South North and Chester le Street were winning national competitions as well, geographically the league covers a wide area and I think the values of the area were reflected in the type of cricketers we all were. I felt that we were carrying the hopes of the area along with us. I think that's also true of the

New Zealand lads, they were very similar to us, and I think that during the time they spent in the Northeast some of those values rubbed off on those lads as well."

I think the same could be said of the other dozen or so England players covered in the book who also played in the NEPL. If you also look at the young players whose progress I have touched upon during the weekly roundup, you will find around half a dozen who have made a mark in senior cricket with Durham this season, this will confirm that the system works, and that McLaurin's ideal is very much alive and well and prospering.

I was sent an alternative view of the origins of The NEPL very early on in the writing process, I think it's worth looking at these observations in full.

"The first thing is to do with the original reason for the advent of Premier Leagues. This reason became redundant before the Leagues came into being, so has been forgotten about. ECB and cricket finances in general were precarious and McLaren and company agreed that second team county cricket was finished. Clubs couldn't afford to employ these players, so a competition was needed so that players not being used in the first eleven could keep themselves ready for the time in which they needed to step up. So Premier Leagues were the answer. Sky then arrived with a lot of cash and this problem disappeared overnight.

I was told that Bishop Auckland were in the original first Premier League roster, but they got cold feet when they became worried as to how much money would be needed to compete. Blaydon were the replacement. I personally thought that Ashington were preferred. I was told by someone within Ashington that they had made a provisional application, but their committee hadn't come to a final decision on whether they wanted to take part or not. Matters were taken out of their hands when Newcastle were selected."

Just another footnote, a lot of people were very sceptical that it (the NEPL) would ever happen, largely due to a perceived hostility from Durham clubs to their inferior Northumberland counterparts.

On the night that the final decision of the NEPL creation was confirmed, one Chairman, on being told what had happened replied "No lad, it'll never happen, the Durham clubs won't agree."

I said "Chairman, they have, it's coming in next season."

He was shocked! I don't think his perspective was unusual, either."

An interesting viewpoint, especially for me, the part about the Sky money solving all the problems of The ECB overnight.

My own opinion, for what it's worth, is that I have been blown away by the quality of cricket and cricketers I have been fortunate enough to photograph for free for the last three years, the only thing that surprises me, is, given the quality on show, how sparse the attendances are and how low the media profile is amongst local news outlets.

For anyone wanting to view my NEPL photos please go to Steve Graham Sports Photos on Facebook, I have included my own favourite photo I have taken after this chapter, to help close the book, as a former fast bowler and now amateur photographer, the photo I'm looking for every photo is the middle stump going flying, Sean Tindale obliged when taking his 200th NEPL wicket.

I have met some lovely people on the boundary edge, hence the covid chapter being what it is, and as a grandad, I hope my eldest grandson Thomas, continues to play cricket, to be one of those juniors that The ECB wanted to give the opportunity to thrive and have a pathway to a cricket career.

As I was writing my first book, Thomas, then aged five, asked his grandma what I was doing,

"Grandad is writing a book about cricket."

"Well, I play cricket, will I be in the book?" came the five-year-old reply.

He was, I put a photo of him batting at All Stars in, and in a moment of sheer indulgence and to remind everyone, one of the main purposes of the NEPL is to nurture junior cricket, to provide the facilities, the safe environment, the coaching and the opportunity for juniors to get involved with our sport and, for the best of them, to rise to the top, the photo of Thomas, now aged nine, at Dynamos, is to make sure that we all remember that, in my opinion, one of the unstated aims of cricket, is to ensure that the future generations have the opportunity to take as much pleasure out of cricket as we all have.

With thanks to all those who have helped write the history of the NEPL and therefore this book, and apologies to those who I have missed in my trawl through its history, and there will be many who have played and deserve to be recognized who I have missed, can I gently lift the bails and call time on the first 25 Years of the NEPL?

Saturday 7th May 2022 South North's Sean Tindale bowls Whitburn's Matt Muchall to take his 200th NEPL wicket.

My grandson Thomas now aged 9, at Dynamo's showing his grandad how batting should be done!

Acknowledgements

As someone who entered this project with practically no knowledge of the history of the NEPL and an appalling memory for what I had learned, I relied very heavily in the writing process of a large number of people, can I thank each and every one of you, without you, this book simply doesn't exist.

In no particular order-

David McKay- Benwell Hill
Duncan Stephen- South North
Russell Perry- Umpire
Ken Waller- Photographer
Peter Young- Umpire and Editor in Chief
Martin Avery- Official NEPL Photographer
Tara Wilson- Photographer and editor of both covers, courtesy of Wilson on the Wall Photography
David McLaren- NEPL Supporter
Mark Wood- Durham and England
Bob Jackson- Durham CCC
Greg Applegarth- Sunderland
Dan Shurben- Chester le Street
Allan Worthy- Burnmoor
Simon Birtwisle- South North
John Graham- South North
Quentin Hughes- Chester le Street
Kevin Ward- Stockton
Richard Waite- Stockton
Lee Crozier- South North
Anthony Trotter- NEPL Secretary
Brian Bennett- "Scoop"- Ashington
Vince Howe- Tynemouth
John Hutton- South North
Phil Hudson- Newcastle
Mark Burdon- Chester le Street
John Oswell- Burnopfield
Chris Youldon- Sunderland
Alec Linsley- Burnmoor
Andy McNally- Felling
John Spellman- Castle Eden
Simon Lunn- Benwell Hill
Oli McGee- South North
Jonathan Wightman- South North
Katherine Robbie- Tynedale
Julie Scott- Grosvenor Publishing

Any unknown photographers whose photos appear in the book.